The Handbook of Secondary Geography

Edited by Mark Jones

Geographical Association

© Geographical Association, 2017

This book is copyright under the Berne Convention. All rights are reserved. Apart from any fair dealing for the purpose of private study, research, criticism or review, as permitted under the Copyright, Designs and Patents Act 1988, no part of this publication may be reproduced, stored in a retrieval system, or transmitted in any form or by any means, electronic, electrical, chemical, mechanical, optical, photocopying, recording or otherwise, without the prior written permission of the copyright owner. Enquiries should be addressed to the Geographical Association. The authors have licensed the Geographical Association to allow members to reproduce material for their own internal school/ departmental use, provided that the authors hold the copyright. The views expressed in this publication are those of the authors and do not necessarily represent those of the Geographical Association.

ISBN 978-1-84377-377-1
First published 2017
Impression number 10 9 8 7 6 5 4 3 2 1

Published by the Geographical Association, 160 Solly Street, Sheffield S1 4BF
Company number 07139068
Website: www.geography.org.uk
E-mail: info@geography.org.uk
The Geographical Association is a registered charity: no. 1135148

The Geographical Association is the leading subject association for all teachers of geography. Our charitable mission is to further geographical knowledge and understanding through education. Our journals, publications, professional events, website and local and online networks support teachers and share their ideas and practice. The GA represents the views of geography teachers and plays a leading role in public debate relating to geography and education.

The GA would be happy to hear from other potential authors who have ideas for geography books. You may contact the Head of Publishing via the GA at the address above.

Copy edited by Fran Royle
Cartography and diagrams by Shark Graphics and Cartography
Illustrations by Dave Howarth
Index compiled by Joanna Penning
Designed and typeset by Ledgard Jepson Ltd
Printed and bound in England by Ashford Colour Press

Disclaimer: Every effort has been made to identify and contact the original sources of copyright material.
If there have been any inadvertent breaches of copyright we apologise.

> Transition from initial discussion of this handbook through to publication is the result of the dedicated support of the GA's publications team (Anna Grandfield, Dorcas Brown, Ruth Totterdell and Elaine Anderson). I am also very grateful to all contributors for their commitment, hard work and support for this publication. In writing the numeracy chapter I would like to thank Alison Fletcher (Director of Cabot Learning Federation Institute), Aidan Farrell and Paul Ryan (PGCE Mathematics Tutors, UWE, Bristol) for their input.
>
> Each of the contributors like you, the reader, will have studied, collaborated or taught with people who have and continue to influence our understanding of what it means to be a teacher of geography – this latest handbook acknowledges all those committed to this endeavour.

Contents

Contributors 4
Introduction *Mark Jones* 6

Section 1

Chapter 1   What is geography? *Alastair Bonnett* 12
Chapter 2   Thinking geographically *David Lambert* 20
Chapter 3   What do we mean by curriculum? *Mary Biddulph* 30
Chapter 4   Progression *Liz Taylor* 40
Chapter 5   Planning for enquiry *Margaret Roberts* 48

Section 2

Chapter 6   Physical geography *Nicholas Clifford and Alex Standish* 62
Chapter 7   Human geography *Peter Jackson* 76
Chapter 8   Teaching geography for sustainability *John Morgan* 92
Chapter 9   Global learning *John Hopkin* 106
Chapter 10 Place and locational knowledge *Denise Freeman and Alun Morgan* 120
Chapter 11 Teaching a good geography lesson *Richard Bustin* 134
Chapter 12 Resources *David Rayner* 150
Chapter 13 Differentiation *Jane Ferretti* 166
Chapter 14 Assessing geography *Paul Weeden* 182
Chapter 15 Literacy *Nicola Walshe* 198
Chapter 16 Numeracy *Mark Jones* 212
Chapter 17 Fieldwork *John Widdowson* 228
Chapter 18 GIS and other geospatial technologies *Mary Fargher* 244
Chapter 19 Post-16 geography *Emma Rawlings Smith* 260

Section 3

Chapter 20 Professional development *Jennifer Hill and Mark Jones* 278
Chapter 21 Researching geography education *Steve Puttick* 292
Chapter 22 Mentoring *Charles Rawding and Andrea Tapsfield* 306
Chapter 23 Leading the geography department *Catherine Owen* 318
Chapter 24 Belonging to a subject community *Alan Kinder* 330

Index 344

Contributors

Mary Biddulph is Lecturer in Geography Education at the University of Nottingham and a member of the Centre for Research in Schools and Communities. She has written widely on the subject of young people's geographies, student agency and curriculum development in geography, and co-led the Young People's Geographies project. Mary was Editor of *Teaching Geography* from 2009 to 2012 and is GA President 2016–17.

Alastair Bonnett is Professor of Social Geography at the University of Newcastle. He is the author of *The Idea of the West* (Palgrave, 2004), *Left in the Past* (Bloomsbury, 2010), *What is Geography?* (Sage, 2010), *Off the Map* (Aurum, 2014) and *The Geography of Nostalgia* (Routledge, 2015).

Richard Bustin is Head of Geography at the City of London Freemen's School. He has published in *Teaching Geography* and *Geography* and is on the *Teaching Geography* Editorial Board. He is the author of the GA's Key Stage 3 Geography Teachers' Toolkit *What's the Use: How can Earth meet our resource needs?* and has completed doctoral research into the capability approach to geography education.

Nicholas Clifford is Professor of Geography and Dean of Social, Political and Geographical Sciences at Loughborough University, with over 25 years of research experience in physical geography and geomorphology. He completed his undergraduate and postgraduate degrees at the University of Cambridge, where he also obtained a PGCE. He is a Chartered Geographer, Managing Editor of *Progress in Physical Geography*, a member of the *Geography* Editorial Collective, and co-ordinating editor of the major international textbooks *Key Methods* and *Key Concepts in Geography* for Sage.

Mary Fargher is a Lecturer in Geography Education at the University College London Institute of Education. Mary was a teacher and head of geography in schools for 19 years and now leads the MA Geography Education at the IoE. Her PhD research was on the relationship between concepts of place and GIS.

Jane Ferretti taught geography in secondary schools in Sheffield until 2003 when she moved to the University of Sheffield, where she is responsible for geography PGDE and works on Masters courses. She is an active member of the Geographical Association and sits on the Publications Board. She edited *Meeting the Needs of Your Most Able Pupils: Geography* (Routledge, 2007) and has written for *Teaching Geography*.

Denise Freeman teaches geography in the London Borough of Redbridge where she has responsibility for professional development particularly with trainee teachers and NQTs. Denise has contributed to a wide range of publications including *Studying PGCE Geography at M Level* (Routledge, 2010), *Teaching Geography* and the *GCSE Bitesize* revision guides and website.

Jennifer Hill is Associate Professor in Teaching and Learning of Geography at the University of the West of England, Bristol. Jenny is passionate about teaching, researching and mentoring. She is a National Teaching Fellow and Principal Fellow of the HEA. She is a former member of the *Geography* Editorial Collective and current member of the *Journal of Geography in Higher Education* International Editorial Board.

John Hopkin was a geography teacher and head of geography in a number of Birmingham schools before becoming a School Improvement Adviser with Birmingham City Council. He has written and edited several geography textbooks and has a particular interest in teaching about global geography, development and the environment. He is currently Head of Accreditation for the Global Learning Programme at the Geographical Association.

Peter Jackson is Professor of Human Geography at the University of Sheffield and was a member of the *Geography* Editorial Collective from 2007 to 2015. He is a passionate advocate of the power of thinking geographically and applies this approach in his teaching and research, which focuses on the geographies of food. Besides his academic work, he also chairs the Food Standards Agency's Social Science Research Committee.

Mark Jones co-ordinates the PGCE Secondary Geography course at the University of the West of England, Bristol. A former geography teacher and curriculum leader with 18 years' experience teaching in secondary schools in Bristol and South Gloucestershire, his interests and publications include cross-phase and cross-curricular collaboration; with David Lambert he co-edited *Debates in Geography Education* (Routledge, 2013), and co-wrote *JumpStart! Geography* with Sarah Whitehouse (Routledge, 2015).

Alan Kinder is Chief Executive of the Geographical Association. He has over 25 years' experience in geography education including as a teacher, school leader, field studies officer, local authority advisor and initial teacher educator. He is the author of a wide range of professional articles and curriculum materials.

David Lambert is Professor of Education at the Institute of Education, University College London, and was Chief Executive of the Geographical Association from 2002 to 2012. A former secondary school teacher and teacher educator, he has written widely on geography in education, citizenship, assessment and the curriculum.

Alun Morgan taught geography in secondary schools in England and Wales for 10 years, and for the past 12 years has been a Teacher Advisor and then Lecturer and Researcher in Higher Education at universities in London and the south-west. He has a long-standing interest in the educational importance of 'place' as a holistic concept.

Contributors

John Morgan is Professor of Curriculum and Pedagogy at the University of Auckland, New Zealand. Before that he worked in geography education at the University of Bristol and the Institute of Education, University College London. His latest book is *Teaching Secondary Geography as if the Planet Matters* (Routledge, 2010). He is a former member of the *Geography* Editorial Collective.

Catherine Owen has 16 years' experience as Head of Geography at The King Alfred School in Somerset, an SGQM Centre of Excellence. She is an active member of the Geographical Association, chairing the GA's International Special Interest Group and writing resources such as *Going Global* and *Introducing India* in the GA's GCSE and Key Stage 3 Geography Teachers' Toolkit series. Catherine is a Chartered Geographer (Teacher) and a GA consultant.

Steve Puttick is Head of Programmes (Secondary/FE/Research Education) at Bishop Grosseteste University, Lincoln. His doctoral research, funded by an ESRC 1+3 Studentship, is an ethnographic study of three secondary school geography departments. A former head of geography, he has published widely on geography teachers' conceptions of knowledge.

Charles Rawding is Senior Lecturer in Geography Education at Edge Hill University, Lancashire. Prior to becoming involved in teacher education, he was head of geography in a large comprehensive school on Humberside. He has written widely on curriculum innovation in geography, including *Effective Innovation in the Secondary Curriculum* (Routledge, 2013). Charles regularly writes for GA publications and presents workshops at the GA's Annual Conference.

Emma Rawlings Smith taught school geography in the UK and the Middle East for over 14 years. Emma is a Consultant to the GA, author of *Top Spec Geography: Changing Places*, a member of the GA's Post-16 and HE Phase Committee, and now PGCE Geography tutor at the University of Leicester.

David Rayner taught and led secondary geography in a variety of schools in London, Medway and Kent for over 30 years. He has been an active member of the GA and RGS-IBG for most of his career. David has run a number of educational websites and published for the GA, the RGS-IBG and the Ordnance Survey. He led the government project to support the introduction of the key stage 3 National Curriculum (2006–2007), and has been Education Lecturer at the Institute of Education, University College London.

Margaret Roberts taught in comprehensive schools in London, Leicestershire and Sheffield before moving to the University of Sheffield where she co-ordinated the PGCE geography course. Her research focused on the geography National Curriculum and 'enquiry'. She is the author of the GA's best-selling *Learning Through Enquiry* and *Geography Through Enquiry*. Since her retirement in 2006, she has edited *Teaching Geography*, been President of the Geographical Association and led courses for teachers in Singapore on geographical enquiry.

Alex Standish is Senior Lecturer in Geography Education and leads the Secondary PGCE Geography Programme at the Institute of Education, University College London. He taught geography and social studies education for six years at Western Connecticut State University in Danbury. Previously, he taught in primary, secondary and special needs schools in the south of England. Alex's publications and research interests include geography education, teacher education and global change.

Andrea Tapsfield is a retired HMI who had responsibility for geography Initial Teacher Training. She is an active member of the Geographical Association and a member of the GA's Teacher Education Special Interest Group.

Liz Taylor is Lecturer in Geography Education at the University of Cambridge, where she co-ordinates the geography PGCE course and supervises at Masters and PhD levels. Liz taught geography for eight years in a large comprehensive school and her research interests include young people's understandings of distant place.

Nicola Walshe was head of geography in three schools before joining the University of Cambridge where she worked for ten years in ITE, ultimately leading the Secondary Geography PGCE course. Nicola is currently a Senior Lecturer in the Department of Education at Anglia Ruskin University and is particularly interested in the concept of sustainability within geography education.

Paul Weeden is a retired lecturer in education who has taught, researched and written extensively in the fields of assessment and geographical education. Previously he taught in a comprehensive school for 20 years. He was Secretary of the GA's Assessment and Examinations Special Interest Group between 2001 and 2014 and for 30 years was actively involved in GCSE examinations (and their predecessors).

John Widdowson is a geography teacher in east London who runs an urban fieldwork project, attracting schools from London and far beyond. He is the author of several geography textbooks at key stage 3 and GCSE level, and is joint editor of the GA's best-selling Key Stage 3 Geography Teachers' Toolkit series.

Introduction

Mark Jones, Editor

'Geography is one of the most important of school subjects and one of the most difficult to teach' (Fairgrieve, 1949, p. 1).

This handbook has been written primarily for all teachers of geography in secondary schools in the United Kingdom. It also speaks to a wider audience, particularly those active and interested in geography education, as many of the choices and challenges of teaching geography in the early 21st century transcend particular locations and educational contexts. Whatever your role and reason for reading this handbook, we hope it provides a useful resource both for understanding the current 'idea' of geography in secondary schools and for discussing and debating possible future directions the discipline might take.

'I found myself wandering between the fields of educational theory and geographical theory and that of practical problems of teaching' (Graves, 1971, p. iii).

In his preface to *Geography in Secondary Education*, Norman Graves (1971) recounts his feelings on undertaking the writing of a book that essentially became a handbook for secondary school geography teachers of the 1970s. What his opening statement captures are the choices to be made about the purpose and guiding principles of such a handbook. In writing *The Handbook of Secondary Geography*, three guiding principles have informed the content, coverage and emphasis between theoretical and practical considerations:

- to offer practical advice and professional development for classroom practitioners
- to encourage scholarly engagement with the nature and purpose of geography
- to signpost the rich legacy of subject-specific literature that geography teachers and the wider geography community can engage with.

Guiding principles

The first guiding principle, of providing practical advice and professional development for teachers, steered much of the writing for this volume. Access to different ideas and approaches to teaching and learning geography is, quite rightly, highly valued by hard-working teachers for its potential transferability into daily practice. I say 'potential', because geography teachers need to carefully scrutinise new ideas, strategies and activities, particularly when applied in different contexts. Such scrutiny has been increasingly important since the 2000s, when generic approaches to lesson structure, the influence of skills-based curricula and 'learning to learn' looked as though they might sideline teachers' subject-specific reasoning and justification for curriculum planning and lesson focus. This is one reason why a handbook written according to subject-specific principles is so important: competing agendas need to be acknowledged, but they should be viewed through a geographical lens. In some chapters, the application of the practical ideas and professional development is obvious; however, a number of chapters suggest 'ways of thinking'; new or alternative perspectives against which existing ways of thinking or current classroom approaches can be problematised. In providing practical advice for readers, we also recognise that we are not always speaking to subject experts: routes into teaching are increasingly diverse and qualified teachers who are non-specialists may be teaching geography in secondary schools, particularly at key stage 3. We strongly encourage these teachers, in addition to reading this handbook, to undertake continuing professional development (CPD) through dialogue with subject experts, through their local school networks and through opportunities provided by the Geographical Association (GA).

The second principle, of encouraging scholarly engagement, is emphasised by James Fairgrieve in the opening chapter to *Geography in School* (1949). He reminds us that, as geography teachers, we must be able to articulate why geography is an important subject. The day-to-day practicalities of teaching can leave precious little time and energy for discussing what Wooldridge and East (1951) have called the 'spirit and purpose of geography'; but if we are to realise the full ambition of geography we need to undertake intellectual engagement with more philosophical and theoretical questions about the discipline: questions such as geography's meaning or spirit, its aims and purposes, conceptual choices and representation; and epistemological considerations such as the origin, authorship and utility of knowledge. This can seem a tall order when the classroom practitioner's immediate priorities are planning and teaching the week's geography lessons, but making sense of such 'big questions' in relation to one's professional practice, and what this means in the context of teaching geography, is important. If we are to consider more critically the complexities of what, and how, to teach geography we must engage with the very purpose of geography: but for this to happen requires us all, teachers and those in the wider subject community, to have both 'a concept of geography and, equally important, a concept of education' (Lambert and Jones, 2013, p. 5).

The third principle, often simply assumed, is to explicitly remind readers of the rich legacy of subject-specific literature that occupies the pages of previous handbooks, books and journal articles. Handbooks, for example those published by the GA, have developed from single authorship (Graves, 1971, 1980) to edited volumes (Boardman, 1986; Bailey and Fox, 1996; Balderstone, 2006; Jones, 2017). These edited volumes provide a range of voices and perspectives; contributors have included practising teachers, teacher educators, university academics, Her Majesty's Inspectorate, members of the Field Studies Council, the GA and independent consultants. This diversity of contexts from which contributors discuss geography is healthy, both for the discipline and the subject community. It encourages us to examine different perspectives on what geography is and how it might be taught; but it also can 'impel us to re-examine current orthodoxies and habitual practices' (Lambert and Jones, 2013, p. 2). Access to the thoughts and ideas of this wider subject community can also help stimulate debate within and between educational contexts and in the wider subject community itself. Looking back, the GA handbooks not only provided invaluable advice at the time; they are also important reminders of the circumstances, choices and challenges that those teaching geography in secondary schools faced during different decades. To make sense of the present and the future, we need to have an informed view of the past.

In alerting readers to the wider literature base available to geography teachers, each contributor has selected key recommended readings, alongside the range of literature referred to in each chapter. Much has been published, both online and in print, in the eleven years between the previous handbook (Balderstone, 2006) and this one. As a subject community we are indebted to those individuals and organisations who contribute to the volume and quality of this material. While there are numerous ways to self-publish through tweets, blogs and websites, it is also worth remembering that the GA actively encourages contributions to its journals *Teaching Geography* and *Geography*, welcoming articles from a range of contexts and from authors at different points in their writing journeys. Many of the chapters in this volume have drawn on articles published in *Teaching Geography* between 2006 and 2015, reminding us of this invaluable source of ideas, activities and CPD.

Secondary geography: priorities and principles

All educational texts are written against a political backdrop, and the educational policies of governments with different political ideologies can significantly affect geography in schools (see Rawling, 2001; 2015). Political discourses promote different agendas at different times, for example 'personalisation' under New Labour, with its emphasis on student experience and pedagogy; or, as in the latest iteration of the National Curriculum (DfE,

2014) the idea of teaching 'core knowledge', introduced by the Liberal-Conservative Coalition (see DfE, 2010) and a tenet of the Conservative Government that took office in May 2015. The previous GA handbook was written at a time when schools were implementing the Labour Government's (1997–2010) National Strategies, local authorities still had geography advisors and geography planning emphasised learning and learners. The government-funded Action Plan for Geography (2006–11), jointly and equally led by the GA and the RGS-IBG, provided much welcome subject-specific CPD for geography teachers at a time when some school approaches, for example 'learning to learn', challenged the very idea of 'subject expertise'. Since 2006, and after two changes of government, the policy emphasis is on 'core knowledge' and comparing educational standards – and teaching methods – with schools overseas. Against a background of constant curriculum change, and especially where CPD is dominated by a whole-school focus or an inspection-facing agenda, geography teachers (both subject experts and non-specialists) have challenging and multi-dimensional roles. This requires teachers to stand firm on the need for subject-specific CPD, and we hope that the chapters in this book will help support this role.

Key stage 3 is an opportunity to present geography to young people in many different ways. The National Curriculum for geography (DfE, 2013) is non-statutory for the increasing number of schools outside local authority control, and even where schools do follow the National Curriculum teachers are encouraged 'to range beyond the National Curriculum specifications' (DfE, 2014, p. 5). However, despite the potential offered by local curriculum making for increased autonomy and interpretation, secondary school geography lessons can be strikingly similar, in both content and approach. The pedagogic principles on which lessons are planned may be strongly rooted in the subject's vocabulary and grammar, but generic approaches imposed by school policies can risk undermining the geography (see Roberts, 2010). This handbook emphasises the importance of putting the geography at the forefront of our planning and teaching. Many of the chapters will support

readers in questioning the nature and purpose of geography both at key stage 3 and beyond. They are intended to be 'at hand'; to be read and re-read; and to initiate and inform discussion in and across the different educational contexts where geography is represented and taught. Figure 1 suggests some thematic questions to help guide your use of the handbook as a CPD tool.

Final thoughts

With new GCSE and GCE specifications being taught from September 2016 for first examination in summer 2018, over the next few years examination classes may become a key focus for geography departments. However, devoting our efforts and energy to this end exclusively implies an exam-led purpose to teaching geography that ignores, or at least marginalises, the ambition and celebration of geography. It is worth reminding ourselves that the word 'geography' is derived from the Greek words *gé* meaning 'Earth' and *graphein* meaning 'to write' or 'to describe'. It was first used by the Greek scholar Eratosthenes in the 3rd century BC; today, geography as 'writing the Earth' can have instant appeal, whether as a permanent reminder of the subject's roots on a classroom display or temporarily, written in the sand on a geography field trip.

Geography, as represented in policy and enacted in practice, is open to interpretation and influence. We can approach 'writing about the Earth' in geography lessons in many different ways: 'in theory at least... the what, the how and the why of teaching is always up for grabs' (Castree, 2005, p. 246). Considering our philosophical position can help make explicit our ideas about what geography is and what it is for, but at the same time we have to accommodate the practical considerations of preparing students for their geography examinations. This is the conundrum that is 'teaching geography in secondary schools'.

Teaching geography can be incredibly rewarding, and every geography teacher aspires to teaching high-quality, relevant and challenging geography. One way of assessing whether this is happening is if young people enjoy and engage meaningfully with the subject while in school, and perhaps most

Before reading the chapter	After (re-)reading the chapter
What do I already understand about this theme or issue?	What has this made me consider/reconsider?
What are my views on this and why?	What did I agree/disagree with and why?
What and who has informed my thinking to date?	What do I want to question and/or know more about?
How does this impact on my professional identity (as a geography teacher)?	How has reading this chapter impacted on my professional identity (as a geography teacher)?
What implications does this have for my professional practice and on others (e.g. pupils, students, teachers, colleagues, others)?	What implications does this have, for my professional practice and for others (e.g. pupils, students, teachers, colleagues, others)?
Have I contributed to work in this field?	Is this an area that I can contribute/respond to (e.g. in meetings, self-publication (tweets, blogs, websites); writing for publication, at TeachMeets, running CPD)?

Figure 1: Questions to accompany the use of this handbook as a CPD tool.

telling is what they say about their geography lessons years after leaving. Their response is, I would argue, mainly down to a teacher's interpretation of the subject. A teacher who embraces the spirit and purpose of geography, and can open students' eyes to geography as 'a fundamental fascination' (Bonnett, 2008, p. 1), is likely to get the response: 'I loved geography at school'.

References

Bailey, P. and Fox, P. (eds) (1996) *Geography Teachers' Handbook*. Sheffield: Geographical Association.

Balderstone, D. (ed) (2006) *Secondary Geography Handbook*. Sheffield: Geographical Association.

Boardman, D. (1986) *Handbook for Geography Teachers*. Sheffield: Geographical Association.

Bonnett, A. (2008) *What is Geography?* London: Sage.

Castree, N. (2005) *Nature*. London: Routledge.

DfE (2010) *The Importance of Teaching: The Schools White Paper 2010*. London: The Stationery Office.

DfE (2013) *National Curriculum in England: Geography programmes of study*. London: DfE. Available at: www.gov.uk/government/publications/national-curriculum-in-england-geography-programmes-of-study (last accessed 02/11/2016).

DfE (2014) *The National Curriculum in England. Key stages 3 and 4 framework document*. London: DfE. Available at: www.gov.uk/government/uploads/system/uploads/attachment_data/file/381754/SECONDARY_national_curriculum.pdf (last accessed 02/11/2016).

Fairgrieve, J. (1949) *Geography in School* (6th edition). London: University of London Press.

Graves, N. (1971) *Geography in Secondary Education*. Sheffield: Geographical Association.

Graves, N. (1980) *Geographical Education in Secondary Schools*. Sheffield: Geographical Association.

Jones, M. (ed) (2017) *The Handbook of Secondary Geography*. Sheffield: Geographical Association.

Lambert, D. and Jones, M. (2013) 'Introduction: geography education, questions and choices' in Lambert, D. and Jones, M. (eds) *Debates in Geography Education*. Abingdon: Routledge, pp. 1–14.

Rawling, E. (2001) *Changing the Subject: The impact of national policy on school geography 1980–2000*. Sheffield: Geographical Association.

Rawling, E. (2015) 'Curriculum change and examination reform for geography 14–19', *Geography*, 100, 3, pp. 164–68.

Roberts, M. (2010) 'Where's the geography? Reflections on being an external examiner', *Teaching Geography*, 35, 3, pp. 112–13.

Wooldridge, S.W. and East, W.G. (1951) *The Spirit and Purpose of Geography*. London: Hutchinson.

The chapters in section one are intended as a stimulus for promoting informed discussion about the discipline: its nature, purpose and representations in academia and schools, and how people's different values and educational beliefs relate to the current idea of geography in secondary schools. Chapters encourage the reader to consider important questions such as: What is geography? What are its aims and purposes? What might be its organising concepts? How can geography be represented in the school curriculum? How can students learn and make progress in geography?

Exploring the ideas presented in these chapters will require us to revisit our 'geographical imaginations' and the current interpretations we hold of geography and geography in the school curriculum as well as the subject's potential, alternative and possible future directions.

Section 1

Chapter 1 – **What is geography?**
Alastair Bonnett

Chapter 2 – **Thinking geographically**
David Lambert

Chapter 3 – **What do we mean by curriculum?**
Mary Biddulph

Chapter 4 – **Progression**
Liz Taylor

Chapter 5 – **Planning for enquiry**
Margaret Roberts

Chapter 1

What is geography?

Alastair Bonnett is Professor of Social Geography at Newcastle University

Introduction

The world is geography's logo. It rolls around the pages of countless geographical societies and school websites. Perhaps it is cut and pasted a little too casually; for this image contains an ambitious argument about geography's scope. It proposes that geography is about the world: that to study geography is to study the world, both near and far. It is a dramatic claim; the most far-reaching and ambitious made by any discipline. In this chapter I show just how important, how necessary, as well as how challenging this claim is; for while it establishes geography as a modern specialism, concerned with environmental and international knowledge, it also suggests that it is a current of human activity and thought that goes much deeper, and is more fundamental, than the nostrums and worries of our own era.

I will be arguing that geography is a modern discipline but one with deep roots. More specifically, geography's fundamental task is identified as seeking order in the world; a task that is a necessity for a species that tries to both survive and find hope in often hostile landscapes. As we shall see, in the eighteenth and nineteenth centuries, this human need was translated into the characteristic concerns of human and physical geography. The translation of ancient needs into modern forms is also apparent in the urge to explore; to discover imaginatively, and sometimes literally conquer, the world 'out there'. This insistent desire is intertwined with the history of geography, conferring upon it a colonial pedigree but also, and more happily, a restless desire to break down the barriers between the classroom and the streets and fields, and to venture outside into the sunshine and the rain.

Ordering the world

Geography seeks to find order and meaning in the diversity and complexity of the world. One of the great monographs of twentieth-century geography is by Clarence Glacken (1976) and has the mysterious title *Traces on the Rhodian Shore*. The title phrase refers to an ancient legend: the Greek philosopher Aristippus, shipwrecked and lost on an unknown island (the island of Rhodes), came across some geometric markings in the sand. 'Let us be of good hope', Aristippus cries out, 'for indeed I see the traces of men'. Glacken's survey of over 2000 years of environmental theories repeats this *cri de coeur*: 'What is most striking in conceptions of nature, even mythical ones', he tells us, 'is the yearning for purpose and order' (1976, p. 3).

The Greek scholar Eratosthenes, who gave us the word 'geography' about 2200 years ago, provides a fine example of this yearning. Not only is he credited with drawing one of the first maps to represent the world, he also devised a grid-based system to locate places on Earth, sketched the route of the Nile and worked out why it flooded.

Eratosthenes's quest to know Earth also prompted him to try and calculate its circumference. It may seem a prosaic statistic (we know today that Earth's equatorial circumference is 24,901 miles), but this quest represented a startling application of pure reason to a geographical problem. Eratosthenes knew that on the summer solstice at Syene (Aswan), the sun's rays left no shadow, falling directly down a well. Eratosthenes knew the distance from this well to Alexandria, the city where he worked as chief librarian, was 500 miles. He also knew that on the summer solstice in that city the sun's rays fell at an angle of 7°. Since Eratosthenes already understood that the light from the sun travels in parallel lines and

Our understanding of the fragility of life gives urgency to our work on environmental management.
Photo © Anna Totterdell.

that Earth was round, he had enough data to calculate the circumference of Earth. He worked it out at 25,000 miles.

However, the need to find order in the world, or to impose order upon it, is not just a question of scientific enquiry, for it taps deeply into the existential function of geography. The search for meaning in the world helps us – personally and as a species – secure our identity within it. The huge variety of geographical knowledge and activities – from constructing borders to changing landscapes; from myths of creation to the Earth Sciences – are unified by this primal and universal ambition. The words 'primal' and 'universal' could equally be applied to a second fundamental driver behind our desire to seek out order in the world, namely the need for a sustainable relationship with Earth. Geography, today as in the past, offers information about landscapes, peoples, routes and resources, and the connections between them, that allows us not only to understand and manage these things, but also to devise ways for our species to flourish, or at least remain alive. Today, when we recognise that we have the capacity to destroy the planet's environmental systems, human survival hovers in the background of many geography lessons. Our new understanding of the fragility of life gives urgency to our work on global conflict and environmental management. Although these particular concerns may appear novel, they are rooted in age-old imperatives.

Modern geography: international and environmental knowledge

Geography has ancient roots but its long history is one of adaptation and change. Modern geography has been shaped by modern ideas and concerns. More specifically, over the last 200 years the increasing need for, and prestige of, intellectual specialisation have combined with the development of the nation state and scientific methods to establish international and environmental knowledge as the two great axes around which geography has come to be defined. It is towards geography that people turn when seeking answers to the questions, 'how and why has the environment altered?' and 'how and why do nations connect and differ?' These questions, transformed into striking images, are postered across school rooms the world over. They are also well represented within television schedules and in the print media. The modern geographical agenda thrives on its global ambitions, on a boldly asserted 'worldliness', but it also asserts 'challenges' and 'problems' as central to the geography student's vocabulary. Indeed, to contemporary ears, the words 'environmental' and 'international' can seem a little incomplete without that pervasive suffix, 'crisis'.

Unique among academic subjects, geography has a roughly equal emphasis on science and social science, yet although we have come to understand geography as comprising two distinct branches; each of them offers forms of world knowledge that spring from the

The rise of Asian power has provoked a new willingness to talk about 'multiple modernities'. **Photo** © Bryan Ledgard.

fundamental human needs that I have already touched on, albeit within a distinct, modern context. In the rest of this section I elaborate on this point, addressing human geography first.

The story of the emergence of industrialised economies, and of the rise of nation states and, subsequently, of international systems, is inseparable from the rise of modern geography. It is a remarkable transition. Well into the nineteenth century one could still find people in Europe whose direct geographical knowledge was confined to their immediate locale. Such peasant and folk communities were part of a fast-disappearing pre-modern relationship to place. Today they are gone, not simply in the West but across the world. Indeed, a very different geographical problem has emerged: that while through the internet many people have access to the world, they know little of their own locale, or even the names of their neighbours. We are all, more or less, plugged into the world economy and world politics. Geography, as in the past, attempts to describe and explain the world and its peoples but increasingly it has come to be imbued with the internationalist qualities of modernity itself. Thus its traditional focus, on depicting discrete and distinct nations and peoples, has come to be overlaid, or overtaken, by an interest in global connections, mobility and development. This shift also means that issues of prejudice, ignorance and stereotype have become defining dilemmas for the discipline.

In the West it has become common, especially within the larger nations, to identify a geographical education with a beneficent cosmopolitanism, yet this chain of association is not as straightforward as it might at first appear. After all, it is easy to be 'cosmopolitan' when the world is being shaped in your image. The rise of Asian power at the start of the twenty-first century is already provoking a new willingness to talk about 'multiple modernities', and threatens to disturb some of the cultural confidence that lies behind Western cosmopolitanism. Western dominance may, finally, be on the wane. It will be interesting to see whether coming realignments of global power act to affirm Western geography's post-national multicultural outlook or create pressures for more defensive versions and visions of 'the world discipline'.

In turning to the physical branch of geography we again witness how the ancient and universal need to find order in the world has come to be shaped by modern concerns. The rise of rational, post-religious explanations of Earth's creation and the systems of nature provided the first and most fundamental step along this path. The birth of modern geology represented a dramatic reconceptualisation of the world. Although rocks and landforms had been the subject of geographical description for thousands of years, the image of an immobile, completed Earth had nearly always held sway. James Hutton (1726–97) shattered this image. His contribution was also early and astute enough to wrestle directly with the challenge it posed to alternative ways of finding order in the world. In his *Theory of the Earth* (2007;

first published 1788), Hutton takes us through different ways of looking at landscape geology in the company of the evidence that he had found of uplift, submersion and slow erosion. He challenged the religious orthodoxy that the world could be understood as a finished, static artefact designed by an omniscient deity. Better, he says, to look at it as 'an organised body …[s]uch as has a constitution in which the necessary decay of the machine is naturally repaired' (p. 15).

Hutton is offering a model of nature not as a mechanism but as a self-regulating system; an active, interconnected set of continuous processes. This vision extinguished the stable, immobile Earth and replaced it with a dynamic planet. Twentieth-century geology and environmental science took Hutton's world vision and applied it to an analysis of how energy and matter shape the Earth, setting the continents and climate into motion. These discoveries not only secularised the notion of an ordered planet but also diminished the role allocated to humans in Earth's long story. They also showed how vulnerable we are to natural and anthropogenic changes.

Thus scientific innovations have worked to remind us of geography's bond with sustainability and survival. It is a bond that, today, is often articulated in the language of environmental crisis. However, another characteristic of modern societies — and hence of modern geography — is that they have convinced themselves that material problems nearly always have a technological fix. Geography, as a consequence, has come to take on the role of a 'solutions forum'; introducing and surveying an ever-extending list of practices and interventions that may assist us in maintaining a habitable planet. It may sound like a common sense thing to do, but it is an orientation that encourages people to believe that they can and should construct their way out of crises. Thus, for the most part, tsunamis have caused us not to stop building in coastal areas but to build better early warning systems. Similarly, knowing that the burning of fossil fuels is damaging the environment is not leading nations to significantly reduce overall energy consumption but, rather, to find other energy technologies, such as cleaner engines and nuclear power.

In his 1887 essay 'On the scope and methods of geography', Halford Mackinder argued that 'Man alters his environment, and the action of that environment on his posterity is changed in consequence' (1996, p.170). An ever more visible component of this cycle is our attempts to ameliorate the impact of the very changes to the environment that we have brought about.

Geography as exploration

Geography surrounds us. We walk, drive and fly over and through it. At the same time, it is distant: geography is the landscape beyond the horizon and the intriguing distance between here and there. Geographical study cannot be contained by libraries and laboratories. It is about our world, and demands that we get out into the world. This makes geography a difficult discipline to institutionalise or corral. Geography wants to take children outside the school gates; it wants to take keyboard tappers out of their gloomy bedrooms and make them confront the raw and diverse world. This yearning for physical sensation and real life makes geography an awkward customer in contemporary societies that tend to be risk averse, remorselessly monitored and highly bureaucratic; but that might just be to its advantage, for it makes geography both unique and refreshingly troublesome.

Geography is constantly urging us to step outside the door, yet isn't exploration dead? '[W]e are now near the end of the roll of great discoveries', Halford Mackinder wrote in his prescient essay of 1887: the 'tales of adventure grow fewer and fewer', yet even in the nineteenth century exploration was never simply about Victorian gentlemen, and a few women, venturing into 'undiscovered' lands. Exploration is a journey into the world in search of the new: it is to physically encounter the world and study and learn from it. My point is that exploration is a basic human trait and that geography is still about exploration, but I am also suggesting that the nature of exploration, what we think it is, keeps changing. Defining exploration generously, as something we all undertake or hanker for, allows us to identify two of its contemporary forms: fieldwork and travel.

The concept of 'fieldwork' originated in land surveying. Fieldwork may be defined as firsthand observations and study carried out outside of laboratories or classrooms. Fieldwork came to be considered a necessary feature of a geographical education with the development of mass education. Some of the key figures who shaped school geography in Britain were also instrumental in asserting the core value of fieldwork. Thomas Huxley's influential early text *Physiography: An introduction to the study of nature* (1877) was unequivocal in claiming that geography was a field-based science 'to be learned in the village and countryside, not read about in books' (cited by Stoddart, 1986, p. 47). Huxley's approach influenced the expectations of school inspectors, who began to insist that the school grounds and the wider locality must be seen as resources for geography lessons. This aspect of 'Victorian' geography, as Teresa Ploszajska (1999) explains, still resonates today, for fieldwork, 'whether in familiar local surroundings or distant unknown areas' (p. 270), was seen as a way of enabling students to see the connections between study and the world outside the school gates. It was, she explains, 'widely considered to be a means of encouraging children to recognise geography' as a form of knowledge 'pre-eminently concerned with the real world' (p. 270). Geography was established as the one of the few slots on the school curriculum that allowed students to escape their stuffy classroom. It has guarded this status – more or less successfully – ever since.

Fieldwork remains a core component of geographical practice. However, with the development of leisure and voluntary-based environmental and international encounters, there is a growing connection between educational and tourist- or experience-based forms of fieldwork. 'Eco-tourism', 'geo-tourism', 'geoparks', and the extensive volunteer schemes that keep many environmental and development agencies staffed, often incorporate fieldwork as a core activity. Ever more landscapes are designated for protection and educational value and growing numbers of students seek out, and are sold and consume, forms of 'fun-learning' that are both active and outward looking. The quality of these fieldwork experiences varies enormously.

However, current trends suggest that fieldwork has become integral to an expanding market of popular, and often extra-curricular, geography.

Something similar can be said of exploration more generally. Most people have an instinctive curiosity about our world. Such yearnings once had to be satisfied by tales from afar and limited forays from our own native spot; the modern era has changed that. A culture of mass travel and mass exploration has grown up. It takes many forms: from gap years to package tourism to feats of endurance in challenging terrain. With these new experiences and opportunities a new global consciousness has emerged: the world is understood to be diverse yet obtainable, exciting but also reachable. It is a world in which one can, for example, live in the USA and imagine India as exotic and distant but also fully expect to be able to be there in a matter of hours (and, moreover, back home, to expect to find people from south Asia living round the corner).

The immediacy and accessibility of the world's nations and environments has encouraged individual biographies to be structured around acts of travel and moments of geographical adventure. Ask someone what they have done over the past year and you are quite likely to hear a roll-call of destinations. It is a striking fact – and I think something that academic geography has not yet appreciated the importance of – that, today, people often talk about their lives in terms of the places they have been to or want to go. One area that has kept pace with this phenomenon is the internet. Blogs, image-sharing sites and social media have turned travel documentation into an everyday activity, both ubiquitous and myriad. The love of exploration is no longer the preserve of the few and is not something that geographers should feel ashamed about: it has emerged as one of the most creative and vibrant aspects of ordinary life.

An ambitious vision for geography

It is a little perverse, but one of the reasons I am anxious to talk about geography as one of humanity's great projects, as something fundamental to culture and identity, is because I have got used to hearing the discipline

Fieldwork remains a core component of geographical practice. **Photo** © John Lyon.

discussed in hesitant and less ambitious ways. The institutionalisation of geography within the National Curriculum, as well as into university degree courses, creates a platform for geography, but it also means that it is vulnerable to being shaped by political and policy forces that narrow its scope and cut it off from its wider purpose and popular constituencies. There are many examples of this, but I will discuss only the two most influential, which can be labelled 'geography as core facts' and 'geography as useful knowledge for global citizens'. Both of these, in other ways dissimilar, viewpoints agree on one thing: that geography provides a handy toolkit for an interconnected, crisis-prone world. And, in this narrow respect, they are both right. Geography can, indeed, deliver useful skills for young people entering a globalised marketplace, yet such a focus on the contemporary utility of geography also betrays something else both approaches share: a lack of ambition. To reduce geography to a helpful gizmo for a changing planet is to turn something profound into something small and transitory.

The 'core facts' approach to geography is almost as old as the idea of geography itself, yet although this heritage is ancient it is also superficial. For at the heart of the work of geographers such as Eratosthenes or, a few centuries later, Strabo, whose 17-volume *Geography* is one of the discipline's founding texts, was something far more important than developing global tick-lists of key facts. At root both men's geography was about studying the world and, more fundamental still, finding and imposing order upon it. The generation of facts was a consequence of this ambition, as it has been many times since, but it would be perverse of any society – especially societies whose claim to modernity is based on a critical approach to tradition – to conflate a geographical education with this particular outcome of geography's will to engage with and understand the world.

The second argument – that geography should be defined in terms of its capacity to create global citizens – also lacks ambition. However, its modern credentials, by comparison with the 'core facts' approach, are unmissable. Indeed, it sometimes appears as if the urge to be 'up to the minute with a changing world' displaces any other consideration. Cheri Lucas, writing for an American teachers' website on geography's relevance, provides a compelling statement of the position: 'In a global society, where communication with someone in a tiny internet café in Nepal is instantaneous, geography skills are more imperative than ever' (Lucas, 2009). Thus geography is identified as a 'twenty-first-century skill'. It is an emphasis that has been developed in many other statements. In a pamphlet from the US-based Gilbert M. Grosvenor Center for Geographic Education, entitled *Why Geography is Important* (no date), it is concluded that: 'Geographic knowledge, skills, and technology provide a means to comprehend the rapidly changing physical and cultural environments of the world and, thus, prepare us to be better global citizens' (p. 4). So geography is identified as a life skill for the early twenty-first century: 'important', to be sure, but something handy for 'now' rather than something of fundamental significance to the human story.

My argument is not that either the 'core facts' or the 'global citizens' approaches to geography are wrong, but that they fall short. Like many issue-based representations of fundamental forms of knowledge, they fail to appreciate the wider and deeper human appeal of the topic they wish to speak up for. This is shown by their insistence that geography can be understood as useful knowledge for the challenges of today. Geography certainly encompasses this urgent agenda. However, it is also necessary to think about geography as something bigger and grander than a crisis response or a 'solutions provider'. Let us not forget that geography has been knowledge for 'now' several times: a century ago, it was knowledge for the 'now' of European imperialism. 'Now' is always important, but when you define a discipline around it you are suggesting that that discipline is a temporary fix. It is a bit like claiming that science matters because it can help us cure cancer. It is not wrong – indeed, it is vital we know this – but it is a superficial way of understanding what science is or what it offers us. To see geography as one of humanity's most ambitious ideas and to define it as 'the world discipline' gives us a bigger and, I think, more truthful portrait of this unwieldy yet utterly necessary and very human project.

Conclusion

A few decades ago the most famous academic definition of geography came from Richard Hartshorne. In *Perspective on the Nature of Geography* (1959) he wrote that 'geography is concerned to provide accurate, orderly, and rational description and interpretation of the variable character of the Earth's surface' (p. 21).

For many years this was, as Peter Haggett notes, the 'best known and most widely used formal definition' of the discipline (1995, p. 8).

It may be formal but it never really sufficed, for it fails to get anywhere near to the beating heart of geography. Indeed, there is not only a dullness of tone but also an intellectual weariness to Hartshorne's definition. Who, after all, ever thought they would set out to 'provide' the inaccurate, disorderly and irrational? Or, indeed, that one could forgo 'description and interpretation'? The 'variable character' of 'the Earth's surface' seems to promise more. But the term 'surface' is misleading, since a lot of geography is concerned with climate or subsurface processes. One might admit 'variable character' if it did not seem like an attempt to turn the obvious into a scholastic achievement (would a historian feel the need to say history concerned the variable character of the past?). What are we left with? One thing: the one thing that lives and breathes and demands our attention under all the waffle. Earth. Young or old, we all recognise it as geography's province. The idea that geography is the world discipline threads its way through many, more verbose, definitions like a vein of gold.

'Geography is the world discipline'. This five-word definition carries complex and challenging claims. Geography arises from the necessity of knowing and making sense of the resources and dangers of our environment, but it also seeks the bigger picture: geography helps us imagine that there is meaning and sense in the world. Geography allows us to see order in what otherwise would be chaos. In the modern era the geographical imagination has been structured into two basic tendencies; namely, the pursuit of international and environmental knowledge. This division reflects modernity's global ambitions and its power to establish nature as a discrete arena for exploitation or wonder. Geography is not just a scholastic venture, it is also an active attempt to engage and encounter the world. Geography will always be associated with exploration. This ambition to explore, to break down the barriers between 'study' and the real world, makes geography a distinctive contribution to bureaucratic and institutionalised systems of education, as well as a challenge to students who can appear a little lost when ripped away from the comforts of mediated, internet-based, experiences. Its wide sweep, its long history and its curiosity about the raw world outside the window, make

Geography should be defined as 'the world discipline'. **Photo** © Bryan Ledgard.

geography a potentially awkward discipline both for schools and school students, but this very awkwardness is also geography's strength: it isn't like other subjects, nor should it try to be. Its ambitions are too big and its horizons too wide. It is an essential component of a good education but it is more than that too, for geography is rooted in some of our most basic and important needs and hopes.

References

Gilbert M. Grosvenor Center for Geographic Education (no date) *Why Geography is Important*. San Marcos, TX: Texas State University. Available at: http://geography.vt.edu/Why%20is%20Geography%20Important.pdf (last accessed 02/11/2016).

Glacken, C. (1976) *Traces on the Rhodian Shore: Nature and culture in western thought from ancient times to the end of the eighteenth century*. Berkeley, CA: University of California Press.

Haggett, P. (1995) *The Geographer's Art*. Oxford: Blackwell.

Hartshorne, R. (1959) *Perspective on the Nature of Geography*. Chicago, IL: Rand McNally.

Hutton, J. (2007, originally published 1788) *Theory of the Earth*. Sioux Falls, SD: NuVisionPublications.

Huxley, T. (1877) *Physiography: An introduction to the study of nature*. London: Macmillan.

Lucas, C. (2009) *Global literacy: geography for the 21st century*. Available at: www.education.com/magazine/article/Global_Literacy (last accessed 12/01/2015).

Mackinder, H.J. (1996, originally published 1887) 'On the scope and methods of geography' in Agnew, J., Livingstone, D. and Rogers, A. (eds) *Human Geography: An essential anthology*. Oxford: Blackwell, pp. 155–72.

Ploszajska, T. (1999) *Geographical Education, Empire and Citizenship: Geographical teaching and learning in English schools, 1870–1944*. London: Historical Geography Research Group.

Stoddart, D. (1986) *On Geography and its History*. Oxford: Blackwell.

Recommended key readings

Glacken, C. (1976) *Traces on the Rhodian Shore: Nature and culture in western thought from ancient times to the end of the eighteenth century*. Berkeley, CA: University of California Press.
In this geographical and historical classic, Glacken gives us an ambitious, and sweeping, survey of the development of Western civilisation's determination to find order in a chaotic world.

Matthews, J. and Herbert, D. (eds) (2004) *Unifying Geography: Common heritage, shared future*. London: Routledge.
An enjoyable survey of the geographical imagination, this edited collection offers excellent essays on the importance of fieldwork and the connections between the branches of the discipline.

Thinking geographically

Chapter 2

David Lambert is Professor of Geography Education at University College London Institute of Education

Introduction

Curriculum authorities frequently place a lot of emphasis on developing young people's capacity to 'think geographically'. However, there are enormous divergences in what is meant by this phrase, why it matters and how to promote it. This chapter opens up a discussion guided by these questions in a way that will be useful and productive to teachers of geography. It borrows heavily from the Geographical Association's (GA's) innovative and influential work on thinking geographically as a means of orienting and underpinning localised geographical curriculum making in schools. Much of this work was accomplished in the context of the 2014 National Curriculum revision in England (and revisions of GCSE and A level examinations) that anticipated a 'knowledge turn' in curriculum thinking in England (Lambert, 2011a).

Renewed emphasis on knowledge is overdue. We may have been careless, collectively, about what we teach in geography, as if the content of geography lessons was not all that important. Ofsted has made this point (Ofsted, 2011) but so has Margaret Roberts who, drawing on a career-long perspective of scholarship and practical experience, has observed the disappearance of geographical knowledge from geography lessons (Roberts, 2013). Bill Marsden warned about this possibility nearly 20 years ago (Marsden, 1997), arguing that political, social and pedagogic influences can lead us inadvertently to 'taking the geography out of geography education'. A refocus on geographical knowledge does not require us to throw out adventurous and active pedagogies, or turn back to the futility of rote learning. To focus on thinking geographically is one way to embrace the value of geographical knowledge in the school curriculum partly because it evokes active intellectual effort. It also implies a distinctive kind of thought – geographical thought – that presumably is less available to those who lack geographical knowledge (and understanding).

Why 'thinking geographically'?

Thinking geographically is not 'everyday thinking'. If we thought these were the same, there would be little point in having geography lessons, or specialist geography teachers who are grounded in – and indeed part of – the discipline of geography. Neither are schools everyday places: they introduce students to the world as an 'object of thought' rather than as a 'place of experience' (Young, 2008; Young and Muller, 2010; Young et al., 2014). Subjects help organise this thinking by relating concepts systematically. For example, when students learn about 'the city' as an object of thought they are taken beyond the realm of their experience by learning about form and function, or about economic and social processes. They are therefore introduced to 'theoretical' concepts that are systematically related to each other and which require different thought processes from those of everyday learning: they enable us to make links, comparisons and generalisations. Sometimes we use models to help frame such thinking, and when used effectively – with an emphasis on the processes they were designed to illustrate rather than the model as a 'fact' to be learned – they can be helpful thinking devices. Used badly, taught as 'facts' or as if they somehow represent 'reality', they can be arid, confusing and almost useless.

To introduce the world to students as an object of geographical thought requires pedagogic ingenuity, for subject knowledge may otherwise remain unconnected and 'inert'. This gets to the heart of both the value of subject-specialist

As teachers, we induct students into making sense of the world through geographical thinking. **Photo** © Bryan Ledgard.

teaching and the intellectual and practical challenges that face teachers every day. To have an overall sense of professional identity as a geography teacher certainly helps us meet such challenges. This identity is provided in part, but crucially, by a clear framework of organising concepts that offer an enduring vision of what lies at the conceptual 'heart' of the subject. It provides the subject resource and the conceptual map teachers require in order to induct students into making sense of the world through geographical thinking. It is helpful to be able to express such a framework in a manner that is relatively straightforward to grasp – by parents at parents' evenings; by head teachers allocating subject time and/or making judgements about the merits of fieldwork (see Lambert and Reiss, 2014); and by students, not least at options time.

Inevitably, by dint of its specialist orientation, we cannot avoid the use of some technical and precise terminology. However, there are ways to help us do this. For example, if we were to imagine learning to think geographically to be a bit like learning a language, then we need both geographical vocabulary and grammar. In 2011, I argued that the subject's 'core knowledge' can be thought of as geography's vocabulary – the extensive, factual basis of the 'world subject' (Lambert, 2011a). If core knowledge is geography's vocabulary, geography's conceptual framework forms its grammar.

Core geographical knowledge under this remit was said to be typically the information presented between the covers of any school atlas. This aspect of geographical knowledge is in itself fascinating to many, but as a gazetteer, has limited educational value. As the GA (2012) stated at the time:

> *'We need facts in order to think, but we also need concepts to enable us to group bits of information, or facts, together. Simply absorbing lists of geography's vocabulary does not amount to much more than a dramatic feat of memory: impressive, but is not in itself a sign of the intellectual development that we could regard as geographical thinking. For this, we are looking for a form of conceptual knowledge development which links facts together through geographic thought'.*

Thus, thinking geographically is a really important and useful means of capturing the significance of what we do in geography classrooms. However, if we want this idea to gain traction and to carry sufficient weight to be convincing then we need to think even harder as to what it really means.

In what ways do geographers 'read' landscapes differently from other specialists?
Photo © Jeremy Buckingham, reproduced under Creative Commons licence (CC BY 2.0).

What do we mean by 'thinking geographically'?

As already discussed, there are strong reasons for expressing the idea in a clear and communicable way. But there are also strong reasons to avoid offering a definition that is so bland as to be useless, so tight as to be restricting, or so 'of the moment' (or idiosyncratic) as to have limited shelf-life. This section, therefore, is in three parts: after some ground clearing, it takes some steps towards making a response to the question through the Geographical Association's 2009 'manifesto' *A Different View* and then presents almost *verbatim* the GA's 2012 framework on how to think geographically.

Clearing the ground

John Morgan (2013) stressed that it was impossible to write a 'once and for all' definition of geography – and therefore, of what it means to think geographically. His main point was that geography as an idea and as a system of thought is not timeless. It is rather, like all subject disciplines, a social construct, 'refracted' through its particular socio-political context. Thus, he concluded that although:

'there is something coherent about the idea of geography, [we need to be] cautious about rushing to "define" the subject once and for all, or even its "core" of essential knowledge, concepts and skills. More productive is the need for continued thought and reflection on the aims and purposes of teaching geography in schools' (Morgan, 2013, p. 281).

Hence, we still have to say what 'thinking geographically' means, even if we remain cautious and open to revision. Morgan offers a number of alternatives, showing through a series of examples how different accounts of – and disputes about – geography have emerged. These do not necessarily run sequentially through time but often occur concurrently:

Geographical knowledge

- Can geography portray the objective 'real world' (a singular geography)?
- To what extent is geographical knowledge 'socially constructed' (multiple geographies)?
- What is geographical knowledge for (to what uses can it be put)?

Geography as a way of seeing

- To what extent is geography (after Mackinder, 1890) a 'trained capacity' for thought (rather than an assemblage of information)?
- In what ways do geographers 'read' landscapes differently from other specialists, such as biologists or artists?
- In what manner do geographical ways of seeing contribute to our potential to 'live sanely' in the world (to paraphrase Fairgrieve, 1926)?

Geography as an integrated approach

- To what degree is geography an attitude of mind to keep things connected – not least, between classroom learning and the real world outdoors?
- What is the significance of geography's refusal to separate the physical and the human (and what are the consequences if it fails)?
- How successfully does geography provide a 'bridge' between the humanities and the sciences?

Geography as a fundamental (modern) idea

- To what extent is the ancient need (after Bonnett, 2008) to 'explain the world and its people' a question, ultimately, of human survival?
- How do the questions geography asks change as contexts change, for instance through developments in communication technologies?
- If geography really is a 'fundamental' idea, can it really be 'owned' solely by academics and be seen only as an academic discipline?

Geography through the everyday

- What status should be afforded to geography in the popular imagination (including that which inhabits quiz shows)?
- To what extent do the popular geographies provided through travel guides, novels and films undermine or strengthen geography?
- What attention should we pay to students' everyday lived experiences as a source of geographical knowledge (and/or meaning making)?

Although it is not meant to suggest a sequential development in a particular direction, the list nevertheless does present a broad transitional sweep from specialist 'knowledge' towards the looser conceptual frame of the 'everyday', finishing with a commitment to take seriously 'the popular wisdom of everyday life' (Jackson, quoted in Morgan, 2013, p. 280). This position accepts that 'children have valid ideas and interpretations, and that academic geographers (and by extension teachers) do not have a "uniquely critical insight" into… cultural texts' (Morgan, 2013, p. 280).

Morgan shows that most of the elements in the list above can be associated with formal geographical thought. It was Halford Mackinder (1890) who introduced the idea of geography as a 'trained capacity' for thought. It was also his generation of geographers who encouraged us to see the world from the British point of view – including the story of Empire. Adjusting this lens somewhat, James Fairgrieve (1926) urged us to think of geography as a means for greater international understanding. The long-standing integrated approach to geographical knowledge is appealing to the present day (sometimes, as with Rawding (2014), referred to as 'holistic' thinking). Matthews and Herbert (2008) have developed a modern integrated approach, but rather differently from Alastair Bonnett's (2008) arguably more inclusive response to the question 'What is geography?'. Bonnett points to the benefits of responding to the question in a multi-perspective manner – requiring us to think of geographies in the plural rather than a singular discipline in content or approach. Included in this of course is the notion of 'everyday geographies', which we can trace to the interventions of highly influential contemporary UK geographers such as Peter Jackson and the late Doreen Massey who have also outlined their understanding of the notion of 'thinking geographically' (see Jackson, 2006; Massey, 2006). The latter in particular has been consistent in encouraging geographers to 'take on the world' (Massey, 2014), promoting 'a sense of the global' – that is, of the planet as a whole, the globe as a place in which divisions and boundaries are understood to be more porous and flexible than previously thought. Not all agree with this of course, and Alex

Figure 1:
Cover of *A Different View: A manifesto from the Geographical Association*
Source: GA, 2009.

Geography holds together ideas such as place and space.
Image © NASA.

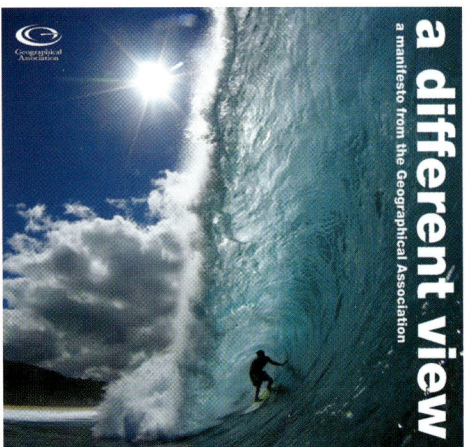

Standish (2012), for example, is keen to warn us of the 'false promise' of global learning. Right or wrong, arguments as fundamental as this are important as they show the very purpose of disciplinary communities.

The development of the discipline of geography as portrayed by the highly compressed account above is but one version of events. Tim Cresswell (2013), has recently provided a different and very much more detailed history of geographic thought, drawing on the various paradigm shifts that have occurred in geography. Though different, such versions of events are not necessarily inconsistent. It is enough for us to understand and concede that geography is not a discipline with hard edges and generally agreed procedures or even purposes. We might say the discipline is dynamic, or simply unruly. Basil Bernstein, the influential education theorist, would say geography is a subject that lacks the 'verticality' of subjects like physics, and that it is weakly 'framed' (Bernstein, 1999). This diagnosis is hard to deny: and why would anyone even try to? Geography's 'horizontality' is in many ways its signature and its appeal.

What do we conclude from this? Do we conclude that geography is so complicated that it does not lend itself to a single (and fixed) definition? And that to try to produce one would be at best a waste of time – or worse, needlessly restrictive? To be fair, when it comes to saying what is meant by 'thinking geographically', Morgan argues that simply to resort to that well-worn adage that 'geography is what geographers do' is also 'a deeply unhelpful response and an avoidance rather than an answer' to the question (Morgan, 2013, p. 273). So, can we come to an answer worth sharing?

Coming to an answer

In 2009, the GA published a 'manifesto' (Figure 1). It can be explored in full on the GA website. In sum, it was an attempt by the GA to make a strong and perhaps provocative statement about geography, expressed as a 'subject resource', and an approach to education articulated partly through Richard Peters' (1963) concept of 'initiation' using his well-known position that to be educated is not so much to arrive at a destination, but to 'travel with a different view' (Slater, 1992).

A fundamental component of the manifesto was 'curriculum making'. This explicitly recognised the role of specialist teachers in creating a 'curriculum of engagement' (Young *et al.*, 2014) based on developing the capacity to think geographically. In short, pedagogic competence and a respect for children's experiences and prior knowledge, though important, are not enough in themselves. In addition, teachers need to draw from and interpret the selections of geographical knowledge in the curriculum. Crucially, it did not advocate turning the clock back to inert and 'given' earlier versions of geographical knowledge – the Gradgrind lists and definitions that have become the very shorthand of 'boring school'.

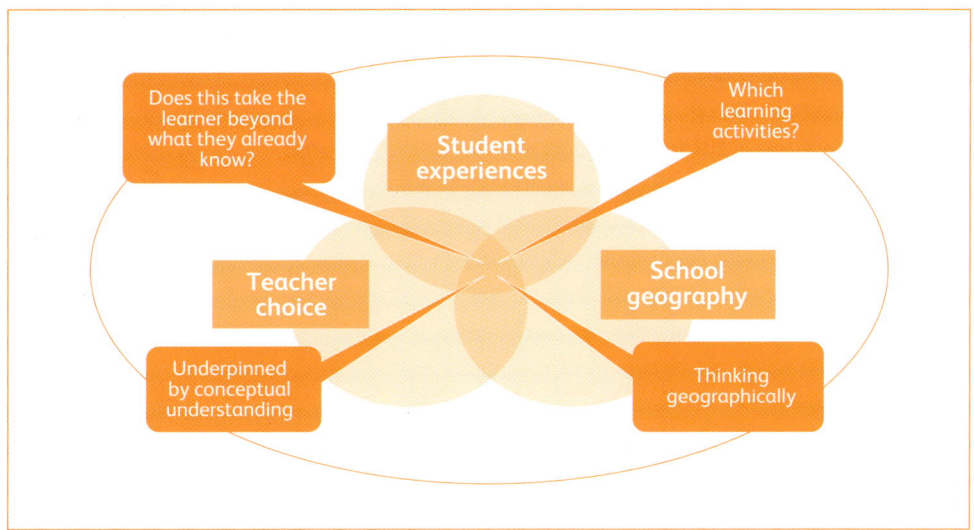

Figure 2:
Curriculum making.
Source: GA, 2016.

Figure 2 attempts to illustrate curriculum making. The diagram is readily interpreted in terms of its self-evident invitation to work towards 'balance' in the midst of the competing priorities – to serve student needs, to demonstrate practical classroom knowledge and skill, and to impart knowledge. Of course, these categories are rarely as distinct from each other in practice as this model implies. However, teaching that is too focused in any one of these domains risks being inadequate:

- Too child-centred, and the teaching runs the risk of failing to move children beyond their pre-existing everyday knowledge.
- Too subject-centred, and the risk is we fail to enable all students to access specialised subject knowledge; we are not sensitive enough to the importance of connecting with children's pre-existing knowledge.
- Too teacher-centred, and the risk is that lessons become defined solely by aspects of the teacher's 'performance'.

In this sense the model describes the practical act of curriculum making in terms of merging – and applying appropriate balance to – the conceptually distinct categories of curriculum and pedagogy (that is, the 'what' and the 'how' of teaching). What is important to the present discussion, however, is that the broad outcome of successfully making the geography curriculum was expressed in the GA's manifesto as the growing capacity of students to think geographically. This was referenced almost exclusively to Peter Jackson's (2006) article, which discussed the idea mainly in terms of the importance in geography of 'relational thinking': holding together pairs of ideas such as place and space, local and global, people and environment, and physical and human.

In a separate but clearly connected line of work I published a tentative article (Lambert, 2011a) that discussed the possible 'reframing' of school geography using a capabilities approach (see also Solem *et al.*, 2013; Lambert *et al.*, 2015). This was a further attempt to pin down thinking geographically as an educational outcome. In asking how school geography may contribute to the growth of children's and young people's capabilities I suggested a three-part framework:

- the acquisition and development of deep descriptive and explanatory 'world knowledge'; we can think of this as geography's core knowledge, its 'vocabulary'
- the development of the relational thinking that underpins geographical thought; we can think of this as geography's conceptual subject identity, its 'grammar'
- a propensity to ask questions, explore and apply analysis to alternative social, economic and environmental futures in particular place contexts; we can think of this as 'geographical enquiry'

(adapted from Lambert 2011a; 2011b).

This formulation is readily communicable to parents, colleagues and students. It provides a sophisticated but clear view as to what thinking geographically entails. It would be interesting to use this as a device for evaluating teaching units – for both content and pedagogy. However, it clearly needs some further work – the relational thinking that underpins geographical thought is in need of some unpacking, but Jackson (2006) offers a good start.

A conceptual framework for relational thinking in geography

The GA's support for school geography has been sustained and consistent for over a century. As curriculum thinking always has to be underpinned by a sense of the goals or purposes of teaching geography, it is inevitable that the GA has invested considerable energy in clarifying the organising concepts of geography as it applies to the school curriculum. The following section rests heavily on this effort.

A few large organising concepts underlie a geographical way of investigating and understanding the world. These are high-level ideas that can be applied across the subject to identify a question, guide an investigation, organise information, suggest an explanation or assist decision making.

An enduring suite of main organising concepts of geography is place, space and environment. Of course, beneath this level of 'big ideas' there is a multitude of substantive concepts – e.g. from river basin to glacial ice; from city to rural fringe; from production to consumption – but by using the big ideas carefully and accurately we have a means of identifying what it means to think geographically about the substantive material.

So, what is meant by these three 'big' organising concepts? How do these link to a definition of geographical thinking?

Place (the importance of context)

A place is a specific part of Earth's surface that people have named and given meaning to (although these meanings may differ between people). Places range in size from the home and locality to a major world region; as we have seen, Doreen Massey even urged us to see the planet as a place. Places are usually interconnected with other places, often in complex ways. Places are unique, but do not have to be studied as if they were singular, for in seeking understanding geographers often study general processes and look for similarities as well as differences in how these are played out in particular place contexts. In studying place in school we can:

- progress from describing the characteristics of places to explaining them. These characteristics include population, climate, economy, landforms, built environment, soils and vegetation, communities, water resources, cultures, minerals, landscape, and recreational and scenic quality. Some are tangible, such as rivers and buildings, while others are less so, such as wilderness and socio-economic status
- explore people's aesthetic, emotional, cultural and spiritual connections with places; the role of places in their feelings of identity, sense of place and belonging; and the ways they experience and use places
- recognise that places may be altered and remade by people, and that changes promoted by one group may be contested by others. The values and beliefs of people and groups are variables that contribute to our understanding of why change in places is often controversial
- use the uniqueness of places to explain why the outcomes of universal environmental and human processes may vary, and why similar problems may require different strategies in different places.

Space (the importance of the spatial dimension)

Space in geography is the three-dimensional surface of Earth. While historians study change over time, geographical study emphasises differences across space. This is of particular importance in understanding the rich diversity of environments, peoples, cultures and economies that exist together. In geography we develop a deeper understanding of space (the 'spatial') by:

- investigating the spatial distribution of phenomena and explaining them, often by looking for a spatial association between several distributions

- learning how to evaluate the environmental, economic, social and political consequences of particular spatial distributions
- studying the influence of absolute and relative location on the characteristics of places and on people's lives
- recognising that improvements in transport and communication systems have greatly reduced the time taken to send goods, capital and information between places, which has increased the speed at which economic and cultural impacts spread around the world
- investigating the ways that space is structured, organised and managed for different purposes
- recognising that people perceive and use space differently, and may feel accepted and safe in some places and unwelcome or unsafe in others
- understanding the role of values and beliefs in influencing decision making about how space may be used in the future
- exploring the ways space is represented, such as by maps, art, literature, films, songs, stories and dance, and the influences of these representations on people's perceptions.

Environment (the importance of the processes that make our surroundings)

The term environment refers to our living and non-living surroundings. The features of the environment can be classified as natural, managed, or constructed (the built environment). However, we also recognise that these categories are fuzzy: there is much interaction and cross-over. The concept of environment provides a powerful way of understanding, explaining and thinking about the world. In geography we do this by:

- recognising the environment as an ecosystem – with environmental benefits, such as genetic diversity, nutrient cycling, water and energy stores
- investigating the structure and functioning of environments as systems: of weather, climate, hydrology, geomorphology, biogeography and soils
- examining the ways that people use, alter and manage environments (intentionally and unintentionally)
- exploring different world views about the relationship between people and the environment, and applying ideas such as stewardship and sustainability in their studies of the environment
- recognising that studies of environmental change have an ethical dimension, succinctly captured by the question: who gets what, where and why (and why care)?
- investigating the effects of the environment on people and places through the opportunities and challenges it presents for economic development and human settlement
- reflecting on the extent to which the environment contributes to people's sense of identity.

The lists above provide an account of the broad organising concepts of geography. They are not to be 'read off' as a syllabus: they are a device to underpin thinking about what a teaching programme looks like when it is directed by broad subject-based aims or goals. When we operate with a clear sense of geography's big ideas we are more able to demonstrate the value of the discipline. Rather than a curriculum of compliance, which compels us to 'cover the content', what is needed is a curriculum of engagement, where we can move children and young people, step by step, into a world of ideas: this is what the GA implied by calling its manifesto *A Different View*. It is very close to what Michael Young has called a Future 3 curriculum (Young *et al*., 2014). In a Future 3 curriculum, subjects are not 'given' and static (as in Future 1), but neither are they arbitrary and dispensable, as in the skills-oriented Future 2 curriculum that has often replaced the traditional notion of a knowledge-led curriculum. Instead, a knowledge-led Future 3 curriculum introduces students to 'the epistemic rules of specialist communities' to provide ways to understand the world objectively, and take students beyond their everyday experience (see also Young and Muller, 2010). It seeks to induct students into the idea of better knowledge (not 'anything goes') and the arguments, procedures and processes that help us discern and decide what this is.

Although places are unique they are connected to other places.
Photo © Tim Peel.

Final thoughts

Peter Jackson (2006) writes that 'thinking geographically offers a uniquely powerful way of seeing the world and making connections between scales, from the local to the global' (p. 119). If we accept place, space and environment as the irreducible 'heart' of school geography it is possible, desirable even, to build a structure such as Jackson's that captures, perhaps even more concisely, the relational thinking that characterises distinctively geographical perspectives. Jackson's list, slightly adapted, is as follows:

- Space and place: This reminds us that although places are unique they are not isolated but connected to other places. The flows between places and through places are important.
- Scale and connection: This is the 'zoom lens' attribute of geography that shows how decisions and events at a local level can have global consequences, and global processes can have differential effects locally.
- Proximity and distance: This means not just physical distance as expressed in kilometres, but perceptions of distance as well. Geographers have had to adopt more flexible understandings of distance, especially in the electronic age.
- People and environment: This stresses the propensity geographers have to link the physical and human world; to keep the world 'whole'. Geography, through its abiding interest in difference and diversity, tells us how challenging this is, but at the same time how important it is to try.

Former President of the American Association of Geographers (AAG) Susan Hanson (2004) also makes a strong claim about the distinctive benefits of thinking geographically, referring to what she calls the 'geographic advantage', communicating 'the truth that geographers have something to offer that others do not'. Geographers consider, she argues:

- relationships between people and the environment
- the importance of spatial variability (the place-dependence of processes)
- processes operating at multiple and interlocking geographic scales
- the integration of spatial and temporal analysis (Hanson, 2004, p. 720).

Although Hanson's list is slightly different, it does not take much to get the main point about the relational thinking that perhaps lies at the heart of thinking geographically. The argument in this chapter is that developing young people's capacity to think geographically serves as a broad educational goal for teachers. And for teachers this goal is their means to make sense of content-heavy National Curriculum lists and examination specifications.

References

Bernstein, B. (1999) 'Vertical and horizontal discourse: an essay', *British Journal of Sociology of Education*, 20, 2, pp.157–73.

Bonnett, A. (2008) *What is Geography?* London: Sage.

Cresswell, T. (2013) *Geographical Thought: A critical introduction*. Oxford: Wiley-Blackwell.

Fairgrieve, J. (1926) *Geography in School*. London: University of London Press.

GA (2016) *Curriculum making*. Available at: www.geography.org.uk/cpdevents/curriculum/curriculummaking (last accessed 02/11/2016).

GA (2009) *A Different View: A manifesto from the Geographical Association*. Available at: www.geography.org.uk/resources/adifferentview (last accessed 02/11/2016).

GA (2012) *Thinking Geographically*. Available at: www.geography.org.uk/news/2014nationalcurriculum/introducingnc (last accessed 02/11/2016).

Hanson, S. (2004) 'Who are "we"? An important question for geography's future', *Annals of the Association of American Geographers*, 94, 4, pp. 715–22.

Jackson, P. (2006) 'Thinking geographically', *Geography*, 91, 3, pp. 199–204.

Lambert, D. (2011a) 'Reframing school geography: a capability approach' in Butt, G. (ed) *Geography, Education and the Future*. London: Continuum, pp. 127–40.

Lambert, D. (2011b) 'Reviewing the case for geography, and the "knowledge turn" in the English National Curriculum', *The Curriculum Journal*, 22, 2, pp. 243–64.

Lambert, D. and Reiss, M. (2014) *The Place of Fieldwork in Geography and Science Qualifications*. London: University College London Institute of Education.

Lambert, D., Solem, M. and Tani, S. (2015) 'Achieving human potential through geography education: a capabilities approach to curriculum making in schools', *Annals of the Association of American Geographers*, 105, 4, pp. 723–35.

Mackinder, H. (1890) 'On the necessity of thorough teaching in general geography as a preliminary to the teaching of commercial geography', *Journal of the Manchester Geographical Society*, 6, 4, pp. 1–6.

Marsden, W.E. (1997) 'On taking the geography out of geographical education: some historical pointers', *Geography*, 82, 3, pp. 241–52.

Massey, D. (2006) 'The geographical mind' in Balderstone, D. (ed) *Secondary Geography Handbook*. Sheffield: Geographical Association, pp. 46–51.

Massey, D. (2014) 'Taking on the world', *Geography*, 99, 1, pp. 36–39.

Matthews, H. and Herbert, D. (2008) *Geography: A very short introduction*. Cambridge: Cambridge University Press.

Morgan, J. (2013) 'What do we mean by thinking geographically?' in Lambert, D. and Jones, M. (eds) *Debates in Geography Education*. Abingdon: Routledge, pp. 273–81.

Ofsted (2011) *Geography: Learning to make a world of difference*. Available at: www.gov.uk/government/publications/geography-learning-to-make-a-world-of-difference (last accessed 02/11/2016).

Peters, R.S. (1963) 'Education As Initiation'. Inaugural lecture delivered at the University of London Institute of Education, 9 December.

Rawding, C. (2014) 'The importance of teaching "holistic" geographies', *Teaching Geography*, 39, 1, pp. 10–14.

Roberts, M. (2013) *Geography Through Enquiry: Approaches to teaching and learning in the secondary school*. Sheffield: Geographical Association.

Slater, F.A. (1992) '…to travel with a different view' in Naish, M. (ed) *Geography and Education: National and International Perspectives*. London: Institute of Education, pp. 97–113.

Solem, M., Lambert, D. and Tani, S. (2013) 'Geocapabilities: toward an international framework for researching the purposes and values of geography education', *Review of International Geographical Education*, 3, 3, pp. 214–29.

Standish, A. (2012) *The False Promise of Global Learning: Why education needs boundaries*. London: Continuum.

Young, M. (2008) *Bringing Knowledge Back In: From social constructivism to social realism in the sociology of education*. London: Routledge.

Young, M. and Muller, J. (2010) 'Three educational scenarios for the future: lessons from the sociology of knowledge', *European Journal of Education*, 45, 1, pp. 11–27.

Young, M., Lambert, D., Roberts, C. and Roberts, M. (2014) *Knowledge and the Future School: Curriculum and social justice*. London: Bloomsbury.

Recommended key readings

Cresswell, T. (2013) *Geographical Thought: A critical introduction*. Oxford: Wiley-Blackwell.
Geography is a notoriously ill-disciplined discipline, in that it can be perplexing to find the common thread between all that is carried out in the name of geography in universities and beyond (including the contents of the National Geographic Channel for example!). This book does a very good job indeed in giving geographic thought a sense of overall shape and direction. Strictly speaking the book is not about the act of thinking geographically, but about the value of engaging with geographical ideas. A particular strength is the historical dimension Cresswell provides and the sense of a discipline of rich and contested theoretical perspectives.

Morgan, J. (2013) 'What do we mean by thinking *geographically?*' in Lambert, D. and Jones, M. (eds) *Debates in Geography Education*. Abingdon: Routledge, pp. 273–81.
John Morgan's interest is closer to the act of thinking in a geographical manner – and in this short but helpful chapter cautions us against trying to define this too closely. Historical perspective is a great strength of this chapter too, as Morgan illustrates how thinking geographically has changed over a period of 130 years – roughly its lifespan as a university discipline in English universities.

Chapter 3

What do we mean by curriculum?

Mary Biddulph is a Lecturer in Geography Education at University of Nottingham

'It seems that the desire and need for knowledge of the world is a basic human attribute… We are all, more or less, plugged into our planet. Its availability and accessibility have created a mass cosmopolitanism. Our wired-up, footloose, travel-bugged world is a stage to expanding and mutating forms of global geographical awareness' (Bonnett, 2008, p. 5).

Bonnett's quote reveals much about the complex world we inhabit. It reminds us that we are all, in known and unknown ways, connected to each other, interacting at a range of scales, and to greater or lesser degrees, with the demands of rapid globalisation and 'mass cosmopolitanism'. Making sense of this 'wired-up, footloose, travel-bugged world' is challenging; navigating the minefield of contradictions, ambiguities and inconsistencies leaves many of us dazed and confused, struggling to find ways to locate ourselves in the world. However, it often seems that young people cope very well with the wired-up, footloose, travel-bugged bit of being in the world; that they seem to adapt effortlessly to the expanding and mutating forms of global geographical awareness, generally enabled by the unique combination of social media and technological change. However, while many may appear to pass through this world of complexities and contradictions without much trouble, making sense of it is a different matter. Helping young people to develop their knowledge and understanding of the world, supporting their capacities to engage with it, and enabling them to appreciate the implications of their own actions and those of others on the planet, is the stuff of school geography. In this chapter I will discuss the ways in which different constructions of two of education's big ideas, 'curriculum' and 'geography' can contribute to the process of making sense of the world.

It is important to state at the outset that this chapter is not about telling you what the curriculum 'should' look like, or suggesting curriculum plans to meet statutory requirements. It is a problem-posing chapter, in so far as the discussion that follows is designed to raise questions in your mind about the kind of geography curriculum you teach to your students, and why. This critical thinking about the geography curriculum is important: the curriculum is far more than lists of content, tables of teaching strategies and folders of schemes of work stored in 'the cloud' or on the school's shared drive. The school curriculum reveals much about what a society feels is the purpose of education. Is the aim of a national education system simply to train the current and future workforce and ensure national economic stability? Or should it serve another, and quite different, purpose? If we wish to preserve the democratic tradition in a liberal and open society, then what might a school's curriculum comprise? Many commentators argue that these questions place enormous moral responsibility on the shoulders of teachers (Lambert and Morgan, 2010; Pring, 2012; Biddulph, 2013). They require teachers to examine their own educational values and consider what they believe is important in teaching – in our case, teaching geography. This raises the curriculum stakes significantly.

As you read this chapter, the following questions are worth considering:

- What is a curriculum?
- What are the forces that impact on the curriculum?
- What is the role of teachers in making the curriculum?
- What is the role of geography in making the curriculum?

What do we mean by curriculum?

In its simplest form, curriculum refers to what we teach students in schools. A curriculum can be defined in a number of ways, but in essence it is the sum total of students' learning experiences: assessed and non-assessed elements, inside and outside the classroom (Rawling, 2007; Kelly, 2009; Oates, 2011). These authors also agree with the government (DfE, 2010) that there is a difference between the prescribed curriculum (whether the National Curriculum or examination specifications) and the learned curriculum and that the former is only a part of the curriculum picture (DfE, 2013).

Looking more closely at the elements that make up a curriculum, Kelly (2009) identifies the curriculum as five distinct but interrelated categories: the National Curriculum/national subject criteria; the planned curriculum; the received curriculum; the informal curriculum; and the hidden curriculum (see Figure 1).

These headings are helpful reminders that 'curriculum' is a complex concept, characterised by discrete and overlapping aspects, each of which is significant in shaping how the geography curriculum functions in individual schools. In your own context you might like to consider the relationship between these different aspects of the curriculum – for example, how does the hidden curriculum shape/inform what you teach? What provision is there in your school for an informal geography curriculum? What is the relationship between the planned and the received curriculum in your school? How could you find out about such a relationship? These explorations (and there are many more you could pursue) are a good opportunity to critique our own geography curriculum: they oblige us to consider and reconsider the subtle interplay between different aspects of the curriculum, revealing the influences that underpin the geography we teach.

The following section begins to explore one aspect of the curriculum relationship considered in Figure 1, which is the relationship between the prescribed and the planned curriculum. The intention is to provide a context against which other curriculum relationships can be explored.

National prescription – the big picture

The historical relationship between national education initiatives, political ideology and the geography curriculum is mapped in detail by Eleanor Rawling (2001) in her definitive text, *Changing the Subject: The impact of national policy on school geography, 1980–2000*. The book tells an interesting story of the consequences for the geography curriculum of political influence on the national educational system. It is not the intention here to re-tell the story in any detail, but more to consider the interplay between changing societal conditions and political ideologies and what this means for the current state of the school geography curriculum in England.

In the 1970s academic geography was turning towards more conceptual ways of thinking, and these fed into schools via three inspiring Schools Council projects: Geography for the Young School Leaver 14–16, Geography 14–18 (the Bristol Project) and the Geography 16–19 project. Through projects such as these (and there were others) teachers' curriculum roles shifted significantly, and a new era of teacher professionalism began. No longer simply 'curriculum deliverers' and 'transmitters of knowledge', teachers found themselves central to the curriculum-making process. The Schools Council projects, through the examination boards, provided a subject framework for planning, and teachers were free to develop their own geography curriculum, tailoring the geography they planned to teach to the needs and interests of their students.

The passing of the Education Reform Act in 1988 marked the start of a long period of centralised control over education and diminished curriculum freedoms for teachers and educators (Kelly, 2009). The first National Curriculum was virtually aims-free, so it was not at all clear what it was actually trying to achieve in terms of broader educational goals. Its overall structure was criticised for comprising the same subjects as those listed in the 1944 Education Act (see White, 2003) and the first geography National Curriculum (DES, 1991) was denounced for being too content-heavy (183 statements of attainment) and overly prescriptive. Any reference to 'attitudes and

Curriculum aspect	Description	Geography example
National Curriculum/ national subject criteria – the prescribed curriculum	Content as specified by associated bodies such as Ofqual and authorised by central government.	Geography National Curriculum (e.g. QCA, 2007; DfE, 2013). Geography GCSE, AS and A level subject content (DfE, 2014a, 2014b).
Planned curriculum	Departmental longer-term frameworks for the curriculum, medium-term schemes of work, team/ individual teachers' lesson plans. Fieldwork – residential and non-residential.	Whole school framework for a school's geography curriculum demonstrating how learning will progress over time. Schemes of work for different age groups, also capturing how geographical learning will progress. Teachers' individual plans detailing geographical teaching and learning in individual lessons – the planned curriculum becomes the taught curriculum.
Received curriculum	Students' learning as evidenced through classroom dialogue, students' work such as written work, display work, presentation work etc.	Over time students 'reveal' their geographical understanding through the range of learning opportunities a school/department provides. There can be a mismatch between the planned/ taught curriculum and the received curriculum
Informal curriculum	Activities that take place outside the formal curriculum such as clubs and societies, school visits (residential and non-residential).	Clubs and societies such as a geography club or an environment club. Residential and non-residential visits where unintended geographical learning may take place, e.g. through language exchange visits. Informal learning as an aspect of formally planned fieldwork.
Hidden curriculum	Learning that occurs as a by-product of the way a school/curriculum/individual classroom is organised and operates, e.g. the school timetable. organisation of teaching groups (streamed, setted, mixed-ability), curriculum priorities. Also social/peer networks, cultural understanding and social inclusion/exclusion.	How is geography taught and what kinds of geographies are taught to different groups of students? What is the status of geography within the whole school curriculum – where is it situated within subject priorities? How do students feel their own geographies are valued within the geography curriculum?

Figure 1: Five categories of the curriculum. **After:** Kelly, 2009.

values' was removed from the Order by the then Secretary of State for Education, Kenneth Clarke, his argument being that the National Curriculum should emphasise knowledge and understanding and 'place less emphasis on attitudes and values' (Clarke, 1991, cited in Rawling, 2001, p. 60). In the new curriculum teachers were positioned as custodians of objective knowledge and teaching was reframed as an act of induction, namely inducting young people into the recognised and understood social and cultural order of the day.

Since 1988 rapidly changing societal conditions, nationally and globally, have captured the political imagination. In a new discourse about global social inequalities, education has become the context for many agendas including poverty alleviation, national economic development and sustaining individual social and emotional well-being (Ball, 2008). When Tony Blair was elected prime minister in 1997, education was at the top of New Labour's policy agenda. The change in government heralded an about-turn in curriculum policy, away from the traditional subject-based curriculum of 1991, towards a curriculum emphasising basic skills and competencies. While geography remained a National Curriculum subject, the curriculum agenda was dominated by policy initiatives such as the National Strategies, Every Child Matters, personalised learning and work-related initiatives. While the New Labour curriculum had the veneer of a radical model for education, in reality it was intentionally more utilitarian; teachers were no longer just teachers of geography, history or whatever; they were now positioned as 'multi-professionals' taking on increasing responsibility for the social and emotional care as well as the education of young people.

A subsequent curriculum revision in 1999 (DfEE/QCA) placed greater emphasis on geographical enquiry (see Roberts, 2003) and content. The fourth version of the geography National Curriculum, published in 2007, was a radical departure from previous incarnations, comprising a framework of seven overarching geographical concepts with no prescribed content. Teachers were offered the tantalising prospect of once again taking responsibility for curriculum decision making. Planning a geography curriculum using this conceptual framework required teachers to 'think geographically' (Jackson, 2006; GA, 2009): in order to develop an interesting, relevant and challenging curriculum for students, teachers themselves had to draw on their own specialist disciplinary knowledge.

Such curriculum freedom was not without its problems. The 2007 curriculum was a clear invitation to the curriculum table, i.e. teachers could again exercise some professional judgement, at least over their key stage 3 curriculum. The reality was that while some schools seized the opportunity for curriculum renewal and change, relishing the opportunity to re-focus their curriculum on new geographies and developments in the discipline, others did not. What were the drivers behind this inconsistent picture? Both the 2008 and 2011 Ofsted reports (Ofsted, 2008, 2011) identified several contributory factors (see Figure 2). To what extent did/do these factors characterise geography in your school?

Over half the schools visited by Ofsted had reduced time for geography in key stage 3 over the previous years. In addition, poorly planned and taught integrated humanities units of work in year 7, often linked to general skills-based initiatives, had resulted in less geography being covered (Ofsted, 2011, p. 6).

In some schools this loss of teaching-time was accompanied by a rise in generic skills-based curricula, such as the RSA's Opening Minds competency-based curriculum or schools' own versions of 'learning to learn'. Couched in the language of functional skills development and thinking skills, these curricula resulted in what Biesta (2012) calls the 'learnification' of education. Teachers' curriculum roles changed again: the traditional caricature of 'teacher as knowledge transmitter' was substituted by a new caricature – teachers were still in 'delivery' mode, but now they were delivering 'three-part lessons', activity learning and 'starters and plenaries'. In this new utilitarianism teachers could be forgiven for thinking that 'what' students learned was less important than 'how' they learned; the focus on learning *per se* undermined the contribution of disciplinary thinking to young people's 'sense making'. Increasing accountability in schools (referred to by Hope (2010) as 'the surveillance curriculum'), and the importance attached to Ofsted inspections, GCSE and A level results and school league tables, reinforced this view. It seemed that the curriculum had become a battleground for competing, and often incompatible, educational agendas.

This messy picture of school geography explains the lack of curriculum renewal in some schools, especially at key stage 3. It may also explain the decline in the number of students studying geography at GCSE between 1996 and 2010 (Weeden, 2012) (see RGS-IBG (no date) for shifting trends in geography examination outcomes at GCSE and A level).

Following the election of a coalition government in 2010, the utilitarian curriculum of New Labour was replaced by yet another curriculum model. The new government's first White Paper, *The Importance of Teaching* (DfE, 2010), identified 'core' or 'essential knowledge' as being at the heart of curriculum reforms. While the White Paper made no attempt to define what core or essential knowledge meant, concern in the geography education community mounted that, yet again, the curriculum would comprise lists of content to be taught.

Issue identified	Reason
Lack of subject specialists teaching geography (especially at key stage 3).	Greater accountability for attainment at GCSE and A level meant that subject specialists prioritised teaching examination classes.
Sustained lack of subject-based professional development for many geography teachers.	CPD agenda dominated by 'other' educational agendas (e.g. Every Child Matters) at the expense of subject-focused professional development, leading to what Ofsted described as a curriculum of 'neglect' (2008, p. 23). The 2006–11 Action Plan for Geography and the awarding bodies became key subject-specific CPD providers.
Too rigid an adherence to the national strategies guidance (objectives-led teaching, three-part lessons).	Period of intense local authority support and pedagogical 'tool kits' to meet the expectations of the national strategies. Perceptions that the Ofsted inspection process required prescribed lesson formats led to formulaic lesson structures.
Too much attention on the *how* of teaching and learning and not enough consideration of the *what*. Teaching and learning, particularly in year 7, often linked to general skills-based initiatives.	Increased emphasis on 'learning to learn' and learning skills, framing how geography teachers approached subject teaching. Easing the transition between primary and secondary school led to a range of generic curriculum initiatives, at the expense of subjects such as geography and history.
Curriculum decisions at key stage 3 were driven by developments at key stage 4 and A level.	Key stage 3 seen as a 'seed-bed' for GCSE and possibly A level, leading to a certain degree of content repetition at each key stage.
Reduced time for geography in key stage 3.	The gradual reduction in time to teach geography, in favour of more generic curricula or in order to provide addition curriculum time for subjects such as English, maths and science.
Poorly planned and taught integrated units of work in the humanities.	Schools with a history of 'humanities' provision often retained a humanities structure at key stage 3, resulting in many non-specialists teaching geography.

Figure 2: The state of geography in secondary schools in England. **Sources:** Ofsted, 2008; 2011.

Teachers and other professionals and organisations such as the Geographical Association (GA) took the opportunity to engage in important debates about the contested nature of knowledge. Indeed, since 2010, the GA's journals *Geography* and *Teaching Geography* have dedicated considerable space to exploring what is meant by geographical knowledge and how teachers can develop the concept.

Following a period of consultation and much angst on the part of the geography education community, the final version, despite the prescribed detail, signalled creative opportunities for teachers' curriculum thinking. While the rationale for the inclusion of certain places and themes in the new curriculum is unclear (Russia and soils stand out), the Order does leave room for interpretation; there is scope for localised curriculum making (Brooks, 2006).

In concluding this section, while politics and ideology seem to be at times overpowering forces in the curriculum debate, and while the curriculum is undoubtedly, on one level, shaped by broader educational ideologies, it is teachers who breathe life into the prescribed curriculum, making geography accessible and interesting for students to learn; and it is teachers' willingness to critically engage with education's two big ideas – geography and curriculum – that will ultimately have significant influence over what and how we teach geography.

The school curriculum: planning, development and making

The discussion above illustrates the ways in which national politics and education interact with each other, with significant consequences for the geography curriculum. In this section we consider curriculum planning, curriculum development and curriculum making as distinct entities in the curriculum process. Understanding these distinctions is important if we are to effectively utilise such tools in bringing the curriculum to life.

Before we get into the details of how a school's curriculum is constructed there are some fundamental questions to consider:

- What are the aims of your school's geography curriculum?
- How do they relate to the prescribed aims of the curriculum and your school's overall aims?
- How do they present geography, as a discipline, to students?
- Why do you teach the geography you teach? Why is it important/significant/essential for students to learn the geography in your curriculum?

It is impossible to engage in any meaningful curriculum decision making until you attend to aims and rationale; without some sense of what you are trying to achieve educationally and why, your geography curriculum will lack purpose. The two big concepts at the start of this chapter – 'curriculum' and 'geography' – are crucial here. You have to 'think geographically' and ask questions not just about 'Why do students in my school need to learn about/are interested in', for example, volcanic activity on Etna, or European migration, but also 'Why are geographers interested in these issues, events and experiences?' The latter question is highly significant in articulating geography's distinctive contribution to the whole curriculum and rationalising with students why geography is an important discipline in making sense of the world.

Curriculum planning

Having considered your aims and rationale for school geography you next have to get to grips with the messy process of bringing the curriculum to life.

Curriculum planning is a technical, intellectual and moral process. Pragmatically you organise material (content, teaching approaches, resources) into a form that you feel will make sense to your students. You decide an appropriate teaching sequence that is progressive in terms of students' learning. You create year-by-year plans, termly plans and shorter, more manageable, units; all ensuring that students have opportunities to learn a range of different geographies at a range of different scales. By these means students develop important geographical skills and explore their own, and others', values and attitudes.

Making these planning decisions requires intellectual rigour and moral judgements about what to teach, when and why. Why teach about rivers instead of glaciation? Why 'map skills' in year 7? Why 'Brazil' in year 8? Even, why study these themes/areas of the world/issues at all? While there will be pragmatic reasons for some of your choices, ultimately you are also exercising intellectual and moral judgements too, and exercising such judgements cannot be a haphazard process. Kelly's (2009) work on the curriculum offers a useful benchmark for your thinking. He proposes the notion of an 'educational curriculum', arguing that education in a democratic society is founded on principles such as, among others, 'the pursuit of personal freedoms, independence of thought, social and political empowerment, acceptance of the freedom of others' (p. 8). A curriculum that embodies such principles is therefore, he argues, 'justifiable in educational terms' (p. 7).

What does this mean for school geography? It means your curriculum must be justifiable in educational terms, not just in relation to 'what goes into it', but in terms of how you frame it. Roberts (1997), Kelly (2009) and Smith (2000) all consider different models for curriculum 'planning'. These are not frameworks, grids or tables to complete; they are ideas, principles and value positions to debate. Each model has significant implications for the kind of curriculum you plan and the kind of geography you teach and each will be considered below.

The cultural transmission model

The cultural transmission model presents geographical knowledge as absolutist; a list of incontestable facts to be acquired along the educational route. Teachers are 'deliverers' of content and students are passive recipients of that content. As a curriculum for a democratic society, this model is deeply flawed. In presenting geographical knowledge as static it fails to take account of the changing nature of knowledge and associated developments in academic geography. A student's understanding of, for example, Russia (a country prescribed for study in the 2014 geography National Curriculum) is likely to be limited to simplistic locational information rather than including any sense of Russia's international trade patterns, the impact of climate change on North Siberian export opportunities, the environmental and sustainability issues surrounding the Sochi Winter Olympics, or, even more controversially, Russia's contested borders. The cultural transmission model may support the acquisition of general geographical knowledge, but as a theoretical perspective for shaping young people's geographical understanding, it fails to meet Kelly's principles for an educational curriculum.

The objectives-led model

This model presents geographical knowledge as tightly-prescribed and pre-determined. In the objectives-led model, curriculum planning is an entirely rational process where teachers 'select and use educational strategies designed to help learners acquire the behaviours prescribed by the curriculum' (Impolite Geography, 2010). Students are expected to demonstrate that they can meet the requirements of a specific objective, such as their capacity to use six-figure grid references in order to locate features on an Ordnance Survey map, and then the outcomes are 'measured' in order to judge 'success'. Clear learning objectives and outcomes can provide your school's curriculum with a sense of direction, i.e. we (teachers and students) know where we are going. However, such a model lacks flexibility and takes no account of students' existing knowledge. It also sets more store by the development of generic skills and competencies than learning geography, and positions teachers as deliverers not of content, but of measurable outcomes (Pring, 2012). The objectives-led curriculum model is very popular in schools, possibly because it is systematic in terms of curriculum design and hot on the measurement so beloved of senior managers, school data collectors and Ofsted (Smith, 2000). On the other hand, it is weak in terms of educational potential because it favours predictability of outcomes over developing students' understanding of substantial, complex geographical concepts – a much messier, unpredictable and therefore harder-to-'measure' process.

The process model

This model starts, before any detailed planning, with the educational principles that underpin teaching and learning. Jerome Bruner (cited in Roberts, 1997, 2003), an early proponent of the process model, identified seven key principles that he felt should underpin a process curriculum. These were:

- to initiate in students a process of question-posing (the enquiry method)
- to teach a research methodology where students can look for information to answer questions they have raised
- to help students develop the ability to use a variety of first-hand sources as evidence from which to develop hypotheses and draw conclusions
- to conduct classroom discussions in which students learn to listen to each other as well as express their own views
- to legitimise the search: that is, to give sanction and support to open-ended discussions where definitive answers to many questions are not found
- to encourage students to reflect on their own experiences
- to create a new role for the teacher, in which they become a resource rather than an authority

(adapted from Bruner, cited in Roberts, 2003, p. 23).

Geographical enquiry is something akin to the process model advocated by Bruner. Through geographical enquiry, geography is problematised rather than presented as facts, and students are encouraged to critically examine and explore geographical ideas and issues. A process-orientated geography curriculum would emphasise students' critical explorations of spatial, environmental and cultural issues

You have to balance what you teach with the needs and interests of your students and how you set about the task of teaching.
Photo © Barking Photographic.

and question evidence, ideas and arguments. To do this in ways that are educationally valuable Roberts (1997, 2003, 2013) and Smith (2000) highlight the significance of the teacher's role in the process model:

> 'The approach is dependent upon the cultivation of wisdom and meaning making in the classroom. If the teacher is not up to this, then there will be severe limitations on what can happen educationally' (Smith, 2000).

What this means is that it is the responsibility of teachers (in this case geography teachers) to ensure that the 'process' of learning safeguards students' capacity to develop critical geographical understanding – learning processes, abstracted from context or concepts rooted in disciplines such as geography, are not enough.

A now widely recognised model for making sense of the process model in school geography is that of 'curriculum making'. Presented by the GA in its manifesto entitled *A Different View* (2009), and discussed by Lambert and Morgan (2010), the idea provides a useful tool to think with. Lambert and Morgan articulate curriculum planning and curriculum development as precursors of 'the practical business of curriculum making' (p. 49), which they describe as the 'in-between work of translating a curriculum plan into lessons' (p. 50). What they are saying is that between curriculum development and planning and individual planning and teaching there is a highly significant space: the space in which you, the teacher, have to balance what you teach with the needs and interests of your students and with how you set about the task of teaching. This model takes as key that ephasis on just students' experience and the curriculum will fail to take them beyond what they already know. Likewise, too much emphasis on just the subject and the curriculum will fail to engage students and meet their needs – it becomes an irrelevant curriculum. Finally, too much emphasis on just teaching approaches and the curriculum becomes a 'pedagogic adventure' (Lambert, 2004, p. 83). Curriculum making as described by Lambert and Morgan (2010) (see here page 25) is possible within a process model: but it is impossible within a cultural transmission model or an objectives-led model, simply because the space between a curriculum plan and teaching and learning does not exist.

Curriculum development

Curriculum development is a close relation of curriculum planning, but it is also distinctively different. Curriculum development is cyclical: reviewing current content (geographical content, teaching approaches, learning resources); deciding what and where to change; then implementing and reviewing your ideas. However, it is not a neat and tidy process: just as with curriculum planning, your own geographical education, your interests, your expertise, your passions and your broader educational values (for example, how you take account of students' needs and perspectives), all influence the choices you make regarding innovation, change and development.

An additional layer of complexity to the development process for school geography, though a welcome one, has to be the unpredictable dynamics of a changing world. Recent (at time of writing) flooding on the Somerset Levels in England, or the Intergovernmental Panel on Climate Change report (2014), or proposals for a wind farm in your local area illustrate these dynamics. The big question for geography teachers is what to do with these world-changing dynamics? Do you ignore them because you have a scheme of work to get through? Do you 'save them for later'? Or do you seize the opportunity they present to bring real events into lessons? The latter option, although the more creative and imaginative response, also requires a great degree of curriculum flexibility. There is also a risk here, which is that in an attempt to guard against teaching 'irrelevant content', as reported in the 2011 Ofsted report, the selection of what to teach, based in current events, creates a curriculum that is in danger of becoming media/popular culture-driven, potentially jeopardising the 'geography' in geography education (Biddulph, 2014). The following example illustrates the point. While observing a student teacher teaching a lesson on the 'geography of crime', centred around a news report on the local area, I was struck by the absence of any geographical content – the lesson comprised plenty of social theory and some human psychology, as students considered crime victims' experiences, but where was the geography? Margaret Roberts's (2011) article 'What makes a geography lesson good?' reminds us how easy it is to lose sight of what we are teaching in our pursuit of other agendas such as 'relevance'. The choices we make are ultimately a question of professional judgement: some opportunities are worth seizing; others are not.

Conclusions

In writing this chapter I have tried to achieve two things. First, I have attempted to explore the impact of different ideologies on the school geography curriculum and expose for analysis the geography/ideology/curriculum relationship. This 'exposing' is important if we are to keep a watchful eye on any future plans for the curriculum and feel equipped, when the time comes (and it will), to play a full part in the decision-making processes. Understanding the shifts in curriculum decision making at a national or even international level is more likely to ensure you retain a critical eye on curriculum debates and therefore work to secure a geography curriculum capable of holding on to its broader educative potential.

Second, the chapter is intended to identify possible ways of framing your own work as a curriculum maker. Examining your own beliefs and values is important because of the role they play in decisions about what your students learn; and decisions about what students learn are important if we believe geographical education is a significant player in building young people's capacity to make sense of our 'wired-up, footloose, travel-bugged world'.

None of the questions raised here has a clear-cut answer. Rather, the intention is to provoke thought, and perhaps cause you to re-examine how you think about the curriculum – its vulnerabilities, its pressure points, its influences and its potential.

References

Ball, S. (2008) *The Education Debate*. Bristol: The Policy Press.

Biddulph, M. (2013) 'Where is the curriculum created?' in Lambert, D. and Jones, M. (eds) *Debates in Geography Education*. Abingdon: Routledge, pp. 129–42.

Biddulph, M. (2014) 'What kind of geography curriculum do we really want?', *Teaching Geography*, 39, 1, pp. 6–9.

Biesta, G. (2012) 'Giving teaching back to education: responding to the disappearance of the teacher', *Phenomenology and Practice*, 6, 2, pp. 35–49.

Bonnett, A. (2008) *What is Geography?* London: Sage.

Brooks, C. (2006) 'Geography teachers and making the school geography curriculum', *Geography*, 91, 2, pp. 75–83.

DES (1991) *Geography in the National Curriculum (England)*. London: HMSO.

DfE (2010) *The Importance of Teaching: The Schools White Paper 2010*. London: The Stationery Office.

DfE (2013) *The National Curriculum in England: Framework document*. Available at: www.gov.uk/government/uploads/system/uploads/attachment_data/file/210969/NC_framework_document_-_FINAL.pdf (last accessed 07/11/2016).

DfE (2014a) *GCE AS and A Level Subject Content for Geography*. Available online at: www.gov.uk/government/publications/gce-as-and-a-level-geography (last accessed 07/11/2016).

DfE (2014b) Geography: *GCSE subject content*. Available at: www.gov.uk/government/publications/GCSE-geography (last accessed 07/11/2016).

DfEE/QCA (1999) *The National Curriculum: Handbook for Secondary Teachers in England*. London: DfEE/QCA.

GA (2009) *A Different View: A manifesto from the Geographical Association*. Sheffield: Geographical Association.

Hope, A. (2010) 'Student resistance to the surveillance curriculum', *International Studies in Sociology of Education*, 20, 4, pp. 319–34.

Impolite Geography (2010) *The ideology of school geography*. Available at: http://impolitegeography.wordpress.com (last accessed 07/11/2016).

Intergovernmental Panel on Climate Change (IPCC) (2014) *Climate Change 2014: Impacts, adaptation and vulnerability. Working Group II Contribution to the Fifth Assessment Report of the Intergovernmental Panel on Climate Change*. New York, NY: Cambridge University Press.

Jackson, P. (2006) 'Thinking geographically', *Geography*, 91, 3, pp. 199–204.

Kelly, A.V. (2009) *The Curriculum: Theory and practice* (6th edition). London: Sage.

Lambert, D. (2004) 'Geography' in White, J. (ed) *Rethinking the School Curriculum*. London: Routledge Falmer, pp. 75–86.

Lambert, D. and Morgan, J. (2010) *Teaching Geography 11–18: A conceptual approach*. Maidenhead: Open University Press.

Oates, T. (2011) 'Could do better: using international comparisons to refine the National Curriculum in England', *Curriculum Journal*, 22, 2, pp. 121–50.

Ofsted (2008) *Geography in Schools: Changing practice*. Manchester: Ofsted.

Ofsted (2011) *Geography: Learning to make a world of difference*. Available at: www.gov.uk/government/publications/geography-learning-to-make-a-world-of-difference (last accessed 07/11/2016).

Pring, R. (2012) *Bring Back Teaching*. Nottingham: Nottingham Jubilee Press.

QCA (2007) *Geography: Programme of study for key stage 3 and attainment target*. London: HMSO.

Rawling, E. (2001) *Changing the Subject: The impact of national policy on school geography 1980–2000*. Sheffield: Geographical Association.

Rawling, E. (2007) *Planning Your Key Stage 3 Geography Curriculum*. Sheffield: Geographical Association.

RGS-IBG (no date) *Results analysis*. Available at: www.rgs.org/OurWork/Schools/Running+a+successful+department/Results+analysis.htm (last accessed 07/11/2016).

Roberts, M. (1997) 'Curriculum planning and course development: a matter of professional judgement' in Tilbury, D. and Williams, M. (eds) *Teaching and Learning Geography*. Abingdon: Routledge, pp. 35–48.

Roberts, M. (2003) *Learning Through Enquiry: Making sense of geography in the key stage 3 classroom*. Sheffield: Geographical Association.

Roberts, M. (2011) *What makes a geography lesson good?*. Paper based on a lecture given at the 2011 Geographical Association Annual Conference. Available at: www.geography.org.uk/projects/makinggeographyhappen/teachertips (last accessed 07/11/2016).

Roberts, M. (2013) *Geography Through Enquiry: Approaches to teaching and learning in the secondary school*. Sheffield: Geographical Association.

Smith, M.K. (2000) *Curriculum theory and practice* in The Encyclopaedia of Informal Education. Available at: www.infed.org/biblio/b-curric.htm (last accessed 07/11/2016).

Weeden, P. (2012) 'An investigation of changing patterns of entry for GCSE geography: choice, diversity and competition'. Unpublished PhD Thesis, University of Birmingham.

White, J. (2003) *Rethinking the School Curriculum: Values, aims and purposes*. Abingdon: Routledge.

Recommended key readings

Rawling, E. (2001) *Changing the Subject: The impact of national policy on school geography 1980–2000*. Sheffield: Geographical Association.
This book charts the changing course of school geography, mapping in fine detail the role of government and other stakeholders in the curriculum process, before and after the arrival of the first National Curriculum for geography. It will add both depth and detail to some of the ideas introduced in this chapter and enable you to make sense of many of the contemporary curriculum debates.

Lambert, D. and Morgan, J. (2010) 'What does it mean to be a teacher of geography?' in *Teaching Geography 11–18: A conceptual approach*. Maidenhead: Open University Press, pp. 37–52.
In this chapter, the authors argue that geography teachers need to critically engage with questions concerning school geography: its content, audience and purpose. These fundamental questions are central to the concept of teachers as 'curriculum makers' and need to be 'grappled with', not just in times of curriculum change but in helping teachers and students to clarify the purposes and goals of teaching geography in schools.

Chapter 4

Progression

Liz Taylor is Lecturer in Geography Education at University of Cambridge

What is progression?

As a trainee or practising geography teacher, you will have gained considerable experience and expertise in the subject. As you reflect on your career as a learner of geography, you are probably able to recall times when you found an aspect of the subject hard to learn. For example, perhaps you found it hard to understand how and why the atmosphere changes with distance from Earth's surface, and how this influences the weather. Or perhaps at university you found it difficult to understand complex ideas like postmodernism or post-structuralism. How did you recognise that you were making progress over time? Maybe you could look back from year to year and realise that you could do or understand things now that you couldn't before. Perhaps you remember a particular 'breakthrough' with something you were finding challenging, assisted by a teacher, some friends or something you read or watched. Or maybe the pieces just came together in a new way when you were writing or revising.

As geography teachers, we want our students to make progress. That sounds simple, but because geography is varied and complex, and people are also varied and complex, it can be difficult to achieve. Once we start to unpack what is meant by geography and what is meant by progress, it can even be difficult to obtain agreement on aims and processes within groups of geography teachers, let alone with other stakeholders involved in education, such as the government or parents.

Bennetts (1995) suggests that progression:

> 'focuses on how pupils' learning advances. It can be applied to both the design of a curriculum, in particular how the structure of content and sequence of learning activities are intended to facilitate advances in learning, and to the gradual gains in knowledge, understanding, skills and competencies which pupils actually achieve' (p. 75).

Thus, Bennetts is suggesting that the term 'progression' may describe two things: first, a series of gradual advances in certain aspects of learning, which teachers may plan for, and second, to the actual gains in learning that students are making. While use of the words 'progress' and 'progression' overlaps in education literature, 'progression' tends to be used to emphasise the act of moving on, so is more often used in relation to the technical aspect of planning for progression.

Various strands of progression in learning geography – aspects of the subject young people should get better at over time – have been proposed. One set of proposed strands can be found in Figure 1.

- Demonstrating greater fluency with world knowledge by drawing on increasing breadth and depth of content and contexts.
- Extending from the familiar and concrete to the unfamiliar and abstract.
- Making greater sense of the world by organising and connecting information and ideas about people, places, processes and environments.
- Working with more complex information about the world, including the relevance of people's attitudes, values and beliefs.
- Increasing the range and accuracy of investigative skills, and advancing their ability to select and apply these with increasing independence to geographical enquiry.

Figure 1: One set of strands in progression.
Source: GA, 2014.

Other lists vary from this one in some details (Taylor, 2013) but they tend to share some key features. First, they signal the need for students to both broaden and deepen their knowledge and understanding of geographical content over time. Breadth refers to students' learning about more aspects of geography, usually more places and themes (ecosystems, natural hazards, urban geography, etc.). Depth refers to the level of detail and sophistication of understanding that students can express regarding any particular place or theme. Second, there is some form of movement from concrete, tangible concepts and processes to abstract ones, so whereas early in their schooling a student might learn about the shops in their local area, later on they might consider global consumption trends and the impact of these on different places. This example also brings in the dimension of scale, which is usually seen as progressing from the student's immediate environment towards things further away; the 'expanding horizons' approach. Third, there is usually an element of increasing complexity in terms of interlinkage within and between different aspects of the subject, or different places. This involves students in synoptic thinking as they increasingly come to see connections and inter-relations. Fourth, there tends to be a geographical skills dimension, whether this is expertise in use and construction of maps, ICT, fieldwork or enquiry/investigative skills. There is an emphasis not only on gaining more of these skills, but also on increasing independence in their selection and effective deployment. Fifth, mastery over an increasingly technical geographical vocabulary is either stated or assumed.

To what extent are these commonly-proposed strands inherently geographical? Sometimes the content proposed is geographical (places, themes) but the progression is seen in more cognitively sophisticated ways of handling it (for example moving from describing to explaining), common to all subjects. However, there may also be progression in a set of distinctively geographical ways of thinking, perhaps including interconnection, interlinkage between scales, or diversity over space (see Chapter 2 here, pages 20–29). Progression in thinking geographically would enable a student to deploy more powerfully their knowledge of themes and places as their education progresses.

How do young people make progress?

In order to be able to plan for progression effectively, we need to know how young people make progress in their geographical learning. While there is a great deal of educational and psychological research on how students learn, there is relatively little specifically on how they learn geography. Probably the most influential ideas on learning in general are from the theories of 'social constructivism'. The idea of constructivism is basically that children and young people actively 'construct' their own understandings by relating new information to their existing ideas about a topic. This information either adds to their existing thinking in a straightforward way, or it may prompt a wider change in their way of thinking. Sometimes, a misconception can get in the way of new ideas being integrated. A key theorist of constructivism was Jean Piaget. His research was not based on learning in a classroom situation, and there are a number of issues with applying it to formal education (see Moore, 2000), although the idea of active, student-centred learning has been very influential over time. However, social constructivism gives greater weight to the involvement of other people in the learning process, with learning being primarily mediated through language. An important idea in social constructivism is the 'zone of proximal development' (ZPD). This is the difference between a child's actual developmental level (problems they can solve on their own) and their potential level (problem solving with guidance from an adult or more capable peer). A teacher often intuitively gauges students' current level and what they can do successfully with support. For example, they will pose different questions to different students, aiming to pitch appropriately within the students' ZPDs. Lev Vygotsky's work on the social context of learning continues to be important in inspiring collaborative problem-solving and group work in schools (see Moore, 2000).

Another social constructivist, Jerome Bruner, coined the term 'scaffolding' to refer to the intervention that extends a young person's understanding into their ZPD on a particular issue. A large part of teaching involves successfully deploying scaffolding in the classroom, for example when designing a worksheet, structuring a task or setting up an activity. Of course, a builder's scaffolding is only useful while something is being built – the aim is for the building eventually to stand on its own. In the same way, the use of scaffolding for a particular task should be reduced over time, with the aim of students being able to undertake that task independently. More recently, work by psychologists on the structure and processes of the brain has provided new insights into how young people make progress (Goswami, 2008).

Compared to subjects like mathematics and science, the way young people learn geography is relatively under-researched. There is some work on students' understandings of aspects of physical geography, such as tectonic processes or ecosystems, where there is a particular interest in misconceptions, linking with science education research (for example, Dove, 1999). There is also quite a selection of small-scale research on children and young people's understandings of different places (see Taylor, 2013). However, relatively little of this work concentrates on processes of learning, tending instead to look at outcomes of learning at a particular point in time. There is also very little work on some aspects of human geography, such as young people's understandings of trade or development. This makes it difficult to plan in an informed way for progression in many of the geographical themes. Certain elements of geographical skills, such as younger students' understandings of maps, have received a little more attention (see Matthews, 1992, for a useful summary).

Without significant amounts of empirical work to inform understanding of how young people progress in specific areas of geography, much planning for progression tends to draw on three sources: learning theory more generally, teachers' experience of 'what works', and logical thinking about the steps involved in learning about a particular topic. Whether the source of insight is one of these or research, you will find that thinking about the process of learning a particular element of geography is valuable. For example, in his discussion of the popular 'Maps from memory' strategy, Nichols (2001) suggests that:

> 'the process of making use of maps and diagrams involves three steps. Firstly, identifying the component parts by detecting one kind of symbolic representation from another. The second is recognition of what the symbols represent and the third step is interpretation of what the spatial distributions of the symbols mean (e.g. that a trunk road links place x to place y along a valley)' (p. 22).

As an experienced geographer, when faced with a map, you are likely to move through all three of these stages practically simultaneously, and certainly without thinking about them. However, your students may well get stuck at one or other of the stages. Knowing that these stages exist will help you diagnose where your students are getting stuck and put in scaffolding to support them (even if this is just a matter of informal questioning).

Planning for progression

Planning for progression takes place over a range of timescales. Short-term planning focuses on the scale of the individual lesson, though it is also possible to consider progression within an individual activity, and it is important not to neglect lesson–homework or homework–lesson progression. For example, what element(s) of progression can you see in Figure 2?

1. List 20 different services, giving examples from the different groups such as education, healthcare and retail.
2. From the point of view of your family, put your list in order with the least frequently used services at the top and the most frequently used at the bottom.
3. Which of the services are specialised and which more general? Colour code your list to show which is which.
4. Is there any relationship between how specialised a service is and how frequently it is used?

Figure 2: Activity designed to help students explore the relationship between frequency of use and degree of specialisation in services. **Source:** Taylor, 1998, p. 26.

Chapter 4: Progression

1. Lesson introducing diversity within Japan	2. Lesson on coastal processes
Lesson objectives LO1: to develop skills in photograph analysis (identifying features that give clues to location). LO2: to recognise that different parts of Japan have distinctive climates, landscapes and population densities. LO3: to evaluate the extent of this diversity.	**Lesson key questions** KQ1: In what ways has the coastline at [example] changed over time? Why? KQ2: How might it continue to change in the future?
Start to lesson Quick quiz: Japan or not? Show ten photos illustrating diversity within Japan. Whole-class hands-up response. Answers not revealed yet.	**Start to lesson** Slowly reveal photo of [example], visited on recent field trip. Students guess location, then think-pair-share on features they can see.
Learning activity 1 (LO1, LO2) Choose two (hard copy) photos. Annotate features and justify initial choice of Japan or not (modelling by teacher if needed). Discuss examples as a class. Reveal answers.	**Main learning activity** (KQ1, KQ2) Students create a simulation of change in this coastline over time (past–present–future) with justification for changes (may need to recap processes learnt in earlier lessons). Produce either 'freeze-frame' Play-Doh animation or a photo modified in image processing software to show past, present and predicted future. Voiceover (recorded or live) to describe and explain changes.
Learning activity 2 (LO2) Find and examine map of Japan in atlas (whole class). In pairs, find location for photographs selected in Learning activity 1. What elements of diversity within Japan do these illustrate (e.g. climate, landscape, population density)?	
Recap on learning (LO2, LO3) Line up: How diverse is Japan? Students position themselves from 'not at all' to 'very' and explain reasons for their choice of where to stand. Teacher prompts or reinforces different elements of diversity and evaluative vocabulary.	**Recap on learning** Show one example of work and use to recap key changes and processes.

Figure 3: Illustrative lesson ideas.

Planning for progression within lessons has received much attention from geography teachers in recent years, for example through devising and sharing ideas for engaging starts to lessons, thinking carefully about lesson objectives and how/whether to share these with students, mediating the learning journey of the lesson effectively and bringing the lesson to a suitable conclusion that reinforces learning and provides a satisfying end. Most geography departments use a lesson planning template that includes space for learning objectives, however these are formulated, as well as timings and learning activities. In planning for students' progression at this scale, it is important to ensure that learning activities are consistent with learning objectives. Often this is an iterative process of refining both the objectives and the activities you deploy to ensure that the emphasis on geographical learning is the same between the two. Figure 3 shows some examples of what this might look like.

In planning for progression over the short term, it is helpful to draw on the theories of learning described in the previous section and any available research on how students learn about the geographical topic. Work on students' misconceptions can be useful in alerting you to common confusions, for example between global warming and the hole in the ozone layer (Dove, 1999), or between pairs of countries whose characteristics young people tend to confuse, such as Japan/China or Australia/New Zealand (Taylor, 2014). If you are alert to possible misconceptions at the planning stage, you can look out for them during the lesson, or even plan activities to respond to them. One of the key findings of the misconceptions research, and constructivist learning theory in general, is that students do not turn up to lessons as blank slates – each will already have a more or less complex set of understandings on a particular topic. This means that it is always important to spend time eliciting these prior understandings through pair/class discussion, brainstorms, quizzes, drawings or other methods (Roberts, 2013). Of course, once you are aware of these prior understandings, the challenge is to respond to them. You may need to change what you have planned, when you realise that students know more about it than you expected, or when particular interests emerge and can be followed up.

Medium-term planning is concerned with the scale of a cohesive set of lessons. The timescale is greater than one lesson and less than a year. For most schools, the medium-term planning timescale will be a scheme of work that gives coherence and direction to a set of perhaps five to ten lessons. Constructing the medium-term plan has been a particular focus of attention at key stage 3, as various changes in the National Curriculum (QCA, 2007; DfE, 2013), and new developments in the subject such as the cultural turn, have been a catalyst for change in existing practice in schools (see Chapter 3 here, pages 30–39; Rawling, 2007). The medium-term plan is a key way of planning for progression in geography. Sometimes, the only type of progression evident within a medium-term plan is breadth (gaining knowledge about a wider range of topics). While subject knowledge is very important, aggregation of knowledge alone does not give a very satisfactory level of intellectual challenge. The learner may know more stuff, but are they thinking in more sophisticated ways about it? At this point it can be helpful to consider different levels of cognitive challenge. Bloom's taxonomy of educational objectives is often referred to in this context. Bloom's taxonomy (a taxonomy is a naming system) was published in the USA in 1956 as a tool for categorising the level of cognitive challenge in test items. It was revised to respond to some issues with the original taxonomy (Krathwohl, 2002). While not designed for curriculum planning, the revised taxonomy can be helpful as a tool for evaluating the level of cognitive challenge across the learning objectives for an entire scheme of work (see Figure 4). If all learning objectives fall in the left-hand boxes, there is likely to be a problem with lack of challenge across the unit, and it would be useful to think about how some activities could be reworked to achieve a greater degree of analysis, evaluation and creative opportunity.

While is it helpful to think about cognitive challenge in planning a scheme of work, this is not inherently geographical. In what ways could we plan for a students' geographical thinking to become more sophisticated over a scheme of work? How could they become more effective at making links between different aspects of the subject, or more sophisticated in their handling of big ideas such as change or diversity? More research on the processes of development of geographical thinking would be helpful here, but some work on planning using an enquiry approach has experimented in this area (Taylor, 2008; Roberts, 2013).

Planning for the development of geographical skills is perhaps easier, as some logical steps can be proposed. However, without considering the underlying ways of geographical thinking that these facilitate, it can be easy to focus on aggregating mastery of skills in the same way as aggregating mastery of knowledge. While gaining these can give some satisfaction, and the learner has clearly progressed, there is more to the discipline of geography than gaining sets of skills or knowledge. A key question for future development is: How can we plan for progression in students' geographical thinking over the medium and long term?

Long-term planning for progression (within and between key stages) has perhaps been the most neglected timescale in schools over the past few years, as teachers have understandably focused on implementing whatever new specification or initiative has taken effect within the key stage, rather than on the student's overall career as a geographical learner. The related ideas of continuity and progression are important in long-term planning. Bennetts (1995) defines continuity as 'the persistence of significant features of geographical education as pupils move through the school system. Such features could include aspects of content, particular types of learning activity or common assumptions about the nature of the subject' (p. 75).

The idea that students should revisit key aspects of geography over time, to develop their understandings at a progressively higher level, is linked to Bruner's idea of spiralling. This 'describes the process by which the learner constantly returns to "previous" learning and understandings in the light of new learning and new experience' (Moore, 2000, p. 23). With such a varied subject as geography, how can we plan in opportunities for this to happen? Building on Bruner's ideas, teachers sometimes talk about the 'spiral curriculum', in which key elements of geographical content and skills are progressively revisited at a higher level over time.

The knowledge dimension	1. **Remember** (recognising, recalling)	2. **Understand** (interpreting, exemplifying, classifying, summarising, inferring, comparing, explaining)	3. **Apply** (executing, implementing)	4. **Analyse** differentiating, organising, attributing)	5. **Evaluate** (making a judgement, checking, critiquing)	6. **Create** (generating, planning, producing)
A. Factual knowledge (e.g. examples of volcanic eruptions)						
B. Conceptual knowledge (e.g. theories of capital flow)						
C. Procedural knowledge (e.g. map skills)						
D. Metacognitive knowledge (learning strategies)						

For example, from the first lesson plan in Figure 3, Lesson objective 1 might fit in boxes C1 and C4, Lesson objective 2 in A1 and A4, then Lesson objective 3 in B5. Such classification can be helpful in checking whether the wording of objectives correctly reflects their planned purpose, but there is always an extent to which the positioning depends on the teacher's vision for that particular activity and their interpretation of the key words, hence two people may disagree about the precise positioning of any one objective.

Figure 4: Revised Bloom's taxonomy in grid form. **After:** Krathwohl, 2002.

However, it is not easy to achieve a genuinely spiral curriculum in practice. Continuity and progression between key stages 2 and 3 in geography are notoriously challenging, especially when students may enter year 7 from a wide range of partner primary schools (Wood, 2006). If key stage 3 geography teachers are not familiar with what has been taught at key stage 2, there is a real danger that topics such as the Amazon rainforest are revisited at a very similar level in key stage 3 as key stage 2, and the curriculum can become a circle rather than a spiral. This highlights the need for elicitation of prior knowledge to inform planning at the medium term, alongside, whenever possible, liaison with key stage 2 teachers to inform long-term planning.

A geography department can consider both continuity and progression when selecting a GCSE and A level specification for their students, and when choosing between any optional sections within those specifications. Is it better to include a theme such as coastal landforms and processes at key stage 3, GCSE and A level, to enable continuity and progression, or if it is on the specification at GCSE, could it be omitted from key stage 3 to avoid repetition and create space for other topics? What about students who do not continue with geography beyond key stage 3? These are difficult decisions, and it can be helpful for a department to share their ideas of the desired characteristics of a good geography student at age 18, and then to work backwards through the activities and experiences that should be provided over their secondary school career to get them to that point. Similarly, what would they want for a student who did not take geography beyond key stage 3? This type of discussion of long-term progression can also be very helpful when planning for more general skills and competencies, such as the ability to write a good geography essay independently by age 18, or becoming a competent user of basic GIS by age 16.

Figure 5: The plan–teach–assess–plan cycle.

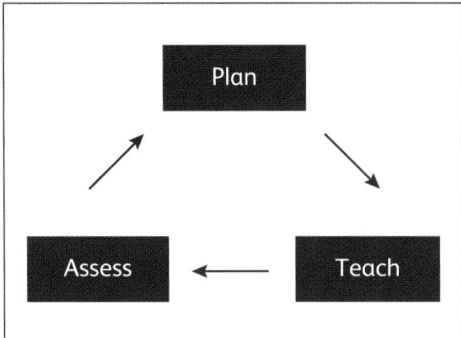

Progression and assessment

All teachers should be constantly asking themselves 'What have the students learned? How do I know?' These questions are equally valid over short-, medium- and long-term timescales. Careful analysis of any outcome of student work (whether a written paragraph, oral responses or a piece of project work) gives useful information on what they know and can do at a particular point in time. Of course, it is important that such methods of assessment give the student the opportunity to express what they actually know or can do, rather than what they have simply copied. Over time, these outcomes can build up into a picture of progression for the student concerned. Teachers are constantly engaged in a process of informal assessment of learning, as they gauge progress of individuals and groups within the lesson. It can be useful to note an evaluation of learning against the objectives on the lesson plan, including any information which can inform planning of the next lesson (Figure 5). In addition, most departments use a set of common tasks to conduct more formal assessment of learning between the milestones of external examinations.

Departments tend to use a commonly agreed set of criteria for assessment of such pieces of work, and may also use internal moderation to standardise judgements. In recent years, many schools have worked hard on ensuring a suitable balance between formative assessment (assessment for learning) and summative assessment (assessment of learning). Following the seminal work of Black and Wiliam (Assessment Reform Group, 1999), increasing attention has been given to the ways in which assessment can aid a student's learning. Their research found that assessment promotes learning when:

- 'it is embedded in a view of teaching and learning of which it is an essential part
- it involves sharing learning goals with pupils
- it aims to help pupils know and to recognise the standards they are aiming for
- it involves pupils in self-assessment
- it provides feedback which leads to pupils recognising their next steps and how to take them
- it is underpinned by confidence that every student can improve
- it involves both teacher and pupils reviewing and reflecting on assessment data'.

(Assessment Reform Group, 1999, p. 7).

This research, and initiatives that followed in its wake, has led to more attention being given in schools to the ways teachers feed back to students, for example by taking care to show what has been successful in the work, as well as signposting areas for improvement. Feedback on aspects for improvement also now tends to be more precise, involving small steps and sometimes setting up a short activity so that students can immediately put the feedback into practice. In addition, the role of the form tutor in many schools has broadened, developing from the traditional pastoral role to more of an academic guide, responsible for reviewing outcomes from assessment with students, and sometimes parents, and discussing past and future progress.

Practice in peer- and self-assessment has also been a focus of attention, in order to help students gain ownership of their learning and increase their understanding of the means of progress. It can be challenging to create a classroom ethos where students can undertake self- and peer-assessment in a mature and thoughtful manner, avoiding superficial feedback or parroting stock phrases. Even simple mechanisms such as a traffic light system for student feedback, so you can check their confidence with a new term or aspect of subject knowledge, can be helpful once they have become established. The process of students assessing their own or a peer's work effectively using shared criteria can be time-consuming, and it may be useful to start by modelling the process, then for the students to try with work mocked up or saved from a previous year before going on to their own.

Conclusion

Progression is a complex but vital aspect for teachers to grapple with. Students' overall progress as developing geographers will not necessarily be visible within individual pieces of work, but should be evident from a range of sources over a longer timescale. While we can draw on research and learning theory in general, the specifics of progression in geographical learning are under-researched. The nature and processes of progression in students' understandings on geographical topics are therefore an ideal focus for small-scale classroom research, though they would also benefit from some large-scale, funded projects. Planning for progression should form an important element of discussion for geography departments, as they seek to draw on the research on learning that does exist, and to share ideas on effective practice. Planning for progression in students' geographical learning, and how this is most usefully assessed, should be a focus of attention over the short-, medium- and long-term timescales.

References

Assessment Reform Group (1999) *Assessment for Learning: Beyond the black box*. Cambridge: University of Cambridge School of Education.

Bennetts, T. (1995) 'Continuity and progression', *Teaching Geography*, 20, 2, pp. 75–9.

DfE (2013) *National Curriculum in England: Geography programmes of study*. Available at: www.gov.uk/government/publications/national-curriculum-in-england-geography-programmes-of-study (last accessed 07/11/2016).

Dove, J. (1999) *Theory Into Practice: Immaculate misconceptions*. Sheffield: Geographical Association.

GA (2014) *An Assessment and Progression Framework for Geography*. Sheffield: Geographical Association.

Goswami, U. (2008) 'Principles of learning, implications for teaching: a cognitive neuroscience perspective', *Journal of Philosophy of Education*, 42, 3–4, pp. 381–99.

Krathwohl, D. (2002) 'A revision of Bloom's Taxonomy: an overview', *Theory into Practice*, 41, 4, pp. 212–18.

Matthews, M. (1992) *Making Sense of Place: Children's understanding of large-scale environments*. Hemel Hempstead: Harvester Wheatsheaf.

Moore, A. (2000) *Teaching and Learning: Pedagogy, curriculum and culture*. London: Routledge Falmer.

Nichols, A. (ed) with Kinninment, D. (2001) *More Thinking Through Geography*. Cambridge: Chris Kington Publishing.

QCA (2007) *Geography: Programme of study for key stage 3 and attainment target*. London: HMSO.

Rawling, E. (2007) *Planning Your Key Stage 3 Geography Curriculum*. Sheffield: Geographical Association.

Roberts, M. (2013) *Geography Through Enquiry: Approaches to teaching and learning in the secondary school*. Sheffield: Geographical Association.

Taylor, L. (1998) *Hodder Geography: Population and settlement*. London: Hodder and Stoughton.

Taylor, L. (2008) 'Key concepts and medium term planning', *Teaching Geography*, 33, 2, pp. 50–54.

Taylor, L. (2013) 'What do we know about concept formation and making progress in learning geography?' in Lambert, D. and Jones, M. (eds) *Debates in Geography Education*. Abingdon: Routledge, pp. 302–13.

Taylor, L. (2014) 'Diversity between and within: approaches to teaching about distant place in the secondary school curriculum', *Journal of Curriculum Studies*, 46, 2, pp. 276–99.

Wood, P. (2006) 'Building on young people's experience of geography in primary schools' in Balderstone, D. (ed) *Secondary Geography Handbook*. Sheffield: Geographical Association, pp. 488–95.

Recommended key readings

Bennetts, T. (2005) 'The links between understanding, progression and assessment in the secondary school curriculum', *Geography*, 90, 2, pp. 152–70.
A classic introduction to the complexities of different elements of progression, based on Bennetts' research in this area.

Taylor, L. (2013) 'What do we know about concept formation and making progress in learning geography?' in Lambert, D. and Jones, M. (eds) *Debates in Geography Education*. Abingdon: Routledge, pp. 302–13.
A more detailed overview of progression in geography, with particular focus on conceptual development, drawing on a range of empirical research and parallel work in history education.

Chapter 5

Planning for enquiry

Margaret Roberts was a Geography Teacher Educator for over 20 years at the University of Sheffield

Introduction

When I carried out some research into teachers' understandings of the term 'enquiry', I found that it meant different things to different people (Roberts, 1998). Some thought it meant that students had to work independently. Some thought about enquiry as a sequence of skills, starting with identifying questions and finishing with reaching conclusions. Some thought that it was essential to have a hypothesis to test. Some associated it with mainly with fieldwork. My own understanding is broader than any of these and, although it could include these ways of thinking, it would not be limited to any one of them. I understand 'enquiry' as an umbrella term, incorporating a range of approaches to teaching and learning that can include both those that are strongly guided by teachers as well as those in which students have more independence.

Essential characteristics of enquiry

For me, regardless of whether enquiry is teacher-guided or student-led, learning geography through enquiry has four essential characteristics that are applicable in the classroom as well as in the field:

- Enquiry is question driven. It encourages curiosity and a questioning approach to knowledge throughout a unit of work: it does not mean simply identifying questions at the start of a piece of work, or answering them at the end of it.
- Enquiry is supported by evidence from the 'real' world, not from invented people and places. Students use geographical information presented in a wide variety of forms, e.g. text, maps, statistics, photographs, film. This can be used as evidence to answer the enquiry questions.
- Enquiry requires thinking geographically. Students make sense of information in geographical source materials by reasoning, weighing evidence and considering different viewpoints. Making sense requires the development of conceptual understanding.
- Enquiry is reflective. Students reach conclusions, make judgements and develop their own viewpoints. Enquiry encourages students to think critically about what they have learnt.

Essentially, in my opinion, developing an enquiry approach to teaching and learning is about developing a questioning attitude to geographical knowledge and enabling students to investigate that knowledge critically and to think geographically. It is not simply about acquiring skills. Although enquiry-based learning helps students develop a range of valuable skills, some specifically geographical and some generic, I do not see these skills only as ends in themselves. I also value them because they can enable students to engage critically with geographical knowledge, to deepen their understanding of complex geographical patterns and processes and to consider conflicting viewpoints.

Why use an enquiry approach?

I justify the use of an enquiry approach to geographical education in four ways. My first justification is related to constructivism, a widely accepted theory of learning. Its central idea is that we can learn about the world only through actively making sense of it for ourselves. How we see and understand the world depends on existing ways of thinking; we make sense of the world not with empty minds but with assumptions about how things are and how things work. We get to know the world through participating in it and sharing how we understand it with others (Barnes, 2008). When students learn something new, they are not simply adding bits of knowledge to what they already have, like adding extensions to a building. To make sense of new information they have to incorporate it into what they already know, reconstructing (and sometimes correcting) their existing knowledge, like modifying a building in order to extend it. Knowledge cannot be transmitted or 'delivered' ready-made to students; students have to engage with knowledge and an enquiry approach can help them do this.

My second justification is related to the nature of geographical knowledge. When students learn geography they are learning to see and understand the world as geographers do. Through an enquiry approach, students learn about the kinds of questions that geographers ask and how these shape the knowledge that they construct. Whereas traditionally geography was concerned with the questions what, where, why and how, geography in the twenty-first century asks, additionally, what might, with what impact, what ought; so geography, as well as describing and explaining patterns and processes, now has a futures and a values dimension. Through an enquiry approach, students learn that geographers use both qualitative and quantitative data as evidence and that all data need analysis and interpretation. Studying like a geographer enables students to construct well-evidenced arguments. Through an enquiry approach, students learn about the different ways in which geographers look at the world. For example, in the past geography tended to treat 'people' as a homogeneous group. Cultural geographers have recognised that different groups, e.g. related to gender, ethnicity, age or class, experience the world differently. By focusing on these different geographies, students can extend their understanding of the world beyond the ways in which they experience it themselves. Students also learn that some aspects of the world studied by geographers, e.g. climate, sustainability or urbanisation, are studied by other disciplines and that our understanding of the world can be increased by working across subject boundaries.

My third justification is related to the broader purposes of education. I believe that school education has to be relevant to the needs of both society and the individual. The kinds of skills thought to be required by citizens and valued by employers have been termed '21st-century skills' and include: using information presented in different forms, media and digital literacies, problem solving, collaborating and communicating. Learning geography through enquiry can develop all these skills in ways in which a more didactic style of teaching cannot, but it can do more than this. It can enhance the present and future lives of individuals. As stated in the National Curriculum for geography, 'A high quality geography education should inspire in pupils a curiosity and fascination about the world and its people that will remain with them for the rest of their lives' (DfE, 2013). An enquiry approach can help students see, understand and appreciate the world differently. It encourages them to think more critically about the geographical information presented to them and enables them to make more sense of the local, national and international issues they encounter.

A fourth justification for adopting an enquiry approach to learning geography is that it is required by public examinations. Some aspects of enquiry have been included in successive specifications for GCSE and A level examinations in England. The geography GCSE subject content (DFE, 2014) makes several references to 'enquiry':

'GCSE specifications should enable students to… develop their competence in applying sound enquiry and investigative approaches to questions and hypotheses (study like a geographer)' (p. 3).

'Formulating enquiry and argument: The ability to identify questions and sequences of enquiry, to write descriptively, analytically and critically, to communicate their ideas effectively, to develop an extended written argument, and to draw well-evidenced and informed conclusions about geographical questions and issues' (p. 6).

'Understanding of the kinds of questions capable of being investigated through fieldwork and an understanding of the geographical enquiry processes appropriate to investigate these' (p. 8).

Figure 1: Brainstorming ideas about what geography to include in a unit of work.

Which of geography's big ideas could underpin this unit?

Place; space; scale; environment; landscape

Physical processes; human processes

Change and development; globalisation; sustainability; inequality

Interdependence

Which specialist concepts do students need to understand?

e.g. a unit of work on coasts might include: abrasion, attrition, hydraulic action, longshore drift, swash, backwash, etc.

What aspects of geography should be included?

Context and locational knowledge

What contexts (local, national, international) will be referred to?

What place names and locations will be referred to?

Which case studies might be used?

Taking into account:
- availability of source materials
- availability of up-to-date statistics
- risks of stereotyping places

Ten questions to consider when planning for enquiry

If you are planning an enquiry-based unit of work or an enquiry-based lesson, even if you want students to work fairly independently, you need to have thought about the following questions, though not necessarily in this order. Often your ideas for a lesson or a unit of work start with a stimulating resource or an activity you might use for investigating a theme, place or issue, and you develop your thinking from that.

1. What aspects of geography should be included?

One starting point could be thinking through the aspects of geography the students are to study. You may be restricted by curriculum and examination requirements. These might specify, in relation to the theme or place being studied, what questions need to be addressed, what key ideas need to be understood or what particular examples need to be studied. On the other hand, there might be scope for you to use some of your own ideas about the theme. You might want to incorporate ideas you have gained from recent academic study of geography, following the example of Bustin (2011) who incorporated activities exploring the concept of 'thirdspace' into a key stage 3 unit of work. You might want to use your own knowledge and resources accumulated during experiences of working or travelling in other parts of the country or world.

A spider diagram can be useful for brainstorming initial ideas. The categories I would use to consider what to include are shown in Figure 1.

2. What is your role to be?

Your role in enquiry-based learning can vary along a continuum with strong guidance at one end and minimal guidance at the other. There is a corresponding change in the role of the student, from less student self-direction at one end to more at the other. In Figure 2, I have divided this continuum into three categories, which I have termed strongly guided, framed and negotiated, and have applied these categories to aspects of enquiry identified above.

You might feel, because of examination and time constraints, that you have to be in control of the enquiry; but even at this strongly guided end of the continuum, you can make students aware that they are investigating something. You can make them aware of the questions framing a unit of work, that the geographical data they use are sources of evidence and that the activities help them make sense of this evidence and reach conclusions.

In the framed category, students are introduced explicitly to the types of questions geographers ask, to the kinds of source material that can provide evidence, and to the ways of analysing and interpreting geographical data. They can begin to identify their own questions, use criteria to select their own data and become aware of choices available to them in representing and analysing data. They are learning to operate geographers' frames of thinking and are participating more fully in the enquiry.

In the negotiated category, students might make all the key decisions, identifying their own

Chapter 5: Planning for enquiry

	Strongly guided	Framed	Negotiated
Role of teacher and student	More teacher guidance/less student self-direction	Some teacher guidance/some student self-direction	Less teacher guidance/more student self-direction
Enquiry is question-driven	Focus of enquiry and questions decided by teacher	Teacher devises activities to encourage students to identify questions or sub-questions	Students devise questions and sub-questions and negotiate them with teachers
Using geographical sources as evidence	Geographical sources chosen by teacher	Students select some sources or select relevant data from given sources	Students given support by teachers to find own sources
Thinking geographically	All activities devised by teacher	Teacher introduces students to techniques and conceptual frameworks, which they learn to use selectively	Students decide how to analyse and interpret data
Conclusions and reflections	Teacher checks conclusions reached	Students discuss conclusions they have reached	Students reach own conclusions and evaluate them critically
Summary	Teacher controls the construction of knowledge by making all decisions about content, data, activities and conclusions	Teacher inducts students into ways in which geographical knowledge is constructed. Students are made aware of choices and are encouraged to be critical	Students are enabled, with teacher guidance, to investigate questions of interest to themselves and to evaluate their conclusions critically

Figure 2: The role of the teacher in enquiry-based approaches to learning geography.

questions to investigate, selecting their own case studies to investigate and searching for their own data on them. Although this approach has been used in geography mainly for A level courses, teachers have shown how it can be applied at key stage 3 in geography (e.g. Norman, 2014) and history (e.g. Burnham, 2007). However, even in this category, if the student is to gain from your greater geographical understanding, there is an essential role for you. Students might need support or approval in identifying questions and appropriate sources of information and in using these to develop understanding. The risk at this end of the spectrum is that students might simply find answers to questions without developing conceptual understanding or being critical about the data they collect. You have a crucial role, carried out through discussion with individuals and groups, in ensuring that students are thinking geographically as well as collecting information.

Your role might vary during the course of a unit of work. Instead of deciding to provide strong guidance throughout the unit, you might, for example, present students with the overarching enquiry question and the sub-questions, but give them a choice of which volcano or earthquake to study. Or you might invite students to discuss the questions framing the enquiry and negotiate which ones the class are going to investigate, but then present them with a particular case study you want them to study. Or, when studying a controversial issue, e.g. 'should the UK carry out fracking for shale gas?', you might devise the questions and provide all the data, but ask the students to reach and justify their own conclusions.

3. What kinds of questions should frame a unit of work?

To encourage an investigative approach to knowledge, it is preferable for each unit of work to be framed by a question rather than a topic heading. Some examination specifications provide overarching questions, e.g. How can the growing demand for energy be met without serious environmental consequences? (Edexcel, GCSE (9–1), Geography B). Some provide both key questions and sub-questions, e.g. 'What evidence is there to suggest climate change is a natural process?' with one of the sub-questions being 'Why is climate change a global issue?' (OCR, GCSE Geography B). Where the questions are not provided, it is worth devising a good

Figure 3: The route for enquiry. **Source:** Rawling, 2007.

Questions	Geographical thinking
What?	Observation and perception
What and where?	Definition and description
How and why?	Analysis and explanation
What might happen? What impact? What decision?	Evaluation, prediction and decision making
What do I think? What will I do next?	Personal evaluation and response

overarching question for each unit of work. Michael Riley (2000) used this approach for school history and argued that the key enquiry question for a unit of work should:

- capture the interest and imagination of students
- place an aspect of historical thinking, a concept or a process at the forefront of students' minds
- result in a tangible, lively, substantial, enjoyable outcome activity (at the end of the unit of work).

Key questions he suggested for key stage 3 history included: 'Does Robespierre deserve his reputation as a bloodthirsty tyrant?' and 'Why did it take so long for women to get the vote?'(Riley, 2000, p. 13).

Riley's approach can be applied to geography. When you devise an overarching question you could consider:

- why might students be interested in this aspect of geography? How can I make the question intriguing and puzzling in order to fire students' curiosity?
- how can the overarching question help students focus on one of geography's big ideas (e.g. place, scale, environment, interdependence)?
- does the question ask students to think and argue geographically (e.g. about cause and effect, about comparisons, about geographical impacts of events and decisions, about contradictory evidence, about meanings of terms such as 'sustainability')?
- how can students communicate what they have learnt in this unit of work in an interesting and rigorous way?

You can see how these criteria have been applied to particular aspects of geography in the titles of the GA's *Key Stage 3 Geography Teachers' Toolkit* series. For example, the book *A Thorny Issue: Should I buy a Valentine's rose?* (Ellis, 2009) raises an issue to which students can relate and presents a puzzling dilemma. The question helps students focus on the concepts of sustainability and interdependence and on the ethical aspects of what is investigated. Students could communicate their findings on this in a whole-class debate or role-play activity. The book *Changing My World: What difference can we make to the climate?* (Batchen, 2009) raises an open question that relates to students' future lives. The question helps student focus on the concepts of physical and human processes and change. It, too, raises ethical issues. Students could communicate their findings in a report or podcast.

It is important for students that the key question framing a unit of work becomes their own and that they are aware throughout the unit of work that this is what they are investigating. Once the key question has been decided, you may want to decide subsidiary questions to frame individual lessons yourself. Or you might discuss or negotiate them with students in the first lesson of the unit, helping them by providing question starters such as what, where, why, when, who, what ought, what might and how (7Ws and an H) or providing frameworks such as the Development Compass Rose or the Route for Enquiry (Figure 3).

4. What knowledge and skills do students already have related to this unit of work?

One of the three circles on the 'curriculum making' diagram (GA, 2016; see Chapter 2 here, page 25) is labelled 'student experience' and

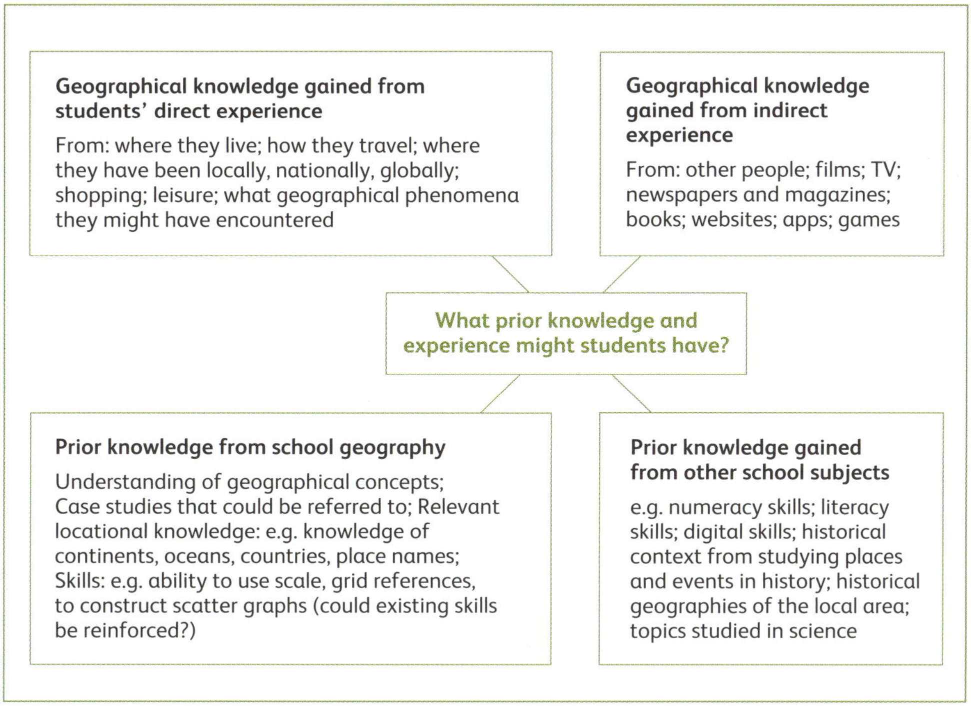

Chapter 5: Planning for enquiry

Geographical knowledge gained from students' direct experience
From: where they live; how they travel; where they have been locally, nationally, globally; shopping; leisure; what geographical phenomena they might have encountered

Geographical knowledge gained from indirect experience
From: other people; films; TV; newspapers and magazines; books; websites; apps; games

What prior knowledge and experience might students have?

Prior knowledge from school geography
Understanding of geographical concepts; Case studies that could be referred to; Relevant locational knowledge: e.g. knowledge of continents, oceans, countries, place names; Skills: e.g. ability to use scale, grid references, to construct scatter graphs (could existing skills be reinforced?)

Prior knowledge gained from other school subjects
e.g. numeracy skills; literacy skills; digital skills; historical context from studying places and events in history; historical geographies of the local area; topics studied in science

Figure 4:
Brainstorming ideas about students' prior knowledge.

asks the crucial question 'How does this take the learner beyond what they already know?' I have found that 'student experience' is the most neglected aspect of curriculum making both in lesson planning and within the classroom.

In my view it is as important to think through this aspect of planning as to think through what content is to be included; students need to be able to relate new knowledge to what they already know. In geography, prior knowledge means much more than what geography students have learnt in primary school or in earlier lessons, although it does include this. All students bring to school their own knowledge and understandings of the world, acquired through direct and indirect experience. From the earliest age, they make journeys outside the home, get to know their own neighbourhood and visit shops and open spaces. They experience different kinds of weather, eat food originating in different places, use different kinds of transport and visit relations. Many have experience of day trips and/or holidays to places and environments that are different from their own local areas. They encounter, indirectly, a world beyond their experience through other people, through toys, stories, information books, magazines, information technology and television programmes. As they get older their experience becomes more extensive. People's everyday knowledge of the world is saturated with their experience and provides a rich source of information. Through their direct and indirect experiences, young people develop their own personal geographies, i.e. their own, sometimes erroneous, knowledge and understandings of place, space and environment. Almost everything studied in geography can be related to personal geographies.

The categories shown in Figure 4 can help you to plan activities that give you opportunities to elicit prior knowledge, and give students opportunities to connect what they know with new knowledge, so that you can sort out any misunderstandings. You might consider involving students in the curriculum-making process, applying one of the principles of the Young People's Geography project: 'using [students'] own experience, ideas and issues… with their teachers to turn these into a focus for curricula' (Biddulph, 2011, p. 50).

5. What sources of geographical information can students use as evidence?

In the classroom, students typically use secondary sources of information, i.e. data and representations collected and compiled by others for other purposes. This could include text, maps of all kinds, statistics, graphs, and visual information, presented either in books or resource sheets or on websites. If you are providing a strong structure for the unit, the students are likely to study relatively few sources of geographical information, so it is important that these are well chosen. If students are to be given some independence, more demands are placed on you: in order to provide guidance where needed, you need to be aware of a greater range of information and a greater number of appropriate websites.

Questions to consider when selecting sources of information include:

- Is the source material interesting and is it likely to stimulate curiosity?
- Are the data relatively unprocessed, so that students have to think about it for themselves rather than rely on the thinking of others, e.g. identifying positive and negative impacts rather than being presented with lists of advantages and disadvantages?
- Are statistical data as up to date as possible?
- Is the source material reliable? Who produced it and why? What assumptions underpin it?
- Does the source material provide evidence to help students answer the overarching question for the unit of work?
- Does the source material demand or encourage the development of conceptual thinking? What concepts need to be understood in order for students to analyse and interpret it? Can it be used not only as a source of factual information but also as a source of ideas?
- Do students need to study conflicting sources of information, e.g. on controversial issues? If so, which views should be presented to them?
- How accessible is this resource to students? Do they have sufficient literacy, numeracy, graphicacy or ICT skills to use it or will they need support, individually or as a class?

It is important for students to learn that source materials can provide only partial evidence and that they learn to probe it and question it. One way of doing this is by using the layers of inference framework (Figure 5) in which students answer questions related to a particular source, which could be, for example, a map, photograph, piece of text, graph or set of statistics.

Another way of encouraging students to examine evidence closely is the Five Key Points strategy, in which students, in pairs or groups, identify five key points from the source material. This encourages them to study the source materials carefully and learn to interpret them. Their ideas are then shared and discussed. Issues such as reliability of data, the extent to which they provide sufficient evidence, and what more evidence might be needed to answer the enquiry questions, can be explored in a class discussion.

6. Will students work as a class, in groups or individually?

It is worth trying, during the course of a unit of work, to give students opportunities to work in different ways: as a whole class; in small groups; and individually. Each has its advantages for learning through enquiry.

Whole-class teaching can be valuable at all stages of an investigation, for:

- sparking curiosity – you can use your own enthusiasm for the subject and interest in what is being investigated to get the students involved
- looking at evidence – students can study geographical source materials together, whether they are images on a screen or printed resources such as maps, graphs or tables of statistics. Through class discussion you can consider the reliability of the source and the extent to which it provides evidence to answer the enquiry question; you can also introduce any techniques needed to analyse or interpret the information
- reflecting on learning – at the end of a unit of work it is valuable to share and reflect on findings in a whole-class discussion.

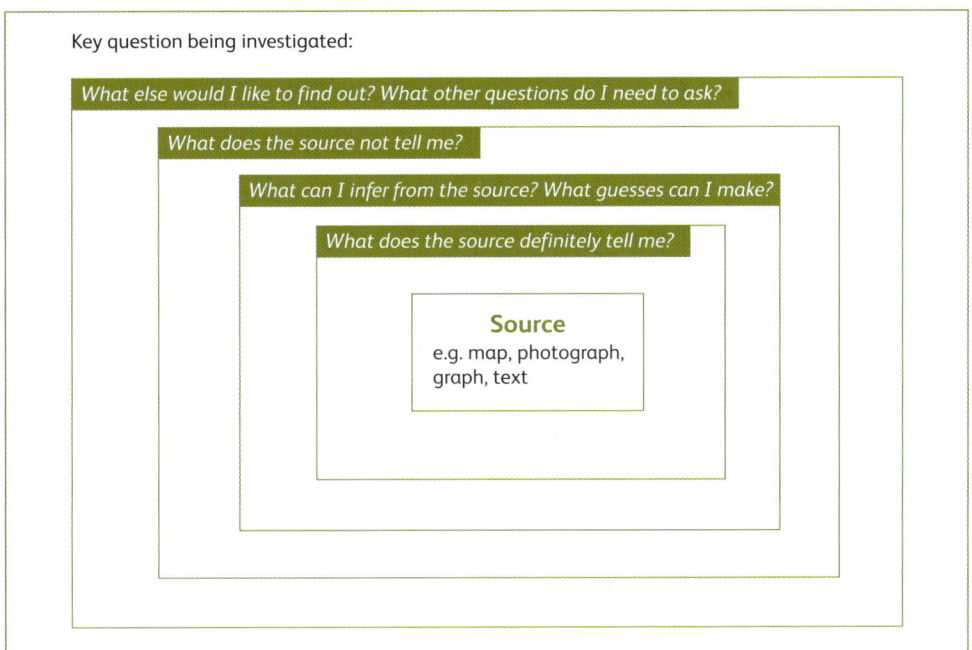

Figure 5:
Layers of inference.
Source: Roberts, 2013.

The advantage of using paired and small group work is that these ways of working give students greater opportunities to talk and to voice their ideas than they would have in whole-class discussion. Research has shown that discussion helps students 'work on their understanding' (Alexander, 2006; Mercer and Dawes, 2008). In small groups or pairs, students can suggest and share their ideas tentatively, question each other, probe each other's ideas and prepare presentations. Small group work is more focused and easily managed if there is some tangible outcome from the activity, e.g. documenting their thinking on paper, perhaps in a layers of inference framework, a concept map or a diamond ranking activity; or preparing something to present to another group or to the whole class.

The advantage of students working individually at some stage during a unit of work is that it requires them to think for themselves rather than rely on the thinking of others. Individual work, e.g. generating sub-questions for a unit of work or identifying key points in a piece of evidence, could be followed by sharing ideas with a group or with the whole class. Students might be expected to write their own individual conclusions following whole-class or small-group discussion. It is important that each student develops the techniques and skills required for a particular unit of work rather than relying on others in the group. This might be particularly applicable for students working at a computer.

7. What kinds of classroom activities would be appropriate for this unit of work?

A wide range of activities can be incorporated into an enquiry-based unit of work, varying from structured activities that will help students develop particular skills to more open-ended activities which will help students explore ideas. Figure 6 suggests some activities for different aspects of enquiry. To get the most out of any of the activities, both whole-class and small-group discussion is important. Research has shown that what students learn from activities is related as much to the strength of teacher/student dialogues about the activities as to the nature of the activities themselves (Webster et al., 1996). The discussion should always keep in mind the key question or sub-questions framing a unit of work and how the activity helps students understand what is being investigated. It needs to deal with the question that I once heard in a classroom: 'Why are we doing this?'

Aspect of enquiry	Possible activities				
Eliciting prior knowledge	Brainstorming	Spider diagrams	KWL grids and variations	Drawing diagrams to show existing understanding	Diagnostic survey
Sparking curiosity	Presenting and discussing stimulus	Generating questions: 5Ws; 7Ws and an H; compass rose; big questions; little questions	Speculating: What is this? How was this formed? How did it get like this? Where is this?	Intelligent guesswork	Choice of what to study, e.g. which volcano, glacier or choice of how to present it
Using evidence	Five Key Points	Photo Editor	Layers of inference	Analysing using spider diagrams and mind maps	Statistical analysis of data, e.g. scatter graph
Making sense	DART (directed activity related to text)	Exploring meanings: contradictions (e.g. sustainable development) different uses of term (e.g. globalisation)	Concept mapping	Applying criteria	Argumentation
Presenting/ reflecting on findings	Sharing findings through discussion	Public meeting role-play	Whole-class debate	Written work: e.g. essay, project folder, newspaper	Producing a display

Figure 6: Some suggested activities focused on different aspects of enquiry. **Note:** More details of these activities and examples can be found in *Geography Through Enquiry* (Roberts, 2013).

8. What are students expected to learn?

The objectives for a unit of work might be determined by examination specifications or guided by key stage 3 requirements. Although I think that enquiry-based units of work and individual lessons are best introduced by questions that stimulate curiosity rather than lists of objectives, you might be expected to identify objectives at the start of lessons. In any case you will need to consider what you want students to have learnt by the end of the unit of work. You could categorise objectives under the following headings:

- Facts, locational knowledge and case study information to be remembered – it is important for students to know what they are expected to remember as distinct from detailed information given to them for analysis and interpretation, e.g. indices of development.
- Understanding of geographical processes, concepts and ideas.
- Geographical skills: analysing and interpreting geographical source materials including maps, GIS, reports, statistics, graphs, visual information, collecting and using fieldwork data.
- Generic enquiry skills: identifying questions, selecting sources, selecting data, using questionnaire surveys, using evidence, making connections, reaching conclusions.
- Other generic skills: literacy, numeracy, ICT, communicating, collaborating.
- Developing awareness of values and ethical dimensions.

9. How is learning to be assessed?

Formative assessment

I think of formative assessment as getting inside students' minds so that they can be given the necessary help. I think it is as important to know about students' misunderstandings and confusions as to know what understand correctly. The purpose of formative assessment is to identify what students already know, understand and can do, to identify any difficulties and to help them progress further. I suggest four strategies that could be used throughout an enquiry-based unit of work.

Chapter 5: Planning for enquiry

Questions that seek clarification: trying to understand what others are saying	Questions about viewpoints and perspectives
What do you mean by…?	Whose points of view are represented?
What is the main point you are making?	What different ways are there of looking at it?
Is your main point…?	Who benefits from this? Who loses?
Could you put it another way?	Why is it better than…?
Could you give me an example of…?	What are the strengths and weaknesses of…?
How does it relate to what we have been talking about?	Is there another point of view we should consider?
Could you explain that a bit more?	What is the counter-argument?
Questions that probe assumptions	**Questions that probe implications and consequences**
Are you assuming that…?	When you say…, are you implying…?
Is that always the case?	But, if that happened, what else would happen as a result? Why?
Does your reasoning depend on the idea that…?	What effect would that have?
Are you taking for granted…?	Would that necessarily happen or only probably/possibly happen?
What else could we assume?	What would be the consequences of that?
Why might someone make that assumption?	What are the implications of that?
Questions that probe reasons and evidence	**Questions about the question**
How can we find out if this is true/accurate?	Why is this issue important?
Why do you think that is true?	How can we find out?
What evidence are you basing that on?	Are there other questions we need to ask?
Do you have any evidence for…?	Can we break the question down a bit?
What are your reasons for saying…?	How far have we got?
Are these reasons enough?	Are we any nearer to answering the question?
Why do you say that?	
Is there any reason to doubt the evidence?	
Why is that happening?	
Are these reasons a good enough explanation?	
Can you explain your reasoning?	
Could there be another explanation?	

Figure 7: Categories of Socratic questions. **Source:** Roberts, 2013.

1. Observe and listen

Devise some activities in which students work in pairs or groups. This gives you the opportunity to listen. Make mental or written notes of what you learn generally and what you learn about individuals. Decide whether you need to intervene or whether you could discuss some of the points you have noted with the whole class later.

2. Intervening and scaffolding learning

When you intervene in a small-group discussion you can scaffold the learning in various ways. You can ask students to explain what they are doing and why, you can probe their thinking, reassure them, correct them if necessary, provide additional information or suggest new ideas. Socratic questions are useful for probing students' thinking (Figure 7). It is through these kinds of dialogues that you can help students progress beyond their present knowledge and understanding. Aim to have geographical, rather than evaluative, dialogues with students.

3. Learning logs

Sometimes called journals or diaries, these are completed by students either during a unit of work or at the end. They enable students to let you know what they have understood, what they are still unclear or puzzled about and whether they can relate what they have learnt to what they already know (headings might help them). The time allocated to such diaries could vary from 5 to 15 minutes, or they could be completed for homework.

4. Applying criteria: self- and peer assessment

If students are to evaluate their own and each other's work, they need to be aware of the criteria by which work (both oral contributions to discussion and written work) is judged. Criteria should be negotiated or presented to students before they start a piece of work.

Summative assessment

The purpose of summative assessment is to establish what students have learnt by the end of a unit of work or course of study. An enquiry-based unit of work could be assessed through:

- presentations to the rest of the class
- a coursework folder
- a written assignment
- a test or examination.

10. How can final activities and reflection help students learn through enquiry?

At the end of a unit of work, bringing together all aspects of the enquiry gives students opportunities to make connections between what they have learnt in each lesson and to reflect on their learning.

Riley (2000) recommended that units of work in history should end with 'a tangible, substantial, enjoyable "outcome activity" through which pupils can genuinely answer the enquiry question' (p. 8). In geography, such outcome activities could include: student presentations to the rest of the class or to a wider audience, possibly using multimedia; debates; public meeting role-plays; and the production of a multimedia resource.

It is important that you leave time – possibly a whole lesson – for students to reflect on what they have learnt. If learning is to be rigorous, then students' work during the unit needs to be open to critical scrutiny and evaluation. They need to reflect on what they have investigated, by considering:

- to what extent have the key questions been answered?
- were the sources of information sufficient and appropriate? What further evidence could be looked for?
- were the skills and techniques used to analyse and interpret data useful?
- could the investigation of this theme/place/issue be improved or further developed in any way?

They also need to reflect on their own learning:

- What have they learnt in terms of knowledge and understanding? Are there still things they don't quite understand? (They need to articulate their confusions rather than simply hold up a red traffic light.)
- Which activities have helped them learn most and/or made them think most?

Conclusion

This chapter has justified and emphasised enquiry as an approach to teaching and learning in which students are actively engaged in investigating geographical questions and issues. Although it has referred to many activities that can be incorporated into a unit of work, the use of one or two of them does not mean that an enquiry approach is being adopted. Nor does the use of questions as headings for units of work, or as chapter headings, necessarily mean that the work that follows is investigative. If students are to learn geography through enquiry, then it is important to establish a culture of enquiry in the classroom within which students are encouraged to question, to examine geographical sources critically and to think geographically for themselves. This rigorous investigative approach, in which students are expected to engage with geographical evidence and ideas, needs to permeate everything you do in the classroom. It influences how you introduce and debrief activities, how you carry out classroom discussion and dialogues with individual students and how you respond to what students write.

There are tensions between the kind of classroom culture that I am advocating and the current culture of education in England. Using evidence from Ofsted reports, Ferretti (2013) mentions three aspects of the current culture that might explain why enquiry is not more widespread in geography classrooms. First, she is concerned that rigid adherence to a three-part lesson consisting of starter, development activities and plenary might stifle geographical enquiry. Second, she is concerned that the managerial/accountability culture in which schools operate, measured by test and examination results, has encouraged teachers to focus on the content and skills they think are required for success, rather than enquiry approaches. Third, in some schools, the focus of the key stage 3 curriculum on generic skills, rather than subjects, has limited investigative work in geography.

However, despite the constraints of time, school expectations and examination specifications, you can still incorporate the essential aspects of enquiry into your units of work. There is scope in the key stage 3 geography curriculum to incorporate enquiry, and the GCSE geography (9–1) specifications are required to include enquiry. The challenge for you, within the culture in which you work, is to find ways to encourage students to develop a questioning approach to geography and a critical attitude towards knowledge. Enquiry-based learning does not simply happen; you need to plan for it to happen.

References

Alexander, R. (2006) *Towards Dialogic Teaching*. York: Dialogos.

Barnes, D. (2008) 'Exploratory talk for learning' in Mercer, N. and Hodgkinson, S. (eds) *Exploring Talk in School*. London: Sage, pp. 1–16.

Batchen, N. (2009) *Changing My World: What difference can we make to the climate?* Sheffield: Geographical Association.

Biddulph, M. (2011) 'Young people's geographies: implications for secondary school geography' in Butt, G. (ed) *Geography, Education and the Future*. London: Continuum, pp. 44–64.

Burnham, S. (2007) 'Getting year 7 to set their own questions about the Islamic Empire, 600–1600', *Teaching History*, 128, pp. 11–15.

Bustin, R. (2011) 'Thirdspace: exploring the "lived space" of cultural "others"', *Teaching Geography*, 36, 2, pp. 55–57.

DfE (2013) *National Curriculum in England: Geography programmes of study*. Available at: www.gov.uk/government/publications/national-curriculum-in-england-geography-programmes-of-study (last accessed 03/11/2016).

DfE (2014) *Geography: GCSE subject content*. Available at: www.gov.uk/government/publications/gcse-geography (last accessed 03/11/2016).

Ellis, L. (2009) *A Thorny Issue: Should I buy a Valentine's rose?* Sheffield: Geographical Association.

Ferretti, J. (2013) 'Whatever happened to the enquiry approach in geography?' in Lambert, D. and Jones, M. (eds) *Debates in Geography Education*. Abingdon: Routledge, pp. 103–15.

GA (2016) *Curriculum making*. Available at: www.geography.org.uk/cpdevents/curriculum/curriculummaking (last accessed 03/11/2016).

Mercer, N. and Dawes, L. (2008) 'The value of exploratory talk' in Mercer, N. and Hodgkinson, S. (eds) *Exploring Talk in School*. London: Sage, pp. 55–72.

Norman, R. (2014) 'Creating crazy enquiry questions', *Teaching Geography*, 39, 1, p. 25.

Rawling, E. (2007) *Planning Your Key Stage 3 Geography Curriculum*. Sheffield: Geographical Association.

Riley, M. (2000) 'Into the key stage 3 history garden: choosing and planting your enquiry questions', *Teaching History*, 99, pp. 8–13.

Roberts, M. (1998) 'The nature of geographical enquiry at key stage 3', *Teaching Geography*, 23, 4, pp. 164–67.

Roberts, M. (2013) *Geography Through Enquiry: Approaches to teaching and learning in the secondary school*. Sheffield: Geographical Association.

Webster, A., Beveridge, M. and Reed, M. (1996) *Managing the Literacy Curriculum*. Abingdon: Routledge.

Recommended key readings

Roberts, M. (2013) *Geography Through Enquiry: Approaches to teaching and learning in the secondary school*. Sheffield: Geographical Association.
This book provides a wealth of examples of enquiry as classroom practice; many of the chapters focus on practical activities such as mind maps, concept maps, DARTS and the layers of inference framework.

Ferretti, J. (2013) 'Whatever happened to the enquiry approach in geography?' in Lambert, D. and Jones, M. (eds) *Debates in Geography Education*. Abingdon: Routledge, pp. 103–15.

While chapter titles in section two are comfortably familiar, the content asks us to consider how current practice in schools has been arrived at and is being influenced at present; it also encourages us to question how practice might change in the future. In considering the wide range of styles and strategies available to how we teach geography, useful questions include: How can I approach teaching this aspect of geography? Why should I use a particular approach and what will be the intended outcomes? How useful are the approaches being discussed in the context of my school or educational environment?

Such discussion may also raise questions concerning 'generic' pedagogy compared with teaching through a geographical lens, which encourages 'geographical thinking' and places the 'geography' of lessons firmly in the foreground.

Section 2

Chapter **6** – **Physical geography**
Nicholas Clifford and Alex Standish

Chapter **7** – **Human geography**
Peter Jackson

Chapter **8** – **Teaching geography for sustainability**
John Morgan

Chapter **9** – **Global learning**
John Hopkin

Chapter **10** – **Place and locational knowledge**
Denise Freeman and Alun Morgan

Chapter **11** – **Teaching a good geography lesson**
Richard Bustin

Chapter **12** – **Resources**
David Rayner

Chapter **13** – **Differentiation**
Jane Ferretti

Chapter **14** – **Assessing geography**
Paul Weeden

Chapter **15** – **Literacy**
Nicola Walshe

Chapter **16** – **Numeracy**
Mark Jones

Chapter **17** – **Fieldwork**
John Widdowson

Chapter **18** – **GIS and other geospatial technologies**
Mary Fargher

Chapter **19** – **Post-16 geography**
Emma Rawlings Smith

Chapter 6

Physical geography

Nicholas Clifford is Professor of Geography at Loughborough University, and
Alex Standish is Senior Lecturer in Geography Education at UCL Institute of Education

Introduction

This chapter provides a brief definition and history of the discipline of physical geography, and some current research directions evidenced in university-level research and benchmarks for university teaching. It is hoped that these markers for advanced study will set a context for the teaching and the curriculum in schools, and also offer some stimulating avenues to explore with students at secondary school level. It suggests some points of contact between GCSE and A level curricula and the university subject, and makes the case for strengthened systematic teaching of basic science and concepts in physical geography.

Physical geography itself combines many areas of foundational scientific enquiry, most frequently considered in terms of the character and dynamics of Earth's surface, climate and vegetation, and a range of human, economic and environmental issues. Our increasingly complex and globalised world has prompted concerns about environmental and resource sustainability, uneven development and climate change, which offer tremendous opportunities for physical geography to address large-scale political and societal agendas, and to deeply engage students with the subject. Various newer ways of conceptualising environment-society interactions are outlined here as illustrations of this: sustainability studies, Earth system science, and Anthropocene and nexus studies. Teaching physical geography today can make use of diverse styles (from classroom to more active and participatory learning) and of diverse media (from personal encounters in the classroom, field or laboratory, through to computer simulation, social networking and virtual worlds). At the same time, concern is increasingly being expressed that teaching more basic knowledge of the science components and foundations of the subject has been neglected. This is reflected in specification changes over the last 25 years, which are briefly presented and reviewed here. A rationale for teaching physical geography as discrete sub-disciplinary units helps redress perceived deficiencies in fundamental knowledge, and informs the knowledge synthesis that more integrated approaches demand. It also provides a partial means of restoring subject knowledge to a curriculum that has been increasingly driven by practical and vocational agendas.

Definitions and history of physical geography

Physical geography may be defined as:

> 'the characterisation and explanation of geological, hydrological, biological and atmospheric phenomena and their interactions at, or near, Earth's surface. This is often, but not exclusively, in relation to human occupation and activity' (Clifford, 2009, p. 6).

Physical geography represents, therefore, a very broad range of enquiry, bringing together a range of natural and physical sciences to bear at and near Earth's surface. Its longer traditions, and its range and scope, reflect very much a late eighteenth- and nineteenth-century sense of optimism and eclecticism for science and modernity, where Earth's environment, people, and animal and plant populations had to be described, ordered and mapped. Physical geography defined both a set of characteristics and attributes of Earth's environment and an emerging field of intellectual enquiry.

In the early years of the formal subject, until about the mid-20th century, geography as a whole had a more unitary, regional focus, and distinctions between the human and the physical were less marked. Physical geography was an

Human geography	Physical geography	Environmental geography	Technology and methodologies
Cultural geography	Biogeography and ecology	Environmental management	Cartography
Development studies	Climatology	Hazard studies	Fieldwork
Economic geography	Earth system science	Regional management	GIS
Gender studies	Geomorphology	Rural geography	Modelling
Historical geography	Hydrology	Sustainable development	Qualitative methods and analysis
Political geography	Meteorology	Tourism studies	Quantitative methods and analysis
Social geography	Quaternary science	Transport studies	Remote sensing
Urban geography	Soils		Spatial analysis

Figure 1: Components indicative of human, physical and environmental geography and their methodologies. **Source:** QAA, 2014, p. 21.

essential background to regional geographical enquiry, providing a natural definition of regions: for example, areas bounded by mountain regions or rivers, or areas characterised by tundra or steppe. Often, economic and social activity was presented in relation to the natural environment, so physical geography was part of an early 20th-century environmental determinism. When this lost popularity, as being over-simplistic and possibly racially or ethnically biased, geography itself changed, to a much more overt separation of the physical and human aspects of the subject. In the mid-1960s, 'the Quantitative Revolution' of geography attempted to construct a new, integrated approach around systems theory and quantitative spatial science, but this lacked traction; by the 1980s geography had broken up into many more or less distinct sub-disciplines with relatively little association or connection. Physical geography was itself fragmented into more specific sub-fields, with more emphasis on hydrology, geomorphology, biogeography and Quaternary studies, and less on local meteorology and synoptic climatology, which had previously been mainstays. This fragmentation process was often associated with a change in the nature and methods of enquiry. Advances in computing, environmental dating and instrumentation all facilitated a growing emphasis on the small scale and fine detail of process studies – a trend, then towards scientific reductionism and specialisation – which held sway until roughly the end of the 20th century, when some newer approaches, and a re-visiting of older projects, emerged. Matthews and Herbert (2004) note a disciplinary fragmentation and argue forcefully for a unifying approach.

The Quality Assurance Agency for Higher Education (QAA) provides university departments in the UK with benchmark statements that describe the nature of the subject and what graduates on completing their studies might know, do and understand in the subject. Figure 1 is taken from the 2014 Geography Benchmark Statement for use in UK universities (QAA, 2014).

This statement emphasises human-environmental-landscape interaction; fundamental concepts are 'knowledge of environments being the result of biophysical processes' and 'knowledge of environments and landscapes as the result of human activity'. It follows from this that physical geography is popularly approached via 'issues' exemplifying human-environment impacts (for example with natural hazards), human impacts on biophysical systems (for example air pollution, deforestation, desertification, and on components of the climate system), and also the management of environments and landscapes (see QAA, 2014, pp. 8–9).

Some key directions

Geography has always reflected the society within which it has been defined and taught, and the present day is no exception. From the 1980s onwards, concerns emerged at an international scale with issues of environmental degradation, resource limitation, development and sustainability; these have now been joined by climate change and 'nexus studies', which address the combination and complexity of water, food and energy security. All of these issues hold potential for renewing and

Physical geography may be approached at all scales.
Photo © John Lyon.

revisiting physical geography as a subject at the interface between science, society and environment. Each has physical, social and economic dimensions – the problems we now face are global in scale, but manifest most severely locally; they involve not just traditional science or development economics, but demand news way of study – they are transdisciplinary and globalised. Alongside this, new possibilities in Earth observation, together with hugely increased capacity in data availability, storage, manipulation and visualisation, have reinvigorated some longer-standing questions and ambitions. Physical geography may thus be approached at all scales – local, regional and global – and through a wide range of methodologies. Three key integrating themes, representing possible directions for pursuing physical geography, are sustainability studies, Earth system science and the Anthropocene and nexus studies. Each of these provides integrating themes and connects physical geography with bigger environmental, social and political agendas. Each is exemplified by a range of issues or problems that easily capture the imagination and commitment of students. However, each of these themes raises, in turn, a key area of debate and tension in the teaching of physical geography. Can foundational concepts and the basic science be taught separately? If they can, should they be taught within or beyond the geography curriculum? These questions are addressed after a short introduction to each of the integrating themes.

Sustainability studies

Sustainability as a topic of study is a response to the issues of sustainability, development and the political ecology of a North–South divide, and is associated with the period leading up to the announcement of the United Nations Millennium Development Goals (MDGs) in 2000. Kates *et al.* (2001) provide a formal, short definition of a new socio-political-environmental agenda, which, they argue, demands a new form of science that is regionally and locally sensitive and does not apply science or science policy simply from the 'top down'. The divide between the North and South is not simply in terms of wealth, but in terms of lifestyle, development priorities and with respect to their nature–society–environment relations (Clark and Dickson, 2003). Sustainability studies reflect deeper thinking about the ways in which globalisation acts on people and place and is itself formed and changed by and in them, and it is also the clearest example of how environmental science and physical geography are necessary and fundamental parts of the globalisation syndrome (Clifford, 2009). Butzer (2002) places concern for environment and development at the heart of a reinvigoration of physical geography, arguing that the subject has been able to shape and enact globally significant agendas outside, as well as within, academic circles.

Some of the core questions of this new approach may be summarised as follows (Kates *et al.*, 2001, p. 642):

Chapter 6: Physical geography

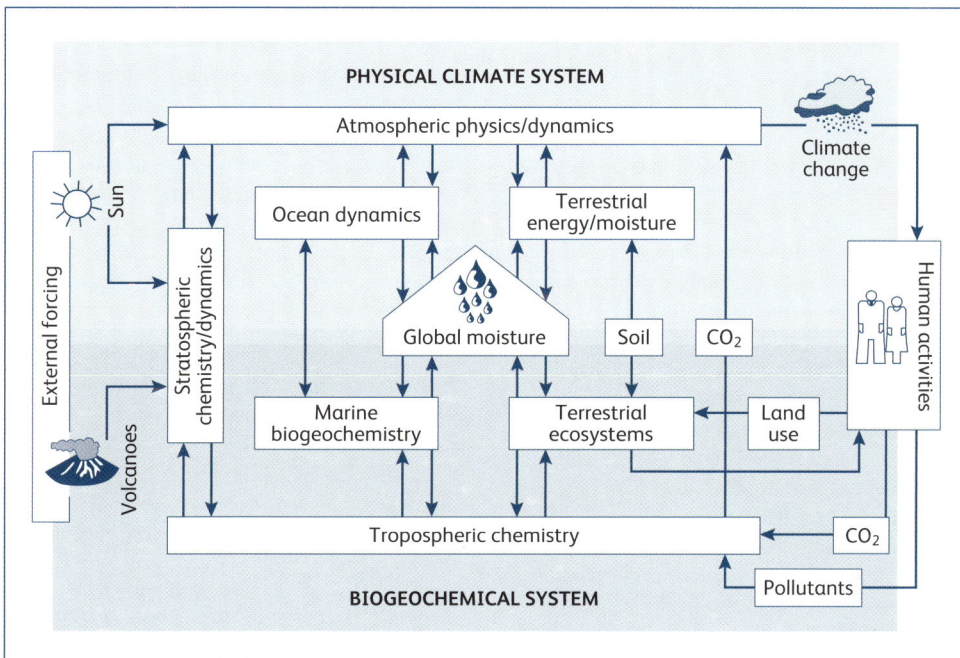

Figure 2: Schematic diagram of the Earth system and its interactions, encompassing the physical climate system, biogeochemical cycles, external forcing and the effects of human activities. **Source:** NASA Earth Systems Science Committee, 1988.

- 'How can the dynamic interactions between nature and society be better integrated into the emerging models and conceptualisations that incorporate the Earth system, human development and sustainability?

- How are long-term trends in environment and development, including consumption and population, reshaping nature–society interactions in ways relevant to sustainability?

- What determines the vulnerability or resilience of the nature–society system in particular kinds of places and for particular types of ecosystems and human livelihoods?

- How can today's systems for monitoring and reporting on environmental and social conditions be integrated or extended to provide more useful guidance for efforts to navigate a transition toward sustainability?'

Earth system science

Earth system science (ESS) appeared formally in the 1980s and was an attempt by NASA, first to structure its range of Earth observation activities, and then to link Earth observation technologies and programmes to the essential dynamics and functioning of oceanic and climatic systems, and to the wider field of geophysics (NASA Earth Systems Science Committee, 1988). ESS now, however, is a much broader emerging discipline, encompassing much of the historical territory of physical geography and much of what might be termed 'integrated geography' – that is, consideration of both physical–environmental and human–social phenomena as linked systems. The term ESS is now widely used in universities, research funding bodies, environmental agencies and scientific publishing. In many US institutions, for example, the term ESS has replaced 'physical geography' in foundational undergraduate level courses.

Figure 2 illustrates the key defining characteristics of ESS. Interactions between component systems (spheres or cycles) of the natural world, linkage and feedback between both natural and social sub-systems, and a concern with the global scale – in terms both of the science and political awareness and issues – are all crucial to the approach. In a recent summary, Gregory (2010) has identified more than 20 spheres spanning environment, geology, climate, soils and socio-economic processes and phenomena, and in many ways, ESS and the Anthropocene and nexus studies are really inseparable.

There are both positives and negatives in this approach. On the positive side, it has an ambition and scale that address globally significant questions of environment, development and sustainability. Using ESS we can connect physical geography with some of the big questions of today. Similarly, there are positives in the connection between these substantive questions and technologies of observation – ESS lends itself readily to studies using remotely sensed imagery and GIS, and to those which use computer simulation and advanced visualisations. It is, then, a kind of 'physical geography meets big science'. On the other hand, ESS is more difficult to address first hand and at smaller scale – what, for example, does it do for the case study or for fieldwork? Just as with sustainability studies, it provokes questions about the local vs the global – what of individuals, or local variations, smaller-scale interactions and individuality? For some, ESS is too abstract, too mechanistic and too totalising; for others it represents the only viable way to address longer-term issues of Earth sustainability. Perhaps, for teaching and learning, it provides a further excellent example of how different approaches should be tailored to linked questions that are manifest at various, and widely different, scales – from, for example, the fate of a raindrop landing on Earth's surface, right through the hydrological cycle and up to the global moisture balance; or soil formation in peatlands, issues of peatland conservation, extraction and burning and thus the global carbon cycle. ESS can be truly enabling in bringing together topics that are pure and applied science, environmental, social, human and physical. Clifford and Richards (2005) and Richards and Clifford (2008) provide introductory critiques of ESS.

The Anthropocene and nexus studies

The term Anthropocene has achieved rapid acceptance as the umbrella term for the phase in Earth history where the geological record is significantly affected by human activity. It is still without a formal time boundary: most accept the Industrial Revolution of c.1800 as its beginning; others argue for the presence in the archaeological record of widespread early hominid activity as a starting point; yet others for the advent of the nuclear era. All of these suggestions are united by the interaction between physical and human aspects of Earth environment – they vary, perhaps, only in scale, with an environmentalist strand in Anthropocene studies stressing mass extinctions, pollution and atmospheric modification as key components of the epoch. Anthropocene studies are ideally addressed within ESS, whether as a concept or by the use of multiple technologies of monitoring, modelling or analysis, and they fit closely with key globalisation and environmental sustainability debates.

One way of viewing physical geography within a human-modified and human-centred environmental framework is summarised in Figure 3. Gregory (2005) associates foundational science and conventional sub-disciplines with a series of problem-orientated themes: the overlapping circles defining subject expertise represent the need for multi-disciplinarity; the outer circle emphasises the need for a holistic and integrative approach containing the various human-environment, physical-social interfaces – in other words, the subject matter and character of physical geography.

Approaches to the teaching and learning of physical geography

In this section we move from a consideration of new disciplinary directions at university level to an exploration of methods for teaching physical geography in schools. Practically, teaching physical geography can be approached through the classroom, the laboratory or the field; in smaller and larger groups, and through individual project work. Each of these encounters with the subject demands one or more teaching and learning styles that call for different skills as students interact with concepts and ideas, exploring data or the real world. The return of the individual project for assessment at A level, requiring students to conduct their own enquiry (see DfE, 2014a, para 27) is a positive development. At this stage in their education, students have the knowledge and skills to develop more independent study, which will help prepare them for degree-level work.

With regard to the delivery and experience of physical geography beyond the textbook and classroom, laboratory work has perhaps been

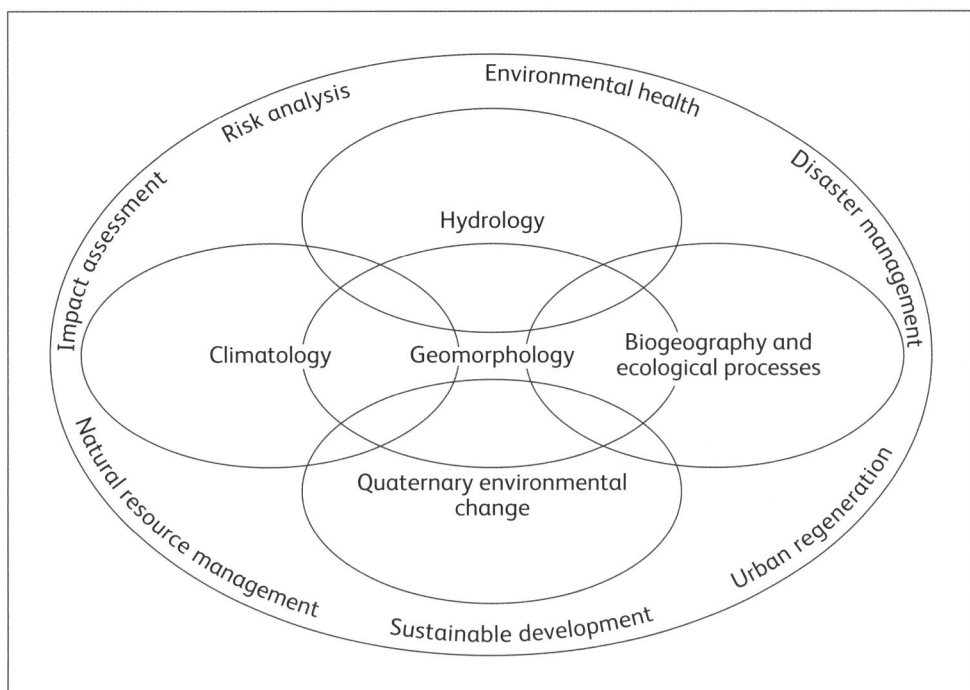

Figure 3:
The five overlapping sub-disciplines of physical geography in the context of multi-disciplinary and problem-orientated themes.
Source: Gregory *et al.*, 2002, p. 136–54.

underdeveloped in schools: basic chemical and physical processes can be encountered here, such as processes of erosion, as can foundational concepts in soil, plant and animal biology. Principles of experimental design, such as observation, replication and trials, can also most easily be appreciated in the lab. Using the lab as a focus for basic science principles and methods in physical geography also fosters welcome linkage between geography and the sciences. The laboratory can also be a workshop, with a focus on the design and build of observation and measurement apparatus, which increasingly extends to smaller-scale and lower-cost electronic sensors to measure light, temperature or moisture.

Fieldwork remains the mainstay of most encounters with a more formal appreciation of the environment – often undertaken as residential trips to 'classic' environments where physical processes, landscapes and regions are most marked and perhaps more exotic than the familiar local environment. Fieldwork activity lies on a spectrum from the fully participative and active – as students generate their own data and explore their own values, meanings and senses – to demonstration exercises and simple show-and-see tours, where the student receives explanations, but does so in the presence of the subject of interest, first hand rather than through the classroom.

GIS, computer models and simulations offer teaching possibilities for physical geography of all styles and applied at all scales, from the neighbourhood up to the planetary. The advent of open source GIS, and open source data such as Google Earth and QGIS, offers possibilities that are in many ways analogous to traditional mapping activities, but with much-enhanced analytical and data manipulation capabilities. Local environments are increasingly approachable to students through online resources, which provide environmental data at the postcode level – for example, the Environment Agency flood-risk maps – and through a growing number of applications on mobile devices to grade environmental quality, take basic measurements and record and share data. Technology, therefore, together with moves from open access through to crowd sourcing and cloud computing, blur the boundaries between primary and secondary data, between fieldwork and the classroom, and, for the student, between being an

Some geography students come through the education system never having studied topics such as glaciation. **Photo** © Bryan Ledgard.

active learner and researcher, and a trainee in methods, techniques and interpretation. Even less formal ways of creating and sharing knowledge – social networking, blogging communities and online gaming communities – are yet to be fully explored or harnessed as a resource for exciting and engaging students, and will doubtless figure more strongly, and very quickly, in the educational experience.

Teaching physical geography in UK schools today – a case of neglect?

It is fairly well established that physical geography has been neglected in the school geography curriculum over the past two or more decades. Some geography students and new teachers now come through the education system never having studied topics such as glaciation, geology or soils. Hawley (2013a) suggests that things began to change in the 1980s with the rise of humanistic geography and environmental issues – a trend that continues to be emphasised in the integrative and emerging key themes outlined above. Evidence for the neglect of physical geography can be found in the geography National Curriculum, GCSE and A level specifications and examinations, and in literature on geographical education (Hawley, 1997; Birnie, 1999; Keylock, 2006; Ofsted, 2011). The outcome for students of this decline is that 'their knowledge base is reduced' (Birnie, 1999); they have a weaker understanding of geographical phenomena and are therefore less well prepared to study at university or teach geography. Chris Keylock (2006) even suggests that students wishing to study physical geography at university may be better prepared if they took subjects other than geography at A level:

> 'The lack of sufficient scientific grounding at A level means that we may serve the interests of our students better by telling them that if they wish to succeed in a physical geography degree, they should pursue maths, physics, chemistry or biology instead of geography, at least in their A2 year' (p. 272).

Drawing on literature and curricular documentation, it is possible to examine how this situation has come about, before turning to an examination of the essential contribution of physical geography to a young person's geographical education, and to the possibilities for the recognition of discrete knowledge-based enquiry as a foundation to facilitate more integrative perspectives.

Issues-based teaching

Themes such as sustainability studies, ESS and nexus studies are exemplars of attempts by academics and policy-makers to link across subjects, so as to address increasingly complex issues of increasingly global concern. In relation to the teaching of geography, they also correspond to changes in the style and emphasis of geographical education in schools during the last quarter of the twentieth century. Something of a revolution took place in A level teaching (Birnie, 1999), with the rise of issues-based teaching and assessment, and decline of systematic sub-disciplinary coverage. This meant that geography is taught through an 'issue' of perceived importance, such as climate change, extreme weather events, globalisation or immigration; or a particular hazard such as an earthquake; rather than as a series of discrete areas of knowledge, such as soils, vegetation, climatology or geomorphology.

Issues-based geography was pioneered by the University of London Syllabus B, part of a Schools Council project. In 1996, the University of London Examinations and Assessment Council merged with the Business and Technology Education Council to become Edexcel. Today, along with some of the other examination boards, Edexcel continues to take an issues-based approach to geography. Its 2013 A level specification (Pearson Education, 2013) was divided into four units: global challenges, geographical investigations, contested planet and geographical research. The language used (World at Risk, Going Global, Crowded Coasts, Unequal Spaces, Extreme Weather, Biodiversity Under Threat and Water Conflicts) illustrated the human-centred approach. The same language prevails at GCSE level in the Edexcel specification (Global Georgaphical Issues, UK Geographical Issues, and People and Environment Issues) and to a lesser extent in other specifications, e.g. AQA (Living with the physical environment, Challenges in the human environment).

Teaching through issues can be engaging and offers opportunities for the application and synthesis of knowledge, when this approach is taught well. It is clear that we need to introduce the problems and challenges people face in diverse environmental settings around the globe, and teaching through issues can set a demanding agenda for more advanced students. Such issues certainly have their place in the curriculum (Standish, 2009). However, in order to synthesise knowledge across different areas of geography, students need to have a basis of knowledge from which to make connections. Issues can also be a way into a topic, perhaps stimulating a need to acquire more knowledge about an area of geography like long-term climatic change or atmospheric forcing. Curriculum innovation is important, and the bigger issues allow space for teachers to devise creative ways to approach the geography curriculum. However, moving straight to complex issues has its dangers and limitations, as this brief example illustrates.

Flooding is a frequent topic for a key stage 3 unit of work, and floods are something that many students will have experience of, either directly or indirectly. In order to properly understand flooding, students need knowledge of weather systems, drainage basins, drainage patterns and density, hydrology (including how rivers respond to storms), land use and its effects upon infiltration/run off, underlying geology, human modification of the drainage basin and river channels, and the effects of these modifications upon discharge. In key stage 3, students are unlikely to have acquired all this knowledge. Flooding may well be a way into developing such knowledge, but if it is taught simply as an 'event' with an emphasis upon human impact, students will lack the theoretical understanding that can be applied to other issues or events later on. This problem was identified in the 2011 Ofsted report on geography teaching: 'The students were expected to understand places and issues but they did not know where the places were, what they were like or the characteristics of their landscapes' (p. 22).

Problems arise from the assumptions that sometimes lie behind the increased emphasis on issues in the curriculum. Returning to the University of London Syllabus B, Birnie observes that 'It was designed, and has been highly successful, as a better preparation for life after school than a conventional A level' (Birnie, 1999, p. 50). In other words, the issues-based approach was seen as more 'relevant' for less

Figure 4: Contrasting representations of physical geography.

Key directions in higher education

Sustainability studies – Examining ways in which human activity impacts on the environment, issues of uneven development and how resources are allocated.

Earth system science – Exploring and representing the interconnections between climate and the biophysical and human spheres in an integrated approach.

Anthropocene – (advocating a new human-induced geological epoch) **and nexus studies** (here, linking geography to the study of food, water and energy security).

GCE subject content (DfE, 2014a, pp. 6–8)

At A level, two of the four core themes are:

Water and carbon cycles – a study of the physical processes that control the cycling of both water and carbon between land, oceans and the atmosphere. This should take place within a systems framework emphasising the integrated nature of land, earth and atmosphere.

Landscape systems – an integrated study of Earth surface processes, landforms and resultant landscape... through study of one landscape system chosen from either: drylands, coastal landscapes, or glaciated landscapes. This should take place within a systems framework, focusing on transfers of energy and movements of materials.

GCSE subject content (DfE, 2014b, p. 6)

4. Physical geography: processes and change

15. Geomorphic processes and landscape – How geomorphic processes at different scales, operating in combination with geology, climate and human activity, have influenced and continue to influence the landscapes of the UK. This should include detailed reference to at least two different and distinctive physical landscapes in the UK.

16. Changing weather and climate – The causes, consequences of and responses to extreme weather conditions and natural weather hazards, recognising their changing distribution in time and space and drawing on an understanding of the global circulation of the atmosphere. The spatial and temporal characteristics of climatic change and evidence for different causes, including human activity, from the beginning of the Quaternary period (2.6 million years ago) to the present day.

Geography National Curriculum (DfE, 2013)

* understand, through the use of detailed place-based exemplars at a variety of scales, the key processes in physical geography relating to: geological timescales and plate tectonics; rocks, weathering and soils; weather and climate, including the change in climate from the Ice Age to the present; and glaciation, hydrology and coasts.

academic students. While there clearly is a place for vocational study post-16, the idea that an academic curriculum or theoretical geography is not relevant to some students lies at the heart of an enduring educational separation in our school system: some students follow an academic route and others do not.

In fact, Michael Young (2008), among others, has noted that doubts about the relevance of theoretical knowledge to young people pervade much of the educational system. In a survey of 226 university students, Birnie found that those students who had studied the University of London Syllabus B had gaps

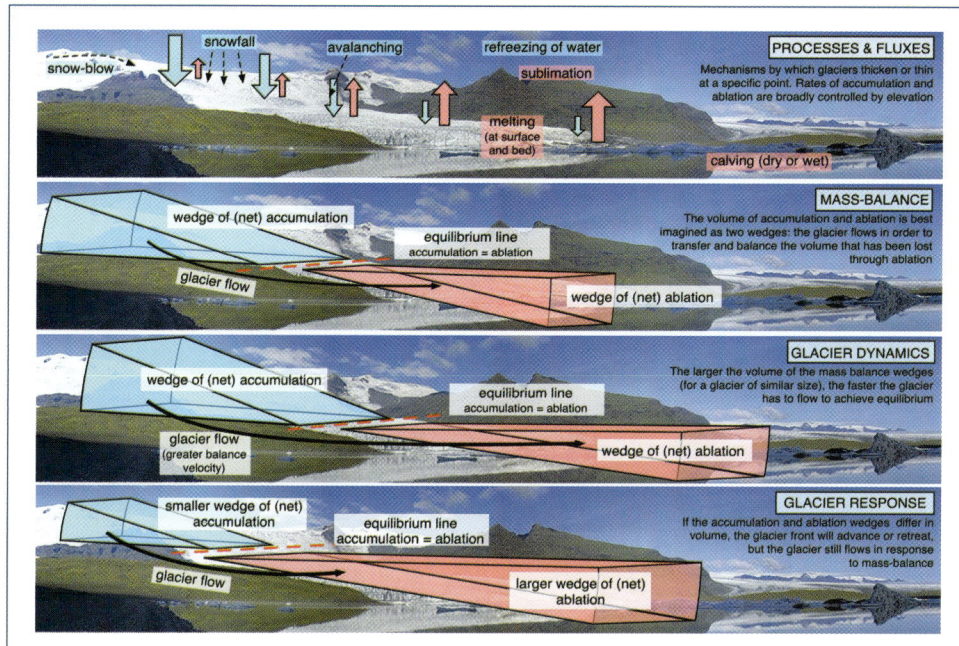

Figure 5: Glacier mass-balance and dynamics – Fjallsjökull, southern Iceland. **Source:** Reproduced with kind permission from Dr Simon Carr.

in their geographical knowledge, a poorer understanding of science and a weaker understanding of geographical terminology. However, the study also revealed that this trend was not confined to students who followed this syllabus, as other examination boards were following its lead. She concludes that 'Although the "16–19" [University of London B] syllabus was not designed with the needs of higher education in mind, higher education is now receiving its product in increasing numbers' (Birnie, 1999, p. 51).

Some teachers have suggested that issues-based teaching or 'extreme geography' like hazards has become more prevalent as departments try to attract more students by glamorising their curriculum. While there is probably some truth in this, the deeper problem is in the assumption that teaching physical knowledge is not sufficiently engaging or interesting in itself. As Rachel Atherton (2009) suggests, for some teachers physical geography must pass the test of 'how does this apply to humans?' yet both the GCSE (DfE, 2014b) and A level (DfE, 2014a) subject content for geography, which were used by awarding bodies to inform specification content and approach, include discrete sections emphasising knowledge of geomorphological processes and landscape evolution in the past and present (Figure 4).

More than one teacher we spoke with responded to the publication of the 2014 geography National Curriculum by suggesting that 'glaciation will not be of interest to my pupils'. It is important to recognise that this attitude is coming from both theoretical constructions of physical geography (see, again, Figure 3) and an increasingly prevalent societal view that the only valuable education is one that is directly relevant to a career or a practical application. Academic study can, of course, be of interest and value in its own right, and following from this, there is a strong argument for the component sub-fields of physical geography to be studied as discrete elements.

For an example of a systems approach to glaciers, as proposed in the A level specifications, we can look at their dynamics in terms of the balance between accumulation and ablation (Figure 5). Here, students can begin to see glaciers as a system of inputs and outputs that may or may not be in equilibrium, and how this influences the movement of ice.

In physical geography students study how natural forces shape the surface of Earth. **Photo** © Jeremiah LaRocco.

Re-visiting teaching through discrete sub-fields

Becoming a geographer means understanding how people are influenced by their physical environment and how they in turn act upon the natural world. Geography is thus a holistic discipline, but knowledge of the distinctiveness of physical and human phenomena is logically prior to understanding the ways in which they are connected.

In important respects, the natural sciences are fundamentally different from the human sciences and geography students need to be schooled in both. In physical geography, for example, students study how natural forces (tectonic, atmospheric, biological, hydrological, glaciological) shape the surface of Earth, in the past and present. This facilitates an understanding of how the landscapes we inhabit, or don't inhabit, have come into being. To the physical geographer, landscapes offer evidence of form, processes and patterns, and the potential to predict future change. It is different for human geographers. Humans are less predictable because we are conscious beings with agency to effect change in the world; we experience a range of feelings and emotions – the affective domain – which often has no tangible realisation but is absolutely essential to our existence. We are driven by ideas, desires and emotions, all of which are shaped by the societies in which we live. Human geographers, therefore, must delve into patterns of culture, social structures, economic structures, political processes and contemporary ideas. These are the social forces that give rise to populations, settlements, urban processes, migration, economies, territories and resource use.

Because the nature of the object of study is thus qualitatively different for physical and human geographers, their procedures and methods of enquiry are different. Physical geographers seek to comprehend and model the effects of natural forces. They must find ways to observe, measure and predict change in physical phenomenon. Human geographers can also study the physical, constructed environment, but this is ultimately a product of conscious thought. It is the human mind and social processes that human geographers must access, so they are likely to employ methods that directly interrogate human consciousness (e.g. surveys, interviews, etc.) or measure the products of human decisions (e.g. trade or urban form). While most academic geographers choose to specialise, teaching geography in school means developing an appreciation for both natural and human phenomena, including their distinctive natures, ways of thinking and modes of enquiry.

The very nature of geography is to explore links between phenomena (both natural and human) so that we can comprehend spatial variation and the uniqueness of places across the surface of Earth (Standish, 2014). Whether we are studying the spatial variation of one aspect of geography (systematic geography) or how human and physical phenomena combine to make a place or an area unique (regional geography), geographers are interested in the links between different areas of knowledge, 'thus no account of the geography of an area would be complete without an initial consideration of the nature and distribution of its rocks, landforms, soils, climate, rivers, minerals and vegetation' (Hawley, 1997, p. 81). Moreover, it is the very structure of geographical knowledge that gives rise to the necessity for discrete knowledge of natural phenomena. Physical geography is essential for students to be able to 'read the landscape' because the 'physical layer (landforms, materials and processes) provides the foundation for superimposed biological and cultural layers that make up the landscape' (Hawley, 2013b, p. 49).

What is often lost with a solely issues-based approach to geography is an understanding of the specialist conceptual frameworks needed to reach a deeper level of knowledge. For instance, in an article about developing conceptual understanding of rocks, Hawley notes that 'the inductive approach is poor at helping students to recognise the fundamental generic characteristics (defining attributes) that categorise different rock groups' (Hawley, 2002, p. 364). By themselves, students are likely to focus on the different colours, textures or mass of rocks. However, this will not lead them to an understanding of the processes by which different rocks types come into being, or a deeper understanding of their properties. When students are introduced to classification systems used by geologists (sedimentary, igneous, metamorphic) 'the scientific conceptual understanding… will form the basis for questioning, reasoning, speculating and inferring about rocks' (Hawley, 2002, p. 365). It is in this sense that theoretical knowledge is powerful. It enables predictions, such as susceptibility to weathering and porosity. It subsequently also helps students to understand how people interact with their environment.

Finally, sub-disciplinary components of physical geography have their own value, irrespective of their application to the human dimension. They take us on journeys into strange and even sublime worlds. For children, geography may be their first encounter with an ice landscape, a tropical rainforest, an ocean trench, geological time, karst landscape or limestone caverns. Geography is often commended for its ability to inspire awe and wonder. Iain Stewart observes that although modern Earth science is 'ripe for public consumption… this ripeness stems less from "pressing social relevance" than from an inherent sense of narrative' (Stewart, 2012). Professor Stewart has contributed to the modern media success of tapping into an audience that has a natural curiosity about how the natural world works. Awe and wonder, however, only capture one aspect of education: sparking curiosity. Yale Professor of Law Anthony Kronman notes that education also ends in wonder. Here, our wonder about things has been replaced by our wonder at them: 'amazement at the structures of things and our capacity to grasp this structure ourselves' (Kronman, 2007, p. 216). In between these two senses of wonder lies education: the process of acquiring concepts, ideas and theories that enable us to conceptualise that which was previously unfathomable.

Physical geography offers the chance to connect and engage with issues of sustainability, e.g. the Amazon rainforest. **Photo** © Neil Palmer (CIAT).

Conclusion

Teaching physical geography today offers several unprecedented opportunities: the chance to connect and engage students with issues of environmental and societal sustainability, at all scales from the local to the global; the chance to encounter the environment in locations as diverse as the classroom, field, laboratory or even virtual worlds; to capture and manipulate increasing quantities of high-quality data, which are themselves increasingly in the public domain; and to create, through such new media as social networking and crowd sourcing, completely new ways of approaching and influencing environmental problems and agendas, at all scales. At the same time, these opportunities imply a scale of ambition which may not so easily be fulfilled: foundational knowledge of science components for the subject is still needed to configure, analyse and solve more complex environment–society problems. A longstanding trend has been to neglect more traditional, discrete teaching of the sub-fields of the subject, which has reinforced the trend towards an implicitly more vocational, rather than academic, curriculum. At a time when subject-specific support and advice in many local authorities has also been removed (Iwaskow, 2013), and for a generation of teachers who are meeting more demanding knowledge-based syllabus changes with little or no physical geography training, then capitalising on new opportunities for the subject will be a demanding, but rewarding, challenge.

References

Atherton, R. (2009) 'Living with natural processes – physical geography and the human impact on the environment' in Mitchell, D. (ed) *Living Geography: Exciting future for teachers and students*. London: Chris Kington Publishing, pp. 93–112.

Birnie, J. (1999) 'Physical geography at the transition to Higher Education: the effect of prior learning', *Journal of Geography in Higher Education*, 23, 1, pp. 49–62.

Butzer, K.W. (2002) 'The rising cost of contestation: commentary/response: Turner's "Contested Identities"', *Annals of the Association of American Geographers*, 92, 1, pp. 75–86.

Clark, W.C. and Dickson, N.M. (2003) 'Sustainability science: the emerging research program', *Proceedings of the National Academy of Sciences*, 100, 14, pp. 8059–61.

Clifford, N.J. (2009) 'Globalization: a physical geography perspective', *Progress in Physical Geography*, 33, 1, pp. 5–16.

Clifford, N.J. and Richards, K.S. (2005) 'Earth system science: an oxymoron?', *Earth Surface Processes and Landforms*, 30, 3, pp. 379–83.

DfE (2013) *National Curriculum in England: Geography programmes of study*. Available at: www.gov.uk/government/publications/national-curriculum-in-england-geography-programmes-of-study (last accessed 07/11/2016).

DfE (2014a) *GCE AS and A Level Subject Content for Geography*. Available at: www.gov.uk/government/publications/gce-as-and-a-level-geography (last accessed 07/11/2016).

DfE (2014b) *Geography: GCSE subject content*. Available at: www.gov.uk/government/publications/gcse-geography (last accessed 07/11/2016).

Gregory, K.J. (ed) (2005) *Physical Geography*. London: SAGE.

Gregory, K.J. (2010) *The Earth's Land Surface*. London: SAGE.

Gregory, K.J., Gurnell, A.M. and Petts, G.E. (2002) 'Restructuring physical geography', *Transactions of the Institute of British Geographers*, 27, 2, pp. 136–54.

Hawley, D. (1997) 'Cross-curricular concerns in geography: Earth sciences and physical geography' in Tilbury, D. and Williams, M. (eds) *Teaching and Learning Geography*. Abingdon: Routledge, pp. 80–92.

Hawley, D. (2002) 'Building conceptual understanding in young scientists', *Journal of Geoscience Education*, 50, 4, pp. 363–71.

Hawley, D. (2013a) 'What is the rightful place of physical geography?' in Lambert, D. and Jones, M. (eds) *Debates in Geography Education*. London: Routledge. pp. 89–102.

Hawley, D. (2013b) 'Physical geography: constructs and questions relating to curriculum and pedagogy', *Didáctica Geográfica*, 14, pp. 37–55.

Iwaskow, L. (2013) 'Geography: a fragile environment?', *Teaching Geography*, 38, 2, pp. 53–55.

Kates, R.W., Clark, W.C., Corell, R., Hall, J.M., Jaeger, C.C., Lowe, I., McCarthy, J.J., Schellnhuber, H.J., Bolin, B., Dickson, N.M., Faucheux, S., Gallopin, G.C., Grübler, A., Huntley, B., Jäger, J., Jodha, N.S., Kasperson, R.E., Mabogunje, A., Matson, P., Mooney, H., Moore, B. 3rd, O'Riordan, T. and Svedin, U. (2001) 'Environment and development: sustainability science', *Science*, 292, 5517, pp. 641–42.

Keylock, C. (2006) 'Reforming AS/A2 physical geography to increase geographic scholarship', *Geography*, 91, 3, pp. 272–79.

Kronman, A. (2007) *Education's End: Why our colleges and universities have given up on the meaning of life*. New Haven, CT: Yale University Press.

Matthews, J. and Herbert, D. (eds) (2004) *Unifying Geography: Common heritage, shared future*. Abingdon: Routledge.

NASA Earth Systems Science Committee (1988) *Earth System Science: A closer view*. Washington, DC: NASA.

Ofsted (2011) *Geography: Learning to make a world of difference*. Manchester: Ofsted.

Pearson Education (2013) *Edexcel Specification GCE Geography*. Available at: http://qualifications.pearson.com/content/dam/pdf/A%20Level/Geography/2013/Specification%20and%20sample%20assessments/UA035234_GCE_Lin_Geog_Issue_4.pdf (last accessed 07/11/2016).

Quality Assurance Agency for Higher Education (QAA) (2014) *Subject Benchmark Statement. Geography*. Available at: www.qaa.ac.uk/en/Publications/Documents/SBS-geography-14.pdf (last accessed 07/11/2016).

Rees, J. (2013) 'Geography and the nexus: Presidential Address and record of the Royal Geographical Society (with IBG) AGM 2013', *The Geographical Journal*, 179, 3, pp. 279–82.

Richards, K.S. and Clifford, N.J. (2008) 'Science, systems and geomorphologies: why LESS may be more', *Earth Surface Processes and Landforms*, 33, 9, pp. 1323–40.

Standish, A. (2009) *Global Perspectives in the Geography Curriculum: Reviewing the moral case for geography*. London: Routledge.

Standish, A. (2014) 'Some important distinctions for geography educators', *Geography*, 99, 2, pp. 83–89.

Stewart, I. (2012) *Tell me a story*. Available at: www.geolsoc.org.uk/Geoscientist/Archive/March-2012/Of-maps-means-ends/Tell-me-a-story (last accessed 07/11/2016).

Young, M. (2008) *Bringing Knowledge Back In: From social constructivism to social realism in the sociology of knowledge*. Abingdon: Routledge.

Recommended key readings

Clifford, N.J. (2009) 'Physical geography' in Gregory, D.J., Johnston, R., Pratt, G., Watts, M. and Whatmore, S. (eds) *The Dictionary of Human Geography* (5th edition). Chichester: Wiley-Blackwell, pp. 531–38.

A short synopsis of the history, concepts and scope of physical geography in relation to its parent discipline.

Hawley, D. (2013) 'What is the rightful place of physical geography?' in Lambert, D. and Jones, M. (eds) *Debates in Geography Education*. Abingdon: Routledge, pp. 89–102.

This chapter explores debates about the place of physical geography and what counts as knowledge in physical geography.

Chapter 7

Human geography

Peter Jackson is Professor of Human Geography at the University of Sheffield

Introduction

As I was beginning to write this chapter, the UK's leading supermarket chain had just launched its Eat Happy Project, described as 'a major new food education programme', designed to help young people have 'a happier and healthier relationship with food' (Tesco, 2014). Over the next year, the website announced, Tesco aimed to take one million school children on educational 'Farm to Fork' trails around their stores and on visits to some of their suppliers' fields, farms and factories (see Figure 1). Tesco is not alone among Britain's major food retailers in launching such initiatives. Morrison's Let's Grow campaign has provided gardening equipment to thousands of schools across the UK (in exchange for vouchers based on in-store purchases) and Sainsbury's recently relaunched their Active Kids campaign, featuring David Beckham making fruit smoothies in a series of TV adverts. But what lies behind this recent outbreak of corporate social responsibility and how should geography teachers react to such developments?

For a geographer whose research focuses on the UK food industry, and as someone who has used the 'farm to fork' metaphor in my own work, Tesco's initiative (and others like it) clearly has its attractions. The initiative plans to take pupils out of the classroom and into the field (or, more often, the supermarket). The project website shows lots of happy pupils wearing fluorescent yellow jackets emblazoned with the slogan 'I'm learning where my food comes from' (including one who had just learnt that potatoes are dug up from the ground and don't grow on trees). Despite their commitment to fieldwork, many schools struggle to support this kind of outdoor learning activity and Tesco's website provides a range of free resources including 'teaching toolkits' and instructions about how to book free store trails and farm visits to Tesco's suppliers. However, one cannot help questioning what motivated this apparently benign project and whether educating pupils about the contemporary food system can be safely entrusted to major corporations whose primary objective is commercial.

Most UK supermarket chains suffered significant reputational damage in 2013 through their involvement in the horsemeat scandal: the widespread adulteration of beef and pork products with cheaper undeclared ingredients. In one batch of Tesco's Everyday Value burgers, horsemeat was found to comprise approximately 29% of the burger's total meat content, leading consumers to question the integrity of the extended supply chains on which firms like Tesco have come to depend (see Figure 2). During 2013, Tesco made a series of public apologies for its role in the horsemeat scandal and took a range of initiatives to help restore customer trust (see Figure 3). In these circumstances, one might ask whether initiatives such as the Eat Happy Project were designed to help regain consumer confidence in the brand, rather than being a purely altruistic effort 'to improve the next generation's relationship with food'.

These news stories and corporate initiatives offer geography teachers a valuable opportunity to raise questions about environmental sustainability, animal welfare and food security, all of which reflect the growing disconnection between food producers, retailers and consumers in a highly industrialised agri-food system that government sources have described as increasingly 'dysfunctional' (Policy Commission on the Future of Farming and Food, 2002). As an everyday necessity that we tend to take for granted, food can be used to show the

Chapter 7: Human geography

Figure 1:
TV presenter Gabby Logan helps launch Tesco's Eat Happy Project in January 2014. **Photo** © Bethany Clarke/ Getty Images Europe.

Figure 2:
How the tabloids reported the horsemeat scandal in 2013. **Photo** © Mikey, reproduced under Creative Commons licence (CC BY 2.0).

Figure 3:
Tesco apologises for its role in the 2013 horsemeat scandal.
Source: Newsworks website.

With the world's population estimated to reach 9 billion by 2050 and with demand for food projected to rise by 70% over the same period, food security has become an increasingly pressing problem. According to the UN Food and Agriculture Organisation, food security exists 'when all people, at all times, have physical, social and economic access to sufficient, safe and nutritious food which meets their dietary needs and food preferences for an active and healthy life' (FAO, 2009). Note how the definition moves from issues of physical and economic access to cultural questions of food preference and lifestyle. On a global scale, as Raj Patel argued in his aptly-titled book *Stuffed and Starved* (2007), food security is fundamentally an issue of unequal access and inequitable distribution, with around one billion people chronically undernourished (mainly in the Global South) and a similar number overweight or obese (mostly in the Global North). Periodic 'spikes' in agricultural commodity prices, such as those that occurred in 2008, combined with severe environmental events such as droughts and floods or natural disasters such as tsunamis or hurricanes, put thousands more at risk each year, even in the world's most affluent countries. Food security therefore raises fundamental questions about the relationship between environmental and social systems bridging the interests of human and physical geography.

Such issues are at the very heart of contemporary human geography and require new ways of thinking about the subject. Using food as a central motif, this chapter explores the scope of contemporary human geography and its ability to address some of the most pressing issues confronting humanity today. It identifies some common themes and unifying principles in terms of the discipline's commitment to relational thinking, transcending boundaries and working across scales. The chapter also challenges geography teachers to think about the conceptual underpinning of their subject as well as its substantive content.

The scope and diversity of contemporary human geography

When prospective students attend university Open Days they are often surprised by the breadth of human geography at degree level.

value of a geographical perspective on issues of truly global significance. The new specifications for geography at AS and A level have placed greater emphasis on food. For example, food issues appear within one of the three human geography options in the AQA A level and there is a unit on the Future of Food in OCR's specification covering security, causes, threats, impacts and future prospects. Food can also be used as an example of the operation of global systems and global governance, demonstrating the connectivity between people, places and environments. Now is therefore a good time for geography teachers to reflect on the nature of their subject, including the role that food might play in exemplifying new approaches and developing revised content.

While they may feel familiar with some themes, such as urbanisation, migration and international development, other aspects are completely new to them – geographies of gender and sexuality, music and art for instance. They are often surprised at what counts as geography and intrigued by the range of methods that geographers employ in the course of their work, including statistics and GIS, remote sensing and environmental modelling but also qualitative methods like ethnographic observation, focus groups and interviews, and techniques for analysing media representations and other visual images.

While the diversity of the subject can seem perplexing and the pace of change within the discipline can be quite breathtaking, geography at university is much less hidebound by tradition than many other subjects and its breadth is a major attraction to prospective students. Undergraduate geography students are actively encouraged to read beyond the discipline (though sometimes it might also help if they had a better grasp of their subject's intellectual history).

The health of the discipline was confirmed by an International Benchmarking Review of Human Geography (ESRC, 2012), which concluded that UK human geography was empirically and conceptually innovative, diverse and vibrant, setting the intellectual agenda in many sub-disciplinary areas. Reviewing the evidence in terms of student quality and publication data, the Review concluded that UK human geography ranks first in the world, setting a global standard. This is heartening news for UK human geographers in an environment where research funding is ever-more competitive, but how do geography students and teachers perceive the scope and diversity of the subject? If you were asked to describe human geography to a non-specialist, would you be more likely to reel off a list of topics (such as population and migration, natural resources and international development) or would you emphasise the subject's core concepts (such as space and place, scale and environment)? Why would you answer the question in this way?

The field of human geography – its broad scope, wide range of theoretical concepts and diversity of methodological approaches – can be daunting, especially for those encountering the discipline for the first time. One recent introduction to the subject (*Introducing Human Geographies*, Cloke et al., 2014) was organised around eleven thematic chapters, nine dualisms and four new 'horizons' in geographical thinking (see Figure 4). *The Dictionary of Human Geography*, now in its fifth edition (Gregory et al., 2009), is equally impressive in its scale and scope. Importantly, though, neither book claims to be definitive or to exhaust the breadth and vitality of the discipline, for there can be no final, comprehensive catalogue of the subject. Human geography is constantly evolving, subject to ongoing contestation and critique. For all its diversity and dynamism, is it still possible to identify any unifying principles and common themes?

Common themes and unifying principles

Many human geographers would be prepared to rally around the idea that their discipline addresses the relationship between people and place or, more abstractly, the interplay of society and space. While they are part of our core vocabulary, 'place' and 'space' are both elusive terms that defy easy definition. Place is often understood as space 'made human' through the many ways in which people make Earth their home (cf. Cresswell, 2004), but place is itself a contested concept as people vary in terms of the degree to which they feel in or out of place and geographers have a long tradition of studying processes of social exclusion and marginalisation (Sibley, 1985; Cresswell, 1996). Place, then, is defined in terms of subjective feelings of belonging as much as it refers to a specific location or territory. The boundaries of place are often fluid, challenging those who seek to establish and police more bounded notions of territorial belonging such as are implied in notions of citizenship and nationality. Place tends to be conceived on a more localised scale than space and to be concerned with embodied and affective notions of belonging as conveyed by the elusive idea of a 'sense of place'. Place involves an embodied and experiential feeling of being at home, though this feeling can extend from the domestic scale to the regional or national scale (and beyond).

Figure 4: Contrasting representations of human geography.

Contrasting representations of human geography

Introducing Human Geographies (Cloke *et al.*, 2014)

Themes: Bio-geographies, Cartographies, Cultural geographies, Development geographies, Economic geographies, Environmental geographies, Historical geographies, Political geographies, Population geographies, Social geographies, Urban and rural geographies.

Dualisms: Local–Global, Society–Space, Human–Non-human, Modern–Postmodern, Self–Other, Masculinity–Femininity, Science–Art, Explanation–Understanding, Representation–Reality.

Horizons: Non-representational geographies, Mobilities, Securities, Publics.

GCE subject content (DfE, 2014a)

At A level, four core themes:

1) Water and carbon cycles

2) Landscape systems

3) Global systems and global governance

4) Changing place; changing places.

(3) Global systems and global governance

Greater connectivity between people, places and environments across the globe means that movements of goods, people, technology and ideas have become easier and the systems which facilitate and direct these flows have become truly global in reach and impact. AS and A level specifications must require students to undertake study of the way in which global systems shape relationships between individuals, states and environments. They must also investigate the increasing numbers of norms, laws and conventions, referred to here as 'global governance', that aim to regulate the consequences of globalisation for people, places and environments around the world.

(4) Changing place; changing places

Relationships and connections between people, the economy, society and the environment help to explain why places are constantly changing. In addition, the meanings and representations attached to places help to shape actions and behaviours affecting that place. AS and A level specifications must require that students undertake study of the way in which these factors (relationships, connections, meaning, representation) affect continuity and change in the nature of places and our understanding of place.

GCSE subject content (DfE, 2014b)

A requirement that all students study the geography of the UK in depth:

Human geography: processes and change

19. Cities and urban society – An overview of the causes and effects of rapid urbanisation and contrasting urban trends in different parts of the world with varying characteristics of economic and social development. At least two city studies, one economically advanced/one poor and understanding of the causes and impacts of national and international migration on the growth and character of these cities.

20. Global economic development issues – The causes and consequences of uneven development at global level as the background for considering the changing context of population, economy and society and of technological and political development *'in at least one poorer country or one that is within a newly emerging economy. Country study should include examination of the wider political, social and environmental context within which the country is placed, the changing nature of industry and investment, and the characteristics of international trade, aid and geo-political relationships with respect to that country'*.

Geography National Curriculum (DfE, 2013)

Understand… the key processes in **human geography** relating to:

population and urbanisation; international development; economic activity in the primary, secondary, tertiary and quaternary sectors; and the use of natural resources.

'Space' is a more abstract term, concerned with the relations between objects and events rather than with the fixed co-ordinates of conventional cartography. In Henri Lefebvre's (1991) terms, space is produced through specific social processes rather than having any a priori or absolute existence. Doreen Massey's *Spatial Divisions of Labour* (1984) provides an extended exploration of these ideas, showing how capitalist social relations are responsible for the development of successive regional geographies whereby each new round of economic investment or disinvestment impacts differentially on places, depending on the impact of previous rounds. Massey's pioneering work has been finessed by subsequent theorising about space, inspired by philosophers such as Foucault and Deleuze, leading to a dynamic view of space as 'the dimension of the social', similar to the conception of time as the dimension of change (Massey, 2005). Massey's work also highlights the connections between space and power, as in her concept of 'power geometries' whose political potential remains to be fully explored.

Thinking relationally

Massey's work is also pivotal in terms of its advocacy of relational thinking, emphasising the connections between scales (such as local and global) and spaces (such as urban and rural). Rather than thinking of these terms as bounded and absolute, relational thinking explores the complex ways in which one produces the other (urban/rural, local/global etc.) where each term can only be understood in relation to the other. So Raymond Williams, for example, in his classic account of *The Country and the City* (1973), begins by demonstrating that 'country' and 'city' both evoke simultaneously positive and negative feelings. The country is celebrated for 'peace, innocence and simple virtue' while also being disdained for 'backwardness, ignorance and limitation' (as in Marx's oft-quoted comments on 'the idiocy of rural life'). Simultaneously, however, the city is celebrated as 'an achieved centre of learning, communication, light' while being loathed as 'a place of noise, worldliness and ambition' (Williams, 1973, p. 1). Williams does not stop at identifying the linguistic ambiguities and contradictions of these terms but proceeds to show how, through the course of the Industrial Revolution and its aftermath, these feelings have been (re)produced through the material and symbolic connections between the country and the city. In his analysis of Hogarth's *Gin Lane*, for example, he reveals how an image of urban dystopia was shaped by the over-production of grain in the surrounding countryside, sold as cheap liquor to the urban poor (see Figure 5), or how pastoral visions of an idyllic rurality conceal the hidden labour that shaped the countryside for the benefit of a privileged few. Exploring these relational connections yields a completely different historical geography from the familiar iconography of the English country house and landed estate, including their literary and artistic representation (as explored in John Barrell's (1980) *The Dark Side of the Landscape*).

So, too, in Edward Said's exploration of culture and imperialism, which he described as 'a kind of geographical inquiry into historical experience' (1993, p. 6), the principal aim is to think relationally about the connections between Self and Other, centres and margins, metropolis and empire. In one of his most compelling examples, Said demonstrates the relational connection between the polite domestic world of Jane Austen's *Mansfield Park* and the wealth on which the house and its imposing estate were built, derived from a plantation economy based on slavery in the Caribbean. Nor are these examples confined to the historical past or to the analysis of literary and artistic representation, as suggested by Neal Fox's recent parody of Hogarth's *Gin Lane*, which features a mix of ironic references to contemporary 'foodie' culture in a gentrified inner London urban landscape (Figure 6). This way of thinking might offer a refreshingly different way of teaching about gentrification and urban change, for example.

Said's deployment of relational thinking offers a radical critique of the geographical conceit that 'we' in the economically developed West are at the centre of the universe, that 'our' way of doing things is the best or only way. By contrast, Said insists that none of us is outside or beyond geography. Rather, we are all involved in the struggle over geography (whether this is defined in physical terms as territory, or in terms of our geographical

Figure 5: William Hogarth's *Gin Lane* (1751). **Source:** Licensed under Public Domain via Wikimedia Commons – https://commons.wikimedia.org/wiki/File:GinLane.jpg#/media/File:GinLane.jpg

imaginations, including the kind of Orientalist ideologies about which Said also wrote so powerfully. In his study of Orientalism, Said (1978) argued that an imagined 'Orient' provided Europeans with their deepest and most recurring sense of 'the Other': 'East assumes West; the Orient assumes the Occident. The two geographical entities support and reflect each other' (p. 5).

Said's work challenges us to recognise that geography's history has been preoccupied with drawing boundaries and defending territory rather than searching for common ground, overcoming barriers and challenging exclusions. As teachers, then, we might reflect on how these ideas and approaches impact on the way we talk about national sovereignty and territorial integrity as outlined in the A level specifications.

The idea of relational thinking can also be applied to other key debates in human geography such as the nature of globalisation and the interconnections between the local and the global, providing an opportunity to teach familiar topics in new ways. Globalisation is often thought of as a linear and irreversible process whereby powerful forces in the Global North are relentlessly extending their influence throughout the world, but geographers like Doreen Massey have provided searching critiques of this simplistic argument, insisting that globalisation is an incomplete and deeply contested process; that 'global' forces emanate from specific places (such as Wall Street or Brussels); and that such forces have a differential impact in different places, depending on their prior geographical and historical circumstances.

Figure 6:
Gin Lane Revisited, Neal Fox (2013).

Just as 'global' forces emanate from specific places, so can 'local' struggles have an impact worldwide, as examples like the fall of the Berlin Wall, the Occupy movement or the 'Arab Spring' uprisings all testify. Approached in this relational manner, Massey argues, it may be possible to identify a more progressive or global sense of place where localities are defined through their particular connections with other places, rather than as the passive recipients of 'global' forces, always originating elsewhere. In this view, 'global' and 'local' are not separate geographical scales but mutually interconnected forces that shape places in distinctive ways.

A final example of the power of thinking relationally in contemporary human geography is the question of how we, as human beings and members of society, define our place in the world. If geography sees itself as a purely social science, then it is tempting to locate ourselves 'outside' or 'beyond' nature – our humanity defined through our assumed superiority to other species that have been progressively subordinated to meet our human needs. From this perspective, 'nature' is often defined as a social construction, subject to specifically human ways of framing it. While this approach has been successful in challenging essentialist constructions of race and gender, for example, repudiating the way these concepts are conventionally assumed to be rooted in nature, the assumptions on which such an approach are based have been criticised by those who see humanity's place as located within nature rather than outside or above it. Thinking in terms of a 'more-than-human' world provides a radical alternative to the traditional view of 'Man and Nature', promising to transcend existing distinctions between the social and environmental sciences, including those between human and physical geographies. Thinking geographically in this relational way about the connections between scales and the transcendence of boundaries might also encourage us to teach traditional issues such as international development or the rural-urban fringe in radically new ways. Geography teachers may wish to consider the possible implications for human geography of thinking of 'our' place in the world as inside rather than outside nature (see Whatmore (2002) for some specific examples).

Returning to the example of food geographies, we might think about the way plants and animals have been domesticated for human consumption. Many animal species are now unrecognisable from their pre-domesticated form, their transformation into objects for human consumption having been subject to agricultural intensification and selective breeding. While this has produced abundant, year-round, relatively cheap food, it has severed the connection between food and farming for many consumers, defying the ecological logic that 'eating is an agricultural act' (Berry, 1992). Periodic 'food scares' and farming crises like BSE ('mad cow disease') or Foot and Mouth Disease serve as constant reminders that the natural world cannot be entirely subordinated to human control and that 'nature' can assert itself in ways that pose serious risks to public health and to the commercial exploitation of plants and animals. What vision of our place in nature, for example, is conveyed by the conditions in which battery eggs are produced, or by the Concentrated Animal Feeding Operations (CAFOs) that are replacing conventional dairy farms across the American Mid-West? What happens to the human relationship with other animal species when the connection between food and farming is strained in this way, as supply chains are extended around the world and as the links to seasonality and locality are increasingly severed?

Transcending boundaries, crossing scales

Geographers have a predilection for working across boundaries, whether in terms of different disciplinary perspectives or geographical scales. Like the search for connections that is intrinsic to geographical thinking (Jackson, 2006), transcending boundaries is part of our geographical DNA. Geography shares with other social sciences a commitment to making the familiar strange (by showing how many of the things that are taken for granted in the relatively affluent Global North are not universally shared). Conversely, geographers and other social scientists often strive to make what at first sight might seem strange more comprehensible by seeking to understand the cultural context of apparently 'exotic' social practices and behaviours.

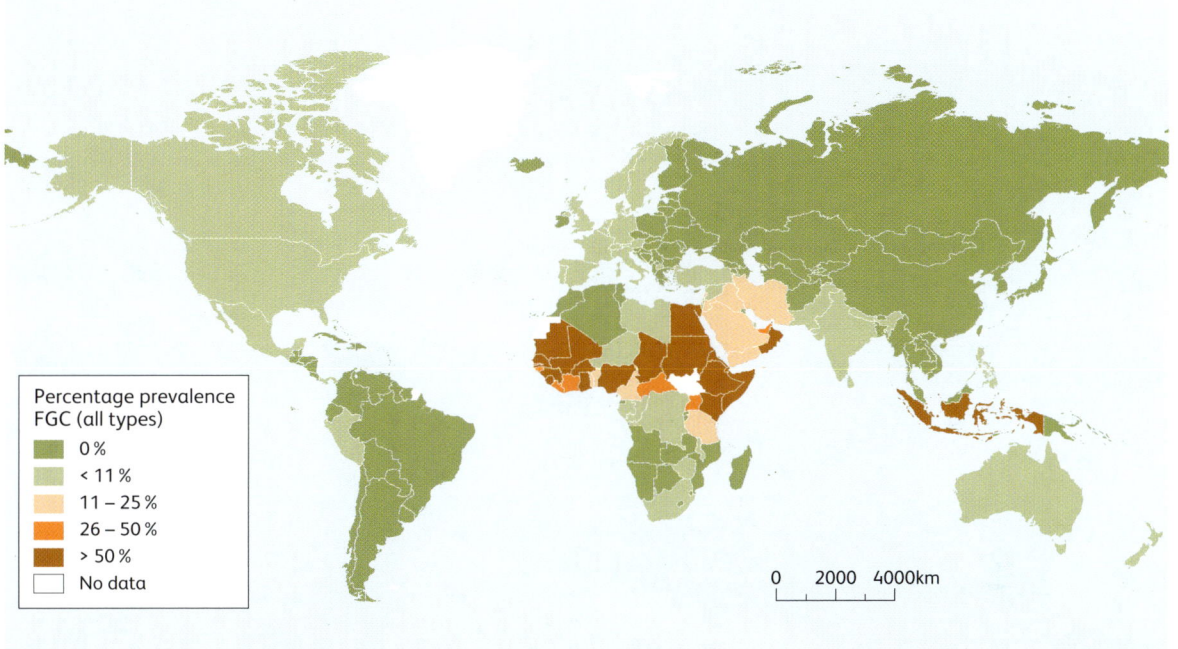

Figure 7: World-wide prevalence of female genital cutting, 2011. **Source:** Barrett, 2014, after Women's Database, 2011.

Understanding the social mores and sexual attitudes that underpin the transmission of HIV/AIDS in different cultural contexts is already addressed in some A level specifications in terms of the study of infectious diseases. A similar approach could be taken to even more emotive issues such as Female Genital Cutting (FGC), sometimes called female genital mutilation or female circumcision, about which Hazel Barrett (2014) has marshalled a range of telling evidence. The practice is widespread in Africa and the Middle East, despite the United Nations' condemnation of FGC as a violation of human rights (see Figure 7). Attempts to outlaw the practice have so far proven largely ineffective. Rather than simply condemning FGC, therefore, Barrett seeks to understand how it is 'made sense' of in different cultural contexts – in terms of concepts of purity and hygiene, spiritual cleanliness and family honour, for example – in order to intervene more effectively. Understanding the cultural contexts and systems of meaning that sanction such practices is a powerful example of the need to work across epistemological boundaries, raising challenging questions about the limits of moral relativism and the efficacy of universal human rights in a radically multicultural world.

As examples like this illustrate, geographers engage in endless acts of translation, like social anthropologists who define their field in terms of the 'interpretation' of other cultures (Geertz, 1973). Food provides a further example of how the 'exotic' might be better understood as a point of view rather than as a reference to a specific geographical or cultural location. Here, for instance, is Rosamund Grant, a Caribbean food writer, talking about the nature of 'exotic' food as part of the Food Stories project (British Library, no date) with which I was involved:

> 'I think Europeans tend to see Caribbean food in a particular way, and they would say it's ackee and salt fish, rice and peas or curried goat and mutton… I like people to be clear about, you know, how they think about it because they stereotype it and "all Caribbean food is spicy" and… "all of it is ackee and saltfish". You know, and so I try and broaden out people's way of thinking'.

Asked why this is important, she continues:

> 'It's important to me because I hate stereotyping, I hate being put in a box, I hate being limited, and I hate being seen through the eyes of Europeans. I don't like defining myself through the eyes of

Quintessentially British Stilton: a symbol of national identity? **Photo** © Sterling College.

somebody who's white or is European. I have my own definition of myself and I think that is really important for me, you know, as a black woman… And because I suppose there's a lot of passionate feeling left over from slavery and the impact of slavery and migration and displacement and all that kind of stuff, and I just think, you know, ok it's time to speak for ourselves … And so it does irritate me when people talk about "exotic food", you know, exotic through whose perspective, is it mine or somebody else's?' (British Library, 2008)

This is a good example (and there are several more on the Food Stories website) of the relationship between food, culture and national identity. For Rosamund Grant, there is no single definition of 'Caribbean food'. Its meaning cannot be confined to certain ingredients or dishes ('ackee and saltfish', 'rice and peas'), though it is sometimes marketed in this way. Nor is 'Caribbean food' reducible to particular tastes (such as those associated with spices and peppers). Grant rejects such stereotypical ways of thinking, refusing to be seen 'through the eyes of Europeans'. From this perspective, what has come to be defined as 'Caribbean food' reflects the particular historical and geographical connections between Britain and the Caribbean. It is a relational construction rather than something that can be defined in absolute terms.

Jamaican-born cultural studies professor Stuart Hall wrote about these connections over two decades ago in the context of what were then described as 'new ethnicities', emerging in hybrid fashion from Britain's connections with its former colonies. Writing about the way tea drinking had become a symbol of British national identity, Hall exposed the many ironies of this connection in 1992:

> 'Because they don't grow [tea] in Lancashire, you know. Where does it come from? Ceylon, Sri Lanka, India. That is the outside history that is inside the history of the English. There is no English history without that other history… People like me who came to England in the 1950s [from the Caribbean] have been there for centuries; symbolically, we have been there for centuries… I am the sugar at the bottom of the English cup of tea. I am the sweet tooth, the sugar plantations that rotted generations of English children's teeth. There are thousands of others… that are… the cup of tea itself' (Hall, 1992, pp. 48–9).

Similar stories could, of course, be told about other quintessentially 'British' foods whose complex geographical and historical origins make the idea of a 'hybrid' mixture of two distinct cultures seem wholly inadequate.

The kind of geographical thinking I am advocating here also encourages the crossing of geographical scales and historical temporalities. Note, for example, how quickly, in the second extract from Rosamund Grant, she moves from a discussion of contemporary food to the 'passionate feeling left over from slavery' including questions of international migration and displacement. I have written about similar kinds of connection in my own work on the British sugar industry, raising questions about the ethical responsibilities that arise when different geographical and historical connections are recognised (Jackson et al., 2009). Consider, for example, the following extract from an interview with a British sugar beet farmer, talking about the impact of the Common Agriculture Policy on sugar growers in the UK and different parts of the world:

> 'The object of the Common Agricultural Policy… was to lift European farmers out of peasantry, which they were soon after the war, and give them the same standard of living as people in the towns and cities.
> That was the original object of the CAP but I think I'm entitled to a price that allows me to grow a crop and make a modest profit so that my wife too can feed my kids the same as anybody else. Now you might say well, and so why can't the Mozambique farmer have the same thing, and I agree, why can't he?' (quoted in Jackson and Ward, 2008, p. 241).

This extract raises a series of interesting political and ethical questions the answers to which depend, to a large extent, on the scale of analysis. What can be defended as ethical at one scale (the national or regional scale) in which the farmer asserts his 'entitlement' to grow a crop and to make a modest profit to feed his family under rules set by the European Union, looks rather different when viewed from a global scale (where the same policies may deny a similar livelihood to sugar cane farmers in places like Mozambique).

Geographers are adept at making connections across scales, thinking of scale not as a series of disconnected layers, moving successively outwards from the local to the global, but in terms of the way each scale is implicated in the production of other scales. The photographic analogy of 'zooming in' and 'zooming out' is a powerful way of thinking about this process of geographical analysis, rather than holding the camera steady, permanently focused at one particular scale.

Current challenges and future directions

While the GCSE and GCE subject specifications strive to represent human geography as a coherent discipline (interpreted in different ways by each awarding body), at university level the subject often appears to be in danger of fragmentation, splintering into a series of narrow sub-divisions, each with its own specialised journals and conferences and very little common ground among the sub-divisions, much less between exponents of the subject's human and physical branches. The kind of relational thinking outlined above and the impetus to make connections and work across geographical scales are some of the ways that these divisions might be transcended. This tendency might also be encouraged by

The British landscape bears the imprint of successive rounds of European agricultural policy. **Photo** © Raquel M.

by the increasing emphasis being placed on interdisciplinary research programmes at university level, funded by government agencies and research councils. Current research programmes in the UK, for example, emphasise integrating themes, such as global food security or living with environmental change, seeking to encourage cross-disciplinary thinking about the 'nexus' of issues connecting energy, water and food security. Geography seems ideally placed to take advantage of these developments but has, so far, been slow to react, with other disciplines rapidly moving in on this inviting middle ground between the natural and the social sciences (Rees, 2013). To address this issue effectively geographers might ask themselves what specific skills and concepts they bring to the table of multi- or interdisciplinary research, rather than assuming that we occupy this space by divine right. One response might be to emphasise our use of integrative methodologies such as GIS and remote sensing, but we should also, in my view, emphasise our distinctive conceptual and theoretical orientation as outlined in this chapter.

Human geography has been transformed within the last few decades by its encounter with social theory, whose impacts have been at least as profound as previous 'revolutions' such as those that were driven by quantitative methods or the radical geographies associated with Marxist thought. It is easy to criticise social theorists for their obscure language which sometimes verges on the impenetrable, but subtle ideas cannot always be expressed in

Figure 8:
Wasted food destined for landfill.
Photo © Starr, reproduced under Creative Commons licence (CC BY 2.0).

everyday language and few theorists set out to be obscure. Indeed some, such as Stuart Hall or Edward Said, managed to write in lucid prose, communicating complex arguments in a highly accessible manner. Human geography has been enriched by a succession of new theoretical ideas from the postmodern to the postcolonial (summarised in Jazeel, 2012a, 2012b), providing a rich array of philosophical insights and conceptual vocabulary from which to draw.

There are encouraging signs within contemporary human geography of a desire to reunite the analysis of the symbolic and the material, bringing together moral and political economies and transcending sub-disciplinary divisions such as those between the cultural and the economic. To take the example of food geographies again, analysis is now focusing on food's material as well as its symbolic dimensions. Some foods are limited in their commercial exploitation by their tendency to discolour or rot when not sufficiently refrigerated while others mature and improve in taste as they age. Its material properties also influence the huge amount of food that is wasted as it passes along the supply chain, with current estimates suggesting that around one-third of total food production goes to waste (Stuart, 2009; IME, 2013) (see Figure 8). What crosses the line from 'food' to 'waste' is fundamentally shaped by social and cultural conventions as well as by its physical properties. This can be readily demonstrated by using time-lapse photography of rotting food (of which there are many examples on YouTube), asking students at what point they would regard the food as inedible. In this case, an analysis of food waste would require us to attend to the affective register of embodied, emotions such as desire and disgust as well as to aesthetic considerations of taste, smell and visual appearance in deciding how and when food is configured as waste.

Let me conclude with a final extract from the Food Stories website where Kath Dalmeny, who works for the campaign group Sustain (the alliance for better food and farming), is thinking about a more sustainable attitude towards contemporary food consumption. As you read this interview extract you may want to analyse it in terms of the concepts deployed in this chapter: materiality and sustainability, local and global scales, etc.

> 'The way I think about it is that I look at the planet and I think this is the most miraculous, amazing place. We live on a rock that is circling the sun, that has created for us carrots, and beef, and chocolate pudding, and lettuces, and sandwiches and just wonderful, wonderful things that are just great to eat. The trouble is, we seem to have slightly screwed that system up by thinking of all of those things as commodities, as things that we can get from anywhere with no consequences whatsoever'

She then asks us to think geographically about one particular type of food:

> 'If you think about something like raspberries – they're very soft, they go off in two days, they get furry and mouldy quite quickly but we get them from half way across the planet sometimes. They've come probably by air because they can't last very long otherwise; they're in plastic packaging; they've had to be refrigerated on the way. When they get to the UK, when they arrive in an airport then they're going to be transported by truck all the way around the UK as well – this is just so you can put them in a bowl and have a quick raspberry for your supper. Now that's very nice, but think of all the fuel that's been used to get that to you. What happens to the plastic afterwards? If you just had raspberries a few times a year when it's raspberry season and you got it from the farm down the road – wow, what a wonderful relationship with raspberries'

She concludes:

> 'It would be perfectly ok for us to think that we can have any kind of fruit and vegetables at any time of the year if it were not for the fact that we live on a planet that has limits. If we could carry on expanding, carry on using fuel and carry on using plastic with no environmental impact at all, there wouldn't be a problem – the problem is that the planet really can't take us doing this for very much longer' (British Library, 2008).

What better example could there be of the power of thinking geographically, inviting us to move between geographical scales from the planetary to the personal and challenging us to think creatively about the way our dietary tastes and cultural preferences relate to broader questions of social responsibility and environmental sustainability?

Conclusion

Taking food as a recurring motif, this chapter has explored the wide-ranging nature of contemporary human geography. This single example has been used to show how geography teachers might open up the curriculum to teach in new ways about familiar subjects from 'primary industries' such as agriculture to migration and international development. Many other examples could have served equally well, but even with this single focus, the richness and diversity of contemporary human geography is already apparent. Within this diversity of subject matter and conceptual approach, it has been possible to identify some common themes and unifying principles, including geography's insistence on making connections and thinking relationally about space and place. The chapter has also made a case for transcending boundaries and thinking across geographical scales. The vitality of human geography can scarcely be in doubt, nor can its ability to contribute to questions of truly global significance. To our mutual advantage, the discipline remains open-ended and constantly changing, its concepts and ideas forever contested and permanently in review.

References

AQA (2013) *GCE AS and A Level Specification: Geography*. Available at: http://filestore.aqa.org.uk/subjects/specifications/alevel/AQA-2030-W-SP-14.PDF (last accessed 07/11/2016).

Barrell, J. (1980) *The Dark Side of the Landscape*. Cambridge: Cambridge University Press.

Barrett, H. (2014) 'Female genital cutting: crossing borders', *Geography*, 99, 1, pp. 20–27.

Berry, W. (1992) 'The pleasures of eating' in Curtin, D.W. and Heldke, L.W. (eds) *Cooking, Eating, Thinking*. Bloomington, IN: Indiana University Press, pp. 374–79.

British Library (2008) *Food Stories*. Available at: www.bl.uk/learning/citizenship/foodstories (last accessed 07/11/2016).

Cloke, P., Crang, P. and Goodwin, M. (eds) (2014) *Introducing Human Geographies* (3rd edition). Abingdon: Routledge.

Cresswell, T. (1996) *In Place/Out of Place: Geography, ideology and transgression*. Minneapolis, MN: University of Minnesota Press.

Cresswell, T. (2004) *Place: A short introduction*. Oxford: Blackwell.

DfE (2013) *National Curriculum in England: Geography programmes of study*. Available at: www.gov.uk/government/publications/national-curriculum-in-england-geography-programmes-of-study (last accessed 07/11/2016).

DfE (2014a) *GCE AS and A Level Subject Content for Geography*. Available at: www.gov.uk/government/publications/gce-as-and-a-level-geography (last accessed 07/11/2016).

DfE (2014b) *Geography: GCSE subject content*. Available at: www.gov.uk/government/publications/gcse-geography (last accessed 07/11/2016).

Economic and Social Research Council (ESRC) (2012) *International Benchmarking Review of Human Geography*. Swindon: ESRC.

Food and Agriculture Organization of the United Nations (FAO) (2009) *Declaration on the World Summit on Food Security, WSFS 2009/2*. Rome: FAO.

Geertz, C. (1973) *The Interpretation of Cultures*. New York, NY: Basic Books.

Gregory, D., Johnston, R., Pratt, G., Watts, M. and Whatmore, S. (eds) (2009) *The Dictionary of Human Geography* (5th edition). Oxford: Wiley-Blackwell.

Hall, S. (1992) 'New ethnicities' in Donald, J. and Rattansi, A. (eds) *Race, Culture and Difference*. London: Sage, pp. 252–59.

Institute of Mechanical Engineers (IME) (2013) *Global Food: Waste not, want not*. London: IME.

Jackson, P. (2006) 'Thinking geographically', *Geography*, 91, 3, pp. 199–204.

Jackson, P. and Ward, N. (2008) 'Connections and responsibilities: the moral geographies of sugar', in Nützenadel, A. and Trentmann, F. (eds) *Food and Globalization*. Oxford: Berg, pp. 235–52.

Jackson, P., Ward, N. and Russell, P. (2009) 'Moral economies of food and geographies of responsibility', *Transactions of the Institute of British Geographers*, 34, 1, pp. 12–24.

Jazeel, T. (2012a) 'Postcolonialism: Orientalism and the geographical imagination', *Geography*, 97, 1, pp. 4–11.

Jazeel, T. (2012b) 'Postcolonial spaces and identities', *Geography*, 97, 2, pp. 60–67.

Lefebvre, H. (1991) *The Production of Space*. Oxford: Blackwell (trans. D. Nicholson-Smith).

Massey, D. (1984) *Spatial Divisions of Labour*. London: Macmillan.

Massey, D. (2005) *For Space*. London: Sage.

Patel, R. (2007) *Stuffed and Starved*. London: Portobello Books.

Policy Commission on the Future of Farming and Food (2002) *Farming and Food: A sustainable future. Report of the Policy Commission on the Future of Farming and Food*. London: Cabinet Office.

Rees, J. (2013) 'Geography and the nexus: Presidential Address and record of the Royal Geographical Society (with IBG) AGM 2013', *The Geographical Journal*, 179, 3, pp. 279–82.

Said, E.W. (1978) *Orientalism*. New York, NY: Pantheon Books.

Said, E.W. (1993) *Culture and Imperialism*. London: Chatto and Windus.

Sibley, D. (1985) *Geographies of Exclusion*. Abingdon: Routledge.

Stuart, T. (2009) *Waste: Uncovering the global food scandal*. London: Penguin.

Tesco (2014) *Eat Happy Project*. Available at: www.eathappyproject.com (last accessed 07/11/2016).

Whatmore, S. (2002) *Hybrid Geographies*. London: Sage.

Williams, R. (1973) *The Country and the City*. London: Chatto and Windus.

Recommended key readings

Cloke, P., Crang, P. and Goodwin, M. (eds) (2014) *Introducing Human Geographies* (3rd edition). Abingdon: Routledge.

A comprehensive and richly illustrated introduction to human geography, written by research-active authors for first-year undergraduates.

Gregory, D., Johnston, R., Pratt, G., Watts, M. and Whatmore, S. (eds) (2009) *The Dictionary of Human Geography* (5th edition). Oxford: Wiley-Blackwell.

An indispensable work for teachers and students of human geography, with fully-referenced essays on human geography's keywords, plus suggested further reading.

Chapter 8

Teaching geography for sustainability

John Morgan is Professor in Curriculum and Pedagogy at the University of Auckland, New Zealand

An inconvenient controversy

In 2007 the Department for Education and Skills distributed a copy of the film An Inconvenient Truth (dir. Guggenheim, 2006) to all secondary schools in England and Wales. The distribution reflected the growing consensus among scientists and the wider public about the existence of anthropogenic climate change and the need for societies to act to reduce global warming. Indeed the Qualifications and Curriculum Authority's (QCA) (2009) publication *Sustainable Development in Action: A curriculum planning guide for schools* indicated how far the environmental challenges society is facing were reflected in 'official' curriculum discussion:

'We need to find a way to live on Earth that enables all people to satisfy their basic needs and enjoy quality of life, without compromising the ability of future generations to meet their own needs' (p. 4).

The QCA publication made special mention of the issue of climate change, echoing the (then) Labour government's view that this represents 'one of the greatest challenges facing our generation'. It argued that cutting the levels of greenhouse gases we produce is one of the most important steps necessary to slow climate change:

'Learning about climate change at school has inspired many children and young people to take their messages to the wider community to try and bring about change. They believe that the key to success lies in working as a community and that we can all be part of the solution' (QCA, 2009, p. 5).

Watching An Inconvenient Truth it is easy to see why it might be a popular teaching resource in schools. The film has high production values, contains a hard-hitting and dramatic narrative, and presenter Al Gore is a charismatic figure. However, a more critical perspective suggests that An Inconvenient Truth is seductive in the way it provides just enough sensation to appeal to the idea that there is a need for change, while at the same time suggesting that the solution lies in reform, rather than transformation, of the present system. Towards the end of the film, Gore lists things that individuals 'can do to save the planet', which is likely to appeal to schools who are seeking to encourage future environmentally aware and responsible 'citizens'. This, it might be argued, is ideology masquerading as education. Joel Kovel in *The Enemy of Nature* (2007) pointed out that:

'An Inconvenient Truth fails to mention the word "capitalism"... it oozes with technological determinism, does not take into sufficient account the Global South, never questions the industrial model, promises his approach will generate a lot of wealth, and offers no way out beyond voting the proper people, i.e. people like himself, into office. Thus neither capital, nor the capitalist state, is at all questioned, nor is any authentic democratization offered' (pp. 166–67).

An Inconvenient Truth presents the ideology that we are all part of the problem, and that it is individuals who hold the key to reducing greenhouse gas emissions. Pointing to the 'things we can do' is, as Kovel says, understandably popular, since these 'comprise a risk-free way of feeling good about oneself in the face of overwhelming crisis' (p. 167). However, these strategies offer no real solution. Kovel's analysis implies that geography teachers should seek to help students understand the principles of how capitalism works in order to recognise the link between perpetual economic growth and climate change (see Newell and Paterson, 2010).

A stark reminder of the 'politics' of all this came when, soon after its election in May 2010, a new government took office, and education for sustainable development was removed from the curriculum, the Qualifications and Curriculum Development Agency (QCDA – formerly QCA) was abolished, and the Secretary of State for Education stated his opposition to the topic of climate change being taught in the school geography curriculum (see Figure 1). After much opposition, a suitably neutral wording was found for the curriculum statement:

> '…understand how human and physical processes interact to influence and change landscapes, environments and the climate; and how human activity relies on effective functioning of natural systems' (DfE. 2013).

Defining sustainability

The case of An Inconvenient Truth provides a useful introduction to the themes discussed in this chapter, which is offered as an introduction to the issues involved in teaching about the concept of sustainability in school geography. From the start, readers should be aware that the chapter does not provide a simple set of 'tips' about how to teach about sustainability; there are plenty of these available elsewhere. Instead, the chapter insists on the need to understand and think about (some people would call this 'theorise') sustainability at the conceptual level. This does lead to ideas about practice in school classrooms, especially in terms of curriculum planning or what contributors to this book might call 'curriculum thinking'.

The inclusion of a chapter on sustainability in a geography teachers' handbook now seems unremarkable. Indeed, there are even counter-claims that geography lessons have become a vehicle for foisting upon students moral and behavioural messages about the need to protect the environment and care for Earth

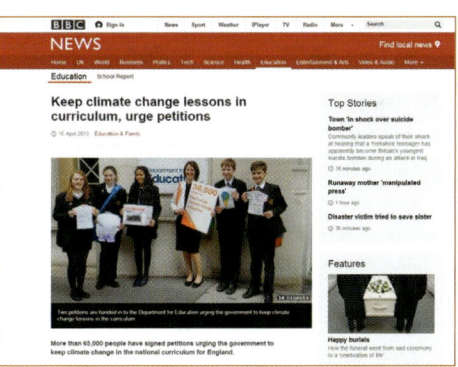

Figure 1: Headlines on climate change and curriculum from 2013. **Sources:** WWF, Guardian and BBC websites.

(see, for example, Williams, 2008). This has to be seen in the light of the widespread acceptance in society – at a general level – of ideas about sustainability. Thus, just as the previous New Labour government published guidance that accepted the need for schools to teach about sustainability, so too are exam boards (perhaps the key arbiters of what counts as 'really useful knowledge' these days!) comfortable with the concept of sustainability, and operate with definitions of the term that are capable of memorisation and recitation by students in written examinations.

Technocentrics believe technological fixes can solve environmental problems. **Photo** © Licence free.

However, it is important to remember that the widespread acceptance of the concept has not been achieved without a struggle, and that some academic geographers are less convinced about its value:

> 'I have not been able to find a single source that is against "sustainability". Greenpeace is in favour, George Bush Jr and Sr are, the World Bank and its chairman (a prime warmonger on Iraq) are, the Pope is, my son Arno is, the rubber tappers in the Brazilian Amazon forest are, Bill Gates is, the labour unions are' (Swyngedouw, 2007, p. 20).

Of course, academics are in the business of contesting and debating the meaning of words, and the concept has been deconstructed to the point where there exist over 150 definitions. Just because there is definitional confusion does not imply that a concept is useless or unimportant. Indeed, according to the cultural theorist Raymond Williams (1976), it is precisely these terms that are important in shaping our culture and society. Concepts change their meaning over time. None of this makes things easy for geography teachers though, since teaching necessarily involves pinning down meaning, if only temporarily, so that students can grasp the significance of ideas. The important point that I want to make here is that as teachers we cannot and should not operate as though a concept such as sustainability has definitional clarity or that consensus exists about its meaning. We must proceed with caution.

Ideologies of sustainability

If, as just suggested, the definition of sustainability is contested, then we can at least identify broad ideologies or discourses that help us to situate statements about sustainability. Although it dates from the mid-1970s, the geographer–environmental scientist Tim O'Riordan's (1976) classification of environmental ideologies remains valuable. O'Riordan identified two broad approaches – the technocentric and the ecocentric (see Figure 2).

Technocentric approaches tend to view environmental issues as technical problems that

Classification of environmental ideologies	
Technocentrics	**Ecocentrics**
Technocentrics believe technological fixes can solve environmental problems. They comprise: • accommodators (educated managerial classes), who encourage management of resources • cornucopians (industrialists), who believe individuals can come up with solutions to environmental problems.	Ecocentrics believe that humans represent only a small part of the planetary ecosystem and should put Earth first. This 'Green fringe' comprises two perspectives: • communalists, who believe small-scale local interventions will allow communities to live an ecologically sustainable existence • Gaianists, who stress the inherent rights of nature and the co-evolution of the human and natural worlds.

Figure 2: Classification of environmental ideologies. **Source:** O'Riordan, 1976.

can be solved given the correct mix of economic and technological tools. O'Riordan identified two distinctive groups of technocentrics – the 'accommodators', who recognise the existence of environmental problems and stress the importance of management of political systems – often through the state as a regulator – to ensure proper use of resources. 'Cornucopians', in contrast, are optimistic about the power of human ingenuity, liberated through individualism and entrepreneurialism, to come up with solutions to environmental problems. Almost four decades later, technocentrism remains the dominant approach to environmental issues and sustainability.

Ecocentrics are convinced that humans represent only a small part of the history and functioning of the planetary ecosystem and should act accordingly. They prioritise Earth over human purposes. Ecocentrics divide into communalists – who stress the importance of small-scale local interventions to allow communities to live an ecologically sustainable existence – and Gaianists, who favour an Earth First approach, stressing the inherent rights of nature and the co-evolution of the human and natural worlds.

A particularly useful feature of O'Riordan's classification is that it set these ideologies in the material contexts that they supported. Thus, cornucopian perspectives were very much associated with industrialists and those who believed in the capacity of the free market to find solutions. Commercial organisations, it was argued, would learn to change their behaviour once they realised it was profitable and sensible to maintain natural capital. This argument is still dominant today, with the 'greening' of capitalism and business, and a faith that we will find technological fixes to future climate change. Accommodators tended to belong to the educated managerial classes who dominate government and politics, and again, this is also common today, where governments seek to convince people that we are playing our part in resolving any environmental problems. For O'Riordan, communalist and Gaianist perspectives were part of the 'green' fringe. The notions of small-scale, decentralised and democratic communities seeking to provide for themselves in ecologically sustainable ways remains attractive, and though these ideas are still relevant today, it is unclear as to the size and extent of these alternative economic spaces. O'Riordan's schema has the advantage of rooting environmental ideas in a broader set of arguments about economy and society. It remains useful for geography teachers seeking to understand the ideas that underpin their teaching about sustainability.

More recently, Hopwood *et al.* (2005) have mapped these environmental discourses, proposing a distinction between two dimensions (Figure 3). The first is concerned with the degree to which environmental concerns reflect technocentric or ecocentric perspectives, and the second is about how far equality and quality of life issues are addressed. This allows them to identify three distinct zones: 'status quo', 'reform', and 'transformation'. Such typologies and mappings are, it is worth reiterating, not finalised or stable, but for the purposes of sustainability in the geography classroom, it gives teachers a starting point for research and clarification.

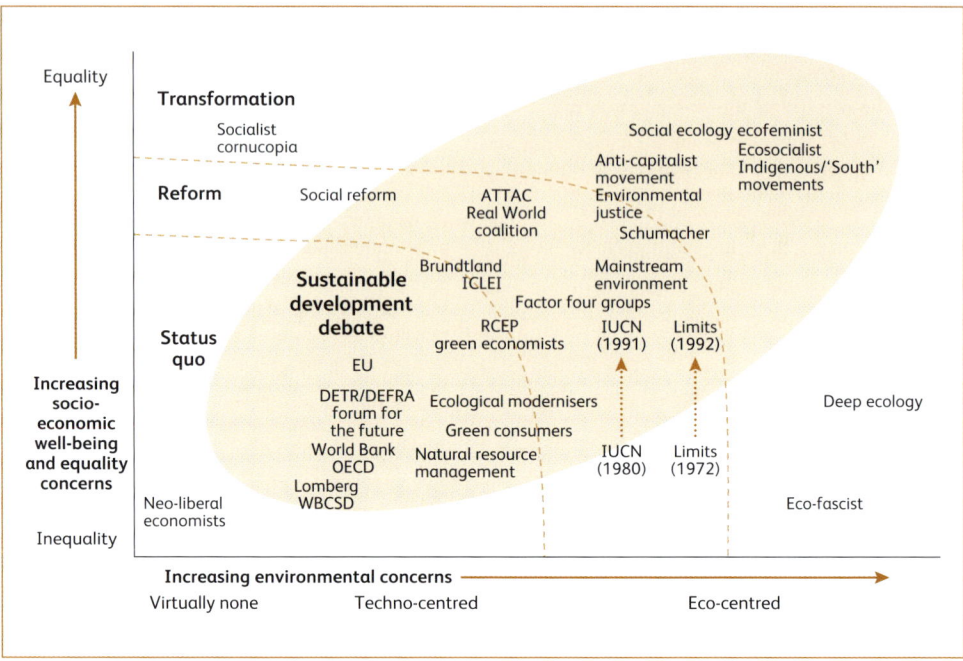

Figure 3: Mapping sustainable development perspectives. Note: IUCN – International Union for Conservation of Nature; WBCSD – World Business Council for Sustainable Development; ATTAC – Association for the Taxation of Financial Transactions and Aid to Citizens. **Source:** Hopwood et al., 2005.

Varieties of education for sustainability

I have suggested that a first step in teaching sustainability is to recognise that the term is open to interpretation and holds a range of different meanings, and this goes some way to explaining the 'inconvenient controversy' discussed at the start of the chapter. In teaching sustainability, are we, as teachers, concerned to teach *about* sustainability (i.e. the concept, its history, its different meanings etc.), *through* sustainability (i.e. developing a series of desirable skills, values and behaviours through a particular set of teaching practices), or *for* sustainability (i.e. ensuring that a particular view of sustainability is disseminated through teaching)? This 'about, through, for' formulation was influential in the early development of environmental education and, as you may already be thinking, has led to some argument and debate about the purposes of teaching (Huckle, 1983; Pepper, 1984; Fien, 1993). As a curriculum subject, geography stands in a close but tense relationship with the fields of environmental education and education for sustainability, and understanding this relationship is an important prerequisite of teaching sustainability in geography. This section is an introduction to these issues.

Modern environmental education dates from the mid-1960s. In 1965, the Keele Conference on Education and Environment called for schools to teach about the coming environmental crisis. It is important to remember that this roughly coincides with the publication of *Silent Spring* (Carson, 1962) and the inauguration of the modern environmental movement. Carson, a scientist, wrote about the damaging effects of pesticide use on the birds and plants of the iconic American landscape. The first Earth Day took place in 1970 (see Figure 4), and the Club of Rome published its report, *The Limits to Growth*, in 1972 (Meadows et al., 1972). In 1973, the economist Fritz Schumacher published *Small is Beautiful* with the subtitle 'economics as if people mattered' and the Ecology Party (a forerunner to the modern Green Party) was established in the UK in 1974. This coincided with a period in which the assumed benefits of the post-war expansion – what the economist J.K. Galbraith (1958) called 'the affluent society' – were being questioned. Galbraith talked of private affluence and public squalor, the way in which the expansion of production and consumption had led to wealth and improved quality of life but brought with it a series of 'externalities' or costs, which were borne by the community as a whole, or, more correctly, by the poorest groups in society.

In Britain, the 1970s saw the emergence of a growing environmental consciousness, registered culturally in a variety of forms. A popular children's TV programme – The Wombles, about a group a furry creatures who lived beneath Wimbledon Common and spent their days picking up litter ('Making good use of the things that we find, things that the everyday folk leave behind') – reflected calls to 'Keep Britain Tidy'. *Watership Down* (Adams, 1972), a best-selling novel, followed by a blockbuster film, told the tale of a group of rabbits whose warren is threatened by a large road-building scheme through southern England. James Herbert's novel, *The Rats* (1974), was set in a London where a refuse collectors' strike has left rubbish on the streets. Less dramatically, the BBC comedy series The Good Life (1975–78) explored the comic tensions between two middle-class couples as one seeks to retreat from consumerism and the corporate rat-race and live off the land in an English suburb. It is important to remember that environmentalism was then widely seen as a fringe activity – hence the jokes about whole-foods and sandals – and this was also the case with environmental education, that took its place as one of a series of 'adjectival studies' (e.g. world studies, peace studies, development education), which challenged the dominance of the traditional curriculum (Dufour, 1990). A sense of the cultural space occupied by early environmental education can be gained by looking at *Teaching Green* (Randle, 1989) which offered a radical critique of schooling and located the alternatives in a radically different set of values. This can be seen from Randle's manifesto describing the characteristics of 'green teachers'. They:

- co-operate with and care for Earth
- co-operate with and care for each other
- grow as independent, self-confident individuals
- design and use technologies that support these aims
- work at new ways of 'doing politics'
- take part in the spiritual transformation that underlies the 'shifted paradigms' (Randle, 1989, p. 54).

'The first Earth Day on April 22, 1970, activated 20 million Americans from all walks of life and is widely credited with launching the modern environmental movement. Growing out of the first Earth Day, Earth Day Network (EDN) works with over 22,000 partners in 192 countries to broaden, diversify and mobilize the environmental movement… more than one billion people now participate in Earth Day activities each year, making it the largest civic observance in the world.'

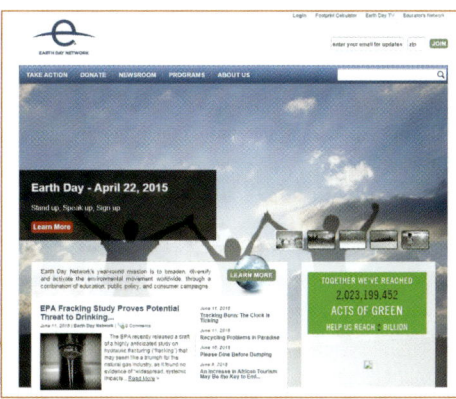

Figure 4: Earth Day. **Source:** www.earthday.org

In this sense, to be a 'green teacher' was to adopt a different paradigm or way of thinking, to define oneself as being against the mainstream and take a radical stance. It is important to remember that at the time there were significant debates about the nature of green politics, especially in relation to the 'Red-Green' debate between the 'socialist' and 'green' elements of the environmental movement. To condense a complex debate into a series of simple statements, greens tended to see environmental problems as resulting from the characteristics of industrial society, and spoke in ecological metaphors of society as a complex living organism. An important question was how change would occur, and many greens, influenced by new age thinking and alternative spiritualities, saw this as coming about through a radical shift in human consciousness. Reds, while recognising the same set of environmental issues, were more inclined to argue that environmental problems were the result of a specific economic system

– capitalism – which was geared to making profits and led to a society divided between the rich and poor. Social change occurred through struggles to change the material organisation of economy and society.

In terms of environmental education, the red-green division offered different analyses of the role of education. Many greens tended to see education as a matter of changing people's minds about the environment and encouraging individuals to change their values and behaviours. Politics mattered, but more important was achieving an environmental awareness or consciousness. It was not the role of teachers or schools to bring politics into classrooms. Red-green environmental educators argued that powerful ideologies shaped people's consciousness, and that political agency was central to bringing about changed environmental practices. Where both red and green environmental educators concurred was over the nature of the school curriculum. For greens the curriculum reflected the fragmented world view of Western society and, in order to remedy this, argued for environmental education that was holistic and integrated. Reds saw traditional subjects such as geography and history as offering ideological perspectives and favoured newer adjectival studies (e.g. development education, peace education) that offered explicit teaching about the environment.

While environmental education was initially a minority interest, it gained respectability as public awareness of the environmental crisis grew from the mid-1980s. Thus Prime Minister Margaret Thatcher, addressing the Royal Society in 1988, recognised the environment as an issue and the Conservative government published the first ever White Paper on the environment – *This Common Inheritance* – in 1990 (DOE, 1990). It commissioned the economist David Pearce and colleagues to devise ways to incorporate the externalities associated with production into economic modelling (Pearce et al., 1989). The Rio Earth Summit of 1992 led to the publication of the UK's Sustainable Development Plan in 1994 (DOE, 1994), and prompted much local government activity on education as part of Local Agenda 21 (UN, 1992). Important discussions took place about the implications of the term 'sustainable development', which many argued was a contradiction in terms. Others favoured 'sustainability', and this has come to incorporate ideas of environmental, social and economic sustainability. The important thing to note here is that environmental education had taken a radical stance, critiquing what it saw as the fragmenting, divided and mechanistic world view upon which Western industrialism has been based, and sought to replace it with a more holistic and organic world view. This had practical implications, since it established education for sustainability (EfS) (a term which has been superceded by 'Education for Sustainable Development' – ESD) as a cross-curricular theme that, almost by default, was marginal to the mainstream curriculum. The growing acceptance of 'environmental modernisation' (in O'Riordan's terms, an 'accommodationist' ideology) within government and society meant that EfS came in from the cold with the election of a New Labour government in 1997, and this led to its involvement in whole-school initiatives. The incorporation or mainstreaming of EfS has had its costs. One of these is that, in line with New Labour's preference for 'learning' over 'teaching', the question of the content of the curriculum has largely been ignored.

At one end of the spectrum is the argument that environmental learning is something that takes place in the myriad spaces of everyday life, such as the supermarket, the cinema or in playing video games (Blewitt, 2006). While it may be the case that such learning takes place any time, anywhere, with anyone, in any form, it is unclear how this is useful in terms of school-based learning, which has to involve more distanced and abstracted understandings of environment. Figure 5 poses a series of key questions for EfS.

In light of the difficulties that EfS has had in establishing itself in a school curriculum geared towards measured attainment, I (along with others) have argued that an intellectually defensible position is to teach about these issues through school subjects (Matthewman, 2010; Morgan, 2011). What this means for geography and geography teachers is the focus of the next section.

What type of geography?

Having asserted the claim that geography matters, it is tempting to sit back with a satisfied smile. However, this is, I think, where the real intellectual work required to engage in curriculum making begins. This is because, as we are used to by now, geography is a huge enterprise; an academic discipline that has burgeoned and fragmented, as well as a popular activity available to all through travel and the media. In the face of this, we need to make some decisions: what type of geography should be taught in schools? In this, I am starting from the assumption that school geography should be derived from and related to its parent academic discipline. I realise that this is controversial for some. Deng (2013) discusses three possible relationships between school subjects and the disciplines. The first is what he calls the 'doctrine of disciplinarity' in which school subjects are condensed versions of academic disciplines. The second is that school subjects are related to, but not derived from, academic disciplines; and the third is that school subjects have their own characteristics and agendas: the broader educational issues take precedence over the discipline. The general movement has been away from the doctrine of disciplinarity, but it is important to remember that disciplines provide intellectual frameworks and concepts for understanding the world, and that without them, the capacity of the school curriculum to educate effectively would be diminished for that part of the world that school subjects seek to describe and explain.

From its inception, geography has been closely concerned with the relationship between people and environment. In its pre-modern form it was concerned with the description of physical environments, and in terms of human–environment relations, the key disputes revolved around environmental determinism and environmental possiblism. In the post-Second World War period, geography underwent a spatial–quantitative revolution, and the effects of this on human geography were profound. The new models of spatial science (e.g. the gravity model, or Central Place Theory) ignored the natural world, so much so that in the 1970s geography teachers were criticised for

- To what extent has a focus on learning been a diversion from the question of curriculum content?
- How far does EfS encourage an idealistic perspective that focuses on the potential for individuals to change the world, as opposed to a materialist perspective that stresses the entrenched interests of powerful organisations?
- How far are schools, with their focus on the production of human capital, spaces where alternative viewpoints and ways of life can be envisioned? Can schools contribute to the process of 'de-growth'?
- How do we handle the growing interest within radical political ecology around the environmental myths that have formed the basis of environmental education?
- How do we cope with the growing influence of business interests and corporations in providing teaching resources to schools?

Figure 5:
Key questions for education for sustainability.

neglecting the looming environmental crisis. However, by the 1980s school geographers were likely to be influenced by a set of paradigm shifts associated with humanistic and radical philosophies. Geographers were increasingly interested in what Noel Castree (2005) called 'the de-naturalisation of nature'. This is a complex process but in understanding this shift it is useful to re-read the seminal article 'Taking the naturalness out of natural disasters' (O'Keefe et al., 1976), which effectively made the case, now widely accepted, that there is no necessary relationship between the frequency and intensity of natural disasters and their impact on people. Economic, political and social processes are more important in understanding and explaining natural events. This implied the need for a radical shift in geography teaching, not least because it challenged the fragmented and partial explanations found in geography lessons:

'The ideas taught in schools too are generally based on an unquestioning view of social change and economic forces. Lessons on environmental problems tend to blame purely natural causes, or regard them as a global or universal problem attributable to such causes as overpopulation, resource scarcity, inappropriate technology, overconsumption, or overproduction' (Huckle, 1988, p. 64).

Castree (2005) characterises the difference between human and physical geographers' approaches to nature as follows:

- Human geographers are concerned with societal representations of nature and de-naturalising nature, whereas physical geographers are concerned with specifying the biophysical properties of the non-human world.
- Human geographers take a constructionist approach to nature while physical geographers hold to the idea that they are producing 'scientific' knowledge.
- Human geographers don't separate fact from value, and question representations of nature that they see as oppressive or disabling.

Castree does not regard the fact that 'physical geographers are from Mars, human geographers are from Venus' (Viles, 2005, p. 26) as a major problem. Indeed, the co-existence of nature-endorsing and nature-sceptical perspectives in the same discipline should be seen as an advantage and a sign of intellectual health. From the perspective of school geography, there are important questions to be discussed about what represents the best selection of 'knowledge' from the academic discipline and how this should be organised. As Castree (2005) shows, contemporary human geography's engagement with nature is concerned with the idea of social nature, or the idea that it is not possible to think of nature without thinking about the social. Nature is a social construction. This is a deceptively simple idea: it represents a major fault line in human geographical studies between materialist positions and the various 'post' approaches to the subject (see Cresswell, 2013).

Amazonian stories

In this section I want to use a common topic in school geography in order to think through the implications of the argument that geography is a divided discipline when it comes to the question of nature. The focus here is on the Amazon rainforest, and I want to set down a series of Amazonian stories that have been told in school geography lessons (a summary is provided in Figure 6).

The first story, which was common in the 1970s and early 1980s, was that of the rainforest as an important ecosystem in which particular ways of life, or ways of making a living, were prevalent. This was linked to a broadly anthropological concern among geography teachers to introduce students to other environments and people's response to them. The building of the Trans-Amazonian Highway was an important part of this story of the shift from traditional to modern societies, and linked well with Rostow's (1949) stages of economic growth model. It involved teaching about the structure and function of the tropical forest ecosystem, and how small farmers utilised the thin rainforest soils through 'shifting cultivation'.

In the 1980s, this story was replaced, or supplemented, by what might be called the 'Decade of Destruction' story, which was literally narrated in Adrian Cowell's eponymous award-winning documentary series (1984–90). This told the tale of the increasing threat to the Brazilian rainforest of road building, cattle ranching, resettlement by the landless poor from crowded cities, and the subsequent impact on indigenous populations and rubber tappers. In many ways this was a story of development and modernisation gone wrong. It very much fitted the shift towards values and attitudes and issues-based approaches in geography, but was also linked to the growing tendency to see ostensibly local or regional issues as having an impact at the global scale. This was a distinctly political ecology, in that it was concerned with the role of multinational corporations and the state in the construction of an environmental problem, as well as focusing on notions of resistance.

Tropical rainforests (1970s)	'Decade of destruction' (1980s)	Dependency (1990s)	Social nature (1990s–2000s)	The 'myth' of rainforests (2000s)
Key ideas: Ecosystem Primary productivity Tropicality Structure and function Nutrient cycles	**Key ideas:** Brazil's Amazon Impact of human activity on biome/ecosystem Biomass, soil nutrients, diversity	**Key ideas:** Brazil as semi-periphery in Wallerstein's (1974) world-system* Exploitation of the Amazon linked to debt-based modernisation Internal problems of Brazilian state – inequality and landlessness, political instability * World divided into core states, semi-peripheral, and peripheral areas. The latter are the least developed; exploited by the core for raw materials and cheap labour	**Key ideas:** Entanglement of social and natural relations There is no 'simple story' 85% of felled timber is consumed within Brazil Amazonia has a complex history of settlement, with different groups having different attitudes to and uses for the rainforest Focus on gender and race as factors shaping activity in the Amazon rainforest	**Key ideas:** Concept of tropical rainforest as a social construction Questions 'complexity' Majority of present-day rainforests are less than 18,000 years old Plant diversity beneath the canopy is actually quite low; not the lungs of the world. In fact, because of their decomposition processes, most rainforests use as much oxygen as they give out, or even more
'Man-Land' tradition	Focus on human (mis-) use of nature Limits and failures of large-scale development projects	The causes of events in Amazonia are not explained by 'local' factors; region is linked to global flows of capital	Post-structural geographies seek to avoid grand narratives; they pay attention to particularity and complexity; recognise historical context; deconstruct or question taken-for-granted categories (e.g. settlers, peasants)	New forms of critical political ecology question the environmental orthodoxies promulgated by Western science and NGOs and both the politics and the ecology of political ecology approaches

A variation of this story was to be found in the materials produced by WWF-UK to support teaching of the decade of destruction (Huckle, 1988). However, in this version the focus is on the wider political and economic forces that shape the development of the Amazon. According to this account, the development within Amazonia must be related to the failed modernisation policies of the Brazilian government from the 1960s onwards. A surplus of capital in the global economy had encouraged developing countries to borrow from the International Monetary Fund and World Bank to invest in large-scale infrastructure projects. However, in the recession of the 1970s and 1980s countries that had borrowed heavily found themselves having to earn foreign currency to service their debts: the Amazonian rainforest was opened up to international investment.

In the 1990s and 2000s, in line with moves within geographical studies in political ecology, the simple narrative of economic development became subject to deconstruction. More attention was paid to the particularity of events, and the 'Decade of Destruction' grand narrative of world systems theory was subject to critique. For example, in *The Fate of the Forest*, Hecht and Cockburn (1995) point out that 85% of the timber felled in the Amazonian rainforest was consumed within Brazil, rather than exported. They provide an account of the complex historical geography of settlement within the forest, especially in relation to migration and gender relations.

Figure 6: Stories about Amazonia in school geography, 1970–2014.

One of the new ideas shown in Figure 7 suggests the link between flooding and deforestation is unclear. **Photo** © Licence free

Problem	Orthodoxy	New ideas
Desertification	The belief that population growth, deforestation and intensive agriculture on the margins is leading to irreversible increase in desert areas, a decline in rainfall and associated famine. This belief leads to policies of limiting livestock and planting trees to act as barriers to sand dune formation.	Long-term fluctuations in rainfall and climate may be of greater significance in drylands. Farming may not be the cause of desertification; there may be multiple causes and farming practices may actually reduce impacts on soil. Drought may be a more effective starting point than desertification for understanding these issues.
Forests and watersheds	Beliefs may include that forests increase rainfall and runoff, and that forests reduce erosion or floods. These beliefs lead to policies to relocate farmers from watershed zones, reforest catchment areas, or convert watersheds into protected zones.	The situation is actually much more complex: the impact of forests on rainfall is small; their impact on erosion is highly variable, depending on type of forest and type of erosion. The idea that forests increase runoff has been widely dismissed (though they may alter the speed and seasonality of discharge). The evidence linking flooding to deforestation is not clear.
Agricultural intensification	The belief that population growth leads smallholders to increase agricultural intensification to unsustainable levels, which may in turn lead to erosion, loss of soil nutrients and water resources.	Intensification does not always leads to deleterious outcomes; it is often accompanied by alternative economic practices (e.g. seasonal migration or finding non-agricultural income); or methods to increase production without environmental degradation (e.g. tree cropping).

Figure 7: Environmental orthodoxies and new ideas. **After:** Forsyth, 2003.

Consider the case of one of the agents of deforestation often raised in geography lessons – the farmer. Farmers are a broad category that includes a wide variety of groups, and there is an important distinction between indigenous and colonist cultivators, who have rather different attitudes to and perceptions of the environment. However, even this binary distinction fails to address the long and complex history of settlement and land use within the rainforest. Such accounts stress that deforestation is not exclusively driven by the capitalist world economy: other, more localised, contexts of social relations are also at work.

The final story is associated with a recent body of work on critical political ecology, which seeks to challenge the types of overarching grand narratives that rainforests are biological wonders of the world, that rainforest clearance is a bad thing, and that we will all suffer if the rainforests are destroyed. Indeed, Stott (2001) argues that 'tropical rainforests' are an invention, the result of a particular way of seeing and interpreting the landscape. Underpinning this approach is a twin concern to problematise the terms 'political' and 'ecology'. In the first instance, this represents a shift from the types of broad political economy approaches that tended to dominate human geography, and in the second instance, it challenges the dominance within biogeography of climax equilibrium ecology.

This type of deconstruction is typical of recent work on critical political ecology, which challenges the prevalence of a whole series of environmental myths or orthodoxies (see Figure 7). These hegemonic (or powerful) myths appear to be Northern (hemisphere), middle-class, white, Anglo-Saxon, and male in their origins. This leads to an important set of questions:

- Who determines environmental narratives?
- How do such narratives become influential?
- What alternatives are there?

Geography as a subject has an important role to play in teaching about pressing environmental issues. Photo © The Value Web.

When presented with these challenges to environmental orthodoxies some geography teachers respond, understandably, that they seem to undermine the whole basis on which teaching about sustainability issues rests. What is happening here is that the science that has underpinned political ecology is now being reassessed, with profound implications. The reassessment challenges the notion of geography as a subject underpinned (even if only in the last instance) by science, and seems to suggest that, in addition to scientific knowledge, geography teaching needs to be based on more sophisticated understandings of nature and environment that draw upon anthropological, sociological, historical and hermeneutical perspectives.

Conclusion

This chapter has sought to provide a wide-ranging introduction to the challenges of teaching sustainability in geography. In writing it, my aim was to convince you that geography as a subject has an important role to play in teaching about the most pressing environmental issues, but that in order for it to do so we need to engage with some complex arguments about the concept of sustainability. The key idea is that geography lessons should draw upon and make available to all students the arguments about sustainability and society–nature relations that are found in geography as an academic discipline. Such teaching is challenging, but so is the scale of the environmental challenge faced by future generations.

References

Adams, R. (1972) *Watership Down*. London: Rex Collings.

Blewitt, J. (2006) *The Ecology of Learning*. London: Earthscan.

Carson, R. (1962) *Silent Spring*. Boston, MA: Houghton Mifflin.

Castree, N. (2005) *Nature*. Abingdon: Routledge.

Cresswell, T. (2013) *Geographical Thought: A critical introduction*. Oxford: Wiley-Blackwell.

Deng, Z. (2013) 'School subjects and academic disciplines: the differences' in Luke, A., Woods, A. and Weir, K. (eds) *Curriculum, Syllabus Design and Equity: A primer and model*. Abingdon: Routledge, pp. 40–53.

DfE (2013) *National Curriculum in England: geography programmes of study*. London: DfE.

DOE (1990) *This Common Inheritance: Britain's environmental stategy*. London: HMSO.

DOE (1994) *Sustainable Development: The UK strategy*. London: HMSO.

Dufour, B. (1990) *The New Social Studies*. Abingdon: Routledge.

Fien, J. (1993) *Education for the Environment: Critical curriculum theorizing and environmental education*. Victoria: Deakin University Press.

Forsyth, T. (2003) *Critical Political Ecology: The politics of environmental science*. Abingdon: Routledge.

Galbraith, J.K. (1958) *The Affluent Society*. Boston, MA: Houghton Mifflin.

Guggenheim, D. (director) (2006) *An Inconvenient Truth* (DVD). Paramount Home Entertainment.

Hecht, S. and Cockburn, A. (1995) *The Fate of the Forest: Developers, destroyers and defenders of the Amazon*. Chicago, IL: University of Chicago Press.

Herbert, J. (1974) *The Rats*. London: New English Library.

Hopwood, B., Mellor, M. and O'Brien, G. (2005) 'Sustainable development: mapping different approaches', *Sustainable Development*, 13, 1, pp. 38–52.

Huckle, J. (ed) (1983) *Geographical Education: Reflection and action*. Oxford: Oxford University Press.

Huckle, J. (1988) What We Consume: *Teachers' handbook*. Godalming: WWF-UK/Richmond Press.

Kovel, J. (2007) *The Enemy of Nature: The end of capitalism or the end of the world?* (2nd edition). London: Zed Books.

Matthewman, S. (2010) *Teaching Secondary English as if the Planet Matters*. Abingdon: Routledge.

Meadows, D.H., Meadows, D.L., Randers, J. and Behrens, W.W. (1972) *The Limits to Growth: A report for The Club of Rome's project on the predicament of mankind*. New York, NY: Universe Books.

Morgan, J. (2011) *Teaching Secondary Geography as if the Planet Matters*. Abingdon: Routledge.

Newell, P. and Paterson, M. (2010) *Climate Capitalism: Global warming and the transformation of the global economy*. Cambridge: Cambridge University Press.

O'Keefe, P., Westgate, K. and Wisner, B. (1976) 'Taking the naturalness out of natural disasters', *Nature*, 260, 5552, pp. 566–67.

O'Riordan, T. (1976) *Environmentalism*. London: Pion.

Pearce, D., Markandya, A. and Barber, E. (1989) *Blueprint for a Green Economy*. London: Earthscan.

Pepper, D. (1984) *The Roots of Modern Environmentalism*. Abingdon: Routledge.

QCA (2009) *Sustainable Development in Action: A curriculum planning guide for schools*. Available at: www.globalfootprints.org/files/zones/teach/Key%20GL%20Documents/QCAsustainabilityinaction.pdf (last accessed 07/11/2016).

Randle, D. (1989) *Teaching Green: A parent's guide to education for life on Earth*. London: Greenprint Press.

Rostow, W. (1949/1960) *The Stages of Economic Growth: A non-communist manifesto*. Cambridge: Cambridge University Press.

Schumacher, F. (1973) *Small is Beautiful: A study of economics as if people mattered*. London: Blond and Briggs.

Stott, P. (2001) 'Jungles of the mind: the invention of the tropical rainforest', *History Today*, 51, 5, pp. 38–44.

Swyngedouw, E. (2007) 'Impossible "sustainability" and the postpolitical condition' in Krueger, R. and Gibbs, D. (eds) *The Sustainable Development Paradox: Urban political economy in the United States and Europe*. New York, NY: Guilford Press, pp. 13–40.

UN (1992) *AGENDA 21 United Nations Conference on Environment & Development*. Rio de Janerio, Brazil, 3–14 June.

Viles, H. (2005) 'A divided discipline?' in Castree, N., Rodgers, A. and Sherman, D. (eds) *Questioning Geography*. Oxford: Blackwell, pp. 26–38.

Wallerstein, I. (1974) 'The rise and future demise of the world capitalist system: concepts for comparative analysis', *Comparative Studies in Society and History*, 16, 4, pp. 387–415.

Williams, A. (2008) *The Enemies of Progress: Dangers of sustainability*. London: Societas.

Williams, R. (1976) *Keywords*. London: Fontana.

Recommended key readings

Morgan, J. (2011) *Teaching Secondary School Geography as if the Planet Matters*. Abingdon: Routledge.

This book develops in detail some of the ideas discussed in this chapter. It argues that school geography has so far failed to develop realistic explanations of sustainability, and suggests how teachers can incorporate environmental perspectives into their planning.

Nicholson, S. and Wapner, P. (eds) (2015) *Global Environmental Politics: From person to planet*. Boulder, CO: Paradigm Publishers.

This book is a collection of short articles, by a wide range of academics, journalists and other writers, that give an up-to-the-minute assessment of debates about the politics of sustainability. It is an invaluable source for teachers to develop their knowledge and understanding of sustainability.

Chapter 9

Global learning

John Hopkin is Head of Accreditation for the Global Learning Programme at the Geographical Association

Introduction

Geography has always had a global view: of where places are and what they are like, how human and physical phenomena are organised in space, and how they are linked together. Global learning, formerly often called 'development education', adds another dimension: it embraces ideas about development and international connections and understanding. It is a challenging aspect of the curriculum to get right, not only because the rate of change in the contemporary world makes it difficult to keep teaching up to date, but also because the concepts involved can be complex, and are commonly used in the context of a variety of meanings and assumptions. As well as having a large and dynamic knowledge base, global learning may also involve a significant values dimension, not least because people have strong, sometimes contradictory, beliefs about what should be taught, how and why. This chapter explores some of this territory, including some key geographical ideas and theory implications for teaching, and evaluates different approaches to global learning.

Global learning in the curriculum

Global learning has supported teachers in educating students about development and the wider world for over 40 years. Internationally and in the UK it has been supported and promoted both within the education system and externally, including by government, universities, non-governmental organisations (NGOs) and, in the UK, by Development Education Centres.

However, attempts to promote an internationalist outlook in education have a considerable history, for example through the interwar League of Nations Union, the post-war Council for Education in World Citizenship, UNESCO and the Council of Europe (see Marsden, 1995). Development education emerged as a feature of the UK school curriculum in the 1960s and 1970s. Although initially focused on learning about international development and aid, differences in emphasis and approach led to the emergence of a range of 'issues-based educations' including citizenship education; race, diversity and multicultural education; and education for sustainable development (see Hicks, 2007; Bullivant, 2010), which also contributed to debate within the geography community.

In the 1990s, the geography programmes of study in the first version of the National Curriculum in England and Wales included some global aspects; although by seeking to establish greater control of the school curriculum and to recast it in 'traditional' terms, the National Curriculum could be seen as an attempt by the state to counter the supposed influence of these broader issues-based approaches.

By the early 21st century the term 'global learning' began to replace 'development education', reflecting increasing economic, social and environmental interconnectedness, a recognition that development processes occur in both 'North' and 'South', and the need for education programmes to include such global perspectives. Particularly under New Labour administrations in the 2000s, the National Curriculum became less prescriptive, and agendas for citizenship and education for sustainable development (ESD) became more visible both in policy and practice. Schools and teachers were encouraged to develop a global dimension across the curriculum through a series of publications (see DfEE, 2000; DfES, 2005; QCA, 2007), while the Department for International Development's (DfID) *Enabling Effective Support* programme (2003) focused on professional development support for teachers in the four UK nations.

Chapter 9: Global learning

Figure 1: Continuity and change in two global learning policy documents.

Developing the global dimension in the school curriculum (DfEE, 2000, updated 2005)
Eight key concepts, with geography exemplification

- **Citizenship:** Inspiring students to think about their place in the world and their rights and responsibilities to other people; studying issues of global significance
- **Conflict resolution:** Explaining how conflicting demands on the environment arise and the difficulties that these can cause
- **Diversity:** Studying people, places and environments in different parts of the world
- **Interdependence:** Explaining why places and people are interdependent
- **Social justice:** Showing how a country's level of development is related to its quality of life
- **Sustainable development:** Teaching the principles of sustainable development, explaining the positive and negative effects of scientific and technological developments on the environment and on people; highlighting the importance of using resources sensitively
- **Values and perception:** Studying less economically developed countries and localities through analysis of sources such as photographs and texts, and raising consciousness of the way these shape the views of students and other.

Developing the global dimension in the school curriculum (DfES, 2005)

- 'Citizenship' became **Global Citizenship**
- **Human rights** was added: Examining how decisions made by governments and organisations can affect peoples' human rights.

Global Learning Programme (GLP-E 2013a, 2013b)
In the GLP there are five curriculum themes, together with more detailed student outcomes

Curriculum themes

Knowledge:

- of developing countries, their economies, histories and human geography
- of the basic elements of globalisation
- of the different ways to achieve global poverty reduction and development and the arguments around the merits of these different approaches
- and understanding of the concepts of interdependence and sustainability.

Supporting enquiry and critical thinking about development and development issues.

Student outcomes

Central elements:

- Understanding of global poverty, development.

Knowledge themes:

- Rights and essential services
- Actions of governments
- Actions of citizens
- Business and technology
- Sustainable development
- Globalisation and interdependence.

Skills and values:

- Critical thinking, Multiple perspectives, Challenging perceptions, Enquiry and discussion, Communication, Teamwork, Planning, Reflection and evaluation.

Values:

- Fairness, Agency, Care, Self-esteem, Diversity, Respect, Social justice, Empathy.

The global dimension and sustainable development was one of seven cross-curricular dimensions that QCA suggested were 'some of the major ideas and challenges that face individuals and society, and help make learning real and relevant' (2009, p. 1).

In the period 2010–15, although many schools continued to include a global dimension in their geography curriculum, the Department for Education's (DfE) commitment to these agendas was less visible. However, the UK government more broadly continued its support for professional development through DfID's Global Learning Programme (GLP), launched in 2013 in England (GLP-E), followed by Wales, Scotland and Northern Ireland. The GLP set out to improve the teaching of global learning in key stages 2 and 3 and to embed it widely in the curriculum, where its aims accord closely with DfID's focus on global poverty reduction:

> 'The GLP will help pupils gain additional knowledge about the developing world, the causes of poverty and what can be done to reduce it. They will also develop the skills to interpret that knowledge in order to make judgements about global poverty' (GLP-E, 2013a).

107

The GLP's emphasis on knowledge and understanding of key concepts, including development, globalisation, interdependence and sustainability, explored through enquiry and critical thinking, confirm a significant curricular role for geography. Comparison with policy documents from the previous decade (Figure 1) suggests some continuity in key concepts, together with a refocusing of global learning in the GLP on knowledge and understanding of development themes and poverty reduction, and a more detailed articulation of a range of student outcomes, especially in skills and values (GLP-E, 2013a, 2013b).

Key ideas in global learning

However visible or not in educational policy, publications and initiatives, most geographers would probably agree that our discipline has an important contribution to make to global learning, particularly in developing students' knowledge and understanding of the contemporary world. In beginning to examine global learning the following five interrelated geographical ideas (see Bennetts, 2005, p. 157) seem particularly relevant; they are some of the big ideas of geography, which in turn may contribute to other more generic aspects of the curriculum such as ideas about local and global cultural diversity and citizenship, and to values education.

1. Space, place, and location

This set of ideas includes where places are, what they are like and how they relate to other places and spaces. Teaching about distant places is an important means of developing students' interest and skills in learning about the world, as well as their framework of place knowledge and sense of place; the foundation of geographical understanding and the cornerstone of geography's contribution to global learning. The way we do so informs their geographical imaginations and creates geography's world view.

In geography we cannot investigate the whole of planet Earth, so we need to select carefully. In the past secondary school geography has tended to use the principles of physical and human geography as the main guide to selecting content, with places often confined to a backdrop of bite-sized case studies chosen to illustrate issues and themes (Hopkin, 1994, 2011). As a result students may gain only a partial view of the world:

> *'All but the best students interviewed were spatially naïve. The mental images they held of the world were often confused and they were not able to locate countries... For example, they understood about development issues in Kenya but had little or no idea of where Kenya was in Africa... Their study of geography was isolated and not set within a context that they could identify with'* (Ofsted, 2011, p. 22).

Although both the 2014 National Curriculum and 2014 geography GCSE subject content (DfE, 2014) emphasise the development of locational knowledge, anchoring students' studies in a systematic framework of place knowledge needs continued vigilance.

The way we represent and frame the world in our teaching also deserves care, particularly through our selection of places, stories of development, and the models we use to describe and explain uneven development (Hopkin, 2011; Taylor, 2011; 2013). Well-used case studies, chosen with the best of intentions to illustrate particular geographical principles, can eventually become typecast and predictable. Examples are the close association between studies of Bangladesh and flooding, and students' knowledge of Brazil often being largely framed by their study of rainforests and favelas. These are places in danger of becoming defined by the issue they are used to exemplify, risking the creation of 'single stories' in students' understanding (Biddulph, 2011). There are many other examples in school geography, not only in the developing world (Roberts, 2009; 2013): exploring the diversity and dynamism of the developing world and its people is surely more geographically literate and culturally insightful. Gary Simmons (2014) describes an approach to planning a scheme of work for teaching about Africa that addresses some of these concerns. Figure 2 provides some prompts for when planning or reviewing sequences of lessons or schemes of work.

2. Human and environmental change

This set of ideas includes the concept of development, how and why it happens (or doesn't), and the idea of sustainable development.

Development is a goal for countries and the world community, as well as a process. Development concerns change, and often implies change for the better, though development may not always lead to improvement – for example an increase in pollution or inequality. The idea of development leading to progress or improvements almost inevitably has a futures dimension.

In 1990 the first report of the United Nations Development Programme (UNDP) set out an idea of human development as 'A vision of economic and social progress that is fundamentally about people enlarging their choices and capabilities' (UNDP, 2013, p. 21). David Lambert (2014) points out that this capabilities approach is linked to Amartya Sen's (1999) work on development and welfare economics, which in turn gives a clear rationale for education, including for intercultural understanding and challenging prejudice. The UN's is one among numerous definitions of development; where the emphasis placed, for example on economic, social/cultural, environmental or political goals, is far from neutral, founded as it is in choices, values and the exercise of political power.

Because people–environment relationships are of central concern to geographers, we also have a significant contribution to make to understanding the linked idea of sustainable development that, recognising the environmental underpinnings of human life and activity, aims to secure the needs of people in the present and in future generations (Huckle, 2011; Morgan, 2011). More broadly, education contributes to international goals for human development and social justice, as expressed in the Millennium Development Goals (MDGs).

What we mean by development, the best policies to achieve it and explanations for uneven development are all deeply contested. For example, is development a process that happens to places and people, or one in which people participate in decisions about change? Katie Willis (2014) reminds us that this is complex territory, and that there were good

- Maintain a geographical focus by using a range of mapping opportunities to locate studies, so ensuring they contribute to students' developing framework of world knowledge. Find space to include topical issues and those in the news from around the world; overall, ensure geography classrooms exude the global dimension

- Plan a variety of studies from different places, some focusing on places, others on issues and themes, and regularly review them to ensure they have not become one-dimensional, helps understanding of diversity. Including studies from high-, medium- and low-income or welfare countries helps explore some of the complexity of development patterns and processes

- Natural and human disasters are among geography's most enduring and engaging staples. There is a danger, often reinforced by images in the media, that these aspects become the 'single story' (Biddulph, 2011) of the developing world, rather than the fulfilling lives of many people who live there. Careful review and critical evaluation of which themes and places are portrayed, including by students, helps avoid this.

reasons why geographers moved on from a view of development based solely on economic modernisation. She provides a useful comparison of three approaches to development:

- Modernisation (1950s to 1970s), modelling development on the experience of the North and defining it in terms of economic growth and improved standards of living, explaining inequalities with reference to stages on a path to development, and operating at national level

- Marxist/structuralist (1960s to 1980s), defining development in terms of economic growth and improved standards of living, explaining inequalities as inherent to global capitalism, and operating at national level within a global economic system

Figure 2:
Global learning: prompts for planning or reviewing work.

Figure 3: Key messages from the 2013 Human Development Report *The Rise of the South*. **Source:** UNDP, 2013, p. 11.

UNDP's 2013 report documents the striking transformation of human development in many developing countries in the previous decade, with faster (albeit uneven) progress in countries with lower levels of human development. Examining the strategies that facilitated these improvements, UNDP noted significant economic growth driven by trade and technology partnerships within the South, supported by 'pro-poor policies and significant investments in people's capabilities' through education and skills, nutrition, and health. It identifies four focus areas to sustain momentum: 'enhancing equity, including on the gender dimension; enabling greater voice and participation of citizens, including youth, confronting environmental pressures; and managing demographic change'.

- Post-structuralist approaches (1990s onwards), recognising multiple definitions of development and a range of factors including gender and ethnicity to explain inequalities, and operating within global networks at local scale.

Willis points out that in practice these categories are often not discrete. This suggests we should be cautious about reflecting or exemplifying only one approach in our teaching. The UNDP's Human Development Reports support a multivariate view in explaining progress in human development; see for example its 2013 report (Figure 3).

3. Patterns of uneven development and human welfare

Ending extreme poverty is a key aim of the international development agenda, and the focus of the MDGs (to 2015) and the SDGs (Sustainable Development Goals) that followed them. The four decades between 1970 and 2010 saw significant improvements in human welfare, economic growth and development. In this period the world averaged a 41% average increase in the Human Development Index (HDI), with striking improvements in education, health and life expectancy (UNDP, 2010, p. 28), with millions lifted out of poverty. However, there are still huge gaps from one end of the continuum of countries to the other, alongside growing inequality within many countries, while over one billion people currently still live in extreme poverty, on less than $1.25 a day.

Because it has a spatial dimension, uneven development is of considerable interest to geographers, while understanding approaches to reducing global poverty through development is also an aim of the Global Learning Programme (Figure 1). This is something of a dilemma: how much emphasis should we place, in our teaching, on the fact of global poverty, risking reinforcing stereotypical views about people and places, compared with global progress and success stories in development? And, of course, consideration of global poverty may well raise issues about poverty and inequality closer to home.

When tackling this complex topic there are opportunities to use personal stories to build understanding of fairness and the commonality between people and the challenges they face, as well as considering concrete and practical ways people, communities and governments have improved the quality of life through development (Figure 4). Investigating the MDGs/SDGs can be a useful framework to focus on progress as well as obstacles to development, and as a way into thinking about the processes that explain development successes and failures.

4. Interdependence and globalisation

The concept of interdependence is a broad one, concerning the interconnections and links between people, places and environments on a range of scales, especially the local, international and global; so it relates closely to important concepts at the core of geography. For Joe Smith (2015), this amounts to a 'ground condition – a description of humanity's state of being in the world' (p. 18). These linkages do not exist on a level international playing field, so learning about interdependence also involves considering uneven power relations in the world, as well as the idea of seeing people in other places as partners in development from whom we have much to learn. It is linked to ideas about global citizenship and solidarity between peoples, as expressed in the UN's SDG 17: 'Global Partnerships for Sustainable Development'.

The linked concept of globalisation can be interpreted in a wide range of ways, but perhaps is used most often to describe the process by which the world is increasingly interconnected by economic activities across international borders, as well as other processes such as cultural exchange, population movements, environmental change and decision making (Figure 5). What seems to distinguish globalisation in the 21st century is the speed of change, often the result of technological development; its widespread impacts on people and environments, both positive and negative, and the de-territorialisation of social, economic and political space. Globalisation is one of the great forces of our time, a source of great controversy and of great interest to geographers (Butt, 2011).

Although almost absent from the 2014 version of the geography National Curriculum (DfE, 2013), developing understanding of global interconnections should surely be part of the curriculum for an educated young person in the twenty-first century.

5. Geographical enquiry and thought

Geographical enquiry is an approach that links a range of practical and intellectual investigative skills and pedagogies with developing geographical knowledge and thinking, and is considered by many geographers to be of fundamental significance in teaching and learning (see Roberts, 2009; 2013). Enquiry has particular value in global learning where, as well as having strong geographical dimensions, much of the territory is dynamic, challenging, and can be thought about from a range of (sometimes contradictory) value positions, so it is potentially controversial:

- Enquiry planned around geographical questions recognises that many global issues are dynamic and uncertain. Moreover, young people are often interested in issues that will affect their futures, and commonly expect to learn about such issues in geography (Ipsos MORI, 2009). Asking questions helps connect their interests and experiences with the real world, motivating and empowering them to investigate in a structured way
- Enquiry supports students' understanding by structuring and scaffolding their learning, helping them actively to make sense of complex concepts such as development or globalisation. Understanding such concepts is much harder than learning straightforward facts about the world, and teaching by simply transmitting information is unlikely to be effective for many students
- Enquiry focuses on investigating and evaluating different types of evidence; this is particularly useful where the subject matter is controversial, and the need to create opportunities to consider a range of perspectives is an important professional responsibility. Investigation and discussion engages students' geographical thinking, so challenging and deepening their understanding.

Roberts presents a useful typology of why issues are controversial (2013, pp. 114–15): the most relevant to global learning include those that are controversial because of differences in interpretation, because of different opinions about what should be done, and for ethical reasons.

Of course whether issues such as these are legitimately part of the geography curriculum may itself be controversial, depending on one's view of the purpose of education. However, it is worth remembering that learning about controversial issues is rooted in a significant strand of geographical thought, the humanistic and welfare tradition, and has also been the subject of considerable professional study and debate, providing both a clear rationale and real challenges for teachers to address (see Mitchell, 2013, and Roberts, 2013, for recent summaries). The study of controversial issues can also be readily justified for a number of educational reasons, including their central role in developing students' understanding of the geography of the contemporary world, the importance of understanding the geographical impact of people's opinions and values, and the utility of using controversial issues to develop and challenge students' cognitive skills and geographical thought (Roberts, 2013, pp. 117–18).

Finally, because students are involved in critically reviewing evidence, studying a range of alternative views and clarifying their own values, a disciplined approach to enquiry and

Figure 4: Global learning teaching approaches: uneven development and human welfare.

Classifying the world

This is still a useful way to think about uneven development, but dividing the world up into North and South, or More and Less Economically Developed, although easier to teach, has limited validity. This is a real dilemma; the terms 'developing' and 'developed' have wider currency, for example with the United Nations, and are probably more dynamic, but are also far from ideal: you might get students involved in discussions about the best terms to use. Students should probably learn that there are different ways to classify places, including countries with high, medium and low incomes or levels of human development; and that development is dynamic, and has a number of meanings. It may be productive to start with investigating individual places as the context for development: what they are like, how they are changing, and how they are linked to the rest of the world. Investigating uneven development and inequality within as well as between countries, for example between rural and urban areas, also helps focus on development processes.

Measuring development

School geography is adept at comparing different measures of development, and teaching students to use and evaluate them. Attention to recent data keeps our teaching in touch with the real world, and teaches students important skills, including cautious scepticism about the nature of evidence. Advocating the Worldmapper website (*www.worldmapper.org*), now sadly rather dated, Dorling and Barford (2006) point out that using 'data concerning people can be brought to life in order in order to highlight how risks, resources and rewards are distributed around the planet, and to feed a geographical imagination that sees people as people' (p. 187). Having a culturally careful approach to data also helps students to question and recognise the variety of people's lifestyles and perspectives about what constitutes quality of life.

Glocal

Development and the 'global' is often assumed to happen in other places and to other people: identifying the interconnected nature of people, places and environments in the 21st century is a key aspect of geographical understanding and thought. For example, investigating the global within the local highlights these connections and relates global issues to students' own experiences, while investigating the processes behind local change helps understand development elsewhere, and makes these processes more concrete and relevant.

Defining development

Explore different models of development, for example giving students opportunities to consider approaches such as small-scale grass-roots changes – perhaps starting with thinking about how change happens in the school or community, compared with change originating from top-down decisions, e.g. from government or business. A focus on individual stories and voices can help provide students with concrete points of reference, and enable real people to speak for themselves, ideally at times through direct communication. Seeing people engaged in development helps counter the assumption that powerful global forces are the inevitable architects of change.

Personal geographies

Many geography teachers and students have first-hand personal experiences of visiting, living in, or family connections in distant places; similarly, many schools are living proof of our globally-connected world. These personal connections are valuable resources for geography that can offer immediately relevant perspectives, but can both challenge and reinforce pre-existing views of the world. Being aware of the limitations of the singular view, the need to look for alternative sources of evidence and training students to recognise these helps avoid this risk.

Reviewing resources
Encourage students to think critically about sources, assumptions and values: do materials from business, NGOs or governments reflect particular agendas? Materials that may reflect particular agendas include teaching resources such as global learning games and simulations, which can be valuable in engaging with complex and abstract ideas (for example about trade), but may also be designed with particular outcomes in mind.

'Right answers'
Similarly, do planning and teaching implicitly lead students to the 'right answers'? Do apparently self-evidently good causes such as fair trade or sustainable development deserve further scrutiny and examination, for example, encouraging a more balanced view of trade? Maintaining a geographical focus, providing a range of arguments and explanations, and promoting critical thinking helps ensure the work does not inadvertently promote pre-determined views.

Learning from each other
Many schools, especially denominational schools, have strong cultures of charitable fund-raising, which can sometimes 'reinforce unfortunate stereotypes' (Ofsted, 2008, p. 46). Similarly, school-linking programmes can make a valuable contribution to students' understanding through direct contact with peers and indirect experience of other places, but they need careful thought to ensure the experience is positive and sustainable for all schools concerned. These are important aspects of global learning: ensuring a strong geographical contribution helps staff and students learn within a framework of knowledge and understanding about development and interdependence, for example by exploring the role and effectiveness of different types of development programmes and comparing charitable giving with approaches to development informed by social justice.

Enquiry
Geography's knowledge base and strength in enquiry make an important contribution to global learning and, in turn, to wider school aims about preparing young people for future study, work and citizenship. Geographical thinking can be particularly effective when linked with other parts of the curriculum through joint work with other subjects: the GA's Secondary Geography Quality Mark recognises these opportunities for geography to take a lead in the whole-school development of global learning.

Future thinking
Global learning in geography has a strong futures dimension; engaging students in thinking about what kind of world they will live in can be a powerful, and perhaps optimistic, motivator: see Roberts (2003, chapter 15) and Hicks (2014).

critical thinking applied to global learning (Roberts, 2015) can be particularly helpful in guarding against the promotion of particular viewpoints or even indoctrination. Most teachers are keen to avoid this, and 'recognition that the purposes of school geography are controversial helps teachers take a critical and morally careful approach to curriculum' (Mitchell, 2013, p. 234) (Figure 6).

Contrasting approaches to global learning

In her article about different perspectives on the geography curriculum, Mary Biddulph (2014) discusses the impact of alternative curriculum aims on what and how we choose to teach. Similar thinking can be applied to different views on the purpose and focus of

Figure 5:
Global learning teaching approaches: interdependence and globalisation.

A focus on interaction and relationship

Connectivity in space and between scales is a fundamental geographical idea, but these are demanding concepts, so progression is a key issue (Hopkin and Owens, 2015). In practice, building up understanding of geographical interactions and relationships through different topics and key stages may be a useful approach, probably starting with concrete and familiar examples before introducing more abstract and complex ideas to older students. For example, work on globalisation will most likely be introduced with concrete examples, perhaps investigating the production, trade and consumption of familiar goods, and looking for the global in the local. Older students may be introduced to more abstract ideas, such as the scale and influence of global financial flows and the cultural and political impacts of globalisation, both challenging and helping to develop fuller understanding.

Understanding values

Learning about international connections and relationships may involve considering uneven power relations in the world and have a strong values dimension, so teaching deserves particular care. For example, investigating globalisation might explore the costs for some people, places and environments, and benefits for others, and compare other approaches to development (which in turn have advantages and disadvantages). The idea that globalisation is an unstoppable force carries its own values and assumptions, as does the binary suggestion that globalisation is a force for good or for ill.

global learning, which in turn may influence the approach individual schools and teachers follow. Here I outline two significant but contrasting approaches to global learning, 'global citizenship' and 'traditional geography'; the remainder of the chapter suggests a third, characterised as a 'knowledgeable geography' approach, with some comparisons between the three developed in the conclusion.

A 'global citizenship' approach

As suggested above, global learning has long had an influence on UK schools. Although there is considerable diversity of approaches, the development of students as global citizens is a common aim of global learning (see, for example, Gadsby and Bullivant, 2010; Bourn, 2014). This 'global citizenship' approach can be characterised as:

- emphasising global learning across the curriculum and through whole-school activities, rather than through individual subjects; indeed this approach can be antipathetic towards subject-based teaching
- prioritising the development of skills – including enquiry and critical thinking – and attitudes and values, rather than what is sometimes characterised as 'reproducing bodies of knowledge'
- focusing on learning, particularly students' active engagement and enquiry, and on developing a range of appropriate pedagogies
- aiming to help students develop a global outlook linked with their own lives, that enables them to challenge dominant assumptions about global relationships, make choices and potentially take action
- a focus on professional development.

This approach can be summarised as emphasising a learning process that promotes more reflective and critical learning about the world. In aiming to develop students as global citizens able to make an active commitment to social justice, to a considerable extent it has moved beyond teaching for understanding about development and the causes of global inequalities to focus on learners themselves. The most significant potential weaknesses of this global citizenship approach seem to be:

- the low priority given to disciplinary knowledge (for teachers and students) and so to the development of students' understanding of global patterns and processes, and a consequent imbalance in favour of pedagogy and developing generic learning skills and values

- the possibility of over-emphasising personal development at the expense of systematically expanding students' horizons through knowledge and understanding of the real world
- the need for teachers to be careful to remain educators, rather than what Marsden (1997) describes as advocates of 'good causes'.

A 'traditional geography' approach

A quarter of a century ago, the development of the first National Curriculum was marked by significant pressure for a return to 'tradition' in the curriculum, most significantly from conservative politicians and think tanks (Rawling, 2001) rather than geographers; in part this was also a critique of aspects of the perceived aims and practices of global citizenship. Recently, the most influential current advocate of what can be (rather simplistically) described as 'traditional geography' is Alex Standish (2009, 2012, 2013, 2014), a geographer who has taken a close interest in global learning.

Standish's critique of global learning, both in general and in geography, is wide-ranging; it centres on the un-bounded nature of global learning, which he argues has helped divorce education and teachers from their core role of transmitting disciplinary knowledge. He argues that this is part of a broad progressive agenda undermining liberal education and standards; thus politicians, educational policy makers and subject associations (particularly the GA) have successfully changed the nature of geography. In this analysis, in the past school geography correctly centred studies on locational and spatial knowledge, concepts and skills, but today it is overly concerned with teaching morality, citizenship and 'trendy' themes rather than independent thought. In his view, this has led geography to become improperly involved in political, social and environmental concerns, thus replacing education with the indoctrination of students into a set of predetermined values, so encouraging them to become involved in matters beyond their responsibility, such as trying to improve the world. Moreover these values (which are positioned as Western and cosmopolitan) also allegedly inhibit global development, for example by prioritising the environment over economic growth.

Characteristics of more careful teaching would include:

- attention to evidence, including a range of evidence and data from different sources
- generating a culture of argument, where different accounts are listened to and, where appropriate, countered
- encouraging a tone of confident uncertainty: confident learners (and teachers) know there is more to know and find out
- including, and addressing, the most difficult geographical questions, such as conflicts, growing inequality and sustainability
- providing opportunities to practice making informed decisions and expressing viewpoints
- opportunities to analyse and reflect on values held by others and self (teacher and student)
- avoiding the ambivalent idea that there are no right or wrong answers, rather than no clear-cut answers
- avoiding teaching that leads to particular conclusions, rather than the means to evaluate a range of outcomes, possibilities or perspectives.

What might be characterised as a 'traditional' approach takes a more fundamental view of global learning, emphasising those aspects concerned with space, place and location, and questioning the focus on contemporary issues and human welfare in the classroom. It can be summarised as:

- having a strong disciplinary focus, within a curriculum organised in subjects
- emphasising students' acquisition of objective facts and theoretical knowledge about the world, founded in 'the wisdom of their forebears' (Standish, 2009, p. 5)
- having a limited view of appropriate geographical skills and sceptical of geographical enquiry and critical thinking

Figure 6: Global learning teaching approaches: careful teaching. **After:** Morgan and Lambert, 2005.

- critical of teaching about or exploring values, and of the idea of relevance, so having significant reservations about teaching contemporary global issues and the concept of interdependence
- a fairly restrictive view of 'the global', in favour of national boundaries as the framework for meaning and study
- promoting a particular view of development, founded in economic liberalism.

Standish makes a number of trenchant criticisms of the theory and practice of global learning, particularly the risks of politicising the curriculum. The critique is in many ways an apt warning to maintain a disciplinary focus and to beware of selecting issues that in reality explore pre-determined value positions; instead we should maintain a sceptical stance towards sources and explore alternative perspectives. The most significant weaknesses of this approach seem to be:

- its reference point is a model of geography from a past 'golden age', where worthwhile subject knowledge was immutable and authorised by experts, rather than recognising subsequent developments in the discipline, including the idea that knowledge is constructed by geographers engaged in investigating the world (Morgan, 2009)
- in a dynamic, interconnected contemporary world, its focus on geographical boundaries and the national scale is limiting
- its scepticism about the role of contemporary geographical issues and of geographical enquiry seems to be based on a misunderstanding of their nature and value in the curriculum, for example in developing knowledge and understanding and challenging students' thinking
- in challenging what is argued to be one orthodoxy, it may seek to substitute a view of the world and of geography education that merely represents a different set of (unacknowledged) interests and values.

A 'knowledgeable geography' approach

The above summary of two different approaches relies on some broad generalisations, not least in designating them 'global citizenship' and 'traditional geography'; moreover the views of individual commentators may vary from the 'model'. For example, the influential Oxfam resource *Education for Global Citizenship: A guide for schools* (Oxfam, 2006), while advocating many aspects of the 'global citizenship' approach, also stresses the importance of building on knowledge and understanding of key concepts.

Both approaches seem to me to have significant weaknesses. By contrast, I think the approach outlined in the first part of this chapter offers improved opportunities for young people to develop deep understanding of the world, so underpinning high standards. This combines:

- a claim for geographical knowledge as having a valuable, foundational role in global learning; and a disciplinary focus that helps students to engage with some big geographical ideas, particularly the centrality of place and the interconnected and dynamic nature of the world
- a recognition of the merits of enquiry in building students' understanding of the geography of the contemporary world, including maintaining a sceptical stance towards sources and exploring alternative perspectives
- a belief that developing students' geographical thinking and understanding by exploring controversial issues has considerable legitimacy (see Roberts, 2013), including the consideration of people's opinions and values.

This approach also makes the case for teachers' active role in developing the curriculum – as argued in the GA's manifesto, *A Different View* (2009). This view is broadly supported by Ofsted, which considers understanding of such ideas to be a significant feature of high-quality geography provision:

'The schools that had a good or outstanding geography curriculum had thought carefully about creating a more relevant curriculum at key stage 3 with a greater emphasis on topical concerns such as sustainability, globalisation, interdependence, poverty and wealth… (here) students were prepared to study a subject which they saw as relevant and with which they could engage' (Ofsted, 2011, p. 32).

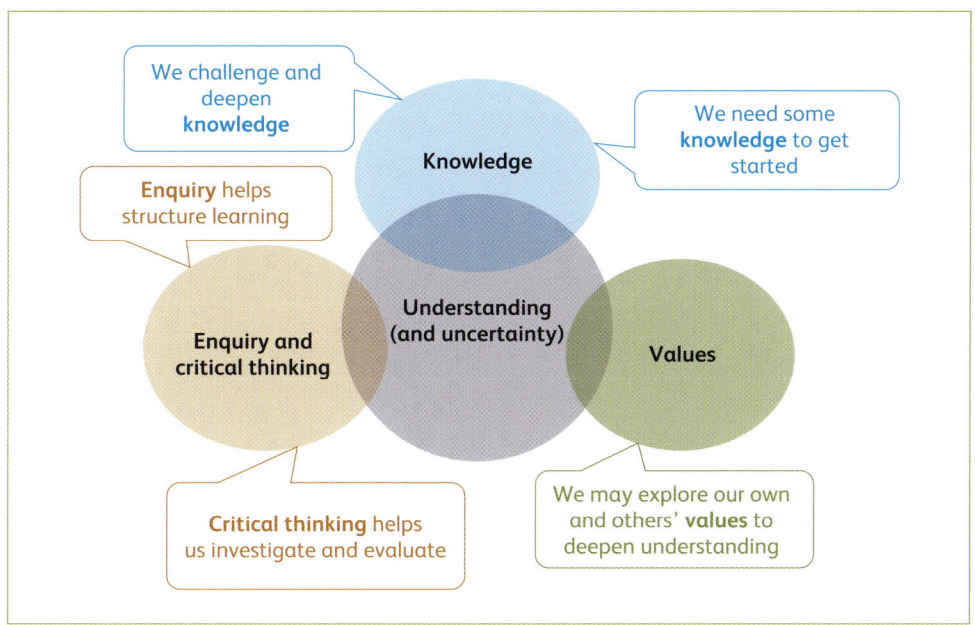

Figure 7: Geographical understanding at the centre of global learning. **Source:** Paula Owens.

This approach to global learning in geography amounts to an assertion of the value of developing understanding about the world to the current learning and future employment and citizenship of an educated young person in the twenty-first century, with knowledge, enquiry and critical thinking and values making a balanced contribution (Figure 7).

Whereas the 'global citizenship' approach may tend to over-emphasise educational and social objectives, and 'traditional geography' lean too far towards narrow subject goals, this approach represents more of a balance between subject, educational and social goals and between geographical traditions (Marsden, 1995).

As well as relating to different ways of organising the curriculum and purposes for learning, the three different approaches outlined here also have some associations with different views of the nature of knowledge (Morgan, 2011). A 'knowledgeable geography' relates to a view of knowledge founded not in 'absolutism' (the tendency for 'traditional geography') or 'social constructivism' (for 'global citizenship') (Firth, 2012; 2013), but rather in 'social realism' where teachers induct students into socially and educationally worthwhile 'powerful knowledge' about global learning through the discipline of geography.

Conclusion

This chapter started by exploring some of the key geographical ideas involved in global learning in geography and their implications for practice, then contrasted the strengths and weaknesses of two approaches to global learning, characterised as 'traditional geography' and 'global citizenship', compared with a 'knowledgeable geography' approach, founded in those key ideas. This alternative approach takes a view of knowledge that is founded in the discipline but, rather than limiting students and teachers, empowers them to investigate and understand the contemporary world, recognising the value of learning about concepts such as development, interdependence and globalisation.

Although these complex issues can be controversial, a disciplined approach helps teachers remain educators, not least by recognising that our subject is steeped in values. Rather than attempting to authorise particular knowledge or prescribe what to study – for example a specific model of development – it suggests that the point of a geographical education is to teach students how to investigate, review evidence and think critically, in order to come to their own conclusions about matters that are both intensely geographical and important to their future lives.

The point of a geographical education is to teach students how to investigate, review evidence and think critically.
Photo © Shaun Flannery.

This is global learning in a curriculum of engagement, including a view of the world and of geography's contribution to education founded in considerations of justice, autonomy and progress: a particular perspective and a set of assumptions and values about which readers can make up their own minds.

References

Bennetts, T. (2005) 'The links between understanding, progression and assessment in the secondary geography curriculum', *Geography*, 90, 2, pp. 152–70.

Biddulph, M. (2011) 'Editorial: The danger of a single story', *Teaching Geography*, 36, 2, p. 45.

Biddulph, M. (2014) 'What kind of geography curriculum do we really want?', *Teaching Geography*, 39, 1, pp. 6–9.

Bourn, D. (2014) 'The theory and practice of global learning', *DERC Research Paper*, No. 11. London: DERC, Institute of Education.

Bullivant, A. (2010) 'Global learning: a historical overview' in Gadsby, H. and Bullivant, A. (eds) *Global Learning and Sustainable Development*. London: David Fulton/Routledge, pp. 6–24.

Butt, G. (2011) 'Globalisation, geography education and the curriculum: what are the challenges for curriculum makers in geography?', *Curriculum Journal*, 22, 3, pp. 423–38.

DfE (2013) *National Curriculum in England: Geography programmes of study*. Available at: www.gov.uk/government/publications/national-curriculum-in-England-geography-programmes-of-study (last accessed 08/11/2016).

DfE (2014) *Geography: GCSE subject content*. Available at: www.gov.uk/government/publications/GCSE-geography (last accessed 08/11/2016).

DfEE (2000) *Developing the Global Dimension in the School Curriculum*. Available at: http://think-global.org.uk/resources/item/883 (last accessed 08/11/2016).

DfID (2003) *Enabling Effective Support*. London: DfID.

Dorling, D. and Barford, A. (2006) 'Humanising geography', *Geography*, 91, 3, pp. 187–97.

Firth, R. (2012) 'Disordering the coalition government's "new" approach to curriculum design and knowledge: the matter of the discipline', *Geography*, 97, 2, pp. 86–94.

Firth, R. (2013) 'What constitutes knowledge in geography?' in Lambert, D. and Jones, M. (eds) *Debates in Geography Education*. Abingdon: Routledge, pp. 59–74.

GA (2009) *A Different View: A manifesto from the Geographical Association*. Available at: www.geography.org.uk/resources/adifferentview (last accessed 08/11/2016).

Gadsby, H. and Bullivant, A. (2010) *Global Learning and Sustainable Development*. London: David Fulton/Routledge.

GLP-E (2013a) *Curriculum framework*. Available at: http://globaldimension.org.uk/glp/page/10706 (last accessed 08/11/2016).

GLP-E (2013b) *Pupil outcomes*. Available at: http://globaldimension.org.uk/glp/page/10724 (last accessed 08/11/2016).

Hicks, D. (2007) 'Responding to the world' in Hicks, D. and Holden, C. (eds) *Teaching the Global Dimension: Key principles and effective practices*. Abingdon: Routledge, pp. 3–13.

Hicks, D. (2014) 'A geography of hope', *Geography*, 99, 1, pp. 5–12.

Hopkin, J. (1994) 'Geography and development education' in Osler, A. (ed) *Development Education: Global perspectives in the curriculum*. London: Cassell, pp. 65–90.

Hopkin, J. (2011) 'Progress in geography', *Geography*, 96, 3, pp. 116–23.

Hopkin, J. and Owens, P. (2015) 'Progression in global learning', *Teaching Geography*, 40, 2, pp. 60–61.

Huckle, J. (2011) 'Bringing sustainability into focus', *Teaching Geography*, 36, 3, pp. 118–19.

Ipsos MORI (2009) *World Issues Survey. Conducted by Ipsos MORI on behalf of the Geographical Association*. Available at: www.geography.org.uk/resources/adifferentview/worldissuessurvey (last accessed 08/11/2016).

Lambert, D. (2014) 'Interculturalism: a sense of the global and a capabilities approach to curriculum making', *Teaching Geography*, 39, 3, pp. 106–7.

Marsden, W.E. (1995) *Geography 11–16: Rekindling good practice*. London: David Fulton.

Marsden, W.E. (1997) 'On taking the geography out of geographical education: some historical pointers', *Geography*, 82, 3, pp. 241–52.

Mitchell, D. (2013) 'How do we deal with controversial issues in a "relevant" school geography?' in Lambert, D. and Jones, M. (eds) *Debates in Geography Education*. Abingdon: Routledge, pp. 29–43.

Morgan, J. (2009) 'Review essay: global perspectives in the geography curriculum', *International Journal of Development Education and Global Learning*, 1, 3, pp. 57–62.

Morgan, J. (2011) 'Knowledge and the school geography curriculum: a rough guide for teachers', *Teaching Geography*, 36, 3, pp. 118–19.

Morgan, J. and Lambert, D. (2005) *Geography: Teaching school subjects 11–19*. Abingdon: Routledge.

Ofsted (2008) *Geography in Schools: Changing practice*. Manchester: Ofsted.

Ofsted (2011) *Geography: Learning to make a world of difference*. Available at: www.gov.uk/government/publications/geography-learning-to-make-a-world-of-difference (last accessed 08/11/2016).

Oxfam (2006) *Education for Global Citizenship: A guide for schools*. Available at: http://policy-practice.oxfam.org.uk/publications/global-citizenship-guides-620105 (last accessed 08/11/2016).

QCA (2007) *The Global Dimension in Action: A curriculum planning guide for schools*. London: QCA.

QCA (2009) *Cross-Curriculum Dimensions: A planning guide for schools*. London: QCA.

Rawling, E. (2001) *Changing the Subject: The impact of national policy on school geography 1980–2000*. Sheffield: Geographical Association.

Roberts, M. (2003) *Learning Through Enquiry: Making sense of geography in the key stage 3 classroom*. Sheffield: Geographical Association.

Roberts, M. (2009) 'Investigating geography', *Geography*, 94, 3, pp.181–8.

Roberts, M. (2013) *Geography Through Enquiry: Approaches to teaching and learning in the secondary school*. Sheffield: Geographical Association.

Roberts, M. (2015) 'Critical thinking and global learning', *Teaching Geography*, 40, 2, pp. 55–59.

Sen, A. (1999) *Development as Freedom*. New York, NY: Oxford University Press.

Simmons, G. (2014) 'How diverse is Africa? Reflections on a new scheme of work', *Teaching Geography*, 39, 3, pp. 110–11.

Smith, J. (2015) 'Geographies of interdependence', *Geography*, 100, 1, pp. 12–19.

Standish, A. (2009) *Global Perspectives in the Geography Curriculum: Reviewing the moral case for geography*. Abingdon: Routledge.

Standish, A. (2012) *The False Promise of Global Learning: Why education needs boundaries*. London: Continuum.

Standish, A. (2013) 'What does geography contribute to global learning?' in Lambert, D. and Jones, M. (eds) *Debates in Geography Education*. Abingdon: Routledge, pp. 244–56.

Standish, A. (2014) 'What is global education and where is it taking us?', *The Curriculum Journal*, 25, 2, pp. 166–86.

Taylor, L. (2011) 'The negotiation of diversity', *Teaching Geography*, 36, 2, pp. 49–51.

Taylor, L. (2013) 'Spotlight On… Case studies', *Geography*, 98, 2, pp. 100–4.

UNDP (2010) *Human Development Report 2010. The Real Wealth of Nations: Pathways to human development*. Available at: http://hdr.undp.org/en/content/human-development-report-2010 (last accessed 08/11/2016).

UNDP (2013) *Human Development Report 2013. The Rise of the South: Human progress in a diverse world*. Available at: http://hdr.undp.org/en/2013-report (last accessed 08/11/2016).

UN Millennium Development Goals: www.un.org/millenniumgoals (last accessed 29/04/2015).

Willis, K. (2014) 'Development: geographical perspectives on a contested planet', *Geography*, 99, 2, pp. 60–66.

Recommended key readings

Bourn, D. (2014) 'The theory and practice of global learning', *DERC Research Paper*, No 11. London: DERC, Institute of Education.

An overview of the history, aims and practices of global learning, linked to the Global Learning Programme, which presents a 'pedagogic framework'.

Lambert, D. and Morgan, J. (2011) 'Geography and development: development education in schools and the part played by geography teachers', *DERC Research Paper*, No.3. London: DERC with the Geographical Association.

A critical review of development education, from a geographical perspective.

Chapter 10

Place and locational knowledge

Denise Freeman is a geography teacher at Oaks Park High School, London, and **Alun Morgan** is a Lecturer in Education at the University of Plymouth

Introduction

It is often said that geography is about places. However, while geography teachers spend a great deal of time teaching students about places, there are few deeper explorations of the term 'place' and its meaning (Taylor, 2005, p. 14). It could be argued that this oversight denies students the opportunity to unpack some of the rich complexities of place as a concept and is a missed opportunity to introduce the work of contemporary academic geographers into the classroom (Taylor, 2005).

This chapter encourages teachers to examine place more critically; to reflect upon their rationale for choosing particular places for study, and the geographical perspectives through which they ask students to explore these places. Students should be given opportunities to undertake individual and collaborative place-based geographical enquiries through which teachers can promote a more critical, reflective and multidimensional understanding of places.

Academic perspectives on place

Before examining place as represented in geography classrooms, it is worth considering how sub-traditions within academic geography approach the study of place. Positivism, associated with the natural sciences, favours gathering knowledge through the 'scientific method' and seeking the 'truth' by adopting the position of an objective observer who explores the material world through a process of reductionism (identifying individual components and exploring their inter-relationships). The value of this approach is undeniable: it led to the explosion in understanding about the natural world that began with the Ages of Discovery and Enlightenment in the fifteenth and sixteenth centuries; and a vast increase in cartographic or locational knowledge. However, from this perspective, place is a clearly bounded and defined part of space that acts as a neutral or passive backdrop for events in the material world. Places can be adequately described both in terms of their spatial extent and particular characteristics and attributes. It presents a single, 'objective', 'true' reading of the place, with scant regard to alternative readings. From this viewpoint, space itself is no more than a boundless, inert field – what is often referred to as Euclidean space – in two or three dimensions. This is useful in as much as it provides Cartesian co-ordinates for location (up/down; left/right; front/back; west/east etc.). However, this positivist approach provides a purely geometric perspective on space and place, devoid of human dimensions, and is therefore very limited.

During the 1970s there was a growing dissatisfaction with positivism: a feeling that it took no account of the inner world of imagination and subjectivity at the individual level, or culture at a societal level. Crucially, it also left out agency – the active potential of people and places to shape reality. It is now widely accepted that people's everyday actions have agency in shaping places, as well as the relations between places. Places themselves can even be considered to have agency: far from being passive backdrops, places have an active role in shaping both the individual's imagination and society's culture. This change in outlook led to the introduction of alternative approaches to the study of geography and places. Sub-disciplines emerged, drawing on the humanities and the social sciences: humanistic geography (underpinned by interpretivism) and social, or cultural, geography – an increasingly 'critical' geography. These post-positivistic perspectives make a distinction between space and place: space being simply parts of the planet that have become associated with events and activities, while place is space that has ascribed meaning. A simple formula, based on the work of the humanistic geographer Tuan (1977), might be: space + meaning = place.

These alternative approaches also acknowledge that there is not necessarily one true reading of place but rather a diversity of idiosyncratic individual and group-based understandings, and corresponding voices and representations; some powerful, some marginalised. This gives rise to an understanding of place that acknowledges and seeks to include a diversity of people and voices, each with their own opinions and perspectives on places, and with the power or agency to shape those places – either deliberately, or through the practices they engage in, in their everyday lives.

More recent developments in geography (Massey, 1997) have presented a 'relational' understanding of place. Places are no longer seen as spaces with inherent characteristics, bounded and discrete, but as the outcome of processes and forces operating over, across and between them; forming an interdependent web of relations. Such a perspective is more likely to see places as 'nodes' in a series of complex networks operating across various types of spaces (economic, political, environmental, etc.).

Using academic perspectives to illuminate school geography

This brief review of developments in academic geography presents us with at least three very different readings of space and place – natural science/positivist, humanistic/interpretivist, and social science. While recognising the limitations of these perspectives, we believe that each one has a valuable contribution to make to the understanding of place. We propose a view of place that acknowledges and applies all of these perspectives; a view that helps young people develop a more rounded or holistic understanding of the world around them.

To help achieve this we propose a simple visual aid – the three lamps model. Imagine these academic sub-traditions as three different coloured lamps – blue, green and red (see Figure 1). When a single lamp is lit, only that colour, or perspective, shines on the place under scrutiny. For example, if blue represents a natural science/positivist perspective, then only spatial and objective aspects of place such as location (latitude and longitude), distance and scale, and identifiable 'features' (such as settlements, mountains etc.) – will be illuminated for study. A positivist lamp is crucial for revealing and developing locational knowledge. By contrast the green lamp, representing a humanistic perspective, picks out individual, personal, subjective responses to place, such as emotional responses (e.g. fear, attraction, attachment, etc.). The red lamp, representing social sciences, illuminates aspects of human-environment interactions at the collective level, and socio-political and/or socio-economic processes at a variety of scales (from neighbourhood to international). Both green and red lamps are likely to reveal fewer objective facts and more subjective representations.

Each of the lamps is essential for illuminating specific aspects, and each has disadvantages and weaknesses. They each leave blind spots: if only that particular light is applied, some aspects of the place remain unilluminated. Consequently it is preferable to explore places by using each lamp in turn, so that each illuminates what the others have missed, leaving no aspect of place unexplored. However, each lamp requires a different approach when reading what the light has revealed. For example, it is not appropriate to apply scientific methods to reading the green or red lights, which require a subtler form of interpretation such as textual analysis or creative writing.

If two or more of the lamps are switched on, the combined light reveals aspects of a place not previously illuminated by the pure wavelength of individual lamps. Switching on the blue and red lights together provides a positivistic approach to sociological phenomena, illuminating 'objective' facts such as demographics, population flows and movements, and socio-economic characteristics. Cultural geographers might combine the green and red lights, integrating humanistic and social approaches, to explore cultural representations. Figure 2 attempts to map out these different approaches. The ideal scenario would be where each light is switched on separately for a detailed and focused analysis, then in

Figure 1: The three lamps model for exploring space and place.

combination to provide synergistic insights, and finally all three together to get closer to 'full spectrum white light' through which a place can be revealed in all its Technicolor, or multidimensional, complexity.

Of course, knowledge about places is also revealed through the daylight of 'lived experience' or ethnogeographies (Martin, 2008). It is important for school geography to explore the ethnogeographies of young people – and understand how students see places. However, the curriculum must move young people beyond these everyday understandings of place towards a more sophisticated understanding, utilising the perspectives and conceptual tools of the discipline. From a constructivist perspective, the enquiry approach to geography (Roberts, 2003) will be most effective, giving learners opportunities to actually explore places for themselves.

Imagine young people exploring a place with an increasingly powerful torch in their hand, applying a variety of coloured filters to guide them in their personal and collaborative explorations. The goal is to bridge the gap between students' everyday engagement with the world and an understanding achieved through the academic discipline of geography.

Shining lights on place in school geography

Teachers play a crucial role in orchestrating the use of lamps to illuminate school geography. The colour of the filtered light will depend upon decisions made by curriculum planners department teams and individual teachers, and are shaped by personal experiences and philosophies. Reflecting upon these decisions and the reasons behind them is a good starting point for practitioners who wish to develop

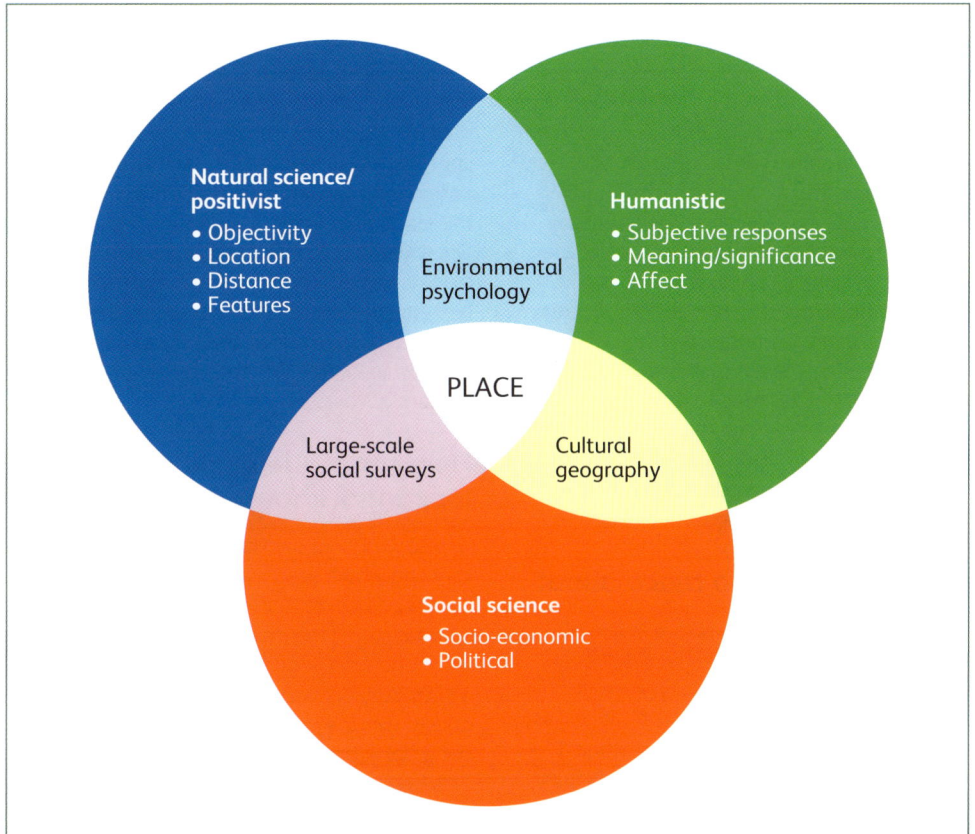

Figure 2: The three lamps model shown in relation to key academic perspectives on place.

a multidimensional approach to teaching about places. Furthermore, there is a powerful argument in favour of devolving some of the decision making to the learners to enable them to undertake increasingly sophisticated place-based enquiry learning.

What follows is a brief discussion of some of the decisions that geography teachers face when considering which places to teach about, and what and how to teach about them. This discussion can be used to support critical reflection (at both the departmental and individual level).

Case study, country study or place study?

Brooks and Morgan (2006) suggest that case studies involve studying a particular aspect of a place, while a country study explores a distant locality. Both approaches are useful tools for teaching geography, but each has potential disadvantages. Case studies can be useful for highlighting a particular theme; however, they can lead to fragmentation, offering students a rather piecemeal view of the world (Taylor, 2013). Additionally, choosing a place for a case study of a particular phenomenon can mean it is presented in a one-dimensional way; for example, flooding may be the main narrative of a Boscastle case study; Haiti is only studied for its earthquake. As Simmons notes, there is 'so much more to know about these places' (Simmons, 2014, p. 110).

Students should be presented with as full a picture as possible, one that includes multiple voices and narratives. Furthermore, Taylor (2013) argues that it is vital to situate any case study 'within its spatial and temporal context' (p. 103), as well as showing how it is linked to other places. She suggests that reflecting upon the way case studies are constructed and taught could help to avoid some of the pitfalls associated with their use.

A country study can provide a wider view of a place and highlight contrasting environments (both human and physical) within a large area. However, Brooks and Morgan (2006) argue that too often such studies take a rather touristic, or superficial and stereotypical, approach. Instead they advocate the use of a place study; this allows students to weave together the many strands of a place in order to see more of the whole picture, and to produce 'a rich and delightful place tapestry' (Brooks and Morgan, 2006, p. 7). While the notion of a holistic place study is appealing, exam specifications (particularly at GCSE) tend to advocate a case study approach to geography, while the National Curriculum (DfE, 2013) advocates a return to studying continents and regions, as well as a focus on several specified countries.

Choosing places to teach about

The concluding comments above highlight some of the external factors that constrain teachers' choices when selecting places for study. The National Curriculum (DfE, 2013) lists areas that should be covered at key stage 3. However, overall, the curriculum remains fairly open to teacher interpretation and choice. The same is true of GCSE and A level specifications, which provide a certain level of instruction on what type of places must be studied and for what reason, but again, there remains a element of choice for teachers on which case study is chosen. This raises questions about the selection of places studied in geography at different key stages, and good practice within geography departments will involve teachers discussing and analysing their responses to these questions (see Figure 3).

Scale: how big are places?

For Tuan (1977) a place can be as small as the corner of a room or as large as Earth itself. Indeed, in school, students may study a small local farm or a continent such as Antarctica. Exam specifications and other curriculum documents often require students to study a range of places and at a range of scales (local, national and global). The issue of scale is crucial because studying places at different scales reveals different geographical forces at work, although some processes, for example those associated with globalisation, will be discernible across all scales. Some critical questions relating to scale are listed in Figure 3. In addition to the size or area of study, there is the question of how we delimit the area being studied. In the contemporary world we are used to politically determined borders around countries. However, there are other ways of delimiting a place. Questioning the origins and representations of place is something that can promote interesting and valuable discussions with young people in the classroom. What do they see as constituting a particular place? Where does this place start and end? Why?

How can students develop locational knowledge?

Developing locational knowledge involves knowing where specific places are (locational facts) and how to locate them on a map or in an atlas (using the index, lines of latitude and longitude, and/or grid references). Until the 1970s/80s, locating places on maps or in atlases was the bread and butter of school geography: the 'capes and bays' approach. This traditional approach has made something of a comeback in recent years, with a renewed emphasis in the 2014 National Curriculum for key stages 1–3 (DfE, 2013) on students being taught about the location of places and features, as well as how to find them on a map. A focus on this set of geographical skills is important: it is crucial that young people are equipped with map skills and locational knowledge. However, there is a danger that such an approach can become rather formulaic, with students learning little more than a gazetteer of places.

To be an effective tool in the study of places, locational knowledge needs to be embedded into a broader curriculum. It is essential to know where a place is and how it fits into the wider world, but as in academic geography, school geography needs to draw upon the work of humanistic, social and cultural geographers to help students develop a deeper understanding of the natural, built and social environment. As well as knowing where places are, students need to understand the forces at work in shaping places, both now and in the past. The schemes of work outlined later in this chapter suggest ways in which locational knowledge can be built into the study of places. Furthermore, with the growth of technology, GIS in particular, this aspect of the curriculum can be exciting and engaging for students.

How can students develop a sense of place?

Since the 1970s subjective, emotional aspects of place have featured more prominently in the classroom, with students being encouraged to develop a sense of place for both local and distant places. They are asked not only to locate places using maps and atlases, but also to consider what it is like to 'be' in a particular place. This can be done using a range of multimedia resources (photographs and moving images) as well as tapping into students' senses through the use of food and sounds from that place.

Another way to help students develop a sense of place is to explore their emotional responses to places. For example, in her work on geographical enquiry Roberts (2003) advocates the use of affective mapping (mapping feelings) to support a broader enquiry into the personal geographies of young people. Building upon this, Jackson (2005) outlines her experience of using affective mapping and memory maps in the classroom to help students reflect on their place in the world around them. Barton (2005) and Dollman (2005) suggest a number of activities aimed at investigating and mapping how students feel about their school and school grounds. Activities such as these can be a starting point from which to develop a deeper sense of place. Affective mapping features in the next section of this chapter, in the exemplar work. All of this work, which was developed in collaboration with a number of schools, was part of the Geographical Association's 'Valuing Places' project (2003–06). Valuing Places puts students at the centre of their learning and highlights the value of their personal, everyday geographies.

Which resources support teaching about places?

With the growth of technology, the number of resources available for teaching students

- Which places are taught about already? Why?
- Which places do students enjoy learning about? Why?
- What resources are available to teach about a particular place? Are these useful/effective/good quality/up to date?
- What new resources are available?
- What places do the students have links with?
- What places to the staff have links with?
- In what way can the teaching of places be made more holistic/multi-faceted?
- What do students already know about these places?
- How can misconceptions about these places be places be addressed?
- Is it best to take a case study approach or a country study? What about a place study?
- What places need to be taught about (due to curriculum requirements)?
- What themes need to be taught about (due to curriculum requirements)?
- What themes would we like to teach about?
- How can themes and case studies be combined? A matrix can be used for planning this (see Lambert and Balderstone, 2000, p. 76).
- How big should the place be?
- How can the students develop a sense of place for this place?
- How can the students develop locational knowledge about this place? What resources are needed for this e.g. atlases, globes, street maps, compasses?
- Are there areas of the world that are over-represented in the curriculum? Are there areas that are under-represented?
- Why is this place significant or special? Does it need to be?

Figure 3: Questions to consider when selecting places in school geography.

about places is almost limitless. Typing the name of a place into an internet search engine will generate an enormous list of video clips, websites, news articles and blogs. These resources can be very helpful when planning lessons and searching for up-to-date examples. However, it is important to treat them with caution. The wealth of resources available at the click of a mouse or touch of a screen has the potential to misrepresent places and create inaccurate geographies, and teachers must ask critical questions about them. Who created them? Why? Are they accurate? Whose voices do they represent? Whose voices are not represented? Furthermore, while digital resources are easily available, teachers should not lose sight of the many tried and tested resources for place study: postcards, leaflets, books, documentaries, photographs, magazines, resources published by charities and NGOs and, not least, students' own experiences.

Despite the ready availability of resources, helping students to develop a deep sense of place for distant places ('other' places) can be a challenge. One way to address this challenge is through collaboration and links with students in other parts of the world. Using the internet to share electronic data (photographs, emails and movie clips), it is possible for students to learn about far-away places from the young people living there. However, the availability of such technology varies from place to place, and it is important to recognise the danger of excluding the voices of those without access to this level of communication technology.

Harrison (2005) discusses the contribution that the Young Lives study (a UK aid project) can make to this learning about the lives of others living far away. The study, related to the Millennium Development Goals, followed the changing lives of 12,000 children in Ethiopia, India, Peru and Vietnam over 15 years from the year 2000. It is a rich source of material about young people living in these countries, with a primary focus on childhood poverty, meaning that the voices of poorer children are represented. However, it is important to avoid presenting a stereotypical view of 'poor children, living in a poor country', which some charity and NGO resources can convey.

Investigating place: year 7

In this part of the chapter we discuss a number of lesson activities that are designed to challenge students' perceptions of places, enabling them to make connections with other, more distant, places and to see how their place fits into an ever more globalised world.

Starting local

Figure 4 provides an outline of a scheme of work focusing on local places. Bearing in mind Taylor's (2005) observation that we should spend more time exploring the concept of place, this sequence of lessons begins by asking students to reflect upon the term 'place' and to consider what it means to them. In this example it was carried out through word association definition tasks: the outcomes revealed interesting perspectives of place among a particular group of young people in an East London school. Students completing the word association task listed a range of places at a range of scales; some intensely local (e.g. home), some much further afield (e.g. Madagascar). For a large number of students the term 'place' meant something far away, something exotic or 'other'. However, the local area was still important, with many listing the city they live in (London) and many simply saying 'home'. When the students were asked to define the word 'place', they saw it as a specific area, somewhere to go, somewhere to be visited. Their definitions of place also evoked a strong sense of being rooted somewhere, of things being fixed in a specific location; a place being 'where someone or something is'.

Having spent time exploring the term 'place', this scheme of work leads into a series of lessons focusing on local geography. A good starting point for a local study is 'where the students are'; establishing which places are important to them, why they are important and how they see these places. Young people and their experiences should be put at the heart of their learning. In the case of local study, students should be given opportunities to explore and share their experiential expertise about their locality (their daily working knowledge of the area). Through careful planning, teachers can build upon this knowledge, adding new layers of information to the existing picture.

Lesson title	Learning activities	Rationale for learning activity/Intended outcomes
What is a place?	Word association task – responses to the term 'place'. Students develop definitions of the term 'place'. Photograph analysis – identifying different characteristics of places (size, personal, official, secret, well known). Extended writing task – journey to school.	To encourage students to analyse the term 'place'. To gain an insight into the way young people see the world around them.
Mapping places	Students compile a personal list of significant/important local places. Students create local memory maps. Significant/important places (from the students' lists) added to the maps. Maps and lists shared and discussed in small groups. New layers of information added to the maps (e.g. 'my friend's places'). Differences and similarities between maps discussed and analysed. **Homework:** students complete survey on positive and negative aspects of their local area.	To understand the characteristics and value of sketch maps. To explore the personal geographies of young people.
Asking questions about places	Geographical questions about places introduced (where, what, why, who, when and how). Students study memory maps of distant place (e.g. Adelaide). Adelaide located in an atlas. Differences and similarities between the two sets of maps are discussed.	To develop atlas skills. To develop a sense of place for a distant place.
Using OS maps	'Real'/official maps introduced (e.g. atlases). Students spend several lessons developing map skills and locational knowledge (including directions, map symbols, scale and grid references). **Homework:** Take a photograph within the local area.	To develop geographical skills, e.g. OS map skills.
Marketing places	*Homework photographs needed* Students study marketing campaigns for a place, e.g. Glasgow. Students use local newspapers and their own photographs to list positive aspects of the locality. Students develop marketing slogans for the locality. Press releases written explaining why the locality is a good place to live and/or work.	To know that places can be marketed. To understand why and how this happens.
Investigating crime	*Homework survey results needed* Students analyse findings of homework survey. Issues of concern identified. Students follow a sequence of lessons about their main issue of concern, e.g. local crime. Crime statistics and crime maps analysed. The geography of crime is explored. Local crime reports written (including data, explanations and prevention ideas).	To explore perceptions of crime. Students help shape the curriculum.

Future development
- Students make simple GIS maps using Google Maps or Umapper.
- Students contact schools in 'other' places via email or video conferencing.
- Local fieldwork introduced.
- Students make video clips marketing their local area.
- Links developed with maths department (for crime graphs/statistics).
- Visit from community or school-based police officer.

Figure 4: Scheme of work on the local area.

Roberts (2003) believes that the first step in this process involves recognising that students' personal geographies are valuable and 'worthy of investigation' (p. 164). She argues that we all possess our own individual personal geographies, made up of 'mental maps, countless images and memories of places and situations, which are constantly being reformed' (Roberts, 2003, p. 164). One activity that can provide insight into how young people see the world around them is to ask students to write a brief account of their journey to school. This reveals a great deal about how young people see their surroundings, the places they know well and landmarks that are important to them. It also says a lot about the parts that go unnoticed, which they deem unimportant.

This journey to school activity can be complemented by asking the students to compile a list of important/significant local places. When asked to complete this activity, students from the East London school produced a long and varied list of local places (Figure 5).

Their lists suggested that family and friends feature strongly in their geographical imaginations, along with work and leisure spaces such as school and the park. As well as naming specific places in the local area they emphasised shopping (various supermarkets, Poundstretcher, the Exchange and Westfield shopping centres) and eating out. These lists of important local places form an essential starting point for many other activities, including memory mapping.

Memory maps can tell us a great deal about how young people view their locality and give us an insight into their geographical knowledge. The maps produced by the East London students (Figure 6) show that their friends' houses are important, along with their school and a small number of other local features. Their maps depict a busy urban area with a strong focus on landscapes of consumption. As a comparison, memory maps produced by students in a school in Adelaide, Australia, also emphasise friends' homes and shopping, but there is a greater focus on outdoor features, e.g. the coast, walking trails and parks. Students should be encouraged to discuss their maps with each other and share their knowledge. Collaborating with students from a contrasting location, whether within the same city, town, area or further afield, and studying each other's maps, is also a valuable learning experience.

The students' local place lists in Figure 5 also provide an opportunity to develop locational knowledge using OS maps. Students can be asked to locate their places on a map. Activities can make use of grid references, directions and scale but with a focus on the students' unique local geographical knowledge. These essential geographical skills are embedded in both schemes of work featured in this chapter (see Figures 4 and 7).

Shining geographical lamps on local places

Having explored students' lived experiences of place and developed greater locational knowledge of their area, the scheme of work outlined above focuses on issues of concern in the local area. Students remain at the centre of their learning: they are asked to identify an issue of concern to be studied. However, in the lessons that follow, the teacher takes the lead, becoming the 'expert' and 'turning on' different geographical lamps to illuminate the issue being studied.

In the London school featured here, year 7 students identified crime as the main issue of concern. In a series of lessons on the geography of crime, students mapped and analysed crime statistics, shining a positivist light on the local area. The use of crime statistics was intended to challenge the students' conceptions of danger in their locality; however, with numbers running in the hundreds or even thousands (depending on the time frame for the data), students can find it hard to contextualise this data.

In an effort to further illuminate this 'dark' aspect of the school locality, the green humanistic lamp was switched on. The students used their memory maps, newspaper clippings and images of the local area to prompt their feelings of fear and safety in their local area. This attempt to unpack their concerns about crime was supported by switching on the red lamp, to shed light on the socio-economic forces at work in the local area. The students analysed how differing land uses and the

Chapter 10: Place and locational knowledge

Figure 5: Wordle generated by young people's list of local places.

quality of the built environment were connected to levels of crime.

Exploring global links and illuminating distant places

It is essential that geography education helps students to understand not only the area in which they live but also how their place connects to other, more distant places. As the world becomes ever more globalised, these connections are increasingly important. However, moving the study of places from the local to the global, the familiar to the unfamiliar, should not exclude the voices of young people: it is important to continue building upon students' existing knowledge and value their lived experiences of the world.

Figure 7 outlines a scheme of work about Brazil, with a focus on Rio de Janeiro. It suggests a series of lessons that aim to further develop students' locational knowledge and challenge any misconceptions. As well as atlas work (including lines of longitude and latitude), there is also the opportunity to use street maps from travel guides or Google Maps. Basic map skills (direction, grid references and scale) are very often taught in year 7; however, it is important to revisit them throughout key stage 3 to embed the skills and prepare students for the use of OS map extracts at GCSE.

The *favelas* are a longstanding feature of a study of Brazil; however, the scheme of work outlined in Figure 7 aims to revisit and represent them in a new light. Having established the location of Brazil and its major features, the work focuses on urban issues, in particular the *favelas*. *Favelas* are often portrayed as places of hardship, lawlessness and poverty; with the added potential for floods and landslides to compound the inhabitants' misery. However, this perspective is very narrow and fails to convey the diversity of such environments. Massey (1991, quoted in Taylor, 2004, p. 15) argues that 'places have multiple identities' and are home to 'multiple communities and individuals, all with different senses of place'. Indeed *favelas* can house vibrant, energetic communities, with pockets of wealth and industry. It is essential to present these different perspectives and allow students to explore each one. The importance of this is echoed by Biddulph (2011, p. 45) who warns against the dangers of presenting a 'single story' to young people and reinforcing place stereotypes.

The Handbook of Secondary Geography

Figure 6: Memory maps produced by students in (a) London, UK, and (b) Adelaide, Australia.

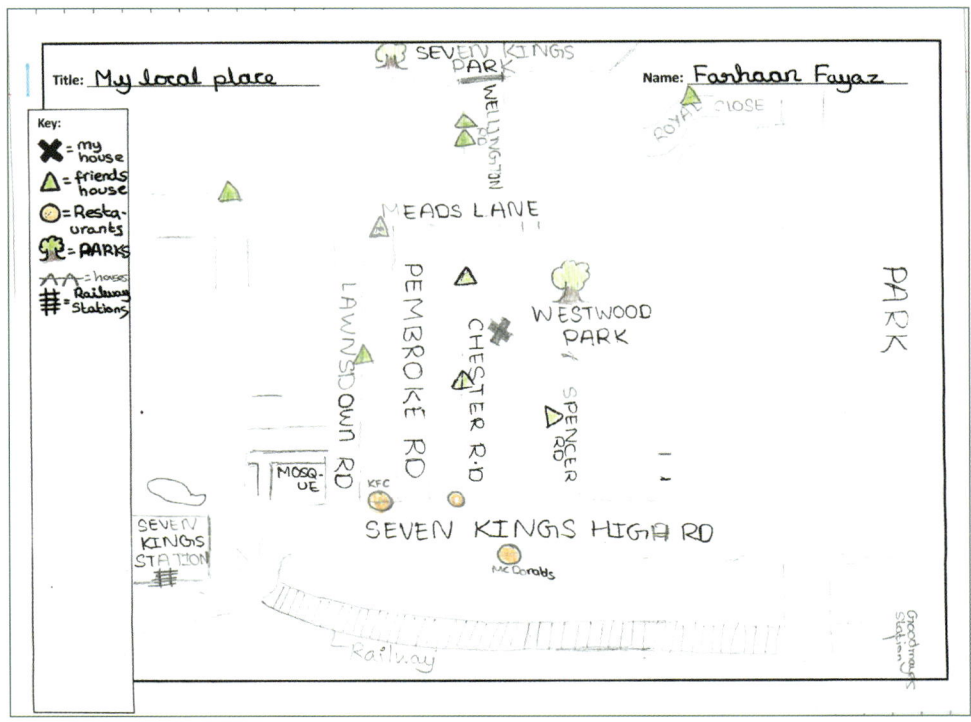

Chapter 10: Place and locational knowledge

Lesson title	Learning activities	Rationale for learning activity/ Intended outcomes
Where is Brazil? **What is Brazil like?**	Introduction to the unit/topic/place using Brazilian food, music, cultural displays, art, etc. Students asked to guess which place they are now studying. Atlas work locating Brazil including latitude and longitude. Key physical features indentified. Scale of Brazil explored (range of landscapes and environments emphasised). Possible drawing of sketch maps of Brazil to show key information (to include the students' existing knowledge of Brazil as well as new knowledge).	To locate Brazil on a global scale and develop a sense of place for the country. Explicit links made to previous learning on asking geographical questions about places (see Figure 5).
Exploring Rio	Rio de Janeiro located. Street maps of Rio used (obtained from Google Maps or from travel guide books). Students start to develop a sense of place for Rio.	Local street maps used to develop locational knowledge and revisit map skills (e.g. directions, scale, symbols and grid references).
The *favelas*	Students introduced to the *favelas*. The historical and geographical context of the *favelas* is explored including rural–urban migration.	Essential background information for next lesson.
Living in a *favela*	Students take part in a *favela* simulation activity: groups of students are given different information packs containing instructions and scenarios for that group, as well as some 'money'. They are also given a map and information about where they live. Different tasks are assigned to each group, e.g. building a house out of very little, designing new artworks for the walls of buildings. Over time the simulation introduces changing fortunes: a landslide destroys some groups' homes, while the life chances of others are improved by the 2016 Olympic Games. Other groups set up community projects and win awards. The groups' feelings and financial status are recorded throughout. At the end students reflect on what they have learnt and evaluate their feelings.	The activity aims to 'immerse' students in *favela* life. The lesson aims to revisit *favela* building (popular in the past) and shine new lights on a popular topic in school geography.
Revisiting Rio	Groups of students feed back on the previous lesson. Film clips and images are used to present a contemporary, and perhaps an alternative, perspective on the *favelas*. Students reflect upon what have they learnt about Rio and how their view of the city has altered.	Builds on positive media coverage of the *favelas* on television and online (after the World Cup 2014 and 2016 Olympic Games). Alternative perspectives on the *favelas* put forward.

Useful links

www.favelapainting.com
www.bbc.co.uk/newsround/27982333
www.bbc.co.uk/news/world-latin-america-27635554

Figure 7: Outline scheme of work entitled 'Learning about distant places: the Brazilian *favelas* revisited'.

Figure 8: Questions about places using the three lamps model.

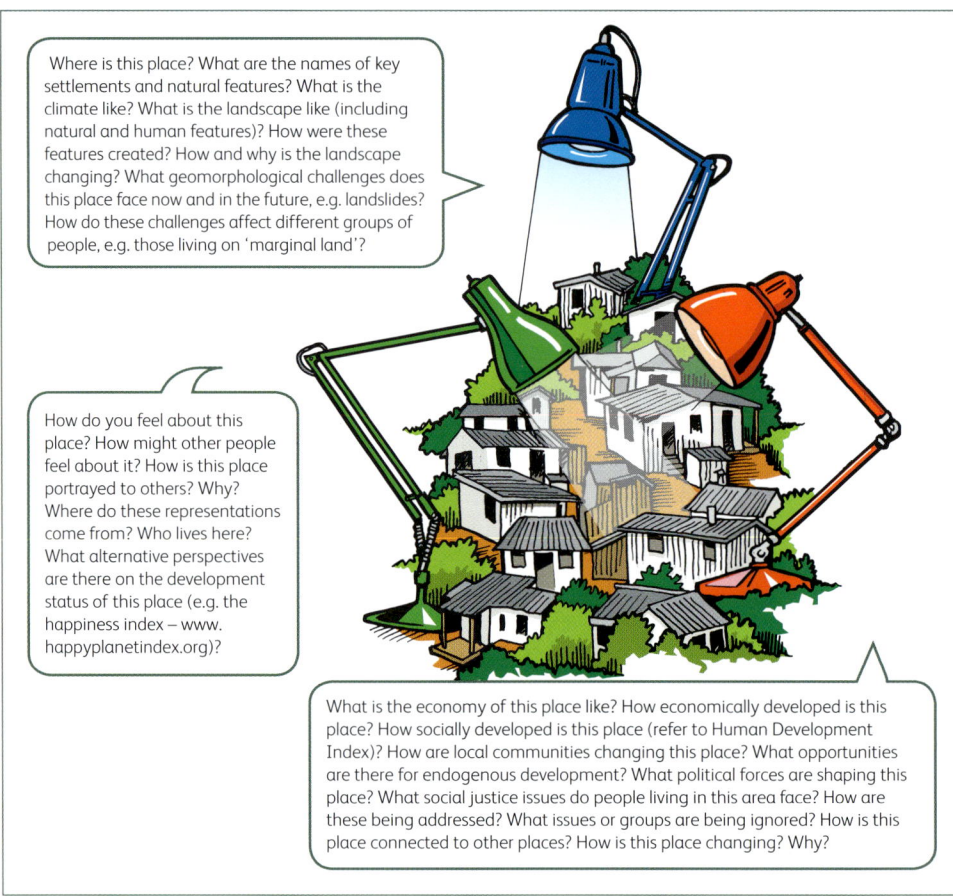

Where is this place? What are the names of key settlements and natural features? What is the climate like? What is the landscape like (including natural and human features)? How were these features created? How and why is the landscape changing? What geomorphological challenges does this place face now and in the future, e.g. landslides? How do these challenges affect different groups of people, e.g. those living on 'marginal land'?

How do you feel about this place? How might other people feel about it? How is this place portrayed to others? Why? Where do these representations come from? Who lives here? What alternative perspectives are there on the development status of this place (e.g. the happiness index – www.happyplanetindex.org)?

What is the economy of this place like? How economically developed is this place? How socially developed is this place (refer to Human Development Index)? How are local communities changing this place? What opportunities are there for endogenous development? What political forces are shaping this place? What social justice issues do people living in this area face? How are these being addressed? What issues or groups are being ignored? How is this place connected to other places? How is this place changing? Why?

The 2014 World Cup and the 2016 Olympic Games have led to increased media coverage of Brazil and Rio de Janeiro. As a consequence many good documentaries and internet-based resources have been developed, some of which challenge the dominant, negative view of the *favelas*. The involvement of sports stars and other well-known figures make these sources of information attractive and engaging to students. However, it is important not to simply replace one single story of negativity and blight with another version of 'colourful poor people'. Instead students should be encouraged to ask critical questions about the place they are studying in an effort to build up as representative a picture as possible (see Figure 8). If we accept that individuals respond to places differently, then the definitive 'truth' about a place is unattainable; what teachers can do is offer students multiple readings of a place to ensure that its diverse voices are heard.

Conclusion

This chapter can be seen as a starting point for considering the study of place in school geography. We hope that teachers find the three lamps model useful, both to reflect upon the way they teach about places and to consider how the work of academics can inform classroom practice. The exemplar schemes of work can be used as a springboard for planning a range of learning activities that explore places and help students develop locational knowledge. Throughout the chapter critical questions have been raised about the teaching of places: questions that should be addressed as part of the planning process. There are no quick answers to these questions, but asking them is vital to ensure places are represented in an ethical, engaging and effective way in the geography classroom and beyond.

Chapter 10: Place and locational knowledge

Teachers can offer students multiple readings of a place to ensure its diverse voices are heard. **Photo** © Bryan Ledgard.

References

Barton, R. (2005) 'Inclusion and emotional mapping', *Teaching Geography*, 30, 1, p. 39.

Biddulph, M. (2011) 'Editorial: The danger of a single story', *Teaching Geography*, 36, 2, p. 45.

Brooks, C. and Morgan, A. (2006) *Theory into Practice: Cases and Places*. Sheffield: Geographical Association.

DfE (2013) *National Curriculum in England: Geography programmes of study*. Available at: www.gov.uk/government/publications/national-curriculum-in-england-geography-programmes-of-study (last accessed 08/11/2016).

Dollman, R. (2005) 'Geography with feelings', *Teaching Geography*, 30, 1, pp. 44–45.

Harrison, D. (2005) 'Young lives, global goals', *Teaching Geography*, 30, 1, pp. 46–49.

Jackson, J. (2005) 'Sharing places', *Teaching Geography*, 30, 1, pp. 28–31.

Lambert, D. and Balderstone, D. (2000) *Learning to Teach Geography in the Secondary School*. (2nd edition). Abingdon: Routledge.

Martin, F. (2008) 'Ethnogeography: towards liberatory geography education', *Children's Geographies*, 6, 4, pp. 437–50.

Massey, D. (1997) 'A global sense of place' in Barnes, T. and Gregory, D. (eds) *Reading Human Geography: The poetics and politics of inquiry*. London: Arnold, pp. 315–23.

Roberts, M. (2003) *Learning Through Enquiry: Making sense of geography in the key stage 3 classroom*. Sheffield: Geographical Association.

Simmons, G. (2014) 'How diverse is Africa? Reflections on a new scheme of work', *Teaching Geography*, 39, 3, pp. 110–11.

Taylor, L. (2004) *Re-presenting Geography*. Cambridge: Chris Kington Publishing.

Taylor, L. (2005) 'Place: an exploration', *Teaching Geography*, 30, 1, pp. 14–17.

Taylor, L. (2013) 'Spotlight On… Case studies', *Geography*, 98, 2, pp. 100–4.

Tuan, Yi-Fu (1977) *Space and Place: The perspective of experience*. Minneapolis, MN: University of Minnesota Press.

Recommended key readings

Hubbard, P. and Kitchin, R. (eds) (2001) *Key Thinkers on Space and Place*. London: SAGE.

A comprehensive overview of the work of key writers on place, including Foucault, Bourdieu, Haggett, Hall and Massey. Their thoughts are presented from a range of perspectives in a multidisciplinary approach, which complements the aims of this chapter. It provides a good springboard for further reading about different perspectives on space and place.

Tuan, Yi-Fu (1977) *Space and Place: The perspective of experience*. Minneapolis, MN: University of Minnesota Press.

While this is rather old now, and might be tricky to get hold of, it is seminal in promoting humanistic geography as an approach to engaging with place. Tuan has been writing for some time on people's subjective relationships to place, and he developed key ideas like 'topophilia' (love of place) and 'geopiety' (positive action towards place).

Chapter 11

Teaching a good geography lesson

Richard Bustin is Head of Geography at the City of London Freemen's School

Introduction

Teaching a good geography lesson has to be the aim of a good geography teacher, but what exactly does a good geography lesson look like? How can teachers make their lessons good? And who decides what is 'good'? This chapter attempts to answer these questions and hopefully will act as a catalyst for reflecting on current and future classroom practice. Experienced geography teachers can recognise a good geography lesson, but even experienced teachers can enhance students' learning by continually refining and updating their professional practice. The chapter begins by considering some features of the geography lesson before discussing different perspectives on the characteristics of 'a good geography lesson'.

What can a geography lesson look like?

In the context of a secondary school curriculum, a lesson is a sequence of activities that aim to promote students' learning. It usually takes place in a classroom, with a specialist subject teacher. Geography lessons can take place both inside and outside the classroom, and for different lengths of time, from a single lesson to a full-day field trip. The location and length of a lesson, therefore, has implications for how teachers plan and prepare it. Some schools have short lessons, sometimes of as little as 30 minutes, while others expect students to remain in a lesson for up to 100 minutes. It is important to be realistic about what students can achieve in the time allocated, and this contextual knowledge needs to inform lesson planning. For longer lessons, activities may need to be varied to maintain students' interest and the pace of the lesson; for shorter lessons there may only be time for one learning activity.

However long or short they are, all lessons benefit from a clear structure. This structure, or sequence of activities, is commonly represented by a lesson plan, although experienced teachers who have internalised their planning can manage with a scheme of work, using detailed lesson plans only when being observed. With the emergence in the late 1990s of the National Strategies and the three-part lesson, many teachers began to structure their geography lessons with a distinct starter, main and plenary – even though Ofsted (2012) advised that 'inspectors must not expect teaching staff to teach in any specific way or follow a prescribed methodology' (p. 33). How a lesson is structured should reflect the nature and purpose of the geography being taught and not necessarily be 'fitted into' three parts (or four of five for that matter). Planning that keeps the geography in mind is exemplified by the enquiry approach; however, this approach has suffered in many schools that adhere rigidly to the three-part lesson (Ferretti, 2013). The dominant model for planning lessons remains linear, although John (2006) argues for a more dialogic approach, with personalised lesson planning, which should 'encourage pedagogical intelligence' (p. 495). Whether you adopt the enquiry approach or an alternative route through a lesson, it is essential to think through the rationale for the activities, their sequence and their progression in each part of the lesson.

Planning a geography lesson

Setting geographical aims

A good geography lesson, or sequence of lessons, has to have clear geographical aims. These aims will need to take account of examination specifications or National Curriculum requirements, and school and departmental learning strategies, but fundamentally they

Ideological tradition	Characteristics	Impact on school geography in England
Utilitarian/informational	• Education primarily aimed at 'getting a job' and 'earning a living'. • A focus on useful information and basic skills.	Emphasis on locational knowledge ('capes and bays'), map skills and useful information about natural resources, travel routes, economic products. Prevalent in the nineteenth century and re-emerged strongly in the 1991 National Curriculum.
Cultural restorationism (as promoted by the New Right in English policy making in the 1980s and 1990s)	• Restoring traditional areas of knowledge and skills (cultural heritage). • Providing students with a set package of knowledge and skills, which will enable them to fulfil well-defined roles in society and the workplace.	Emphasis on aspects of locational, regional and economic geography related to Britain's early twentieth-century Empire and trading links. Strong in school geography in the twentieth century. Re-emerged in 1991 National Curriculum giving a view of a relatively unchanging world.
Liberal humanist (also called classical humanist)	• Worthwhile knowledge as a preparation for life; the passing on of a cultural heritage from one generation to the next. • Emphasis on rigour, big ideas and intellectual challenge.	The development of geography as an academic discipline in the twentieth century resulted in higher status for the school subject. Emphasis on concepts, scientific methods, theories and quantitative techniques. Transferred to schools via the 'new geography' of the 1960s and 1970s and prevalent in GCE O- and A levels.
Progressive educational (also called child-centred)	• Focusing on personal development or bringing maturity to the individual student. • Using academic subjects as a medium for developing skills, attitudes, values and learning styles that will then help them become autonomous individuals.	Emphasis on enquiry, active learning and the development of skills (e.g. communication), attitudes (e.g. respect of others) and values (e.g. care for the environment) through geography. Emphasised in child-centred primary education in the 1960s and 1970s and in Schools Council geography curriculum projects of 1970s. Reappeared in thinking skills in late 1990s.
Reconstructionist (also called radical)	• Education as an agent for changing society, so an emphasis on encouraging students to challenge existing knowledge and approaches. • Less interest in academic disciplines, more focus on issues and socially critical pedagogy.	Geography's involvement with, for example, environmental education, global education, multi-culturalism. Prevalent in the 1970s and 1980s radical geography. Interest by 1997 Labour government in sustainable development education and citizenship seemed to offer opportunities but may have been a utilitarian reaction to societal concerns.
Vocational or industrial trainer (Note: in some ways this cuts across all the other traditions)	• Provides students with knowledge and skills required for work. • Uses workplace and work-related issues as a stimulus for learning skills/abilities. • Uses work-related issues for questioning status quo.	The Geography, Schools and Industry project 1983–91 used work-related contexts in a progressive way for curriculum change and active learning. In the 1990s and 2000s governments promoted careers education, work-related initiatives and key skills, which were utilitarian in character.

derive from a teacher's beliefs or philosophy about the purposes of a geography education. To help teachers clarify their own standpoint it is useful to look at the impact on school geography of 'ideological traditions' as identified by Rawling (2000) (Figure 1).

For example, some teachers may see their role as helping students to develop a traditional academic 'body of knowledge' about places, patterns and processes. Others, espousing a more radical 'reconstructionist' ideology, will encourage their students to think about how their choices have an impact on the world and to actively consider alternative global futures, taking sides on potentially controversial issues. None of these ideologies is necessarily more

Figure 1:
Curriculum ideologies and their impact on school geography 1970–2000.
Source: Rawling, 2000.

Key term	Associated terminology	Purpose	Planning questions
Lesson aim(s)	Purpose of lesson Ideology or philosophy underpinning lesson 'Big picture' of geography curriculum	To provide a rationale for the lesson and to ensure it fits into a teacher's broader ideas about geography education, within the specific topic and scheme of work being studied.	Why are students learning about this? How do I want students to think geographically in this lesson? How does this lesson fit with my beliefs about geography education? How does this lesson fit with the ones before and after?
Learning objectives	Lesson objectives WALT (We are learning to) Differentiated objectives (e.g. all, most, some; must, should, could) Learning intentions Key questions	To narrow down the aim into a workable form. To make clear what students will be learning, e.g. knowledge, understanding, skills, behaviours, values, attitudes. Often objectives are differentiated to take account of varying ability levels, identifying those lesson objectives which: • all students should achieve • most will achieve • some might achieve.	What do I want students to learn: • about • to do • through doing • from each other • and why? Will I be able to evidence the students' geographical learning? How will differentiated objectives affect how and what students are learning in the lesson? Are there other ways to word objectives? How will using key questions be different to stating objectives?
Learning outcomes	Intended learning outcomes Learning outputs WILF (What I am looking for) Differentiated outcomes	To make clear what will show that students have learnt in the lesson and how well. This is measurable, and usually quantifiable. To reflect on the lesson aims and broader ideology, to inform future planning. Did the lesson contribute to the bigger aims?	Will the planned learning outcomes show the objectives were achieved? How will I be able to measure this? How might this inform the next lesson?

Figure 2: Some key terms associated with the lesson planning and reflection process.

correct than any other, although school policies and different national strategies can prefer a particular approach. By acknowledging and discussing these different ideologies geography teachers can arrive at a rationale for the departmental vision, schemes of work and individual lesson aims.

Lesson aims are often translated into achievable, measurable objectives, which set out what students will be learning about. Outcomes are what the teacher wants students to achieve during the lesson, and should be broadly similar to the objectives. Intended objectives should be reflected in actual outcomes, but may not be: students may have made more or less progress than anticipated, and this must be taken into account when planning the aims of the following lesson. Many outcomes are measurable – a tangible assessment of the students' progress in the lesson. This assessment may not take the form of a written test, or formal scrutiny of their work; it can be based on how students answer questions and interact with the lesson content.

At different times, educationalists have used different terminology to describe the processes of planning and structuring lessons, and different teachers may interpret these terms in different ways. Figure 2 attempts to clarify some of the terminology used in relation to lesson aims, objectives and outcomes.

Lesson structure

Having established the overall purpose and geographical focus of the lesson, the teacher must ensure it has a coherent structure, with a clear justification for both individual activities and the sequence of activities.

The beginning

A number of factors influence how a teacher decides to begin a lesson: the success of the previous lesson, the stage in the scheme of work, how the lesson is to be assessed. Sometimes, for instance, to respond to students' curiosity about an event in the news, a teacher will begin by deviating from the plan. However it starts, the beginning of the lesson should get students thinking about geography; it should engage their interest and generate curiosity about the lesson ahead. It is not enough for students to simply enter the classroom and write down the title and objectives. While it is important for students to have a sense of where the lesson is going, and what they are aiming for, using objectives in this way can constrict learning (Roberts, 2011); students may be tempted to think that once they have grasped the objectives – or even simply copied them down – they can sit back and relax. If both teachers and students are restricted to following a number of narrowly defined objectives in a lesson it can also stifle creativity (Davidson, 2006).

How objectives and intended outcomes are expressed and utilised by teachers in lessons can be influenced by an individual teacher's preference or whole school policies, and the latter can require particular approaches to be used. In Figure 3, differentiated objectives that also incorporate the intended outcomes are used. How would you word the objectives and more importantly what is your rationale for using that approach?

The main outcome of this lesson would be the finished annotated diagram, or sequence of diagrams, that can be assessed to see how well students have met the objectives (although this may not necessarily represent what all the students have learnt, or knew already, about waterfall formation).

While it is important for teachers to have a clear sense of a lesson's aim, and the objectives that will assess the success of that lesson,

Aims

For students to understand that waterfalls are dynamic natural landforms created by physical processes.

Objectives

All will be able to draw a labelled cross-section of a waterfall.

Most will be able to draw a short sequence of diagrams to explain the process of waterfall formation using vocabulary such as 'downward erosion', 'underlying geology'.

Some will be able to draw a fully annotated, complex sequence of diagrams to explain the stages in the formation of a waterfall using vocabulary such as 'vertical erosion'. They will understand the links between each stage and see the process as a continuation over time.

Figure 3: Example of differentiated objectives.

these do not always need to be shared quite so obviously with students. Some lessons, particularly based around a 'mystery' activity, may not have an aim shared with the class at all. One way of enabling students to engage with lesson objectives is to express them as a question, which students use as the heading in their exercise books for that lesson's work (e.g. 'How are waterfalls formed?'). This question can be provocative, open-ended and intriguing. A strong enquiry question can drive the lesson, being referred to throughout and answered at the end of the lesson or series of lessons.

A word of warning here: simply rephrasing an objective as a question may not result in a challenging enquiry question or indicate that genuine enquiry is operating in the classroom. The teacher needs to set up activities that reflect stages or aspects of Roberts' (2003) enquiry approach; for instance by creating 'a need to know' at the start of the lesson. Students need to be engaged from the moment they arrive in the classroom, and Figure 4 shows some examples of engaging starter activities.

Beginnings of lessons can be magical moments – students may ask incredibly insightful questions, or make an assertion that needs challenging – and a good geography teacher

Figure 4: Examples of starter activities.

Starter activity	Example	Purpose
Intriguing image displayed to class on arrival in the classroom	Get students to ask simply 'who, what, where, how and why?' Images could be anything! Log in to the GA website for access to photo galleries, particularly the 'A Different View' collection of images (GA, 2009) and 'Photos for enquiry'.	To ask questions that stimulate geographical thinking.
Mind map	Students start with an initial stimulus and branch out into ideas and understanding.	To assess prior knowledge of a new topic, or understanding of previous topics.
Keyword recap	Word searches, crosswords, matching word and definition exercise, odd one out.	To check understanding of vocabulary used in the topic.
Unexpected question	This works particularly well with older students: • Can water ever flow uphill? • Which is better, high birth rate or high death rate? • Why are some places poorer than others?	To stimulate geographical thinking and encourage students to apply understanding to unexpected contexts.

will give time and space for these to be addressed, even if it means a lesson objective has to be shelved until later. Many teachers begin lessons by sharing learning objectives with the class, but while students need to know the point of the lesson this can – depending on the purpose of the lesson – be achieved with an enquiry question.

Main activities

The lesson's main parts or learning episodes, for there may be more than one, is where students actively engage with geographical knowledge and significant learning can take place. The teacher decides whether these episodes are teacher-led, in which the teacher controls the activities, or student-led, to encourage more independent learning. Each approach can bring different benefits and challenges. Teacher-led activities, for instance running a class debate, leading a whole-class review of homework or questioning individuals or pairs, can help students to remain on task. There is also less chance of misunderstanding as the teacher can elicit specific information. Student-led activities, for example peer teaching, individual research projects and presentations to the class, involve students taking control over what they learn and how they learn it. This has greater potential for engaging students: having chosen the activity themselves, they should be interested in it. The downside is that the activity might deviate from the geographical purpose of the lesson, and misunderstandings can go unchallenged.

The main part of the lesson is likely to require most resources. Geographers use a variety of classroom resources, such as maps, atlases and globes, textbooks, newspaper articles, photographs, aerial images, data tables, film and TV clips, blogs and twitter feeds, as well as GIS packages. These need to be selected carefully on the basis of need, and the aims of the lesson. During these episodes teachers need to monitor students' learning to ensure they are engaging with the material and making progress.

The ending

The final part of a good geography lesson can vary in both approach and time spent on what has become commonly called the plenary (DfES, 2004a). Like the *denouement* of a good film, though, the ending of a lesson should be the culmination of the work that precedes it, not a bolted-on activity with only a tenuous link to the lesson, or a 'fun' activity which marginalises the geography, such as watching a humorous video clip or listening to music. A more appropriate approach in common use is to recap and review the lesson content to ensure the students have grasped the concepts and ideas, and to address the learning objectives to see if they have made progress. This part of the lesson offers students the opportunity to clarify anything they are not sure about, and to consolidate their understanding of what has been covered. Younger students enjoy the 'smiley face' or traffic light technique, where they review their level of understanding and record it. If an enquiry question has framed the learning, perhaps the students can answer it, reflecting on how they have learnt and the value of what has been learnt (Roberts, 2003).

On a practical level, there needs to be time towards the end of a lesson to enable students to write down their homework, tidy up, put resources and atlases away and throw paper into the recycling bin. These activities need to be factored in – subject inspection reports frequently identify the lack of time to review the geography of the lesson (Ofsted, 2008, 2011) – so that quality time is available for an effective and meaningful lesson ending.

Homework

Homework should also be seen as a type of lesson, or a lesson extension, and it demands careful consideration in terms of purpose and approach. Homework can take many forms but it should never be just a routine: it should always enhance the students' geographical learning. Where students use the learning from the lesson to work independently on tasks or activities, homework can give teachers a means of assessment to inform future lesson planning. It can also be used to encourage students to research new topics, find news stories on particular themes, engage in creative writing and drawing or bring artefacts to school to represent their personal geographies. Homework can also serve to prepare for the following lesson, rather than consolidate the work of the previous one: in a 'flipped classroom' students research a selected theme at home and bring their findings to the next

Fun activities must be carefully planned so as not to marginalise the geography. **Photo** © Licence free.

lesson to work collaboratively with their new knowledge. The flipped classroom works particularly well with older students, although it demands careful selection by the teacher of both the homework theme and the suggested activities. In the flipped classroom, the teacher's role is to question, challenge and nurture students' understanding, rather than deliver information.

The first part of this chapter has presented some of the choices teachers face when structuring a lesson. But how do teachers, their students and other interested parties decide if the decisions made at a personal and departmental level have resulted in a good geography lesson?

Who decides what a good geography lesson is?

The next part of the chapter considers a fundamental question: 'Who has the right to decide what a good geography lesson should look like?' What makes a geography lesson good has been debated by a number of people, groups and organisations, but they are using different criteria so their views diverge (Roberts, 2011; Ofsted, 2012). The ideas and suggestions presented here draw on relevant literature, inspection findings and the personal experience of teaching and observing geography lessons over a number of years.

Writing from a geography teacher educator's perspective, Margaret Roberts (2011), suggests a good geography lesson has three main components:

1. There needs to be some geography (data, ideas and contexts)
2. There needs to be a connection with learners' minds
3. There needs to be an opportunity for learners to make sense of new geographical knowledge for themselves.

These three components derive from two central ideas: knowledge and pedagogy. Subject knowledge is the first of Roberts' components. Without geography, there is no geography lesson; instead it becomes a generic 'lesson': however well delivered, it cannot enhance students' geographical understanding. Pedagogy is the art of teaching, and here it is centred on the students – how they learn and how they conceptualise ideas. This is Roberts' second point: good teachers need to know their students and understand how their minds work. Her third component is the interaction of the first two: a good geography lesson provides opportunities for students to engage with geographical knowledge so they can make sense of it. A good lesson is centred on the students' learning, not the teacher's performance.

Earlier in the chapter, the lesson was presented as a series of choices about what to teach and how to sequence the different activities. In making these decisions, it is also important for teachers to see lessons as part of a bigger picture, which is often referred to as 'curriculum making' (GA, 2016; see here, page 25). This can be described as the 'in-between work of translating a curriculum plan… into lesson sequences' (Lambert and Morgan, 2010, p. 50) and represented as a Venn diagram with three overlapping influences that a teacher needs to consider: geography the subject; students' experiences of the world; and the teacher's pedagogic choices (GA, no date). This model connects the 'what' and the 'how' of geography teaching, but also takes seriously the students' role in the process. Students do not arrive in the classroom devoid of any knowledge or experience. They come with knowledge and skills gained in previous geography lessons, other subjects and their own experience. Teachers can exploit these personal geographies to take the student beyond what they already know and understand into new areas of knowledge. The combination of the three factors represented in curriculum making creates the ideal space for devising good geography lessons.

Students' learning

For teachers of any subject, understanding how students learn is fundamental. In his work on child development, Vygotsky (1962) argued that as children develop they are capable of understanding increasingly complex ideas, but that at any given age there is a limit to what they can learn on their own. However, given some 'light assistance', children are able to progress much further. He called the gap between what children can achieve on their own, and what they can achieve with help, the 'zone of proximal development' (ZPD). Given assistance within their ZPD they develop mentally, expanding their capabilities and enabling them to tackle the same problems independently in future: 'with assistance, every child can do more than he can by himself… what the child can do in co-operation today he can do alone tomorrow' (Vygotsky, 1962, p. 104). The light assistance Vygotsky referred to does not consist of telling children the correct answers: it is 'providing the first steps in a problem… asking a leading question… explaining… correcting'. This enables children to discover the answer for themselves. In the context of geography teaching, teachers need to be able to help geography students progress

Chapter 11: Teaching a good geography lesson

Kinaesthetic learners like to be active and physically engage with the world. **Photo** © Bryan Ledgard.

through their ZPD – not by giving them the right answer, if there even is such a thing, but by questioning, suggesting and helping them to come up with their own solutions. Of course, students can receive this assistance from abler peers, as well as from the teacher.

Allied to Vygotsky's work is the notion of 'scaffolding' knowledge (Wood *et al.*, 1976). Scaffolding provides a framework to help students build on their knowledge and engage with new ideas. The scaffolding could be as simple as providing a worksheet or a writing frame, or it could involve dialogue between student and teacher. Good questioning by the teacher can enable students to explain their ideas, particularly if the questions are something like 'Why?', 'What does that lead to…?', and 'What might happen if…?'. A good geography lesson will involve students learning, enjoying their learning and making progress within their ZPD. In a poor geography lesson students learn nothing new, or they tackle work that lacks challenge, or which they are fully capable of on their own. Of course, teachers need to understand clearly what the students are capable of achieving on their own, which is why time must be spent at the start of a topic to find out how much the students already know about it. A brainstorming starter activity can help in this regard.

Learning activities

Different people learn in different ways, and another way in which a geography lesson is good – one emphasised by the DfES (2004b) in the National Strategies materials – is when the teacher takes account of students' different learning styles to ensure they all have the opportunity to show what they know and understand about a subject. Two points need discussing here. Firstly, it is very tempting to teach the class in ways you would like to learn yourself, but not everyone will learn in the way you do! One common approach is the VAK model, which identifies learners as visual, auditory or kinaesthetic. Put simply, a visual learner is one who finds visual stimulus most engaging and benefits from the use of images, maps, and diagrams. An auditory learner learns best through talk and thinking through ideas verbally so will prefer questioning and discussion to written or graphic work. A kinaesthetic learner likes to be active and physically engage with the world, and benefits when it comes to fieldwork as they can experience the world directly and make sense of it. Kinaesthetic learners can be catered for in a classroom by card sorting activities, where students have to move pieces of information on paper into piles, or categories, or continuum lines. They will also engage with role play activities.

Figure 5: Thinking Skills activities.

Thinking skills activity	Description	Example
Card sort classification activity	Information is provided on a series of cards and students need to group them into categories, either their own or predetermined.	Categorising the impacts of overfishing as social, economic, political and environmental.
Role play	Students take on stakeholder roles and debate an issue in character.	Planning issues enable students to take key player roles, such as local resident, councillor, etc.
Odd one out	Students are given sets of four key words and have to work out which is the odd one out and why.	In a topic on settlement, four terms could be: city, conurbation, hamlet and urbanisation. Urbanisation would be the odd one out as it is a process; the others are types of settlement.
Taboo, Pictionary	Students have to get the rest of their team to say a key word by using their descriptions (Taboo) or drawings (Pictionary).	In Taboo, students would have to verbally describe the term river without using the words: water, rain, flow or channel.
Living graph	Students are given statements and have to decide which point on the graph the statement refers to.	In a climate graph for a place, a statement could be 'the rivers are in full flow and the temperatures are the lowest of the year'.
Mysteries	Students are presented with a problem and a range of clues to possible solutions. They read the information, maps, graphs and diagrams to solve the problem.	The enquiry question 'Why did Omar move house?' could have information on push and pull factors that students have to read about and unravel.
Most likely to…	This gets students to think about what conditions are likely in a given situation.	In a topic on urban geography, students could be asked which area of a city is most likely to contain the most litter, most pet cats, most foxes, and why.
Predicting with video	A video is played then stopped at a certain point, with students guessing what might take place next, before showing what really happened.	Education videos can work, but better still are films and TV shows based on a geographical idea.

However, the effectiveness of the VAK approach is contested (see Coffield et al., 2004) and more research is needed. Teachers and students might rely too heavily on these styles, or justify a lesson's aims on the basis of them. Although individuals may have a preference for a particular style, students usually learn through a combination of styles, so it is important not to categorise students based on learning styles audits or questionnaires but to enter into a dialogue with them about preferred ways of working, then differentiate to help them increase their confidence and competence in accessing learning through a wider range of learning activities.

A good geography lesson should contain a variety of learning activities. In building up a bank of useful activities, teachers look to different sources including online sharing sites, textbooks, professional journals such as *Teaching Geography*, academic journals such as *Geography*, and specialist teacher publications such as the GA's *Geography Teachers' Toolkit* and *Top Spec Geography* series. Whatever the source, it is important to scrutinise the activity and resources for their geographical accuracy and suitability to the lesson being planned. To provide a well-known example, in the late 1990s geography teachers starting using the 'thinking skills' activities suggested in two successful publications *Thinking Through Geography* (Leat, 1998) and *More Thinking Through Geography* (Nichols, 2001) to help students engage more critically with geography themes and ideas (see Figure 5).

These 'thinking skills' activities do come with a warning. Much like other classroom skills, it is important to ensure they are not the aims of a lesson in themselves. Their purpose is to enable geographical knowledge to be approached through a particular framework for thinking geographically. Just because a student can arrange pieces of paper into piles does not necessarily mean they have understood or engaged fully with the geography, so it is important that the activities are always discussed and followed up to ensure the centrality of the learning. Equally, teachers must critically engage with the rationale behind the activities that were an essential part of the two thinking skills texts, rather than focusing on the resources for the activities; for example, debriefing is crucial (see Nichols, 2006).

Geographical knowledge and skills in the classroom

The key component of curriculum making is the 'subject of geography': the geographical input. Subject specialist teachers are expert geographers and use their 'curriculum-making' skills to present knowledge creatively and constructively in the classroom.

Students like geographical facts: they want to know the tallest mountain or longest river; and teachers can capitalise on this interest to create engaging 'hook' activities at the start of a lesson. However, this type of knowledge is what Bonnett (2008) calls 'popular geography': anyone could find it out with the click of a mouse, and on its own it will not enable students to 'think geographically' (Jackson, 2006). In this thought process students take a knowledge of places, sometimes called geography's 'vocabulary' and link it with geographical ideas, sometimes called geography's 'grammar', to make meaning (Lambert, 2011). Thinking geographically engenders a holistic understanding of the world, and an appreciation of how places evolve and are linked.

This way of thinking is complex, and enables geographical knowledge to become 'powerful' (Young, 2008). 'Powerful knowledge' may use everyday knowledge as a starting point, but it takes a learner beyond the everyday. Powerful geographical knowledge is shaped within the academic field of geography: it is rigorous knowledge, and represents the 'best knowledge' we have now. It is reliable knowledge, but it is also dynamic and open to debate and re-presentation, which can lead to a re-shaping of meaning. A useful way to conceptualise powerful knowledge, and enable geographical thinking in the classroom, is through the idea of geography's 'key concepts'. What makes concepts 'key' (Brooks, 2013) and which are geography's key concepts, is contested (Taylor, 2009), but they can help teachers clarify the conceptual framework supporting the geographical knowledge component of lessons (see Figure 6). The concept-led National Curriculum (QCA, 2007) emphasised seven key concepts, which teachers used at the time to plan their curriculum. Although not explicit in the 2013 National Curriculum (DfE, 2013), 'space' and 'place' recur in the aims, purpose and subject content of the document. Despite different groupings and varying emphases, geography's key concepts can be helpful for teachers thinking about geographical knowledge in the classroom.

The lesson resources prepared by the teacher, which will form the basis of the geography students work with, can come from a variety of sources. They can include data, statistics, newspaper articles, websites, film clips or fact sheets. The more relevant and engaging the material, and the more up to date it is, the better; just as important is to get students to reflect on the accuracy of each source. Where is it from? Why did that source make it available? How reliable is it? Questioning and reflecting on the accuracy and reliability of data they collected themselves during fieldwork is also part of this data evaluation process. It always creates lively classroom debate when two reputable sources of geographical data contradict each other! Case studies from a variety of real places around the world, including places local to the students, should always be used to test theories, models and hypotheses introduced as part of geographical theory.

Leat (1998)	Geography Advisors' and Inspectors' Network (2002)	Rowley and Lewis (2003)	Holloway et al. (2003)	Jackson (2006)	2008 key stage 3 curriculum in England (QCA, 2007)
Cause and effect	Bias	Describing and classifying	Landscape and environment	Proximity and distance	Cultural understanding and diversity
Classification	Causation	Diversity and wilderness	Physical systems	Relational thinking	Environmental interaction and sustainable development
Decision making	Change		Place	Scale and connection	
Development	Conflict	Patterns and boundaries	Scale	Space and place	
Inequality	Development	Places	Social formations		Interdependence
Location	Distribution	Maps and communication	Space		Physical and human processes
Planning	Environment	Sacredness and beauty	Time		
Systems	Futures				Place
	Inequality				Scale
	Interdependence				Space
	Landscape				
	Location				
	Perception				
	Region				
	Scale				
	Uncertainty				

Figure 6: Geography's key concepts as a contested idea. **Source:** Taylor, 2009.

Although geography is split into physical and human domains, good geography teachers will take opportunities to identify the links between these different aspects of geographical knowledge and help students to see the interconnected nature of geography and the real world. This ability to think synoptically is a key feature of most post-16 courses, so applying knowledge across the 'divide' of physical and human geography should be encouraged in earlier key stages.

Helping students to acquire geographical skills is of course central to good geography lessons, but geography teachers also have a responsibility to help students develop their literacy, numeracy, presentation and research skills, and the 'soft' skills of personal confidence and wellbeing. Lesson activities that enhance these skills can contribute to a good geography lesson; however, there is a danger that these skills can be taught without any geography. If a class spends a whole lesson drawing a climate graph, for example, this can develop their numeracy skills, but a climate graph means nothing, geographically, on its own: teachers must give lesson time to helping students make sense of it. What does the graph tell us about that place? Where has the data been collected? It would be helpful to locate and map the place, and ask questions about it, such as 'What might it be like here because of the climate?' Students can think about how the weather in different seasons might impact on people's lives, including working, growing food and obtaining water. This is where geographical knowledge and skills come in: the graph becomes an excellent source of data that students can use to understand the world. As an end in itself, though, drawing a graph is not good geography.

The same can be said of many of the other skills taught in geography lessons. Map skills can give students access to a huge amount of information about the world, and interpreting maps correctly requires a specific skill set, yet using grid references and measuring distance are sometimes taught as skills to master and use adeptly, rather than tools with which to explore the world. GCSE and GCE examinations often require students to demonstrate skills in isolation, but although good geography lessons will develop the key skill of graphicacy – analysing and interpreting spatial information – it will do so with a clear sense of purpose: the skill is being taught in order to help students better understand the world.

Sometimes, a good geography lesson will introduce students to challenging ideas about people and places, and give students a chance to debate potentially controversial issues such as migration, conflict and ethnic segregation. Teachers need to be able to handle these topics sensitively, challenging prejudice and racism but also facilitating discussion to help students form views and opinions of their own. It is very easy for teachers to fall into 'morally careless' teaching, imparting their own views to students, and this is poor geography teaching, yet it is almost impossible for a teacher to remain completely neutral in the classroom: the words and phrases we use unwittingly convey ideas and opinions. Textbooks are not value-neutral either: for instance, using the negative word 'destruction' instead of the more neutral 'deforestation' is designed to make students feel in a particular way about the Amazon rainforest. Students should be encouraged to question and challenge opinions and ideas and a good geography lesson will ensure many sides of a debate are aired.

Another view of good geography lessons

Roberts' (2011) criteria for a good geography lesson relate to every aspect of what happens in a geography lesson – planning, preparation, execution, reflection, review: all aspects familiar to geography teachers. However, the language of 'good' is most often associated with inspection – the external inspection frameworks that arguably perpetuate a checklist culture against individual standards. Formal inspections of maintained schools and colleges are carried out by the Office for Standards in Education (Ofsted) in England, HM Inspectorate of Education in Scotland, the Education and Training Inspectorate in Northern Ireland and Estyn in Wales.

The independent sector is inspected by the Independent Schools Inspectorate (ISI). During inspections lessons are observed and a judgement made as to whether the quality of teaching is 'unsatisfactory', 'satisfactory', 'good' or 'outstanding' (although in the endless drive to raise standards, Ofsted's 'satisfactory' turned into 'requires improvement' (Ofsted, 2012)). Since September 2014, Ofsted no longer grades individual lessons and instead gives general feedback following lesson observations. Looking at lessons across the school inspectors assess the level of challenge, the extent of student engagement with tasks and how students' progress is monitored. These generic aspects are not necessarily features of a good geography lesson, but many schools concentrate on them when being observed by a visiting inspector: external assessors are often not geography specialists and so will be in no position to make judgements about the quality of the geography being taught (see Roberts, 2010). Inspections are never popular with teachers, and in many ways the criteria they use to judge teachers and their lessons are inappropriate. This is problematic. A lesson could be deemed 'good' by a non-specialist inspector that contains very little geography: or worse, contains geography that is uncritical, lacks rigour or is even incorrect.

It is easy to position external inspectors and teachers in different camps; however, Roberts (2010) has alerted teachers to the fact that some school-based mentors observing student teachers also over-emphasise the generic qualities of teaching. Timings, behaviour for learning and building positive relationships often feature at the expense of the quality of the geography being taught. Roberts commented at that time that 'what particularly struck me from written feedback on lessons was the large amount of attention given to generic matters and the very limited feedback on the actual geography' (p. 112). This can also happen in peer lesson observations, where teachers from different subject areas observe each other teaching. While peer observations can provide valuable opportunities to reflect on and improve teaching, what is being observed may be general aspects of good teaching and student engagement, rather than the geographical content. Peer observations can be very useful;

Figure 7: Characteristics of a good geography lesson.

Characteristic	Rationale
Geography the Subject	
Rigorous geographical knowledge and skills	If there is no geography, it is not a geography lesson. Activities in the lesson should provide challenge and promote geographical thinking.
A sense of the geography 'big picture'	Teachers need to have a clear idea of why the geography is being taught and the aims of the lesson.
Engaging geographical material	Students need to be actively involved in the work; they need to be interested and think creatively. This results from engagement with high-quality, well-devised lesson material and resources.
Teaching resources	Well-prepared resources could include images, maps, fieldwork equipment, data tables, graphs, newspaper articles, film clips.
Student Experiences	
Interaction	Students need to share ideas and questions, not just between themselves but with the teacher.
Routine, discipline and boundaries	Teachers need to set clear expectations of behaviour, routines and boundaries. Without this, behaviour may be poor, making learning difficult.
Consolidation time	Students need opportunities to reflect on what they have learnt, and learn to apply their knowledge to new contexts.
Teacher Choices	
Subject specialist teacher	If students are going to learn through a geographical lens, it is vital that they have a teacher who understands the subject's fundamental principles and concepts.
Experience and reflection	A good geography lesson results from teaching experience and from observing other lessons, in both geography and other subjects.
Pace	A lesson should not try to get through too much in one go. It should provide time for critical reflection on the material, but at the same time ensure progression and not allow students to get bored, or bad behaviour can start.
Organisation	A lesson needs to be well planned, with resources created in advance and a clear set of aims and sense of direction.
Questioning	Questioning by the teacher helps students think and this improves their understanding. Open-ended questions with a wide variety of possible responses can enhance student understanding.

observing how students you teach respond to and interact with teachers in other subjects can help inform your own teaching in terms of generic competencies. However, they will not necessarily inform your geography teaching.

The best people to judge the success of a geography lesson are geography subject specialists, particularly those who engage in sustained professional dialogue and development. Most school geography departments will have a formal observation process, and the best departments are those in which mutual support and observation are a regular part of life in school. Not only can other geography teachers, or heads of department, offer support about general aspects of a good lesson, such as behaviour management, they can also offer an informed critique of the quality of the geography.

Figure 7 shows how teachers in one geography department described the characteristics of a good geography lesson. It is not a definitive checklist, but such discussions are a valuable exercise – they could form part of departmental meetings or Inset programmes.

Figure 8:
Students' views about what makes a good geography lesson.

The process encourages teachers to propose and critique the elements of a lesson they consider important, rather than adapting their lesson to meet particular agendas. The ideas generated by the teachers' discussion have been categorised according to the three aspects of curriculum making: geography the subject; the students' experiences; and the teacher's choices. Teachers could critique this table: should anything be added, or left out? Could the ideas be ranked in terms of importance?

With over 20 years of government involvement in curriculum content, and inspection frameworks constraining teachers to teach in certain ways, it is easy to forget that there is another group who observe teachers' lessons all the time. In many ways, students are the most critical observers of all! Ask students what they think of their geography lessons, what they enjoy, what helps or hinders them in lessons: ask them for feedback after each topic. Given genuine opportunities, students can be very honest about the lessons they are taught and will often identify aspects of teaching that teachers may not have considered. Anonymous comments can produce some genuinely interesting feedback. Wider scale research with young people has included how students experience geography lessons (Hopwood, 2014), and how their perceptions of geography influence subject choice post-14 (Adey and Biddulph, 2001; Weeden, 2007) and post-16 (Ferretti, 2007). Small or large scale, such research requires good professional judgement.

When I asked my own students what makes a good geography lesson, many wrote things like 'I like up-to-date case studies', and 'I enjoy learning about real places'. This type of feedback can be helpful in assessing what engages and motivates young people. Figure 8 shows a 'word cloud' created from students' ideas of what makes a good geography lesson (the larger a word appears, the more popular the idea). Interestingly, students thought interactive activities and group discussions were the key elements of a good geography lesson. The student voice can help teachers devise good geography lessons.

Conclusion

External accreditation and good examination results are important, but neither are necessarily benchmarks of a good geography teacher. Teachers themselves, though they are often the most critical, are the most important judges of quality geography teaching. Teaching good geography lessons, day after day, takes effort. Schools are incredibly busy places and teachers have many demands on their time: pastoral commitments, managing behaviour, running activities and clubs and marking students' work. Despite these pressures, making quality time for informed and considered reflection and thorough lesson preparation should be at the centre of what teachers do. Good geography teachers prioritise lesson preparation, and find opportunities for collaborative critical reflection on the geography that is being taught, and how. This chapter cannot fully address every aspect of a teacher's professional activities, but has focussed on some of the most significant aspects of teaching a good geography lesson. The next step is to find the space and time to reflect on some of the ideas presented here.

Good geography teachers prioritise lesson preparation.
Photo © Barking Photographic.

References

Adey, K. and Biddulph, M. (2001) 'The influence of pupil perception on subject choice at 14+ in geography and history', *Educational Studies*, 27, 4, pp. 439–50.

Bonnett, A. (2008) *What is Geography?* London: Sage.

Brooks, C. (2013) 'How do we understand conceptual development in school geography?' in Lambert, D. and Jones, M. (eds) *Debates in Geography Education*. Abingdon: Routledge, pp. 75–88.

Coffield, F., Moseley, D., Hall, E. and Ecclestone, K. (2004) *Learning Styles and Pedagogy in Post-16 Learning: A systematic and critical review*. London: Learning and Skills Network.

Davidson, G. (2006) 'Start at the beginning', *Teaching Geography*, 31, 3, pp. 105–8.

DfE (2013) *National Curriculum in England*. Available at: www.gov.uk/government/collections/national-curriculum (last accessed 15/09/2015).

DfES (2004a) *Pedagogy and Practice: Teaching and learning in secondary schools. Unit 5: Starters and plenaries*. London: DfES.

DfES (2004b) *Pedagogy and Practice: Teaching and learning in secondary schools. Unit 19: Learning styles*. London: DfES.

Ferretti, J. (2007) 'What influences students to choose geography at A level?', *Geography*, 92, 2, pp. 137–47.

Ferretti, J. (2013) 'Whatever happened to the enquiry approach in geography?' in Lambert, D. and Jones, M. (eds) *Debates in Geography Education*. Abingdon: Routledge, pp. 103–15.

GA (2009) *A Different View: A manifesto from the Geographical Association*. Available at: www.geography.org.uk/resources/adifferentview (last accessed 08/11/2016).

GA (2010) *Making geography happen*. Available at: www.geography.org.uk/projects/makinggeographyhappen (last accessed 08/11/2016).

GA (2016) *Curriculum making*. Available at: www.geography.org.uk/cpdevents/curriculum/curriculummaking (last accessed 08/11/2016).

Holloway, S., Rice, S. and Valentine, G. (eds) (2003) *Key Concepts in Geography*. London: Sage.

Hopwood, N. (2014) *Geography in Secondary Schools: Researching pupils' classroom experiences*. London: Bloomsbury.

Jackson, P. (2006) 'Thinking geographically', *Geography*, 91, 3, pp. 199–204.

John, P. (2006) 'Lesson planning and the student teacher: re-thinking the dominant model', *Journal of Curriculum Studies*, 38, 4, pp. 483–98.

Jones. M. (2013) 'What is personalised learning in geography?' in Lambert, D. and Jones, M. (eds) *Debates in Geography Education*. Abingdon: Routledge. pp. 116–28.

Lambert, D. (2011) 'Reviewing the case for geography, and the "knowledge turn" in the English National Curriculum', *The Curriculum Journal*, 22, 2, pp. 243–64.

Lambert, D. and Morgan, J. (2010) *Teaching Geography 11–18: A conceptual approach*. Maidenhead: Open University Press.

Leat, D. (1998) *Thinking Through Geography*. Cambridge: Chris Kington Publishing.

Nichols, A. (2006) 'Thinking skills and the role of debriefing' in Balderstone, D. (ed) *Secondary Geography Handbook*. Sheffield: Geographical Association, pp. 180–97.

Nichols, A. (ed) with Kinninment, D. (2001) *More Thinking Through Geography*. Cambridge: Chris Kington Publishing.

Ofsted (2008) *Geography in Schools: Changing practice*. Manchester: Ofsted.

Ofsted (2011) *Geography: Learning to make a world of difference*. Available at: www.gov.uk/government/publications/geography-learning-to-make-a-world-of-difference (last accessed 08/11/2016).

Ofsted (2012) *School Inspection Handbook: Handbook for inspecting schools in England under Section 5 of the Education Act 2005 (as amended) from September 2012*. Manchester: Ofsted.

QCA (2007) *Geography: Programme of study for key stage 3 and attainment target*. London: HMSO.

Rawling, E. (2000) 'Ideology, politics and curriculum change: reflections on school geography 2000', *Geography*, 85, 3, pp. 209–20.

Roberts, M. (2003) *Learning Through Enquiry: Making sense of geography in the key stage 3 classroom*. Sheffield: Geographical Association.

Roberts, M. (2010) 'Where's the geography? Reflections on being an external examiner', *Teaching Geography*, 35, 3, pp. 112–13.

Roberts, M. (2011) 'What makes a geography lesson good?'. Paper based on a lecture given at the 2011 Geographical Association Annual Conference. Available at: www.geography.org.uk/projects/makinggeographyhappen/teachertips (last accessed 08/11/2016).

Rowley, C. and Lewis, L. (2003) *Thinking on the Edge*. Bowness-on-Windermere: Badger Press Ltd.

Taylor, L. (2009) *Concepts in geography*, GTIP Think Piece. Available at: www.geography.org.uk/gtip/thinkpieces/concepts/#5821 (last accessed 06/05/2015).

Vygotsky, L. (1962) *Thought and Language*. Cambridge, MA: Massachusetts Institute of Technology Press.

Weeden, P. (2007) 'Students' perceptions of geography: decision making at age 14', *Geography*, 92, 1, pp. 62–73.

Wood, D., Bruner, J. and Ross, G. (1976) 'The role of tutoring in problem solving', *Journal of Child Psychology and Psychiatry*, 17, 2, pp. 89–100.

Young, M. (2008) *Bringing Knowledge Back In: From social constructivism to social realism in the sociology of education*. Abingdon: Routledge.

Recommended key readings

Best, B. and Padget, S. (2013) *Secondary Starters and Plenaries: Geography ready-to-use activities for teaching geography*. London: Bloomsbury.

A book with 50 pairs of practical ideas for beginning and ending lessons, covering themes such as managing rural areas, wildlife conservation, resource management and sustainable development. However, as this chapter has emphasised, these ideas need to be carefully considered in relation to the aims and purpose of the lesson you are planning.

Roberts, M. (2011) 'What makes a geography lesson good?'. Paper based on a lecture given at the 2011 Geographical Association Annual Conference. Available at: www.geography.org.uk/projects/makinggeographyhappen/teachertips (last accessed 08/11/2016).

In this article Margaret Roberts discusses constructivism as a learning theory and outlines the value she places on enquiry. It provides detailed consideration of the three elements required for good geography to take place in a lesson. It also makes the case for the quality of lessons to be judged holistically.

Chapter 12

Resources

David Rayner taught geography in secondary schools for over 30 years and was PGCE Tutor at the Institute of Education, University College London

Introduction

Imagine that you are a geography teacher from around 1965 walking into a geography classroom today – what two things might surprise you? The first thing could be that you would still see students sitting at tables, a pen in hand and an exercise book or work folder lying in front of them. In other words, a scene very similar to what you would have observed around 50 years ago. After spending a little time in the classroom, however, you would be astounded to see the geography teacher not regularly handing out textbooks but instead presenting a wide variety of geographical resources in a digital format via an interactive whiteboard (IWB) from the teacher's laptop. On talking to the teacher you are informed that students now are also encouraged to be more independent of the teacher, having access to a rich diet of contemporary information, accessible both in the classroom (via the IWB, PCs and tablets) and at home (via the internet and PCs/tablets/smartphones), using the latest technology.

This scenario demonstrates a dichotomy inherent in many modern classrooms. Despite living and working in a predominantly digital era, the age-old tradition of students developing and demonstrating knowledge, understanding and skills by writing on paper still continues. By contrast, alongside this somewhat static scenario, geography teachers have increasingly exploited various forms of constantly evolving technology to research, create and present digital resources that students now utilise alongside their print resources. In some schools, attempts to digitise students' work involve issuing young students with laptops and tablets, or commissioning bespoke digital classrooms where high-tech workstations have replaced traditional tables. Such radical moves have met with mixed reactions from both staff and students, and research has demonstrated varying degrees of success, particularly in relation to planned improvements in the quality of learning:

> 'the correlational and experimental evidence does not offer a convincing case for the general impact of digital technology on learning outcomes. This is not to say that it is not worth investing in and using technology to improve learning. But it should encourage us to be cautious in the face of technological solutions to educational challenges' (Higgins et al., 2012, p. 3).

It is against this multimedia backdrop that this chapter discusses how geography teachers can make use of both traditional and digital resources in their teaching. Whatever type of resource is being used, we need to ask some critical questions of how we choose, create and utilise resources with students; in particular for what purpose, and what intended geographical outcome? It might, however, be worth pointing out at this early stage in the chapter, the obvious rider to this discussion – it isn't 'what' resources you use but 'how' you use them that has the greatest impact on both the teaching and the geographical learning.

Resources and pedagogy

Geography as a subject has always been very fortunate in terms of the range and quality of resources that we are able to choose from. Good geographers are able to select an appropriate mix of text, photos, statistics and maps alongside audio, video, physical objects (rock and soil samples), 3D models, fieldwork equipment, newspapers, cartoons, poems and much more. Although the technology has changed over the years, for example video streaming replacing video cassettes and DVDs, more pertinent are the ways in which teachers use some of these resources. It could be argued that there were too many instances in the past where students sat passively for whole lessons watching a single 50-minute TV programme. Today, with the so-called 'YouTube generation', a three-minute video clip may seem ideal: but such clips, if not carefully chosen, can lack geographical context and/or depth. It is not enough to just insert short video clips into the lesson plan: as always, we have to search hard for a viable compromise that provides a quality learning experience for our students.

> 'There is no doubt that technology engages and motivates young people. However this benefit is only an advantage for learning if the activity is effectively aligned with what is to be learned. It is therefore the pedagogy of the application of technology in the classroom which is important: the "how" rather than the "what"' (Higgins et al., 2012, p .3).

The Higgins *et al.* (2012) report also identified a chasm opening up between the enthusiastic advocates of a digital education and those sceptics with increasing doubts about the value of each technological wave that engulfs society in general and education in particular; yet at the same time, they recognise that 'it is impossible to imagine that digital technologies will not be used in educational settings as they are now so embedded in wider society' (p. 10).

The ongoing and increasingly polarised debate about the educational value of digital technology is pertinent to this chapter in the sense that geography teachers have, on a daily basis, to make difficult decisions about how and where they source their resources. The advent of the internet and its ease of access to virtually all the information that exists has in many ways made the teacher's job more difficult, rather than easier. A similar argument can be applied to students who, research shows, now use the internet as the key resource for the majority of their homework.

How do we select resources?

An important element of this question lies within the realm of 'media literacy' (Durbin, 2006). The resources selected by teachers of geography inevitably transmit a particular view of the world and there are associated issues of over- and under-representation. Some sources make clear a particular stance or view of the world while others proclaim a neutrality and balance that is nevertheless frequently challenged. Some of the media that we use in classrooms is strongly influenced by commercial interests. It is also important to acknowledge that the various media we use will be interpreted through individual lenses. This is where a student's cultural background and experience of life will play a vital role in how they deal with a geographical resource. As a consequence of these ideas, it is important that as teachers we develop in both ourselves and our students the ability to be 'critical'. As such, when we select resources, we need to ask certain questions:

1. Do we know the original source of the information that we are using?
2. Does the source provide a balanced view of the topic or event with different perspectives?
3. Is the source trying to inform, persuade, entertain or make a profit?
4. Is the source targeted at adults, children or a range of ages?
5. Are there alternative sources that will give a different version of the reality of an event?

One of the most important messages that critical media literacy teaches us is 'to take a second look'. A 'second look' can reveal bias, omissions, hidden messages and so on – students need to be taught that they are also responsible for taking a 'second look' at any media presented by their teacher or researched as part of a project or homework task.

These skills help students not only to successfully negotiate their way through the huge variety of media resources presented to them on a daily basis but also, over time, to develop the necessary skills and understanding to create and present their own media (posters, essays, scripts, poems, etc.). For a more detailed look at this topic see Chapter 11 in Lambert and Morgan (2010).

When selecting media resources, a key question in our minds should always be 'what are the learning outcomes of this lesson?' In this way, we can think carefully about how a video clip, newspaper article or image will support the learning outcome. Experience tells us that all too often what students take from using a resource is not what we expected. It is important, therefore, to think carefully about how we present the resource and how we explain a task if the resource is to serve its intended purpose.

How do we create resources?

When the textbook ruled the classroom, geography teachers acknowledged the work of authors in sifting through large amounts of existing text, photos, maps and statistics and then making professional decisions about the content and layout of the geography appropriate for the age and ability level targeted by the publishers. While the textbook (aimed at a typical student in a typical class in a typical school) can never fully meet the needs of particular students in a particular class in a particular school, many geography teachers in the past at least shared a core set of resources that they could supplement in various ways.

Now, of course, many teachers are doing much of the work of the textbook authors, making those difficult decisions about what resources to select in order to meet the needs of their particular students. At this point, we have to address the uncomfortable question of the extent to which 'media is dominating pedagogy' (Collie and Lewis, 2011). An example is provided in Figure 1.

Having planned the lesson in outline (see Figure 1), the next task is to resource it.

1. A search of the internet for 'immigration into the UK from within the European Union' reveals 127 million items including some posted just six hours ago – you can't get more topical than that!
2. Delving a little deeper reveals that there are lots of very complex reports that deal with both the technicalities and the impact of migration. Not very helpful, however, as these professional documents are somewhat dull and relatively inaccessible.
3. There are also, readily available, hundreds of newspaper reports, many with outlandish headlines, that each provides its own perspective on the topic of EU immigration. How do you as the teacher provide a range of perspectives to give a balanced view to your students?
4. Scrolling through pages and pages of digital images reveals lots of uninspiring photos of flags and politicians (or just very, very offensive images linked to 'immigration').
5. Statistics – only 102 million web links to sort through this time but the first few look promising. There are reports with graphs and raw data from Eurostat – but how to present this information to the students? Can the data be edited/simplified? A good resource from the Migration Observatory (based at Oxford University) provides context, data (already graphed unfortunately) and useful articles including one on the impacts of migration.
6. Video clips – some good clips from news channels such as Channel 4 and Newsnight but a bit long at six minutes and quite complex in places.

So, what have you got so far? Millions of websites containing millions of reports, images and data: but just where are the ideal resources that will underpin your lesson plan? Time is ticking by and unfortunately the technology has not yet been invented that marks your students' books! So where is the compromise? Will the lesson plan stay intact or will the most accessible and most easily modified media resources determine the flow and content of your lesson? Changing the search to 'Geography lesson on EU Migration' may show up a 'ready-made' set of resources from a teacher website or teachers collective such as the *TES*, but this then raises further questions about the provenance and suitability of the resources. Sharing teaching resources and ideas is a very desirable goal but it is not a shortcut that can regularly replace good planning and lesson resourcing.

Looking at such examples, it may be easy to become cynical about the perceived benefits of being able to create your own resources, tailored to the needs and interests of your own classes. Geographers, however, like many other subject teachers, have always had to make compromises when planning, resourcing and teaching lessons. Good teachers take a pragmatic approach and try to get some overall balance into their planning and resourcing over time. It also seems fair to point out that teachers benefit long-term from their current ability to revisit, adapt and update resources stored in a digital format. Sharing is also easier within departments, and more widely, for those willing to support that concept through personal blogs and online resource sharing accounts.

Individual resources

Having established some context for creating and sharing resources, this section looks at individual resources and assesses the benefits and shortcomings of both traditional and digital resources. It also deals with sourcing resources, but as always, it has to be noted that resources invariably come and go over time.

Textual resources

There is an inevitable overlap between purely text-based resources and those that might well include other useful resource material. Obviously, textbooks still provide a key resource for some teachers, particularly those teaching key stage 4 and 5 examination classes. The content of textbooks has been carefully authored and edited to suit the needs and abilities of a particular age group. At key stage 3, the text may often be minimal: in general, the concerns expressed by Walford (1995) in the past over text erosion and dilution, still hold true.

Textbooks used for examination courses have undergone a radical transformation in style and approach. In the past, teachers would have chosen from a range of textbooks and in the sixth form would have utilised a wide range of general and specialist topic texts. Today, each examination specification has a dedicated single textbook that often acts as the sole resource for teachers and students. Accusations abound of using these single textbook resources to 'teach to the test' and rumours of students who have opted to further study geography getting a diluted version of the subject at school undoubtedly have some validity. The reality, however, is that in best practice schools, geographers will enrich the single textbook diet with a wide variety of digital and other appropriate resources.

Imagine yourself planning a typical lesson on migration within the European Union, with a focus on the impact of immigrants on the UK (economy, housing, education, health and welfare). You want some facts, some statistics, some images and some short video clips. You know what resources you want in order to create a stimulating and thought-provoking lesson.

You want to find an engaging video clip or a suitably puzzling image to engage the students at the start of the lesson. Having shared and understood the lesson objectives/learning outcomes, your students will need some text to provide context and some pertinent data to graph and analyse, perhaps working in small groups. Your plan next involves a card sort activity to help them classify the impacts of immigrants arriving in the UK. After a short 'think, pair, share' activity, the students will be expected to feed back their thoughts to the whole class. A homework activity is required, to allow students to draw together all the information from the various resources and answer an overarching question about the positive and negative impacts of EU immigration on the UK.

Specialised e-readers and e-reading apps on smartphones and tablets have gone some way to providing commuters and holiday makers, for instance, with an alternative to carrying large or multiple text-rich tomes; but they are weak when it comes to reading and enjoying media-rich books on relatively small screens. This, of course, then equally applies to a typical geography textbook. The current consensus is that textbooks, magazines and newspapers will be with us (alongside digital alternatives) for some time to come.

How then to best use textbooks? As ever, there should be a balance between spending endless hours creating new resources and being pragmatic about existing resources. Atlases and textbooks contain valuable information and teachers need to be creative in their use of

Figure 1: Planning a lesson on migration within the European Union.

Figure 2: Using photographs to stimulate geographical thinking. **Photo** © Anna Grandfield.

'I always ensured that with both my tutor group and my geography classes, there was a powerful and intriguing geographical image on the newly acquired IWB when it wasn't being used for something else. It got to the point that if I forgot to put up an image or forgot to change it daily, my students would loudly protest.'

these existing resources, using them as a store to be drawn upon where relevant and appropriate alongside other media.

At key stage 3, there has been a strong move towards teachers creating (or at least collating) their own resources, predominantly in a digital format, and presenting these resources to students via the now ubiquitous IWB and data projector. This has been made possible by a strong push by successive UK governments to ensure that schools adopt this particular technology: research has shown that the UK now has the highest percentage of classrooms fitted with IWB and projector. Articles published in *Teaching Geography* suggest a range of innovative ideas for the creative use of IWBs (see for example Bayliss and Collins, 2006; 2007a; 2007b).

When creating lesson resources, some teachers focus on visual rather than textual information. The use of predominantly visual resources, coupled with the trend for teachers themselves to talk less and less to their students, for fear of being labelled didactic and old-fashioned (Didau, 2013), is worrying in that it can lead to students studying topics in something of a textual vacuum. What is needed, as always, is a balance, with well-judged teacher input alongside quality textual resources where students are supported by strategies such as DARTs ('Directed Activities Relating to Texts') to help them access information and remain focused. Having said that, it is important that teachers make appropriate judgements about the length and difficulty of the text they present to students. Well-chosen and edited text should combine accessible everyday language and good geographical terminology, so students learn their geographical vocabulary in context.

Image resources

The term 'images' covers many different visual elements including photographs, line drawings, graphs, maps and paintings. The focus here is on photographs, because they can provide one of the most powerful and engaging resources used in a geography classroom. Photos can be puzzling, shocking, outlandish and dramatic – the list is almost endless – but essentially they are emotive, because they generate an emotional response in students.

Chapter 12: Resources

	Advantages	Disadvantages
Set of images on one PPT slide	Easy to compare/contrast pairs or sets of images or see a sequence.	Detail and impact of individual images may be lost.
Single image on each PPT slide	Students can see details with potential to generate more 'awe and wonder' or intrigue.	PowerPoint gets longer and becomes a larger file size to store.
Using Prezi rather than PPT to display images	Increased flow and connectivity between individual images.	More complex. Time needed to learn new software.
Using high-tech display equipment	Easier for students to share images as a class. Images can be edited, annotated and manipulated.	Time and effort spent in sourcing quality images is wasted by poor visual quality if there are low-tech blackout facilities.

Figure 3: Methods of displaying and using images: advantages and disadvantages.

Geography is about places, people and environments and we need strong visual input alongside the use of our other senses. Although we live in a world dominated by moving images, there remains huge educational value in finding and using good photos in a geography classroom.

Such startling and intriguing images as Figure 2 lend themselves to classic questions such as 'Where?', 'When?' and 'Why?', but it could be argued that the best route to learning comes about when the students themselves shape the questions. What would your first question be?

Most teachers use Microsoft PowerPoint (PPT) as a tool for holding together the resources they want to present to students in a lesson and in many senses (in spite of the proverbial 'death by PowerPoint') it is very good at the job (Figures 3 and 4). Too few teachers, however, have fully utilised the potential of this powerful software. Many teachers move in and out of the PPT presentation to link to a streamed video, visit a webpage, show an animation or to listen to a podcast. All of these resources can be embedded within a PPT presentation to give a much smoother and more professional experience for the students. As far as photos are concerned, every image should be hyperlinked to a slide showing it full size with a link back to the original slide.

As with any other resource used in school, teachers need to be aware of copyright restrictions, particularly if images may be re-used by teachers/students and placed on school networks and/or school websites.

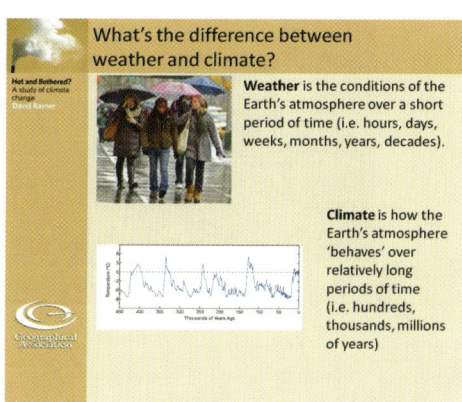

Figure 4: PowerPoint slide incorporating text and images. **Source:** Rayner, 2011.

Teachers are generally aware when photocopying from a book or other publication that there is a limit on how much material can be copied – generally, these restrictions are placed on display next to the photocopier. Fewer teachers are aware that similar restrictions apply to text and images taken from digital sources.

Not only has the law been slow to change in response to the growth of online digital resources, but Web 2.0 technologies have led to an internet dominated not by static web pages available to view but by user-generated web pages that constantly evolve and often have no single author or contributor. Examples of Web 2.0 include social networking sites (e.g. Facebook), blogs (e.g. DigGeog), wikis (e.g. Wikipedia), video sharing sites (e.g. YouTube), web applications (e.g. online video editing), and mashups (e.g. Earthquakes based on Google Maps plus USGS website data).

Figure 5:
A Flickr image search for 'volcano eruption' using Creative Commons.

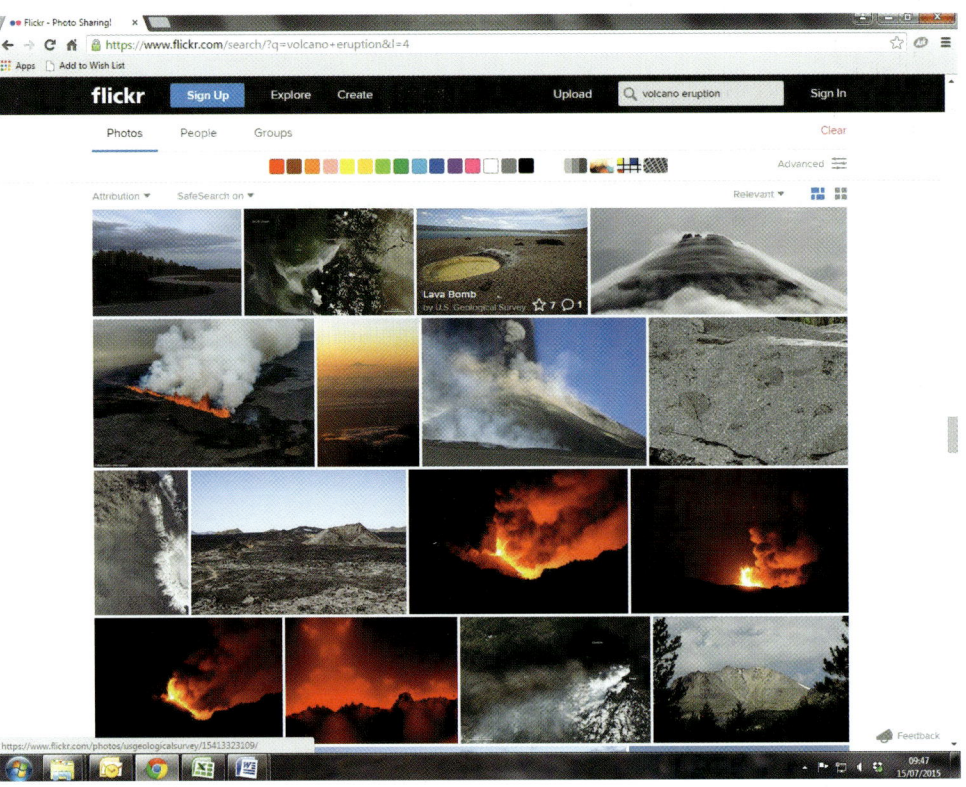

As far as photos are concerned, many online images have a clearly stated copyright restricting their use, but there also exists a new form of less restrictive copyright called Creative Commons (CC). Teachers looking for photos that are under CC licences will find them on a variety of websites. Flickr, for example, used by many geographers, has a special section within advanced search that locates only CC images. Often these have no restrictions at all although some photographers draw the line at commercial use of their images. A simple search at *www.flickr.com/creativecommons* will reveal thousands of excellent high-resolution photos, which can be safely used in the classroom or on school websites, geography blogs, etc. (see Figure 5).

There is a wealth of images available via internet searches on specific websites such as Flickr, The Big Picture, Geograph and Google Images (Figure 6), although the latter remains the default source for many teachers. Once a suitable image or set of images have been sourced how they are used in the classroom depends on the purpose of the geographical learning.

Is the image to stimulate students' questions, such as in the 5Ws approach, or will a tool be provided, such as the Development Compass Rose, to analyse the image from a social, economic, environmental and political perspective? Figure 7 suggests a range of activities for using images and photographs.

Atlases and maps

Under 'Geographical Skills' the 2014 Geography National Curriculum continues to emphasise the importance of these resources: 'pupils should be taught to build on their knowledge of globes, maps and atlases, and apply and develop this knowledge routinely in the classroom and in the field' (DfE, 2013). An atlas is a valuable resource that contains a wealth of geographical data with added text, photos and graphs to enhance the political and thematic maps. However, Lambert and Balderstone (2010) have highlighted the fact that atlases are not an easy resource for students to use and that to be effective, students need to develop a range of skills that allow them to understand map projections and access the data displayed in atlas maps.

Chapter 12: Resources

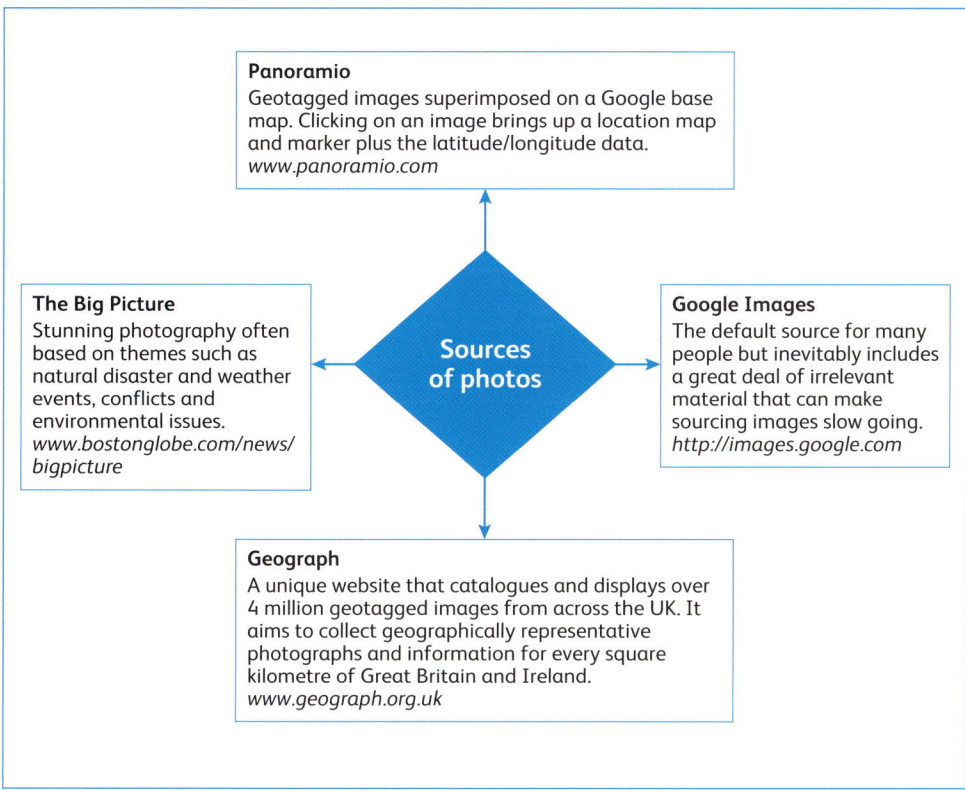

Figure 6: Sources of photographs and images.

One important way of developing understanding about Earth, its people and environments is the ability to use maps to zoom in and out, from local to global and back again. In an atlas, however, this necessitates turning pages and finding maps at different scales. While this may seem straightforward to the teacher, this process can be problematic for younger students as they struggle to move from map to map trying to relate the information on one to the information on another. Similarly, students need to be able to develop relational skills, knowing where places are in relation to the UK and to each other.

If looking at a map of the UK within Europe and then looking on a separate page at a map of the African continent creates a disconnect rather than a transition in students' minds, what then are the alternatives? In spite of some practical difficulties, most school networks permit teachers to access Google Earth, which allows students to witness and experience a smooth transition as we move across the globe from a UK location to a distant case study in India.

Adding layers, such as country boundaries and place names, plus a latitude/longitude grid, allows students to see relevant contextual data similar to that contained within a traditional atlas. A key benefit of using digital data is that we can switch layers of data on and off to simplify maps or to focus on one element. Although still using a 2D screen, at a global scale, the Google Earth software gives the impression of a 3D surface. Specific data and journeys are easily saved and stored for future reference. Unlike an atlas, which inexorably dates year on year, Google Earth provides contemporary data, some of it virtually live (weather data for example) and it makes a virtue of older maps by allowing you to create time lines that show changes in land use, urban areas, deforestation, etc. over time.

Various incarnations of the National Curriculum and different awarding body specifications all require students to develop the skills necessary to view and interpret Ordnance Survey (OS) maps at various scales. In the past, departments collected examination sets of OS maps and used these with students at all key stages.

Figure 7: Activities using photographs and images.

Activity	Description
5Ws, 6Ws, 7Ws	Students try to answer questions (What? Where? When? Who? and Why?; also What next? What if?) verbally or by annotating an image. This can be developed further by getting the students to ask their own questions, e.g. How did they [the government] let this happen? (see Nichols, 2001).
Here or there?	Use a selection of images for two or more places to see if students can suggest where they were taken and justify their choices. Good starting point to a study of place.
Sensing images	Students place themselves in the image and use their five senses to describe the location. Good to compare students' sensory perceptions.
Out of place	Using a composite image see if students can work out if erroneous information has been added to a picture.
Looking in another direction	What would be seen if the camera turned around 90° or 180°, e.g. Pyramids and Cairo, slums and skyscrapers in developing world cities? Can also be instructive to look up or down and think what might be different.
Image within an image	Get students to select smaller frames within an image to make the foci of their work. Cut up one image and give separate parts to students to make sense of before coming back together.
Image hole	Use the IWB to show only a small part of an image – what does the rest of the image show?
Back to back	Describe an image to another person to draw – developing geographical language and vocabulary. Use before and after images of a physical landscape (see Hawley, 2014).
Image bingo	Get students to apply a set of adjectives to an image and use these to create a bingo card (see Hawley, 2014).
Compass rose	Apply the Development Compass Rose to an image: North = Natural; East = Economic; South = Social; West = Who decides (political).

In addition, from 2002–2010, all 11–12-year-old students in English schools were eligible to receive a free Ordnance Survey Explorer map (1:25,000) of their local area. This meant that teachers were restricted in their access to OS maps by virtue of luck in terms of which maps they received and by the sheer cost of buying further paper maps. At the same time, in April 2010, it was announced that the OS was being forced by the government to release in digital form some of their data for non-commercial use. The release of the OS OpenSpace API (programming code) allowed a range of websites, for the first time, to build in free access to OS maps. In this way, schools could access OS maps of any part of the UK at certain scales (including 1:50,000 maps). This led to some innovative resources such as Gavin Brock's Ordnance Survey Map KML overlay for the UK and the website 'Where's the Path?', which

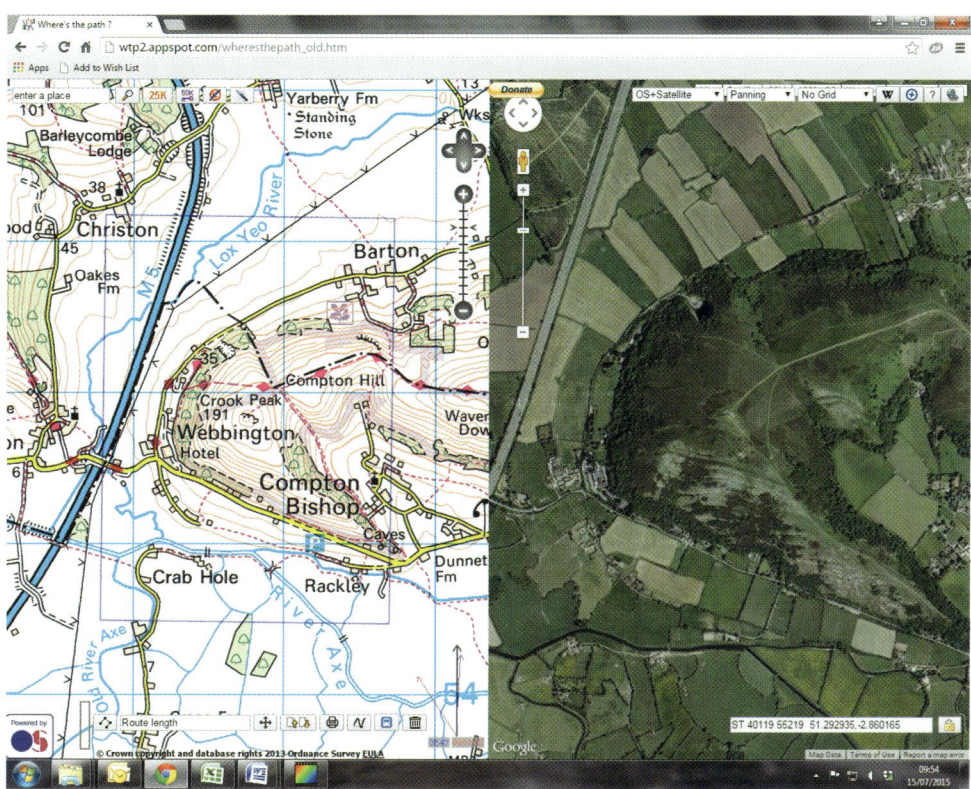

Figure 8: 'Where's the Path?' website.

allowed a mix of current OS maps, historical maps and aerial photos to be shown on screen side-by-side (Figure 8).

Gavin Brock's OS Map KML overlay allows OS maps to be shown as an extra layer in Google Earth. The OS map can be faded in and out and the use of Google Earth 3D terrain tab allows OS maps to be viewed as 3D objects. Previously this required the purchase of bespoke software, such as that produced by Memory Map and Anquet. Using resources such as these, geographers are now able to access for free OS maps of any part of the UK. There is, therefore, no longer any excuse not to incorporate the regular use of high-quality OS mapping into lessons.

The internet also gives us easy access to a wide variety of mapping previously undreamed of in terms of traditional atlas use. Teachers can access maps from a range of organisations such as government agencies, aid organisations, local authorities, etc. A range of mapping websites is highlighted in Figure 9.

Data and statistics

As geographers, we always want the latest data to use with our students. The increased use of modern technology has helped our cause but not removed all the problems inherent in providing high-quality, up-to-date data. Census data is still only collected every ten years in England and Wales: once collected, it is drip fed to the waiting public. The processing of the vast quantities of data is now faster but it still takes time. After the 2011 Census (which cost £480 million), a debate began about abandoning the traditional census, which has been carried out every ten years since 1801, and 'an online survey could replace the study… or information could instead be collated using data already held by government' (BBC News, 2013).

On a more positive note census data, once processed, is freely available in a variety of interesting visual formats that can support work in the classroom. If the original data is required, it can be easily downloaded in Excel format from the Office for National Statistics (ONS) website.

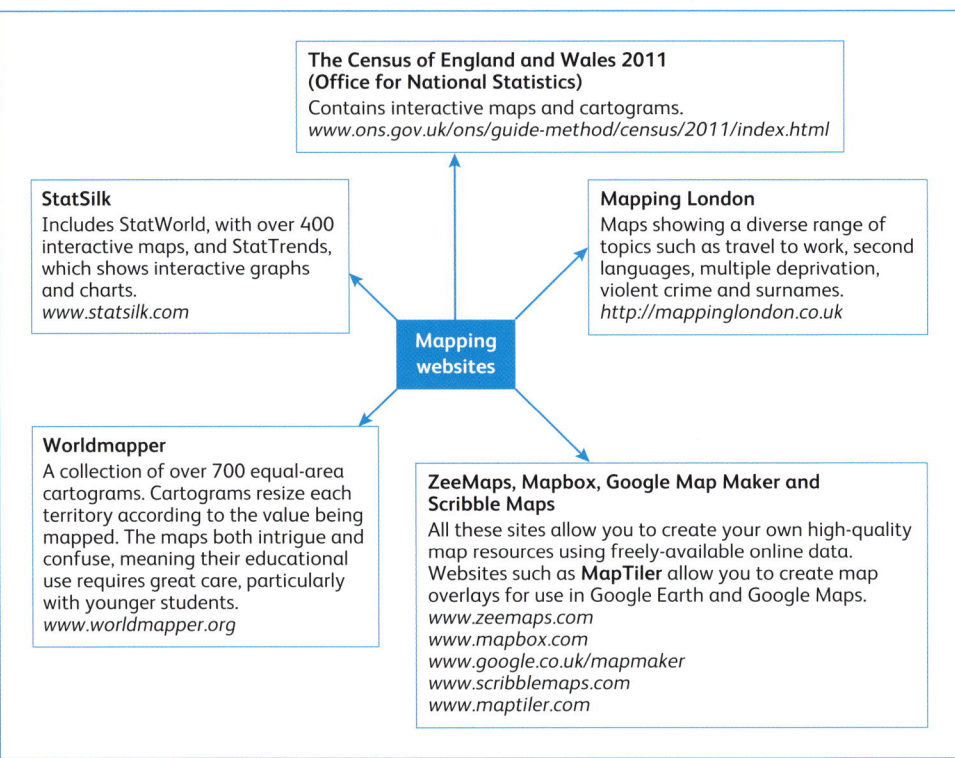

Figure 9: Mapping websites.

Alongside government censuses, most large organisations (United Nations, European Union, World Bank, etc.) and many smaller concerns now publish online a wealth of statistical data. Although there is still an inevitable in-built time lag, the majority of this data is relatively current. The ability to readily source historic data allows change and trends to be recorded and analysed.

The standard for presenting and visualising data has been set by Gapminder (a non-profit venture founded by Hans Rosling in 2005). The Trendalyzer software developed by the company 'sought to unveil the beauty of statistical time series by converting boring numbers into enjoyable, animated and interactive graphics' (Gapminder, 2015). In 2007, the software was acquired by Google who have made it available via Google Charts so that anyone can use their own data to create Gapminder-like animated graphs. Many organisations have utilised the power of this software to provide a more interactive experience for what can be dense data sets, tricky to make sense of. A good example is the annual Human Development Report, which uses its Public Data Explorer (powered by Google) to display data in a user-friendly fashion.

Some websites, such as the Met Office, provide free data alongside specific educational resources (videos, worksheets and posters) that support the use of their data. However, the amount of free data is limited: beyond such usage schools are required to pay a fee. One of the best sources of weather data is WeatherOnline, which has freely available data, well organised, for over 5000 stations worldwide. There are also specialist websites that provide live weather data feeds.

Video and audio resources

Reference has already been made to the 'YouTube Generation' – students (and adults) who seek quick gratification from bite-sized video clips, many of which are generated by those who frequent the various social media websites. For teachers seeking classroom resources, finding suitable video clips can be another stressful experience. Like Google Search, a YouTube search for a simple topic such as 'Fairtrade bananas' throws up almost 15,000 results.

Chapter 12: Resources

	Title	Length	Description	My review	Score
1	'Rapping Bananas'	57 secs	Animation featuring three singing bananas – produced by the Fairtrade Foundation.	Not very funny and the vocals are incomprehensible.	1/10
2	'The Co-operative film about Fairtrade bananas'	8 mins	A video clip produced by the Co-operative supermarket.	A case study format based on Ghana with mainly local people discussing the highs and lows of Fairtrade farming. Some useful visuals but heavy on dialogue – the video title says it all – slightly dull.	6/10
3	'Fairtrade bananas are treated better'	30 secs	Appears to be produced by Fairtrade.org.uk	A clip of a young woman peeling and licking a banana.	0/10
4	'Tipping the balance (what is Fairtrade?)'	5 mins	'Bernadette and Carlos, two personable bananas take us on a journey mixing animation with live footage to discover what being a Fairtrade banana is all about'.	Provides geographical context – deals with the disadvantages of traditional plantation farming and the advantages of small-scale, co-operative Fairtrade farming.	8/10
5	'Stick with Foncho to Make Bananas Fair – Fairtrade Fortnight 2014'	3 mins, 19 secs	Linked to the launch of a Fairtrade campaign in the UK.	The video is punchy, clear and should appeal to children – it is, however, promoting a particular personal stance that asks people to sign a petition and buy Fairtrade.	9/10

Figure 10: Choosing a video clip. Just viewing these five video clips takes a good 20–30 minutes! Which would you choose and why?

As before, this bewildering choice leaves the average teacher with two choices – spend the rest of your life looking through 15,000 video clips featuring bananas or go with the first few in the list. What then do the first five consist of? Figure 10 shows how I would review and score them on classroom viability.

It is perhaps inevitable that teachers fall back on YouTube as the default source, in spite of the danger of dropped internet connections during the lesson and the dreaded 'Comments' column that sits underneath the video window and seems to attract more than its fair share of vile and obscene posts. In early 2014, YouTube was trialling a new system designed to clean up its website but in the meantime it is recommended that geographers either download video resources or use websites such as ViewPure or SafeShare, which de-clutter YouTube and simply show the required video against a plain background.

For pragmatic reasons, many teachers store all the video resources they might want to use in lessons on a hard drive or school network. However, although YouTube clips can be relatively easily downloaded and saved, video clips from other websites, including news websites, are often heavily copyright protected and have to be used 'live'. In the case of video news clips, after a short time these valuable resources are often lost. For teachers who use a lot of video material in their lessons, it might be worthwhile investigating and investing in software that allows some of the less user-friendly websites to be utilised more productively.

Figure 11: Activities using video and films.

Activity	Description
Video without sound	Show video clip without sound and ask questions based only on the imagery, or ask students to write a commentary to accompany the clip (Ferretti, 2009).
Video without picture	Ask students to listen to the sound track with the picture turned off – what do they imagine they are seeing?
Predicting with video	Show part of a video clip and ask students to predict what happens next (Nichols, 2001).
Making videos using compact camcorders/ phones	Provide students with a specific audience and purpose for a 3-minute movie of a geographical issue or place. Or select the same place and ask them to make movies for different audiences.
Event perspective	Ask students to research news clips about an event that shows a particular perspective, e.g. victims, aid workers, government official.
The geography of film: The director's cut	A year 9 scheme of work that uses films to explore several geographical themes: landscape, culture, the film industry, portrayal of LEDCs, changing cities, imagined and future places (Coulson and Mattley, 2013).

Some of this can be done using browser plug-ins or add-ons for Firefox, Chrome and Microsoft Edge. Another possibility is to use Real Player (a free media player) that creates an easy method of downloading video clips but doesn't work with all websites. Figure 11 suggests some activities using video and films.

Few geography teachers use audio in the classroom but it can be a useful and powerful resource. Most audio is available in the form of podcasts, usually in the default mp3 format, which works with a broad range of technology. Podcasts from the BBC and from organisations such as the *Guardian* newspaper are designed to be downloaded and saved so there are fewer problems when compared to video clips. Podcasts are available for a wide variety of topics covering the environment, technology, transport, trade and population among others. Their length varies from bite-sized 3–4-minute clips to full-length 30–60-minute discussions. In the same way that we might ask a class to watch a video with the sound muted in order to focus on the imagery, it can be productive to get classes that you have a good relationship with to sit quietly with their arms folded, heads down and eyes closed in order to focus deeply on sounds and speech – it can be quite powerful and enlightening for students when it works well.

Other resources

Geography teachers have a long history of bringing artefacts into the classroom, often collected during their travels. Students themselves may also provide interesting items. Common examples might include volcanic rocks, small pieces of coral, items of clothing, flags, musical instruments and coins. Such items provide an insight into different cultures and landscapes. They can be used alongside images to create interest and 'a need to know' when starting a lesson or a new topic.

Although physical geography at key stage 3 had declined in popularity since its heyday in the 1991 National Curriculum, there is an increased emphasis and focus on physical geography again in the 2014 National Curriculum, including the requirement to look at rocks and soils. Students are often intrigued by rocks and fossils and it is worthwhile assembling a small collection for a display or to use in some practical work, as was often done in the past. If geology is not a particular strength then a good starting point is two articles in *Teaching Geography* (see Wright, 2009; 2010).

Aside from resources presented collectively to students via IWBs and projectors, the classroom environment itself provides a wealth of opportunities for students to draw from various resources:

- Word wall – displays of geographical terms can be used to familiarise students with the language of the subject, but these need to be used interactively and regularly changed in order to avoid the 'wallpaper effect'.

Chapter 12: Resources

Teachers need to make full use of the potential offered by so much technology in the classroom.

- Hotboards and work displays – in the most effective classrooms, there are always high-quality displays of students' work that not only celebrate achievement but also act as a resource for revision and information for visitors. Creating and maintaining good wall displays requires skill and a great deal of time, but is part of the geographical ambience created by teachers who have ownership of a teaching room. Hotboards are a relatively new (but fairly expensive) method of creating a more flexible wall display that can be integrated more easily into the actual lesson: perspex pockets allow students or the teacher to easily add or remove resources and work from the hotboard display.
- Experiments and games – although used by a minority of teachers, there is merit in retaining a practical element to geography work in the classroom alongside that carried out in the field. Such experiments might include volcano simulations (messy, sticky and dramatic), stream tables or flumes (messy but instructive), and earthquake simulators (simplistic but effective). One of the most dramatic 'experiments' I have witnessed over the years was a tropical rainforest simulation complete with high humidity and temperature, several large household tropical plants and rainforest sound effects – the students loved it. There are many teachers and students who favour a 'hands-on' approach to learning, and the use of modelling materials, both conventional (clay or plasticine) and unconventional (cake or pastry) can lead to some interesting experiments and outcomes. Games and simulations are used less by some teachers although the 'Trading Game' retains a place in many schemes of work. *Teaching Geography* provides examples of teachers sharing classroom activities, such as Spencer's detailed example of a sweatshop production game that she created and trialled with her students (see Spencer, 2014) and Clemens, Parr and Wilkinson's discussion on creating a local version of Monopoly for their urban studies unit (see Clemens *et al.*, 2013).

163

Computer simulations are also now available. A good example is the online simulation 'Stop Disasters!' produced by the UN/ISDR.

- Technology – for a long time, geographers had to seek out and book computer rooms, but increasingly geography rooms have easy access to PCs, laptops or tablet computers that students can use to research and work on. Their use requires careful planning and supervision if 'learning' is to remain the key focus – as is so often the case, using technology in the classroom doesn't guarantee adding value to the learning process. Increasingly, students and teachers carry with them sophisticated technological gadgets – formerly called mobile phones, these multi-purpose gadgets now include cameras, phones, computers and GPS units in a single device. With the right sort of apps installed, these same gadgets can be used as seismographs, as GPS tracking devices, as compasses, as weather stations, as scanners and as audio recording devices. Although we take the use of these gadgets for granted in everyday life, few teachers have managed as yet to make full use of the potential offered by so much technology in the classroom (or in the field). When you do, be sure to share your ideas and thoughts via *Teaching Geography*.

Teacher as 'resource' or as 'facilitator'?

There has been a strong move in recent years to see the classroom teacher as a 'facilitator' rather than as a 'resource'. The well-documented move away from didactic teaching to a student-centred approach has left the notion of 'teacher as expert' adrift in a sea of abandoned approaches. Alongside this change Mitchell and Lambert (2015) identified the 'trend toward interest in the processes of teaching and learning', one that 'emphasised skills development over subject knowledge'. They go on to point out that 'notions of flexibility and soft, transferable skills supported a view of the subject knowledge of "traditional" academic subjects (such as geography) as outdated and of questionable "relevance" to learners'. The work of Young (2013) in espousing the content of traditional subjects as 'powerful knowledge' has gone some way towards balancing the argument and supporting the current 'knowledge turn', i.e. a renewed interest in subject knowledge, particularly 'core knowledge'.

But where does this leave teachers in terms of their role as 'subject expert'? 'The subject discipline provides a resource which informs the teacher's curriculum thinking' (Mitchell and Lambert, 2015) but the teacher in turn acts as a conduit for the 'smaller subset of school geography'. While it could be argued that lesson planning, or the broader curriculum making, is where geography teachers need their subject expertise, students have to be enabled to access, through 'thinking geographically', the geography that lies at the heart of each individual lesson. What better way to develop a student's 'geographical imagination' than for teachers to see themselves, once again, as an integral resource within the lesson plan. Applicants being interviewed for initial teacher training courses are commended for demonstrating their 'passion' for geography. Surely, in order to demonstrate that passion in the actual classroom, teachers must be allowed to become ('guilt-free') one of the many high-quality resources available to students as they learn and enjoy their geography? What does that mean in reality? It means that teachers must be given the time and freedom to talk to their students as and when it is appropriate – to pass on knowledge, to explain complex processes or ideas and to share examples of things that inspired them to become geographers with a genuine passion for their subject.

Alongside 'teacher as a resource', it can be argued that there are two other critical roles to play. The 'resourceful teacher' is able to understand the pros and cons of resource selection and is able to select, create and bring together exciting and relevant student resources that engage and promote geographical learning. Finally, and perhaps most importantly as stated earlier, is the role of 'resource critic'. Both teachers and their students need to understand the importance of critical media literacy in order to think about where resources have come from, how they are viewed in geography and ultimately how they may be best used in a geography lesson where engagement is strong and learning is the focus.

References

Bayliss, T. and Collins, L. (2006) 'Invigorating teaching with interactive whiteboards', *Teaching Geography*, 31, 3, pp. 133–35.

Bayliss, T. and Collins, L. (2007a) 'Invigorating teaching with interactive whiteboards: case studies 3–6', *Teaching Geography*, 32, 1, pp. 56–59.

Bayliss, T. and Collins, L. (2007b) 'Invigorating teaching with interactive whiteboards: case studies 7–10', *Teaching Geography*, 32, 2, pp. 97–99.

BBC News (2013) *Census consultation has option to replace 200-year-old survey*. Available at: www.bbc.co.uk/news/uk-23943490 (last accessed 08/11/2016).

Clemens, R., Parr, K. and Wilkinson, M. (2013) 'Using geographical games to investigate "our place"', *Teaching Geography*, 38, 2, pp. 63–65.

Collie, P. and Lewis, L. (2011) *A Guide to ICT in the UK Education System*. Available at: www.educationimpact.net/media/23170/bett-2011-a%20guide%20to%20ict%20in%20the%20uk%20education%20system.pdf (last accessed 08/11/2016).

Coulson, S. and Mattley, C. (2013) 'The geography of film: the director's cut', *Teaching Geography*, 38, 1, pp. 32–34.

DfE (2013) *National Curriculum in England: Geography programmes of study*. Available at: www.gov.uk/government/publications/national-curriculum-in-england-geography-programmes-of-study (last accessed 08/11/2016).

Didau, D. (2013) *Teacher talk: the missing link*. Available at: www.learningspy.co.uk/english-gcse/teacher-talk-the-missing-link (last accessed 08/11/2016).

Durbin, C. (2006) 'Media literacy and geographical imaginations' in Balderstone, D. (ed) *Secondary Geography Handbook*. Sheffield: Geographical Association, pp. 226–37.

Ferretti, J. (2009) 'Effective use of visual resources in the classroom', *Teaching Geography*, 34, 3, pp. 108–10.

Gapminder (2015) *About Gapminder*. Available at: www.gapminder.org/about-gapminder (last accessed 08/11/2016).

Hawley, D. (2014) 'Looking into the physical future', *Teaching Geography*, 39, 1, pp. 26–29.

Higgins, S., Xiao, Z. and Katsipataki, M. (2012) *The Impact of Digital Technology on Learning: A summary for the Education Endowment Foundation*. London: Education Endowment Foundation.

Lambert, D. and Balderstone, D. (2010) *Learning to Teach Geography in the Secondary School* (second edition). Abingdon: Routledge.

Lambert, D. and Morgan, J. (2010) *Teaching Geography 11–18: A conceptual approach*. Maidenhead: Open University Press.

Mitchell, D. and Lambert, D. (2015) 'Subject knowledge and teacher preparation in English secondary schools: the case of geography', *Teacher Development*, 19, 3, pp. 365–80.

Nichols, A. (ed) with Kinninment, D. (2001) *More Thinking Through Geography*. Cambridge: Chris Kington Publishing.

Rayner, D. (2011) *Hot and Bothered? A study of climate change*. Sheffield: Geographical Association.

Spencer, H. (2014) 'The sweatshop production game', *Teaching Geography*, 39, 2, pp. 68–70.

Walford, R. (1995) *Geographical textbooks 1930–1990: the strange case of the disappearing text*. Available at: http://faculty.education.illinois.edu/westbury/paradigm/Walford.html (last accessed 08/11/2016).

Wright, D. (2009) 'Bringing geology into geography lessons: make sense of solid geology', *Teaching Geography*, 34, 3, pp. 111–13.

Wright, D. (2010) 'Bringing geology into geography lessons: make sense of drift geology', *Teaching Geography*, 35, 1, pp. 23–25.

Young, M. (2013) 'Overcoming the crisis in curriculum theory: a knowledge-based approach', *Journal of Curriculum Studies*, 45, 2, pp. 101–18.

Recommended key readings

Biddulph, M., Lambert, D. and Balderstone, D. (2015) *Learning to Teach Geography in the Secondary School: A companion to school experience* (3rd edition). Abingdon: Routledge.

Aimed at those entering the profession through university and school-based initial teacher training courses, chapter 6 introduces the reader to a wide range of resources available for teaching and learning geography. As well as a wealth of practical suggestions, it covers the important factors that should be considered when creating, selecting and using resources with students in geography.

Balderstone, D. (ed) (2006) *Secondary Geography Handbook*. Sheffield: Geographical Association.

The previous handbook remains a valuable resource with many ideas for using resources to support teaching and learning in geography lessons. Recommendations include Chapter 13: Using geography textbooks; Chapter 14: Understanding distant places; Chapter 19: Media literacy and geographical imaginations; Chapter 22: Let's get physical and Chapter 24: Theatrical geography.

Chapter 13

Differentiation

Jane Ferretti is a PGDE Tutor at the University of Sheffield

Introduction

Differentiation, personalised learning, inclusion: these are all terms used to remind teachers that every class will include students with a range of abilities and that they need to plan and teach lessons that ensure that all their students make progress. These terms are often used together although their meanings are different. This chapter will concentrate on differentiation, which Lambert and Balderstone (2010) define as 'a planned process of intervention in the classroom designed to maximise learning potential based on individual needs' (p. 205).

The expectation for teachers to differentiate for all their students is made clear in the National Curriculum:

> 'Teachers should set high expectations for every pupil. They should plan stretching work for pupils whose attainment is significantly above the expected standard. They have an even greater obligation to plan lessons for pupils who have low levels of prior attainment or come from disadvantaged backgrounds' (DfE, 2014, p. 9).

To make sure that all students are provided for requires careful planning. You must consider both the least able and the most able, those with disabilities and those with English as an additional language (EAL), not forgetting of course what some have referred to as the invisible middle ability students (see Sebba et al., 2007). This is a tall order, and it is not surprising that differentiation remains one of the greatest concerns of experienced teachers as well as those who are training or in the early stages of their career.

Geography teachers are no different to other teachers in facing these challenges but at least we have the advantage of a subject which is about the world we live in, so is intrinsically interesting to young people. The availability of a range of excellent resources, and the variety of ways in which information can be presented, means that geography teachers have the opportunity to introduce new ideas and discuss issues with students, be it challenging the most able or supporting those who find learning geography difficult.

Few teachers would disagree that differentiation matters and in some geography classes it is clearly evident, with resources carefully chosen or adapted to engage all students; teachers using advanced questioning skills to help students to learn; students having elements of choice in the tasks they do; and both group work and talk being used to develop understanding. Well-planned and effective differentiation is not, however, seen in every classroom; there are a number of reasons for this, not least that teachers' heavy workload can mean they do not have enough time to sit back and reflect on what they are doing or plan how they might better support different groups in their classes.

Creating an appropriate learning environment

As a teacher it is important to make sure your geography classroom is one where all individuals feel comfortable to voice their opinion or ask questions and are confident that they can learn and make progress. Building on Evans and Smith's (2006) ideas, there are a number of things you can do to ensure a positive learning environment for all:

- Get to know your students as quickly as possible as individuals: not just their name but a little about them, including their strengths and weaknesses as learners. This will help you to differentiate by the support you give them.

- Make it clear that everyone in the class is expected to contribute and that everyone's views are valued. It is essential that the least able have the confidence to ask and answer questions and to express their opinions without fear of being ridiculed, and equally that the more able are encouraged to discuss or question ideas introduced in the lesson.
- Make sure your classroom is always well presented, for example with colourful wall displays. One way to celebrate the work of your students is by displaying it, making sure you include contributions from all, not just the most able or the neatest. Try to change your displays regularly, as this shows you care about the classroom environment and your students' work.
- Use a wide variety of resources and teaching and learning strategies that encourage all students to actively participate in lessons.
- Adopt an enquiry approach starting with a stimulus that creates 'a need to know' and encourages students to ask geographical questions and think about explanations.
- Think carefully about how you group students in your classes; change seating plans from time to time to ensure different students work with each other. It may sometimes be appropriate to arrange groups by ability so different work can be completed but sometimes mixing abilities encourages more able students to support those needing help. Finding a 'buddy' to work alongside students with EAL can be helpful.
- Encourage oracy and listening skills. This is one of the most useful assessment for learning (AfL) strategies, as it enables you to gauge each student's progress and understanding and consider what type of support they might need.
- Use a reward system that recognises students' achievement at their own level.

Planning for differentiation

The diagram in Figure 1, from the National Strategies programme, illustrates an approach to planning for inclusion for SEN students; however, you might also find it a useful way to think about planning differentiation for all students.

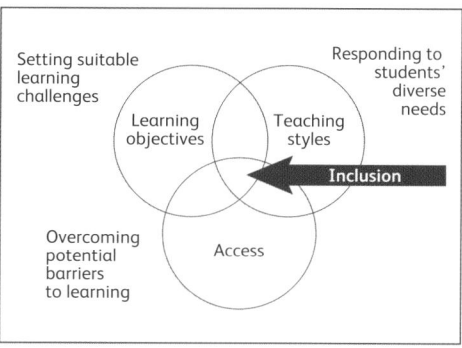

Figure 1: The circles of inclusion. **Source:** DfES, 2006.

Differentiation will not just happen, however experienced you are: it must be carefully planned and prepared for. Nor should it be just an add-on at the end of lesson planning. Learning objectives do not have to be the same for all students nor do they necessarily have to be different as long as strategies are in place to help overcome barriers. Most schools' lesson plans will expect several different learning objectives to be set and include sections asking for differentiation intentions to be clarified. Many will also want students with particular needs to be named and specific strategies indicated. Of course, just writing about differentiation on the lesson plan is only the first step: what count are the intervention strategies you adopt to enable all students to make progress.

Differentiation for the least able

Lower achieving students will always need a great deal of your time and support, and planning for this group is particularly important. Although many teachers will have excellent support from teaching assistants (TAs) or other adults for some of these students, you cannot always rely on this: and there will be lessons when the usual TA support is not there. If you do have such support it is important to think how best to use it and, wherever possible, to plan this in advance with the TA; at the very least, have a quick word before the lesson starts. Make the most of any specific information that TAs may have about students and take every opportunity to learn from them. Where the TA role is specific to a student, the TA can also be very effective in managing groups of students in which 'their' student works. Where their role is not specific, use their time to support as many students as possible.

You may need to set separate and different tasks for the least able students, but if possible it is best to start lessons with an engaging activity and resources that all students can access and differentiate later in the lesson.

There may be students with specific and identified learning needs such as dyslexia, dyspraxia, attention deficit hyperactivity disorder (ADHD) or autism or with a disability such as hearing or visual impairment. There is not enough space here to detail how you might differentiate for each of these particular needs, but publications such as *Meeting Special Educational Needs in the Classroom* (Swift, 2005) provide sound advice. Students with dyslexia, autism or a physical disability, for instance, may be academically able: you must not assumew they will need the same support as the lower achieving students. Some approaches you may find useful are listed below:

- Ask named students questions they will be able to answer and remember to praise them if they do this correctly.
- Speak to students individually to make sure they understand what you have asked them to do. Reassure them so they are confident to tackle the task.
- Make careful use of TAs or other adult help in the class and be clear about the kind of support they need to provide.
- Make sure all resources and worksheets are well presented, colourful and clear. Do not present too much information on one sheet and always use both lower case and upper case letters; capital letters are often more difficult for poor readers, as are underlined and bold type.
- Set structured tasks.
- Provide a writing frame that gives students the first words of each sentence they should write. Lewis and Wray of the University of Exeter have written extensively about the use of writing frames and provided many examples (see Lewis and Wray, 1996; Wray and Lewis, 1997).
- Remember work does not always have to be presented in a written form. Use alternatives such as a poem, a picture or a presentation with or without the use of IT.
- Use plenty of images and video clips to engage students and help them to access the curriculum.
- Set tasks that allow students choice both in the work they do and how it is presented.
- When marking, do not correct every single mistake; concentrate on geographical errors and important grammatical errors, such as not using capital letters at the start of sentences. Remember to set achievable targets and to praise aspects of the work you are pleased with.

Challenging the most able

At one time called 'gifted and talented', those students now called 'more able' or 'higher achievers' need to be stretched in order for them to make progress. Many teachers are tempted simply to give more able students an extra worksheet or more questions about the same topic as an extension, but if possible I feel you should avoid this approach. Rewarding students when they finish by giving them more work that they have already shown they can do is not 'extension': it is just 'more of the same'. Instead you should try to provide challenge by asking them to do something different or to do the same task as the others but do it differently, for example within a time limit or a word limit. For a more detailed discussion see Ferretti (2007). Listed below are some approaches you may find useful:

- Ask named students challenging questions and expect well-developed answers; probe answers to elicit a fuller response.
- Maintain a good pace throughout.
- Set tasks that allow choice and encourage research.
- Set strict word limits to develop the skill of writing concisely.
- Provide scope for good-quality extended writing.
- Expect the use of geographical terminology.
- Encourage more able students to take the lead in group work and discussion and to explain geographical ideas to those who do not understand.
- Encourage the use of high-level geographical skills when analysing data.

- Develop students' metacognition skills by asking them to explain how they approach tasks and articulate how they are 'thinking about thinking'.
- When marking work, make sure you focus on the geographical learning and set targets that will stretch the students; make it clear you have high expectations.

Supporting students with English as an Additional Language (EAL)

There are increasing numbers of students in UK classrooms who are expected to speak and learn in English at school but speak a different language at home. EAL students range from newly arrived migrants, or those in the early stages of learning English, to those who speak and write well; nevertheless all these students need some support. It can take many years for students to acquire the full range of necessary literacy skills and in the early stages many students remain silent in class, even if they can begin to understand some of what is said. It may be possible to make some use of these students' first language, for example by pairing them with another student who speaks the same language or by providing a dictionary. Always make it clear that you value their own language and culture, by showing an interest in their country of origin and focusing on positive aspects of their move to the UK. Even though their English is poor these students are as able as the others and need stimulus and challenge: try to avoid setting tasks in which they simply copy text or listen to conversation they cannot understand. Some approaches you may find useful are listed below:

- Speak to students individually to make sure they understand what you have asked them to do. Reassure them so they are confident to tackle the task.
- Make careful use of TAs or other adult help and be clear about the kind of support they need to provide.
- Make use of contextual support, particularly for EAL students at an early stage, for example using visual clues, making connections with their own experiences and giving them opportunities to talk.
- Use a 'buddy' to sit with and help students to understand tasks they have been set. This may be another student who speaks the same language or alternatively an English speaking student who is a friend or would be willing to support their peer.
- Provide structured tasks that help learners to understand selected new words and phrases.
- Where possible read text with students to help them to match spoken and written words.
- Encourage EAL students to speak both to you as their teacher and to their peers.
- Understand that writing English will almost certainly be the greatest challenge for EAL students and they will need support with this even if their spoken English is fluent.

Approaches to differentiation

You should have good pedagogical reasons for selecting a particular approach to differentiation and take into account the particular needs of the students you wish to support, whether this is to enable lower ability students to participate and achieve or to provide stretch and challenge for the higher achievers. In my view differentiation does not have to mean creating different resources or tasks for different groups in your class, although there may be times when you think this is best.

Figure 2 summarises different approaches to differentiation, suggesting some points for teachers to consider for each and providing some examples.

Differentiation through questioning

According to Wallace (2000) 'the key to differentiation lies in the quality of teacher questioning' (p. 55). Although this was written in to the context of teaching the most able students, in my view it is true for teaching all students. Questions are an immensely important tool for all teachers, but effective questioning is a skill that needs to be worked on. Research suggests that many teachers ask largely low-level, closed questions, so it is important that you plan some more challenging and open questions, particularly for more able students.

Approach	Description	Things to consider
By questioning	Teacher questioning and interaction with students	Probably the most effective way to differentiate for both less able and more able students. Teachers, especially beginner teachers, should incorporate their questions into their lesson planning. (See section on differentiation through questioning, p. 169)
By talk	Teacher explanation and interaction with students	Talk is important, for example to describe and explain ideas. However, you should expect some students to understand more than others; for example to learn and be able to use more geographical terminology. The task you set after your verbal explanation to the class would probably differ for different groups of students. (See section on differentiation through talk, p. 173)
By task	Setting different tasks to different students based on ability and/or interest	This can be effective, but creating a range of different resources is time-consuming. It could be done within a department, by sharing resources and keeping them for future years. Examples of differentiated tasks are 'Layers of Inference' and 'Structured Independent Learning' (see later sections in this chapter).
By feedback	Varying the language and purpose of feedback for individual students	It is important to make your expectations clear when you feed back on students' work, either orally or in writing. Praise is important but should only be given if earned. Teachers will be familiar with providing targets and should tailor these to individuals. Having high expectations is particularly important.
By grouping	Different groups are made up of similar or mixed abilities	Groups should be planned in advance and seating in the classroom arranged accordingly. If groups are mixed ability then the same resources should be used by all; more able students may need to support others in their group. If groups are arranged by ability then different tasks may be set after the initial input. Examples are Shared views, Dragons' Den and Concept maps (see later sections in this chapter).
By support	Teacher time dedicated to individuals or groups Targeted use of learning support staff Peer-to-peer learning support in lessons	Most students respond positively to individual attention; however, it is difficult for teachers working with groups of up to 30 to give this to every student in every lesson. Making careful use classroom support is important – remember, however, that as the teacher you should try to work with all students, speaking to them directly to encourage them to produce the best work they can.
By objectives	'All, most, some'; 'must, should, could'	Differentiated objectives may present the appearance of differentiation and increasing levels of challenge, but may not necessarily mean students' different abilities are planned for: it can mean some students focus only on the simplest objective and are not encouraged to challenge themselves.
By outcome	Setting different students different outcomes based on ability and/or interest Alternatively, allowing students to select the outcome	One of the most frequently used approaches, this allows teachers to use the same resources and set the same tasks for all students. However, they need to be clear about what is expected of them: there is a risk that more able students will not be stretched unless there are clear and challenging expectations. An example is explaining the impact of a volcanic eruption or the process of migration through a storyboard, diagram or oral presentation.
By scale/topic	Setting the same topic for all students but at different scales	This allows more able students to extend their knowledge while working on the same topic as the rest of the class. It requires different resources, so more preparatory work and classroom organisation are needed. An example is a local environmental issue investigated by some learners while others explore recent case studies in another part of the country or worldwide.

Figure 2: Approaches to differentiation.

You should think about the geography you want to develop, whether this is factual knowledge, understanding processes, interpreting data, considering different viewpoints or making decisions.

You probably use questions frequently in your whole-class teaching: they are a quick way of assessing understanding and hence one of the main elements of assessment for learning (AfL). More demanding questions also encourage students to think carefully, to analyse information, to evaluate and to speculate. Skilful questioning can challenge students to consider their own views and the views of others about controversial issues, or to question why certain decisions have been made. Targeted questions are an invaluable way both to assess and to differentiate.

You can and should use your skills as a questioner to differentiate, and the better you know your students the more effective this approach will be. An obvious way to do this is by tailoring questions to the individual needs and abilities of your students. In general simpler questions, often referred to as lower order questions, require recall of information, description or simple explanation; they are usually closed questions that have a 'right answer'. More challenging questions may require analysis, application of knowledge to a new situation or evaluation; these are usually open questions with many acceptable answers. However, as a teacher you need to be careful about these generalisations; do not be misled into thinking that all so-called lower order, closed questions are easy. For example, there is a great deal of difference in terms of difficulty between these questions:

- What is the name of the major river that runs through London?
- What is a spit and how are spits formed?
- What is the jet stream and how does it affect Britain's weather?

These are all reliant on recall of knowledge and understanding so could be considered lower order questions; however, it is clear that the question about the jet stream is by far the most difficult, and personally I would not consider this to be a lower order question. Students need knowledge to answer closed questions, so if a high level of knowledge is needed even recall questions can be difficult. Many schools advise teachers to refer to Bloom's taxonomy to help them to think more carefully about the questions they ask and to distinguish between lower order, usually easier, questions and higher order, more challenging, questions (Figure 3).

Benjamin Bloom proposed his taxonomy in 1956 but it was not widely applied in schools until the National Strategy documents (DfES, 2004) revitalised it, modified to focus on teachers' questions. Bloom's taxonomy was adapted by Anderson and Krathwohl (2001) who changed some of the terms and used verbs instead of nouns (see Figure 4). Despite their popularity in schools, both versions suffer from a number of limitations, including that different levels of difficulty can be present within, as well as between, categories. Some questions categorised as low order, remembering or understanding are much more difficult than others, as illustrated by the examples in Figure 4. Equally, some questions that may be categorised as high order, for example evaluation, may not be very challenging at all. For example, it may be easier to evaluate the advantages and disadvantages of building new houses on the green belt in the local area than it is to analyse complex data about changing global temperatures, or the frequency of extreme weather events, yet according to Bloom's hierarchical sequence analysis is less challenging than evaluation.

Improving questioning for differentiation

- Plan questions in advance, making sure you have questions which are accessible to the least able and more challenging for the most able.
- Where possible, ask open questions, such as 'What do you think about…?' or 'Do you agree with the idea that…?' Remember that not all closed questions are easy and not all open questions are difficult.
- Do not be satisfied with simplistic answers. Probe students' answers to develop their ideas and if appropriate pass or 'bounce' a question from one student to another.
- Use a 'no hands up' approach so students know they may be asked a question at any time; this also helps you to make sure different

Bloom's categories	Bloom's definitions	Bloom's subcategories	Possible examples of questions related to Bloom's categories
Evaluation	Judgements about the value of materials and methods for given purposes	Internal criteria External criteria	Is the data presented in the survey valid and reliable? Does the report on the earthquake deal with all relevant aspects?
Synthesis	Putting parts together to form a new whole	Production of a unique communication Production of a plan Ability to form hypotheses	What would you include in a three-minute TV report on a recent volcanic eruption?
Analysis	Breaking down into constituent elements	Of elements Of relationships Of organisational principles	Identify the social, economic and environmental impacts and possible legacy of the 2012 London Olympics and Paralympics.
Application	The use of ideas in particular and concrete situations	[no sub-division]	How has globalisation influenced this town/area? How could this school be made more sustainable?
Comprehension	Ability to grasp meaning of material	Translation Interpretation Extrapolation	What does the graph show? How would you describe the photograph? What coastal features can you identify on an Ordnance Survey map?
Knowledge	Recall of specifics and universals Remembering previously learned material	Terminology Specific facts Trends Classifications Methodologies Evaluative criteria Methods of 'inquiry' Principles and generalisations Theories and structures	What is GDP? Which is the largest ocean? What different types of soil are there? How is precipitation measured? What is the theory of plate tectonics?

Figure 3: Framework of levels based on Bloom's taxonomy of cognitive objectives. **Sources:** Bloom, 1956; Roberts, 2013.

students are asked questions, not just those who put their hands up. Try to question as many students as possible each lesson.

- By identifying a student before you ask a question you can tailor what you ask to their needs. For example: 'Tina, why does IKEA want to build a new store on the edge of Sheffield and not in the city centre?'; then 'Andrew, can you explain why some people are against IKEA building a new store in Sheffield?'; then 'Nadia, what sort of people might disagree with these views?'
- Use more advanced vocabulary when questioning more able students and expect a more sophisticated response, including the use of appropriate geographical terminology.

Cognitive level	Category	Sub-divisions
High	Creating	Creating, generating, planning, producing
High	Evaluating	Evaluating, checking, critiquing
Medium	Analysing	Analysing, differentiating, organising, attributing
Medium	Applying	Applying, executing, implementing
Low	Understanding	Understanding, interpreting, exemplifying, classifying, summarising, inferring, comparing, explaining
Low	Remembering	Remembering, recognising, recalling

Figure 4: Anderson and Krathwohl's revised taxonomy. **Source:** Anderson and Krathwohl, 2001.

Differentiation through talk

Teachers use talk for reasons other than to ask questions, particularly to explain geographical ideas. This is another area where you can and should differentiate by varying what you say and the way you speak to individuals, small groups or to the whole class.

In explaining geographical ideas you can use the same resource for all students but explain the geographical processes at different levels of complexity. For example, if you displayed the photograph in Figure 5 of a meandering river in Scotland you might expect all students to understand that the river curves, to use the term meander and to be able to describe it, even if only in simple language. Evidence of erosion on the outer side of the bends, where water is flowing more quickly, can be clearly seen, and deposition where water is flowing less quickly. For some students it may be enough to identify these features as sandbanks and steep river banks and label them as such on a diagram. You might expect more able students to annotate their diagram to show they understand how and why these features have formed, and of course some will be able to use geographical terminology such as slip-off slope, deposition, undercutting and bluff. It is possible for you to describe and explain the processes to all students, but expect some to understand more than others and to learn, and be able to use, more geographical terminology. The task you set after your verbal explanation to the class would differ for different groups of students; for example, some might have a diagram to label, others might be expected to annotate the diagram and the most able might also be expected to use key geographical terminology to write an explanation of how meanders develop.

Strategies for differentiation in geography

In general you will find it more manageable and less time consuming to use the same lesson resources for all students and to differentiate through the questions you ask and the tasks you devise. Occasionally you may decide to create different resources that take account of different students' ability to read, understand or interpret material; however, this requires more work in advance and can also be more difficult to organise in the classroom.

Whatever your approach you will need to plan carefully. Sometimes you may decide that you will set the same work for all students but have different expectations of what they will achieve; at other times you may decide that not all students need to do the same work and set different tasks.

Some examples of strategies you could use which start with the whole class working together from the same resources are listed below.

Layers of inference

This activity has been adapted from Margaret Roberts' 'layers of inference' framework in *Geography Through Enquiry* (2013). You could use this approach across all key stages and with students of all abilities. The source could be a photograph (as shown in Figure 6), a diagram, a graph, a table of statistics or a short extract from a newspaper, selected as appropriate for the class. The activity is best organised for small groups of two to four students. It is definitely not an activity to be done individually, because the conversations the students have within the group are important and help them to learn.

Figure 5: Meandering river, East Lothian, Scotland. **Photo** Richard West, reproduced under Creative Commons licence (CC BY-SA 2.0).

If you choose to have mixed ability groups the least able can be supported by others in the group and all should be able to participate.

The photograph in Figure 6 shows a child on the Payatas Garbage Dump in Quezon City in The Philippines. Almost every student should be able to suggest some ideas for each section of the task starting with 'What does the photograph tell me?' As you talk to each group you will be able to indicate that the photograph provides very little factual evidence, particularly if you have not told them where the photograph was taken. Many students will start by putting their assumptions under 'What does the photograph tell me?' and you will need to challenge them about this, asking them how they know something is a fact. If they are actually making assumptions, these should be listed under 'What can I infer or guess from the photograph?'

I have found that most students enjoy this activity and it creates what Roberts (2013) refers to as 'a need to know'; a curiosity to find answers to their questions and the motivation to learn more. You should be ready for students to suggest unexpected questions that may be difficult to answer; all students' questions should be valued. Although you may not initially tell the class where the photo was taken, it is important to have this information for your later discussion. You should also be careful not to perpetuate stereotypical views, in this case explaining that although some people in The Philippines live in shanty towns and are very poor many other people are not, and indeed Quezon City is a prosperous and dynamic place. After this activity you could ask students to carry out research into Quezon City and The Philippines and people who earn a living by picking through rubbish. Quezon City was the capital of The Philippines between 1948 and 1976, and an internet search will provide lots of images showing it as modern, busy and prosperous. There are also plenty of good video clips online showing how families survive

Key question being investigated:

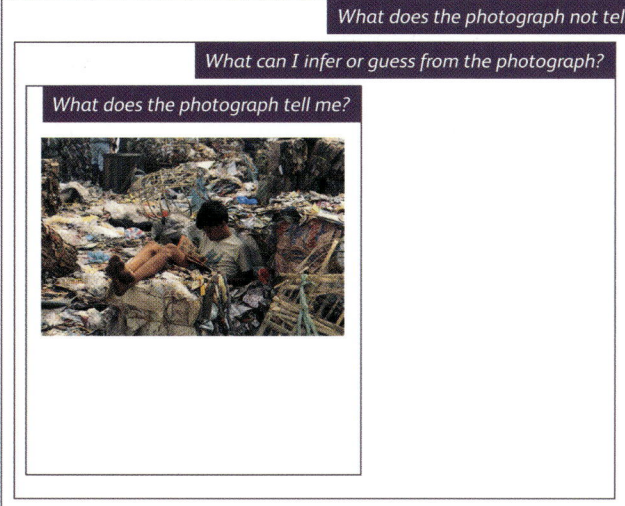

Figure 6:
Layers of inference.
Photo © Licence Free.

by sorting rubbish and the dangers they face doing this work. Alternatively you could select supporting resources of your own and set more structured tasks, perhaps using a writing frame for those who need most support, or you could ask them to act out, or draw or write a poem about, what they have learnt.

This photograph and other ideas about how to use it can be found on the GA website: www.geography.org.uk/resources/adifferentview/imagesandactivities

Storyboard

Don't be put off using a storyboard with more able or older students; it works well with a range of age groups and abilities, so is also useful for differentiation. It is always important to remind students that they do not have to be good at drawing for this exercise as the strategy is designed to help them to understand and remember events, and the process of thinking about how to change words into pictures helps them to do this. You will be able to illustrate this by asking them to re-tell the story at a later date, even in another lesson: most will remember a surprising amount of detail.

Choose an issue or event that has a story or a chronological series of events. The example used in Figure 7 is based on the eruption of Mount Ontake in Japan in September 2014.

It occurred without warning, killing 48 people. The eruption was unusual in being a phreatic eruption, the result of ground water turning to steam and causing an explosion. Storyboards work well for actual events such as this one, or a flood, a hurricane, or an earthquake, but can also be used for stories about changes in employment or migration. Stories focusing on one character usually work best. You can easily write your own text for the story although you should be careful to make it accurate and not too long or complex – six to eight frames works best – and students can either draw their own frames or you can give them a ready prepared sheet divided into frames. Make sure they number each frame in advance so they know where successive pictures should be drawn. Older and more able students can be expected to work faster; whatever the group's ability, this strategy works best if the pace is kept high and there is a time limit – perhaps 90 seconds – for drawing each frame. Similarly, decide how many times you will read each section of text (probably twice) and do not give way to calls for reading it again. It is sometimes useful to leave the final frame for the students to decide for themselves what might happen next. This is also a useful starting point for your questions and discussions once they have finished the task.

Figure 7:
Text for storyboard (Eruption of Mount Ontake, Japan).

Japan, Saturday 27 September 2014, 11.52 a.m. local time: Mount Ontake, an active volcano on Honshu Island, erupted without warning. Gas inhalation, and injuries from impacts with rock and ash bound together in pyroclastic flows, killed 48 hikers and injured 69 other people.

1. It was a beautiful autumnal Saturday morning in September, and Kazuto was up early for a day's hiking. He was wearing warm clothes and strong hiking boots and had extra clothes, food and drink in his rucksack. He set off with three friends, planning to reach the summit of the nearby Mount Ontake.
2. Mount Ontake is just over 3000m high and because it is a volcano it is not surrounded by other mountains. It is a relatively easy climb and Kazuto and his friends made good progress through the trees and up onto the rocky slopes, stopping after two hours at a mountain hut with spectacular views before climbing the final and steepest part of the trail to the top.
3. Thanks to their early start, Kazuto and his friends reached the summit at about 11.15 a.m. A cable car brings less active visitors close to the summit, and there were plenty of other people walking around the crater or simply admiring the view.
4. After a short stop and a quick bite to eat the friends set off back down, passing many other hikers on their way up. There were lots of people on the mountain, making the most of one of the last days it would be possible to climb the mountain before winter snow made it too difficult and dangerous.
5. Suddenly, without any warning, there was a loud explosion and a huge plume of ash and smoke was thrown up into the air from the summit behind them. It was just before 12.00 noon, and the volcano was erupting. Kazuto and his friends looked back and saw a huge black cloud moving towards them. Kazuto managed to take a couple of photos on his phone before they all started to run downhill as fast as they could.
6. The friends soon realised they could not outrun the eruption; already they could feel hot ash beginning to settle on their jackets and hear rocks landing behind them. Kazuto spotted a hut ahead of them and they started to run faster, covering their faces to avoid breathing in the dust and gases.
7. Dozens of people were crammed inside the building. It was being covered by ash and bombarded by rocks, penetrating ceilings and walls and shattering windows. Worried about the risk of toxic gases, everyone kept their faces covered.
8. Create a picture of your own to complete this storyboard.

Shared views

You may have used a strategy in which a group of students works together on a topic; each student becomes 'an expert' in one aspect of the topic, and then returns to the group to complete a task such as creating a poster or presentation about the whole topic. For example, this could be done for a country study, where students become 'experts' about certain aspects of the country before returning to their original group to make a complete country fact file. Alternatively it could be used to look at different areas of land use in a city, with the group presenting a city transect, or for flood management strategies, with the group drawing up a flood protection plan. One problem with this approach is that the individual 'experts' tend to collect written information in the form of notes and once back with the group they simply copy this down or dictate it to others and there is little shared learning. Another problem is that it may be difficult for the least able to keep up or manage this activity and it may not be challenging enough for the most able.

An alternative approach, which I have found works better and is more inclusive, I call 'shared views'.

Figure 8: Coral Cay information sheet.

Photo © Laszlo Ilyes, reproduced under Creative Commons licence (CC BY 2.0).

Photo © Pat Hawks, reproduced under Creative Commons licence (CC BY 2.0).

Coral Cay Conservation

Nicknamed the Emerald Isle of the Caribbean, Montserrat is home to lush green vegetation and sapphire blue waters. Stunning scenery houses a wealth of unique wildlife, with many fascinating species found nowhere else in the world. However, following a series of volcanic eruptions on the island, which began in 1995, Montserrat's tropical forests and coral reefs have come under increasing pressure and now work needs to be done to help preserve these extraordinary ecosystems for the future.

Coral Cay Conservation is delivering an exciting 'ridge to reef' project on Montserrat, working in partnership with the Government of Montserrat and the RSPB. The project has a holistic approach, with scientific survey programmes to collect data from both tropical forests and coral reefs, accompanied by community education programmes and local capacity building.

As a volunteer, you can choose to join either the marine or terrestrial project, or even take part in both. All volunteers get to be involved in survey work specific to their project, as well as have a chance to join the team in delivering community education programmes.

Source: www.coralcay.org/volunteer/montserrat

A maximum of four mixed ability students work together around a table. The resources are chosen around an enquiry question such as 'Is ecotourism sustainable?' or 'What is the best way to protect Exetown from flooding?' Each group is given one resource or information sheet to study (see Figure 8) and every student is given a worksheet to complete (see Figure 9). In addition each table has a marker pen and a large piece of paper (flip chart size) that has the name of the project written on it in large letters. Students read and discuss the information they are given and all complete their own worksheet; then they summarise their views on the paper, perhaps as the beginning of a spider diagram. Each group moves on to the next table to look at a different information sheet, complete their worksheets and add their views to the paper. You can move the groups on as many times as you like but, if time does not allow, it is not necessary for every group to read and respond to every information sheet. While they are working you should go round supporting any students who need help (although their group may also be supporting them) and directing more challenging questions to the more able, who might also be asked to prepare a summary of the views about one of the projects on the paper. Later, you will also be able to differentiate as you question the class about their views and in the follow-up tasks you ask them to complete. This approach is accessible to most students and helps them see a range of views about an issue and to develop their own opinions.

Figure 9: Worksheet for shared views activity, using Coral Cay information. NB The worksheet should have space for information about all of the resource sheets you are working with.

Is ecotourism sustainable?

Name of ecotourism: *Coral Cay Conservation*

Location: *Montserrat, an island in the Caribbean*

Brief description: *This is an activity holiday where volunteers take part in a scientific research project and…*

Sustainable aspects: ....

Unsustainable aspects/other issues: ....

Overall assessment (circle one):

very sustainable   sustainable

unsustainable   very unsustainable

Name of ecotourism: ....
Location: ....
Brief description: ....
Sustainable aspects: ....
Unsustainable aspects/other issues: ....
Overall assessment (circle one):

very sustainable   sustainable

unsustainable   very unsustainable

Concept maps

Thinking Through Geography (TTG) (Leat, 1998) and *More Thinking Through Geography* (MTTG) (Nichols, 2001) introduced geography teachers to a range of approaches and ideas that gave students the responsibility for learning and working through ideas. They were encouraged to think for themselves rather than rely on a teacher giving them facts and telling them what to do and what to think. Concept maps are introduced in the second book (MTTG) as a way of 'helping pupils to make sense of complexity, marshal their ideas and ultimately produce more coherent and sophisticated explanations of geographical patterns' (Nichols, 2001, p. 108). Concept maps are one way of helping students to think about cause and effect and are a useful way to organise ideas, perhaps as a precursor to a written task or even an assessment. Although concept maps are sometimes used at the start of a topic to see what students already know, my view is that they are best introduced at the end of a topic, as they enable students to apply and consolidate their knowledge and understanding.

Arrange your class into groups of three students and give each group a piece of A3 paper, a set of concept cards (an example is given in Figure 10) and a glue stick. The students write the topic ('Factors affecting severity of flooding') on the A3 sheet and stick the concept cards around it. Ask the students to indicate with a line as many links as they can and to write beside the line or as a key what this link is (see example in Figure 11), with explanations (to show the link has been discussed). You can go round the class, prompting groups to consider links they might not have

amount of rainfall	type of bedrock
relief of the land	time (of day, day of week, time of year)
amount of building on the flood plain	agricultural land use
emergency services	wealth of country
access to mobile devices (handheld computers)	river management in place
antecedent rainfall	type of building on the flood plain

Figure 10: Concept cards for factors affecting the severity of flooding. The shaded cards could be given to more able students only.

thought of themselves. You can use concept maps with students of any ability, and mixed ability groups can support each other.

An alternative would be to arrange the groups by ability, giving fewer concept cards to those needing support and more cards, perhaps up to about 12, to higher achieving students. Figure 10 shows 12 cards but you could reserve the four shaded cards for the most able students. As with the other suggested activities, differentiation can also be achieved through your questioning while students are completing their concept maps, your management of any class discussion afterwards, and in the tasks you set following this.

Dragons' Den

Many students enjoy role-play activities and it is an excellent way to help them understand that different groups of people may have very different and sometimes strongly held opinions. My experience, however, is that despite the students' initial excitement at the idea of taking part in a role play the reality can be difficult to manage, not least because students tend to read from prepared notes and don't always present the key points of their argument well. An alternative is to use this Dragons' Den strategy, which follows the format of the BBC programme. This works well as part of a decision-making lesson, such as deciding on the best way to manage a section of eroding coastline, choosing between several locations for a new housing estate or choosing the most appropriate form of aid for a squatter settlement on the edge of a developing world city. Before using this approach you need to be sure students have a good understanding of the topic you are studying so they can make sound decisions. It is a good strategy for involving all students, no matter what their ability, and you might be surprised by the quality of some of the pitches made by your lower achievers, or those with specific learning needs such as Asperger's syndrome or dyslexia.

Having selected your theme you will need to decide how many groups of students you want and prepare information sheets for each, with details about the scheme they will be pitching in the Dragons' Den. For example, for coastal management one group could argue for groynes, one for a sea wall, one for revetments, one for managed retreat, etc. I suggest groups of three or four so you can get all students involved yet still leave enough time in the lesson for all the groups to make their pitch. One group should be designated Dragons; for this you might want to select more able and more confident students. Each of the remaining groups will make their pitch, then answer questions posed by the Dragons. The key to this is that the pitchers prepare in advance and do not use any notes, just as in the BBC programme. Indeed, you could show a short video clip for those not familiar with the show and discuss what makes a good pitch and one likely to get the Dragons' support. At the end of all the pitches the Dragons will make a decision and must justify both why they have chosen this particular scheme and why each of the others was rejected. Follow-up work can be tailored to the needs of the class and will vary depending on your learning objectives.

Figure 11:
Examples of links and explanations.

1. Higher rainfall is more likely to cause floods, and more rain will usually make floods worse.
2. New housing built on the flood plain makes floods worse as there are more impermeable surfaces. Drains might not be able to cope with all the water.
3. If most people have smart phones, they can receive warnings about flooding and be told to evacuate their houses.
4. More people have access to mobile devices in wealthier countries.
5. If people have access to mobile devices, emergency services can send out information about the floods and what they should do if they need help.

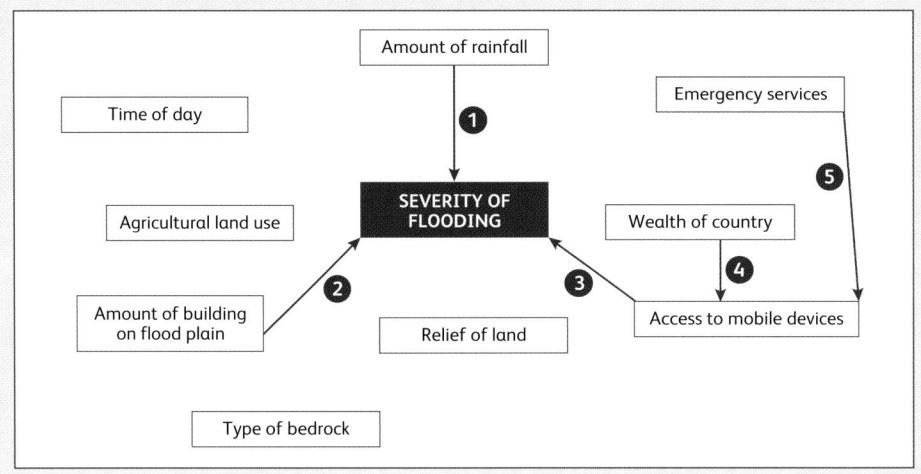

Structured independent learning

The term independent learning has been used in schools and advocated by Ofsted over a number of years. Many teachers are reluctant to try it, thinking it means just letting students get on by themselves and feeling anxious that they will consequently make little progress. This is not the case, because although independent learning involves a transfer of responsibility from teacher to student it does not mean leaving students to their own devices. The process must be scaffolded and supported by the teacher but allow students some autonomy, which encourages them to become involved in managing and organising their own learning. This in turn can increase motivation significantly.

Giving students a choice about what they study is important and you should try to do this on a regular basis. It is also another way for you to differentiate, as you can tailor your support to help individuals according to their needs, be this for extra stretch and challenge or for more specific needs. Some schools incorporate structured independent learning tasks with choice by periodically setting students what might be termed project work: this might be for a limited number of weeks, or lessons, or it might be homework. Either way, projects should not last too long as students either get bored or simply put off doing any work as the deadline is too far away.

Other projects could be based on travel around one country – either the UK or further afield, for example India or Australia – and this would help to consolidate important locational knowledge. Alternatively projects could focus on case studies of volcanic eruptions, earthquakes and tsunamis or extreme weather events. Again, it would be possible to let students choose both the example studied and the way the information is presented. I would emphasise that you cannot just send students off to do this work without any help, but the amount and type of help you provide can vary according to need. With the most able it will also be important for you to make your expectations clear and encourage them to present the best work that they can.

Conclusion

It will always be a challenge for teachers to help all their students to learn and make progress, given the fact that most classes have students of a wide range of ability. However, this is what you must try to do. Planning how to do this is a first step but it is equally important to reflect on your strategies afterwards and modify them as appropriate. Talking to colleagues, especially colleagues or teaching assistants who might have watched the lesson, will help you to evaluate it; it is also important to discuss different approaches with the students themselves.

In his book *Lessons are for Learning*, Hughes (1997) wrote that students should 'leave a classroom at the end of a lesson knowing, understanding and being able to do more than when they came in' (p. 13). You need to strive to meet this challenge in every lesson.

References

Anderson, L.W. and Krathwohl, D.R. (eds) (2001) *A Taxonomy for Learning, Teaching, and Assessing: A revision of Bloom's taxonomy of educational objectives*. New York, NY: Longman.

Bloom, B.S. (ed) (1956) *Taxonomy of Educational Objectives: The classification of educational goals. Handbook 1: Cognitive domain*. New York, NY: David McKay.

DfE (2014) *National Curriculum in England: Framework for key stages 1–4*. London: DfE. Available at: www.gov.uk/government/publications/national-curriculum-in-england-framework-for-key-stages-1-to-4 (last accessed 08/11/2016).

DfES (2004) *Pedagogy and Practice: Teaching and learning in secondary schools. Unit 7: Questioning*. London: DfES.

DfES (2006) *Primary National Strategy: Leading on intervention: a resource to support leadership teams and leading teachers*. London: DfES.

Evans, L. and Smith, D. (2006) 'Inclusive geography' in Balderstone, D. (ed) *Secondary Geography Handbook*. Sheffield: Geographical Association, pp. 332–53.

Ferretti, J. (2007) *Meeting the Needs of Your Most Able Pupils: Geography*. Abingdon: Routledge.

Ferretti, J. and Totterdell, R. (2011) *Life on the Edge: A study of extreme environments*. Sheffield: Geographical Association.

Hughes, M. (1997) *Lessons are for Learning*. Stafford: Network Educational Press.

Jones, M. (2013) 'What is personalised learning in geography?' in Lambert, D. and Jones, M. (eds) *Debates in Geography Education*. Abingdon: Routledge, pp. 116–28.

Lambert, D. and Balderstone, D. (2010) *Learning to Teach Geography in the Secondary School* (second edition). Abingdon: Routledge.

Leat, D. (1998) *Thinking Through Geography*. Cambridge: Chris Kington Publishing.

Lewis, M. and Wray, D. (1996) *Writing Frames: Scaffolding children's non-fiction writing in a range of genres*. Reading: University of Reading, Reading and Language Information Centre.

Nichols, A. (ed) with Kinninment, D. (2001) *More Thinking Through Geography*. Cambridge: Chris Kington Publishing.

Roberts, M. (2013) *Geography Through Enquiry: Approaches to teaching and learning in the secondary school*. Sheffield: Geographical Association.

Sebba, J., Brown, N., Steward, S., Galton, M. and James, M. (2007) *An Investigation of Personalised Learning Approaches Used By Schools*. Nottingham: DfES Publications.

Swift, D. (2005) *Meeting Special Educational Needs in the Curriculum: Geography*. Abingdon: Routledge.

Wallace, B. (2000) *Teaching the Very Able Child*. London: NACE/Fulton.

Wray, D. and Lewis, M. (1997) *Extending Literacy: Children reading and writing non-fiction*. Abingdon: Routledge.

Recommended key readings

Roberts, M. (2013) *Geography Through Enquiry: Approaches to teaching and learning in the secondary school*. Sheffield: Geographical Association.

This book has a wealth of practical examples of many of the strategies for differentiation suggested in this chapter, including layers of inference and concept maps. It also discusses some of the issues facing geography teachers in the classroom and encourages reflection.

Jones, M. (2013) 'What is personalised learning in geography?' in Lambert, D. and Jones, M. (eds) *Debates in Geography Education*. Abingdon: Routledge, pp. 116–28.

This chapter sets out the policy and whole-school context for personalised learning before considering the implications for practice. At the classroom level, different interpretations of differentiation and personalised learning are discussed. In particular it suggests 'differentiation by interest' is possible through providing students with greater choice and 'voice' in geography lessons.

Chapter 14

Assessing geography

Paul Weeden is a retired lecturer in education who has taught, researched and written extensively in the fields of assessment and geographical education

Introduction

The theme of climate change is being explored in a year 9 lesson. The teacher starts by asking the class to write three things they know about climate change. Students share these with a neighbour and then the teacher pulls all their different ideas together and lists them on the whiteboard for the whole class to see. During this early part of the lesson the teacher is collecting and recording ideas while mentally noting common themes and possible misconceptions. In the next phase of the lesson a short video is shown that presents some 'facts' about climate change; then the students are asked in pairs to do a 'card-sort' exercise, categorising statements into human or natural causes of climate change. The teacher then questions selected students, asking them to justify and develop their categorisation. Sometimes other students are asked to help out or to say whether they agree or disagree with the categorisations. In the final task the students are asked to consider their responses to two different opinions – that climate change is the result of people's actions or that it is a naturally occurring phenomenon. They have to write a definition of climate change and then explain potential causes.

The lesson on climate change above shows how informal low-stakes assessment can be used on a day-to-day basis in the classroom to promote learning while still collecting evidence about students' performance. Sadly, discussion about assessment is too often focused on more formal high-stakes examinations. This chapter describes how approaches and attitudes to assessment have changed over time (see Figure 1 for a summary). While some of these changes have been imposed as the result of shifting political opinion many of them have sound educational and social foundations.

The chapter discusses different purposes of assessment and gives examples of assessment strategies that can be used on a day-to-day basis. It discusses the benefits and challenges of using assessment for learning to collect and record evidence of 'progress' in geography.

Assessment and government policy

National assessment structures in England and Wales in the second half of the twentieth century retained and developed many features of the tripartite system of external assessment developed after the Second World War. In the 1960s the top 20% of 16-year-old students took GCE O-levels; the next 40% took CSEs; the bottom 40% took no examinations at all. Students therefore effectively followed academic, vocational or occupational routes through the education system. A variety of factors, including the raising of the school leaving age to 16 in 1975, increased opportunities for higher education, changes in types of economic activity and a desire for a more equitable society, resulted in the aspiration that all students should gain formal external qualifications.

Until the 1980s assessment was largely left to educationalists. Schools decided their curricula and some teachers were involved in setting and marking externally administered examinations through local examination consortia. Little information was available about the relative performance of students in different schools. Since the 1990s there has been increased 'standardisation' and data collection about individual and school performance. Successive national governments have sought to assert their authority over schools by centralised control of teaching, curriculum and assessment, through measures such as prescribed methods of teaching, a statutory National Curriculum, reduced diversity of external assessments and the publication of data about school performance. There is now an increased role for the 'market', both in school choice and school type, allowing parents to compare schools by the outcomes of external assessments such as the General Certificate of Secondary Education (GCSE) and school inspections (by Ofsted). The policy rhetoric has been about personalisation and choice at the individual level alongside increasing accountability for schools and teachers in an effort to raise standards.

The GCSE qualification, introduced in the late 1980s, also increased centralisation. National and subject criteria (standards) were introduced and there was a major reorganisation and rationalisation of the external examination system. In England, the number of examination boards (awarding bodies) was reduced from over 20 to three (AQA, Edexcel and OCR) and the choice of geography specifications was reduced. Students in England can also take specifications set by the Welsh examination board (WJEC Eduqas). However, elements of the tripartite system of assessment were retained, with a grade 'C' becoming the usual criteria for progression into a more academic pathway. In geography this was formalised in 1996 by the introduction of tiered papers, with students taking GCSE Higher Tier, GCSE Lower Tier or Certificate of Achievement examinations. While this had advantages – questions could be targeted at different attainments – it also meant that there were 'ceilings' to performance, for example Lower Tier papers covered C–G grades only. From the 2016–18 examination cycle government regulations require common papers for all GCSE geography examinations (Ofqual, 2015).

The GCSE was based on the premise that all students should be enabled to show what they 'know, understand and can do' so different approaches to assessment were introduced to increase the validity of the assessment. In geography, teacher-assessed fieldwork activities provided students with opportunities to demonstrate their enquiry skills through coursework. Over time, in response to concerns about reliability and fears that parents or teachers were assisting students too much, the value of these assessments was reduced to

1. Formal qualifications
- Movement from a *laissez-faire* approach to assessment to a more formal, structured approach.
- Expectation that all children will be formally assessed throughout their school career.
- Increased use of formal qualifications (GCSE/A level) to measure and certify student performance.
- Increased emphasis on qualifications as an entry to the next stage of lifelong learning.
- Changes to the format and structure of examinations.
- Increased transparency and standardisation of formal assessment structures.

2. Formative assessment
- Focus on improving learning in the classroom by using formative assessment approaches (assessment for learning and assessment as learning):
  a. questioning
  b. peer- and self-assessment
  c. feedback and next steps.
- Increased collection of data on individual progress by many schools.
- Debates about progression and attempts to clarify progression within geography.

3. Evaluation and accountability
- Increased collection of data and its use for accountability purposes for both teachers and schools.
- Political discourse focused on standards and target setting.
- Use of 'league tables' to compare schools.

25% of the final mark; and from 2009 they were conducted in 'controlled' conditions. From the 2016–18 examination cycle GCSE assessment will be through terminal written examinations (DfE, 2014). This illustrates

Figure 1: Changes in assessment practice in England and Wales.

Figure 2: Reliability, validity and standards.

Term	Meaning
Reliability	Reliability is about the assessment performing the same way whenever it is used.
Validity	Validity is about whether the assessment actually measures what it is supposed to measure.
Standards	Standards are difficult to compare over time and between schools because examination format and content changes, contextual factors differ and assessors vary. Awarding bodies spend time and money attempting to make examinations 'fair' but performance is still often strongly linked to school attended and socio-economic factors.

the tension present in any assessment where there is a trade-off between reliability, validity, manageability and educational impact (Figure 2). In this case the assessment has been changed by political decisions that take little account of the educational value of different assessment methods.

The introduction of the National Curriculum in 1988 saw proposals for a national system of assessment (Task Group on Assessment and Testing (TGAT), 1988) that had four purposes: formative, diagnostic, summative and evaluative (Figure 3). The TGAT report is a sophisticated document: it was only partially implemented, but it has had an important impact on assessment in schools. TGAT recognised that capturing the breadth of student capabilities is difficult to achieve by a single assessment method or instrument. Teacher assessment was recognised as providing important information about students. The ambitious national programme of assessment quickly proved to be unmanageable in terms of time and cost; but it did provide opportunities for teachers to meet and moderate work across schools.

Although pilot materials were produced and trialled for geography SATs, national summative tests were restricted to English, mathematics and science. For geography and the other foundation subjects, reporting of teacher assessments at the end of the key stage was introduced. The first revision of the National Curriculum in 1995 replaced the original 183 discrete statements of attainment with criteria-based level descriptors (from levels one to eight, plus exceptional performance) that attempted to provide a broad-brush view of progression. This was not perfect but it did provide a common language for teachers about standards that could be applied nationally. There were still problems about interpretation and consistency between teachers and schools, but exemplification materials from national bodies (SCAA and QCA) provided useful guidelines and assessments. They also encouraged discussion about common national standards.

A further major change in assessment has occurred since 2000. Research evidence (Black and Wiliam, 1998) about formative assessment, often referred to as Assessment for Learning (AfL), as an effective method of raising standards led to the promotion of AfL through the National Strategies (see for example DfES, 2004; DCSF, 2008). Formative assessment is a vital part of your day-to-day work in the classroom. This change has improved the quality of assessment, teaching and learning in many schools because teachers are now less inclined to regard assessment as an afterthought. Instead they systematically seek ways to collect evidence about current performance (baseline and diagnostic assessment) and use this knowledge to help students 'bridge the gap' between their current performance and intended outcomes. Within geography, materials have been produced to assist teachers. These include *Geography Inside the Black Box* (Weeden and Lambert, 2006); the GA's Making Geography Happen project (GA, 2011); *Assessing Progress in your Key Stage 3 Geography Curriculum* (Gardner et al., 2015) and numerous articles in the journal *Teaching Geography*. Strategies such as better questioning, feedback and feed-forward, peer- and self-assessment and formative use of summative tests have helped teachers to support student learning more effectively.

Accountability has meant that successive governments have prioritised the evaluative element of the TGAT proposals. A number of outcome measures have been used to evaluate schools' performance and to set challenging targets in an effort to raise standards. The problem with this is that the high-stakes evaluative performance measures were often relatively blunt instruments, and failed to reflect significant contextual differences between schools. They also had a number of unintended consequences, such as increasing social segregation as aspirational parents moved their children to 'higher performing' schools, and schools being encouraged to 'game' with performance outcomes by focusing on C/D borderline candidates – or entering students for 'easier' subjects. The importance of these outcome measures in modifying behaviour in schools can be illustrated by the increased number of entries for GCSE geography since 2012, which can be largely attributed to the introduction of the English Baccalaureate (EBacc) performance measure in 2010. Schools that previously had a wide range of option choices have encouraged students to take either geography or history to boost the school's EBacc performance score. This trend is likely to continue with the introduction of the Progress 8 performance measure in 2016 and 2017 because geography and history are subjects included in this new measure.

The use of 'big data' has also increased over the last ten years, since the introduction of the National Pupil Database (NPD). On entry to school each student is given a unique number and their performance tracked over time. This data has been analysed by organisations such as RAISEonline and Fischer Family Trust and is increasingly used by Ofsted and schools to measure performance and provide evidence of progress. Schools have used previous performance to predict and track under- or over-performance by individual students. This requires teachers to report progress on a regular basis and led to the sub-division of National Curriculum levels, e.g. L5c, L5b and L5a, which in a subject like geography makes little or no sense (see Hopkin, 2006, for a more detailed discussion). Progress is difficult to summarise using grades or sub-grades because students will almost always have done well on one aspect of the subject and not so well on another.

- Formative, so that the positive achievements of a student may be recognised and discussed and the appropriate next steps may be planned.

- Diagnostic, through which learning difficulties may be scrutinised and classified so that appropriate remedial help and guidance can be provided.

- Summative, for the recording of the overall achievement of a student in a systematic way.

- Evaluative, by means of which some aspects of the work of a school, an LEA or other discrete part of the educational service can be assessed and/or reported upon.

While a number (level) is a simple way of recording performance, it does not help the student make progress. For example, 'description' may occur in any piece of work but will vary in sophistication, so it is too simplistic to tell students that description is a level 4 feature while explanation is at level 5. They need to know which areas of knowledge they are good at and what they can do to improve, in specific terms that relate to geography, not a recording system. Teachers can better help students improve their work by getting them to understand what makes descriptions or explanations better. The SOLO taxonomy (Structure of Observed Learning Outcomes) proposed by Biggs and Collis describes five stages of increasing complexity in a student's understanding of a subject, It has been used to describe differences in the quality of description or explanation in geography moving from simple to more complex relationships (George *et al.*, 2002).

Using levels to record progress has also been challenged by changes to the National Curriculum. From September 2014 National Curriculum levels are no longer required, because they are:

'complicated and difficult to understand, especially for parents. [The levels system] also encourages teachers to focus on a

Figure 3: Purposes of assessment and testing. **Source:** TGAT, 1988, para 23.

pupil's current level, rather than consider more broadly what the pupil can actually do. Prescribing a single detailed approach to assessment does not fit with the curriculum freedoms we are giving schools.

Schools will be able to introduce their own approaches to formative assessment, to support pupil attainment and progression. The assessment framework should be built into the school curriculum, so that schools can check what pupils have learned and whether they are on track to meet expectations at the end of the key stage, and so that they can report regularly to parents' (DfE, 2013).

The dilemma for departments is how to devise a system that more broadly represents both what a student can do now and the progress they have made. The GA (2014) has provided guidance on possible approaches and will continue to work with schools and teachers to update these ideas as teachers get to grips with the implications of these changes. The rest of this chapter highlights some of the issues.

Assessment in the geography classroom

Figure 4 summarises the key features of the main types of assessment commonly used in the geography classroom. The lesson described at the start of this chapter allows us to explore some of the changes and continuities in assessment that have been discussed previously.

- What is the purpose of the assessment?
- What assessment opportunities were there in the lesson on climate change?
- What challenges are there for the teacher in collecting, interpreting, recording and using information about students' responses to the geographical tasks undertaken?

Referring to Figure 4 and the three questions above, the lesson is an example of day-to-day assessment for learning (formative assessment) where the purpose is to use assessment to establish where students are now, identify any misconceptions they may have and help them make progress. There are assessment opportunities throughout the lesson as the teacher finds out what different students know through questioning, observation and dialogue. The lesson has its challenges: difficulties arise because the teacher interacts with many students and cannot formally record or reflect on them all. While some evidence will be recorded in written responses that can be evaluated later, much of the evidence will be ephemeral and only recorded informally in the teacher's memory.

Planning for assessment

To make the most of day-to-day assessment opportunities it is essential to be clear about the differences between the three common purposes of assessment (Figure 4) and the timescale in which they operate (Figure 5). It is also helpful to recognise that many of the interactions that occur in 'normal' teaching are also evidence of student misconceptions, knowledge and progress: what you need is to find ways to use this data more constructively. The rest of the chapter introduces some of the strategies that have been used successfully in geography classrooms. The GA website and publications are a good source of ideas for taking these strategies further.

Formative assessment should be an ongoing, classroom-based, day-to-day affair designed to promote and support student learning, not an afterthought or bolt-on activity. Planning for assessment opportunities should therefore be an integral part of any scheme of work or lesson plan. Teachers should take the opportunities provided by interactions with individual students and classes to assess performance informally and to provide feedback and feed-forward. Assessments tend to be low-stakes in themselves but can be designed to promote beneficial outcomes, such as a better understanding of how to make an answer more 'geographically literate'.

Assessment is too often regarded as remote from classroom activity; something that happens to students at the end of their course in quiet exam halls. In the context of high-stakes public examinations summative assessment (AoL) is separate from teaching and learning: the means of assessment (exam papers) come into the school from outside, the scripts are sent elsewhere to be marked and the student receives a

1. Formative assessment or assessment for learning (AfL)

Data is collected about what the students know, understand and can do before you start a lesson or topic. This helps with planning tasks and activities. For example, you might find out that only a few of the class are able to tell you the difference between weather and climate. This allows you to plan lessons and activities that help the majority understand the difference while including tasks that challenge the minority to develop their understanding. You can use data from the start of the lesson to demonstrate how progress has been made during the lesson. Baseline assessment also helps you identify common student misconceptions so that you can revisit these in different ways to promote better understanding.

Once you have established what the students know, understand and can do you can give feedback to help them improve. It is important that you as a teacher have an idea of intended outcomes so that you can help students 'bridge the gap' between what they know already and what you want them to know. AfL builds on baseline assessment, regularly monitors what students know and can do, is useful in ongoing diagnosis of particular difficulties and provides information for teachers about the effectiveness of their teaching. AfL usually involves relatively informal, day to-day processes designed to inform both teacher and student about progress made and attainment achieved. It can involve strategies such as questioning, self- and peer-assessment, feedback and feed-forward.

It is also important to remember that assessment can have a powerful effect on motivation. Students will react in different ways: some may be spurred on to try harder; others put off by comments that question their attitude or the quality of their work. It is therefore important to find ways to celebrate what individuals can do rather than focusing on what they are not (yet) capable of.

2. Summative assessment or assessment of learning (AoL)

This measures achievement at a moment in time, providing teachers, students, the school, parents and carers, Ofsted and the Department for Education (DfE) with information about students' levels of achievement/attainment at different points. It often occurs at the end of a unit of work, academic year or phase of education. Assessment will be more formal and does not provide feedback beyond the grade achieved.

Summative assessment's most 'high-stakes' purpose is to certificate achievement – to recognise a standard achieved in a particular subject (or area of study) through the award of a certificate, or qualification, which has an accepted currency among students, teachers, parents and employers. The GCSE and A level represent accepted certificates of achievement.

3. Evaluation

This uses assessment data to make judgements about the effectiveness of educational systems. Schools are judged by the performance of their students (percentages of students who 'pass' qualifications at different levels) and the progress they make over time. There is considerable debate about the value of the measures used, but the growing availability of performance data has increased the use of evaluation when comparing the quality of teaching and learning in different schools. In recent years this has been extended to comparing the performance of educational systems in different countries around the world.

Figure 4: Three common purposes of assessment.

summary grade some time afterwards. This certification provides a snapshot of performance at a particular time. It is important for opening (or often, unfortunately, closing) gateways to future opportunities in education or employment but is only of day-to-day significance for teachers if examinations are the only focus of teaching in the classroom. Where 'teaching to the test' is the only priority, summative assessment can become overwhelming.

Figure 5: Timescales for assessment.

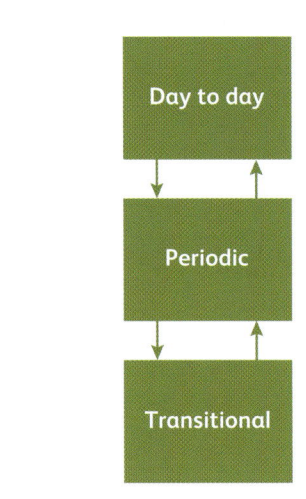

Figure 6 shows how the different purposes and functions of assessment, teaching and learning overlap and are interconnected. It also indicates some of the questions that teachers and students can ask during the assessment process. Importantly, the student being assessed is placed at the centre of the assessment process, and the information collected is used to aid learning through feedback and feed-forward.

Figure 7 is a simple example of how a lesson can be planned to incorporate day-to-day assessment using four key questions:

- What do the students know already? (baseline or diagnostic assessment)
- What are the 'standards' of performance that I want them to achieve?
- How can I help them 'bridge the gap' (scaffold their learning)?
- What evidence is there of progress?

Figure 7 also raises practical issues associated with identifying and recording progress on a day-to-day basis:

- How will we know whether students have achieved their learning objectives if they are not regularly and accurately assessed in the classroom?
- How will they demonstrate what they know, understand and can do if the means of assessment employed do not access this information successfully?
- What types of assessment are valid, reliable and fit for purpose in different learning situations?

In answering these questions, it is important to note that the meaning of 'regularly' will vary dependent on the context. It may be assessment within the lesson, at the end of the lesson, at the beginning of the next lesson or at the end of a module. In terms of the type of assessment to use, different forms of assessment lend themselves to different teaching and learning situations. A multiple-choice format will gather very different information about students' abilities and attainment from assessing them by setting a timed piece of extended writing or a collaborative decision-making exercise. These different forms of assessment are not right or wrong; they simply test different knowledge, understanding, skills and abilities. They may be suitable for certain purposes – possibly the measurement of what students have attained at a particular point – but not for others, such as gauging the effectiveness of the style of teaching used over the past few lessons. This again points to the need for careful thought and action with respect to assessment planning.

The next section gives examples of planning and classroom strategies that use the four key questions. It also discusses some of the benefits and challenges associated with collecting useful assessment information.

Chapter 14: Assessing geography

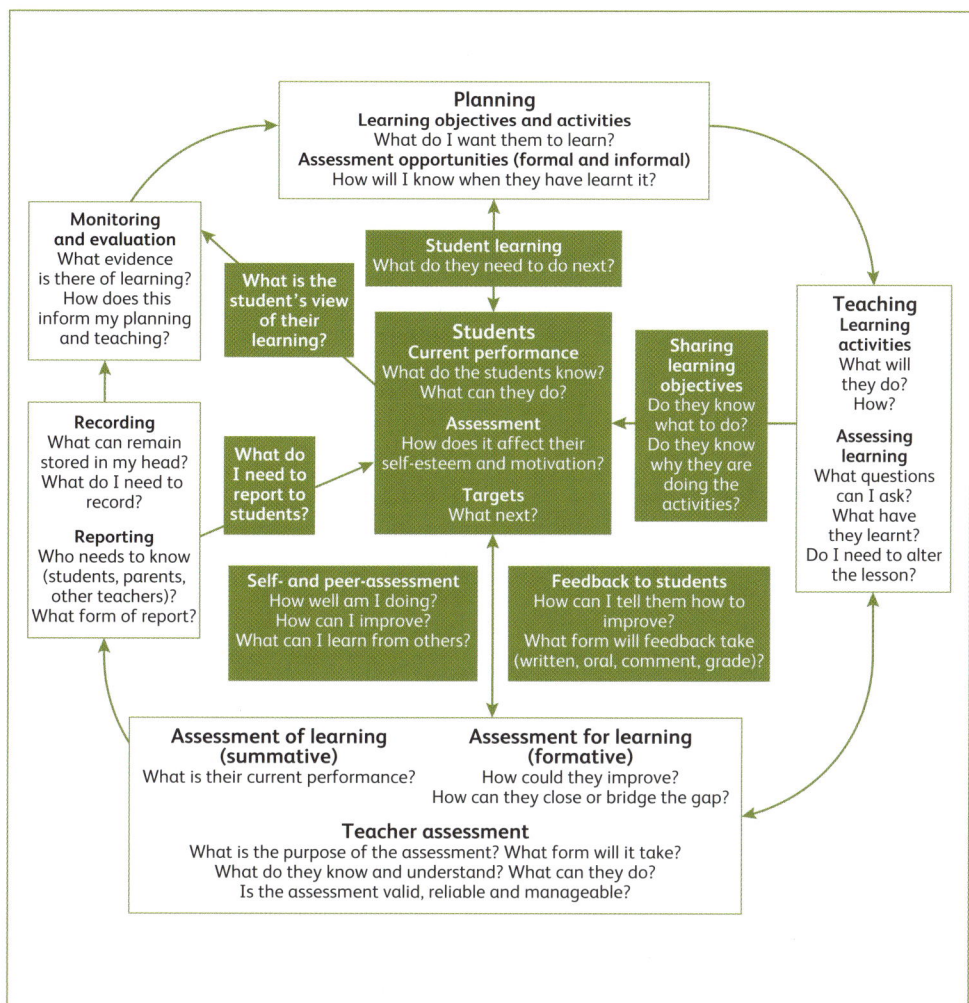

Figure 6:
Teaching, learning and assessment.
Source: Weeden and Hopkin, 2006, p. 415.

What do they know already?

Collecting information about students' prior knowledge should help you identify areas that need to be developed and ones that are less important. Some of the many ways of collecting information include:

- 'Write down three things you know about…' (helps identify knowledge, stereotypes and misconceptions).
- Map skills test, e.g. symbols (establishes which ones the students know already, and how well they have they been learnt).
- Questioning their recall of a previous topic (helps to identify what is remembered and understood or requires revisiting).

- Stimulus picture or task – what does this picture show? (Motivates students and allows you to get a 'sense' of current knowledge.)
- What questions do you have about this? (Can show level of students' understanding of, or personal interest in, current topic.)
- Local issue or problem – mind mapping (helps reveal students' organisational ability and detail of existing knowledge).

The key element in all of these baseline assessments is that you are seeking a better understanding of the existing range of knowledge or skills within the class. This will help you plan the next steps in the lesson or module and also provides a starting point against which evidence of progression can be measured.

189

Figure 7: Lesson on flooding.

> The teacher starts the lesson by asking her students to write down individually three causes of flooding. The lists are then shared in pairs and students are given two minutes to decide on the most important cause and justify their decision. The teacher asks four or five students to tell her their most important cause and allows them to give an explanation. This gives the teacher an indication of the students' current knowledge of the topic (a baseline assessment).
>
> During the lesson a number of activities develop and challenge students' knowledge and understanding. The last activity asks them to use their increased knowledge to analyse the complexity of a recent flood event. The tasks are designed to allow students to demonstrate different abilities, not just copy information. This provides written and oral evidence of their progress during the lesson.
>
> The problem for the teacher is how to identify and record this information for each student. On some occasions evidence will be ephemeral and recorded later. Over time the teacher will accumulate a range of evidence about individual students that can be used to establish their progress.

What are the expected outcomes/standards of performance?

At the start you need to be clear about the expected outcomes. It's not sufficient to say 'I want them to know about flooding'; what do you want them to know? What are the expected 'standards' of performance and what constitutes progress?

The first challenge, therefore, is to identify the 'standards' that individual students have achieved. This has always been a problem. Before the introduction of National Curriculum levels (criteria) and transparency about marking schemes by awarding bodies teachers had no national guidance to help them decide what made better work. There are three main approaches – norm-referenced; criteria-referenced; and ipsative-referenced (Figure 8).

You are marking a written task that your class has done in your lesson: which approach to standard setting will you take? Will you rank students (norm referencing), will you compare each individual with their previous work (ipsative referencing) or will you use a statement of expectations (criteria referencing)? Each of these approaches has advantages and disadvantages and may be used appropriately in different contexts.

While you may feel satisfied with your assessment of students' performance, how do you know that your interpretation of the standard is the same as other teachers in your department or in other schools? Outcomes of national examinations (GCSE and A level) provide one measure but it is important that schools create regular ongoing opportunities to promote a common understanding of standards. The National Foundation for Educational Research (NFER) suggests:

> *'In order to introduce and maintain rigorous and consistent approaches to assessment in schools, novice and established teachers need to develop a culture and discourse of high-quality assessment throughout their careers. The role of professional associations, advisers and schools should be to support this development, so that a shared understanding of assessment can become embedded in classroom practice'* (Brill and Twist, 2013, p. 3).

In the revised National Curriculum, first taught from September 2014, the requirement to report attainment and progress through levels was lifted. This removed a structure that was familiar and usable, if problematic, without providing an alternative vision; a situation that offers both opportunities and challenges for assessment. The opportunities arise from the freedom this provides for teachers to focus on student learning; the challenges arise from the lack of a national structure that provides a shared understanding of assessment.

Norm-referenced	Norm-referenced approaches take the whole cohort and rank them from top to bottom. If the distribution is normal most will group around the mean and there will only be a few at the top or bottom. This works best with large cohorts so the spread represents the whole ability range. In most classes this does not work because the spread of ability is not representative especially when classes are grouped by prior attainment.
Criteria-referenced	Criteria referencing is the use of a statement that describes expected performance. All students, or no students, may be able to achieve this level of performance. Criteria referencing provides a benchmark against which 'standard' judgements can be made. This appears relatively straightforward if we consider something like the high jump: we can set the criterion as being able to jump a height of one metre. However, this does not take account of the age and height of individual competitors. Should allowances be made for these physical differences? It gets even more complicated if we consider more complex standards such as achieving a grade C at GCSE. How can this standard be defined? This has been one of the problems with National Curriculum levels, which are 'best fit' statements about performance that require teachers to make relatively subjective judgements.
Ipsative-referenced	Ipsative referencing compares students' work with their own previous performance so that teachers can assess improved performance.

Figure 8: Three main approaches to assessment.

Bridging the gap: why is understanding progress in geography important?

A further challenge is how to plan for and identify progression. Having found out what students already know, understand and can do, do you have a clear idea of how to develop their knowledge, understanding, skills and values? Will you start with simple ideas (heavy rainfall) or floods they have experienced (recent news items)? How will you make it more complex (introduce ideas about the permeability of different surfaces)? Do you want them to look at floods in different places and at different scales (what impact do floods have on people's lives in different parts of the world)?

Key stage 3 is a crucial time to both support the future 'geographers' in our society and educate geographically-literate citizens, because this may be the only time in their school career that students study geography in a systematic manner. As a geography teacher you need to have a clear idea of how assessment, teaching and learning interact so you can help students acquire and develop geographical capability and use the specialised vocabulary of geography meaningfully. Commonly agreed concepts are the 'language' of geography that give a sense of purpose to learning the subject. The language of geography is held together by the ideas and generalisations (the 'grammar') that geographers have developed to help them better understand and explain the world around them. To make the best use of concepts in assessing performance you will need to clarify your understanding of progression in geography.

What principles of learning underpin progression in geography?

This chapter argues that the integration of assessment, teaching and learning raises standards because both teachers and learners can develop a better understanding of where they are now, what is expected of them, and how to identify the next steps to improve performance. While the approaches to teaching geography may vary, the fundamental ideas or principles of learning and assessment remain the same. Students need opportunities to engage with the subject and teachers should realise that the curriculum is not merely 'content to be delivered' to passive recipients, but a vehicle that can help learners engage with the ideas and concepts of the subject.

Understanding of the subject will change over time as new theories and curriculum priorities emerge. Figure 9 models the process of learning and suggests that personal experiences can be linked to the underpinning ideas and concepts of geography through personal and public

Figure 9: The roots of understanding. **Source:** Bennetts, 2005, p. 154.

Figure 10: Four principles of learning. **After:** Weeden and Lambert, 2006, pp. 6–7.

A first principle of learning is to start from where the learner is and recognise that learning occurs when students have opportunities to connect their personal experiences of the world to the subject of geography and thus reconstruct their understanding. This can be achieved through classroom dialogue – from student to teacher, and teacher to student. If the teacher asks a question that enables students to demonstrate their current thinking, this can be a starting point for the subsequent dialogue about learning and assessment.

A second principle of learning is for students to take an active part in the dialogue – when they are doing the learning. The teacher's role is to create a learning environment where students are prepared to give a range of responses, where either a right or wrong answer is acceptable and where students can be supported in clarifying inconsistencies so they can respond to challenges.

A third principle of learning is that students must know the target they are aiming for. This means they need to know what a good-quality answer looks like and how their work compares with it. Having a grasp of quality criteria helps students take responsibility for their own learning and make judgements about whether the work does or does not meet the criteria. Peer- and self-assessment are essential here, because the process of judging both their own work and that of fellow students encourages active involvement and develops their understanding of expected standards.

A fourth principle of learning is that students should be given opportunities to talk about geographical ideas. This allows them to learn how to actively use the language of geography – the vocabulary and the grammar. This 'scaffolds' their learning, whether in a whole-class dialogue or in peer groups.

dialogue and reflection (Bennetts, 2005). You can help students to make their best progress when you are aware of four principles of learning (Figure 10) and use them effectively in your classroom.

Progression in geography is unlikely to be linear. It happens in fits and starts: light-bulb moments are followed by periods of consolidation before the next 'spurt'. Curriculum planning in blocks of thematic content can also complicate progression because there may be few opportunities for linear development or for synthesis. Broad 'dimensions' of progress, what it means to 'get better at' geography, can be helpful when thinking about both planning and assessment (Figure 11).

When planning a topic it is useful, therefore, to try to identify the progress you expect on some of these dimensions. This will allow you to plan your assessment so that students can demonstrate what they know, understand and can do. This will require the collection of (possibly informal) data throughout the lesson, so you must take note of the evidence provided by students' responses to appropriate tasks.

These dimensions of progress can be applied to lesson plans as well as units of work to show progress on a day-to-day basis, even if the assessment information is more informal and ephemeral in nature. Strategies such as better questioning (challenging questions, rich questions), feedback (including formative marking, with opportunities for students to respond and improve their work) and effective self- and peer-assessment (Black *et al.*, 2002, 2003; Weeden and Lambert, 2006) require teachers and students to understand progress in these terms – not in the shorthand of level numbers. What level descriptions provided was an imperfect common language.

Strategies that have been used effectively are discussed more fully elsewhere – the ideas here provide brief summaries of their potential.

Questioning

'More effort has to be spent in framing questions that are worth asking: that is, questions which explore issues that are critical to the development of students' understanding' (Black *et al.*, 2003, p. 42).

'Questions that are worth answering' encourage students to be involved in developing their understanding. They foster a climate where questions can be considered and responded to fully. Open questions are good at promoting discussion and dialogue and allowing for 'wait-time', so that students can formulate answers, rather than rewarding those students who demonstrate they 'know' the answer the quickest. Ways to develop better questioning include the use of discussion partners, for example using 'think-pair-share' strategies, or the 'snowballing' technique, where larger groups of students take turns explaining their ideas about an issue to each other, expanding their understanding.

- Demonstrating greater fluency with world knowledge by drawing on increasing breadth and depth of content and contexts.
- Extending from the familiar and concrete to the unfamiliar and abstract.
- Making greater sense of the world by organising and connecting information and ideas about people, places, processes and environments.
- Working with more complex information about the world, including the relevance of people's attitudes, values and beliefs.
- Increasing the range and accuracy of investigative skills, and advancing their ability to select and apply these with increasing independence to geographical enquiry.

Feedback

Research into AfL suggests there is a clear link between the use of effective feedback and learning gains. The focus of good-quality feedback, therefore, needs to be on the link between the assessed piece of work and the learning that has taken place. Importantly, the next stage of the learning process should also be considered. Therefore feedback should include:

- the use of formative and effective comments
- verbal feedback in support of the written comments
- time for student reflection.

However, there needs to be a common understanding of what 'effective feedback' means. Figure 12 might be useful in enabling the department to identify areas where practice might change and to discuss any barriers to change.

What improves feedback comments?

Your feedback comments should concentrate on helping students understand and develop the area of the subject they are working on. Making time for students to reflect on your

Figure 11: Dimensions of progress in geography. **Source:** GA, 2014b.

Figure 12: Framework for feedback.

Stage	Reasoning
Assess students' work and give a formative comment without a grade or mark.	Marks get in the way of feedback because: • students often disregard any written feedback if there is a mark • they are more interested in comparing their level of success with others than in the feedback • motivation can be adversely affected and comments intended to improve learning are lost.
Return assessed work as soon as possible after it is completed and give students an opportunity to read the comments.	Students need to have feedback quickly so they still remember what they did, and they need to have time to re-engage their thoughts with the work.
Planned verbal comments to class.	This provides opportunities to: • tackle more general misconceptions with the whole group • revisit core concepts where many students have given poor answers • model the process students should go through in making sense of their comments. You can help them make the link between the objectives, their work and the comments they receive • target comments to groups of students.
Time for student reflection.	Learning gains are greatest when students reflect on the work and make connections with their understanding: • students need time in class to respond to specific questions and teachers' comments – 'dedicated improvement and reflection time' (DIRT) • a homework task might encourage more extended reflection.

written comments is an important part of the feedback process (see below). They should be less about making statements and more about encouraging the students to respond; you should foster an expectation that comments on work are part of a dialogue. For example 'You are right that the image shows the glacier is retreating. Can you suggest why this might be happening?' tells the student what they have done correctly, but then asks them to develop their thinking, thereby building their level of knowledge and understanding.

Another way of extending learning through feedback comments is to set a clear and definable target for further work, for example 'Well done, Jess, you give a clear account of the changes in the South Korean economy over the past 20 years. Now develop your answer by referring to and including quantitative data to support your main arguments'.

Among the many ways of providing effective feedback are two useful frameworks: praise, improve, encourage (PIE) – and praise, error, next steps (PEN) – the requirement to develop work further. Other methods include highlighting three good sections, suggesting an area for development and asking for a response; or using a 'bubble' (improvement prompt) and 'box' (specific praise) followed by a direct request to students for a response (Rooney, 2006, pp. 85–86).

Verbal feedback in support of written comments

Written comments can be supported by verbal feedback to a whole group: this allows you to tackle more general misconceptions and revisit core concepts when necessary. Verbal feedback also provides opportunities to 'model' the process students should follow when refining their work.

Time for student reflection

Assessment needs to be planned as carefully as the lessons and learning it supports. Marking using formative comments takes longer than 'tick and flick' marking: it is better to assess a limited number of pieces of work in depth, feeding back on central concepts and skills, than to write comments on all work. One key element is planning time for student reflection and responses. If you have spent time marking work you should give the students opportunities to reflect on your comments and make a considered – and sometimes extended – response. While it is true that this cuts into teaching time, it is focused learning time. Student learning should be more rapid, especially once the approach becomes second nature to the students and teacher.

Self- and peer-assessment

> 'Students can only achieve a learning goal if they understand that goal and can assess what they need to do to reach it. So self-assessment is essential in learning' (Black et al., 2002, p. 10).

Developing students' ability to assess performance in an increasingly independent way is important for learning. This is where self- and peer-assessment becomes central to the formative assessment process.

Clarke (2005) offers a very clear, simple and useful framework for self-assessment. First, students highlight their successes against clearly defined learning objectives. You then ask students to identify a place where their work could be improved in the context of the learning objective(s). Then you add a suggestion for improvement to which the student responds. This creates opportunities for dialogue between teacher and student in which they are working together to improve learning. Finally the student begins to rely less on the teacher and identifies the parts of his or her work that could be improved. The teacher becomes a 'critical friend' who no longer acts as the marker, but who supports and comments where necessary.

Using summative assessment formatively

While many practitioners can see the positive impacts of AfL, some are still concerned, given the ultimate high-stakes goal of successful exam results, that there is not enough time to develop such strategies. In response to this dilemma Black et al. (2002) devised techniques that allow for the formative use of summative assessments. They outline three main 'innovations' that have positive impacts on summative assessment (Figure 13).

These strategies help to blur the notional boundary between formative and summative assessment, making it easier for you to plan for the use of formative assessment even in 'high-stakes' situations. It will ultimately make the learning of students approaching terminal examinations more focused, useful and, hopefully, enjoyable.

Tracking and recording progress without National Curriculum levels

Levels provided a useful shorthand for recording progress on a school database, a practice encouraged by the increasing focus of Ofsted inspections on performance at the end of key stage 4 and progress over time. For example, the Ofsted guidance in relation to achievement in geography, published in December 2013 after the disapplication of National Curriculum levels, still refers to them in their definition of progress:

> 'Expected progress is defined by the government as two National Curriculum levels of progress between key stages 1 and 2 and three National Curriculum levels of progress between key stages 2 and 4' (Ofsted, 2013).

Schools face an interesting dilemma when it comes to recording progress. Levels did at least provide a 'rough-hewn' language of progression for teachers to employ. If definitions of standards and progression are destined to become local rather than national matters, then the purpose of study, aims and introductory paragraphs for each key stage within the curriculum provide good starting points for defining expectations by the end of each key stage. Schools can use their experience of assessment for learning to strike a healthy balance between advising students on progress and improvement and making summative statements about their overall attainment. Further guidance on this dilemma is available on the GA website (GA, 2014a).

It is worth remembering that these issues are not new and that many teachers and schools will already be defining progress in terms of

Figure 13: Innovations that have a positive impact on summative assessment. **Source:** Black et al., 2002.

Innovation	Activities	Benefit
1. Development of revision It is often assumed that students know how to revise for examinations. These study skills are often underdeveloped so students make poor use of scarce revision time.	This can be done by 'traffic-lighting' key words or questions from past papers. Students can focus on those areas they feel less confident about, rather than 'blanket' revising all of their work, some of which they already understand. Peer groups can research and discuss parts of the subject they all feel unsure about.	Engaging students in discussions and activities focused on revision helps them improve their exam preparation. It also encourages students to explain ideas and concepts to each other, developing their understanding. These activities can cut down on the amount of personal preparation.
2. Generating and answering questions Involvement in the process of question setting, marking answers and giving feedback improves student performance.	Students have the opportunity to write their own questions, mark other students' answers, and give feedback. Reading parts of essays, such as introductions, to suggest possible essay questions. Teachers can use good examples of students' questions as class tests during reflective periods at the end of topics, boosting the students' confidence in their work.	If students are to set appropriate questions they are obliged to focus on the subject content. More importantly, students gain a better understanding of the assessment process.
3. Use of test outcomes for further work Test outcomes are not merely recorded but are built into the learning process.	Students self- and peer-assess practice test questions. Students assessing the relative quality of a selection of introductions or conclusions of exam questions in a focused way instead of blindly working through test questions regardless of whether students have performed well on them or not. For example, students identify questions that are problematic in terms of answers or understanding.	This process helps them to develop a more critical understanding of how they will be assessed in terminal examinations. As with the framework for self-assessment, this gives students a better understanding of assessment criteria and learning objectives.

what students know, understand and can do, not in terms of numbers (levels and sub-levels). Removing levels will provide teachers and schools with the opportunity to focus on helping students make day-to-day progress in geography formatively, rather than recording progress through often dubious sub-level judgements. Further detail about the use and misuse of levels and sub-levels can be found in Weeden and Hopkin (2014).

Conclusion

Until the late 1990s, assessment was often seen as unconnected to learning: it was simply an exercise in measuring the amount that a student had understood. Assessment for learning (AfL) changed this perception, demonstrating that assessment and student learning should be intertwined: in AfL, the main function of assessment is to help students make better sense of the work they are doing and, as a consequence, enable them to do it better. At the same time, their motivation increases and they experience a greater sense of achievement. However, adopting AfL approaches can be a daunting prospect: it requires you to empower students and play a less dominant role in their learning. Allowing such frameworks to emerge and develop in your classroom means you may have to rethink your own preconceptions and practices. Nonetheless, all the evidence leads to the conclusion that AfL approaches improve students' learning experiences, and ultimately their learning outcomes.

References

Bennetts, T. (2005) 'The links between understanding, progression and assessment in the secondary geography curriculum', *Geography*, 90, 2, pp. 152–70.

Black, P. and Wiliam, D. (1998) *Inside the Black Box*. Slough: nferNelson.

Black, P., Harrison, C., Lee, C., Marshall, B. and Wiliam, D. (2002) *Working Inside the Black Box: Assessment for learning in the classroom*. Slough: nferNelson.

Black, P., Harrison, C., Lee, C., Marshall, B. and Wiliam, D. (2003) *Assessment for Learning: Putting it into practice*. Maidenhead: Open University Press.

Brill, F. and Twist, L. (2013) *Where Have All the Levels Gone? The importance of a shared understanding of assessment at a time of major policy change (NFER Thinks: What the Evidence Tells Us)*. Slough: NFER.

Clarke, S. (2005) *Formative Assessment in the Secondary Classroom*. London: Hodder & Stoughton.

DCSF (2008) *The Assessment for Learning Strategy*. Nottingham: DCSF.

DfE (2013) *Assessing without levels*. Available at: http://webarchive.nationalarchives.gov.uk/20130123124929/http://www.education.gov.uk/schools/teachingandlearning/curriculum/nationalcurriculum2014/a00225864/assessing-without-levels (last accessed 09/11/2016).

DfE (2014) *Geography: GCSE subject content*. Available at: www.gov.uk/government/publications/gcse-geography (last accessed 09/11/2016).

DfES (2004) *Assessment for Learning: Guidance for senior leaders*. Available at: http://webarchive.nationalarchives.gov.uk/20130401151715/http://www.education.gov.uk/publications/eOrderingDownload/DfES%200043-2005G%20PDF1.pdf (last accessed 09/11/2016).

GA (2011) *Thinking about progression in geography*. Available at: www.geography.org.uk/projects/makinggeographyhappen/progression (last accessed 09/11/2016).

GA (2014a) *Assessment and the National Curriculum*. Available at: www.geography.org.uk/news/2014nationalcurriculum/assessment (last accessed 09/11/2016.

GA (2014b) *An Assessment and Progression Framework for Geography*. Sheffield: Geographical Association.

George, J., Clarke, J., Davies, P. and Durbin, C. (2002) 'Helping students to get better at geographical writing', *Teaching Geography*, 27, 4, pp. 156–59.

Hopkin, J. (2006) *Level descriptions and assessment in geography: a GA discussion paper*. Available at: www.geography.org.uk/download/ga_aulevelassessmentsingeography.pdf (last accessed 09/11/2016).

Ofqual (2015) *Get the facts: GCSE reform*. Available at: www.gov.uk/government/publications/get-the-facts-gcse-and-a-level-reform/get-the-facts-gcse-reform (last accessed 09/11/2016).

Ofsted (2013) *Geography Survey Visits: Generic grade descriptors and supplementary subject-specific guidance for inspectors on making judgements during visits to schools*. Available at: http://dera.ioe.ac.uk/19125 (last accessed 09/11/2016).

Rooney, R. (2006) 'Effective feedback as a focus for CPD with a developing geography department', *Teaching Geography*, 31, 2, pp. 84–86.

Task Group on Assessment and Testing (TGAT) (1988) *National Curriculum Task Group on Assessment and Testing: A report*. Available at: www.educationengland.org.uk/documents/pdfs/1988-TGAT-report.pdf (last accessed 09/11/2016).

Weeden, P. and Hopkin, J. (2006) 'Assessment for Learning in geography' in Balderstone, D. (ed) *Secondary Geography Handbook*. Sheffield: Geographical Association, pp. 414–33.

Recommended key readings

Weeden, P. and Lambert, D. (2006) *Geography Inside the Black Box*. London: nferNelson.

Part of the 'Inside the Black Box' series, this blends what we know about the power of formative assessment with a restatement of the educational purpose of geography.

Gardner, D., Weeden, P. and Butt, G. (eds) (2015) *Assessing Progress in your Key Stage 3 Geography Curriculum*. Sheffield: Geographical Association.

This pdf e-book explores many of the issues raised in this chapter in more detail.

Chapter 15

Literacy

Nicola Walshe is a Senior Lecturer in Education at Anglia Ruskin University, Cambridge

Introduction

What has literacy got to do with geography? This is a question that has become surprisingly familiar throughout my work with teachers and trainee teachers. Literacy always seems to be of great interest to the teaching profession, government agencies and the general public, and yet the question of its relevance is an important one to ask at the start of this chapter. If we are to incorporate literacy into our geography lessons, we should ask why: what role does geography play in developing students' literacy and, perhaps more importantly, what does literacy contribute to our students' geographical learning?

Traditionally, and in the Secondary Literacy Strategy especially, the purpose of cross-curricular literacy has been to address fundamental issues with students' literacy. In particular, it was argued that poor literacy limited students' ability to access and progress in curriculum subjects at key stage 3 and beyond. At its most basic, the Literacy Strategy responded to this perceived weakness through a framework of 'word', 'sentence' and 'text' level objectives: 'word' level development aimed to improve spelling and vocabulary; 'sentence' level objectives targeted sentence and paragraph construction; and 'text' level objectives aimed to develop the skills of reading, writing, speaking and listening (DfES, 2001). Although governmental approaches to tackling the reportedly persistent 'literacy problem' differ, whatever the political climate it is unlikely that the focus on students' literacy skills will disappear (e.g. Ofsted, 2013). Language is at the core of how students communicate, express themselves and learn across the curriculum, so every subject needs to develop language as a tool for learning. As teachers, we have a vested interest in incorporating literacy into our classroom work.

But what about the geography? How, specifically, can we develop students' literacy through our subject? Geography can be discursive, analytical, descriptive and creative, and, as such, it has the potential to address some fundamental aspects of literacy development. For example, in exploring with students a variety of real-world geographical issues, such as the development of sustainable energy or the ethics of transnational corporations, we ask them to listen, reflect, discuss and debate; they are able to voice their own points of view, and we ask them to empathise with key stakeholders. This enables them not only to develop a more holistic understanding of geographical issues, but also to articulate their thoughts and put forward their point of view eloquently, thereby developing skills of speaking and listening.

Geography's dynamic mix of factual, conceptual and issue-based learning also requires a range of subject-specific vocabulary that contributes to students' ability to express a view, make an argument or clarify meaning in their own extended writing. The use of more creative genres such as poetry may enable students to explore the affective dimension of a range of geographical issues, such as the global fashion industry or water conflict. Finally, geography gives students opportunities to learn about the subject in a range of textual contexts: from newspaper or magazine articles to longer non-fiction texts, novels and even poetry. This not only develops their skills of engaging with written sources in-depth, they also encounter a range of ways of conveying geographical information for different audiences and for different purposes.

Although the scope for developing students' literacy through geography is huge, this chapter focuses on developing the skills of effective speaking and listening, extended writing, creative writing, and reading for geography.

Developing these skills can lead to significant improvements in students' literacy and, perhaps more importantly to us, to their geographical understanding.

Dialogic classrooms: developing effective speaking and listening

A large body of evidence suggests that students learn more effectively when they are actively engaged in discussion, dialogue and argumentation (Wolfe and Alexander, 2008; Alexander, 2012); specifically, it is the 'interaction' promoted by speaking and listening (or dialogue) that appears to be crucial. In dialogic interactions, students are exposed to alternative perspectives and required to engage with another person's point of view in ways that challenge and deepen their own conceptual understandings; knowledge is jointly constructed and learners achieve greater understanding.

Geography has enormous scope for talk, discussion and presentation, and in turn, using talk to explore, question and revise ideas is an extremely effective tool for the learning of geography. The teacher's task is to integrate speaking and listening into classroom work in a well-managed and focused way that optimises learning. Figure 1 gives some examples of how this might be done. For example, on a small scale, undertaking an 'Alien teacher' or 'Think, pair, share' activity is extremely easy to facilitate and yet is ideal for promoting high levels of participation and ensuring that discussions are highly focused. These activities can be useful in the early stages of learning, for students to recall work from a previous lesson or generate questions, or as a 'quick-fire' reflection and review for a rehearsal of ideas before a presentation to the whole class.

At a larger scale, debate as a means of dialogue can be an extremely effective way to structure students' speaking and listening, as well as to develop their geographical understanding. However, particularly if a class is not used to whole-class discussion and debate, it is important to scaffold activities carefully so they can produce the evidence to support their point of view. One example of how to do this is Liz Taylor's (2004) idea of an argument/counter-argument grid (Figure 2), which develops the usual role-play situation by asking participants to not only represent their own role but to predict, and decide how to respond to, the argument of their opposite number. Argument/counter-argument grids could, for example, be used in a debate about the development of a local wind farm or Antarctica's oil reserves.

Being able to predict and respond to a counter-argument is an excellent skill: it involves some complex thinking about the geography, and the ability to see both sides of an issue. However, it is not easy and needs to be well supported, for example by giving students briefing sheets with full details about their role and suggestions for sentence starters and persuasive language, or by re-arranging students with the same role into groups so they can support each other when filling in their argument/counter-argument grids (see Taylor, 2004).

Finally, one approach to developing students' speaking and listening skills, which is particularly useful for controversial issues, is Philosophy for Children (P4C)'s 'community of enquiry'. This introduces students to an issue through a stimulus, such as a video clip or newspaper article, and the students generate questions about that issue; the class then selects one of these questions for discussion. A key role for the teacher, as neutral Chair, is to welcome the diversity of students' initial questions and views and use these to start students on the process of questioning assumptions, developing reasoned opinions and then applying the best reasoning and judgement they are capable of to the chosen question (Lewis and Chandley, 2012).

Developing written conversations through dialogic diaries

When we talk about dialogue or discussion in the classroom we are usually referring to spoken dialogue; however, it is possible that the benefits of effective spoken dialogue – both to students' geographical understanding and relationships between students and teachers – can to some extent also apply to written dialogue between either the teacher and the student, or the students themselves. Using a 'dialogic diary' could be one way of facilitating this written dialogue.

Figure 1: Strategies for developing speaking and listening skills within the geography classroom.

- **Pair talk:** Students discuss the response to a particular question in pairs.
- **Think, pair, share:** Students are given time to think about a question on their own, before working collaboratively to agree an answer to share with the teacher and class.
- **Alien teacher:** Students work in pairs, numbering themselves 1 and 2. A slide from a previous lesson is shown and number 1s must explain everything they can about that slide or topic to number 2s (in 20 seconds). The slide then changes and number 2s must explain everything they can about that slide or topic to number 1s (in 20 seconds). This continues until the slides stop.
- **Verbal rally:** Students sit facing each other and try to score points by, in turn, coming up with vocabulary for a particular topic, e.g. features of a river valley. The rally continues until a student repeats a word or hesitates, upon which their opponent gets the point.
- **Pairs to fours:** Students work together in pairs; each pair then joins up with another pair to explain and compare ideas.
- **Listening triads:** Students work in groups of three, taking on the roles of talker, questioner and recorder. The talker explains something, comments on an issue or expresses an opinion, and the questioner prompts or seeks clarification. To further encourage dialogic talk, Socratic questions could be modelled and incorporated (Roberts, 2013). The recorder makes notes and reports at the end of the conversation. Next time, roles are changed.
- **Envoys:** Students work in groups to complete a given task. Once the groups have completed the task, one person from each group is selected as 'envoy' and moves to a new group, to explain and summarise their work, and to find out what the new group thought, decided or achieved. The envoy then returns to the original group and feeds back. This is an effective way of avoiding repetitive 'reporting back' sessions, as well as encouraging active listening within the group.
- **Snowball:** Students discuss an issue or brainstorm some initial ideas, then double up to fours and continue the process, then into groups of eight to compare ideas and decide which are best. Next, the whole class is drawn together and a spokesperson for each group of eight feed back ideas. This is a useful strategy to promote public discussion and debate.
- **Jigsaw:** A topic is divided into sections. In 'home' groups of four or five, students allocate themselves a section each. They then regroup into 'expert' groups, working together on their section, then return to original 'home' groups to report back on their area of expertise. The 'home' group is then set a task that requires students to combine the different areas of expertise into a joint outcome. This speaking and listening strategy has the advantage that it ensures the participation of all students.

Dialogic diaries are a 'learning journal' in which students reflect on their learning at the end of their geography lessons. However, the learning process does not end there – following each diary entry by the student, the teacher writes a response (hence the dialogic or conversational nature of the diaries). Although the use of dialogic diaries is relatively unresearched, Anthony Ghaye (1989) reported that using this method with his class of year 7 students offered them a format for exploring their understandings, as well as performing a metacognitive function, helping students become more aware of what they were learning. The teacher's response is as important as the student's entry: it forms the basis of a conversation between the adult and the young person. Establishing and maintaining dialogic diaries allows teachers to both explore and develop student understanding.

An example of my own use of dialogic diaries is to develop understanding of sustainability with

Your point	Counter-argument	Possible response
The wind farm will be a source of primary energy, so we will be less reliant on expensive imported energy.	But constructing a wind farm is very expensive.	Yes, but in the long term the money saved will outweigh the initial cost.
We have lots of windy days in our country and the wind is free.	But what about when we have periods of calm days with no wind?	We are developing better ways of storing the energy created by wind power.

Figure 2: Argument/counter-argument grid for a debate about the development of a wind farm. **After:** Taylor, 2004.

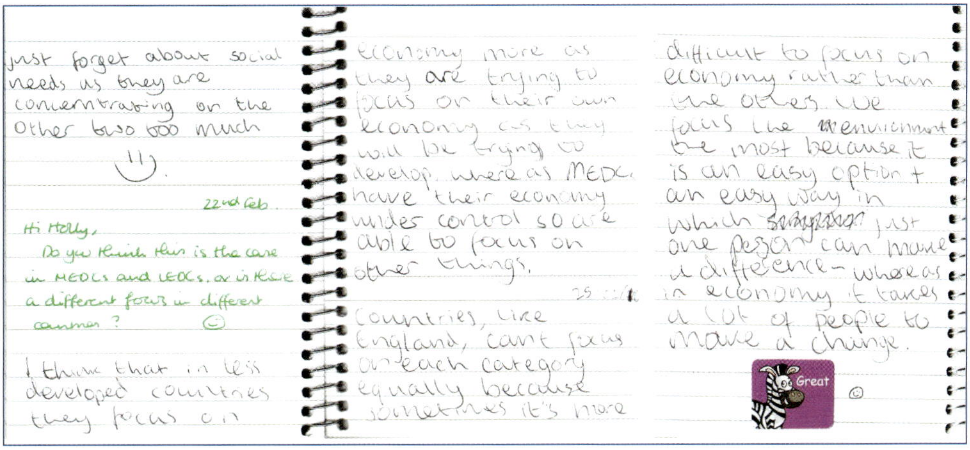

Figure 3: An extract from a dialogic diary.

a class of year 10 students (Walshe, 2012). At the beginning of the school year students were given diaries, with suggestions at the front for the sorts of things they might write about. These included relating the lesson content to sustainable development, saying which activities they thought developed their understanding of sustainability, or considering what their teacher did in particular that helped them to learn. Entries could be made in written or pictorial form and could be as free from literary conventions as the students wanted (I was not going to 'mark' them). Initially, the students' comments were generally short and often descriptive; frequently, students did not 'know what to write'. My written responses included requests for clarification of their meaning, questions about what they had learnt in a lesson (or what they needed more help with), and discussion about the topics or concepts covered in the lesson, as well as responses to the students' written questions. Ultimately, an environment was created in which students felt they could inform and share, rather than merely reply, and in this way the diary became a dialogue.

The dialogic diaries of my year 10 students demonstrated their capacity for reflecting on their learning, for geographical discussion and for developing their subject understanding. Spending time on dialogic diaries had three key advantages:

1. Developing geographical understanding: using dialogic diaries developed students' understandings of sustainable development such that they were better able to explore the tensions within sustainability as a concept, as well as to consider how and why approaches to sustainable development vary between the local, national and global scale (see Figure 3).

2. Developing thinking: by engaging in conversation with me in their diaries, many of the students became better able to think about their learning (metacognition); this became apparent in both class discussion and written work.

3. Developing relationships: as well as revealing quite a lot about the students' responses to their geographical learning, the process of engaging in an ongoing dialogue with me,

Figure 4: Continuum of written conversations between students and teachers from formative feedback on the use of dialogic diaries.

Basic formative feedback	DIRT	TIM	Dialogic diaries
Increase in dialogic nature of conversation →			
The students complete the task. The teacher explains to the students how they could improve their work.	The student completes a piece of work. The teacher (or a peer) provides feedback. The student reads the feedback and, with another colour pen, responds to the comments by making improvements to their work. Specific time is given for this within the lesson.	The student completes a specific task and explains how it meets the success criteria. The teacher uses the success criteria to explain how to improve the work and sets specific tasks for the student to complete. The student reads the feedback, answers the questions the teacher has asked and completes the tasks the teacher has set.	The teacher questions the student (e.g. what did you learn about sustainability today?). This would usually be in a separate location (e.g. in a paper or online 'diary'). The student responds to the teacher's question but is also free to ask further questions or comment on other learning within the lesson. The teacher responds to any questions, prompts the student for further information, and asks further questions. This is not usually related to a specific task, but an overarching concept or topic as it develops across one or more enquiry sequences.

and the kind of informal contact that resulted, appeared to make some students feel valued within the class, so they became more engaged in their lessons generally.

The personalised nature of the diaries is important; with more able students I can engage in high-level discussion of geographical issues, while with less confident learners I can consolidate and develop basic subject understanding. Perhaps more importantly, the diaries enable students to confidently express their concerns (for example, difficulties in understanding population pyramids), or asking questions about the lesson content. Obviously, completing the diaries is very time-consuming, not only in lessons but also writing the responses. However, it does not take significantly longer than we might already spend on formative assessment in the form of written comments, 'green-penning', dedicated improvement and reflection time (DIRT) or triple impact marking (TIM) (see Figure 4), and it has the potential to reap significantly higher rewards in terms of student understanding and development of their written and spoken literacy.

Approaches to extended writing

Figure 5 is the introduction to an analytical-style report, created by a year 8 student. It was written for the Secretary-General of the United Nations (UN), Ban Ki-moon, and coherently introduces some of the key issues of global fashion.

Writing for a specific audience and in a specific style is an important skill, in both the classroom and the world of work. Students should be made aware early on that all writing is created for a specific purpose and aimed at a specific audience,

Report for Ban Ki-moon

Recently I have been researching the global fashion industry and the effect it has on different people around the world. There are many people who believe it is unfair and takes advantage of innocent people, for example the factory workers who are paid next to nothing for hard labour. However, what they don't take into account is what would happen to those people if they didn't have a job? Some money is always better than no money. We need to understand the consequences of any changes we might want to make to the industry because our way of life is so interconnected with it; for example the West is heavily dependent on cheap imports from the East; we wouldn't have nearly as many luxuries, so relatively cheaply. This report explains the various areas of global fashion and how it works. It will also explain who is 'winning' and 'losing' from these situations. In addition to that, it will suggest examples of how to improve the global fashion industry for everyone, some that have already been carried out and others that I have thought of myself.

Aspect of writing	Example
Theme/focus	Global fashion
Audience	Ban Ki-moon (Secretary-General of the UN)
Purpose	To explore the winners and losers of the global fashion industry
Style	Report
Genre/text type	Analysis

Figure 5: A year 8 student's introduction to an analytical piece of writing about the winners and losers of the global fashion industry.

so before they start writing they should be encouraged to reflect on who they are writing for and choose a style of writing appropriate to that particular audience. The role of the teacher is to support students in their use of an appropriate style (Figure 6).

- **Instructions** – to describe how something is done, in a series of sequenced steps *(e.g. how to give a six-figure grid reference).*

- **Recount** – to retell an event/series of events, usually in chronological order *(e.g. the method section of a traditional fieldwork write-up).*

- **Explanation** – to explain the processes involved in natural/social phenomena *(e.g. explanation of processes that lead to rapid urban growth).*

- **Information** – to describe the way things are *(e.g. description of different river features).*

- **Persuasion** – to argue the case for a point of view, make people do/buy something *(e.g. a leaflet for, or against, the development of nuclear power).*

- **Discursive writing** – to present arguments and information from different points of view, to balance argument and counter-argument as fairly as possible, and to come to a reasoned conclusion (attempts to 'stay on the fence' until the conclusion) *(e.g. discussion of reasons for and against limiting immigration).*

- **Analysis** – to analyse or to present a reasoned response to a text/series of texts/other media products *(e.g. essay on 'Should people be allowed to destroy the Amazon rainforest?' following one line of argument all the way through, but also presenting and critiquing counter-arguments).*

- **Evaluation** – to record the strengths/weaknesses of a performance/product *(e.g. reflection on strengths and weaknesses of a fieldwork method).*

A piece of extended writing is likely to involve more than one of these text types, perhaps with sequences of information and explanation within a discursive or analytical framework. Much writing also includes an element of persuasion.

Figure 6: Categories of non-fiction writing. **Source:** DfES, 2001; examples and comments in italics from Taylor, 2004, p. 147.

Figure 7: QUADS grids.

- **Question** – students write their own enquiry questions for their research. Ideally, these should be open ended, e.g. How is the River Nile changing over time? Three or four questions should be spaced out down the grid.
- **Answer** – students write a short, basic answer here. There is not enough space to copy everything out, so they must summarise the big points from their reading.
- **Details** – students provide evidence to back up their main answer, perhaps facts and figures, or explanation, as appropriate.
- **Source** – students cite the source from which the information came. This gets them into the good habit of recording where their information has come from (and, when appropriate, thinking about how reliable this source might be). It also makes it easy to return to the source to check information or refer to a useful diagram or photo.

Extended discursive or analytical writing gives students the opportunity to explore their ideas fully, and to reflect on both their own values and attitudes and those of others. Creating high-quality analytical and discursive writing is not easy, but geography teachers can employ a variety of scaffolding strategies to support students. Liz Taylor (2004) suggests three groups of strategies: those which help students to 'select' the geography, those which help them prioritise and structure their points, and those which help them effectively communicate the geography.

Strategy group 1: Selecting the geography

These strategies scaffold students' developing research skills and help them to focus on the relevant points (avoiding the 'writing everything I know about' problem, which can persist into the sixth form). These strategies are likely to overlap with those suggested for reading for geography but could also include:

- QUADS (Question, Answer, Details, Source) grids to structure students' individual research (see Figure 7)
- modelling research skills (skimming, scanning, efficient web searching, etc.)
- developing the skills of breaking down the question, e.g. highlighting command words, setting their own sub-questions
- producing a concept map at the planning stage and checking that each point on it is directly relevant to the title
- discussing or marking examples of completed work, e.g. by highlighting parts that do and don't refer directly to the question
- a card-sorting exercise, selecting relevant points and discarding irrelevant ones.

Strategy group 2: Prioritising points and structuring the argument

Once students have gathered the information they will need help to arrange it, otherwise they may end up with one long paragraph of disjointed information, jumping from point to point with no logical sequence. A variety of useful strategies will support students in prioritising and structuring their information, including:

- 'Big points, little points' (see Counsell, 1997). Big points are the key organising statement for each paragraph, e.g. 'Water scarcity can have human causes'. Little points add further detail or explanation and evidence from case studies, e.g. 'One human cause of water scarcity is agriculture'. A paragraph is likely to deal with one big point and a number of supporting little points.
- Card-sorting activities to establish sequences or priorities, such as ripple diagrams (e.g. analysing the impact of the 2016 Olympics on different groups or exploring the short-, medium- and long-term impacts of deforestation in Borneo), continuum (or 'it depends…') diagrams (e.g. exploring which physical effects of a volcano are most destructive) and power towers (e.g. who has most power in the global fashion industry) or other card sorts.
- Writing frames for each text type, which make use of generic structures and varying connectives (conjunctions) to help maintain shape and cohesion. These are particularly useful when differentiated to support

students with different levels of expertise, both within and across year groups, and should be used less and less as the students' knowledge of writing forms increases and their confidence in their ability to write grows.

- Essay planners (see Taylor, 2004, Chapter 3.4, which gives two very helpful examples of essay planners and how to use them, with particular reference to sixth form groups).
- Discussing or marking examples of work – if the class is confident with peer feedback, you could use their own work; alternatively, you could use examples from previous years or create your own.

Strategy group 3: Effectively communicating the geography

The final group of strategies encourages students to think carefully about the genre or text type they are writing in. They include:

- Working on signposting, for example focusing on connectives, or cutting an essay into paragraphs and asking students to re-assemble it (using clues from signposting to order it correctly).
- Discussing examples of work showing good/poor communication.
- The teacher modelling the process of writing an introduction and conclusion, and selecting appropriate vocabulary, writing style and grammatical structure. Jones and Fitzgerald (2007) describe how teacher modelling can support students. Before asking students to start their own text, Mark Jones wrote a model text and gave it to pairs of students to de-construct. They used DARTs strategies, such as red underlining for geographical facts and blue underlining for stylistic features, for example the choice of tense, or narrative voice. Students discussed the effect of these linguistic choices on the reader, enabling them to make reasoned decisions about their own subsequent writing.
- Working on visual communication skills, for example how to incorporate effective sketch maps and diagrams into extended writing.
- Use of a 'Why tree', working with students at the planning stage of their writing to elaborate their 'big points' and produce higher quality extended writing (see Rider and Roberts, 2001).

Talking essays

Talking essays enable students to develop their ideas in depth without the need for large amounts of independent writing. They scaffold their progress through the three stages described above, and smooth their way into essay writing. Talking essays can also develop students' extended writing technique, and depending on how you structure the activity it can help them select the geography for their writing, prioritise their key points, or effectively communicate the geographical content.

An example of how I have used talking essays is with a year 10 class preparing to write an essay on 'What is being done to solve the problems of shanty towns in Rio?' In previous lessons, students had considered the variety of housing in Brazil and differences in quality of life between those living in different areas. They then explored ways of increasing quality of life in areas of informal settlement, using a Rio de Janeiro case study. The essay title was introduced at the end of the previous lesson, and for their homework students considered the types of information they might include. The talking essay process is summarised in Figure 8. Of course, although this example relates to informal housing, the technique could easily be adapted for other topics and year groups. For example, to give year 13 greater confidence in selecting relevant case study information for extended examination questions you could provide a wide range of descriptive smaller points relating to a range of case studies: the activity then becomes the more challenging task of selecting and tailoring the information to the overall question.

Creative geography: developing geographical literacy

A range of genres can be explored in the classroom to develop students' geographical literacy. This not only includes the different text types shown in Figure 6, but also more creative genres, such as story-telling and poetry. What is the value of creative writing in geography? How can it be more than a tokenistic 'cross-curricular link' in which we give a nod to English and ask our students to write 'a poem about volcanoes' as a last-minute homework filler? What are the key learning objectives you want students to

Figure 8: The process of working with students to produce a talking essay.

Talking essay: What is being done to solve the problems of shanty towns in Rio de Janeiro?

- Write the title on the board and explain the task, then arrange the students in groups. (Some groups will have more information to deal with than others, so place students appropriately.)
- Discuss the potential structure of the essay as a class – what are the big points? (If they have written the structure for the essay as homework, refer to this.)
- Give each student one of a set of cards describing the problems of *favelas* in Rio and potential solutions.
- Display a set of big points, matching those decided in class, on larger cards.
- Students move around the classroom and allocate their cards to one of the 'big point' categories.
- Each group now adopts one 'big point' and its associated cards. They decide what is the most important point on their cards and why – this nudges them towards a discussion of the significance of one fact *vis-à-vis* another. Any prior knowledge can be incorporated here.
- Discuss as a class what should go in the introduction (signposts for the audience) and pick representatives from each group to write it. Do the same for the conclusion. Writing an introduction or conclusion can be quite challenging, so this is a good opportunity to build in differentiation. Ask another representative from each group to say why their 'big point' is important and record their responses.
- Each group is given time to write their 'big point' paragraph. Everybody in the class should have a part to play, so make sure every group member writes at least a couple of sentences and reads them out.
- Perform the essay as a class, recording it if possible.
- Finally, the class discusses the key points arising from the activity, in terms of both their geographical understanding and the process of putting together the essay. This plenary element is particularly effective if you can watch a recording of the essay performance: it is an opportunity for more extended engagement with the essay (such as students assessing the essay with pre-determined success criteria).

achieve through creative writing? They may extend beyond the cognitive. For example, instead of wanting students to understand the physical processes of a volcano, you may want them to develop an appreciation of what it might be like to experience a volcanic eruption; or when teaching the geography of conflict, you might want students to empathise with an individual refugee rather than explore the geographical causes of a particular conflict. These subtly, but importantly, different learning objectives will reshape your choice of classroom activities. Whatever the example, it is important to scaffold the activities carefully to help students make the jump from creative writing in the familiar territory of the English classroom to a geographical context.

One example of how to do this with students is by starting with an exemplar poem, exploring it (both its structure and its geography) and then using it as a springboard for students to write their own work. There is a wide variety of poetry appropriate for geography lessons, both written specifically for the geography classroom, such as Mark Cowan's anthology *Poems for the Geography Classroom* (2008), or the vast number of poems and anthologies depicting human landscapes (e.g. *The City Breathing* by Andrew Fusek Peters (2011)) or physical (e.g. Philip Gross' *Severn Song* (2009) or Owen Sheers' poems in the anthology *A Poet's Guide to Britain* (2010)). You might even consider writing your own poem to use as an exemplar, for example a three-line Haiku or an acrostic poem. A factor to consider when choosing a poem is the students' age group: it must be accessible to them or it may act as a barrier to, rather than a facilitator of, geographical learning.

I used the poem *Global Fashion* by Mark Cowan (2008) as a stimulus at the end of a year 8 unit on the global fashion industry, then asked students to produce their own poetry in this style. The poem in Figure 9 struck me as being particularly interesting in not only portraying the conditions in sweatshops, but making the reader consider their own role in perpetuating the problem.

An important consideration for teachers when working with creative genres is how to assess students' work: what makes a 'good' poem about a river or a 'good' diary entry by a refugee? While validity assessment criteria may be straightforwardly achieved (i.e. the work provides an opportunity to evaluate aspects of learning that we believe to be important, such as skills of empathy or effective representation of place), reliability criteria are more difficult because responses are so subjective: one teacher may feel a poem conveys a strong sense of place because it chimes with his or her own experience; but it may have no resonance at all for another. This is something that you would need to consider both individually and with students before they complete the work.

Reading for geography

From novels, travel books and poetry to magazine and newspaper articles and, of course, online materials (including websites, tweets and Facebook entries), both fiction and non-fiction have great potential for use in the geography classroom. They offer access to a wide variety of voices, opening up viewpoints beyond the 'speech bubble' snapshots often provided in textbooks. They often introduce and develop interesting characters in interesting situations, such as a rural Chinese migrant working in a factory in Shenzhen or a survivor of

Global Fashion

Behind the clothes we see on the rail,
There hides a much sadder tale.
Of tears and blood and sweat and more,
That fell on to the factory floor.
In Asia workers slaved away,
Earning 60 pence per day.
Shouted at, abused and hit,
They have no power to change it.
Living in a crowded room,
Vermin scurry through the gloom.
Weak young workers live in fear,
So next time you go and shop,
Take a moment and just stop.
Hopefully if you really care,
You'll think twice about what you wear.
Would you rather buy those shoes,
Or save a helpless child: you choose.

Figure 9: A poem written by a year 8 student on the global fashion industry.

Hurricane Matthew, and they can contain a wealth of up-to-date information that goes far beyond textbooks, which have to last a number of years. Whatever the source, the key is to use it to develop deeper learning; encourage students to engage with the information, rather than reading through it mechanically or simply copying it into their books.

As geography teachers, we need to encourage our students to read geographical texts, but how can we best do this? Modelling an interest by reading geographical literature ourselves is important, but how do we share this with our students? One way might be to mount a 'living' classroom display of geographical fiction and non-fiction, contributed to by students and staff alike. Alternatively, you could build into your lessons a specific time for students to read geographical texts. For example, Richard Taylor (2008) suggests incorporating ten minutes of reading into the beginning of lessons, during which students read either a geographical book (he gives the example of the *Horrible Geography* series, but it could come from a wide range of literature chosen either by the students or by you), or a newspaper article with a geographical theme. In his lessons, students read a specific page or topic or a page of their own choice, either silently or aloud in class (each student taking a turn), or a combination. Taylor observes that this strategy served not only to help improve literacy levels (of both lower and higher ability groups), but also to improve behaviour at the beginning of lessons. It also had the effect of enthusing students about geography, either through learning amusing or engaging facts from *Horrible Geography*, or developing an understanding of the relevance of geography to everyday life through the use of recent news items.

As well as promoting reading in the classroom, geography teachers also need to support and develop students as readers. The strategy you use to help your students engage with the text depends on the nature of the text, the prior experience and skills of the students, and your aim in using the text. Is it a hook to engage them at the start of a lesson or enquiry sequence? A key source of information to be used for a series of lessons? Or possibly to illustrate one voice among many, with the focus on comparison between them? The answers to these questions will determine the amount of time you spend on the text and the amount of detail you are hoping the students will get out of it. Whatever the purpose of using a particular text, you may need to help students decode individual words, make meaning of passages of text, or extract information from larger bodies of text when researching particular topics or ideas. These different strategies are considered separately below.

1. 'Decoding' text at word level: vocabulary

Being able to read and understand vocabulary is fundamentally important for understanding the message of a text, so geography teachers have a responsibility to support students' reading and understanding of both subject-specific and generic vocabulary. We already use a range of strategies to help students learn the spelling and the meaning of geographical vocabulary, from the traditional use of wall displays and glossaries in books, to playing adaptations of popular games such as bingo, Pictionary, Scrabble, Taboo and dominoes. However, we are perhaps less conversant with ways of helping students decode the unfamiliar words they encounter while they are reading geographical texts. The following strategies may help students learn new vocabulary and, therefore, help to improve their writing as well:

General supported reading strategies

There are a number of strategies for supporting the initial reading of a text: the teacher can model the reading, the class can listen to a recorded version, students can read in pairs, the class can read aloud, or individuals can read to themselves. If you are modelling reading, you need to be confident in a range of subject-specific and generic terminology, for example helping students read and understand new geographical vocabulary, or literary devices such as alliteration and onomatopoeia.

Wall displays

These will include key geographical vocabulary, but they can also be used to help students with common difficulties. For example, you might display examples of geographic homophones, such as current and currant, or list words that are often misspelt, such 'dessert' for 'desert'. Good geographical classroom displays will support not only students' reading, but also their speaking, listening and writing.

Word mats

Word mats complement wall displays: they can help students learn specific geographical vocabulary for particular topics. They can incorporate a combination of key words, images and definitions (if required), and are easily differentiated to cater for students with a range of needs (such as EAL, or a particularly low, or high, reading age).

Synthetic phonics

Synthetic phonics teaches children to recognise the sounds that each individual letter makes and the sounds that different combinations of letters (such as 'sh' or 'oo') make, and blend these together to make a word. They should be able to use this knowledge to decode new words. Since its introduction into primary schools (DfES and PNS, 2006), students have come into year 7 having been taught to read using synthetic phonics (see Jolliffe *et al.*, 2012). It is the expectation of the DfE that teachers in the secondary phase will continue to use synthetic phonics, although in practice it might be more helpful to see it simply as one of several strategies to support your students' reading.

Reconstructive activities	• Text sequencing: the teacher cuts an article into pieces, which the students then have to re-order, giving their reasons. • Word deletion (cloze test): students are given a text with significant words missing and are asked to restore it to its original state. • Text matching: a text might have certain features, such as headings or illustrations, removed. Students are given these missing elements separately and asked to put them in appropriate places. • Prediction: the text is divided into sections; at the end of reading each section students discuss what they think is most likely to happen next, from evidence of their own former reading. Mind movies, a thinking skills strategy devised by David Leat (1998), encourages students to engage with texts in this way.
Processing activities	• Text marking: students annotate the text using underlining, pens of different colours, or brackets to indicate separate or related sections. • Re-presenting text: students convert text into a different form, for example turning a piece of prose into an illustration or a timeline, or a different genre, for example rewriting a story as a play, or explanations as instructions. • Statements: students are given statements about the text, some true, others not, and have to establish which have a clear relationship with the original.

Figure 10: Examples of reconstructive and processing DARTs activities.

2. Reading for meaning: comprehension strategies

Any teacher introducing a text to a class is responsible for ensuring that the text has meaning for all students. Across primary school and within English lessons at secondary level, students are taught that texts are constructed for particular purposes, for identifiable audiences and within recognisable text types or genres (see Figure 6). If we give students time to engage with geographical texts, seeking their purpose and considering how the meanings have been made, this should not only help them to better understand the texts they are working with, but may also encourage them to pay closer attention to their own written efforts. Through this association, they might better see how reading and writing are integrally linked (Dean, 2003).

One important way to develop students' understanding of text is through directed activities related to text (DARTs), in which students read and re-read text closely to extract its meaning. DARTs can be separated into reconstructive activities, involving a text modified by the teacher, which students are expected to reconstruct to its original state, and processing activities, which involve students processing the information in some way (Dean, 2003; Figure 10).

3. Reading for information: research strategies

Geography teachers often ask students to skim and scan text for potentially useful passages, to read and re-read passages to establish and check meaning, or to summarise its content. While some DARTs strategies can help students with this, Wray and Lewis (1997) produced an alternative model to encourage students to engage with written texts. The EXIT (extending interactions with text) model specifically maps out the stages that students may pass through when using written resources (see Figure 11). The overarching EXIT model can incorporate a range of other strategies (such as DARTs) and is particularly useful for researching information for extended writing (stages 7–10 in Figure 11).

In addition to the EXIT model, layers of inference diagrams can also be very useful, when students are engaging with longer texts, to extract details on a certain theme, to consider the wider significance of these details (the inference) and to devise questions that may structure further work. The range of strategies for 'selecting the geography' for extended writing, such as QUADS grids (Figure 7), might also be useful here.

Figure 11: The EXIT model: stages, questions and teaching strategies. **Source:** Wray and Lewis, 1997.

Process stage	Questions	Teaching strategies
1. Activation of previous knowledge	What do I already know about this subject?	Brainstorming, concept mapping, KWL grids (where the letters KWL are an acronym for what students already know, what they want to know, and what they ultimately learn)
2. Establishing purpose(s)	What do I need to find out and what will I do with the information?	Question setting, QUADs grids, KWL grids
3. Locating information	Where and how will I get this information?	Situating the learning
4. Adopting an appropriate strategy	How should I use this source of information to get what I need?	Metacognitive discussion, modelling
5. Interacting with text	What can I do to help me understand this better?	DARTs, text marking, text restructuring, genre exchange
6. Monitoring understanding	What can I do if there are parts I do not understand?	Modelling, strategy charts, grids
7. Making a record	What should I make a note of from this information?	Modelling, writing frames, grids
8. Evaluating information	Which items of information should I believe and which should I keep an open mind about?	Modelling, discussing biased texts
9. Assisting memory	How can I help myself remember the important parts?	Revisit, review, restructuring
10. Communicating information	How should I let other people know about this?	Writing in a range of genres, writing frames, publishing non-fiction books, drama, etc.

Learning through cross-curricular collaboration

Geography teachers can use a range of approaches to develop their students' literacy skills in geography lessons, but we should not neglect the potential of collaborating with our English colleagues. This may simply be through dialogue and discussion, but perhaps more importantly could include cross-curricular, collaborative projects, from small-scale, one-off activities to more well-developed events, for instance a 'collapsed curriculum' when departments work together for a day on a chosen theme. Examples of these larger-scale ventures (Jones and Fitzgerald, 2007, 2010; Walshe, 2013) make it clear that both students and teachers learn more through these collaborative experiences. Could you speak to your colleagues in the English department about opportunities for closer collaboration, with the aim of enhancing both the geography and English programmes of study?

Conclusion: the potential of literacy for developing geographical understanding

Whether it is a journalistic piece of extended writing aimed at persuading the reader that the 2012 London Olympics was 'the best ever', or a class debate about local flood defences, literacy is integral to geography. Geography provides a meaningful and relevant context through which to successfully introduce students to effective ways of learning with a range of texts. The strategies considered in this chapter are appropriate across all key stages.

Teachers would need to model activities carefully for younger students, but as they achieve familiarity and proficiency, gradually adjust the level of modelling and scaffolding until students are able to engage in activities independently. Regardless of the students' age, it is my opinion that true understanding of any geographical topic would be difficult to achieve without the appropriate literacy skills. Conversely, I believe that geography has a significant part to play in developing students' literacy; from a more sophisticated understanding of discussion and debate to the ability to understand and explore a range of genres in their reading and extended writing.

References

Alexander, R.J. (2012) *Improving oracy and classroom talk in English schools: achievements and challenges*. Presentation given at the DfE seminar on oracy, the National Curriculum and educational standards, 20 February. Available at: www.robinalexander.org.uk/wp-content/uploads/2012/06/DfE-oracy-120220-Alexander-FINAL.pdf (last accessed 09/11/2016).

Counsell, C. (1997) *Analytical and Discursive Writing*. London: Historical Association.

Cowan, M. (2008) *Poems for the Geography Classroom*. Blackburn: Educational Services Printing Limited.

Dean, G. (2003) *Teaching Reading in Secondary Schools*. London: David Fulton.

DfES (2001) *The Key Stage 3 National Strategy*. London: DfES.

DfES and Primary National Strategy (PNS) (2006) *Phonics and Early Reading: An overview for head teachers, literacy leaders and teachers in schools, and managers and practitioners in early years settings*. London: DfES.

Fusek Peters, A. (2011) *Leaves are Like Traffic Lights*. London: Salt Publishing.

Ghaye, A. (1989) 'A teacher, an adult or a friend' in Slater, F. (ed) *Language and Learning in the Teaching of Geography*. Abingdon: Routledge, pp. 175–211.

Gross, P. (2009) 'Severn Song' in Gross, P. *The Water Table*. High Green: Bloodaxe Books Ltd, p. 64.

Jolliffe, W., Waugh, D. and Carss, A. (2012) *Teaching Systematic Synthetic Phonics in Primary Schools*. Exeter: Learning Matters.

Jones, M. and Fitzgerald, B. (2007) 'Landscapes of language: geography across the curriculum', *Teaching Geography*, 32, 1, pp. 22–28.

Jones, M. and Fitzgerald, B. (2010) 'Town as text', *Teaching Geography*, 35, 3, pp. 96–99.

Leat, D. (1998) *Thinking Through Geography*. Cambridge: Chris Kington Publishing.

Lewis, L. and Chandley, N. (2012) *Philosophy for Children Through the Secondary Curriculum*. London: Continuum.

Ofsted (2013) *Improving Literacy in Secondary Schools: A shared responsibility*. Available at: www.gov.uk/government/publications/improving-literacy-in-secondary-schools-a-shared-responsibility (last accessed 09/11/2016).

Rider, R. and Roberts, R. (2001) 'Improving essay writing skills', *Teaching Geography*, 26, 1, pp. 27–9.

Roberts, M. (2013) *Geography Through Enquiry: Approaches to teaching and learning in the secondary school*. Sheffield: Geographical Association.

Sheers, O. (2010) *A Poet's Guide to Britain*. London: Penguin Classics.

Taylor, L. (2004) *Re-presenting Geography*. Cambridge: Chris Kington Publishing.

Taylor, R. (2008) 'Using "Horrible Geographies"', *Teaching Geography*, 33, 1, p. 28.

Walshe, N. (2012) 'Dialogic diaries: having conversations to develop students' geographical learning', *Teaching Geography*, 37, 1, pp. 26–29.

Walshe, N. (2013) 'Exploring sustainable development through poetry and moving image', *Teaching Geography*, 38, 3, pp. 119–21.

Wolfe, S. and Alexander, R.J. (2008) *Argumentation and dialogic teaching: alternative pedagogies for a changing world*. Available at: www.robinalexander.org.uk/wp-content/uploads/2012/05/wolfealexander.pdf (last accessed 09/11/2016).

Wray, D. and Lewis, M. (1997) *Extending Literacy: Children reading and writing non-fiction*. Abingdon: Routledge.

Recommended key readings

Taylor, L. (2004) *Re-presenting Geography*. Cambridge: Chris Kington Publishing.

In this valuable book, Liz Taylor explores a range of ways of supporting students in their developing literacy. Organised into three broad themes: Whose view? Whose world? and Writing the World, the latter considers how students represent their world through constructing their own written texts, and how teachers can support them. It provides exemplar enquiry sequences with photocopiable resources for teachers, as well as giving the theoretical context behind them and suggestions for further reading.

Wray, D. and Lewis, M. (1997) *Extending Literacy: Children reading and writing non-fiction*. Abingdon: Routledge.

David Wray and Maureen Lewis explore the linked questions of how children's literacy skills may be extended and how they can be taught to read and write non-fiction texts more effectively. The book is the result of the Exeter Extending Literacy (EXEL) project and contains examples of practical classroom strategies, as well as a coherent, theoretical framework for them. This book is aimed primarily at developing children's literacy across key stages 1, 2 and 3, but the strategies could be equally useful when adapted for older children and even sixth form groups.

Chapter 16

Numeracy

Mark Jones is a PGCE Geography Tutor at University of the West of England, Bristol

Introduction

In geography lessons, numerical data is a source of important contextual information that can help students make sense of the geographical theme, event or phenomenon being studied. In a lesson I observed recently, students were answering a GCSE examination question that compared data for the earthquakes in Port-au-Prince, Haiti, 2010 with Christchurch, New Zealand, in 2011 (Figure 1). Data on the impact helped the students understand the scale and significance of these disasters and provided a means for comparison, analysis and evaluation. In geography lessons like this one students can handle many different types of primary and secondary data, from numbers in text, tables and diagrams to data presented visually through charts, graphs, maps and online visualisations. Using geographical data gives students the opportunity to develop numerical, graphical, cartographical and statistical skills.

However, although working with quantitative data can improve students' geographical understanding, its potential can sometimes be reduced to that of mere numbers to be plotted on a graph or numerical facts to support case study answers in examinations. While these types of activity may serve revision purposes, at other times such superficial appreciation of the origin, reliability and validity of data would be a concern. In an age of 'big data', geography and geography teachers have a key role in educating students to become critical consumers of the information they are presented with, both inside and outside school.

In this chapter we consider different interpretations of numeracy and the relationship between geography and numeracy. Practical examples of how to integrate numeracy in geography are provided, making the case for both 'numeracy through geography' and 'numeracy for geography'. While the former encourages geography and mathematics teachers to consider the mutual benefits of closer collaboration and dialogue, the latter reminds us that, when correctly applied and appropriate for context, numeracy skills can extend and deepen students' geographical understanding.

Figure 1: Data for earthquakes in Port-au-Prince, Haiti, in 2010 and Christchurch, New Zealand, in 2011. **Source:** DEC, no date; Vervaeck and Daniell, 2012; Anderson, 2014; CNN, 2015.

Data	Port-au-Prince, Haiti	Christchurch, New Zealand
Date	12 January 2010	22 February 2011
Magnitude on Richter scale	7.0	6.3
Focus (distance from surface)	13km	5km
Distance from epicentre	25km	10km
Loss of lives	316,000	185
Injured	300,000	2164
Homes collapsed or severely damaged	250,000	181,000
Commercial properties collapsed or severely damaged	30,000	70% of CBD buildings
Homeless	1,500,000	40,000

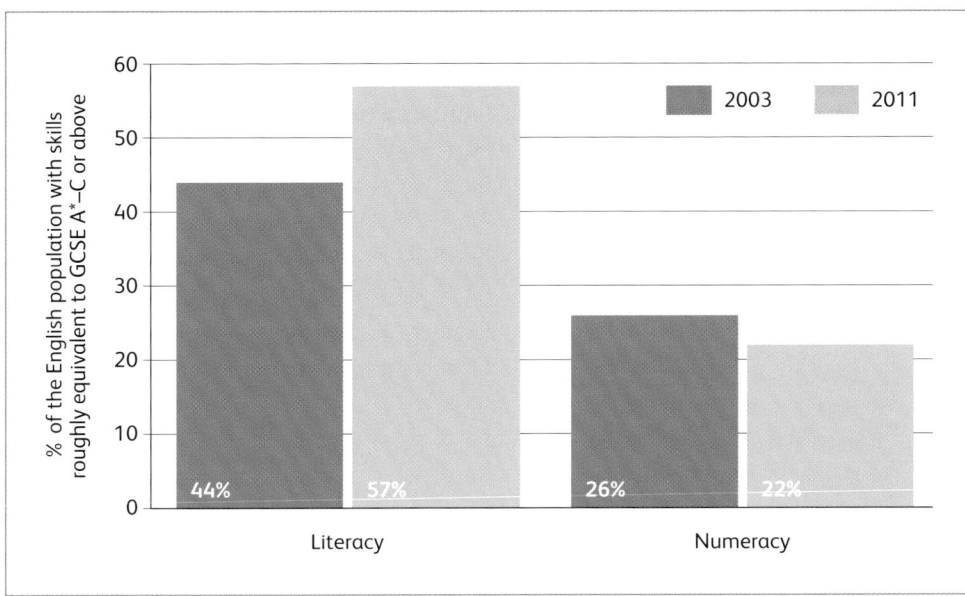

Figure 2: Bar chart showing the percentage of the English population with literacy and numeracy skills roughly equivalent to GCSE A*–C or above. **Source:** National Numeracy, 2014, p. 4.

Why a focus on numeracy?

Before exploring what we understand by numeracy it is worth reminding ourselves why there is such an emphasis on developing students' numeracy. The Skills for Life Survey 2011 revealed that 17 million adults in England have numeracy skills roughly equivalent to those expected of primary school children (DfBIS, 2012). Figure 2 graphically illustrates how the literacy and numeracy skills of English adults compare with those expected of GCSE students.

In addition to concerns about the numeracy skills of the general population, the British Academy (2012; 2013) has reported a 'quantitative skills deficit' in humanities and social science degree courses. Their position paper (British Academy, 2012) reported that 'too many students enter higher education with poor numerical skills' and that they 'feel anxious about quantitative methods, mathematics and numeracy' (p. 3). However, Harris et al. (2013) offer some evidence that geography 'remains in a position of relative strength' (p. 1). Their report, based on surveys in 2012–13 of school teachers, university students, university instructors and heads of UK geography departments, calls for increased communication and connectivity between employers, universities and schools.

If students are to be adequately prepared for higher education, employment and society, improving their numeracy and mathematical competence is a prime concern for both the UK government and schools. Over thirty years ago the Cockcroft Report (Cockcroft, 1982) made recommendations for addressing students' poor numeracy skills, and in the following two decades ongoing concerns resulted in the National Numeracy Strategy (NNS) (DfEE, 1999), which recommended a dedicated 'mathematics lesson' every day in primary schools. In secondary schools, the drive to raise numeracy standards has since the 1970s advocated 'mathematics across the curriculum' (Ling, 1977; Cockcroft, 1982) rather than viewing the problem as the preserve of mathematicians. In a similar vein the NNS expected all secondary teachers to contribute to 'numeracy across the curriculum' (DfES, 2001). More recently, the National Curriculum (DfE, 2014a) requires that 'teachers should develop pupils' numeracy and mathematical reasoning in all subjects' (p. 9). This renewed focus may reflect governmental dismay at the results of the fifth international Programme for International Student Assessment (PISA) tests, which compare the mathematics scores of 15-year-old students in different countries: the UK was ranked 26th out of 65 (OECD, 2012).

One of Ofsted's grade descriptors for judging the quality of teaching as 'outstanding' in the school inspection framework (Ofsted, 2015) is that 'the teaching of... mathematics is highly effective and cohesively planned and implemented across the curriculum' (p. 61). In pursuit of this outcome, schools strongly encourage all teachers to focus on numeracy. However, whereas promoting literacy clearly appears in the Teachers' Standards (DfE, 2013) and teachers are required to 'demonstrate an understanding of and take responsibility for promoting high standards of literacy, articulacy and the correct use of standard English, whatever the teacher's specialist subject' (DfE, 2013, p. 11), there is no corresponding statement about numeracy. Despite this obvious omission numeracy is firmly embedded in whole-school agendas and should feature in the departmental policies for all subjects (although there can be significant variation between policy and practice).

What is numeracy?

One way to think of numeracy is as a contraction of 'numerical literacy'. The term 'numeracy' appeared in the Crowther Report (Ministry of Education, 1959), and was presented as a complementary set of skills to literacy that required students to 'think quantitatively' (p. 270). Forty years later, the NNS defined numeracy as 'a proficiency which involves confidence and competence with numbers' (DfEE, 1999, p. 4), but numeracy is more than working with numbers; it requires an ability to use numbers and mathematical concepts for different purposes and in different contexts. It is also important to note that numeracy and mathematical competence are not synonymous (Westwood, 2008).

When geographers are asked about numeracy, and opportunities for numeracy in geography lessons, our responses will reveal not only what we consider 'counts' as numeracy – for example measuring, using graphs and problem solving – but also how we view numeracy's relationship with geography. Interestingly, when numeracy in key stage 3 geography is discussed, it can sometimes be viewed as an 'add-on' to the geography lesson – possibly the result of the waves of external advice and strategies that have promoted the concept of 'numeracy across the curriculum'.

Numeracy across the curriculum

The National Curriculum (DfE, 2014a) states that 'teachers should use every relevant subject to develop pupils' mathematical fluency' (p. 9). In the key stage 3 mathematics National Curriculum (DfE, 2014a), geography is specifically mentioned as one of three subjects to which students should apply their mathematical knowledge. Geography provides valuable 'real-world' contexts for developing numeracy skills and geography departments make a significant contribution to numeracy across the curriculum: the point to emphasise is that *geography* should be the main focus of geography lessons.

A whole-school focus on numeracy will result in subject audits, school and departmental numeracy policies and classroom displays showcasing, for example, 'numeracy in geography'. However, the impetus generated by these activities needs to be maintained, otherwise the opportunity to embed a more sustained dialogue between colleagues about geography's ongoing relationship with numeracy and mathematics will be missed. We might at this point define sustained collaborative engagement as 'geography through numeracy': the numeracy and mathematical skills that are being applied in geography lessons benefit from ongoing cross-subject conversations between geographers and mathematicians. Of course, for this to be mutually beneficial, schools must devote curriculum space and professional development time to the process: precious commodities in schools, particularly during times of curriculum change.

What a discussion of numeracy at school or departmental level reveals is the different interpretations of, and emphasis on, the concept. Figure 3 provides some starting points for thinking about how numeracy may be conceptualised within the department/school and when planning geography lessons. Of course the interpretations overlap and the status given to numeracy often depends on a combination of, at one level, national policy and school inspection frameworks and, more

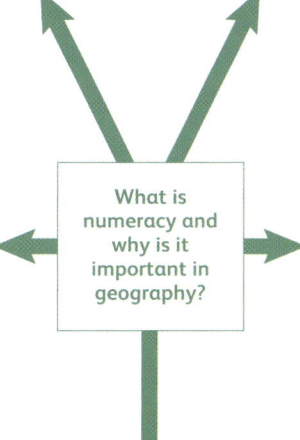

Figure 3: Ways of thinking about numeracy in geography.

Numeracy across the curriculum
A whole-school focus on numeracy, in response to national concerns and policy. This can result in the appointment of a numeracy co-ordinator, a whole-school numeracy policy, subject audits, working groups, cross-subject projects, corridor displays, numeracy checklists on lesson plans and numeracy logos on resources, tutor time activities, numeracy champions, departmental policies, etc.

Numeracy through geography
Numeracy as an essential skill for learning geography. Departments consider what numeracy skills are employed in geography lessons and what students may find difficult. Geography teachers have a positive attitude to mathematics and engage in ongoing conversations with mathematics teachers. Mathematicians teaching some lessons through 'real-world' geographical contexts.

Numeracy for geography
Using numeracy to enhance geographical thinking. For instance, considering how geographers use and make sense of quantitative data; reflecting critically on all stages of the data-handling cycle; understanding the role of graphicacy in representing and interpreting data for geographical purposes; developing statistical literacy and the role of numeracy skills in geography for moral purposes.

Numeracy for examinations
Numeracy as defined by GCSE and GCE subject content (DfE 2014a, 2014b). These documents were used by awarding bodies to inform the content of specifications for first teaching from September 2016. Teachers will select specific numeracy skills to support students' performance in national examinations.

What is numeracy and why is it important in geography?

Numeracy for lifelong learning
Numeracy as 'multiple numeracies'. Teaching students to use numerical skills confidently in different contexts and for different purposes; helping them understand current and future economic, social, environmental and political issues; helping them develop as successful learners, informed members of society and active citizens, with the skills required for economic wellbeing, employment and travel; helping them develop the skills to critically analyse media and governmental numerical and statistical representations of local to global events and issues.

locally, the school, departmental and individual commitment to the pedagogic potential of numeracy, both within and across subjects.

Numeracy in geography

Most geography teachers will regard numeracy simply as those aspects of mathematics that support students' geographical skills and understanding: for instance, using co-ordinates and scale on maps to help students navigate between places and search for spatial relationships, and the visual representation of geographical data through charts and graphs to identify geographical patterns, trends or relationships. These useful cartographical and graphical skills, along with numerical and statistical skills, are often subsumed under the broader heading of 'geographical skills'. These skills appear in checklists on departmental websites, in key stage 3 textbooks and online resources, or as required content in GCSE and GCE specifications. However, these checklists are designed for different purposes, and terms such as numerical data, quantitative data, statistics, graphicacy and 'big data' have slightly different and potentially overlapping meanings: this can complicate the relationship between numeracy, mathematics and geography. The glossary of terms in Figure 4 reveals the subtle but sometimes important differences between these terms.

Figure 4: Glossary of numeracy terms.

Term	Definition
Big data	Massive digital datasets of spatial information that have four Vs – volume, variety, velocity and veracity (see Graham and Shelton, 2013; Kitchin, 2013). Big data are produced by, and available to, numerous individuals, organisations and companies.
Categorical data	Data in categories, including non-numeric, or that have been grouped into categories.
Correlation	A connection or relationship between two variables: • positive correlation (both variables increase) • negative correlation (as one variable increases, the other decreases) • causal (one variable influences the other) • non-causal (any relationship is due to another variable not represented).
Continuous data	Data on a continuous scale of measurement. Continuous data can take any value within the range, as on a number line or ruler.
Data	Facts, statistics or information used as evidence for analysis and decisions. Data can include images, words, numbers, statistics.
Discrete data	Separate or distinct data. Discrete data can only take particular values, and interim points between data values have no meaning.
Geographical data	'This includes published statistics, data gathered from fieldwork, literature, biographies, travel writing and information generated by GIS' (QCA, 2007, p. 105).
Graphicacy	The ability to use graphical techniques to construct and understand spatial information through maps, plans, charts, graphs, photographs and sketches at a variety of scales. 'Graphicacy and Visual Literacy' was one of four key processes listed in the geography National Curriculum (QCA, 2007).
Numeracy	'…a proficiency which involves confidence and competence with numbers and measures. It requires an understanding of the number system, a repertoire of computational skills and an inclination and ability to solve number problems in a variety of contexts. Numeracy also demands practical understanding of the ways in which information is gathered by counting and measuring, and is presented in graphs, diagrams, charts and tables' (DfEE, 1999, p. 4).
Numerical data	Data, collected in the form of numbers, that include measurable information about a place, event or phenomenon. Numerical data can be discrete or continuous.
Statistics	The maths or science of collecting and analysing numerical data in large quantities, especially for the purpose of inferring proportions in a whole from those in a representative sample. Statistics can be: • descriptive, e.g. mean, median, mode, range, standard deviation • inferential, e.g. Spearman's rank correlation co-efficient, chi-squared.
Qualitative data	Data that are typically descriptive; that approximate or characterise attributes or properties, but do not measure them.
Quantitative data	Data that can be quantified and verified; which can be counted or measured.
Quantitative skills (QS)	'The ability to handle data and use numerical evidence systematically… Quantitative skills (QS) can include anything from the ability to design surveys or experiments to assessing and using quantitative evidence from surveys, digital media, archives or open data' (British Academy, 2013, p. 1).

Developing a departmental glossary of numeracy terminology can benefit students (and trainee teachers) as they start to consider what numeracy means and which skills it includes.

Geography provides a meaningful and potentially highly motivating context for developing numeracy skills. Drawing on geography-focused primary and secondary school inspections between 2007 and 2010, Ofsted (2011) commented that a feature of effective teaching in schools at that time included units of work that 'identified opportunities for students to consolidate and enhance cross-curricular skills such as… numeracy' (p. 25). However, having a numeracy statement in a departmental policy or a 'tick in a box' for numeracy in a scheme of work or a lesson plan is not necessarily evidence of thinking carefully or critically about the relationship between numeracy and the geographical context.

First, while it is good practice to identify opportunities for working with numbers, graphs or statistics, these opportunities need to be translated into practice rather than remaining 'possible approaches'. Second, the approaches need to enhance students' geographical understanding, as well as their numeracy skills. It is worth considering whether students are being encouraged to look at their work through a numerical, rather than a geographical, lens. Numeracy is not a set of skills to be developed in isolation: the choice and application of particular numeracy skills should relate to the particular geographical context.

Key stage 3

The geography National Curriculum specifies the skills required for key stage 3, although not all schools are required to follow it. The descriptions of skills incorporating numeracy and mathematical concepts have varied in detail and terminology in the different versions of the National Curriculum. The first geography National Curriculum (DES, 1991) dedicated one of the five attainment targets to 'Geographical Skills', an extensive list of 'levelled' statements of the skills students should learn. This, although content-heavy and unworkable in terms of assessment, did at least give teachers a detailed reference point. Subsequent revisions have reduced the prescribed content for skills although enquiry, fieldwork and using geographical data remain. The third revision of the geography National Curriculum (QCA, 2007) identified geographical skills through four 'key processes'; one of these, 'graphicacy and visual literacy', emphasised using graphical techniques to present evidence and provided examples of 'geographical data' (see Figure 4). The National Curriculum (DfE, 2014a) provides little guidance on specific skills beyond the aims and content, which require students to learn how to 'communicate geographical information in a variety of ways, including through maps, numerical and quantitative skills' (p. 91). Figure 5 suggests one approach to reviewing which numerical and quantitative skills should be covered at key stage 3.

GCSE and GCE

The GCSE and GCE specifications determine the geographical skills that post-key-stage 3 students should acquire. The awarding bodies develop their specifications based on the subject content for GCSE (DfE, 2014b) and GCE (DfE, 2014c). It is interesting to compare the terminology across the key stages, and also the progression of the numerical, graphical, statistical and cartographical skills expected of students.

Whereas in GCSE and GCE specifications specific numeracy skills may be explicit, at key stage 3 these tend to be subsumed under the broader term 'geographical skills', which can encompass a wide range of mathematical skills, although even the term 'geographical skill' is open to debate (see Wood, 2013).

Numeracy in geography lessons

In the next part of the chapter we consider some examples of numerical and mathematical knowledge and skills that teachers and students regularly employ in their geography lessons: handling data in their numerical, graphical, cartographical and statistical forms.

At the start, it is worth reminding ourselves of the different forms through which new geographical knowledge or skills can be introduced. Particularly valuable here is Roberts' (2013, pp. 56–57) suggestion that psychologist Jerome Bruner's (1966) three modes of representation – enactive, iconic and symbolic

Figure 5: Geography department review of geographical skills at key stage 3. Note: Stages 3 and 4 represent a 'numeracy through geography' approach that suggests that closer collaboration between teachers can be mutually beneficial and support whole-school improvement plans.

Stage 1
Audit the geographical skills currently covered at key stage 3. Identify coverage and establish the extent of continuity and progression of skills between topics and across key stage 3. Discuss how the current set of skills was arrived at. For example, was there liaison with partner primary schools or the mathematics department? Is the terminology used for specific skills the result of previous geography National Curriculums, published resources or another source?

Stage 2
Discuss as a geography team how well the geographical skills currently taught at key stage 3 prepare students for the range of cartographic, graphical, numerical and statistical abilities required at GCSE (see DfE, 2014b). Are there opportunities to carry out student voice activities with GCSE students through questionnaires and/or focus groups?

Stage 3
Ask colleagues in the mathematics department how your key stage 3 audit, and possible additional skills required for GCSE, relates to what students cover each year in mathematics. This also enables you to check whether numeracy terminology is used consistently across the school: for example, the use of bar chart and bar graph, as charts and graphs have different considerations.

Stage 4
Consider comments from colleagues in mathematics (ideally through meeting face-to-face), seek clarification and/or identify opportunities to update or adapt the scheme of work. Once a range of skills is identified, consider whether the choice of a particular numeracy skill is helping to deepen or extend students' geographical understanding. Are students looking primarily through a geographical or a numerical lens?

Stage 5
Build this process into the departmental cycle of curriculum review.

– are a useful starting point for geography teachers planning to introduce students to data-handling processes and different types of data. The simplest and most accessible mode – enactive – is where new knowledge is introduced through action, e.g. during fieldwork. In the iconic mode, the next most accessible, knowledge is represented visually, for example in photographs or videos. The symbolic mode – representing knowledge through words or symbols, e.g. tables, graphs and statistics – is more challenging, and can act as a barrier to learning. When presenting students with data in symbolic form, we need to carefully consider their prior experience of the data type.

Number

The numerical data students encounter in geography will vary widely in both type and size (see Figure 6). Numbers will range from very large, e.g. Earth's population of over 7.3 billion people, to the very small, e.g. the sizes of the smallest soil particles. Students will be expected to work with and between positive and negative values, e.g. temperature; decimals, e.g. fertility levels; percentages, e.g. employment sectors; and fractions, e.g. land use. Sometimes the sources they work with will contain a combination of whole numbers, fractions and decimals, and some students may need more time or additional support to make sense of them.

One way to help students understand the significance of very large or small numbers is to use comparisons and analogies with contexts students can easily relate to. Different soil sizes could be discussed in terms of the students' fingernails, for instance; with larger numbers, features in the school grounds or local landmarks could be used for comparison. Buildings are particularly good for comparing heights and depths, and known distances, such as the 100m track or regular travel routes, are good for comparing distances and the length of physical features. Having some numeracy facts on display, or hanging as mobiles, can also help when making comparisons. Where students have no direct experience of the physical features in question, it helps to make a comparison with a place or feature they know. For example, to help students in Bristol understand the scale of the 410-mile-long reservoir created by the Three Gorges Dam in China, they were told that it was approximately the distance from Bristol to the city of Luxembourg.

A word of warning here, though, about analogies. Some analogies can become enshrined in students' and teachers' minds, for example tropical rainforest destruction in Amazonia has often been associated with the claim in geography textbooks that 'an area the size of Wales disappears every year'. We should encourage students to question the accuracy of such a claim; they could compare the raw data for the size of Wales (20,779 sq km) and the annual deforestation figures to make their own meaningful comparisons. In fact, the worst reported year for Amazonian rainforest deforestation was in 2004 when 30,000 sq km were lost. However, between July 2012 to July 2013 this was just 6000 sq km (BBC News, 2014). Interestingly the environmental charity 'Size of Wales' has turned this negative association of the country's size with deforestation on its head, reaching its target of £2 million to protect a number of rainforests worldwide, which together equal the area of Wales, approximately 2 million hectares. This analogy also reminds us that numbers often are combined with different units of measurement, relating to area (e.g. sq km, hectare, acre), weight (e.g. kilograms, tonnes), volume (e.g. cubic metres, litres) speed (e.g. m/sec, miles per hour, km per hour, cm per year) as well as specific geographical terminology such as quantifying a river's discharge in m^3/sec or cubic metres per second (cumecs). These units of measurement may be unfamiliar and hard to estimate or 'picture' for students, and further complicated where texts or resources move

Current world population – 7,320,172,722		
	Today	This year
Births	182,564	59,967,114
Deaths	75,328	24,743,151
Population growth	107,236	35,223,963

Family size in 2012

- There were 7.7 million families with dependent children in the UK in 2012, one in seven of whom had three or more dependent children.
- Married couples had a higher average number of dependent children in their families than other family types, at 1.8 children per family compared with 1.7 on average.

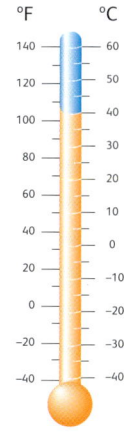

Boulders		>200mm
Cobbles		60–200mm
Gravel	Coarse	20–60mm
	Medium	6–20mm
	Fine	2–6mm
Sand	Coarse	0.6–2.0mm
	Medium	0.2–0.6mm
	Fine	0.06–0.2mm
Silt	Coarse	0.02–0.06mm
	Medium	0.006–0.02mm
	Fine	0.002–0.006mm
Clay		<0.002mm

Figure 6: Examples of numerical data in geography.

Figure 7:
How well do you know your area?

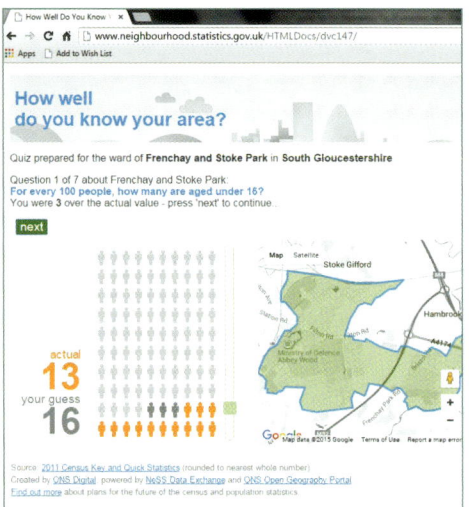

between metric and imperial units. Students therefore need to have meaningful comparisons and analogies to support them in building up their knowledge and understanding of the different units of measurement encountered in geography.

Numbers are often used for comparative reasons, but before students can make sense of comparisons Roberts (2003) suggests the strategy of 'Intelligent Guesswork' as one way to encourage 'a need to know' as part of the enquiry process. In her original example students make intelligent guesses of the life expectancies for a selection of 16 countries; these are then shared and discussed before the answers are revealed and debriefing occurs. The 'Intelligent Guesswork' approach can be used for other geographical purposes such as exploring students' perceptions of place or for suggesting causes or effects of changing circumstances in a location (Roberts, 2013). The Office for National Statistics has interactive maps, charts and graphs for the 2011 Census and the 'How well do you know your area?' website (Figure 7) can be used with students to try 'Intelligent Guesswork' for any postcode area. While this activity involves guessing percentages and other areas of numeracy, such as the median, there is questionably little in terms of numeracy skills being developed. The debriefing is therefore the crucial part of the activity, and adequate time needs be set aside for discussing why students' guesswork was

higher or lower for different characteristics, and for the significance of the variation between the guesses and actual data to be explored if a stronger numeracy focus is desired.

Data-handling cycle

Guidance about numeracy in geography is thin on the ground compared to that for literacy in geography, but two teacher educators (Roberts, 2003, 2013; Brooks, 2006) have written about the significance of 'the data-handling cycle' (DfES, 2001) to both geography and mathematics. Students at all key stages will encounter this process in geography lessons that take an enquiry approach, and particularly in fieldwork for independent investigations. The data-handling cycle (Figure 8) requires both the overall process and each of its stages to be considered in depth, particularly as regards data origin, representation, reliability and validity. Stage 1 of the process is very important, in both geography and mathematics: if students are to engage with the process it must investigate real and relevant contexts and make worthwhile enquiries.

Depending on the nature and purpose of an enquiry, and the extent of student ownership, students may have to collect primary data or they may be presented with secondary data to process or interpret. Whereas fieldwork at GCSE and the independent investigation at GCE require students to complete all stages of the data-handling cycle, at other times students

Chapter 16: Numeracy

5. Evaluating the results
- How reliable were the methods used to collect the data? What factors could have affected how data was collected at each point or each time?
- How could you mitigate against this happening next time? What other methods may have helped?
- How valid are the results? How truthful are they? How well do they represent reality? What did you do to reduce potential bias or mis-representation?
- How confident are you in drawing conclusions based on the reliability and validity of the data?
- What questions are left unanswered?
- What new lines of enquiry have been generated?
- What have you learnt through undertaking this enquiry?

1. Specifying the problem and planning
- What are you interested in and why?
- What is the purpose of the enquiry?
- How will you represent this – as an enquiry question? As a hypothesis?
- Why did you decide on this approach?
- What do you already know about the issue, theme or problem you wish to investigate? How reliable is this prior information?
- What geographical concepts, models or theories relate to the enquiry? Why are these relevant? Are there others?
- What different approaches will you use to help answer the question or hypothesis (e.g. use of primary and/or secondary data; quantitative and/or qualitative data)?
- What methods of data collection will you use? Is each method appropriate and will it help to answer the 'actual' enquiry question/hypothesis?
- What risks are involved to you and others in undertaking this enquiry? How will you minimise these so the enquiry can proceed?

2. Collecting data from a variety of sources
- How will you make each data collection method reliable, so that if you repeated the method it would provide similar results?
- How will you eliminate bias in collecting the data?
- Is the sample size appropriate in terms of significance?
- Will data be collected manually and/or digitally?
- How will data be stored?
- Is the data collection feasible in the planned time frame?

4. Interpreting and discussing data
Interpreting
- What does the data tell us (describe) and why (explain)?
- Does the data show any emerging themes, trends, patterns, relationships or anomalies? Can you explain these?
- What can and cannot be interpreted from the data?

Discussing
- What does the data tell you in relation to the original question or hypothesis?
- How does the data support or challenge aspects of the underpinning geographical concepts, models or theories?
- What conclusions can be drawn?

3. Processing and representing data
Processing
- Which approaches to sorting, classifying and making sense of the data are most appropriate?
- What is the most suitable sequence for processing the data?
- Can data be combined in any way? Why would you want to do this? How might it help?
- Can ICT and digital technologies help to process and represent the data? What are the advantages and disadvantages of different forms of ICT/digital technologies?

Representing
- What types of visual representations are most appropriate and why? What are the implications of using particular approaches?
- In what sequence and in what ways will the represented data be shown/written about?

Figure 8: Data-handling cycle. **After:** DfES, 2001, p. 180.

may be operating within particular stages in a lesson or learning outdoors. Allowing time for meaningful debriefing activities on what has been learnt should occur in all scenarios.

Maps, charts and graphs

In lessons students may be required to partially/completely construct and/or analyse a wide range of maps, charts and graphs. However, if working with data is too complex or too time consuming, students can lose interest, and potentially lose sight of the geography. Imagine a year 8 class is producing annual climate graphs from the monthly data for mean temperature (°C) and total precipitation (mm) for two locations. Do they need to complete all 24 data entries for both locations if that means there is insufficient time to help them make sense of it? A minority of examination questions still require partial completion of data, but reading data 'for geographical meaning' on maps, charts and graphs is a skill required from key stage 3 to GCE.

If we approach these types of data as visual texts to be read, then Curcio's (1987) work in the field of mathematics is helpful. This approaches reading data in three ways:

- reading the data: what does the data tell us? e.g. highest, lowest, specific values or plots
- reading between the data: what relationships are there within and between the data? e.g. groups, trends, peaks, troughs, anomalies
- reading beyond the data: what can we extrapolate or infer from the data? e.g. future trends, for a different context.

We might expect students to have few problems with reading the data, e.g. identifying the month with the highest temperature on a climate graph, or the GNP (US$) per capita and life expectancy (years) for a specific country on a scatter graph, although they will need to have had prior experience of the graph form (e.g. line, scatter), mathematical content (scale, percentages, positive and negative integers) and the geographical context. Difficulties with reading between the data can occur through errors 'related to mathematics knowledge, reading/language errors, scale errors, or reading-the-axes' (Friel *et al.*, 2001, p. 132). Reading, and reading between, the data are required by examination questions, which routinely ask students to 'describe and comment on' data. Reading beyond the data is more challenging: students might be asked to predict or make a generalisation from the data, which requires them to draw upon contextualised background knowledge. A final, important, fourth level is reading behind the data, in order to make 'connections between the context and the data' (Shaughnessy, 2007, p. 991).

As well as teaching about the different types of maps, charts and graphs and their suitability for specific contexts, we also need to examine common errors and misconceptions (see Figure 9). This can help us plan for appropriate interventions and support for individual students, but is also a fundamental ingredient of good teaching, in both geography and mathematics.

Requiring students to justify the advantages and disadvantages of different approaches to representing data visually in charts, graphs and on maps, e.g. a dot distribution versus a choropleth map for population density, is a common focus of GCSE and GCE questions. Many geography departments maintain a library of past examination papers to prepare students for discussing the benefits and limitations of different approaches.

The 'human graphs' strategy can help some students master charts, graphs and even theories and models. In human graphs, students become the data and the axes are provided by the walls of a classroom or marked on the playground. This works well with bar charts, line graphs and scatter graphs, where students can be given exact data to locate; or they can create their own graphs for others to interpret. Even a human line of best fit can help some students understanding this construct. The strategy is more effective when authentic data are used, as in the following example of Butler's model of tourist development. Having researched the history of tourism in Weston-super-Mare, students went to the seaside resort's beach and made axes in the sand for the year (x axis) and number of tourist arrivals (y axis). Then they 'performed' the graph, plotting themselves at various points, explaining their position on the graph and in relation to surrounding plots, and relating this to the human and physical factors operating at that point in history. This enactive mode of representation can make particular forms of data representation more accessible to many students, and the memorable nature of the strategy helps recall.

Co-ordinates and scale

Map work can appear in skills-based units in key stage 3, as a backdrop to case studies or in exam preparation; however, maps should feature throughout a scheme of work and at all key stages. As with graphs, enactive representation is a useful strategy for learning map skills: large-scale maps can be replicated, preferably outdoors. Chalking up a playground area with grids, or using string or rope to make a temporary 2-D plan view, can help students learn to use positional language, follow compass directions and begin to understand how co-ordinates relate to a grid square or specific point in space; all through 'being on the map'. Remember that as well locating a

Bar charts are often wrongly constructed by students confused about the difference between discrete and continuous data and whether the bars should have gaps between them or not **(a)**. Line graphs, too, can be wrongly constructed by students giving the x axis a category, rather than a numeric or temporal scale **(b)**. Equally misleading, axes can distort the significance of data, and where symbols in pictograms are not of a uniform size it can affect how we read the data **(c)**. Scatter graphs with lines of best fit with a positive correlation always being attracted to (0,0) **(d)**, and misspelling choropleth as 'chlropleth' **(e)**, are two further common errors.

Figure 9: Maps, charts and graphs: some common misconceptions and errors.

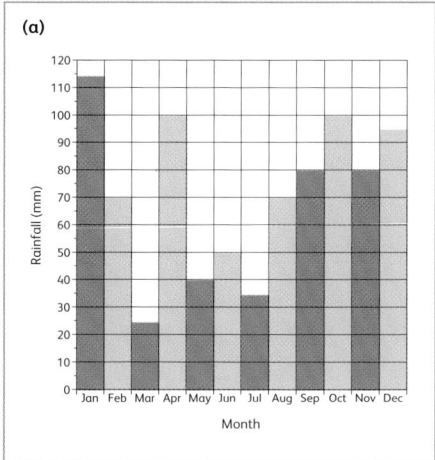

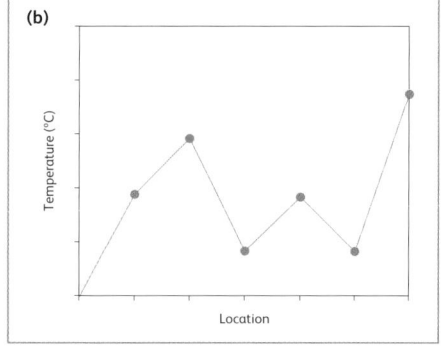

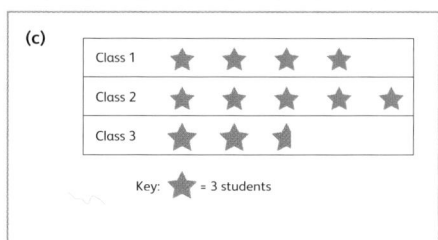

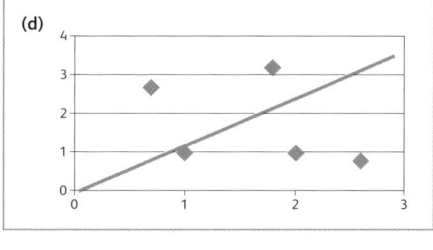

specific grid or feature from a grid reference, students need to be able to work back from a randomly selected grid or feature to identify the corresponding grid reference.

Comparing reality with maps, or scale models for that matter, requires students to develop what Wiegand (2006) calls 'scaling ability'. He suggests that when students represent reality through a drawn map, they may show close angular configuration of separate elements, e.g. on a map of the school the pond, bike racks and school gates are approximately correctly located in relation to each other, but the scale relationship is lost. Understanding scale is closely related to the ability to measure and to perceive and estimate distances in real scenarios. Again, enactive representation outdoors with maps or photographs of the school at different scales can help some students understand scale. Scale also requires students to understand its associated language of numbers and ratio. Maps come at different scales, from small-scale (such as 1:50,000) to large-scale (such as 1:1250). 'One to fifty thousand' requires students to understand that 1cm on the map represents a distance of 50,000cm/500m/0.5km on the ground. While online visualisations and mapping websites have the advantage of easy access for numbers of students in terms of moving between scales and seeing beyond the edge, physical copies of maps are still an important resource. Each Ordnance Survey 1:50,000 Landranger map covers an area of 40km by 40km (25 miles by 25 miles) and for some students seeing their locality physically unfold before their eyes can help them not only to understand scale but also to compare land coverage and distances.

A statistic, and statistics

'Nuclear power currently provides 20% of the UK's electricity' (Source: DECC, 2014, p. 66).

A statistic is a numerical fact or datum, whereas statistics is the analysis of numerical data. Rather than simply accepting a statistic, students should be encouraged to subject it to scrutiny, by asking questions such as: What is the source of this statistic? How reliable is the source? How is this statistic calculated? Who else produces statistics on this theme? This encourages a form of 'reading behind the data' (Shaughnessy, 2007), whether the statistics are presented as in the quotation above, as charts, graphs or maps, or as an outcome of statistical analysis.

The final part of this chapter examines the use of statistics and statistical analysis in school geography, an approach that first gained momentum as a result of the 'quantitative revolution' in the 1960s. There has been helpful guidance over the years on using statistics in school geography, which geography teachers have drawn upon (see Richardson, 1996; St John and Richardson, 1996; Sutton, 2007). Geography teachers now routinely teach a range of descriptive and inferential statistical techniques when analysing data. The most commonly taught statistics reflect GCSE, and particularly GCE, specification requirements. Harris *et al.* (2013, p. 3) reported that the most common types of statistics taught by geography teachers were the mean (92%); Spearman's rank (83%); median (74%); mode (68%); standard deviation (57%); interquartile range (51%); chi-squared test (51%) and the Mann-Whitney U test (46%). In the report 58% of teachers agreed that students' mathematical confidence and ability was 'an important challenge limiting effective teaching of quantitative methods' but also that '42% of teachers identified their own lack of confidence' (Harris *et al.*, 2013, p. 3).

With this final statistic suggesting that nearly one in every two geography teachers lacks confidence in quantitative methods, we would want to look more closely at the original research and any related literature, something we would actively encourage our students to do. For example, the data sample comprises 97 geography teachers, 45% of whom taught in an independent school (Harris *et al.*, 2014). Despite its small scale, this research is valuable, raising as it does questions not only about how quantitative skills and statistics are understood and taught in school, but also their purpose: is this simply a means to an end, i.e. for examinations, or is it intended to equip students to be critical consumers of statistics? Where school students, and in some cases geography teachers, do lack confidence with particular quantitative skills or techniques, any opportunities for teachers and university geographers to communicate and collaborate on resources and approaches for developing students' statistical skills is to be encouraged.

Spearman's rank correlation co-efficient is taught at GCSE and GCE and is often used to see if relationships identified on scatter graphs are statistically significant. Common errors occur when students misunderstand correlation and causation or fail to appreciate the difference between the dependent and the independent variable. A strong positive correlation between, for example, the sales of ice cream and the incidence of sunburn during August in the UK does not mean that one caused the other (causation); the intensity and duration of sunshine on each day is responsible. The independent variable is the sunshine, whereas the dependent variables are ice cream sales and the incidence of sunburn. Students can also confuse the two wholly unrelated quantities of correlation coefficient and the gradient of the line of best fit. Because it ignores the size of the data, Spearman's rank means that an extreme value can affect the final calculation; it might be sensible to discard it. More importantly, Spearman's rank does not measure linearity. You could, for example, have a set of data, which when graphed shows that each successive x co-ordinate is greater than the previous one and each successive y co-ordinate is also greater than the previous one. However, these points could very easily lie

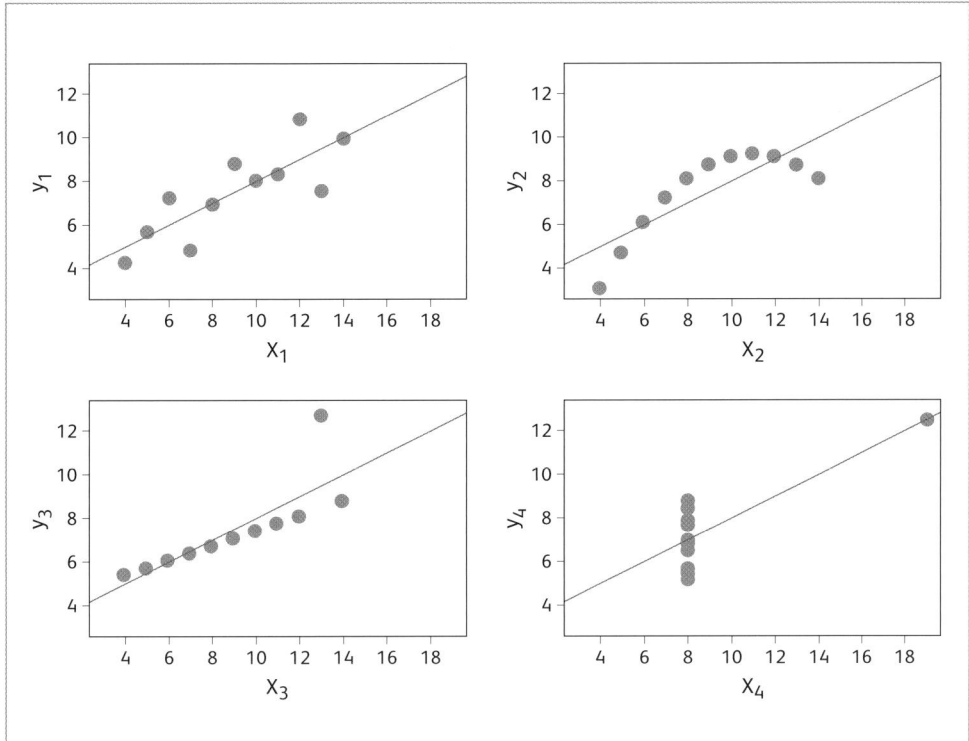

Figure 10: Anscombe's quartet.

on anything but a straight line. Students should not therefore rely on the calculation of the correlation coefficient; they should examine the graph too. Statistician Frank Anscombe devised four sets of data (Anscombe's quartet) to demonstrate both the importance of graphing data before analysing it and the effect of extreme values on statistical properties (Figure 10). Each of the datasets had a correlation coefficient of 0.816, but looking at the graphs reveals significant variation in the plots.

A final point relates to students' (and teachers') access to statistical analysis and to the massive geo-located digital datasets known as 'big data' (Graham and Shelton, 2013; Kitchin, 2013). In 2012, the Royal Statistical Society expressed concern that levels of 'statistical literacy', both in students and the population at large, are not sufficient for the data-rich world we live in. Their report, on the future of statistics in education (Porkess, 2012), reminded us that whereas 'computers produce data; it is up to people to decide how to analyse and interpret them, and indeed what data to seek' (p. 5). With the rise of 'big data' we have access to a significant volume and variety of online data from numerous sources, each with their own agendas. In preparing students to be critical consumers of data we must teach them to read behind the data, to question the way they are presented, to investigate their authenticity, audience and purpose, and to consider possible bias, over-, under- and even mis-representation of data.

Ways forward

Nearly 20 years ago, Davidson et al. (1998) made two important recommendations for geography teachers in relation to numeracy: that they adopt a positive attitude to numeracy, and that they liaise with their colleagues in mathematics. Returning to the research by Harris et al. (2014), 63% of teachers in their study agreed that students get anxious when asked to work with data: a positive attitude to mathematics reassures students that the numeracy in geography lessons will help develop their geographical understanding. Many geographical skills are valid techniques for developing students' proportional reasoning, ability to select appropriate ways to represent data, and application of mathematical reasoning to new contexts. However, many of the data presentation and analysis techniques used in geography are not necessarily covered in school mathematics, so students may not have encountered them before.

In many schools, working with mathematics colleagues to help teach aspects of numeracy in geography is an underutilised resource. Cross-subject conversations to gather intelligence on students' mathematical experience can start to address concerns expressed nearly 40 years ago that 'teachers of related subjects often do not know the mathematical capabilities of their pupils – which topics they have met and how far they understand them' (Ling, 1977, p. 4). Davidson *et al.* (1998), writing during the NNS pilot phase, exemplify a more collegiate approach to numeracy; a message reinforced by Roberts (2013) who suggests that liaison with the mathematics department can help geography teachers to understand specific numeracy skills and the 'issues related to developing them' (p. 59). In schools where such a collaborative culture is possible and sustainable it can certainly enhance students' geographical learning. However, it need not be a one-way street; geography provides real contexts for the collection, handling, presentation and analysis of numerical data, and geography schemes of work may provide a rich environment for mathematicians to work with.

The Geographical Association (2002) has made a strong case that 'geography provides unequivocal real-life contexts for numeracy' and that 'numeracy enhances geographical understanding' (p. 3). This chapter has offered examples of both; it has also emphasised that the latter is only possible when numeracy is used in a meaningful and purposeful way to examine data for a geographical purpose. Rather than seeing numeracy as a set of skills to be learnt, we should understand clearly why we are using a particular mathematical concept or numerical approach, and its advantages and disadvantages; crucially, perhaps, we should understand how a specific approach might influence how the geography is represented and understood. This we might call 'numeracy for geography': using numeracy skills effectively for questioning, discussing, analysing and thinking geographically about geographical phenomena. The challenge, of course, is to find the time and resource, both within the geography department and with colleagues who are mathematicians, to develop aspects of numeracy through and for geography.

References

Anderson, C. (2014) *Christchurch: after the earthquake, a city rebuilt in whose image?* Available at: www.theguardian.com/cities/2014/jan/27/christchurch-after-earthquake-rebuild-image-new-zealand (last accessed 02/11/2016).

BBC News (2014) *Figures confirm Amazon rainforest destruction rate.* Available at: www.bbc.co.uk/news/world-latin-america-29151977 (last accessed 02/11/2016).

British Academy (2012) *Society Counts: Quantitative skills in the social sciences and humanities.* Available at: www.britac.ac.uk/policy/Society_Counts.cfm (last accessed 02/11/2016).

British Academy (2013) *Stand Out and Be Counted: A guide to maximising your prospects.* Available at: www.britac.ac.uk/policy/Stand_Out_and_Be_Counted.cfm (last accessed 02/11/2016).

Brooks, C. (2006) 'Cracking the code – numeracy and geography' in Balderstone, D. (ed) *Secondary Geography Handbook.* Sheffield: Geographical Association, pp. 134–45.

Bruner, J.S. (1966) *Toward a Theory of Instruction.* Cambridge, MA: Belkapp Press.

CNN (2015) *Haiti earthquake fast facts.* Available at: http://edition.cnn.com/2013/12/12/world/haiti-earthquake-fast-facts (last accessed 02/11/2016).

Cockcroft, W.H. (1982) *The Cockcroft Report: Mathematics counts.* Report of the Committee of Inquiry into the Teaching of Mathematics in Schools under the Chairmanship of Dr W.H. Cockcroft. London: HMSO.

Curcio, F.R. (1987) 'Comprehension of mathematical relationships expressed in graphs', *Journal for Research in Mathematics Education*, 18, 5, pp. 382–93.

Davidson, G., Stevens, B. and Williams, A. (1998) 'Developing numeracy through geography', *Teaching Geography*, 23, 4, pp. 174–78.

DECC (2014) *Delivering UK Energy Investment.* Available at: www.gov.uk/government/uploads/system/uploads/attachment_data/file/331071/DECC_Energy_Investment_Report.pdf (last accessed 02/11/2016).

DES (1991) *Geography in the National Curriculum* (England). London: HMSO.

DfBIS (2012) *The 2011 Skills for Life Survey: A survey of literacy, numeracy and ICT levels in England.* BIS Research Paper 81. London: DfBIS.

DfE (2013) *Teachers' Standards: Guidance for school leaders, school staff and governing bodies.* London: DfE.

DfE (2014a) *The National Curriculum in England. Key stages 3 and 4 framework document.* London: DfE.

DfE (2014b) *Geography: GCSE subject content.* Available at: www.gov.uk/government/publications/gcse-geography (last accessed 02/11/2016).

DfE (2014c) *GCE AS and A Level Subject Content for Geography*. Available at: www.gov.uk/government/publications/gce-as-and-a-level-geography (last accessed 02/11/2016).

DfEE (1999) *The National Numeracy Strategy: Framework for teaching mathematics from reception to year 6*. Sudbury: DfEE publications.

DfES (2001) *National Numeracy Strategy: Unit 7 Handling data in key stage 3*. London: DfES.

Disasters Emergency Committee (DEC) (no date) *Haiti earthquake facts and figures*. Available at: www.dec.org.uk/articles/haiti-earthquake-facts-and-figures (last accessed 02/11/2016).

Friel, S., Curcio, F. and Bright, G. (2001) 'Making sense of graphs: critical factors influencing comprehension and instructional implications', *Journal for Research in Mathematics Education*, 32, 2, pp. 124–58.

GA (2002) *Developing the Case for Geography*. Sheffield: Geographical Association.

Graham, M. and Shelton, T. (2013) 'Geography and the future of big data, big data and the future of geography', *Dialogues in Human Geography*, 3, 3, pp. 255–61.

Harris, R., Fitzpatrick, K., Souch, C., Brunsdon, C., Jarvis, C., Keylock, C., Orford, S., Singleton, A. and Tate, N. (2013) *Quantitative Methods in Geography: Making the connections between schools, universities and employers*. London: RGS-IBG.

Harris, R., Tate, N., Souch, C., Singleton, A., Orford, S., Keylock, C., Jarvis, C. and Brunsdon, C. (2014) 'Geographers count: a report on quantitative methods in geography', *Enhancing Learning in the Social Sciences*, 6, 2, pp. 43–58.

Kitchin, R. (2013) 'Big data and human geography: opportunities, challenges and risks', *Dialogues in Human Geography*, 3, 3, pp. 262–67.

Ling, J. (1977) *The Mathematics Curriculum: Mathematics across the curriculum*. London: Blackie.

Ministry of Education (1959) *15 to 18 Report of the Central Advisory Council for Education (England) (The Crowther Report)*. London: HMSO.

National Numeracy (2014) *Manifesto for a Numerate UK*. Available at: www.nationalnumeracy.org.uk/sites/default/files/media/manifesto_for_a_numerate_uk.pdf (last accessed 02/11/2016).

OECD (2012) *PISA 2012 Results in Focus: What 15-year-olds know and what they can do with what they know*. Available at: www.oecd.org/pisa/keyfindings/pisa-2012-results-overview.pdf (last accessed 02/11/2016).

Ofsted (2011) *Geography: Learning to make a world of difference*. Manchester: Ofsted.

Ofsted (2014) *The Annual Report of Her Majesty's Chief Inspector of Education, Children's Services and Skills 2013/14*. London: HMSO.

Ofsted (2015) *School Inspection Handbook*. Available at: www.gov.uk/government/publications/school-inspection-handbook-from-september-2015 (last accessed 02/11/2016).

Porkess, R. (2012) *The Future of Statistics in Our Schools and Colleges*. London: The Royal Statistical Society and the Actuarial Profession.

QCA (2007) *Geography: Programme of study for key stage 3 and attainment target*. London: HMSO.

Richardson, D. (1996) 'Using statistics' in Bailey, P. and Fox, P. (eds) *Geography Teachers' Handbook*. Sheffield: Geographical Association, pp. 151–63.

Roberts, M. (2003) *Learning Through Enquiry: Making sense of geography in the key stage 3 classroom*. Sheffield: Geographical Association.

Roberts, M. (2013) *Geography Through Enquiry: Approaches to teaching and learning in the secondary school*. Sheffield: Geographical Association.

Shaughnessy, J.M. (2007) 'Research on statistics learning and reasoning' in Lester, F. (ed) *Second Handbook of Research on Mathematics Teaching and Learning*. Charlotte, NC: Information Age Publishing, pp. 957–1008.

St John, P. and Richardson, D. (1996) *Methods of Statistical Analysis of Fieldwork Data*. Sheffield: Geographical Association.

Sutton, R. (2007) *Understanding Geography Fieldwork 1: Statistics for geographers*. Telford: Field Studies Council.

Vervaeck, A. and Daniell, J. (2012) *Christchurch – 1 year after the devastating quake*. Available at: http://earthquake-report.com/2012/02/21/christchurch-1-year-after-the-devastating-quake (last accessed 02/11/2016).

Westwood, P. (2008) *What Teachers Need to Know about Numeracy*. Melbourne: Acer Press.

Wiegand, P. (2006) *Learning and Teaching with Maps*. Abingdon: Routledge.

Wood, P. (2013) 'How is the learning of skills articulated in the geography curriculum?' in Lambert, D. and Jones, M. (eds) *Debates in Geography Education*. Abingdon: Routledge, pp. 169–79.

Recommended key readings

Roberts, M. (2013) *Geography Through Enquiry: Approaches to teaching and learning in the secondary school*. Sheffield: Geographical Association.

An essential text for the geography department. Particularly relevant to this chapter are Chapter 6, Using source materials: an evidence-based approach, Chapter 13, Intelligent Guesswork and Chapter 14, Five Key Points, which provide classroom activities and strategies relating to aspects of numeracy and graphicacy.

St John, P. and Richardson, D. (1996) *Methods of Statistical Analysis of Fieldwork Data*. Sheffield: Geographical Association.

This text, and its sister volume *Methods of Presenting Fieldwork Data* by the same authors, are excellent reference guides, both for teachers developing their own subject knowledge and for those wanting to encourage their students to select the most suitable methods of data presentation and statistical analysis.

Chapter 17

Fieldwork

John Widdowson is a geography teacher and author, and runs an urban fieldwork project in east London

Introduction

This chapter is about learning geography through fieldwork: its purposes, approaches, benefits and future possibilities. It makes the case that fieldwork is an essential ingredient of geography, whether the learning outdoors occurs in close proximity to the school for a couple of hours or further afield and over an extended period. The chapter has a particular focus on how we can approach planning for and running fieldwork activities. It begins, though, with a personal reflection, since fieldwork is above all a highly memorable experience for students and teachers alike!

A personal reflection on fieldwork

It was my first school fieldwork trip at the age of 16 that subsequently led to my career as a geography teacher. I remember the trip to Pembrokeshire in west Wales vividly (Figure 1). I was a city kid and, up to that point in my life, my only experience outside London had been holidays at the seaside. I had never travelled anywhere in Britain that could remotely be described as wilderness, but as we tramped the coastal path, climbed hills and combed rocky shores, it aroused a new curiosity within me. It made me want to explore more of the world.

Figure 1: Pembrokeshire – a memorable fieldwork experience for an urban teenager. **Photo** © NH53, reproduced under Creative Commons licence (CC BY 2.0).

Broad educational purpose	Geographical fieldwork aim	Positive outcomes from Learning Outside the Classroom Manifesto
Conceptual	Develop knowledge and understanding of geographical processes, landforms, issues.	• Improved academic achievement. • A bridge to higher-order learning. • Opportunities for informal learning.
Skills-related	Develop skills in data collection, presentation and analysis with real data.	• Skills and independence in a widening range of environments. • The ability to deal with uncertainty.
Aesthetic	Develop sensitivity to and appreciation of natural and built environments.	• Stimulation, inspiration and improved motivation. • Nurture of creativity.
Values-related	Develop empathy with views of others and care about/for the environment.	• Development of active citizens and stewards of the environment.
Social and personal development	Personal, learning and thinking skills such as independent enquiry, critical thinking, decision making, team working.	• Engaging and relevant learning. • Challenge and the opportunity to take acceptable levels of risk. • Improved attitudes to learning. • Reduced behaviour problems and improved attendance.

Figure 2: The purposes of geographical fieldwork. **Source:** Kinder, 2013, after Caton, 2006; Job, 1996; DfES, 2006.

As a geography teacher, I have since been privileged to lead field trips to many places, some remote and others less so. I have seen the eyes of many students opened to a different world for the first time and, each time, it reminds me why I decided to become a geography teacher in the first place.

Things have now turned full circle and I find myself leading fieldwork visits to east London, the area in which I was brought up. Schools come here from all parts of the country to see the changes that are happening, many inspired by the 2012 Olympics. It may be the opposite of my teenage experience – discovering a new world in the city rather than beyond the city – but the principle is the same. Fieldwork has the power to broaden students' horizons and even to change the direction of their lives.

What is the purpose of fieldwork?

Like me, you probably need little persuasion that fieldwork is a worthwhile activity. Most geography teachers would concur with former Schools Commissioner for London Tim Brighouse's comments, that 'one lesson outdoors is worth seven inside' (quoted in May *et al.*, 1993, p. 2). Brighouse's view is supported by the Field Studies Council (FSC) who commissioned the National Foundation for Educational Research (NFER) to undertake a review of the research on outdoor learning. They concluded:

> *'substantial evidence exists to indicate that fieldwork, properly conceived, adequately planned, well taught and effectively followed up, offers learners opportunities to develop their knowledge and skills in ways that add value to their everyday experience in the classroom'* (Rickinson *et al.*, 2004, p. 5).

Properly conceived, geography fieldwork can incorporate a range of purposes, some subject-related and others related to broader educational objectives. These broader objectives are linked to a range of positive outcomes for young people listed in the *Learning Outside the Classroom Manifesto* (DfES, 2006) and identified by geographers working with young people (see for example Job, 2002; Caton, 2006). The specific purposes may vary from one field trip to another but it is important, when planning any field trip, to consider in advance what the purposes are (Figure 2).

Unfortunately, the temptation for teachers, when organising fieldwork, is to revert to what worked last time, without considering the purpose of the fieldwork. As educational objectives and the geography curriculum change, so we need to consider how the fieldwork we offer should change too.

It would be easy to deduce from the table above that the benefits of fieldwork are self-evident. However, it is worth pausing to consider what it is about fieldwork that brings about these benefits.

Firstly, we would do well to note the caveats in the NFER conclusions quoted earlier, that fieldwork 'properly conceived, adequately planned, well taught and effectively followed up' (Rickinson *et al*., 2004, p. 5) adds value to students' experience in the classroom. Not all fieldwork meets these criteria. For example, a minimalist version of fieldwork that focuses merely on data collection, at the expense of developing a real sense of place, may have little lasting benefit. On the other hand, merely being outside the classroom, in a setting that stimulates new sensory experiences, can have a positive impact on students' long-term memory (MacKenzie and White, 1982). In a study of fieldwork in primary schools, Nundy (2001) observed that affective gains reinforced the cognitive gains and vice versa, with each influencing the other and providing a bridge to higher-order learning. A more recent study of secondary school geography in the Netherlands suggests that for fieldwork to be a rich and powerful teaching strategy, there should be a balance between cognitive and affective development (Oost *et al*., 2011).

There is some conflicting evidence that bringing students into an unfamiliar setting can be a barrier to learning, unless they are given time to adjust to the new situation. This goes against the natural inclination of most field trip organisers, who like to keep students busy to make maximum use of limited time outside the classroom. Many of the teachers involved in the NFER study on outdoor learning acknowledged that while their initial emphasis in fieldwork was on cognitive development, other affective benefits emerged. These included developing students' values and attitudes, learning about themselves and working with others.

What is fieldwork and where do we do it?

Fieldwork can be any learning or research undertaken outside the classroom. It is not exclusive to geography. However, geography, uniquely among subjects taught in schools, can claim fieldwork as an essential ingredient. Fieldwork begins when you walk out the classroom door and start to explore the school grounds. Often, this happens in primary schools where teachers encourage their pupils to use the immediate surroundings in various ways, for example, to study nature or cultivate a school garden. At secondary level the school grounds are fertile territory for investigating geographical topics like mapping, microclimates and physical processes at work. The advantage of using the school grounds is that it can be done within lesson time and involves little extra administration.

Beyond the school gates, geography teachers can make use of the local environment for fieldwork. This is to be encouraged and, indeed, the local area is a valuable training ground for more distant fieldwork in less familiar surroundings. There is a surprising amount of geography that can be done locally, yet the opportunities are all too easily overlooked. Familiarity can breed contempt. Local fieldwork has the additional benefit of encouraging students to reflect on their own environment and to see it in new ways. It is also cheaper than organising a long-distance field trip and the work can usually be done within a morning or afternoon.

Further afield, fieldwork can be undertaken as a one-day visit or a residential trip. Obviously, residential trips take longer and will be more expensive, so the costs have to be weighed against the potential benefits. While local fieldwork has its advantages, there is no substitute for taking students to new locations to study geography. Depending on your familiarity with a distant location, there is the option of running a teacher-led trip or using an external provider. The advantage of a teacher-led trip is that it allows you to focus on the needs of your students, to build on what has been done in lessons and, of course, it is cheaper. However, unless you are already familiar with the location's geographical potential, as well as its risks, you will need to

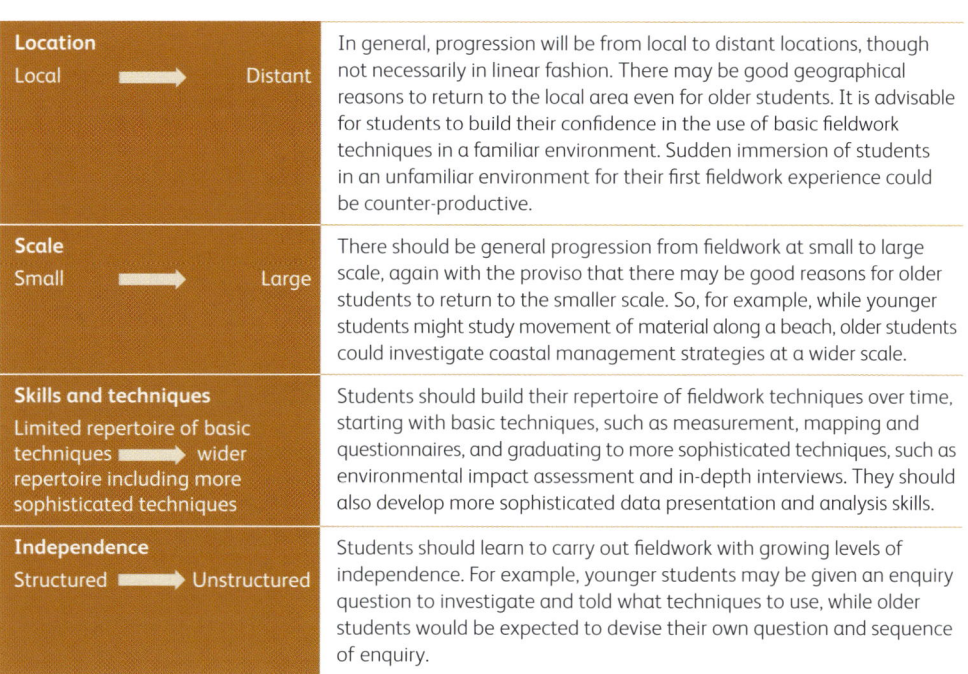

Figure 3: Progression in secondary geography fieldwork.

prepare by visiting and planning before the field trip. The other option of using an external provider also has advantages. Often, with residential trips, the accommodation and tuition come as a package, reducing the amount of preparation and administration the teacher has to do. The provider will have expert local knowledge and can create a new learning environment to stimulate students' learning and participation. This frees you, as the teacher, to take on a supportive and supervisory role, reducing the amount of stress involved.

There is a noticeable trend for schools to organise fieldwork in foreign, not to say exotic, locations. This has happened over the past few years with the benefit of cheaper flights. Often geography departments use such trips to promote the subject within their schools. While any attempt to increase the uptake of geography is to be applauded, the increased use of overseas fieldwork locations does raise questions about sustainability and the extent to which opportunities for fieldwork in the UK are being missed.

Conversely, while some schools are undertaking overseas trips, at a wider level, geography fieldwork is under threat. Internal and external pressures on the school timetable make it harder to fit fieldwork into the hours available. Reduced school funding for activities such as fieldwork means parents are expected to pay, and in times of austerity that is less likely to happen. Anxieties about health and safety, and the increased administration involved, are further barriers to organising fieldwork. As a result of these threats, it does seem that the number of key stage 3 students who experience fieldwork is falling (Ofsted, 2011). Given that key stage 3 is the only point at which all secondary students study geography, it is sad to think there will be many who leave school without any experience of doing fieldwork.

Progression

In the same way that progression is built into other aspects of the geography curriculum there should also be progression in fieldwork. We would not expect A level students to be doing fieldwork at the same level as students at key stage 3. Unfortunately, for reasons outlined in the paragraph above, the first opportunity many students get to do fieldwork is when it becomes a requirement for their GCSE or A level course. We should not be surprised if their achievements are not so great as they might have been with greater fieldwork experience.

Figure 4: Classification of fieldwork strategies. **After:** Job, 1996.

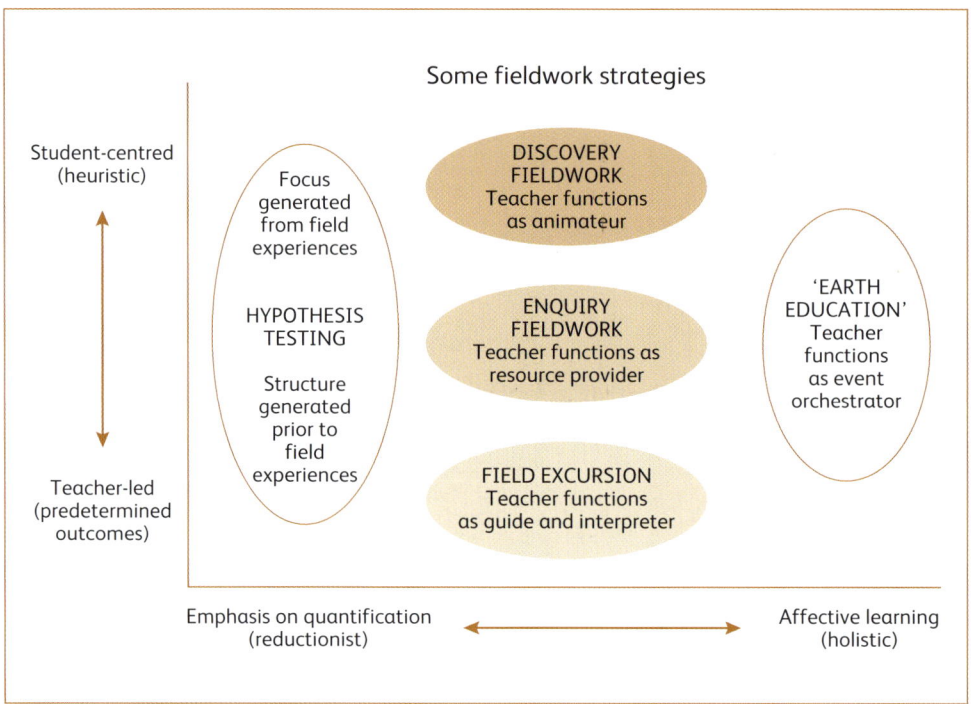

Assuming there are opportunities for fieldwork throughout a student's time at secondary school, their progression could be summarised in Figure 3.

What are the different approaches to fieldwork?

One of the most influential thinkers in recent times on the different approaches to fieldwork is David Job, who came up with a classification of fieldwork strategies (Job, 1996). It still provides one of the most useful ways of thinking about fieldwork. The classification applies two parameters (Figure 4). The vertical axis shows the degree to which the fieldwork can range from being teacher-led to student-centred. The horizontal axis shows the amount of emphasis on either quantitative methods or affective learning. Five categories of fieldwork strategy emerge from the analysis, although it should be noted there can be variation within as well as between categories.

Field excursion

Somewhat frowned upon these days, the traditional field excursion is also sometimes known as the 'Cook's Tour' or 'look and see'. This approach to fieldwork usually takes the form of a local expert – who might be the teacher – leading the group on a predetermined tour. The expert describes the features that are seen and then offers an explanation. Meanwhile, the students may be asked to take notes, draw sketches or take photos and there may be opportunities for questions and answers. Critics of the field excursion approach point out there is a low degree of engagement and autonomy among students and that it makes the assumption that complex knowledge and understanding can be transmitted through teacher exposition. This is not always the case, particularly with younger students. However, with pressure of time, or an environment that is too hazardous to allow students to explore independently, there is still a place for this approach.

I have seen the traditional field excursion being used successfully with a group of British A level students in Iceland. In this case the group leader was Icelandic, with extensive local knowledge and the ability to capture and hold the students' attention with anecdotal stories. As A level students, they had the capacity to

Hypothesis testing in a small area can help students think critically about a particular geographical idea. **Photo** © John Lyon.

absorb the information given. The priority for the teacher was for the students to see as much of Iceland as possible in a relatively short time. Under such circumstances, there is no reason why this strategy should not work.

Hypothesis testing

The 'scientific' approach to geography fieldwork, epitomised by hypothesis testing, was developed during the quantitative revolution in the subject in the 1970s. It is still probably the dominant approach used by school geography departments today, not least because exam boards often expect fieldwork to be structured around the testing of hypotheses. Typically, the teacher, sometimes in collaboration with students, sets up one or more hypotheses that can be tested through fieldwork. The hypotheses are generated from geographical models or theories and applied to specific locations. Following Job's model (Figure 4), hypothesis testing can be either teacher-led or student-centred. If teacher-led, it is organised deductively, with the teacher formulating a hypothesis from the theory. If student-centred, it is organised inductively, with students developing their own hypothesis from initial observations in the field. However, in most instances, it tends to be the former rather than the latter.

There are several benefits of hypothesis testing that make it a popular approach to fieldwork:

- When used to test a particular model or theory within a small area, it makes the fieldwork more manageable. It can also help students to focus on, and think critically about, a particular geographical idea.
- Students are actively involved in data collection, helping them to develop a range of skills, not just in data collection techniques, but also in subsequent data presentation and analysis.
- The process of hypothesis testing is well-structured and promotes a logical and sequential approach to fieldwork, allowing students to make sense of a complex world.

In recent years, the orthodoxy that has grown up around the 'scientific' approach to fieldwork has come into question. While in the 1970s hypothesis testing was seen as an innovative way to actively involve students in fieldwork and a welcome departure from the traditional, passive field excursion, it has itself become the new norm. The debate has moved on to consider just how engaged students really are when using repetitive data collection techniques yet ignoring the real-world context in which they are using them.

Taylor (2004) asks, 'How often do we take students to interesting places, perhaps far removed from their normal range of experience, and then get them to spend most of their time looking at a clipboard or measuring instrument?' (p. 53). This is probably the main criticism of hypothesis testing, but it is far from being the only one:

- The focus is usually pre-determined by teachers rather than arising from students' own experiences or perceptions. Limited use is made of students' prior understanding.
- Much hypothesis testing involves pseudo-scientific fieldwork where measurements are taken but the outcome is probably already known (at least by the teacher!)
- The amount of conceptual learning from quantitative fieldwork can be limited. Often the learning happens later, rather than when the students are in the field; back in the classroom they cannot always make the connections.
- Hypothesis testing typically focuses on measurable patterns and processes but does not consider values and opinions that are less amenable to measurement.
- The narrow focus can also limit the student's understanding of the links between human and physical processes and the wider geographical context.

The classic example of the hypothesis testing approach to fieldwork is the ubiquitous river study, which I have organised myself, many a time. In what has become a well-rehearsed routine, students are given a hypothesis along the lines that 'A river becomes wider, deeper and faster along its course'. They are then let loose, armed with an array of tape measures, ranging poles and flow meters, to prove exactly the same hypothesis that generations of students before them have proved. The spectacle of a group of students, standing knee-deep in a river, noisily wielding equipment and shouting out numbers, might lead the casual observer to believe that a lot of learning is happening. However, closer observation may reveal it is a small number of students actually doing the work, while the majority are getting cold, writing down the numbers, and not really engaging in the process. Even those doing the work may have lost a sense of the purpose of the activity. Listening to the teacher can also be illuminating. This may be the umpteenth time they have done this fieldwork and they know full well that a river becomes wider, deeper and faster along its course. The sense of intrigue and anticipation they might have conveyed to the first group of students who did this fieldwork has been lost years ago. It is hard for them to hide the fact that the outcome of the fieldwork is a foregone conclusion and this message is transmitted subliminally to the students.

Nonetheless, it is not always the means, but the ends, that are important. As previously mentioned, sometimes what students take away from fieldwork are not the intended benefits. The student getting bored writing down numbers may be taking in the breathtaking landscape around the river. The students measuring the width of the river may be learning how to work together as a team. Never underestimate the power of fieldwork – even if the outcomes aren't quite the objectives!

Enquiry

An enquiry-based approach to fieldwork emerged in the late 1970s, partly in response to some of the criticisms of hypothesis testing. In a fieldwork enquiry, students start with a geographical question or issue that might require them to draw on a breadth of geographical knowledge, rather than focus on a particular model or theory. So, for example, they might be asked to investigate the question, 'Where should a wind farm be built?'

Job *et al.* (1999) suggest that enquiry is the most appropriate approach for local fieldwork where students already have prior knowledge and experience of their locality. This can help them to formulate their own questions or issues as the basis for enquiry. The role of values and opinions is more readily appreciated in a local context where students are familiar with the communities and cultures. Also, where the issues being investigated have local immediacy, students can see the relevance and apply their findings to their own personal decision making.

The enquiry approach has also been adopted at a wider level by the geography exam boards, who often require students to undertake a fieldwork enquiry as part of their exam assessment. The term 'geographical enquiry' or 'independent investigation' is now used to refer to a discrete piece of work, often

Chapter 17: Fieldwork

Investigating 'is London a city for people or for profit?' through fieldwork. **Photo** © Bryan Ledgard.

submitted for an exam. Such investigations require the collection of primary data in the field and have been refined into a sequence of so-called enquiry skills (Figure 5).

Of course, the enquiry-based approach is not the sole preserve of fieldwork. It is also extensively used in the classroom as an approach to learning in geography. Whether in the classroom or in the field, the secret of a successful geographical enquiry lies in posing the right questions. Perhaps the most helpful guide in posing a good enquiry question in geography comes from a history publication! Riley (2000, p. 8) suggests that a good enquiry question is one that:

- captures the interest and imagination of students
- places an aspect of [geographical] thinking or concept at the forefront of students' minds
- results in a tangible, lively, substantial, enjoyable outcome activity.

The questions that are most likely to 'capture the interest and imagination of students' are the questions they pose themselves. Even if the teacher poses the question – and, practically, it is not always possible to run a fieldwork trip where each student poses their own questions – reference should be made to the needs and interests of the students. Too often, the questions asked in geography limit the possibilities of enquiry. For example, a more interesting question than 'Where should a wind farm be built?' could be 'Should a wind farm be built?'

In London, Urban Geography East London runs a range of one-day, enquiry-based fieldwork programmes for schools *(www.urbangeogeastlondon.org)*. Each one-day programme is structured around a single enquiry question. All the activities and fieldwork techniques throughout the day are designed to enable students to gather the data they need to come up with their own answer to the question. The answer is never a foregone conclusion!

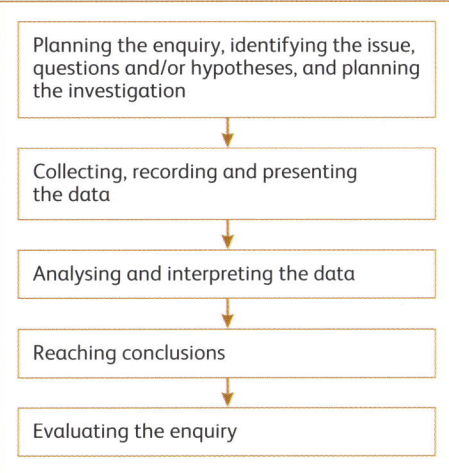

Figure 5: Flow chart showing sequence of enquiry skills.

235

Figure 6:
A mission from Mission:Explore.
Source: *www.missionexplore.net*

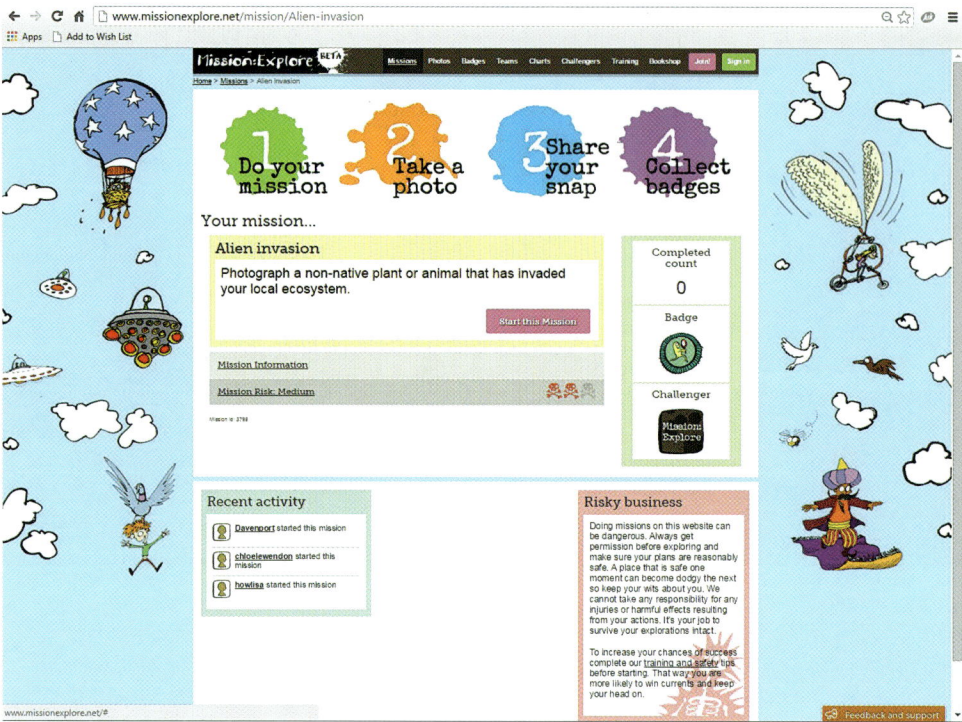

One A level programme, 'London – a world city', poses the question 'Is London a city for people or for profit?' It considers how the rapid growth of the financial services industry has led to London's reinvention as a world city, changed the city skyline and accelerated the process of gentrification around the city. The question is one that captures students' interest and imagination, places the concepts of a world city and equality/inequality at the forefront of their minds and can be investigated through a variety of tangible, lively and substantial activities.

Students start the day at Tower Bridge sketching the new buildings onto a view of the former London skyline. They compare how the types of people working in the City of London reflect the make-up of London's population. Then, walking outwards from the City through Spitalfields, they attempt to replicate Booth's nineteenth-century map of poverty in London by identifying evidence of wealth and of deprivation. Finally, further east in Stratford, they assess whether the legacy promise of the 2012 Olympics – to bring living standards in east London up to the average across the city – is being realised.

Discovery

Discovery is an 'experiential', open-ended approach to fieldwork that encourages students to explore an environment for themselves. Of course, this requires the teacher to take a calculated risk by relinquishing some control. However, it need not be the recipe for chaos that some teachers might fear. As with all fieldwork, adequate preparation, including a visit by the teacher to build their familiarity with the environment, is essential. Some structure can be incorporated into the fieldwork by providing the students with maps, photos, secondary data and even worksheets for the area. One technique that will be familiar to primary teachers – the scavenger hunt – would fit into the category of discovery fieldwork.

Job (1999) describes how discovery can be used as the starting point for an extended piece of fieldwork, to familiarise students with their surroundings. They get to know the area by using drama, old photos, chatting with local people and making landscape models with natural materials. By these means the questions and issues for more conventional fieldwork emerge but the result of these experiences is that students are more likely to be engaged with, and see the relevance, of the fieldwork.

A recent phenomenon has been the *Mission: Explore* book (The Geography Collective, 2010) and website (www.missionexplore.net). Aimed directly at students, rather than teachers, it encourages them to interact with their environment, wherever that may be:

> 'Geography is about curiosity, exploration and discovery. It gives you the power to see places in new ways, even imaginary ones. Geography also helps you to understand and make sense of the world.
>
> To be a successful geographer you should:
> - think of your own questions
> - search for your own answers
> - talk, watch, listen to people, animals, plants and places
> - think about who you are and the effect of your actions'
>
> (The Geography Collective, 2010, p. 25).

Such has been the impact of Mission:Explore that teachers now use some of the ideas (Figure 6) in their own fieldwork and set 'missions' for students to do in their own time as homework. It has certainly tapped into an approach to fieldwork that, until now, has not been fully exploited.

I understand the reluctance of some teachers to let students loose in an unfamiliar environment. I had that experience at Westfield, Stratford City – the largest urban shopping centre in Europe! We wanted GCSE students to experience shopping there through the eyes of different types of shopper, including a banker, a parent with young children, an OAP and a Muslim woman, so we asked them to get into character and go on a 'virtual shopping trip' around Westfield. Of course, they were asked to stay in small groups, armed with a guide to the centre (any excuse to get in some map practice!) and each group was given an imaginary budget with which to 'virtually' buy the things they wrote on their shopping list.

The first time we did this I didn't know what to expect. Would the students get lost, attract the attention of one of Westfield's ever-vigilant security guards or, (most likely I thought) forget about the task in hand and indulge in some real shopping? Actually, they all found their way back, having taken the task absolutely seriously, brimming with thoughts about how Westfield did, or didn't, meet the needs of their character. It is an activity we have since repeated many times, with equal success. It just took that first leap of faith to trust the students.

Earth education

Otherwise known as 'sensory fieldwork', Earth education aims to reconnect students with the natural environment through greater use of all their senses; smell, touch, hearing and taste, as well as sight. Students can be encouraged to focus on one sense by depriving them of others, for example, with a blindfold. Such sensory fieldwork is likely to effect a deeper, emotional response to the environment than mere field observation, data collection or even fieldwork enquiry. The implication of the name, 'Earth education', is that sensory fieldwork is most likely to happen in more natural or remote wilderness environments, but there is no reason why it might not also happen in an urban environment.

Earth education has a long tradition and van Matre (1979), writing in reaction to the quantitative revolution of the 1970s, says:

> 'Many of life's most rewarding, enriching and heartfelt experiences can barely be put into words, let alone placed on a scale. If we relied too much on the usual processes of collecting and testing, what would happen to our goals of instilling a sense of wonder, a sense of place and a reverence for life?'

House *et al.* (2012) describe a modern take on Earth education. They characterise such fieldwork as being 'risky', pointing out that 'the outcomes are not guaranteed: aims and objectives are clear, but the outcomes are unpredictable' (p. 60). However, they go on to say that the 'risks' of conventional fieldwork approaches can be even greater: 'the risk of an unsuccessful learning experience increases significantly as practitioners and learners become disengaged' (p. 60). They exhort teachers to use the opportunities during fieldwork not only for students to collect data, but also

Figure 7: Creating geo-squishes encourages students to think about their environment. **Photo** © Jon Ley.

to engage them in active learning outdoors. They suggest ways to encourage learners to think in the field. Teachers could use videos to interview students about the places they are in and students can take photos or 'geo-squishes' to encourage them to think about the landscape around them (Figure 7). While in the field, they can display the data they collect using 'human graphs' where individual students represent the data on a giant graph marked out with tape measures.

Going even further, they suggest not just using innovative fieldwork techniques in familiar locations, but regularly changing the locations too. Unpredictable learning outcomes for the student and teacher are often the most rewarding. This returns to a criticism of hypothesis testing – that the outcomes are so predictable that the teacher, and consequently the students, can lose interest.

How can you make the most of fieldwork?

Preparation

Preparation is essential for effective fieldwork, whatever approach you decide to use. Though the emphasis so far in this chapter has been on the various approaches to fieldwork and the teaching and learning that will take place, the importance of planning the logistics of a field trip should not be overlooked. Many a field trip has been spoiled because the bus did not turn up on time, no one checked where the toilets were, or the students came inadequately dressed for fieldwork in that environment.

Paramount, among all the factors that have to be taken into account, is student safety. Some schools have been deterred from organising fieldwork because of the perceived inherent dangers. The function of a risk assessment is to anticipate, minimise and manage possible risks. This will require a visit to the proposed fieldwork site or sites, and this can conveniently be combined with preparation of the fieldwork content.

Having identified the risks it is then essential to:

- set clear expectations and responsibilities, both for teachers and students
- make sure everyone is aware of the expectations and responsibilities
- have appropriate materials and contingency plans to cope with minor accidents or emergencies
- have effective procedures for dealing with major incidents.

Figure 8 gives an example of a risk assessment for fieldwork in an urban setting.

However time-consuming the logistical preparations for a field trip can be, it is important not to lose sight of the educational/geographical objectives of the fieldwork. These also need to be planned for. Students need to have the prior knowledge and skills to enable them to understand and carry out activities in the field. To make best use of time in the field this ought to be done in the classroom beforehand. If it is a long-distance trip, students may need to be prepared for the sort of environment and culture they may encounter.

Students should also be encouraged to take responsibility for their own preparations. This may involve background reading or revision of work covered in class, and they could be encouraged to find out more about the sites they will be visiting through online research. At the very least, students should be aware of the likely weather and physical conditions in which they will be working and come adequately dressed with the right equipment.

Risk/hazard	Risk severity 1–5 (1=low, 5=high)	Risk likelihood	Control measures	Risk likelihood with control
Falls, slips and trips, cuts, abrasions, minor injury	3	High	School to advise groups on appropriate footwear and clothing in advance. Tutor to make groups aware of any uneven surfaces, verges, steep steps, sharps and other hazards while walking or undertaking fieldwork activities. Tutor to make groups aware of expected behaviour while moving and undertaking activities. Tutor has recent first aid training and first aid kit.	Low
Traffic accidents, road crossing collisions with cyclists	5	Medium	Tutor to brief groups on arrival on procedures for walking in a group, including teacher/supervising adult roles. Tutor to advise groups of particular local traffic hazards. Tutor to advise groups on road crossing procedures and need for groups to stay in discrete group except when instructed otherwise.	Low
Use of public transport, Docklands Light Railway	5	Medium	Tutor to brief groups on journey details before travel. Tutor to advise all students to travel in single designated carriage except when instructed otherwise. Tutor to brief groups regarding student separation procedure. Tutor to ensure students hold handrails. Tutor to give notice while on train of destination station. Tutor to ensure headcount at destination station.	Low
Hazards in busy urban area, contact with general public, crowds, antisocial behaviour, 'stranger danger'	5	Medium	Tutor to brief group regarding expected behaviour, nature of locations where activities will take place. Tutor to advise on designated area where activities are to take place and the time allotted. Tutor to ensure students are in appropriate groups and have appropriate adult supervision at all times. Tutor to ensure provision is made for toilet stops and there is clarity about visiting/not visiting shops etc. Tutor to advise groups on dealing with antisocial behaviour. Tutor to ensure regular head counts take place. School to ensure a minimum student teacher ratio of 15:1, therefore with UGEL tutor approx. 10:1.	Low

Teaching and learning

With such a range of fieldwork approaches to choose from, these need to be carefully considered before embarking on a field trip, to decide which would be most appropriate to the fieldwork setting and the students you will be working with. Whichever fieldwork approach, or combination of approaches, you decide to adopt, Kent *et al.* (1997) maintain that the 'overriding objective should always be the maximisation of the students' engagement and the educational benefit from the work' (p. 321).

Though writing for teachers in higher education, the principles outlined by Kent *et al.* (1997) to maximise the educational benefits could well be applied to school fieldwork:

- Deep knowledge of a locality is most effectively acquired through multi-sensory experience and participation in activity. However, a high degree of student autonomy and plenty of time is required.
- Conversely, if a very specific learning outcome is desired, some aspects of the fieldwork must be carefully controlled, through explicit objectives, worksheets and guidance.
- Supporting material, such as field guides, maps and data collection sheets, have a powerful influence on the success of fieldwork and need careful design.
- Enquiry-based fieldwork (as with any enquiry-based learning) can provide a very

Figure 8: Extract from a risk assessment for fieldwork in an urban setting. **Source:** Urban Geography East London website.

Fieldwork topic and key enquiry question	Quantitative strategies	Qualitative strategies
A local planning issue: How will the development of a new superstore affect a town?	Environmental impact assessment – students give positive and negative scores to likely impacts of a proposed superstore. Traffic flow count – students count traffic flow at site of proposed superstore and predict likely change after it is built.	Sketch visualisation – students draw a sketch, superimposed onto a photo of the site, to show their impression of the new superstore. In-depth interviews – students identify stakeholders who will be affected by the superstore and devise their own questions to carry out interviews.
Urban regeneration: Who are the winners and losers in an urban regeneration project?	Environmental quality survey – students complete a bi-polar chart to score aspects of environmental quality in regenerated and non-regenerated areas. Homes and jobs survey – students investigate house prices and wage rates at local estate and employment agencies to calculate who can afford to live in the area.	Stakeholder role-play – students, in role as stakeholders in the area, identify the changes that would most affect them. Dragon's Den decision – students choose a business and decide on the best location to set it up within the regenerated area.
River environments: How does the relationship between a river and people who live nearby change along its course?	River geometry – students measure and record channel width and depth at intervals along the river's course. River flow – students measure river velocity using flow meters at intervals along the river's course.	Ecosystem services – students identify the natural benefits of a river along its course, including provisioning, regulating, supporting and cultural. Residents' flood risk questionnaire – students visit communities along the river's course and question residents about their experiences/perceptions of flooding.
Investigating National Parks: How do visitors to a National Park affect a particular village?	Village health check – students rate the state of village services and functions by giving positive or negative scores. Vehicle license survey – students use license plate tags to identify the city or area where visitors' vehicles come from.	Request a stop – students ask to stop the bus at interesting sites on their journey to the village to write, record or photograph their impressions of the National Park. Village issues – students match characters in the village with the issues that would most affect them and decide how relevant each issue is in that village.

Figure 9: Examples of quantitative and qualitative fieldwork strategies. **Source:** Widdowson and Parkinson, 2013.

effective vehicle for learning. Students answer an enquiry question by collecting and analysing field data.

- Skills can be acquired only through students' direct participation and taking responsibility for their own work.

Returning briefly to Job's (1996) classification of fieldwork strategies (Figure 4), there is a broad distinction between those strategies described as 'quantitative' (reductionist) and those described as 'qualitative' (affective). As teachers, we tend to be more reluctant to experiment with qualitative strategies, as these are perceived as being more 'risky'. Job (2002) suggests that this may be a consequence of exam specifications that offer 'little encouragement to work with qualitative data, demonstrate a sense of place or focus on issues of social or environmental concern' (p. 131). Of course, it is possible to make use of both quantitative and qualitative strategies during the same fieldwork experience (Figure 9), as demonstrated in the text *Fieldwork through Enquiry* (Widdowson and Parkinson, 2013). If we are to maximise students' engagement and the educational benefits of fieldwork, we should be prepared to make use of the full repertoire of fieldwork strategies available to us.

Follow-up

Once the field trip is over there is a natural inclination to breathe a deep sigh of relief that everything went according to plan and then relax. However, it's not over yet! Follow-up is a critical, but often neglected, part of the fieldwork experience.

Follow-up should take place as soon as possible after the fieldwork experience. Of course, teachers carrying out fieldwork with students for the purpose of examination assessment will already know the importance of follow-up at the earliest opportunity to ensure the most effective sharing of data and writing up fieldwork while the ideas are still fresh in students' minds. It is only after data has been shared and analysed that overall conclusions can be drawn about any hypothesis that has been tested or the findings from any geographical enquiry. It is unlikely that every student will have had exactly the same experience, so they should be encouraged to recall and share experiences. It is even better if there can be short cycles of activity and follow-up throughout the fieldwork, with instant feedback from the students at the end of each activity. This accords with House et al.'s (2012) advice to make greater use of active learning strategies in the field.

In the longer term, the fieldwork experience should also be integrated within the curriculum's overall learning objectives. Some teachers plan the fieldwork to precede the coverage of the relevant part of the curriculum in the classroom, while others plan it to follow curriculum coverage in class. Both strategies can work, so long as consideration is given to how the fieldwork ties in with, and enhances, learning in the classroom. It is through linking the fieldwork with the curriculum as a whole that the learning outcomes will be maximised.

What is the future of fieldwork?

Sustainable fieldwork

Geography plays a major role in raising awareness of sustainability among students and fieldwork is central to this role. Fieldwork can raise sustainability awareness in at least two ways, which could be summarised as the medium – the way the fieldwork is organised and managed – and the message – what the students actually learn about sustainability through fieldwork. This resonates with the 1980s environmental education concepts of 'learning through the environment' and 'learning for the environment'.

In organising fieldwork, teachers need to exercise care and concern for the environment. This is important, to help students recognise their responsibilities to the environment and to future generations. Many of the sites geographers use for fieldwork are in fragile environments. As responsible teachers, we need to monitor the impact that fieldwork activities have on these sites and recognise where they are being overused. The same might be said of local communities; we should ensure they are not inundated by large numbers of students on field trips.

Another issue is the mode of transport used to reach the fieldwork location. In my early years as a teacher, I would think nothing of driving students from London to Wales in a minibus. We would then drive around Wales from one fieldwork location to another. It would be hard to justify that use of transport now, given the carbon emissions of the minibus and the fact that there are alternative fieldwork locations much closer to home that could be used. Incidentally, there is also the question of how much time on the field trip is wasted travelling to and between sites, not to mention the cost. This creates a real dilemma for geography teachers who, understandably, want their students to experience different environments, but are also conscious of the environmental impacts of travel. It is an even bigger dilemma if they are thinking of an overseas field trip. The environmental costs of flying have to be weighed against the educational benefits of the trip. The question is, could the same learning be achieved locally, or within the UK, without the need to fly? Of course, there is additional conflict here with the desire to promote geography to students and parents as an exciting subject with the prospect of overseas travel. I do not have an answer, but think the question needs to be raised.

Sustainability is an essential part of the geography curriculum and, as such, can also be a focus for fieldwork. Job et al. (1999) see particular potential in utilising the local area for studying sustainability because students can more easily apply their findings, both in terms of personal decision making and in influencing policy decisions. They suggest energy use in school buildings, local traffic and the origins of food on supermarket shelves as suitable topics for investigation. Furthermore, use of the local area for fieldwork about sustainability avoids the need for any form of long-distance travel.

However, sustainability can be studied anywhere, not just in the local area. Many popular fieldwork themes, such as river flooding, coastal management and tourism, lend themselves to considering sustainability. Sustainable urban living is one of the fieldwork topics in *Fieldwork Through Enquiry* (Widdowson and Parkinson, 2013) in which a sustainable community assessment was used to assess sustainability in much the same way as an environmental quality survey is often used as a fieldwork technique. Other features, such as land use, retail diversity, building design, air quality and noise can also be investigated as aspects of sustainable urban living.

The case for fieldwork

'We are all aware, education is more than the acquisition of knowledge. Improving young people's understanding, skills, values and personal development can significantly enhance learning and achievement. Learning outside the classroom is not an end in itself, rather, we see it as a vehicle to develop the capacity to learn' (DfES, 2006, p. 3).

There is widespread agreement among teachers, parents, school administrators and politicians that fieldwork is beneficial. However, widespread agreement alone is not enough to guarantee the place of fieldwork in the curriculum. There has been a marked decline in the provision of fieldwork, particularly in primary schools and at key stage 3 (Ofsted, 2011). Prior to 2016 there had been a weakening of the link between fieldwork and the coursework required for post-14 examinations, making it harder to justify field trips to parents and school managers. Kent and Fosket (2002) argue that geography teachers need to remake the case for fieldwork with each new curriculum review. At least part of the contemporary case must be the increasingly sedentary and online existence of young people – the so-called 'nature deficit disorder'. Another element of the case for fieldwork is the need to raise students' awareness of sustainability issues, discussed in the previous section. Unless we can engage young people with their natural environment it is hard to know how they will be able to take long-term responsibility for it.

In their study of secondary school geography teachers in the Netherlands, Oost *et al.* (2011) identified ways in which geographers could use fieldwork as a rich and powerful teaching strategy. They advocate fieldwork that is:

- enquiry-driven and student-centred
- structurally integrated on a classroom level – with thorough preparation and follow-up
- structurally integrated on a curriculum level – linking fieldwork goals with the wider curriculum
- balanced between the cognitive and the affective – including raising students' awareness of sustainability issues and level of social responsibility.

However, Oost *et al.* (2011) discovered that, although 71% of geography teachers do fieldwork, most do not succeed in meeting these conditions.

It is all too easy for geographers to be confident that the case for fieldwork is self-evident, particularly when fieldwork has been a statutory and examination requirement. At GCSE the DfE (2014a) subject content used by awarding bodies to inform their 2016 geography specifications 'require that fieldwork is carried out, outside the classroom and school grounds, on at least two occasions' (p. 8). Post-16 specifications 'must require students to undertake fieldwork which meets the minimum requirements of two days of fieldwork at AS, and four days of fieldwork for A level' (DfE, 2014b, p. 13). However, nothing is certain and future changes to the National Curriculum or exam specifications might challenge our complacency. If we are to present a convincing case for fieldwork and ensure its future place in the curriculum, we need to consider the purpose of the fieldwork and what the most suitable strategies should be.

In their 2014 subject survey criteria for geography, Ofsted (2013) recommend that:

'Fieldwork is well planned and clearly identified as an integral part of the schemes of work. Pupils experience fieldwork on a regular basis, with activities that offer clear progression rather than repetition and include diverse landscapes and varied locations' (p. 10).

That would serve as a suitable benchmark for geography departments to aim towards and to help us make, or even remake, the case for fieldwork.

References

Caton, D. (2006) 'Real world learning through geographical fieldwork' in Balderstone, D. (ed) *Secondary Geography Handbook*. Sheffield: Geographical Association, pp. 60–73.

DfE (2014a) *Geography: GCSE subject content*. Available at: www.gov.uk/government/publications/gcse-geography (last accessed 09/11/2016).

DfE (2014b) *GCE AS and A Level Subject Content for Geography*. Available at: www.gov.uk/government/publications/gce-as-and-a-level-geography (last accessed 09/11/2016).

DfES (2006) *Learning Outside the Classroom Manifesto*. Nottingham: DfES. Available at: www.lotc.org.uk/wp-content/uploads/2011/03/G1.-LOtC-Manifesto.pdf (last accessed 09/11/2016).

House, D., Lapthorn, N., Moncrieff, D., Owens-Jones, G. and Turney, A. (2012) 'Risky fieldwork', *Teaching Geography*, 37, 2, pp. 60–62.

Job, D. (1996) 'Geography and environmental education' in Kent, A., Lambert, D., Naish, M. and Slater, F. (eds) *Geography in Education: Viewpoints on teaching and learning*. Cambridge: Cambridge University Press, pp. 22–49.

Job, D. (1999) *New Directions in Geographical Fieldwork*. Cambridge: Cambridge University Press/Queen Mary Westfield College.

Job, D. (2002) 'Towards deeper fieldwork' in Smith, M. (ed) (2002) *Aspects of Teaching Secondary Geography: Perspectives on practice*. London: Routledge Falmer/The Open University, pp. 128–45.

Job, D., Day, C. and Smyth, A. (1999) *Beyond the Bikesheds: Fresh approaches to fieldwork in the school locality*. Sheffield: Geographical Association.

Kent, A. and Fosket, N. (2002) 'Fieldwork in the school geography curriculum: pedagogical issues and development' in Smith, M. (ed) *Teaching Geography in Secondary Schools*. London: RoutledgeFalmer, pp. 160–81.

Kent, M., Gilbertson, D. and Hunt, C. (1997) 'Fieldwork in geography teaching – a critical review of literature and approaches', *Journal of Geography in Higher Education*, 21, 3, pp. 313–32.

Kinder, A. (2013) 'What is the contribution of fieldwork to school geography?' in Lambert, D. and Jones, M. (eds) *Debates in Geography Education*. Abingdon: Routledge, pp. 180–92.

MacKenzie, A.A. and White, R.T. (1982) 'Fieldwork in geography and long-term memory structures', *American Education Research Journal*, 19, 4, pp. 623–32.

May, S., Richardson, P. and Banks, V. (1993) *Fieldwork in Action: Planning fieldwork*. Sheffield: Geographical Association.

Nundy, S. (2001) *Raising Achievement Through the Environment: The case for fieldwork and field centres*. Doncaster: National Association of Field Studies Officers.

Ofsted (2011) *Geography: Learning to make a world of difference*. Available at: www.gov.uk/government/publications/geography-learning-to-make-a-world-of-difference (last accessed 09/11/2016).

Ofsted (2013) *Geography Survey Visits: Generic grade descriptors and supplementary subject-specific guidance for inspectors on making judgements during visits to schools*. Manchester: Ofsted.

Oost, K., De Vries, B. and Van der Schee, J. (2011) 'Enquiry-driven fieldwork as a rich and powerful teaching strategy – school practices in secondary geography education in the Netherlands', *International Research in Geographical and Environmental Education*, 20, 4, pp. 309–25.

Rickinson, M., Dillon, J., Teamey, K., Morris, M., Choi, M.Y., Sanders, D. and Benefield, P. (2004) *A Review of Research on Outdoor Learning*. Slough: National Foundation for Education Research/King's College London.

Riley, M. (2000) 'Into the key stage 3 history garden: choosing and planting your enquiry questions', *Teaching History*, 99, pp. 8–13.

Taylor, L. (2004) *Re-presenting Geography*. Cambridge: Chris Kington Publishing.

The Geography Collective (2010) *Mission:Explore*. London: Can of Worms Kids Press.

van Matre, S. (1979) *Sunship Earth: An acclimatization program for outdoor learning*. Martinsville, IN: American Camping Association.

Widdowson, J. and Parkinson, A. (2013) *Fieldwork Through Enquiry*. Sheffield: Geographical Association.

Recommended key readings

Job, D. (1999) *New Directions in Geographical Fieldwork*. Cambridge: Cambridge University Press/Queen Mary Westfield College.

A valuable contribution to thinking about fieldwork for sustainability. It is particularly helpful for teachers wanting to plan more qualitative experiences involving discovery, sensory exploration, and personal interpretations of environments.

Kinder, A. (2013) 'What is the contribution of fieldwork to school geography?' in Lambert, D. and Jones, M. (eds) (2013) *Debates in Geography Education*. Abingdon: Routledge, pp. 180–92.

This chapter provides a detailed analysis of the practical choices that geography teachers are presented with when designing fieldwork experiences. It also benefits from an extensive literature base, invaluable to those completing assignments or research on fieldwork.

Chapter 18

GIS and other geospatial technologies

Mary Fargher is Lecturer in Geography Education at University College London Institute of Education

Introduction

In this chapter, I want to explore the wide range of options that geography teachers have to help their students learn about geographical information systems (GIS) and other geospatial technologies. The chapter will explain how such technologies can help students to a better understanding of geography, and also how factors inhibiting their use can be overcome. The chapter focuses on three possible choices of geospatial technologies: GIS, Earth viewers and digital mappers. Each area of discussion is supported by illustrative case studies and highlights the opportunities and challenges associated with particular routes into geospatial technology in school geography.

GIS and geospatial technology

Geospatial technology refers to technology that is used for the visualisation, measurement and analysis of features on the surface of Earth. 'Geospatial technology' covers a number of different technologies Including global positioning systems (GPS), GIS and remote sensing (RS) – see Figure 1.

Geography teachers sometimes use the term 'GIS' to refer to geospatial technologies that are technically not 'true GIS', by which we mean a geographical information system which has the capacity to analyse geographical data sets. 'True GIS', such as ESRI ArcGIS, can be accessed via software packages and online, and are powerful tools for the visualisation and spatial analysis of geographical information. While 'true GIS' is an exciting tool to use in the classroom, it is important to acknowledge the key role that other geospatial technologies, in particular Earth viewers, can play in geography teaching (see Figure 2). Earth viewers are usually accessed free online and include Google Earth, Bing Maps and Earth Viewer. These applications have less to offer than a true GIS in terms of in-depth analytical capabilities, but they do offer other impressive ways of visualising places. The digitisation of spatial data has transformed the ways in which geographical information can be represented. This 'geovisualisation' involves the use of a range of geo-technologies to support geographical knowledge construction. The rapidity with which web-based geovisualisation has become ubiquitous is demonstrated by Google Earth, launched in 2005: school geography should reflect and make full use of the wide range of geography-related applications available. Using the internet allows us to interact with 'digital worlds' through an immensely diverse range of application programming interfaces (APIs). Since 2005 geography-related APIs have grown exponentially, including the now familiar Bing Maps, Google Earth and NASA's World Wind, and the proliferation of volunteered geographic information (VGI – see Boyd and Foody, 2014) and 'neogeography' (Turner, 2006) has further increased the volume and range of these applications.

Of course, GIS and Earth viewers can be used to map geographical data in a number of ways; however, there is another exciting option – digital mapping. Maps have always been a mainstay of good geography and while this chapter focuses on the use of digital tools, paper maps still have an important role to play in geography departments, and geography teachers are familiar with the use of maps in the classroom as a beneficial resource for learning.

Chapter 18: GIS and other geospatial technologies

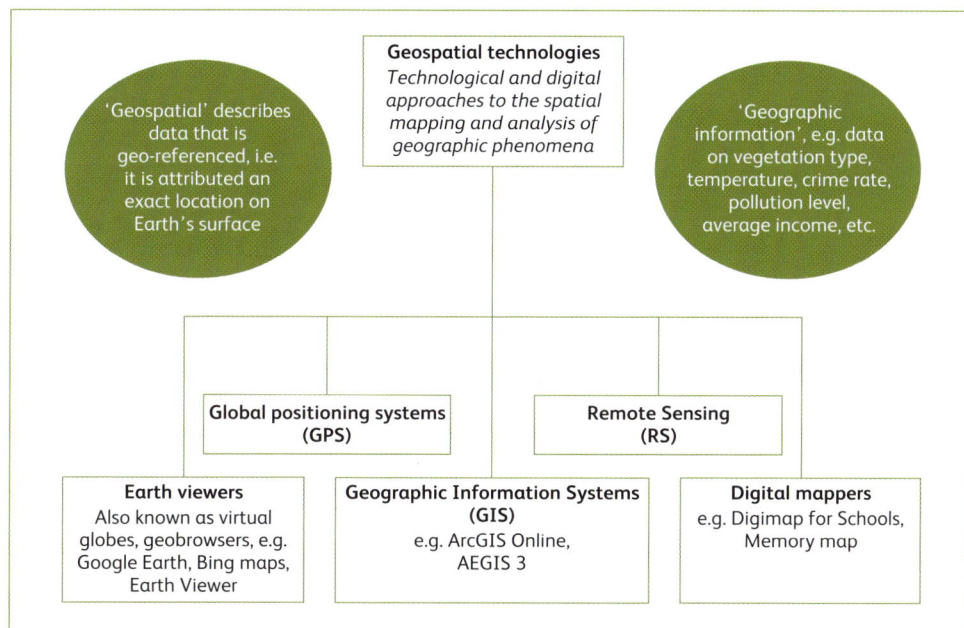

Figure 1: Geospatial technologies.

Geospatial technology	Benefits	Challenges
GIS, e.g. ArcGIS A powerful tool, accessed via software packages and online, which provides visualisation and in-depth spatial analysis of geographic information.	• In-depth analysis possible through multiple tools and layers. • High-quality mapping and visualisation. • Available online. • Access to big data sets. • Spatial analysis of data sets, e.g. measuring distances and areas, examining distributions, finding appropriate locations for new developments, making predictions.	• Takes longer to get to grips with than Earth viewers or digital mapping services. • Cost. • Requires internet access. • Need to be critical of online data sources. • Need to check PC/tablet compatibility. • Students require clear instructions linked to geographical enquiry.
Earth viewers, e.g. Google Earth Displays satellite images as 3D views of Earth's surface. Users can zoom in and out of locations, and additional information can be viewed by adding layers.	• Easier to use than GIS. • Range of tools appropriate for geography lessons e.g. virtual tours, 3D viewing – wider range than digital mapping. • Powerful visualisations of Earth's surface. • Updated regularly. • Enhances quality of teachers' visual presentations. • Valuable resource for student enquiries. • Online tutorials available. • Geography community share ideas and lessons plans.	• Lacks the in-depth analytical tools of 'true' GIS. • Requires internet access. • Students require clear instructions linked to geographical enquiry. • Need to check PC/tablet compatibility. • Can require subscription.
Digital mapping, e.g. Digimap Allows users to access maps online and use tools such as zoom, annotation and measurement.	• Easier to get to grips with than GIS. • Easy to access. • Current and historical maps available. • Variety of scales available. • Growing community of users.	• Requires subscription. • Requires internet access. • Need to check PC/tablet compatibility.

Figure 2: An overview of the benefits and challenges of GIS, Earth viewers and digital mapping.

However, what I hope this chapter will demonstrate is that using digital maps in geography lessons is probably now easier than ever.

Having outlined the nature of geospatial technologies, the remainder of the chapter examines three examples available to teachers, considers both the theoretical and practical rationales for using them in contemporary school geography, then reviews their emergence and evolving status in the school geography curriculum. Throughout, the chapter aims to showcase best practice by using examples from geography practitioners (both in schools and in geography teacher education) with a view to engaging us more practically in the debate about where innovation through geospatial technologies can really benefit geographical learning.

Geographical information systems – 'true GIS'

GIS can be defined in a number of ways according to whether one considers a geographical system to include its physical components (hardware and software) solely or whether we acknowledge its human components (Figure 3).

Longley *et al.* (2001) provide this useful definition of GIS:

> *'Many definitions of GIS have been suggested over the years, and none of them is entirely satisfactory, though many suggest more than a technology. Today, the label GIS is attached to many things: amongst them, a software product that one can buy from a vendor to carry out certain well-defined functions; digital representations of the world in the form of datasets, a community of people who use and perhaps advocate the use of these tools for various purposes; and the activity of using GIS to solve problems or advance science'* (Longley *et al.*, 2001, p. 10).

This definition hints at the complexity surrounding GIS, and it can be argued that the recent proliferation of new, particularly web-based, geo-technologies has further complicated this situation. It is interesting to note that many 'in the know' now reject the narrower scope of the term 'GIS' and refer to 'geospatial technologies'. Today 'geospatial technologies' is increasingly used as an umbrella term to describe the fuller range of geography-related digital systems now available. This includes GIS as Longley *et al.* (2001) describe it and other related technologies that teachers might want to use such as Earth viewers and digital mapping services.

True GIS can be used to input, store, analyse and display a wide range of geo-referenced data such as maps, satellite images, tables and graphs. As a result, using GIS in the classroom is attractive for most geography teachers: where GIS is being used effectively, it can support high-quality geographical learning. However, many teachers continue to find this daunting; partly due to lack of experience, but often due to one or more of the following challenges: time, training, cost and access (although the latter is now less of an issue because of the wide availability of online GIS). Later parts of the chapter explore the significance of this development for teachers, and ways in which teachers and students can explore online GIS opportunities together. This is genuinely an exciting time to be exploring GIS!

The use of geographical information systems allows the user to ask questions of data about spatial relationships that simply could not be posed without the considerable processing capacities of a GIS (Schuurman, 2004). What is particularly relevant here for geography teachers is the emphasis on representing and analysing the spatial dimension of geographical information – the main function of GIS and the key reason many of us want to use it to study geographical patterns. Indeed, when we look at the evolution of GIS over the years, it is clear that using its processing power to display and map geography has always been its main attraction. This is relevant for teachers because it can provide valuable ways to use GIS to structure enquiry learning – a well-recognised pedagogy in high-quality school geography (Roberts, 2013).

As well as having impressive visual and analytical capabilities, GIS is significant in the way it represents and communicates geographical information. Many of the ways we represent important geographical concepts such as place,

Chapter 18: GIS and other geospatial technologies

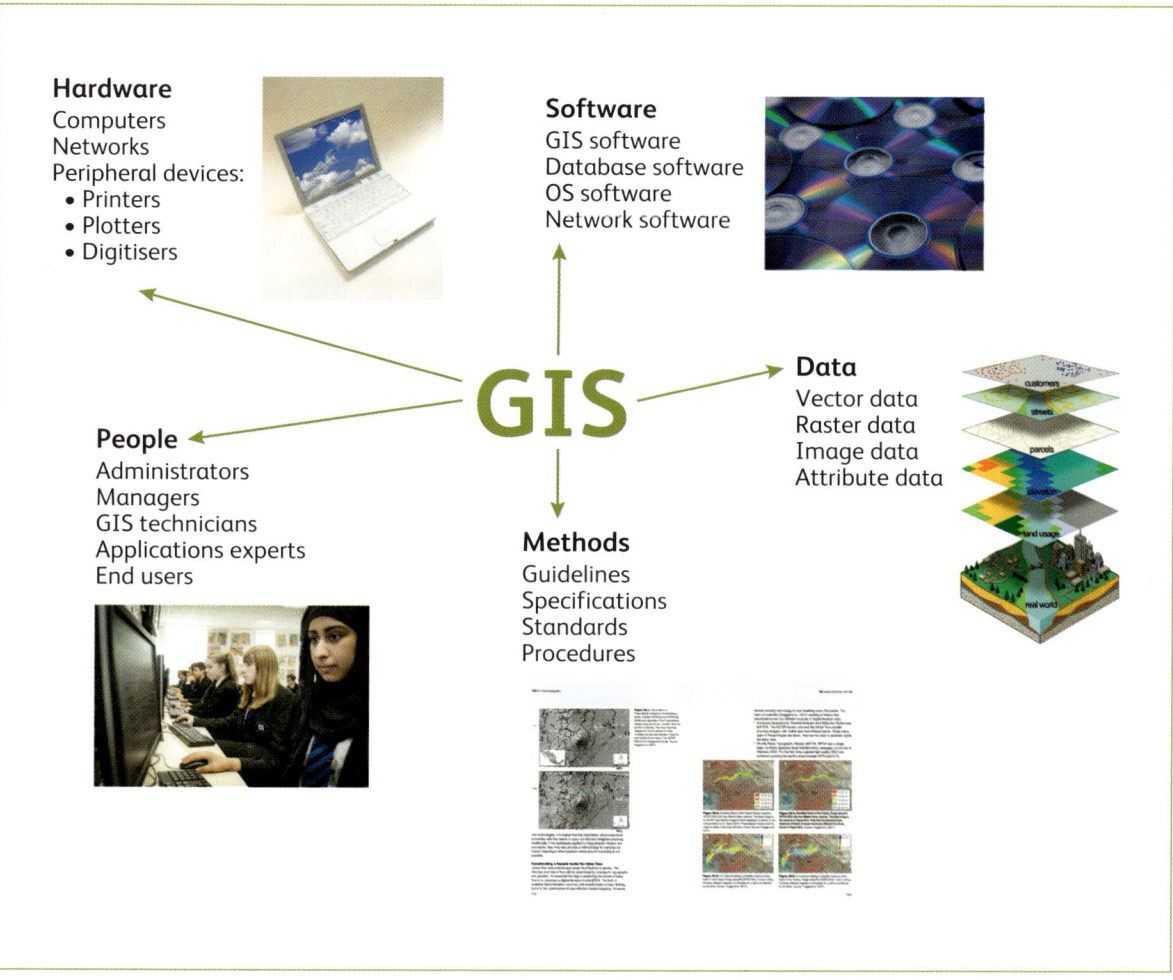

Figure 3: Components of GIS.

space and scale rely heavily on the closely inter-related disciplines of geography and cartography. In both, mapping plays the central essential part in how we come to represent and know the world, so it is important to establish the parameters that are placed on geographical representation by two cartographical processes: abstraction and generalisation.

Abstraction

All maps, including GIS representations, select or 'abstract' certain elements of any viewed reality that they represent. This involves deciding which phenomena we wish to represent in a map or any other geographical representation of Earth. As a result, some observed elements are simplified and others exaggerated depending on the purpose or function of the map.

Generalisation

To make the purpose of a map or GIS representation clearer, geographers and cartographers follow certain principles and conventions that help them to generalise about the complexity of the world (Harvey, 2008). This involves processes such as simplification, for example reducing a building's complex shape to a rectangle, or symbolisation, for example representing a place of worship through a symbol, as the circle or square topped by a cross on an Ordnance Survey map.

GIS in the school curriculum

Although the term GIS was not specifically mentioned in the first three versions of the geography National Curriculum in 1991, 1995

247

and 1999, the use of ICT was encouraged, including suggestions in the second revision (DfEE/QCA, 1999) that at key stage 3 'pupils could use the internet to obtain Earth observation, satellite and other information about rainforest depletion and sustainable use' (p. 101). Of course, this advice was before the launch of Google Earth in 2005; subsequently, more Earth viewers have become available and GIS choices for teachers have broadened considerably. In the 2007 revision of the National Curriculum (QCA, 2007) it was suggested that 'pupils learn to think spatially and use maps, visual images and new technologies, including geographical information systems (GIS), to obtain, present and analyse information' (p.101). With the implementation in September 2014 of the revised geography National Curriculum (DfE, 2013a) GIS appears more prominently in the aims for the programmes of study for key stages 1, 2 and 3:

> '…the National Curriculum for geography aims to ensure that all pupils: interpret a range of sources of geographical information, including maps, diagrams, globes, aerial photographs and Geographical Information Systems (GIS)' (DfE, 2013a, p. 198).

However, with no definition or exemplification for what counts as 'GIS' in the National Curriculum, geography teachers have interpreted this as using a range of geospatial technologies, particularly Earth viewers and digital mapping, at these key stages.

At GCSE, the DfE (2013b) geography subject content, which informed awarding body specifications for first teaching from September 2016, stipulates that students must be able to demonstrate how to use GIS in carrying out geographical investigations. A level students are also expected to use technologies such as GIS to synthesise geographical information in a number of forms from different sources. The GCE subject content (DfE, 2014), used by awarding bodies to produce GCE specifications, requires students to demonstrate they 'understand what makes data geographical and the geospatial technologies (e.g. GIS) that are used to collect, analyse and present geographical data' (p. 13). These curriculum developments clearly indicate that digital geographic information is now considered to have an important part to play in representing and integrating geographical knowledge in contemporary school education, particularly as regards their role in viewing, analysing and interpreting places and data. It is also now acknowledged in the geography National Curriculum (DfE, 2013a) that GIS plays an important part in interpreting a range of sources of geographical information, including maps, aerial photographs and imagery. In particular this implies a use of GIS that leads to students becoming competent in gathering, analysing and discussing geographical data and communicating their findings and applications of these in sophisticated ways.

In meeting National Curriculum aims and examination specification requirements 'true GIS' offers geography teachers huge potential as it can be used to input, store and display a wide range of geo-referenced data as maps, satellite images, tables and graphs. As a result, the classroom potential of GIS is attractive for most geography teachers. However, the 2011 Ofsted report *Geography: Learning to make a world of difference*, noted that GIS use in UK schools is often limited and that only a few schools are using GIS to its full potential (Ofsted, 2011). More recently and optimistically, while more conventional and costly GIS still remains difficult to access for many teachers, the proliferation of free online GIS on a range of platforms (PC, laptop, network, mobile) has started to make digital geographical information more readily available (Elwood, 2009). In addition geography teachers are using a range of geospatial technologies including Earth viewers and digital mapping services alongside or instead of 'true GIS' to fulfil specification requirements. Teachers and students are at last beginning to gain more access to the use of these technologies in the formal curriculum (Fargher, 2013).

As this short review of the emergence and status of GIS in school geography has shown, GIS in schools is characterised by two significant aspects, which are important for geography teachers if they are to be given the opportunity to realise the full educational potential of geospatial technologies. These are:

- Spatial thinking, enquiry learning and GIS
- Technical challenges for teachers using GIS.

Spatial thinking, enquiry learning and GIS

While acquiring geographical knowledge with GIS is no substitute for real experience of different localities, it can be a very useful pedagogic tool for fixing geographical significance to specific locations. Though evidence on the use of GIS (particularly Earth viewers such as Google Earth) is not yet substantial, there are clear indications that some geography teachers are beginning to make more use of GIS in the formal school curriculum, particularly in schools in the United States (Baker et al., 2009). Evidence reflecting the educational benefits of using GIS to enhance spatial thinking continues to grow. By far the largest proportion of research on the use of GIS in schools has been carried out in the US, and it emphasises the role of GIS in the development of spatial literacy (Kerski, 2003; Bednarz and van der Schee, 2006; Lei et al., 2009). The US report 'Learning to think spatially' (National Research Council, 2006) considers GIS an example of a high-tech system that can help students become spatially literate. It recommends developing education programmes that enable students to develop 'a habit of mind of thinking spatially… practise spatial thinking in an informed way, and… adopt a critical stance to spatial thinking' (p. 4). The latter emphasises students' evaluation skills and their ability to question the reliability and accuracy of spatial data in answering geographical questions.

A growing body of literature, particularly regarding the use of GIS in US schools, also indicates that effective use of GIS can complement enquiry-based geography education (Fargher, 2013), and, as Ofsted (2011) has reported, the best school geography is often enquiry-based. The rigorous and highly-structured nature of GIS lends itself to constructing knowledge through a set of stringent spatial querying procedures, similar to those illustrated in Rhind's classification (1992). His method contends that this leads a user to ask five generic questions, outlined in Figure 4.

Figure 5 takes the five types of knowledge construction and illustrates the enquiry steps most usually followed in the classroom use of GIS. The process is designed to mirror the way in which geographical information is processed in GIS. In a similar way to Rhind's classification (1992), this process involves gathering and storing data in a form appropriate for digital processing but starts by asking a 'geographical question'. This is usually connected with proving or disproving an hypothesis; predicting a spatially-orientated pattern or solving a well-defined problem. Key to this process is that the activities involved in it produce data that can be mapped, turned into tables and graphs and/or quantified.

Use of GIS in schools is largely dominated by the US company ESRI (originally the Environmental Systems Research Institute), which publishes a wide range of educational resources to support and encourage the use of its commercially available ArcGIS software (Malone et al., 2005). Figure 5 illustrates the application of the concept of spatial querying in GIS (after Rhind, 1992) to enquiry learning with GIS in schools as advocated by the ESRI literature.

In GIS use in schools where enquiry learning is of a high standard, geography has become more interested in the 'whys of where' rather than pure accumulation of geographical facts (Kerski, 2003).

Research into how learning can be enhanced by using GIS enquiry has focused on two main learning theories: constructivism and 'optimal flow theory'. The theory of constructivism in education advocates learning where students create and adapt their own knowledge and skills; an approach that is often associated with the use of GIS in schools. The teacher acts as a facilitator and student peers are often engaged in collaborative learning (Bednarz, 2001).

Question	Type of knowledge construction
What is at…?	Inventory
Where is…?	Monitoring
What has changed since…?	Inventory and monitoring
What spatial pattern exists?	Spatial analysis
What if…?	Modelling

Figure 4: Spatial querying in GIS. **After:** Rhind, 1992.

Figure 5: Steps in enquiry learning with GIS. **After:** ESRI, 2003.

Steps in enquiry	What to do	Type of knowledge construction
Ask geographical questions	Ask questions about the world around you.	Inventory
Acquire geographical resources	Identify data and information that you need to answer your questions.	Monitoring
Explore geographical data	Turn the data into maps, tables and graphs and look for patterns and relationships.	Inventory and monitoring
Analyse geographical information	Test a hypothesis, carry out map, statistical, written analysis.	Spatial analysis
Act upon your geographical knowledge	Reach geographical conclusions, inform a decision, solve a problem.	Modelling

Specifically within the UK context, enquiry is identified as one of the key aspects of the geography National Curriculum (Roberts, 2003). In conjunction with GIS, a constructivist approach to learning allows the student to generate a range of digital data, which they can manipulate and adapt as they decide and require. Linking and layering geospatial information becomes part of the overall learning process but also a pivotal aspect of a student's own understanding. A growing body of literature indicates that effective use of GIS can augment enquiry-based geography education (Bednarz, 2001; Fargher, 2013).

Another benefit of enquiry learning through GIS relates to 'optimal flow theory'. Optimal flow theory (Csikszentmihalyi, 1991) describes the cognitive processes associated with an individual's motivation to become involved in a task. To achieve a state of flow there needs to be a balance between an individual's skill level and the level of the challenge presented by an activity; otherwise a learner may become bored if a task is too easy or anxious if it is too challenging, as shown in Figure 6.

With specific reference to GIS, Smith (2005) suggests that effective teaching and learning in often problem-based 'real-world' GIS-related activities tends to encourage a 'state of flow' in involved individuals. Through engaging directly with their own knowledge construction and following the GIS enquiry process, students become engrossed in their learning. As students become more familiar with GIS, their skill levels improve alongside their broader geographical thinking. Once students have grasped the technical elements of using GIS they can become more motivated to learn and potentially enter a 'state of flow' similar to that described by Csikszentmihalyi (1991).

Figure 7 shows Smith's (2005) framework for exploring the relationship between GIS and learning. This connects 'flow theory' and constructivism with acquiring geographical knowledge and skills through the medium of GIS. Here GIS is central to the relationship, but in creating optimal GIS environments for students, Smith (2005) also acknowledges potential obstacles to the proposed framework, including students' varying abilities and the steep learning curve involved in learning to use GIS.

Using GIS

Even though GIS in schools is usually a simplified version of the industrial standard package, it still requires quite considerable prior knowledge and skill to operate it successfully. In order to access even its most basic functionality, users have to be conversant with at least the six main tasks required by 'general purpose GIS' (ESRI, 1996): input, manipulation, management, query, analysis and visualisation.

- Input: Before any geographical data can be used in GIS it needs to be in an appropriate format. While contemporary GIS includes much data that are already compatible, some still require converting via a process of digitisation.

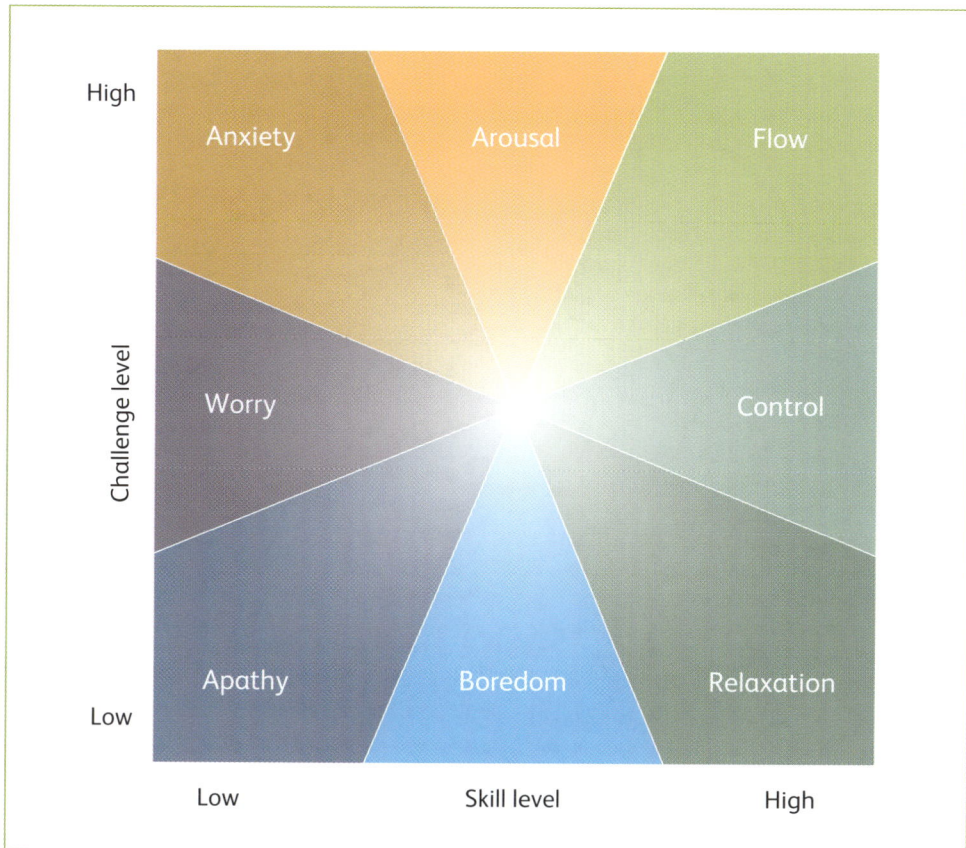

Figure 6: Optimal flow theory. **After:** Csikszentmihalyi, 1991.

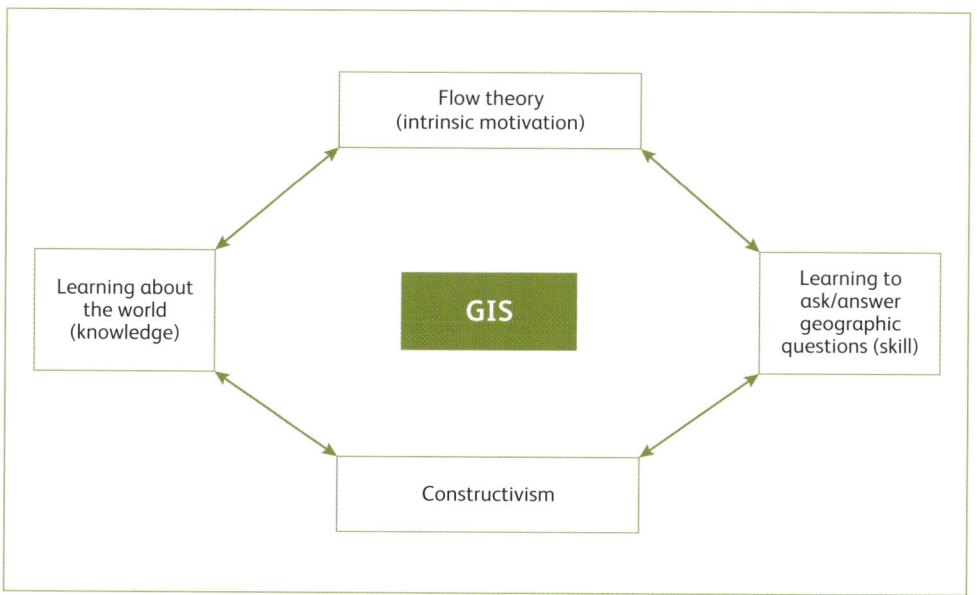

Figure 7: Learning theory, geographical knowledge and GIS. **Source:** Smith, 2005, p. 228.

- Manipulation: Using GIS to manipulate digital data requires the user to perform a number of important routine tasks, including transforming datasets to the same scale in data overlay operations and aggregating data to specific areas on a map.
- Management: Geographical information used to involve managing large amounts of data requiring huge storage capacities (ESRI, 1996). Today, with storage available online, GIS users are no longer constrained by data storage limitations.
- Query: One of the most significant functions that a GIS user needs is to query data. At its simplest level this might involve choosing a feature on a map and examining its associated attribute table. At a more complex level, users can query based on a number of attributes to contribute to a deeper level of spatial analysis in the work undertaken (Harvey, 2008). Although querying can be defined as a form of analysis (Harvey, 2008), it is useful in this context to consider analysis as a separate category of task that a GIS user needs to master.
- Analysis: Complex GIS can involve a range of procedures, but in school GIS there are most commonly two distinct forms of analysis: distance analysis, which explores proximity relationship of data, and overlay analysis, which may be at a simple or more complex level, where layers are related and joined.
- Visualisation: Displaying data visually, as a map or graph, which can benefit from a range of multimedia including three-dimensional views, photographs and videos.

To become knowledgeable users of the basic ArcGIS (formerly ArcView) or ArcGIS Online, geography teachers need to set time aside for learning how to perform the tasks outlined above. *GIS for A level Geography* (O'Connor, 2008) offers teachers both the theoretical background to GIS and practical exercises using, at that time, ArcView 9.2. Enquiries include investigating flood risk and patterns of crime across England and Wales. Courses on using ArcGIS and open-source GIS, such as QGIS, for fieldwork and expeditions are available from the Royal Geographical Society (RGS-IBG).

The greatest benefits of investing time in learning GIS are realised when geography teachers, university geographers and geography teacher educators share their experiences and publish 'ready to use' tried and tested examples.

Example: Using ArcGIS Online

Online GIS can provide a rich diversity of maps and satellite imagery for use in the geography classroom. By combining reference and thematic maps with a range of different geographical topics, online GIS can allow students to explore a wealth of geography-related information and also create their own map layers.

Fred Martin (2014) uses the example of flooding on the Somerset Levels to provide some insights into how the digital maps and satellite imagery of online GIS can support a geography case study. The Somerset Levels resource (see Figure 8) contains a map and a contents list including a range of layers of information on history, rivers and drainage, flood villages and railway flooding. The resources are designed to help secondary school students understand 'causes and effects of the 2014 flooding on the Somerset levels' (Martin, 2014).

Garry Simmons uses ArcGIS Online to significantly improve the quality of geographical learning in his key stage 3, GCSE and post-16 level classes. Garry advocates the use of ArcGIS Online because the software is easy to use and can be accessed straight from your browser. He says one of the greatest benefits for his teaching is the impressive data visualisation that he can bring into his class and fieldwork, which includes:

- charting the progress of glacial retreat globally
- mapping the latest Multiple Deprivation Index data for London and the South-East
- mapping global earthquake and local crime data
- creating heat maps, isoline maps and drawing proportional symbol maps
- creating 'story maps' to support local fieldwork
- students adding primary and secondary data to their own fieldwork maps.

Chapter 18: GIS and other geospatial technologies

Villages under water

Several villages have been in the news because they have been badly flooded. Two of these villages are at **Muchelney** and **Moorland**.

It should be possible to find these villages by using the **Search** tool (Find address or place). Unfortunately, neither of them are listed in the program's database because they are too small.

Click on the **Flood villages** item in the Contents list. The location of the villages are shown by marker pins.

Click on the pins to find out more.

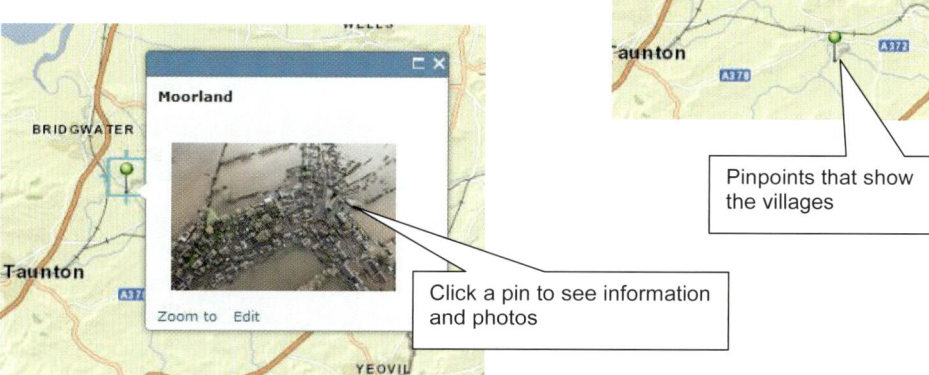

Pinpoints that show the villages

Click a pin to see information and photos

Zoom **in** to show details of each village. You can look at several map layers to do this, e.g. the World Imagery layer.

- About how big are they in area?
- About how many houses are in each?
- What road access is there to them?
- What do the photos show about how much of the villages have been flooded?

Click on the **Railway flooding** item in the Contents list. Find the location on the map.

- Describe what the photo shows.
- How will flooding affect places outside the Somerset Levels?

A village in closeup

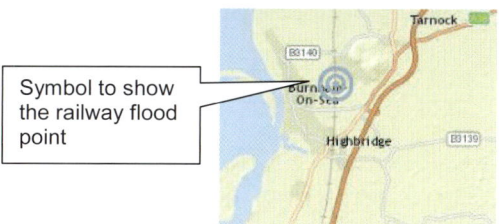

Symbol to show the railway flood point

Figure 8: Using ArcGIS Online to study flooding on the Somerset Levels. **Source:** Martin, 2014.

Figure 9:
Disappearing glaciers: Aletsch Glacier, Switzerland.
Photo © Tony Lewis.

One of Garry's key tools is ESRI's 'story mapping'. Story maps are easy-to-use, open-source web applications. They use web maps created using ArcGIS Online and ESRI's cloud-based mapping system, with a broad range of multimedia content that teachers and their students can use to enhance their story maps. These can include text, photos, video and audio sources, which help the user tell their geographical story. In his Disappearing Glaciers story map Garry charts the alarming rate at which the world's glaciers are retreating (Figure 9). His year 11 students use the measuring tool in ArcGIS Online to measure and annotate retreat rates at a number of famous glaciers worldwide including the Aletsch in Switzerland, the Athabasca in Canada and the Upsala in Argentina.

As an alternative or in addition to using the ArcGIS Online subscription service, geography teachers often make use of free online GIS, which allows for exciting visualisation and spatial analysis of familiar geographical themes such as flood risk, crime investigations or hurricane tracking. A useful starting point for key stage 3 is *GIS Made Easy: Geography lessons using GIS* (Lang, 2012), which provides resources and ideas for nine lessons.

Chapter 18: GIS and other geospatial technologies

Geospatial technology enables students to acquire a range of skills. **Photo** © Raphael Heath.

While GIS is an exciting tool to use in the classroom, it is important to discuss the key role that other geospatial technologies available to teachers can play in geography. The next section describes the role of Earth viewers and digital mapping in supporting geographical teaching and learning.

Using Earth viewers

Earth viewers give users access to a 3-D world in the form of a 'virtual globe'. Three are in common use in geography classrooms: Google Earth, Bing Maps and Earth Viewer. These applications are available free online and provide some impressive ways of visualising geography in the classroom. The free online CPD course *GIS: Get it sorted* (Geographical Association, no date.) asks teachers to consider 'GIS or visualisation?', and thus 'identify the areas where Google Earth falls short of being a "true GIS"'. Even though both are digital geographical representations, they possess quite different capacities: contrast the analytical functionality of conventional GIS and the largely Earth-viewing capacities of geobrowsers. However, although Earth viewers lack the more complex multi-criteria analysis

Figure 10:
Using Google Earth to study changes in the River Severn. Map data © Google, Digital Globe.

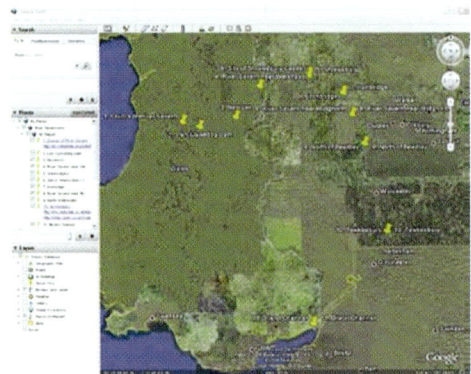

available in true GIS, they have made digital geographies 'virtually accessible' to the individual internet user in ways that were not previously feasible. As Elwood (2009) explains:

'In the world of geospatial technologies, change is afoot. In the past five years, we have seen the emergence of wide array of new technologies that enable an ever-expanding range of individuals and social groups to create and disseminate maps and spatial data' (Elwood, 2009, p. 256).

Easier access to a wider range of new types of online maps and spatial data was then beginning to change the way in which many geographers (and the general public) looked at digital geographical information (Elwood, 2009). Geography teachers now routinely incorporate Earth viewers into their lessons as alternatives to more complex GIS programmes, to the extent that Earth viewers are becoming the 'default meta-geography of the media'.

Example: Using an Earth viewer – Google Earth

Lucy Mitchell uses Google Earth in an enquiry learning framework to study changes in the physical geography of the River Severn. Using a series of Google Earth 'markers', her year 7 students examined changes in the shape and features of the drainage basin, the characteristics of the river's course and processes of erosion and deposition downstream (Figure 10).

Comparing a similar lesson she had previously taught using video extracts, Lucy spells out exactly how beneficial she found using Google Earth (Mitchell, 2010): her students developed a stronger sense of place, the panning maps developed their sense of spatial orientation, and the experience encouraged them to help each other learn how to use Google Earth tools. She also commented on how much her students enjoyed lessons based on Google Earth and how this helped them develop as independent learners.

Lucy provides a number of useful questions for teachers considering using Google Earth:

- what do we want students to learn – about the geography, and in terms of Google Earth skills?
- what enquiry questions should we ask them in order to achieve this?
- what opportunities are there for us to assess their learning through GIS?
- are there any ICT limitations? For example, does the system run slowly with multiple users?

She summarises the benefits of using Google Earth thus:

'Google Earth is available free and is easy to use. My experience showed how easily it can be incorporated into existing schemes of work. Using GIS created a palpable sense of excitement among the students, while undertaking an enquiry allowed them to be more independent learners. In the words of one year 7 student I worked with, "I find it [Google Earth] interesting as you can find out things for yourself"' (Mitchell, 2010, p. 20).

Using digital mapping

Digital mapping services offer teachers another route into using digital geographical information. Bespoke digital mapping services such as Digimap and Memory Map provide a range of historical and contemporary digital maps that can be used in the classroom. In the UK the most frequently used digital mapping service is provided by the Ordnance Survey in the form of Digimap for Schools. The importance of using comprehensive sources such as the Ordnance Survey was confirmed in the 2014 geography National Curriculum:

'At Key Stage 2 pupils should be taught:
- *Four-figure grid references, symbols and key (including the use of Ordnance Survey maps) to build their knowledge of the United Kingdom and the wider world.*

At Key Stage 3 pupils should be taught to:
- *Interpret Ordnance Survey maps in the classroom and the field, including using six-figure co-ordinates and scale, topographical and other thematic mapping, and aerial and satellite photographs'* (DfE, 2013a).

The Digimap for Schools subscription service was launched in 2010 and reached a milestone in November 2014 with 2000 primary and secondary schools signed up to it. The great advantage of using Ordnance Survey maps in Great Britain is the level of detail provided, which allows teachers the flexibility to map local and more distant locations at both small and large scales. A range of free online resources, including the *Basic User Guide* (Digimap for Schools, 2014) and *Quick Ideas for Using Digimap for Schools* (Parkinson, 2013), support teachers making use of this subscription service.

Example: Using a digital mapping service – Digimap for Schools

Lydia Williams uses Digimap with her year 7 students to complete postcode activities, finding places in London and describing surrounding areas. Her students use Digimap to print base maps for local fieldwork and then use annotation tools post-fieldwork to produce maps of site observations. She encourages students to use Digimap for Schools for research, for geography homework and for projects.

Lydia describes the benefits to her students of using Digimap regularly in their lessons:

'In year 7, students do a "mystery postcodes" activity, looking up places in London and describing the surrounding human geography (using the map key). In year 10 we include a "virtual journey along the River Thames" to understand how a river changes and in year 12 it is useful for our tourism surveys for "crowded coasts"' (Williams, 2013).

Conclusion

This chapter has looked at three ways of using geospatial technologies in school geography: GIS, Earth viewers and digital mapping, and has provided some examples of how geography teachers and teacher educators have used them with students. These examples, and new geospatial technologies becoming available, have a number of implications for practice.

Teachers must consider which route into geospatial technologies is appropriate for them and their students. For instance, do they need full-blown GIS – what I have referred to as 'true GIS' (a software package or online) – or will an Earth viewer such as Google Earth suffice? Digital mapping services now often have more manipulation tools; for example Digimap for Schools allows users to select specific areas of the map to analyse (a process called 'buffering'), annotate both contemporary and historical maps, and work on and print out maps at different scales.

Whichever you choose, geospatial technology has many advantages for good geography teaching and learning:

- It enables students to acquire a range of map skills – choosing an appropriate scale, processing data to represent geographical phenomena and patterns, and creating appropriate map keys.
- It enables students to create professional-looking maps.
- The range of different platforms – PCs, tablets, phones and other portable devices – can improve students' access to mapping.

The move towards digital mapping opens up new opportunities for both teachers and students: teachers have a wider choice of ways in which mapping can enhance their students' geographical knowledge and understanding, and as the case studies indicate, students are enthused by the potential of geospatial technology for independent working. Mapping, whether paper-based or digital, remains an essential element of good school geography.

Photo © Sheffield Park Academy.

References

Baker, T.T., Palmer, A.M. and Kerski, J.J. (2009) 'A national survey to examine teacher professional development and implementation of desktop GIS', *Journal of Geography*, 108, 4, pp. 174–85.

Bednarz, S.W. (2001) *Thinking spatially: incorporating GIS in pre and post secondary education*. Online paper for the GA's Spatially Speaking project. Available at: www.geography.org.uk/projects/spatiallyspeaking/furthermaterials (last accessed 09/11/2016).

Bednarz, S.W. and van der Schee, J. (2006) 'Europe and the United States: the implementation of geographic information systems in secondary education in two contexts', *Technology, Pedagogy and Education*, 15, 2, pp. 191–205.

Boyd, D. and Foody, G. (2014) 'Volunteered geographic information', *Geography*, 99, 3, pp. 157–60.

Csikszentmihalyi, M. (1991) *Flow: The psychology of optimal experience*. New York, NY: Harper Perennial.

DfE (2013a) *National Curriculum in England: Geography programmes of study*. Available at: www.gov.uk/government/publications/national-curriculum-in-england-geography-programmes-of-study (last accessed 09/11/2016).

DfE (2013b) *Geography: GCSE subject content and assessment objectives*. Available at: www.gov.uk/government/uploads/system/uploads/attachment_data/file/206145/GCSE_Geography.pdf (last accessed 09/11/2016).

DfE (2014) *GCE AS and A Level Subject Content for Geography*. Available at: www.gov.uk/government/publications/gce-as-and-a-level-geography (last accessed 09/11/2016).

DfEE/QCA (1999) *Geography: The National Curriculum for England*. London: DfEE/QCA.

Digimap for Schools: *http://digimapforschools.edina.ac.uk* (last accessed 09/11/2016).

Digimap for Schools (2014) *Digimap for Schools: Basic user guide*. Available at: http://digimapforschools.edina.ac.uk/schools/Resources/allstages/userguide.pdf (last accessed 09/11/2016).

Elwood, S. (2009) 'Geographic information science: new geovisualization technologies – emerging questions and linkages with GIScience research', *Progress in Human Geography*, 33, 2, pp. 256–63.

ESRI (1996) *GIS Tasks*. Available at: http://healthcybermap.org/HGeo/res/esri_what_is_a_gis.pdf (last accessed 09/11/2016).

ESRI (2003) *Geographic inquiry: thinking geographically*. Available at: www.esri.com/industries/k-12/education/~/media/Files/Pdfs/industries/k-12/pdfs/geoginquiry.pdf (last accessed 09/11/2016).

Fargher, M. (2013) 'Geographic information (GI) – how could it be used?' in Lambert, D. and Jones, M. (eds) *Debates in Geography Education*. Abingdon: Routledge, pp. 206–18.

GA (no date) *GIS: Getting it sorted*. GA online CPD course. Available at: www.geography.org.uk/cpdevents/onlinecpd/gis (last accessed 09/11/2016).

Harvey, F. (2008) *A Primer of GIS Fundamental Geographic and Cartographic Concepts*. New York, NY: The Guildford Press.

Kerski, J.J. (2003) 'The implementation and effectiveness of geographic information systems technology and methods in secondary education', *Journal of Geography*, 102, 3, pp. 128–37.

Lang, R. (2012) *GIS Made Easy: Geography lessons using GIS*. Sheffield: Geographical Association.

Lei, P., Kao, G., Lin, S. and Sun, C. (2009) 'Impacts of geographical knowledge, spatial ability and environmental cognition on image searches supported by GIS software', *Computers in Human Behaviour*, 25, 6, pp. 1270–79.

Longley, P.A., Goodchild, M.F., Maguire, D.J. and Rhind D.W. (2001) *Geographic Information Systems and Science*. Chichester: Wiley & Sons.

Malone, L., Feaster, L., Napoleon, E., Palmer, A. and Voigt, C. (2005) *Mapping Our World: GIS lessons for educators, ArcGIS® Desktop Edition*. Redlands, CA: ESRI Press.

Martin, F. (2014) 'Flooding on the Somerset Levels – ArcGIS Online', *GA Magazine*, 28, pp. 24–5.

Mitchell, L. (2010) 'Why use GIS?', *Teaching Geography*, 35, 1, pp. 18–20.

National Research Council (2006) *Learning to Think Spatially: GIS as a support system in the K–12 curriculum*. Washington, DC: The National Academies Press.

O'Connor, P. (2008) *GIS for A level Geography*. Sheffield: Geographical Association.

Ofsted (2011) *Geography: Learning to make a world of difference*. Available at: www.gov.uk/government/publications/geography-learning-to-make-a-world-of-difference (last accessed 09/11/2016).

Parkinson, A. (2013) *Quick ideas for using Digimap for Schools*. Available at: http://digimapforschools.edina.ac.uk/schools/Resources/Secondary/quick_ideas.pdf (last accessed 09/11/2016).

QCA (2007) *Geography National Curriculum*. London: QCA.

Rhind, D.W. (1992) 'Data access, charging and copyright and their implications for geographical information systems', *International Journal of Geographical Information Systems*, 6, 1, pp. 13–30.

Roberts, M. (2003) *Learning Through Enquiry: Making sense of geography in the key stage 3 classroom*. Sheffield: Geographical Association.

Roberts, M. (2013) 'The challenges of enquiry learning', *Teaching Geography*, 38, 2, pp. 50–52.

Schuurman, N. (2004) *GIS: A short introduction*. London: Blackwell.

Smith, J.S. (2005) 'Flow theory and GIS: is there a connection for learning?', *International Research in Geographical and Environmental Education*, 14, 3, pp. 225–30.

Turner, A.J. (2006) *Introduction to Neogeography*. Available at: http://highearthorbit.com/neogeography/book.pdf (last accessed 09/11/2016).

Williams, L. (2013) *Using Digimap for Schools*. Available at: http://digimapforschools.edina.ac.uk/schools/Resources/newsletters/newsletter_issue2_2013.pdf (last accessed 09/11/2016).

Key recommended readings

Lang, R. (2012) *GIS Made Easy: Geography lessons using GIS*. Sheffield: Geographical Association.

This provides teachers with a practical toolkit for using GIS in the geography classroom without the need to become a GIS specialist. A series of lessons showcases how GIS can be used in the key stage 3 classroom.

Milson, A., Demirci, A. and Kerski, J.J. (2012) *International Perspectives on Teaching and Learning with GIS in Secondary Schools*. New York, NY: Springer.

This offers teachers a broad international perspective on the pedagogical value of using GIS technology in classrooms. Through a series of case studies from 34 countries (including the UK) it assesses the opportunities for teaching and learning with GIS both now and in the future.

Chapter 19

Post-16 geography

Emma Rawlings Smith has taught school geography in the UK and abroad and is a member of the GA's Post-16 Committee

Introduction

This chapter sets out the specific challenges and opportunities that teaching Advanced Subsidiary level (AS level) and Advanced level (A level) geography present to teachers and students in schools and further education colleges. It will provide a brief historical perspective, outline the process of curriculum planning and development, review different approaches to teaching and learning, and suggest how students can prepare effectively for examinations. The chapter concludes by outlining the purpose, beyond examinations, of a post-16 geography education.

Curriculum change

Established in 1951, the A level was introduced as a two-year linear qualification with examinations at the end of the course. Although there had been adaptations and amendments during the previous half-century, it was the reforms of Curriculum 2000 that ushered in modular examinations and the new AS level qualification – an attempt to encourage candidates to study a wider breadth of subjects. The election of a Conservative-Liberal Democrat Coalition government in May 2010 saw the end of New Labour's progressive education policies: the newly elected government's first education White Paper (DfE, 2010) set in motion a 'root and branch' review of the English education system. It was based on the premise that A levels should prepare students for both Higher Education (HE) and the world of work, while bearing comparison with the highest educational standards internationally. New specifications for first teaching in 2016 were developed based on the requirements of the DfE (2014) geography subject content.

The Curriculum 2000/2008 A level reforms, and the more recent 2016 specifications, are significant: not only in terms of updating subject content and the balance of core curriculum content, but also in the shifting format of assessment towards individual investigations and fieldwork (Figure 1).

Subject content

The complexity and rapidly changing nature of human society is having a profound effect on the planet and yet post-16 geography subject content, as written in successive curriculum documents, is failing to keep up with the times. China's rapid transition to a market economy, migration within an enlarged European Union, conflict and humanitarian crises across the Middle East and the global financial crisis have significantly altered the socio-economic landscape in which A levels are being taught, but new content is slow to reach the classroom. The core content introduced in the 2016 specifications requires students to study a balance of human and physical geography, with more emphasis on the application of knowledge rather than knowledge itself. Core content comprises two human and two physical themes. The human themes are Global Systems and Global Governance, and Changing Place, Changing Places. The physical themes are Water and Carbon Cycles, and Landscape Systems.

Skills

In 2008 fieldwork-based coursework disappeared and was replaced with a requirement for fieldwork experience or research to be assessed in a controlled examination. During the recent A level review Ofqual revoked this change – 'geography fieldwork skills are hard to demonstrate in a written exam' (Ofqual, 2013) – and a teacher-assessed investigative report worth 20 per cent of the qualification was reintroduced.

Chapter 19: Post-16 geography

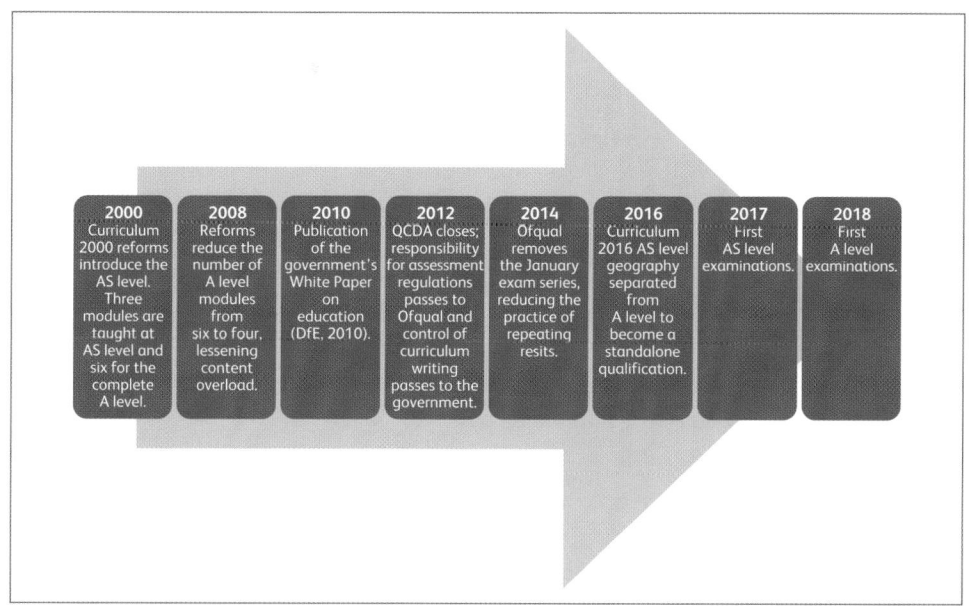

Figure 1: Timeline of A level reforms from 2000 to 2018.

The delivery of Level 2 quantitative methods is now an integral part of the A level course. Methods include quantitative and qualitative data collection, calculating and interpreting statistics and analysing geographical relationships using appropriate statistical tests.

Format of assessment

Curriculum 2008 saw the introduction of one specification per examination board for England and Wales, a reduction from seven to just four specifications, a move from six units to four, the introduction of greater stretch and challenge at A level, and the introduction of the A* grade. The modular nature of Curriculum 2008, developed to reduce students' assessment load (QCA, 2006), meant students could try for better exam grades in both the June and new January series in Year 12 and Year 13. Students achieved better results and this made examinations appear to be getting easier, ultimately undermining qualification standards. Concerned about grade inflation, in March 2012 the government reverted to a linear structure for GCSE, AS and A level assessments, with all exams to take place at the end of the of the course. The AS level is again a standalone qualification that no longer contributes towards, and may not be 'co-teachable with', the new A level. We will not be able to judge whether these measures have been a success until summer 2018, when the first cohort sit their terminal examinations and the A level system can be fully evaluated.

Curriculum development

In 2014, the government stipulated a rich, relevant and challenging geography curriculum at A level. The curriculum encompasses all the activities that take place in a school or college, from timetabled lessons to less formal activities such as field trips and GA Branch lectures. As such, the concept and content of curricula is much contested and debated, because it reflects society's different views about the purpose of education (see Kelly, 2009; Biddulph, 2014). Curriculum development is the process by which we decide what to teach and how to organise teaching and learning. In a broad sense, curriculum development is a school-based process that begins before teaching, is evaluated during teaching, and reflected upon and developed after teaching, it includes the stages of design, development, implementation and evaluation of all that is taught. Rawling (2007) describes it as:

> 'the experiences that pupils are to receive in schools in order to help them make progress in geography, enjoy the experience and appreciate the relevance of geography to their own lives' (p. 7).

The Geographical Association (GA) uses the term 'curriculum making' to describe the planning and development process:

> 'There are three main ingredients in the curriculum making process. Teachers make it happen in the classroom by drawing from their knowledge of:
> - teaching approaches and specific teaching techniques
> - students and how they learn
> - the subject – geography – and what it is for' (GA, no date).

Since the key outcome of post-16 education is to obtain qualifications, we must turn to the awarding organisations to find out what to teach. All geography examination specifications have these common features:

- aims and objectives
- subject content and concepts
- assessment.

The next section will focus on each of these dimensions of assessment-led curriculum development.

Aims and objectives

In an era of competition for both students and funding, schools and teachers are under considerable pressure to get results: positive value-added scores move schools up league tables and good grades give students access to Russell Group universities. However, results should not be the only measure of a successful education: they should be seen in the context of more general educational aims (Butt, 2002), including 'intrinsic' aims (for the good of the individual) and 'instrumental' (for the good of the state or society). Before choosing a specification it is worth comparing the formal aims and objectives of the 2013–16 AS and A level reforms (Figure 2) with the aims and objectives of your own geography department and school.

The aims and objectives of a school or college geography department are represented below in the form of questions (adapted from Rawling, 2007), each of which is useful to consider as curriculum development progresses.

Rationale
- What is the purpose of education in the school?
- What is the rationale for geography in the school?
- How can the geography curriculum contribute to the school's aims and ethos?

The school context
- How can you build on the special features of the school and its locality?
- What teaching expertise is available to the department? e.g. Chartered Geographers, GA members, Google Certified Teachers or SSAT Lead Practitioners.
- Which existing community links and contacts can support the new specification? Do you need to source new links (e.g. university researchers and lecturers, planning experts or National Park education officers)?
- What new technologies have already worked well and how can these be embedded in new practice? Is there a need for different technology to aid teaching?

The geography department
- What content will we select in order to develop the required concepts, skills and processes?
- How will we sequence it?
- Which resources and approaches to learning are successful and should be retained? (in response to the views of both teachers and students)
- What can we learn from past experiences? What experiences do new department members bring?

The students
- Within the constraints of the examination specifications, what approaches to geography best meet the needs of the students (e.g. an enquiry approach, a people/environment approach)?
- How might the current post-14 student performance level influence curriculum making?
- Can students interact face-to-face with professional geographers such as RGS Ambassadors and guest lecturers or Skype interviews with geographers in the field?

Statutory and Awarding Organisation (AO) requirements

- Can government initiatives and moral agendas, including Eco-Schools and the Global Dimension, be incorporated into the formal geography curriculum or might this 'corrupt' the curriculum?

There should be stronger progression from GCSE to A level, following the GCSE geography reforms (DfE, 2013b) in terms of concepts and new material. When a key concept or geographical theme such as tectonics or urban environments is revisited as students move through their school career, it should be studied at a higher level of complexity (cf. Bruner's (1966) spiral curriculum).

Selecting a specification

Success at A level requires careful planning. Once progression, aims and objectives have been considered you can make the all-important decision about which specification to teach. The four core themes common to all GCE geography specifications, as set out by the DfE (2014), represent 60 per cent of the A level qualification. AOs have created a variety of content to attract different cohorts of students for the remaining 40 per cent non-core people-environment content, with some including tectonics. Your choice of specification may depend on existing department resources, students' desire for vertical progression from GCSE, availability of published schemes of work, or teacher preferences and expertise. Some choices are more important than others; for example, when there are fewer teachers in a geography department, or expertise is lacking for essential curriculum development, the availability of published schemes of work and resources may take priority over preferred non-core subject content or student preferences.

Resourcing your chosen specification

Once you have selected your chosen specification it is worth consulting AO publications, which include past training content, teacher support material and transition documentation. Registering with your AO will give you access to past question papers, mark schemes, examiners' reports and details of face-to-face or online teacher support meetings.

AS and A level specifications in geography must encourage learners to:

- develop and apply their understanding of physical and human geographical concepts and processes to understand and interpret our changing world
- develop their awareness of the complexity of interactions within and between physical and human environments at scales from local to global
- develop as global citizens who recognise the challenges of sustainability and the implications for their own and others' lives
- improve as critical and reflective learners aware of the importance of attitudes and values, including their own
- become adept in the use and application of skills and new technologies through their geographical studies both in and outside the classroom
- be inspired by the world around them, and gain enjoyment and satisfaction from their geographical studies and understand their relevance.

Finally, talking to the AO's Subject Advisor or colleagues who already teach the specification may resolve any specific issues you have. If available, it may be useful to follow the AO's published schemes of work when first teaching a new specification; they can be easily adapted, provide further guidance and offer useful links to alternative resources. Textbooks are one such resource: they can provide helpful theoretical information, but the subject content and case studies can quickly date so it is essential to maintain a bank of fresh resources – such as documentaries, published case studies and journal articles – to keep knowledge current. However, published schemes of work rarely include specific details about your locality and they may not address your particular students' needs, so you must consider carefully whether they are suitable for use in your department. The GA and Royal Geographical Society

Figure 2: The formal aims and objectives of the AS and A level reforms. **Source:** DfE, 2013a.

Figure 3: Four conceptual frameworks as represented in formal curricula and by geographers.

Formal curriculum frameworks		Geographers' curriculum frameworks	
2016 GCE specifications (DfE, 2013a)	Geography National Curriculum (DfE, 2013c)	Thinking Geographically – linking 'big ideas' through pairs of concepts (Jackson, 2006)	Linking everyday experience with higher-level geographical ideas (Taylor, 2008)
The representation of technical and abstract ideas	The spiral curriculum, revisiting concepts and developing complex links	• Space and place • Scale and connection • Proximity and distance • Relational thinking	* Diversity * Change * Interaction and * Perception and representation
• Space • Place • Interdependence • Diversity • Physical and human processes • People-environment interaction • Changes over time	• Place • Space • Interdependence • Similarities, differences and links • Human and physical processes • Change over time		

(RGS-IBG) offer a range of publications, journal articles and continuing professional development opportunities to help plan and teach post-16 geography. Many teachers tend to 'play safe', using published schemes of work and AO-endorsed resources, but you can create your own schemes of work. This can be time-consuming, but it does give you freedom of choice about what students learn (content and concepts), how they learn (skills and approaches, e.g. research skills, essay writing, data analysis and fieldwork) and the nature of their learning (intrinsic/instrumental). Your own material can include local case studies – these will be more relevant to students, and therefore more memorable. Taking on the role of expert curriculum-maker can help to develop teacher confidence and bring much-needed professionalism back into the classroom (Rawling, 2007).

Subject content and concepts

When interpreting your chosen specification, it is important to establish the conceptual framework and context before selecting the specific subject content or essential knowledge and processes to be taught. It is also important to be able to distinguish between the subject content and concepts, or 'big ideas' (see Bonnett, 2008). An idea is 'big' if it both helps us to make sense of our own geographical knowledge and helps us to make sense of the world. Concepts are the understanding, the cement if you like, that bonds seemingly discrete areas of knowledge. Some concepts are concrete and easy to grasp; others are more abstract. To avoid schemes of work that are just accumulations of 'content' (Jackson, 2006) it is worth spending some time drawing out the concepts that frame learning.

Key concepts

Some key concepts (Figure 3) are so big that they cross disciplinary boundaries. In order to make sense of these concepts, students must link them with other, smaller, concepts. The water cycle, for example, is a concrete concept that helps to explain where water goes when it evaporates, how water moves around the planet and why lowland areas flood. Although most students would be able to show a basic understanding of the water cycle, it might take a college student to explain the influence of complex Earth-atmosphere concepts such as the jet stream, global climate change and global weirding that contributed to the extreme British flooding of January 2014.

In the same way, an explanation of why present-day Sahara and Antarctica are both deserts and yet have a plentiful supply of water underground requires an understanding of both physical processes and change over time. These concepts are even more abstract and difficult to grasp than the previous example, so students need more time to learn about them.

Developing conceptual understanding by framing learning with 'big ideas' helps students to think in more abstract ways and make connections between everyday and theoretical concepts (see Brooks (2013) for a categorisation of hierarchical, organisational and developmental concepts, and Roberts (2013) for developing conceptual understanding).

Subject content

What awarding organisations think students should learn is tied closely with what can be assessed. Subject knowledge is easier to measure than either skills or competencies. In the Edexcel 2008 A level specification, for example, half the marks were based on knowledge alone. The change in government in 2010 brought with it a change in both curriculum language and conceptions of knowledge. New Labour's neo-liberal approach to education, which prioritised pedagogic process and generic skills-based curricula such as 'learning to learn' over subject specialisms, were swept away; the Coalition government favoured a return to traditional subject-based teaching, with a focus on core knowledge and subject-based concepts. Access to this powerful knowledge – concepts peculiar to academic subjects (Young, 2008) – allows students to make sense of the world and make informed decisions while looking at the world through a geographical lens (Lambert, 2011; Firth, 2013). With the ever-increasing processing power of modern technology, there is now more than ever a need for knowledgeable geographers able to understand and analyse the wealth of available geospatial data. Knowledge – and more importantly the understanding of knowledge, balanced and integrated with skills, concepts and pedagogy – is fundamental to geographical education (see Figure 4).

Many of the challenges of teaching post-16 geography, particularly for new teachers, stem from a lack of detailed knowledge of human and physical geography. High-quality resources and CPD can address such challenges, providing subject updates and opportunities for teachers to develop new skills and tackle subject areas not covered during their own undergraduate experience and to actively engage in the curriculum-making process.

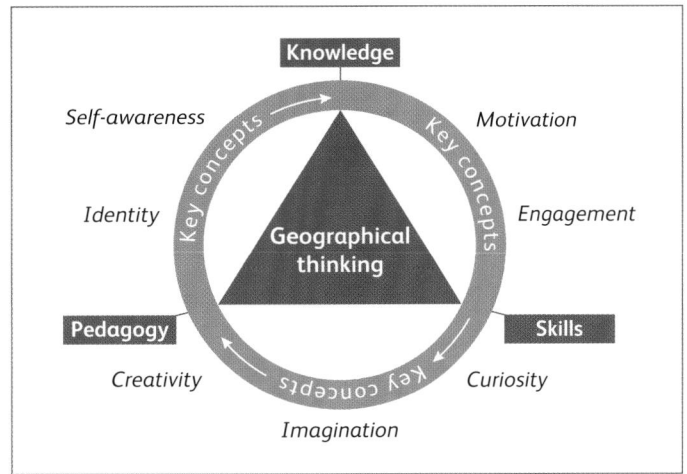

Figure 4: The dynamic process of learning.
Source: Scoffham, 2011, p. 129.

Approaches to learning

We all know that successful students start preparing for their final exams long before they walk into the examination room; however, their success also depends on their teachers choosing the right teaching and learning strategies. This section outlines the different approaches to learning, what students say helps them in post-16 lessons, some effective teaching and learning strategies and exam preparation.

A number of dichotomies are used to describe the learning process; the most common is that of teacher-led/student-centred learning (Figure 5). New Labour's educational discourse implied that teacher-led learning was outdated and irrelevant compared to student-centred learning with its progressive and personalised approach to education. Under the Coalition government the tide turned, with calls for a return to didactic teaching methods and the encouragement of teacher talk as being vital to introduce students to the language of geography and develop their geographical understanding (Roberts, 2013). When used appropriately, teacher talk, rote learning, recitation and knowledge recall all merit a place in the classroom. Indeed, Ofsted's lesson observation framework was amended after concerns were raised about the inspectors' support for too narrow a range of preferred learning activities (Burns, 2013). The message for teachers in a changing political landscape is simple: providing both teacher-led and student-centred learning opportunities will give students the best chance of success.

Figure 5: Teacher-led and student-centred learning.

Teacher-led learning	Student-centred learning
Teacher decides what is to be learnt	Students have a say in what is learnt
Teacher delivers the curriculum	Students explore the curriculum
Teacher is the subject expert	Teacher is the facilitator
Students receive knowledge	Teacher provides learning opportunities
One-way transmission of education	Co-construction of knowledge
Learning outcomes are predetermined and fixed	Learning is shared by teachers and students and learning activities are flexible
Focus on summative assessments	Continual formative assessment
Power rests with the teacher	Students are empowered

Student voice

It is good practice to involve post-16 students in the learning process; informing them about what they are learning and why can enable them to take ownership of their learning. Spend time outlining the specification's 'big picture' – its subject content, skills and assessment structure – and get them, for example, to build their own conceptual frameworks in which to fit new knowledge. This will help them successfully navigate their way through the specification. In the early stages students will have to be carefully supported to assist their transition from GCSE to A level. In an education system that prioritises exam results over any other educational outcomes, we should nevertheless teach students how to learn: how to engage with knowledge and develop a range of skills and competences in preparation for life-long learning. When rating the success of your own teaching it is a good idea to ask your students what they think. I asked 30 sixth-form students firstly, what helps them learn, and secondly, what were the characteristics of a successful lesson: their answers were wide-ranging and very insightful:

'Collaborative work has helped me develop some really useful skills, for example using Dropbox to share files, Google Docs Forms to collect survey data and blogging to spread my ideas to other geographers.'

'Developing a mature essay style in preparation for exams can take time, so start practising early! A strong paragraph starts with a clear point, includes real evidence and a helpful explanation and ends with a link to the next point (the PEEL approach).'

'Enjoyable lessons involve the use of innovative teaching methods and stimulating resources or an element of competition or challenge. When I enjoy a lesson I work really hard!'

'This year has provided the opportunity to learn from each other through peer presentations, role plays, decision-making exercises and debates – challenging but empowering.'

'To reduce exam stress, it is worth being organised and prepared for exams by writing revision notes, keeping neat notes and re-drafting exam answers and essays on a weekly basis.'

The characteristics of a successful lesson as perceived by my students (Figure 6) correspond closely to psychologist Mihaly Csikszentmihalyi's 'flow' theory (1990). This asserts that what makes an experience genuinely satisfying is complete absorption in an activity, a state of consciousness he called 'flow'. In the classroom context, flow is achieved when subject knowledge and understanding are central to the learning process, lessons are active and engaging, and levels of challenge and skill stretch every student.

Enquiry approach

Having completed my PGCE under the tutorage of Margaret Roberts, my teaching was underpinned by her advocacy of the enquiry

Figure 6: The characteristics of a successful lesson according to 30 sixth-form students (produced using Wordle.com).

1. Knowledge	2. Comprehension	3. Application	4. Analysis	5. Synthesis	6. Evaluation
Define	Explain	Demonstrate	Classify	Combine	Appraise
List	Summarise	Show	Compare	Compose	Criticise
Identify	Interpret	Operate	Contrast	Construct	Critique
Describe	Rewrite	Construct	Distinguish	Create	Debate
Match	Convert	Apply	Deduce	Design	Judge
Locate	Give examples	Illustrate	Infer	Suppose	Support

Figure 7: Bloom's taxonomy keywords.

approach (Roberts, 2003), at a time when 'delivering' the textbook double-page spread was the more usual approach. The enquiry approach can give students the opportunity to work 'in flow' and to show independence, initiative and imagination; it can prepare them for the next stage of their education or training or for the world of work. These three strategies, based on an enquiry approach, are designed to promote questioning, deeper thinking and literacy:

- Using higher order thinking skills – questioning
- Supporting an enquiry with a range of geographical information
- Thinking geographically – concept mapping, concept grids and writing frames.

Using higher-order thinking skills – questioning

A taxonomy is a hierarchical list of instructional words. Bloom's taxonomy (1956), originally designed for assessment objectives, was modified by Anderson and Krathwohl (2001) into lower- and higher-order thinking skills (1 easier – 6 harder) to frame questioning (Figure 7). So often a majority of questions asked in the classroom are lower-order closed questions, requiring simple recall and one-word answers, yet with careful planning you can generate a much greater variety of questions to help ensure all orders of thinking are exercised in students' learning.

What better way to foster a culture of thinking than with key questions or 'big ideas' (Bonnett, 2008) that engage students in the learning process and get them thinking critically about their learning?

Question grids, another adaptation of Bloom's taxonomy, can help students to construct questions. Working collaboratively, students can generate extremely challenging questions, which often need very little re-drafting. Question grids can incorporate geographical images to spark curiosity, and the questions can be displayed around the interactive whiteboard as a visual reminder. John Sayers has produced a number of helpful question grids, two of which are shown in Figure 8.

Figure 8a has instructions for use, and the version shown in Figure 8b can include images, theoretical models or even Twitter feeds as stimulus material. Using the questions generated by the students, teachers can develop a series of lessons that students find intrinsically interesting and motivating, because they were part of the process of creating them.

Socratic questioning

The Greek philosopher Socrates believed that questioning was at the root of all learning. Socratic questioning is a very simple but important strategy for helping students to acquire conceptual understanding, to probe the meaning of data and to formulate further questions (Paul, 1993). The six steps of Socratic questioning encourage students to think harder to develop more challenging questions:

1. Get students to clarify their thinking: Why do you think this? Who else might think this?
2. Challenge students' assumptions: Is this always the case? Does this assumption hold true?
3. Probe reasons and evidence: Why do you say that? Is there reason to doubt this evidence?
4. Question viewpoints and perspectives (great when learning about key players): What is the counter argument for…? Does anyone see this another way?
5. Challenge implications and consequences (to help students analyse a topic): If that happened, what else would result? How does … affect…?
6. Question the question: Why is this question important? Why do you think I asked that question?

Hinge point questions

Each of the questioning techniques described so far has been designed to extend students' thinking in a structured way. The last example, hinge point questioning, can be used to establish straight away whether students understand an important concept. The hinge question, asked halfway through the lesson, can take any form as long as the teacher can collect and interpret the responses quickly (see Wiliam, 2011); student response apps or mini whiteboards work well for this. The background for the example below is a study of the causes of climate change and the reasons for the rapid global rise in temperatures. It is important to ensure that all students understand the range of factors that cause temperatures to increase rapidly in the Arctic.

Hinge question: Which two of the following ideas do *not* help us to understand the rapid rate at which Arctic ice is melting?

A. Melting of the permafrost releases methane, itself a greenhouse gas, which traps more heat in the atmosphere.

B. The expansion of the ozone hole over the Arctic allows more solar radiation to heat the surface of Earth, especially over the Arctic where the atmosphere is thinner.

C. Melting of sea ice exposes vast areas of darker sea surface, absorbing more solar radiation.

D. Melting of Arctic sea ice will slow the thermohaline circulation and increase the sea temperature.

E. Humans are burning more fossil fuels and releasing more carbon dioxide, itself a greenhouse gas, which traps more heat in the atmosphere.

This question is ideal because the distracters B and D have both been offered as explanations in past examination scripts; they are wrong, but if a students' conceptual knowledge is weak they can appear plausible. If students get this question correct, learning can move on; if some students get it wrong, more time needs to be spent improving their conceptual understanding.

Supporting an enquiry with a range of geographical information

The geographical information in textbooks can be out-of-date even before it is published. It is therefore important to teach students how to search and filter information to make sure it is accurate and relevant, and to give them opportunities to make sense of it. Vast quantities of online data, often available as raw data ready to be manipulated, are easily accessible. Planning web enquiries can be really rewarding; however, if the teacher creates the key questions, researches relevant websites and devises meaningful learning tasks, they can also be hugely time-consuming. Students find independent internet research exciting, and this element can be lost if the teacher always does it for them. Why not encourage students to

Chapter 19: Post-16 geography

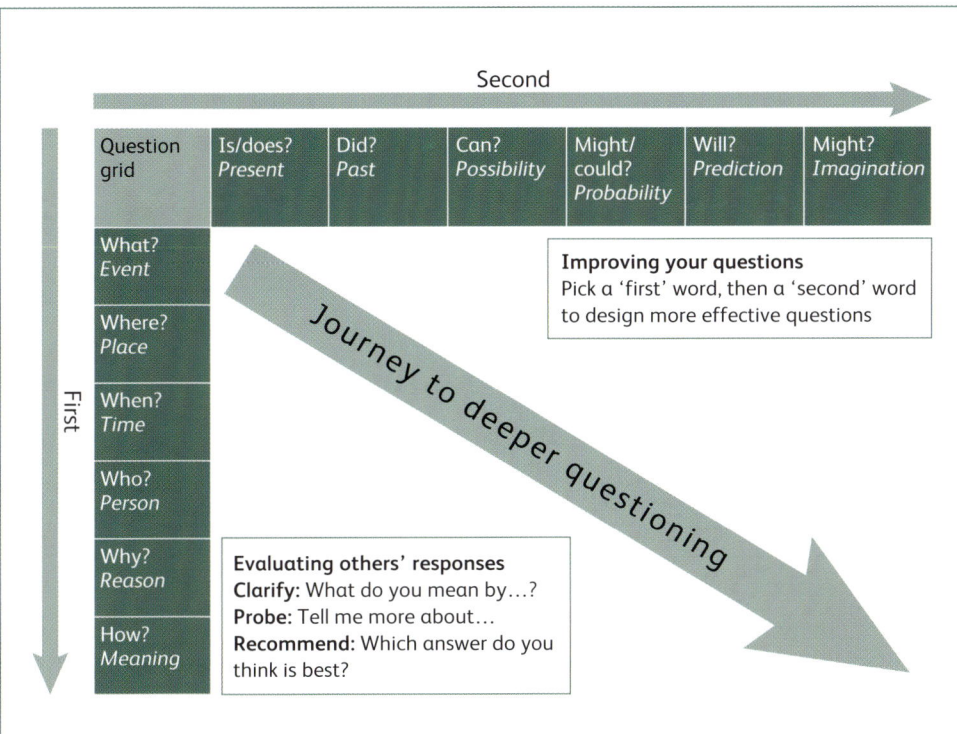

Figure 8: (a) A question grid based on Bloom's taxonomy; **(b)** A question grid with stimulus. **Source:** @JohnSayers. **Photo:** licence free image.

Figure 9: Learning grids to support concept mapping.

	1	2	3	4	5	6
1	Birth rate	Emigration	Pull factors	Dependency ratio	State pension fund	Fertility rate
2	Tax-free earnings	Internal migration	Spending the grey pound	Ageing population	Population structure	Push factors
3	Economic opportunities	Reduced childcare provision	Death rate	Raising retirement age	Urbanisation	Remittance payments
4	Immigration	Rapid population growth	High demand for public services	Life expectancy	Rapid population growth	Increased poverty
5	Reduced workforce	Accession 10 countries	Unlimited immigration	Asset-rich, income poor	Encouraging family planning	Working family tax credits
6	Net migration balance	Shrinking state pension fund	Encouraging larger families	Controlling birth rates	Winter fuel subsidy	Baby boom

employ Web 2.0 technology or 'user-generated content' to source online resources ready for publication on social media platforms such as Scoop.it or Flipboard? It is worth creating separate publications for each of the main themes in the specification and associated keywords can be tagged to pull content. Each time you visit the site relevant news stories, videos and other media sources are waiting to be curated to the platform: within minutes a contemporary magazine-style publication can be put together and shared with other users.

Thinking geographically – concept mapping, concept grids and writing frames

Making sense of new knowledge, and relating it to existing knowledge, can be effectively achieved by using conceptual frameworks. At their simplest, frameworks can be a continuum onto which smaller concepts are organised: opinion lines are a good example of this form of concept mapping. For example, if students are investigating the attitudes of various key players to the impact of climate change on the Arctic, Russian energy giant Gazprom, who would benefit from an ice-free Arctic because drilling for oil would be easier, might sit at one end of the continuum; environmental groups such as Greenpeace, who protest against the loss of fragile Arctic ecosystems, might be found at the other.

With progression, students can develop their own complex frameworks for learning. The process of organising information and concepts such as place, space and scale can encourage analytical thinking and reasoning skills: an excellent precursor to essay writing.

Figure 9 shows a learning grid to support concept mapping. Students start by discussing the geographical concepts. Then, working in pairs or small groups, students roll a pair of dice to select a concept from the learning grid and use it to start a concept map. Then they roll the dice again and add a new concept to the map. Finally, they annotate the map to link the two concepts. This is a great revision tool, because students must use higher-order thinking skills and reasoning to link concepts. Learning grids can also be used for concept analysis: instead of linking concepts students can compare and contrast the new concept with the previous one. Picking 'Accession 10 countries' after 'Reduced workforce', a student might link them with 'consequences of European migration for the donor country'. See Griffith and Burns (2012) for more examples of how to use learning grids.

Finally, there is a whole range of activities to support the effective transmission, retention and revision of conceptual understanding and knowledge; Figure 10 lists some for a unit on climate change.

- List and define the key words for the unit from your chosen specification.
- Complete a spelling quiz for the key words using Socrative.com or test using the Brainscape iPad app.
- Identify glacial and interglacial periods on a long-term climate graph.
- Describe the natural causes of climate change including sunspots, volcanoes and Earth's orbit.
- Match the main greenhouse gases and their proportions with their natural or human sources.
- Compare and contrast the different characteristics of natural and enhanced climate change, using a HOT Solo taxonomy writing frame (Biggs and Collis, 1982).
- Order the different proxy temperature reconstruction methods according to their accuracy and reliability.
- Mindmap and collate examples of the direct impacts of climate change (a warmer world with more variable weather) across the world and across one continent, such as Africa.
- Listen to a summary of the Stern report and write notes. Reconstruct the original speech as accurately as possible.
- Read aloud in class recent newspaper articles about the indirect impacts of climate change (sea level rise) and locate the affected coastal places on a map of the world.
- Categorise the impacts of climate change using a framework such as the Development Compass Rose (Tide~DEC, 1995, p. 19)
- Use the World Resources Institute's Extreme Weather and Climate Events Timeline (*www.wri.org*) to research last year's extreme weather, for example the hottest, coldest, wettest and driest events.
- Answer multiple-choice hinge questions and write new examples, including using distracters, in pairs. Questions should test conceptual understanding: for climate change, they might focus on feedback mechanisms such as the permafrost melting or a reduction in surface albedo.
- Create Top Trumps with vulnerability data, including population density and structure, GDP, hazard risks, insurance, hazard mapping and awareness, education, hazard-proof homes etc., for different countries.
- Sort the different consequences of climate change by magnitude – the worst last.
- Prioritise the needs for a range of societies as a consequence of climate change. This may focus on low-lying islands such as the Maldives and vulnerable countries such as the Philippines.
- Appraise the mitigation and adaptation responses to climate change of a range of countries.
- Design a home adapted to sea-level change for the people of Tuvalu or coastal Bangladesh.
- Develop a concept map for the unit and add links between the big ideas.
- Write a paragraph outlining one method of climate change mitigation and have a second student read it and devise questions about it. Compare two methods and evaluate which one works better and why.
- Answer examination questions, peer/self-mark these and redraft model answers.
- Write an analytical report on one aspect of climate change. It could focus on why a place struggles to cope with climate change, or why geo-engineering is not the best solution for the future.
- Research the key players in the fight against climate change and role-play a debate about who is responsible and how they should respond. Key players include governments, energy companies and NGOs.
- Combine information about climate change effects and responses into a persuasive speech from the viewpoint of environmental refugees, or those affected by extreme weather, advocating the need for global action.
- Redraft an essay/speech/case study/report with corrections and subject updates from the news.

Figure 10: Climate change: activities to support the effective transmission, retention and revision of conceptual understanding and knowledge.

Building up to exams

The preparation for linear A level exams should be integrated into the course from day one. By sticking a summary of the course structure in the front of files, students can date and chart their own progress through the specification. Providing model answers, low-level exam responses and mark schemes can help students to understand how exams are marked. This activity is essentially what happens at AO examiners' meetings and it allows students the opportunity to think about how to write a good exam response. Peer- and self-assessment should be used regularly for marking exam-type questions, to familiarise students with the examination process. Introducing students to feedback from examiners' reports, one question at a time, can provide further opportunities for exam talk. A good exam essay requires a student to understand the subject matter, and also be able to interpret the command words used on the question paper. It is good practice to regularly use a range of command words in class. 'To what extent…?' or 'Consider the view that…' can initiate lively discussions when used as starter tasks and to structure extended writing. Delivering past-paper questions for homework on a weekly basis, alongside the active use of command words and specification terminology in class talk, will familiarise students with exam language; it is also an opportunity to develop their essay-writing skills. Finally, time-management skills (or the lack of them) can have a significant impact on the results of students following linear courses. Students should know the mark allocation for each exam they sit, and the number of minutes per mark. End-of-topic assessments can be used not only to test students' subject knowledge but also their time management.

Final exam preparation

A level exams assess only a narrow range of knowledge and skills, so students will need guiding carefully through the revision process. A revision activities checklist (Figure 11) can be a really useful tool.

Post-16 teaching beyond examinations – what are we teaching for?

At a time of high youth unemployment, A level choices can be critical. Enjoyment, past success and peer-group influences can seem less important than whether a particular choice is a 'facilitating' subject, as defined by the Russell Group (2015). Studying facilitating subjects, such as geography, at A level opens up a wide range of options for undergraduate study. At both AS and A level, geography is the eighth most popular subject (JCQ, 2015) and it is the least gender imbalanced of all subjects (GA, 2014). Candidate numbers for geography examinations have been fairly stable since 2006. The three years 2012–2014 saw an increase in entries, during a period when total A level entries fell (GA, 2014), due, in part, to the introduction of the English Baccalaureate, which is encouraging the take-up of geography and history at GCSE and therefore a greater supply of post-16 geographers.

Ofsted (2011) rate post-16 geography highly because of the quality of the learning: it is often taught by experienced subject-specialists, in smaller classes, with motivated students, and it offers the opportunity for more frequent fieldwork than in lower age groups. A quality geography education develops communication skills, problem-solving, the ability to work in teams and ICT skills, making the subject inherently valuable to young people – these are the skills employers want from their workforce in a globalised world (OECD, 2013). Perhaps this is the reason why geography graduates are also highly employable. Even so, geography students can find the transition to university difficult. That they feel under-prepared for degree-level study is well documented (Hill and Jones, 2010; Tate and Sword, 2013). It is hardly surprising: as well as new content and a different approach to study, they have to contend with a significant amount of extended writing and investigative writing, skills that in school were sidelined in successive restructurings of A level specifications (Pointon, 2008). The move from modular to linear A levels and recent A level reforms have provided the impetus for a much-needed reintroduction of theoretical learning, cognitive and critical thinking skills and a return to rigorous geography. Hopefully this will narrow the gap that has opened up between school and university geography. Figure 12 outlines opportunities and activities that may also help teachers to narrow this divide.

1. Goal is in focus	You have a clear goal of exam success	
	You are willing to receive advice	
	You are in a position to act on advice	
	You know where to seek advice	
2. Revision context	You are able to devote sufficient time to revision	
	You have a suitable place in which to revise	
	You have committed to a revision programme	
	You have the subject materials you need to revise from	
3. Revision programme	You know the dates and times for all your exams	
	You know what is on each exam and the question types	
	You know what skills you may be required to show	
	You have created a varied revision timetable	
4. Revision process	You are aware of a range of revision techniques	
	You have selected techniques that work best for you	
	You self-check to ensure revision techniques are effective	
5. Applying the revision	You have access to past exam papers and mark schemes	
	You have attempted past papers and marked your answers	
6. Tackling exam questions	You interpret questions accurately	
	You follow command words such as 'Assess' and 'Explain'	
	You make a sufficient number of points to be awarded all marks	
	You make specific, not generalised, statements, using examples	
	You refer to information provided in maps, photos and graphs	
	You link points 'as a result of this…' 'because of this…'	
	You do not miss out questions, either accidentally or on purpose	
	You use exam time effectively; all questions get equal attention	
7. Writing to get your ideas across effectively	You write answers using the lines/space effectively	
	Your writing is legible and easy to read	
	You use full sentences and SPaG rules accurately all the time	
	You use geographical vocabulary accurately all the time	
	Diagrams are in pencil, clearly labelled and stating the source	
	You sustain focus throughout the paper: last answers as good as first	
8. Well-being	You are getting sufficient sleep	
	You are eating the right kind of food	
	You are able to handle the stress	
	You have an effective support network when it is needed	
	You are able to derive satisfaction from the exam preparation process	

Figure 11: A level geography: personal preparation game plan. **After:** Andy Day (@Andyphilipday).

Figure 12: Opportunities and activities to help teachers bridge the school-university divide.

Activities for school teachers	Activities for geography teacher trainees and new teachers
Attend GA Branch lectures and RGS Monday night lectures.	Share knowledge and skills learnt at university with the geography department and school network.
Attend school conferences, Teach Meets and twilight CPD and evaluate them where possible.	
Sit on a Geographical Association Phase Committee or Special Interest Group.	Write a scheme of work based on a contemporary theme adapted from undergraduate course.
Read *Teaching Geography* and *Geography*, published by the GA.	Participate in RGS-IBG and GA conferences.
Read *Geographical*, *Area* and *Transactions*, published by the RGS-IBG.	
Use your teaching experience to write journal articles for the GA or *Geography Review*.	Invite student ambassadors from university, subject associations or past alumni to teach or talk about different aspects of geography.
Organise university taster days for GCSE and A level students.	
Complete formal qualifications (Masters, EdD, PhD) in geography education.	Establish a buddy/mentor system between school and university students.
Follow updates from the GA Post-16 and HE Phase Committee.	
Complete Massive Open Online Courses (MOOCs) to update geography knowledge and skills.	

Conclusion

The challenge of teaching post-16 geography is to make sure learning happens. It is unsurprising that the best geography, observed by Ofsted (2011), occurs in schools with strong professional development programmes, where geography is a specialist subject, where the school shares good practice in local networks, and where schools have built strong links with local universities to provide opportunities and activities (see Figure 12) to cross the school-university divide. The growing uptake of geography at GCSE should generate increasing numbers of A level candidates. If we continue to actively engage and motivate young people through creative, rigorous and exciting geography, and if students perceive the relevance of the subject to their own lives, then the future for geography education looks bright. The relevance of geography cannot be underplayed in our rapidly changing world; it has intrinsic value and equips students with an appreciation of wider educational agendas such as global citizenship, environmental education and sustainable futures. In a world where 80% of jobs require no specific degree, a geography education is perfectly placed – with equal access to the worlds of art and science – to develop essential life skills. In our fast-changing global society, geography really does matter.

References

Anderson, L.W. and Krathwohl, D.R. (eds) (2001) *A Taxonomy for Learning, Teaching, and Assessing: A revision of Bloom's taxonomy of educational objectives*. New York, NY: Longman.

Biddulph, M. (2014) 'What kind of geography curriculum do we really want?', *Teaching Geography*, 39, 1, pp. 6–9.

Biggs, J. and Collis, K. (1982) *Evaluating the Quality of Learning: The SOLO taxonomy*. New York, NY: Academic Press.

Bloom, B. (ed) (1956) *Taxonomy of Educational Objectives: The classification of educational goals. Handbook I: The cognitive domain*. New York, NY: David McKay.

Bonnett, A. (2008) *What is Geography?* London: Sage.

Brooks, C. (2013) 'How do we understand conceptual development in school geography?' in Lambert, D. and Jones, M. (eds) *Debates in Geography Education*. Abingdon: Routledge, pp. 75–88.

Bruner, J.S. (1966) *Toward a Theory of Instruction*. Cambridge, MA: Belknap Press.

Burns, J. (2013) *Ofsted warns schools not to fake it during inspections*. Available at: www.bbc.com/news/education-21777940 (last accessed 09/11/2016).

Butt, G. (2002) *Reflective Teaching of Geography 11–18: Meeting standards and applying research*. London: Continuum.

Csikszentmihalyi, M. (1990) *Flow: The psychology of optimal experience*. New York, NY: Simon & Schuster.

DfE (2010) *The Importance of Teaching: The Schools White Paper 2010*. London: The Stationery Office.

DfE (2013a) *Proposed GCE AS and A Level Subject Content for Geography*. London: DfE.

DfE (2013b) *Geography: GCSE subject content and assessment objectives*. London: DfE.

DfE (2013c) *National Curriculum in England: Geography programmes of study*. London: DfE.

DfE (2014) *GCE AS and A Level Subject Content for Geography*. London: DfE.

Firth, R. (2013) 'What constitutes knowledge in geography?' in Lambert, D. and Jones, M. (eds) *Debates in Geography Education*. Abingdon: Routledge, pp. 59–74.

GA (no date) *Curriculum making*. Available at: www.geography.org.uk/cpdevents/curriculum/curriculummaking (last accessed 09/11/2016).

GA (2014) *2014 A level results*. Available at: www.geography.org.uk/news/geography-gcse-and-a-level-exam-results (last accessed 09/11/2016).

Griffith, A. and Burns, M. (2012) *Engaging Learners*. Carmarthen: Crown House Publishing.

Hill, J. and Jones, M. (2010) '"Joined-up geography": connecting school-level and university-level geographies', *Geography*, 95, 1, pp. 22–32.

Jackson, P. (2006) 'Thinking geographically', *Geography*, 91, 3, pp. 199–204.

Joint Council for Qualifications (JCQ) (2015) *A, AS and AEA Results, Summer 2015*. Available at: www.jcq.org.uk/examination-results/a-levels (last accessed 09/11/2016).

Kelly, A.V. (2009) *The Curriculum: Theory and practice* (6th edition). London: Sage.

Lambert, D. (2011) 'Reviewing the case for geography, and the "knowledge turn" in the English National Curriculum', *The Curriculum Journal*, 22, 2, pp. 243–64.

OECD (2013) *OECD Skills Outlook 2013: First results from the survey of adult skills*. Paris: OECD Publishing.

Ofqual (2013) *New A Level Regulatory Requirements – October 2013*. Coventry: Ofqual.

Ofsted (2011) *Geography: Learning to make a world of difference*. Available at: www.gov.uk/government/publications/geography-learning-to-make-a-world-of-difference (last accessed 09/11/2016).

Paul, R. (1993) *Critical Thinking: How to prepare students for a rapidly changing world*. Santa Rosa, CA: Foundation for Critical Thinking.

Pointon, V. (2008) 'Changes in A-level geography and their implications for HE', *Planet*, 19, pp. 9–11.

QCA (2006) *GCE AS and A level Subject Criteria for Geography*. Coventry: QCA.

Rawling, E. (2007) *Planning Your Key Stage 3 Geography Curriculum*. Sheffield: Geographical Association.

Roberts, M. (2003) *Learning Through Enquiry: Making sense of geography in the key stage 3 classroom*. Sheffield: Geographical Association.

Roberts, M. (2013) *Geography through Enquiry: Approaches to teaching and learning in the secondary school*. Sheffield: Geographical Association.

Russell Group (2015) *Informed Choices: A Russell Group guide to making decisions about post-16 education*. Available at: www.russellgroup.ac.uk/media/5320/informedchoices.pdf (last accessed 09/11/2016).

Scoffham, S. (2011) 'Core knowledge in the revised curriculum', *Geography*, 96, 3, pp. 124–30.

Tate, S. and Sword, J. (2013) 'Please mind the gap: students' perspectives of the transition in academic skills between A-level and degree level geography', *Journal of Geography in Higher Education*, 37, 2, pp. 230–40.

Taylor, L. (2008) 'Key concepts and medium term planning', *Teaching Geography*, 33, 2, pp. 50–54.

Tide~DEC (1995) *Development Compass Rose: A consultation pack for teachers*. Birmingham: DEC.

Wiliam, D. (2011) *Embedded Formative Assessment*. Bloomington, IN: Solution Tree Press.

Young, M. (2008) *Bringing Knowledge Back In: From social constructivism to social realism in the sociology of education*. Abingdon: Routledge.

Recommended key readings

Elder, Z. (2012) *Full on Learning: Involve me and I'll understand*. Carmarthen: Crown House.

Zoë Elder's 'full-on' book is rich with reflection, synthesis and practical tips, helping us to explore the what, when and how of creating successful learners with deep learning and quality engagement.

Rawding, C. (2013) 'How does geography adapt to changing times?' in Lambert, D. and Jones, M. (eds) *Debates in Geography Education*. Abingdon: Routledge, pp. 282–90.

This chapter discusses the changing nature of geography and how the subject is influenced by both academia and society. It is just one chapter in a book rich with key debates that geographers should understand, reflect on and engage in.

The chapters in section three provide discussion of the opportunities and challenges that professional development, through being part of a geography department and wider geography community, can present. They encourage readers to see the importance of contributing actively to subject-specific practice, discussion and debate. Chapters raise important questions such as: How can professional development impact on professional practice? How can research-related activities contribute to our understanding of what makes effective teaching and learning? What are the essential requirements for excellent geography leaders, mentors and departments?

The chapters highlight areas of teachers' wider professional responsibilities considered important to sustaining high-quality geography training and teaching in secondary schools and academies. School-based and other geography colleagues need to meaningfully engage with these aspects of practice if educational principles and priorities are to maintain a focus on subject pedagogy and subject-specific professional development.

Section 3

Chapter **20** – Professional development
Jennifer Hill and Mark Jones

Chapter **21** – Researching geography education
Steve Puttick

Chapter **22** – Mentoring
Charles Rawding and Andrea Tapsfield

Chapter **23** – Leading the geography department
Catherine Owen

Chapter **24** – Belonging to a subject community
Alan Kinder

Chapter 20

Professional development

Jennifer Hill is Associate Professor, Geography and Environmental Management at UWE, Bristol, and former member of the editorial board of the GA's journal *Geography*, and **Mark Jones** is PGCE Geography Tutor at UWE, Bristol

'All teachers should have a professional responsibility to be engaged in effective, sustained and relevant professional development throughout their careers' (Training and Development Agency for Schools, 2007, p. 3).

What is professional development?

Whether you are more familiar with the term 'professional development', 'continuing professional development (CPD)' or 'professional learning' (O'Brien and Jones, 2014), we begin this chapter by asking some questions:

- What professional development have you engaged in recently?
- Where did this take place?
- What did it involve?
- Who was involved?
- What impact has it had on you and on the students you teach?

How teachers and others in the world of geography education answer these questions is important because it reveals how we conceptualise the purpose and priorities of professional development: its relevance to ourselves, our students and the educational contexts we work in. Some responses can reflect a somewhat restricted notion of professional development; involving one-off courses, twilight meetings and in-service education and training (Inset) days, perhaps with short-term benefits and varying impact on practice. Other answers reflect a more sustained and extensive range of opportunities incorporating these activities, from professional learning through peer coaching and collaborating online to engaging with the wider subject community and researching one's practice. In this chapter, we define professional development as all the formal and informal learning opportunities with which geography teachers engage over time, causing them to reflect critically upon and consequently enhance their practice, ultimately for the benefit of their students' development (Avalos, 2011). We suggest that professional development must be 'ongoing' but, to be of benefit, it requires those involved in creating, contributing to and consuming these experiences to consider more critically its relevance, effectiveness and transformative potential for practice.

The political context within which teachers' professional development is afforded status at the national level is significant, since some educational policy environments are more conducive to professional development than others. The provision of ongoing CPD opportunities for teachers in England became a priority under the Labour government between 1997 and 2010. A government CPD strategy for teacher professional development was instituted (GTC, 2000) and expanded (GTC, 2007), with aspirations to develop teachers as part of an integrated approach to improve students' lives. In addition, the National Strategies (1997–2011) meant maintained schools in England prioritised training in whole-school approaches to literacy (DfEE, 2001a) and numeracy (DfEE, 2001b), pedagogy and practice (DfES, 2004) and, in particular, assessment for learning (DCSF, 2008). This emphasis on 'generic' pedagogic principles and technical competence meant geography-specific discussion and debate became marginalised in some schools. Where subject-focused activity was prioritised, this was mainly through established local and regional networks, the work of local authority geography advisers and organisations such as the Geographical Association (GA) and the Royal Geographical Society with the Institute of British Geographers (RGS-IBG). A government-funded collaborative project between the GA and RGS-IBG, 'The Action Plan for Geography' (2006–11), produced a diverse range of activities and resources that were of enormous benefit to geography teachers' professional development during the period (see GA and RGS-IBG, 2011).

More recently, the Coalition government (2010–15) in the UK stepped back from the notion of funding national strategies for professional development, preferring instead to let schools take greater responsibility for teacher professional development. While this structure enables less mandated and standardised forms of professional development, it partly explains why the development of teachers tends to be uneven over space and time – across schools and over career life cycles (Huberman, 1995). There are also differing needs for teacher professional development depending on the history, traditions and cultures of schools, the educational needs of their students, the working environments of teachers, and the learning opportunities that are open to teachers. Equally, schools do not offer comparable expertise in organising and/or managing teachers' professional development. This situation has brought calls for a radical reform of current practice from those who find it 'hard to justify much of the current CPD practice as either "continuous", "professional" or even "developmental"' (Kempton, 2013, p. 7). There is consequently a continuous need to review and refresh teacher professional development in order to ensure its effectiveness for specific times and contexts.

Why is professional development important?

Professional development has a range of benefits, both for teachers and the students who benefit from their expertise (Figure 1). During their careers teachers face continuous demands to update their knowledge and skills due to the introduction of new curricula,

- Ensures that teachers are doing the best possible job they can and are confident and prepared in all situations.
- Provides long-term career prospects and enhances professional standing.
- Acknowledges teacher commitment to innovation and sharing their work with others.
- Provides documented evidence of teacher commitment to their own professional development and to the professionalism of the discipline.
- Provides material that can be used to support job applications – enhances career portfolios and employability.
- Encourages collaboration with colleagues, both within school and within the wider geographical community.
- Introduces innovative ideas into teaching.
- Helps teachers to develop their role within their department.
- Identifies strengths and weaknesses.
- Introduces new staff to school policy.

advances in technology, changes in learning needs of students and in light of emerging pedagogic research. Professional development calls for teachers to engage in new learning and this keeps their subject knowledge current, although it has been argued that knowledge gains from professional development generally erode after teachers return to the classroom and that the gains are unlikely to impact significantly on uneven distribution of teacher quality across schools (Goldschmidt and Phelps, 2010). Professional development does, however, encourage teachers to think reflexively about their teaching practices (Schön, 1983), building competence over time and prompting teachers to use reflection (sometimes in conjunction with self-assessment tools or reflective portfolios) as a trigger for change (Vescio et al., 2008). Supporting effective professional development for teachers is, therefore, a very important component in supporting student learning and in fostering achievement gains. Additionally,

Figure 1: Benefits of professional development for teachers. **Source:** RGS-IBG website.

Figure 2: Attributes for effective professional development. After: Hawley and Valli, 1999; Timperley *et al.*, 2007.

Effective professional development:
- is informed by differences between goals for student learning and student performance
- involves teachers in identifying their learning needs and opportunities
- is based in schools and wider learning communities (both face-to-face and e-learning)
- is organised around collaborative enquiry, problem-solving and reflection – with access to 'competent others'
- is a continuous, long-term and supported process over the teacher's career cycle
- provides progressive, challenging and relevant opportunities to develop theoretical understanding, as well as practical application in school contexts
- goes hand-in-hand with teacher autonomy and choice in work roles
- forms part of a comprehensive and integrated change process that is, in turn, consistent with wider policy trends and research.

Having established the recent history, nature and relevance of professional development for teachers, this chapter will now examine some of the different models of professional development, considering the 'who', 'how', 'where' and 'when' of delivery. In so doing, it will provide an analysis of the strengths and weaknesses of the key approaches. The chapter will offer specific examples of professional development available to geography teachers and will finish by highlighting the key questions that remain with respect to ensuring relevant professional development for geography teachers in the future.

Approaches to teacher professional development – is there a favoured model?

Teacher professional development is a complex and multi-faceted activity that requires a range of different approaches if it is to be effective. The modern conception is that professional development is not a short-term intervention, but a long-term process extending from initial teacher education to Inset in the workplace and formal and informal opportunities beyond the workplace. Professional development that comes about through practice, reflection and further exploration serves to transform the novice into the expert, but this process needs to be ongoing over 'at least 10 years of deliberate practice' (Wiliam, 2013, p. 55).

Effective professional development has a number of attributes (Figure 2) and, from these, three important foundational principles can be drawn. First, we must refrain from 'deficit' models where participants are seen as presenting skills and knowledge gaps that need to be plugged (Day and Sachs, 2004). Such deficit models, where 'experts' attempt to deposit information in the mind of 'novice' practitioners (Freire, 1970), fail to recognise teachers as sources of knowledge or as active participants in their own professional growth. Instead, we should see professional development as an opportunity for all teachers to engage in ongoing learning in learning communities (Lieberman and Miller, 2008). Second, we must avoid thinking of professional development as something that is delivered to a passive audience of teachers by internal

professional development tends to motivate teachers and engage them in metacognition (thinking about their own learning) (Flavell, 1979) and self-authorship (Baxter Magolda, 1999). Self-authorship defines learning as a collaborative exchange of perspectives that requires interaction between a diversity of individuals in order to reflect on alternative viewpoints, to shape self and to help shape others. Such critical self-reflection results in teachers who are sensitive to context and empowered to take control of their learning, leading them towards increased self-efficacy and regulation over their professional behaviour. Thus, to be effective, teacher professional development requires that individual teachers develop in three distinct ways: professionally, personally and socially (Bell and Gilbert, 1996). This process should involve 'not only the use of new teaching activities in the classroom, but also the development of the beliefs and conceptions underlying the actions' (Bell and Gilbert, 1996, p. 15).

	Internal to school		External to school	
	Formal	Informal	Formal	Informal

	• Workshop/conference
	• Mentoring and coaching
	• Peer and team teaching
	• Classroom observation (self and colleagues)
	• Curriculum and assessment reflection and development
	• Departmental meetings
		• Self-directed learning
		• Collaborative problem solving
		• Sharing experiences (story-telling, brainstorming), materials, innovations
		• Co-planning and co-teaching
		• Classroom observation
			• Workshop/conference
			• Mentoring and coaching
			• Teachers' networks as:
			  - national groups
			  - part of a federation or chain of academies
			  - within a local authority or county
			  - with a local HEI
				• Self-directed learning
				• Teachers' networks through online communities

Figure 3: Generic forms of professional development.

or external facilitators. Teachers must be seen as, and see themselves as, active agents in the development process, consciously shaping their learning and practice through genuine dialogue and collaboration with others. Third, professional development should not be conceptualised as distinct events, disconnected from previous professional learning and actual work settings. Safe professional environments need to be established where teachers can share experiences and learn with and from each other, integrated into the contexts and routines of their schools (James et al., 2007). Professional development must speak to the classroom, field or laboratory where teaching occurs to ensure it is perceived as authentic. It must offer relevance, challenge and progression to individuals if it is to be transferred back into the school environment on an ongoing basis. This is notwithstanding the fact that there must be resonance between the professional development of individuals and institutional culture and aspirations.

Models of professional development – the 'who', 'how', 'where' and 'when' of delivery

For optimum professional development, access to widely distributed knowledge is important. The challenge here is to link internal with external support – to promote and strengthen activities within a subject department while also capitalising on external communities of practice to advance professional development. This is particularly important to avoid fragmentation, something that policies promoting Teach First and Teaching Schools might unwittingly bring about because of localism (Cordingley, 2013). Professional development can also adopt a formal or informal character. It can be delivered as structured workshops, but can also take place during a school day when, for example, an experienced teacher shares experiences with a newly qualified teacher, when a teacher tries to find a solution for a problem he or she is confronting, or via classroom observations between colleagues (Figure 3).

Internal to schools/departments

Professional development has to be organised within the constraints of existing teaching duties and the financial costs of its implementation (e.g. paying for replacement teachers, travel to and participation in workshops). One way to minimise these costs is for schools to offer localised opportunities for individuals to develop, working with and learning from each other collaboratively on an ongoing basis. School departments are prime sites for professional learning through daily practice. Self-directed learning, arising from the teachers' own initiative, can take place as a result of day-to-day teaching, supported by the use of available resources (such as teacher magazines and journals, internet sources), but the experiences gained must be processed to lead to development of new knowledge that, in turn, can contribute to developing competence. Thus, teachers must learn from their own experiences and include them in the planning of future practice. An effective way to encourage this is through exploring their experiences with others, gaining a meta-perspective of their own teaching practice.

Collaborative CPD, teachers learning from each other, can take the form of discrete in-school workshops for teachers on a collective basis or more prolonged one-to-one mentoring (Hobson *et al.*, 2009). Collaborative models of professional development engage teachers in joint enquiry about teaching as a means of shifting practice. Groups of teachers work together locally, within schools, or peripherally, for example in meetings separate from immediate practice, to develop new ways of teaching. Individually or collectively, teachers try out new ideas in classrooms and monitor the success of their efforts. They come together to review their instruction, talk about outcomes and critically reflect on their teaching.

Collaboration among teachers provides several benefits. Cognitive benefits include the opportunity for teachers to gain access to new information, clarify their ideas and beliefs, examine different ways of thinking about teaching and reflect on their own practice. Emotional benefits of collaboration include support for teachers' struggles with new approaches, their willingness to experiment with ways of teaching for which they may not be very skilled, and the courage to take risks in the face of organisational pressures against experimentation. Collective participation in workshops can form the foundation for subsequent teamwork among school colleagues. Issues to consider are that the personal experiences and beliefs of teachers play an important role in the way they react to these in-house learning opportunities. Equally important are the learning opportunities created within schools, making it possible for teachers to work constructively with the learning opportunities provided. Schools should operate a support system for teachers' professional development across all levels of leadership and teachers should be given the opportunity to plan, implement and evaluate their practice in collaboration with colleagues (Figure 4).

Since the 1980s and 1990s, in-school mentoring has provided a structured sustained process for supporting teachers through induction and in their early careers. Mentoring and coaching can be effective means for professional development for teachers at different stages of their career, although there is some evidence that for those who have been teaching longer the impact may not be as great (Walker *et al.*, 2011). There is potential benefit in the partnership not only for the mentee but also for the mentor, who gains experience of peer management and enhanced responsibility. For the mentoring relationship to be effective the mentor must be committed to and value the role. Equally, the mentee should play an active role in the relationship, trusting the mentor, and being willing and able to talk about their strengths and weaknesses. He/she should not become dependent on the mentor and should be able to end the relationship after the defined time. Between them, the mentor and mentee must find the appropriate balance of support and challenge for the mentee. Beyond the dynamics of the individual learning partnerships, schools face additional challenges with respect to delivering effective mentoring, including mentor selection, support and evaluation, making time for coaching in busy school timetables, and allocating appropriate resources to the mentoring process (Stansbury and Zimmerman, 2000).

External to schools/departments

Teachers' networks can act as important communities of practice (Lave and Wenger, 1991; Wenger, 1998; Lieberman and Miller, 2008), supporting continuous professional growth and moving away from the traditional Inset model. Such communities have been defined as groups of individuals bound by shared practice, related to a set of problems or tasks, sharing and creating knowledge reciprocally through participation. Community members exchange ideas, collaborate, and learn from one another. In so doing, these communities help to shape personal identity, develop cognitive knowledge and skills, and progress inter-personal skills such as building trust, recognising multiple perspectives and resolving differences. These networks can be informal, comprising groups of teachers from different schools (sometimes with

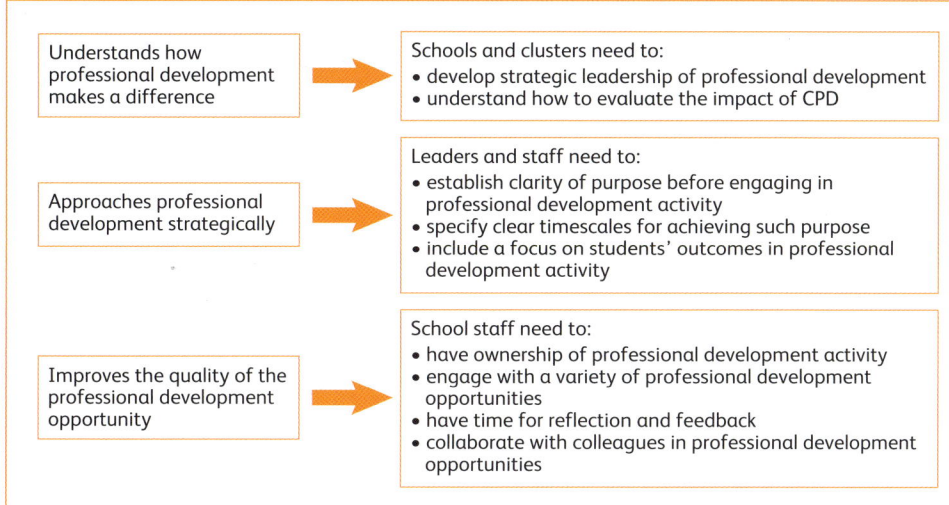

Figure 4: Maximising the impact of professional development in schools through leadership. **Source:** Earley and Porritt, 2014.

other education professionals) who have a common interest or goal. They allow teachers to engage in dialogue, and to negotiate and co-construct understandings of policy, practice and identity (Knight, 2002; Hofman and Dijkstra, 2010). They acknowledge and integrate the tension between individual and group (between autonomy and collegiality), and they incorporate strategies of conflict resolution. Such communities make it safe to ask questions, using uncertainty positively to help shape adaptations.

It must be remembered with respect to networks, however, that their usefulness depends on the extent and quality of the resources they provide, i.e. the group of teachers and the ideas that are created and disseminated in the network. There needs to be a critical mass of experienced teachers participating over time in order to keep discussions and materials current. Group membership must be flexible, but there should nevertheless be overall group stability.

Examples of teachers' (and more broadly-based) networks include localised face-to-face networks and online communities like nings (short for network**ing**); for example where teachers follow the same awarding body specification (see *http://aqaageog.ning.com*) or are part of a regional group. While some networks are virtual (Figure 5), many combine online activity with face-to-face events and meetings, such as The Geography Collective (see *http://thegeographycollective.wordpress.com/*). Networks can also be organised formally through membership of organisations such as the Geographical Association (GA) (*www.geography.org.uk*) and Royal Geographical Society (with the Institute of British Geographers) (RGS-IBG) (*www.rgs.org*) (Figure 6). As members of these organisations, teachers and students can benefit from a wealth of online resources as well as attending national, regional and local events such as competitions, lectures and conferences.

Models of professional development – the role of technology

There has been increasing emphasis on technology to deliver and/or support professional development. Technology can give teachers access to distributed expertise that has previously been inaccessible due to limitations of cost and time. A notable form is e-learning communities related to online forums, which help teachers to engage in conversations and share teaching materials. The Staffordshire Learning Net (SLN) Geography (*www.sln.org.uk/geography*) is a good example of such a website, started by Chris Durbin and Kate Russell, former Geography Advisers with Staffordshire Local Authority, and dedicated to 'the collaboration of geographers and a celebration of geographical education' (SLN, no date). The website remains live, although resources

Figure 5: Case studies of informal teachers' (and more broadly-based) networks.

The Geography Collective

The Geography Collective is an ever-expanding group of geography teachers, freelance educators, academics, artists, activists, therapists and others, who come together to encourage young people to engage with the world in innovative, creative and exciting ways. Their approach is embedded in exploring, questioning, playing, experimenting and experiencing our planet, while developing critical thinking around the interconnected, multiple and dynamic geographies that every aspect of our lives entails. The Collective began as the Guerilla Geographer movement, encouraging more young people to be passionate about place. The group created the *Journey Journal*, a passport-sized booklet for school pupils (aimed roughly at 7–12 year olds), with a collection of space-based activities to encourage them to (re)think the places that they visit on holidays and during field trips. They then developed *Mission:Explore*, an interactive book intended to get young people to (re)claim their right to play and explore outdoors through setting a range of tasks to be completed across local neighbourhoods (see www.missionexplore.net). Inspired by positive feedback from Mission:Explorers, the Collective has so far created four more books (*M:E Camping*, *M:E On the Road*, *M:E Food* and *M:E Water*).

The Geography Collective has branched out into other projects such as the Urban Earth ning, a collaborative project to explore and (re)present our habitat. The purpose of this website is to bring together people who are interested in joining urban adventures and sharing their experiences. It offers a space for planning explorations and sharing them with other members of the community (visit *http://urbanearth.ning.com*).

By using the Geography Collective's books, website and materials in the classroom, teachers can encourage children and young people to explore geographical inequalities and their own sense of place.

The Bristol Region Inter-District Geography Educators Network (BRIDGE)

BRIDGE is an example of how a more formal network has evolved and adapted more widely. In 1996, South Gloucestershire Local Education Authority (LEA) initiated CPD opportunities in the form of three face-to face meetings, co-ordinated by a humanities advisor and led by two heads of humanities. With two Advanced Skills Teachers (ASTs) for geography, the network continued to thrive; a ning was established, and increased collaboration with geography lecturers and teacher educators at the University of the West of England (UWE) meant the formal core benefitted from more informal and wider connections. In 2004, the third meeting of the year became a one-day conference at UWE open to undergraduates, pre-PGCE and PGCE students, teachers and academic geographers from across the region. The GA and RGS-IBG have been particularly supportive, offering a long list of keynote speakers. University geographers (from UWE and other local HEIs), specialists in their fields, provide valuable CPD for teachers in connecting university and school geographies. The benefit of this cross-phase and local authority-school-university collaboration is the variety of expertise, experience and perspective that participants can draw upon, both formally and informally, as a source of CPD.

are no longer updated. The SLN Forum, where teachers respond to each other's questions and contribute ideas for resources, also remains active with over 40,000 posts to date. Whereas this forum has been successful, elsewhere research into such virtual communities has questioned their support of higher order skills such as querying and responding to questions, and engaging in general reflection (Yang and Liu, 2004). Mentors are crucial to the success of network-based communications. Mentors can initiate and sustain the conversation when the network first starts and provide information and resources, raise questions or offer ideas, direct

Figure 6: Case studies of formal teachers' networks.

The Geographical Association (GA) CPD courses

In addition to its journals, online access to resources/courses and Annual Conference, the Geographical Association has been the prime player in offering a range of professional development activities and resources for primary, secondary and post-16 geography teachers across the UK (see www.geography.org.uk/). Notably, its annual CPD training courses, following a model of regional delivery, act to link sub-disciplinary and skills facilitators with teachers from diverse backgrounds and experiences. The intent is to supplement, rather than replace, any schools-based teaching courses in which the delegates might also participate. These workshops sometimes link school and university domains, affording time and space for academic geographers to converse with school teachers. Building on existing knowledge and understanding, the workshops have aimed to heighten enthusiasm for teaching specific components of curricula, to update subject knowledge, to provide up-to-date case studies and to demonstrate a range of creative teaching and learning approaches. This is achieved by engaging participant teachers actively in practical exercises, allowing them to share their ideas, knowledge and experiences with each other. Time is also allocated for structured reflection on subject content (challenging existing perspectives and offering alternatives), how this content might be delivered and assessed, and how the participants might engage differently with such material in the classroom after the workshops. Thus, these events do not provide a top-down model of what constitutes good practice; rather, guided collaboration between participants leads to a process of problem-solving and forward planning.

Royal Geographical Society (with Institute of British Geographers) (RGS-IBG) Chartered Geographer (Teacher)

The RGS-IBG is committed to enhancing the development of individual teachers by recognising subject-focused advancement and standards through their Chartered Geographer (Teacher) accreditation. Chartered Geographer (Teacher) is the only ongoing professional accreditation linked to CPD in geography and is relevant to the Training and Development Agency (TDA) framework of professional and occupational standards for teachers. The accreditation provides access to a wide range of regional continuing professional development and mentoring opportunities (see www.rgs.org) and online CPD resources for use during departmental Inset sessions or during teachers' own time. Chartered Geographer (Teacher) is available to teachers who can demonstrate competence, experience and professionalism in the use of geographical knowledge or skills in and out of the classroom, and who are committed to maintaining their professional standards.

enquiries, and connect groups with similar interests and needs as the network becomes better established.

Online courses, some of which require payment and others of which are free, are another means of professional development. The GA has developed a number of free online CPD courses designed to support both primary and secondary teachers in developing their subject expertise. These courses provide guidance on embedding themes such as 'global learning' and 'sustainability' into curriculum plans, learning new skills such as GIS, and subject leadership. While the GA online courses guide teachers through their use, many online materials are not actually courses although they do provide the opportunity for professional development when teachers engage with the ideas, discussions and resources. When reviewing individual resources, such as lesson ideas or schemes of learning online, it is important to know the authorship of, or at least the rationale behind, the material. For example, the RGS-IBG hosts many of the 'Geography Teaching Today' resources created by teachers, geography educators and

Choosing the best CPD for you may be through formal face-to-face conferences. **Photo** © Bryan Ledgard.

geography consultants as part of the joint GA and RGS-IBG Action Plan for Geography. These resources were developed during the period when the concept-led National Curriculum (QCA, 2007) was being rolled out in schools, hence the focus on the associated seven key concepts, but also the starter, main and plenary approach to the lessons. Materials added to the RGS-IBG website based on the DfE (2013) curriculum, such as 'glaciation and geological timescales' and 'Russia's regions and roles' have authors' details included. If you are using online materials, consider the rationale for the way geography or discussion of an educational issue has been presented. If you are creating a resource, which subsequently might inform another teacher's thinking, does it have a clear accompanying rationale that will help the teacher interpret it in the way intended?

As well as accessing lesson resources and images, another form of supporting technology is video – for example Teachers TV, a government-funded TV and online video service available through TES Connect, which operated until April 2011. Using video clips of teaching can capture the richness and complexity inherent in classroom situations, depicting teachers from a variety of backgrounds and contexts in terms of class composition and size, school resources, and locations.

Where video footage is produced for professional development it should contain overviews that address the background of the teachers, classrooms and curriculum shown. There should also be commentary by teachers about their intents, constraints, rationales and understandings. Video can help create visions of alternative practice that are more powerful than text alone. Watching video of others struggling with and resolving dilemmas encourages teachers as they face the difficult task of modifying their practice.

Technology also means that individuals can benefit from and contribute to professional development through social media such as blogs, Twitter and TeachMeets. Like the internet itself, the vast choice of whose blog to 'favourite' or who to follow on Twitter is one of personal choice. For blogs, a useful starting place is the GA's 'Geography Blogs A–Z' hyperlinked list; additionally, many teachers will have sites recommended to them by colleagues or other online users. Since Twitter began in 2006, many individuals, school and university geography departments and organisations use this micro-blogging tool to update followers of their activities or to link to relevant news stories, resources and upcoming events. The use of Twitter can form part of a teacher's personal learning network (PLN) by following or

More informal CPD may also be the right route for you. **Photo** © Rose Ledgard.

connecting with other individuals, groups and organisations (for some suggestions for which geography teachers and educators to follow see Watts, 2012 and Marsh, 2014). While some geography teachers may make infrequent or limited use of these forms of technology, for others it has become a significant feature of their professional networks (Parkinson, 2013). Since 2006, when Ewan McIntosh first used the term 'TeachMeet', these face-to-face 'unconferences' have provided a valuable opportunity for professional networking. Contributors at TeachMeets usually have between five and seven minutes to share their ideas and activities related to teaching and learning. Technology enables users to follow these events either through video streaming, delegates' tweeting or later when videos can be posted online. Locally organised geography-specific TeachMeets are a growing source of professional development in many areas. The GA launched its first ever TeachMeet at its Annual Conference in Manchester in 2015.

How do I choose what is best for me?

In this section we return to thinking about the competing demands and interests teachers encounter when deciding on professional development priorities and approaches. One of the four key themes of successful CPD identified by Ofsted (2010, p. 4) is 'successful balancing of individual and institutional needs'. Whole-school priorities may be driven by inspection frameworks or previous reports, changes in the student demographics of the school community or national priorities, but attention will most likely be on improving students' performance against the recognised performativity measures of the day. As a result, whole-school professional development may focus on developing students' literacy or numeracy skills, or supporting teachers to make better use of student data to plan more effectively for interventions. While this can benefit a geography teacher's professional development, opportunities for more subject-specific foci may be marginalised as a result and this means teachers have to seek additional space and time within their institutions and beyond. Of course, wanting students to be successful in their examinations is a prime concern for all teachers but they will also have other professional development needs, some subject-specific and others relating to wider professional roles and responsibilities. Figure 7 may be useful in helping to reflect on the origins and priorities for our professional development. It may also be useful during the appraisal or performance management process where discussion must also consider individual CPD needs.

Figure 7: Origins of and priorities for professional development.

Geography department:

Name:

Professional development priorities for year:

Priority 1:

Priority 2:

Priority 3:

Questions	Prompts
Where have your PD priorities originated?	National priority, curriculum change, whole-school focus, inspection feedback, Awarding Body focus, observation feedback by line manager/SLT/colleague, self-review, annual review meeting, performance management, appraisal, promotion, seeking promotion/new role, collaborative project, network meeting, personal interest, reading research, doing research.
What is the focus of each PD priority?	Student performance, student wellbeing, student inclusion, departmental focus, area of responsibility, whole-school theme/approach, individual class, group of students, teacher performance, aspect of teaching (generic/subject-specific), teacher use of assessment, teacher subject expertise, teacher subject knowledge.
What is the current situation and why?	National agenda, policy change, school organisation, faculty or departmental structuring, roles and responsibilities of self and colleagues, changes to curriculum or pastoral system, school reorganisation, change to specifications, change to school policy, new role, lack of experience or expertise in an area, experience of expertise in area, restricting of school day, rooming or timetable.
What are the intended outcomes for your PD?	Improved student engagement, improved student attainment in GCSE/GCE, increased take-up of subject at GCSE/GCE, improved level of teacher performance, reduction in student misbehaviour, updating of teachers' subject knowledge, renewal of scheme of learning.
What approaches will be used?	Formal/informal, in-school/external support, whole-school Inset, departmental meetings, additional PPA time, observations, coaching, mentoring, self-guided learning, collaborative network, research, visits to other schools, attending courses, online courses.
What time-scale and review dates will be set?	Weekly, termly, half year, end of year, review dates set within a longer two- to three-year period for ongoing professional development.
How will the impact of the PD be evaluated in the short, mid and long term?	Written evaluative statement of activity, written report, self- and peer-learning, journals, teacher blog, student questionnaires/interview/focus groups (pre- and post-activities associated with PD), observation notes/video, peer-review of videos, scrutiny of students' exercise books/online learning logs, learning walks by SLT, student voice, students as co-researchers, school records of students behaviour/engagement/attainment.

Ofsted (2010) reported that schools' evaluation of the impact of professional development remained the weakest aspect of their provision. We might respond by asking if all professional development actually needs evaluating: much of it is informal, self-directed and personally fulfilling. Where evaluation is required it is important to consider what is meant by impact – impact on whom and with what outcomes? Student outcomes, represented by quantitative data on progress and attainment, might appear an appropriate measure but impact, like 'progress', is a slippery concept. Making claims that particular professional development or newly adopted approaches to teaching have brought about gains in students' attainment can be problematic. Noticeable improvements in students' behaviours or engagement in geography lessons may follow a period of coaching and the structured peer support may be one ingredient contributing towards the changed behaviours. If claims about the impact of particular professional development are to be made, the potential impact through specific outcomes needs identifying and then monitoring, with careful attention to the process of data collection. Data can be acquired through observation, analysis of students' work and through feedback via questionnaires, focus groups or interviews. However collected, data to evaluate the effectiveness of professional development need to reflect a range of voices, particularly students, alongside those of teachers and other adults. A newly acquired approach to providing student feedback, for example via QR codes, may be easily transferrable from one context to another and initially seem to engage students in terms of their interest, i.e. 'it had an immediate impact', but the value and purpose of providing feedback in this way needs to be situated within teachers' existing conceptions of what makes effective feedback and not simply bolted on as 'innovative practice'. Making time for teachers' reflection and discussion during and following professional development is therefore vital.

Professional development: the future

Professional development, in its various forms and contexts, has positive effects to some degree on teachers and learners. But we still know little about how pervasive these changes are and to what degree they sustain continuous efforts to move ahead. The optimum framework for the development of teachers' classroom practices and student learning appears to be teacher professional development in formal contexts (such as courses and workshops), continuing through networking and interchange among schools, and combined with informal practice-oriented reflection with other teachers – supported by a school administration that promotes social learning (Parise and Spillane, 2010). There is a clear need for a system of professional development in which sustained and critical dialogue takes place between teachers, principals, in-service providers and their trainers. It is necessary to create mutual trust, respect and productive relationships within and across schools and between schools and universities and other CPD providers. An optimal mix of activities can then be provided, which suits particular teachers at different stages in their individual development. Multiple activities offer a greater prospect of engaging diverse individuals with varying interests and values. In addition, varied opportunities foster the development of a culture that supports continuous enquiry into practice.

Looking to the future, we are left with a number of unanswered questions:

1. How do we construct a system of professional development that best enables dialogue between teachers, principals, and in-service and external facilitators?
2. How do we extend engagement with professional development beyond those teachers already interested in enhancing teaching and learning?
3. How do we use resources for continuing professional development to make more 'spaces' for CPD, e.g. departmental libraries, communal areas, networking facilities?
4. How do we encourage cascading of professional development learning from one teacher to another?
5. How can we better understand the complex and situated interactions that occur between teacher development and improvement in teaching and learning in different institutional contexts?
6. How do we establish an effective framework for evaluating the outcomes of both formal and informal professional development?
7. How do we successfully support sustained professional development over career cycles – development that does not limit teacher learning progression, but supports teachers to be active lifelong learners?
8. How do we strengthen the relationship between teacher professional development and retention of teachers in education?

Increasingly, the role of research and its relationship to teachers' professional development may help us to better understand what makes effective professional development.

The BERA-RSA Inquiry into teacher education and research summarises a number of research reviews into the characteristics of effective CPD. Common characteristics are summarised as:

- *'Sustained collaboration with professional colleagues, including both making use of specialist expertise and structured peer support for embedding specialist contributions.*
- *An understanding of and commitment to professional learning, including enquiry-oriented learning and learning to learn from looking.*
- *A focus on refining teaching and learning, working towards aspirations for specific pupils side-by-side with theory.*
- *Effective scaffolding and modelling of learning by both teachers and leaders for colleagues and for pupils'* (Cordingley, 2013, pp. 1–2).

Engagement in and with research is also advocated by Wiliam (2013) who advises teachers to avoid 'fads like learning styles and Brain Gym®, and instead focus on the improvement of classroom practices that research indicates are likely to improve learning' (p. 55).

Conclusion

Teaching geography brings immense personal and professional satisfaction for teachers, but challenges can occur in a variety of professional contexts and at different points in a career. Quality professional development for geography teachers provides them with the tools to deal with and find solutions to these professional challenges. In a rapidly changing world, it is important to make it possible for geography teachers to continue to broaden their outlook, to learn collaboratively and continuously about changing pedagogy and to apply effective pedagogies in their classrooms. It is therefore important that, collectively, professional development is given the time, space and resource for those involved to shape its direction so that it has meaningful educational outcomes for teachers and students.

References

Avalos, B. (2011) 'Teacher professional development in *Teaching and Teacher Education* over ten years', *Teaching and Teacher Education*, 27, 1, pp. 10–20.

Baxter Magolda, M.B. (1999) *Creating Contexts for Learning and Self-Authorship: Constructive-developmental pedagogy*. Nashville, TN: Vanderbilt University Press.

Bell, B. and Gilbert, J. (1996) *Teacher Development: A model from science education*. London: Falmer Press.

Cordingley, P. (2013) *Research and Teacher Education: The BERA-RSA inquiry. The contribution of research to teachers' professional learning and development*. Available at: www.bera.ac.uk/wp-content/uploads/2013/12/BERA-Paper-5-Continuing-professional-development-and-learning.pdf (last accessed 14/11/2016).

Day, C. and Sachs, J. (2004) 'Professionalism, performativity and empowerment: discourses in the politics, policies and purposes of continuing professional development' in Day, C. and Sachs, J. (eds) *International Handbook on the Continuing Professional Development of Teachers*. Milton Keynes: Open University Press, pp. 3–32.

DCSF (2008) *The Assessment for Learning Strategy*. Nottingham: DCSF Publications.

DfE (2013) *National Curriculum in England: Geography programmes of study*. Available at: www.gov.uk/government/publications/national-curriculum-in-england-geography-programmes-of-study (last accessed 14/11/2016).

DfEE (2001a) *Literacy Across the Curriculum*. London: DfEE.

DfEE (2001b) *Numeracy Across the Curriculum*. London: DfEE.

DfES (2004) *Pedagogy and Practice: Teaching and learning in secondary schools: leadership guide*. London: DfES.

Earley, P. and Porritt, V. (2014) 'Evaluating the impact of professional development: the need for a student-focused approach', *Professional Development in Education*, 40, 1, pp. 112–29.

Flavell, J.H. (1979) 'Metacognition and cognitive monitoring: a new area of cognitive-development inquiry', *American Psychologist*, 34, 10, pp. 906–11.

Freire, P. (1970) *Pedagogy of the Oppressed*. New York, NY: Continuum.

GA and RGS-IBG (2011) *The Action Plan for Geography 2006–2011: Final report and evaluation*. Available at: www.geography.org.uk (last accessed 14/11/2016).

General Teaching Council (GTC) (2000) *Continuing Professional Development: Advice to government*. London: GTC.

GTC (2007) *A Personalised Approach to Continuing Professional Development*. London: GTC.

Goldschmidt, P. and Phelps, G. (2010) 'Does teacher professional development affect content and pedagogical knowledge: how much and for how long?', *Economics of Education Review*, 29, 3, pp. 432–39.

Hawley, W.D. and Valli, L. (1999) 'The essentials of effective professional development: a new consensus' in Darling-Hammond, L. and Sykes, G. (eds) *Teaching as the Learning Profession: Handbook of policy and practice*. San Francisco, CA: Jossey-Bass, pp. 127–50.

Hobson, A.J., Ashby, P., Malderez, A. and Tomlinson, P.D. (2009) 'Mentoring beginning teachers: what we know and what we don't', *Teaching and Teacher Education*, 25, 1, pp. 207–16.

Hofman, R.H. and Dijkstra, B.J. (2010) 'Effective teacher professionalization in networks?', *Teaching and Teacher Education*, 26, 4, pp. 1031–40.

Huberman, M. (1995) 'Professional careers and professional development: some intersections' in Guskey, T.R. and Huberman, M. (eds) *Professional Development in Education: New paradigms and practices*. New York, NY: Teachers College Press, pp. 193–224.

James, M., McCormick, R. and Black, P. (2007) *Improving Learning How to Learn: Classrooms, schools and networks*. Abingdon: Routledge.

Kempton, J. (2013) *To Teach, To Learn: More effective continuous professional development for teachers*. Available at: www.centreforum.org/assets/pubs/teacher-cpd-web.pdf (last accessed 14/11/2016).

Knight, P. (2002) 'A systemic approach to professional development: learning as practice', *Teaching and Teacher Education*, 18, 3, pp. 229–41.

Lave, J. and Wenger, E. (1991) *Situated Learning: Legitimate peripheral participation*. New York, NY: Cambridge University Press.

Lieberman, A. and Miller, L. (2008) *Teachers in Professional Communities*. New York, NY: Teachers College.

Marsh, J. (2014) *Geography teachers on Twitter: who should I follow?* Available at: www.theguardian.com/teacher-network/teacher-blog/2014/aug/18/geography-teachers-twitter-follow (last accessed 14/11/2016).

O'Brien, J. and Jones, K. (2014) 'Professional learning or professional development? Or continuing professional learning and development? Changing terminology, policy and practice', *Professional Development in Education*, 40, 5, pp. 683–87.

Ofsted (2010) *Good Professional Development in Schools*. Manchester: Ofsted.

Parise, L.M. and Spillane, J.P. (2010) 'Teacher learning and instructional change: how formal and on-the-job learning opportunities predict change in elementary school teachers' practice', *The Elementary School Journal*, 110, 3, pp. 323–46.

Parkinson, A. (2013) 'How has technology impacted on the teaching of geography and geography teachers?' in Lambert, D. and Jones, M. (eds) *Debates in Geography Education*. Abingdon: Routledge, pp. 193–205.

QCA (2007) *Geography: Programme of study for key stage 3 and attainment target*. London: HMSO.

Schön, D. (1983) *The Reflective Practitioner: How professionals think in action*. New York, NY: Basic Books.

SLN (no date) *SLN Geography Forum*. Available at: http://learningnet.co.uk/geoforum (last accessed 14/11/2016).

Stansbury, K. and Zimmerman, J. (2000) *Lifelines to the Classroom: Designing support for beginning teachers*. San Francisco, CA: WestEd.

TDA (2007) *Professional Standards for Teachers*. Available at: www.rbkc.gov.uk/pdf/standards_core.pdf (last accessed 14/11/2016).

Timperley, H., Wilson, A., Barrar, H. and Fung, I. (2007) *Teacher Professional Learning and Development: Best evidence synthesis iteration*. Available at: www.educationcounts.govt.nz/publications/series/2515/15341 (last accessed 14/11/2016).

Vescio, V., Ross, D. and Adams, A. (2008) 'A review of research on the impact of professional learning communities on teaching practice and student learning', *Teaching and Teacher Education*, 24, 1, pp. 80–91.

Walker, M., Jeffes, J., Hart, R., Lord, P. and Kinder, K. (2011) *Making the Links between Teachers' Professional Standards, Induction, Performance Management and Continuing Professional Development* (DFE Research Report 075). London: DfE.

Watts, J. (2012) *Twitter for geography teachers/students*. Available at: www.slideshare.net/nefertari_1984/twitter-for-geography-teachers-and-students?ref=http://sharegeography.co.uk/2012/04/14/twitter-for-geography-teachers-and-students (last accessed 14/11/2016).

Wenger, E. (1998) *Communities of Practice: Learning, meaning, and identity*. Cambridge: Cambridge University Press.

Wiliam, D. (2013) 'The importance of teaching' in Clifton, J. (ed) *Excellence and Equity: Tackling educational disadvantage in England's secondary schools*. London: Institute for Public Policy Research, pp. 50–57.

Yang, S.C. and Liu, S.F. (2004) 'Case study of online workshop for the professional development of teachers', *Computers in Human Behaviour*, 20, 6, pp. 733–61.

Recommended key readings

'Chapter 10: Professional Development' in Biddulph, M., Lambert, D. and Balderstone, D. (2015) *Learning to Teach Geography in the Secondary School: A companion to school experience* (3rd edition). Abingdon: Routledge.

Written primarily for beginning teachers and teachers in the early parts of their careers, this chapter provides practical advice and raises questions concerning teacher reflection and the importance of continuing the professional development experienced during Initial Teacher Education.

Cordingley, P. (2013) *Research and Teacher Education: The BERA-RSA inquiry. The contribution of research to teachers' professional learning and development*. Available at: www.bera.ac.uk/wp-content/uploads/2013/12/BERA-Paper-5-Continuing-professional-development-and-learning.pdf (last accessed 14/11/2016).

A paper that draws on empirical evidence from a number of reviews and presents eight common characteristics of effective CPD and CPDL (Continuing Professional Development and Learning). It emphasises the need for teachers to engage in and with research as part of their professional development but recognises we need to develop 'a shared language for and about CPDL that includes a role for theory and criticality' (p. 9).

Chapter 21

Researching geography education

Steve Puttick is Head of Programmes (Secondary/FE/Research Education) at Bishop Grosseteste University, Lincoln

Introduction

We often tell students that geography is enquiry-led, and much geography teaching seeks to introduce students to the habits (or disciplines) of enquiry: asking good questions, finding and assessing evidence, drawing conclusions and developing further questions. This chapter considers how we, as teachers, also enquire: what questions are we asking about geography education? Where do we go to find reliable evidence? What kinds of standards do we require of this evidence, and what might we do with it?

Research is defined here broadly as 'systematic enquiry that is made public and exposed to collective criticism' (Stenhouse, in Rudduck and Hopkins, 1985; Winch *et al.*, 2013, p. 2). There are many traditions of educational research, each with different assumptions about knowledge (epistemology: what we can know, and how we might acquire knowledge), the nature of being (ontology: what constitutes fundamental reality, or what can be said to exist) and the aims of research. Geography education research (GER) is a sub-field of educational research, and a sub-field of geography. GER connects, in different ways, the concepts of geography, education and research: 'big ideas' (Lambert, 2010, p. 85) that are important, highly contested and emergent from multiple traditions.

Readers of this chapter will be at different places in their research journeys, and some may be in the very early stages; we all have to start somewhere (see Figure 1). To begin the chapter, a brief summary of different geographical traditions is presented below, followed by an outline of significant perspectives in educational research. Asking what makes 'good' research across traditions and perspectives, I argue that research needs to make sense on its own terms: different approaches are necessary for asking different questions, and addressing different problems. I then present three areas of GER:

1. Research *about* geography education
2. Research *for* geography education
3. Geography *of* education.

The chapter concludes with some practical suggestions for ways in which you might become (more) involved in research.

> My experiences with GER began during my PGCE year. The dissertation I wrote about predicted grades and student motivation was, for me at least, an exciting thing to do. Later, I studied part-time (in the evenings and weekends) for an MA in Educational Leadership and Innovation. My main motivation for doing this (I certainly needed motivation on Tuesday evenings, after teaching a full timetable, to drive for an hour and sit through several hours of lectures) was to make our geography department more efficient and more effective. I was also interested in promotion, being keen for a head of department role, and possibly to become a head teacher in the future. However, my plans to do research that would tell us 'what works' unravelled, and the research process raised hard questions about the purposes and aims of education. Engaging with research, and seeking 'truth', may reveal surprising answers, and you might find your assumptions, priorities and questions reframed.

Figure 1: My early encounters with geography education research.

Period	Summary
1900s	'Regional recitation', characterised by exploration, mapping, imperialism and areal differentiation.
1960s	Highly modernist quantitative revolution, moving beyond the descriptive to a law-making and explanatory science.
1970s	Humanist critique of positivism, with (renewed) interest in Marxist analyses of social justice and inequality (Harvey, 1973).
mid-1980s	Prime significance given to locale and place, structure and agency, and the socio-spatial dialectic (Soja, 1989).
1990s	Cultural turn in geography (Barnett, 2002).
2000s	Affective turn in geography (Leys, 2011).

Figure 2:
Brief summary of the history of geography. **After:** Taylor, 2009, p. 653.

Research traditions

A snapshot of research interests in geography is presented in Figure 2, with space to add future 'turns' as they develop.

The summary in Figure 2 is very broad, and within each trend are disagreements. Summaries such as this also underplay the enduring influence of 'past' positions. Aspects of the quantitative revolution, far from being left in the 1960s, have grown more accessible as powerful statistical software has developed. Marxist analyses of social justice, such as those by David Harvey (1973), continue to attract significant interest and implications of the cultural turn continue to be discussed (Winter, 2011).

Across traditions different terms are used to describe the aims, claims and quality of research, revealing something about each tradition's epistemological and ontological assumptions. In Biesta's (2005) terms:

'Just as language makes some ways of saying and doing possible, it makes other ways of saying and doing difficult or even impossible. This is one important reason why language matters to education, because the language or languages we have available to speak about education determine to a large extent what can be said and done, and thus what cannot be said and done' (p. 54).

GER has developed from a range of traditions, drawing on a variety of sources of evidence from:

'personal experience through the outcomes of designed investigations, based on such approaches as observation, hypothesis testing and experimentation to rational and creative argument and perspectives' (Catling, 2010, p. 97).

A summary of contrasting positions is shown in Figure 3, although it is emphasised that 'qualitative' and 'quantitative' approaches are found – albeit to differing degrees and for different purposes – across all traditions: the false dichotomy of 'qualitative' and 'quantitative' approaches should be avoided.

Throughout this chapter different types and examples of research are discussed, and it may be helpful to refer back to, and locate them on, Figure 3.

What might 'good' research look like?

Research needs to make sense on its own terms. There may be general principles that all research aspires to, including trustworthiness, contribution to knowledge and transparency (discussed below). However, the ways in which traditions understand, interpret and articulate these principles vary considerably. In their review of criteria for excellence in applied research, Oancea and Furlong (2007) 'emphasize the principle that research in education ought to be assessed in the light of what it wants and claims to be, and not through a rigid set of universal "standards"' (p. 122). Understanding research on its own terms is liberating: you do not have to follow a predetermined approach and can develop whatever kind of research is best suited to the

Figure 3:
A simplified diagram of possible methods of data collection and research processes.
Source: Perks and Prestage, 2009.

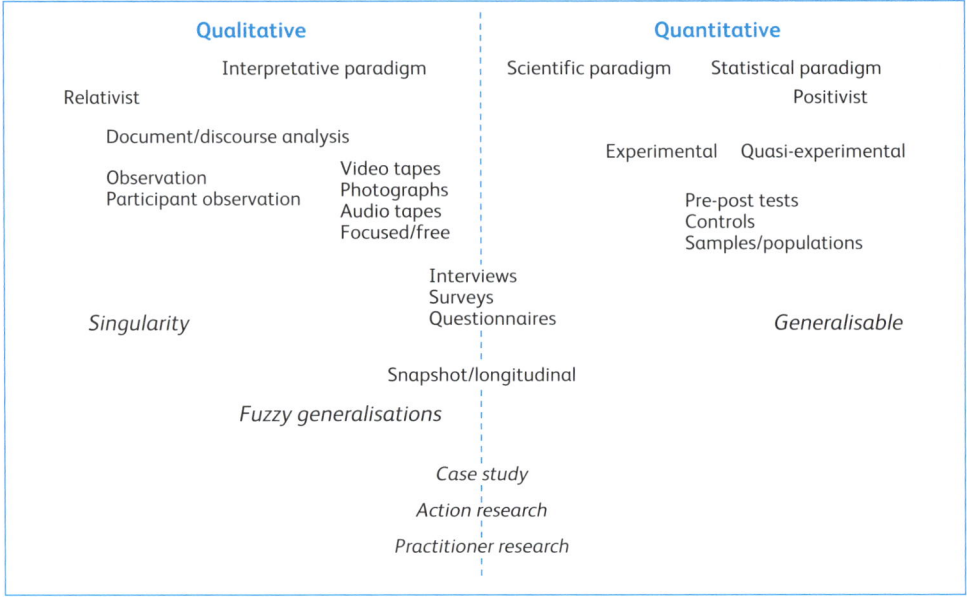

issues you are interested in. However, not having a tick list of standards can also be uncomfortable. As you design a study, and face questions about samples and data collection methods, it may be reassuring to hear that there is a right approach. However, good answers to these questions often begin 'it depends…'. Oancea and Furlong's (2007) position also means that consistency between aims, questions, methods and claims is very important: is the evidence presented appropriate and sufficient for the claims made?

Although the definitions vary between research traditions, these general descriptors of good research have been offered:

- trustworthiness (what reasons are there for trusting their findings?)
- contribution to knowledge (what do we learn from the research? How does it challenge or contribute to our previous understanding of the issues?)
- transparency and explicitness in design and reporting (is what they did, how they did it and their reasons for these methodological decisions clear?)
- paradigm-dependent considerations (including locating the research in relation to the categories suggested in Figures 2 and 4) (Oancea and Furlong, 2007).

Interpretations of these concepts are explored below in the context of examples from GER. Three areas of research are discussed (summarised in Figure 4): research *about* geography education, research *for* geography education and geography *of* education.

Research *about* geography education

Research about geography education is that which seeks to understand and describe 'geography education' better. Geography education is an expansive notion. In the context of the current chapter 'geography education' refers primarily to the formal secondary school subject. However, 'geography education' is bigger than this (Catling, 2010). Research about geography education is not explicitly aimed at changing or improving geography education (although it may later be used to do that). Observing, questioning and measuring are used to describe, summarise and represent. The majority of educational research is of this kind, primarily based on reflection and interviews, and mostly small-scale and qualitative (Menter, 2011). Hopwood's (2012) research on students' conceptions of geography is one example. He developed an 'ethnographic' approach (which we might locate on the left of

	About geography education	*For* geography education	Geography *of* education
Types of aims	Developing understandings, describing, analysing.	Effecting change, improving situations, causing action.	Integrating research from academic geography. Very broad range of specific research aims, potentially foregrounding the ways wider spatial and social processes shape (and are reshaped through) formal and informal spaces of education, and how this is experienced, embraced and contested by students and teachers.
Types of claims	Descriptions of what geography education is like. For example: *These particular aspects of geography education (such as year 9 students' conceptions of the subject) are like this…*	Recommendations about how to improve situations. For example: *These aspects of geography education (such as homework) can be improved by doing this (change/intervention), which we found to have these effects (such as improvements in engagement and uptake)…*	Very broad range of possible claims, including description, recommendation as appropriate to particular problems, aims and questions.
Examples of research	Hopwood (2012) Catling (2013)	Van der Schee *et al.* (2006) Karkdijk *et al.* (2013) Duffy (2013) Puttick (2013)	Valentine (2004) Taylor (2009) Jeffrey (2010)

Figure 4: Areas of geography education research.

NB. Research in these three areas – *about*, *for* and *of* – is not necessarily related to particular types of educational research (outlined in Figure 3); Butt (2010) argues that GER is primarily small-scale and qualitative due to structural issues.

Figure 4) to explore the ways in which students understand what geography is. An earlier article (Hopwood *et al.*, 2005), based on some of this research, is now discussed. It is chosen because it is an interesting example of a 'close relationship between the researcher and the teachers involved' (p. 92). They describe their study as:

'small-scale and detailed research into year 9 students' conceptions of geography. It is in contrast to the more large-scale and quantitative approach used by Norman and Harrison (2004). Such contrasts in approach should be viewed as healthy, providing comparisons of both findings and methodology' (Hopwood *et al.*, 2005, p. 91).

Contrasting their study with another helps to locate their work, and hints at the kind of research tradition they are seeking to be a part of. Hopwood *et al.* anticipate a possible critique of the 'small scale' of their study by suggesting that the contrast between it and a larger scale study is healthy: 'Norman and Harrison's findings relate to a larger number of students, whereas the data from [Hopwood *et al.*'s] study is more detailed, in-depth and context-specific' (p. 93). Here, Hopwood *et al.* acknowledge a strength of larger-scale research, and place alongside that a strength and weakness of their own work. They describe their research design in terms of sample 'two year 9 classes (nearly 60 students)', and data collection methods. They asked these students to:

As teachers, what questions are we asking about geography education? Where do we go to find reliable evidence?
Photo © Alex Brylov Shutterstock.

'produce a poster showing what they think "geography" is… students were also asked to complete a short questionnaire… a selection of closed and open-ended questions about topics studied in geography, skills learnt and the ways the subject can be useful, interesting or important (Hopwood et al., 2005, p. 91).

The claims made in their paper relate their findings again to the literature they previously introduced, concluding that:

'the prominence of countries, cultures and natural hazards in terms of content in both studies is striking… map reading and understanding world events and environmental issues also emerged as issues in both studies' (Hopwood et al., 2005, p. 93).

Hopwood went on to develop this area of research through a doctoral study taking an even more in-depth approach, studying six students over a longer period of time (Hopwood, 2006).

Research questions *about* geography education are not proposing change, but are focused on accurate, detailed description. This description might be used to inform discussions identifying areas to address through further research and in policy. Rich descriptions of specific cases, shared and made available to public scrutiny – particularly by other geography teachers – are potentially an important source for professional reflection and development.

Well-founded understandings about geography education also provide an important premise for developing research that might seek to improve these situations: solutions are more likely to succeed if the 'problems' are thoroughly, and accurately, clarified.

Research *for* geography education

In contrast to largely descriptive studies, research *for* geography education is explicitly designed to seek change and improvements, and might be described as emancipatory. This research still needs to offer rigorous descriptions, but further understanding of problems is gained in order to then change situations. Randomised Control Trials (RCTs), experimental and quasi-experimental designs are also types of research designed to effect change, often by testing the effectiveness of an intervention. RCTs are often used in medical research, in which they are relatively straightforward: give participants different interventions (such as pills) and measure which work best. They are powerful methodologies, which can be politically influential. It is significant that the Department for Education (DfE) commissioned Ben Goldacre, a popular science writer with a medical background, to conduct a review of research in education. He advocates far greater use of RCTs in education research, claiming that in medicine it is '*only* by conducting [RCTs]… that we've been able to find out what works best' (Goldacre, 2013, p. 7, emphasis added).

The phrase 'what works' is significant, and is discussed further below. RCTs are rarely used in GER, possibly because of the costs involved. Their wider use in educational research has also been controversial, and there have been lively debates about their adoption, with some arguing that RCTs ought to be seen as a gold standard (Hargreaves, 2003) and others contending that 'big science' models of research become politicised and 'marginalize or rubbish other research traditions without even attempting to explore the complexity of their positions' (Furlong, 2004, p. 351). Furlong takes this position because he believes that: '(a) the disagreements between the different communities are important and are genuine, and (b) the different research traditions have a great deal to contribute to the core purposes of research' (p. 351). One rare example of a quasi-experimental study in GER is critically discussed below, after a brief discussion of some philosophical issues related to research about 'what works', and a discussion of action research, one of the main types of research for geography education used by geography teachers.

What works?

As geography teachers we make a huge number of decisions about what we should do. Research can play an important role in helping us to make decisions, but can it tell us 'what works'? Asking what I *should* do is a normative question. It is value-laden and involves ethical issues. It is important to appreciate that many social scientists have taken very strong positions on the relationship between what research can tell us about the world (what *is*) and what it can tell us about how we should then act (what we ought to do). In Max Weber's (1949) terms, there is a logical distinction between 'existential knowledge' (of what is) and 'normative knowledge' (of what should be). He argues that:

> 'it can never be the task of an empirical science to provide binding norms and ideals from which directives for immediate practical activity can be derived... An empirical science cannot tell anyone what he should do' (Weber, 1949, pp. 52–54).

More recent discussions have explored the relationships between evidence and action, critiquing simplistic notions of research as something that is able to simply tell us 'what works' (Thomas and Pring, 2004; Biesta, 2007, 2009; Bridges *et al*., 2009). These debates are worth exploring further, although there is not space to do so here beyond saying 'beware!' of jumping too quickly between what research suggests *is* and what we *should* do.

Action research

Action research always intends to change situations. It is not happy to simply describe (although description is an essential aspect of all research), but seeks to effect improvements. For Duffy (2013) this means 'identifying a problematic issue, imagining a possible solution, trying it out, evaluating it and changing practice in the light of the evaluation' (p. 66). For her, the problem was about homework; she found that 'students often failed to hand in this meaningless task' (p. 66). Her research question asks 'How can I improve the homework situation in geography?'. She imagined several solutions, including making the academic purpose clearer and giving students greater ownership. She gives examples of the particular strategies trialled in her department and describes her engagement with action research as 'empowering', having given her greater 'professional confidence' (p. 67). The outcomes are reported as extremely positive; the home learning is now so popular that 'the majority of learners... invest much thought and energy into their independent research [and] students and parents/carers now rank geography as their favourite foundation subject' (p. 68).

The role of action research in developing geography teachers' 'professional judgement' (Winch *et al*., 2013, p. 2) is potentially significant, and high-quality partnerships between school geography teachers and other, probably university-based, geography education researchers may enhance both:

> 'Engagement with/in research and awareness of research processes and findings may contribute to the richness of reflection required in practical deliberation, while also enriching research itself through bringing it closer to the fluidity and immediateness of practice' (p. 2)

However, action research without critical reflection on what counts as 'success', or sufficient engagement with theory (that is, with existing research and established concepts

Figure 5: Action research summary. **Source:** Puttick, 2013, p. 26. ('CD' here stands for 'Compact Disc'.)

> **What revision strategies are most effective for GCSE geography students?**
>
> *Step one*
> Focusing on year 11: Questionnaires to find out: What is revision? What strategies do they find most effective? What do they need to help them? Similar questionnaires to teachers.
>
> **Action**: Revision CD developed. Text message revision started.
>
> **Next stage planned**: To observe geography revision lessons, focusing on the types of activities engaging different groups of students.
>
> *Step two*
> Geography revision lesson observations: What activities are used? What types of students are engaged? Discussion in department.
>
> **Action**: Develop central stores of resources. Share differentiated strategies more effectively.
>
> **Next steps**: Investigate specific revision strategies and evaluate through student feedback.
>
> *Step three*
> Teach and evaluate two revision lessons: What strategies do students find most effective? What do they still need to help with revision?
>
> **Action**: Refine revision CD for next year. Share findings within department and at academic board. Trial social media (Twitter and blogging) to develop revision.

to question the original premise. One action research project I conducted while head of department is reported in *Teaching Geography* (Puttick, 2013). The aim was to develop 'more effective revision strategies that worked', asking 'what types of revision strategies are most effective for GCSE geography students?' (p. 26). The action research model of asking questions, taking action, reviewing this action, and planning next steps is often illustrated in a cyclical form but is represented here on a line (Figure 5).

This kind of research is small-scale and highly practical, enhancing work teachers are already doing. Action research is often associated with the statement 'Research that produces nothing but books is inadequate' (Lewin, 1946). I found that my study reframed this question and returned it to me: what about revision that produces nothing but grades? This research project began with the intention of increasing the effectiveness of revision strategies to boost GCSE grades but instead raised critical questions about the nature of geographical knowledge fostered by current approaches towards revision, and I found myself facing a more fundamental question: 'what counts as an educated 19-year-old in this day and age?' (Pring *et al.*, 2009, p. x). I argued that revision, because of its chronological position as the culmination of formal geography courses, has a symbolically significant place in students' experience of geography, teaching students about the nature of geography in ways that contradict other (better?) visions of geography education. I concluded that my research *for* geography education ought to take a more critical view and seek to develop distinctively educational and geographical language (discussed further below, in the geography *of* education). This action research effected change and, I would argue, improvement, but it was not the change I had anticipated.

Quasi-experimental designs

The political importance currently attached to RCTs and experimental designs means we need to understand them, even if you might be less likely to be directly involved in such research or regularly encounter them in GER. Some examples of similar research do, however, exist in GER and the discussion below focuses on an

relevant to the problem or topic) is in danger of, in McNiff's (2013) terms, being 'domesticated' into merely 'telling stories' (p. 6). Firth and Morgan's (2010) call for GER to engage in more critical research is relevant to this discussion: it is not enough to make something more efficient, or more effective, leaving more fundamental questions about its purpose and goodness unexplored (Biesta, 2009).

The open and inherently reflexive, nature of action research offers exciting potential for research to take unexpected turns, and even

Experimental group (N=76)	School 1 (N=21)	Pre-test	TTG strategies	Post-test
	School 2 (N=28)			
	School 3 (N=27)			
Control group (N=77)	School 1 (N=24)	Pre-test	Regular geography lessons	Post-test
	School 2 (N=28)			
	School 3 (N=25)			

Figure 6: Quasi-experimental pre-test and post-test control group design. **Source:** Van der Schee et al., 2006, p. 127.

interesting project seeking to understand the effect of teaching thinking skills.

Quasi-experimental designs often carry out some kind of measurement on participants before and after an intervention. In the example discussed here the interventions are strategies from a series of popular publications emphasising 'thinking skills' (Leat, 2001). A statistical test is carried out on the results of the measurements (such as the t-test, ANOVA [analysis of variance between groups], and multilevel regression models). This methodology is called 'quasi'-experimental because in educational settings it is impossible to control for variables in the laboratory-type ways required of experimental designs. The research of Van der Schee et al. (2006) aims to 'explore the effect of using ['Five Ws', 'Reading Photographs' and 'Mysteries'] on thinking skills of students in lower secondary education' (p. 126). They also aim to 'help pupils understand' (p. 124) and to 'aid the intellectual development of pupils' (p. 125): action-oriented aims, seeking to improve situations. The study (summarised in Figure 6) is a quasi-experimental pre-test and post-test control group design, carried out in three Dutch lower secondary school classes.

The intervention is highlighted, and this box is what the study is all about: do the students receiving this intervention do better than those not receiving it? The 'doing better' is judged by statistical comparison of the differences between the pre- and post-test scores.

I am now going to be critical of the claims made by Van der Schee et al. Before I do this, I want to emphasise that I do not wish to critique quasi-experimental designs in general, nor *Thinking Through Geography* (TTG) in general. The TTG resource books continue to be hugely popular, and I continue to enjoy using a wide range of the strategies they describe. However, it is partly because of the extent of TTG's influence on geography education that it is worth thinking about critically.

Van der Schee et al. report that their 'results are complex' (2006, p. 130). It is hard to know what this means, because on one level their data and results are simple: a list of means and standard deviations, and the differences between these. Partly to illustrate the kinds of results reported in these studies, I have presented results from Schools 2 and 3 (Figures 7 and 8). The pre- and post-tests consisted of 14 open questions, based on the 'Odd One Out' strategy. The total score is the number of correctly identified 'odd ones', plus the number of correctly described connections between the other three, 'not-odd' options. The relations score refers only to the latter.

The t-value represents the difference between means; the larger this value, the larger the difference. The p-value tells you how likely you are to get this result (the difference between means) by chance. A p-value – or 'significance value' – of less than 0.05 normally means the null hypothesis is rejected. In this case, the null hypothesis is that there is no difference between pre- and post-test results.

You can read their results by looking down the right-hand column. The group given TTG strategies seem to improve more than the control in School 2, but in School 3 the control group improves between pre- and post-tests. While acknowledging that 'the results of this research project are not unambiguous' (Van der Schee et al., 2006, p. 130), nevertheless, the authors maintain their belief in TTG's ability to improve students' learning: 'although hard evidence is lacking, the role of the different teachers and different materials in the control groups may explain some of these differences' (p. 130).

299

Figure 7: Results of the pre-test and post-test at School 2. **Source:** Van der Schee et al., 2006, p. 130.

Group	Score	Pre-test M	Pre-test SD	Post-test M	Post-test SD	Progression
Experimental group N=28	Total score Max=14	9.81	3.71	11.15	4.15	$t=2.09, p<0.05$
	Relations score Max=7	1.59	1.89	3.52	2.53	$t=4.17, p<0.00$
Control group N=28	Total score Max=14	10.07	3.21	10.85	4.57	$t=0.96, p<0.35$
	Relations score Max=7	2.30	2.15	3.26	2.64	$t=2.74, p<0.01$

Figure 8: Results of the pre-test and post-test at School 3. **Source:** Van der Schee et al., 2006, p. 130.

Group	Score	Pre-test M	Pre-test SD	Post-test M	Post-test SD	Progression
Experimental group N=28	Total score Max=14	10.12	3.52	12.52	4.05	$t=4.33, p<0.00$
	Relations score Max=7	1.08	1.47	1.92	2.22	$t=2.11, p<0.05$
Control group N=28	Total score Max=14	9.82	3.25	12.41	4.25	$t=3.19, p<0.00$
	Relations score Max=7	1.27	1.58	2.18	2.34	$t=3.36, p<9.00$

It is interesting to note the way in which Van der Schee et al. position TTG as a 'new way of learning', and an 'alternative view', which they contrast against 'normal' lessons, which are 'safer' and 'more predictable' (p. 132). Having rhetorically positioned TTG as something new and exciting, and attributed their inconclusive results to the teachers, the authors conclude that 'it is through collaborative models of professional development that such approaches as [TTG] are likely to achieve their greatest impact' (Van der Schee et al., 2006, pp. 132–33). One of the co-authors is David Leat, editor of TTG, which raises possible issues about potential conflicts of interest. Research, as systematic enquiry made public, should not advocate particular teaching strategies, but seek to be open to all possibilities, including that teaching 'thinking skills' actually may not offer a more effective approach to teaching and learning than what they describe as 'normal' textbook lessons.

A more recent study of the effects of using one of the TTG strategies offers a more descriptive account, using a larger sample, a more refined test (reporting just relations) and a more sophisticated multi-level regression statistical analysis (Karkdijk et al., 2013). They found:

'a significant effect of teaching with mysteries on students' skills to make geographical relations. So, there seems to be some empirical evidence for the effects of teaching with mysteries on fostering students' geographical thinking' (p. 188).

The differences between the 2006 and 2013 papers, particularly in terms of methods, language, and the types of claims made, are fascinating, and together they offer a good example of the development of knowledge: of a scholarly conversation being taken forward. They are interesting to explore together; read them side by side, analysing the different methodologies and the differences in language used to describe the aims and claims of each.

I have presented research *for* geography education as action-oriented, involving change and effecting improvements to the teaching of geography. The types of research involved are diverse, including small-scale action research, and studies using larger samples and statistical analysis. Action research might be used to develop your own practice in your classroom. The highly situated specific findings such research may develop have the potential to powerfully inform your practice. However, it is important to communicate these findings carefully and transparently, making claims and suggestions for improvement that are justified and acknowledging the situated nature of the

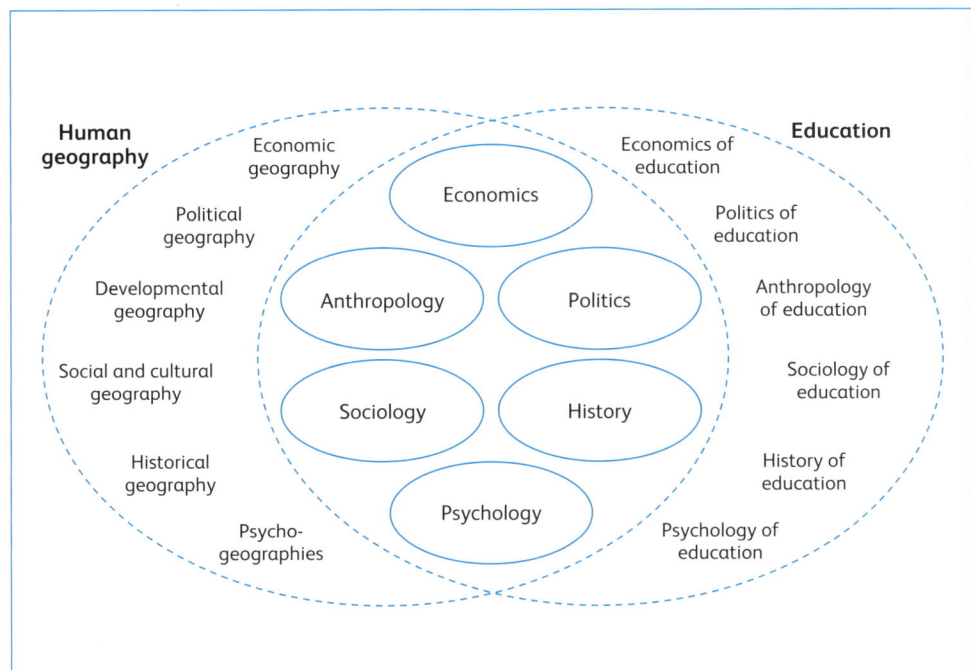

Figure 9:
The multi-disciplinary foundations of geography and education. **Source:** Taylor, 2009, p. 654.

research. It is equally important to acknowledge the danger of large-scale studies over-claiming the extent to which their highly generalised conclusions might apply to your specific classroom situation. Research *for* geography education raises important questions surrounding notions of 'what works', where, and for who:

> *'Just because we have evidence for something working does not mean it is a good thing, and what "works" means here is inevitably contentious. We need to ask what "works" for what, and in the service of what? Morphine works to alter our moods. It is a bad drug for anyone destructively hooked on heroin and a good drug for pain control for the terminally ill'* (Heilbronn, 2008, p. 170).

Geography *of* education

GER is uniquely positioned at the interface between school and academic geography, and there may be much to be gained from developing the geography *of* education. Taylor (2009) offers an important argument that geography has the potential to make significant contributions to our understanding of education. His representation of the broad intersections between geographical and educational research is shown in Figure 9.

Taylor's work focuses on large-scale analysis of spatial distribution and access to schools. Dorling's (2014) research on inequality in education also offers a powerful example of what geography might 'bring to the party' (Massey, 2014, p. 38). Beyond these important large-scale geographies of education, Taylor argues that psychogeographies and geographies of emotion offer interesting areas, as do geographies of 'consumption – affecting how learners behave and react to learning as consumers of education – and globalisation' (Taylor, 2009, p. 661). An account of the emergence of children's geographies is also presented by Schäfer (2012); an area of interest to academic geographers with perhaps the most obvious connections to school geographies. Workplace geographies, such as Crang's (1994), also hold considerable potential for teachers to conduct geographical ethnographic research on the workplace geographies of their own geography departments. Related to this are McCormack and Schwanen's (2011) calls for research into the space-times of decision making (Puttick, 2014). As Figure 9 indicates, these suggestions are a drop in the ocean of possible lines of enquiry.

Reading is an essential part of research. **Photo** © University of Illinois Library.

Practical suggestions

Imagine you have been lured into accepting something of my position – that research is important and potentially exciting. How might you get (more) involved in it, and at what level? Below are three practical suggestions: read research, further study, and publish; which might be described as 'using research, engaging in research and *being* a researcher' (Brooks, 2010, p. 115).

Read research

Reading is an essential part of research, and there are good reasons for placing it here as the first suggestion:

> 'The best writers are always the most diligent readers. By reading voraciously and widely you will begin to understand how [research-based] writing and argument "works", the truths it conveys, and the forms of rhetoric and style it relies on' (Mills and Morton, 2013, p. 23).

Find research articles to read: joining the GA and subscribing to one of their journals is a good place to start. Academic journals such as *International Research in Geographical and Environmental Education*, and the *Journal of Geography in Higher Education* are also aimed at disseminating GER. General education research journals might also be of interest, for example the *British Educational Research Journal*, *The Curriculum Journal* and the *Oxford Review of Education*. Google Scholar is also an extensively indexed source of articles.

Find others to read with; maybe dedicate every other departmental meeting to discussing a piece of research, circulating it for everyone to read beforehand. You could host a termly discussion, extending the invitation to other local geography departments. You could also approach your local university geography department, GA Branch, or geography PGCE tutor; they might be interested in attending, hosting or publicising such a group. These kinds of reading groups are very informal; there is no commitment, and by circulating the article beforehand people can drop in on those sessions they are most interested in. They also require little preparation; just find an article and circulate it (suggestions for finding articles are below, but you could even just start with this chapter). You could use the suggestions of Oancea and Furlong (2007) on pages 293–4 to give the discussion more structure.

Further study

Further study might include formal accredited courses with universities and other continuing professional development (CPD) opportunities. Both approaches complement – and offer a development from – reading research, by providing explicit education and training in research methods. Several Masters courses are now available on a part-time basis, designed specifically for teachers. Most are general education courses, although within these there is potential to make your research geography-specific. For example, Oxford University offers a part time 'MLT' (Masters in Learning and Teaching) course; the Open University offers a Masters degree in Education; and there are many others from a wide range of institutions. The Institute of Education in London offers an MA specifically in geography education. If you would like to continue formal study beyond Masters courses there are a range of options at doctoral level, including full- and part-time options to gain a Doctor of Philosophy (PhD) or Doctor of Education (EdD) degree, each with different assessment criteria and expectations. As well as giving you accreditation in recognition of your research, formal study has other advantages: university access to journal articles, supervisor support from an experienced researcher, critical feedback on your writing and research, methodology and study design, and discussion and networking with peers also engaging in research.

Publish

Research was defined above as 'systematic enquiry that is made public and exposed to collective criticism'. If one of the aims of research agreed upon by different research traditions is developing knowledge, then publishing, or more broadly communicating, is important. Knowledge is only developed when it is shared, and conversations about research happen through your writing (part of the purpose of academic referencing is to articulate something of the conversation that you are contributing to). Your writing needs to be made accessible in order for others to engage in this conversation, so that your contribution not only responds to the existing voices of others but stimulates further responses and so moves the conversation on. Publishing or communicating research is easier now than at any point in history. Social networks, blogs and websites are (once you are online) free and relatively easy. You do not need a publishing contract or to pass peer review in order to get your research 'out there', and these online tools can all help conversations to develop in interesting ways.

Social networks and online self-publishing offer an interesting addition to more traditional publishing options, although they are unlikely to replace established methods of publishing, particularly in academic journals. Reading an article in a journal, as opposed to a blog, does not necessarily mean that it will be better. What it does mean is that others (normally anonymous peer reviewers) have critically read the research and its claims before approving the article; something that has not happened with a blog post.

Conclusion

Geography education research is a diverse field. Hopefully the three areas – *about*, *for* and *of* – presented in this chapter offer a sense of the diversity of this research and also of the possibilities. A broad conception of research – that is, systematic enquiry that is made public and exposed to collective criticism – has been presented, and I have argued that research should be understood on its own terms, being scrutinised for internal consistency between aims, questions, methods, data and claims. GER represents a potentially powerful source of knowledge for teachers, helping us both understand and improve geography education, and doing so in a way that is informed by an ongoing dialogue with academic geography. However, research has limitations and cannot un-problematically tell us 'what works': it needs to be engaged with thoughtfully, reflectively and critically.

Communicating your research responds to the existing voices of others, stimulates further responses and moves the conversation on. **Photo** © Bryan Ledgard.

References

Barnett, C. (2002) 'The cultural turn: fashion or progress in human geography?', *Antipode*, 30, 4, pp. 379–94.

Biesta, G. (2005) 'Against learning: reclaiming a language for education in an age of learning', *Nordisk Pedagogik*, 25, pp. 54–66.

Biesta, G. (2007) 'Why "what works" won't work: evidence-based practice and the democratic deficit in educational research', *Educational Theory*, 57, 1, pp. 1–22.

Biesta, G. (2009) 'Good education in an age of measurement: on the need to reconnect with the question of purpose in education', *Educational Assessment, Evaluation and Accountability*, 21, 1, pp. 33–46.

Bridges, D., Smeyers, P. and Smith, R. (eds) (2009) *Evidence-Based Education Policy: What evidence? What basis? Whose policy?* Oxford: Wiley-Blackwell.

Brooks, C. (2010) 'How does one become a researcher in geography education?', *International Research in Geographical and Environmental Education*, 19, 2, pp. 115–18.

Butt, G. (2010) 'Which methods are best suited to the production of high-quality research in geography education?', *International Research in Geographical and Environmental Education*, 19, 2, pp. 103–7.

Catling, S. (2010) 'Sources of evidence for conducting research in geography education', *International Research in Geographical and Environmental Education*, 19, 2, pp. 97–101.

Catling, S. (2013) 'Teachers' perspectives on curriculum making in primary geography in England', *The Curriculum Journal*, 24, 3, pp. 427–53.

Crang, P. (1994) 'It's showtime: on the workplace geographies of display in a restaurant in southeast England', *Environment and Planning D: Society and Space*, 12, 6, pp. 675–704.

Dorling, D. (2014) *Is the British education system designed to polarise people?* Available at: www.theguardian.com/education/2014/feb/04/education-system-polarises-people-economic-inequality (last accessed 14/11/2016).

Duffy, M. (2013) 'Home learning: how can we make this more meaningful?', *Teaching Geography*, 38, 2, pp. 66–68.

Firth, R. and Morgan, J. (2010) 'What is the place of radical/critical research in geography education?', *International Research in Geographical and Environmental Education*, 19, 2, pp. 109–13.

Furlong, J. (2004) 'BERA at 30: have we come of age?', *British Educational Research Journal*, 30, 3, pp. 343–58.

Goldacre, B. (2013) *Building evidence into education*. Available at: http://media.education.gov.uk/assets/files/pdf/b/ben%20goldacre%20paper.pdf (last accessed 14/11/2016).

Hargreaves, D. (2003) *Education Epidemic: Transforming secondary schools through innovation networks*. London: Demos.

Harvey, D. (1973) *Social Justice and the City*. Baltimore, MD: Johns Hopkins University Press.

Heilbronn, R. (2008) *Teacher Education and the Development of Practical Judgement*. London: Continuum.

Hopwood, N. (2006) *Pupils' Conceptions of School Geography: A classroom-based investigation*. DPhil. thesis, University of Oxford.

Hopwood, N. (2012) *Geography in Secondary Schools: Researching pupils' classroom experiences*. London: Continuum.

Hopwood, N., Courtley-Green, C. and Chambers, T. (2005) 'Year 9 students' conceptions of geography', *Teaching Geography*, 30, 2, pp. 91–93.

Jeffrey, C. (2010) *Timepass: Youth, class and the politics of waiting in India*. Stanford, CA: Stanford University Press.

Karkdijk, J., Van der Schee, J. and Admiraal, W. (2013) 'Effects of teaching with mysteries on students' geographical thinking skills', *International Research in Geographical and Environmental Education*, 22, 3, pp. 183–90.

Lambert, D. (2010) 'Geography education research and why it matters', *International Research in Geographical and Environmental Education*, 19, 2, pp. 83–86.

Leat, D. (2001) *Thinking Through Geography* (2nd edition). Cambridge: Chris Kington Publishing.

Lewin, K. (1946) 'Action research and minority problems', *Journal of Social Issues*, 2, 4, pp. 34–46.

Leys, R. (2011) 'The turn to affect: a critique', *Critical Inquiry*, 37, 3, pp. 434–72.

Massey, D. (2014) 'Taking on the world', *Geography*, 99, 1, pp. 36–39.

McCormack, D.P. and Schwanen, T. (2011) 'Guest editorial: The space-times of decision making', *Environment and Planning A*, 43, 12, pp. 2801–18.

McNiff, J. (2013) *Action Research: Principles and practice* (3rd edition). Abingdon: Routledge.

Menter, I. (2011) 'Teacher education research – past, present, future', *Research Intelligence*, 116, pp. 11–13.

Mills, D. and Morton, M. (2013) *Ethnography in Education*. London: SAGE.

Norman, M. and Harrison, L. (2004) 'Year 9 students' perceptions of school geography', *Teaching Geography*, 29, 1, pp. 11–15.

Oancea, A. and Furlong, J. (2007) 'Expressions of excellence and the assessment of applied and practice-based research', *Research Papers in Education*, 22, 2, pp. 119–37.

Perks, P. and Prestage, S. (2009) *Masters in Education (MEd): Coursebook*. Birmingham: School of Education, University of Birmingham.

Pring, R., Hayward, G., Hodgson, A., Johnson, J., Kepp, E., Oancea, A., Rees, G., Spours, K. and Wilde, S. (2009) *Education for All: The future of education and training for 14–19 year olds*. Abingdon: Routledge.

Puttick, S. (2013) 'GCSE geography revision: an action research project', *Teaching Geography*, 38, 1, pp. 26–27.

Puttick, S. (2014) 'Space-times of teachers' journeys for knowledge', *Teaching Geography*, 39, 3, pp. 114–15.

Rudduck, J. and Hopkins, D. (1985) *Research as a Basis for Teaching: Readings from the work of Lawrence Stenhouse*. Harlow: Heinemann.

Schäfer, N. (2012) 'Finding ways to do research on, with and for children and young people', *Geography*, 97, 3, pp. 147–54.

Soja, E.W. (1989) *Postmodern Geographies: The reassertion of space in critical social theory*. London: Verso.

Taylor, C. (2009) 'Towards a geography of education', *Oxford Review of Education*, 35, 5, pp. 651–69.

Thomas, G. and Pring, R. (eds) (2004) *Evidence-Based Practice in Education*. Maidenhead: Open University Press.

Valentine, G. (2004) *Public Space and the Culture of Childhood*. Aldershot: Ashgate.

Van der Schee, J., Leat, D. and Vankan, L. (2006) 'Effects of the use of *Thinking Through Geography* strategies', *International Research in Geographical and Environmental Education*, 15, 2, pp. 124–33.

Weber, M. (1949) *The Methodology of the Social Sciences*. New York, NY: The Free Press.

Winch, C., Oancea, A. and Orchard, J. (2013) *The Contribution of Educational Research to Teachers' Professional Learning – Philosophical understandings*. London: BERA/RSA.

Winter, C. (2011) 'Curriculum knowledge and justice: content, competency and concept', *The Curriculum Journal*, 22, 3, pp. 337–64.

Recommended key readings

Butt, G. (ed) (2015) *Masterclass in Geography Education: Transforming teaching and learning*. London: Bloomsbury.

This book combines stimulating discussion about research, knowledge, the curriculum and theory with practical applications for engaging with research. Structured around themes, the discussion sections provide a particularly insightful commentary, helping the reader to locate the chapters in relation to one another, and wider debates, and provoking further questions.

Punch, K. and Oancea, A. (2014) *Introduction to Research Methods* (2nd edition). London: SAGE.

In the crowded marketplace of 'research methods' texts, this book stands out. It combines sharp philosophical analysis of issues surrounding educational research with clear discussion of specific methods, and the study questions posed at the end of each chapter are powerful in facilitating a deeper engagement with the concepts presented.

Chapter 22

Mentoring

Charles Rawding is Senior Lecturer in Geography Education at Edge Hill University, and **Andrea Tapsfield** is a retired HMI who had responsibility for Geography Initial Teacher Training

Introduction

The purpose of this chapter is to explore ways to mentor geography teachers throughout their professional careers. It discusses the nature of mentoring and looks at strategies for developing effective mentor-mentee relationships.

What is mentoring?

A mentor works with teachers to support their professional development and encourage them to improve their practice. There are different forms of mentoring. In initial teacher education (ITE), the mentor's responsibility is to train a new geography teacher. They must ensure that a trainee becomes an effective teacher with the ability to reflect on and evaluate their own practice and that they are equipped to develop their own professional expertise. An ITE mentor is also an assessor, who judges whether a trainee teacher meets the Teachers' Standards and is fit to join the profession. In the departmental context, a mentor acts as a critical friend who observes teaching, reviews planning and provides advice. A mentor may also provide support for non-specialists, for the induction of newly qualified teachers (NQTs) or for those facing significant challenges.

Mentors can also take the role of a coach to support an individual's professional development. Mentoring and coaching both involve similar approaches and skills, and the terms are often used interchangeably: however, coaching has a narrower remit and usually focuses on specific areas of performance (Lord et al., 2008). Both mentoring and coaching encourage teachers to be analytical about their teaching and to experiment with new classroom strategies. They do not seek to promote one right way; rather to help teachers find the most effective approach in a particular context.

Mentoring can be an extremely rewarding professional experience and a mentor benefits from insights into their mentees' practice. However, prospective mentors need to reflect carefully on their own suitability before they take on the role. Figure 1 sets out some self-reflective questions for doing this.

Mentors should be knowledgeable, experienced and successful teachers, respected by their colleagues. The key skills of mentoring are effective questioning and active listening. Good mentors ask questions that motivate, clarify, encourage reflection and enhance problem solving. They listen actively to a mentee's contribution to ensure they understand accurately the messages they wish to convey and resist the temptation to always impose their own ideas on a mentee. A mentor's role requires insight, flexibility, empathy, tolerance and the ability to develop an effective working relationship. Mentors must be genuinely interested in their mentees, with realistic expectations of their progress. They must aim to foster reflection and analysis, guiding their mentees to recognise issues and find solutions themselves. They should resist the temptation to impose their own ideas.

Preparation for becoming a mentor can take a number of forms. Some mentor training, through a university-run accredited course in mentoring, may be available locally. There are also courses that can support the development of mentoring skills such as observing, reflecting, target setting and action planning (see *www.goodcpdguide.com* or *www.hotcourses.com*). If you intend to become a mentor for a trainee teacher, find out what training and support an

> Are you an effective teacher who consistently teaches good or outstanding lessons?
>
> Can you provide a good role model for others?
>
> Do you have a clear understanding of what is high-quality challenging geography teaching?
>
> Are you up to date in your own knowledge of geography and pedagogy?
>
> Are you committed to supporting and training others?
>
> Can you explain and analyse your own classroom practice?
>
> Are you an approachable person who can establish a trusting relationship with colleagues?
>
> Can you inspire colleagues?
>
> Do you have effective communication skills?
>
> Are you prepared to learn from others?

Figure 1: Requirements for effective mentoring.

ITE scheme provides: most provide face-to-face or online training specifically for new mentors. In addition to an individual ITE scheme's support, the Geographical Association (GA) website provides an extensive range of support materials for geography mentors. Informal discussion with experienced mentors, and working with colleagues who have experience of mentoring, can be invaluable.

Mentoring for different purposes

Mentoring in ITE

There are several different training routes into teaching; some are led by universities, others by schools. In all cases the geography mentor plays a key role, although the specific responsibilities differ from scheme to scheme. A mentor's role in ITE can be underestimated. Trainee teachers in school are not just doing 'work experience' or 'teaching practice': they are participating in intensive professional training. Mentors are responsible for managing a programme of experiences for trainee teachers to develop their teaching expertise. The National Standards for school-based initial teacher training (ITT) mentors (Teaching Schools Council, 2016) are a set of non-statutory standards for the mentoring of trainee teachers, which provide a framework for the professional development of current and aspiring mentors.

A mentor in a university partnership will have the support of a university geography tutor. In school-based schemes, there is usually an experienced geography mentor or a consultant who co-ordinates and leads the geography training. A senior member of staff will have overall responsibility for trainee teachers across all subjects. As well as approaching departmental colleagues for advice and support, geography mentors can find it useful to discuss common issues and collaborate with subject mentors from other departments (Bott, 2012).

To sustain good geography teaching across the country, new entrants to the profession require the best geography teachers and departments to help to train them. Involvement in ITE offers numerous benefits to mentors: developing the skills of coaching and mentoring constitutes excellent professional development and is an opportunity for the mentor to reflect on and develop their own teaching. It also facilitates working with other geographers, both university tutors and mentors from different schools. Above all, it provides intellectual challenge and increased job satisfaction.

Mentoring a trainee teacher challenges all members of a geography department to model excellent teaching. Teachers will get used to being observed by a trainee, and it provides a stimulus to discuss and develop practice. Trainee teachers can ask difficult questions, which acts as a catalyst for experienced teachers to self-reflect, analyse and justify their approaches. Consequently, involvement with a trainee can invigorate a department and introduce both pedagogical and curricular innovations.

Ideally, the whole geography department should be involved in mentoring, so trainees receive a variety of experiences. However, mentees regularly report that they receive conflicting advice from different teachers, particularly on aspects of lesson design and behaviour management, so it is important to discuss alternative approaches with them and reconcile any inconsistencies.

There are other advantages to getting involved in geography ITE. For example, a mentor observing a trainee teacher has the opportunity to observe how students respond to lessons and learn – something that is difficult to do when teaching a class. Trainee teachers are often recent geography graduates, and should be encouraged to contribute fresh ideas and perspectives, especially about current developments in the subject. They can create new resources for a department and provide extra support, such as with fieldwork, with students with special needs or with GCSE intervention. Mentoring trainee teachers also provides an opportunity to recruit a good trainee!

Mentoring takes dedication, patience and time. A mentor spends time in planning, undertaking training and carrying out assessments, as well as discussing with the trainee the lessons they have taught and those they are planning to teach. The time commitment far exceeds the hour a week that most schools allocate for mentoring. Most trainee teachers have been carefully selected and turn out to be good teachers, but there are no guarantees. The training year is extremely demanding and stressful and a mentor needs to be prepared to face all eventualities. Figure 2 summarises what geography trainees consider to be indicators of an effective mentoring experience.

Mentoring NQTs

All NQTs in maintained schools must complete a statutory induction period during which they should have a designated induction mentor. These mentors need a clear understanding of the professional requirements for the induction year. They must monitor the NQT's progress in relation to the Teachers' Standards, identify development needs and adopt effective intervention strategies when required.

The best induction practice is to ensure that the new teacher has a personalised action plan that is regularly reviewed and revised. The mentor also needs to gather a wide range of evidence to make decisions on the assessment of the NQT.

Mentoring NQTs is not usually as demanding as supporting a trainee teacher, but it does require a personalised programme of professional development activities, including regular observation and feedback. The induction year should lay down a firm foundation for the new teacher's continuing professional development: it is essential that NQTs continue to develop as reflective professional practitioners.

The NQT year can be very pressured and stressful, and empathy with the mentee's perspective is an essential prerequisite for effective mentoring. Mentors must be ready to provide a wide range of appropriate advice, encouraging their mentees as well as professionally evaluating the quality of their work. Most NQTs will need support in particular aspects of teaching (see Figure 3), especially in developing their expertise in meeting individual needs, assessing students' progress and managing tasks in which they have only limited experience, such as report writing and taking parents' evenings. NQTs may also find the higher expectations of a fully-fledged teacher somewhat daunting. With more classes and more teaching, behaviour management is often a challenging issue for an NQT.

Mentoring for professional practice within a department

The purpose of mentoring within a geography department is to respond to developmental needs and goals. It can take a variety of forms. It may be part of a strategy to support someone new to the department, or newly promoted. Here a mentor's responsibility is to ensure that the new person receives an effective orientation into their job, the department and the context within the school. Mentoring can be used to challenge and stretch teachers with high potential or re-motivate those who are experiencing difficulties. It can also help to embed change and establish new systems or approaches within the department, such as for assessment or GIS.

Chapter 22: Mentoring

- Being valued and feeling they are 'part of the geography team'.
- Receiving constructive critical feedback on lessons.
- Being set clear, achievable, but challenging targets.
- Being provided with clear and informative schemes of work.
- Having access to well-organised school resources.
- Getting advance notice of what they are expected to teach.
- Receiving clear and precise explanations of school and departmental systems.
- Having good links identified between their geography and professional training.
- Being given the opportunity to try out new ideas.
- Benefiting from informal chats and advice.
- Having supportive peers, i.e. other trainees they can work with in their school.
- Having access to physical space to work in and keep their resources.

Figure 2: Trainees' perceptions: indicators of an effective mentoring experience.

- Provide guidance on writing schemes of work.
- Provide guidance on planning field trips.
- Suggest marking GCSE past papers.
- Share the planning of new topics.
- Provide opportunities to observe examination classes.
- Provide opportunities to observe colleagues in other departments.
- Try co-teaching of a class.

Figure 3: Strategies for supporting NQTs.

When establishing a departmental mentoring programme, the mentor should secure the commitment of all teachers by ensuring that they understand its purpose. The mentor should find time within the department's day-to-day activities to provide the mentee with a range of different experiences. Mentoring for professional development should be undertaken within a culture of mutual support and agreed confidentiality. It should take place in a context of mutual learning, self-evaluation and critique of professional practice, as part of a support culture that has improving students' learning at its heart. Some geography departments use a peer review approach. For the peer review process to be effective and mutually beneficial, pairs of teachers will need to work collaboratively, holding regular meetings to sustain continuous improvement. When planning mentor interventions it can be useful to consider the preferred learning styles of different members of the geography department, as set out in Figure 4.

Activists like to get involved in new experiences, tend to be open-minded and enthusiastic and enjoy challenges. They are often outgoing people who like to be at the hub of things and are likely to work positively at peer-coaching activities.

Reflectors tend to ponder deeply and think things through. They listen to others and respond carefully. They are likely to respond positively in discussions with a mentor and should be encouraged to go through their thinking, explaining the pros and cons.

Theorists thrive on facts and have a linear, rational approach to problems; they need things to 'make sense'. They are likely to analyse events to establish what can be learned from them. They could usefully design an approach, maybe as a flowchart, which others can use.

Pragmatists are practical and down to earth. They like seeing if things work in practice and respond to problems as a challenge. They will try out new ideas and experiment but tend to be impatient with long-winded discussion and often benefit from demonstrations.

Figure 4: Learning styles. **Source:** Honey and Mumford, 1986.

Peer coaching is a partnership between teachers who are comitted to reciprocal learning. **Photo** © Bryan Ledgard.

Coaching established teachers

Coaching is a more structured form of mentoring for a specific purpose. It may be appropriate, for example, for a non-specialist teacher or a teacher returning to the classroom to be coached in order to develop their understanding of current geography teaching, to review and refine their practice, or to develop and extend their teaching and learning repertoire. Peer (or collaborative) coaching is a partnership between teachers who are committed to reciprocal learning.

Coaching is a commonly-used strategy for supporting established teachers who are experiencing challenges in the classroom. In a climate in which school leaders take accountability and Ofsted inspection very seriously, coaching is often adopted to support teachers who are considered to be 'underperforming'. As Lofthouse and Leat (2006) point out, one consequence is that coaching can be perceived negatively, as colleagues coming to 'tell me what to do'. Indeed, it is important to avoid what has been termed 'judgementoring' (Hobson and Malderez, 2013, cited in Lofthouse and Hall, 2014, p. 759). To dispel this impression they suggest starting with volunteer 'good' teachers, rather than struggling teachers, to convey the message that coaching is not a cure for professional ailments.

A mentor-coach needs to have knowledge and expertise relevant to the difficulties the teacher is experiencing. Building trust and confidence are of prime importance; and the use of non-judgemental questioning and support will help the teacher to take control of the learning process. The mentor-coach and teacher must agree the learning goals and a programme of activities and shared experiences to achieve these goals. An essential element is to discuss and analyse practice together – as a collaborative activity. When observing a lesson, the mentor-coach should record what occurs without making evaluative comment. The record should be analysed in a post-lesson discussion and 'key elements' identified to inform subsequent analysis and reflection (for a more detailed discussion of the possible elements of professional dialogue see Lofthouse and Hall, 2014, pp. 760–62). Video can assist this process, allowing both participants to review particular phases or 'critical moments', both within the lesson and between lessons.

If, as a mentor, you are asked to take on the role of a coach to help a teacher to improve, you should reach a clear understanding with school managers of your specific role. You should not be 'reporting' on teaching quality for performance management purposes; you are evaluating performance in order to advise a teacher objectively. Your role is to empower – to help a teacher build their teaching capacity and learn and develop new skills to improve their teaching. Empathy and building trust are very important here.

Working with teachers who have been deemed to be underperforming or who are demotivated can be difficult and uncomfortable for a coach. The teacher concerned may be in denial about their problems and they will almost certainly be experiencing high levels of stress. The coach may meet resentment or even aggression and will need to combine clarity with sensitivity. It is important to encourage struggling teachers to reflect on their teaching and see the problems they face. The coach should encourage them to develop solutions to their problems and engage in constructive discussion as a way of enhancing their self-esteem and confidence. Teachers can be reinvigorated when they see there are ways forward. However, coaching is not therapy and it is important to present objective data and evidence for discussion. Figure 5 sets out some techniques for effective coaching.

With peer coaching, relationships are rather different. Peer coaching involves non-hierarchical observation and feedback between pairs of teachers. The key benefit of peer coaching is that teachers have control over their own development and develop a mutual understanding through experiences shared with colleagues. Such an approach offers shared insights into classroom practice and is often used to introduce and experiment with alternative teaching and learning strategies. It can be part of classroom-based research in which peers provide a perspective from someone with similar experience. Peer coaching enables all staff to be 'mentors' and can be a cost-effective means of improving departmental performance and creativity. The coaching partners support each other and might seek out specialist input from a consultant or a text resource. Video is useful to review practice; it also helps teachers develop and enhance the skills required for peer coaching (Charteris and Smardon, 2013).

- Encourage teachers to reflect on their teaching and identify the problems themselves.
- Let the teachers know that you respect their ability to develop solutions.
- Ask open-ended questions to encourage analysis and draw out suggestions; be prepared to challenge teachers with your questions.
- Good coaching questions are 'Can you tell me more about that?', 'Why do you think that happens?', 'How might you manage this differently?'
- Be sensitive in your tone and body language.
- Give constructive feedback – people learn more quickly if they know what they are doing well.
- Try to avoid using the word 'but' after you praised an aspect of the teacher's work; this signals that criticism is coming and may make the teacher defensive.
- Silence can be a great tool; it indicates that you have asked a significant question. Don't feel compelled to fill the void immediately!
- At the end of a discussion/meeting, summarise the key points to clarify understanding and agree appropriate actions.

Figure 5: Effective coaching techniques.

Coaching is popular among teachers and has significant potential for improving professional learning (Lofthouse *et al.*, 2010; Lofthouse and Hall, 2014). Coaching shares many of the characteristics identified with successful, effective professional development; there are opportunities for experimentation, observation, feedback, collaboration and dialogue, and the process has a strong focus on classroom pedagogies. Interestingly, evidence collated by the Centre for the Use of Research and Evidence in Education (CUREE) (2005) has shown that in general the benefits to the coach outweigh those of the teacher. On this basis, enabling teachers to become coaches themselves is likely to improve their own performance.

Figure 6: Approaches to co-teaching. **Source:** Friend and Cook, 2010.

1. **Teacher as support assistant.** One person teaches while the other teacher supports the students by circulating the classroom and offering assistance when needed.
2. **Station teaching.** Teachers divide the lesson content and students into two groups; the teachers meet with each group for half of the lesson time, delivering different content.
3. **In parallel.** The class is divided into two groups and each teacher teaches the same content to one group in different parts of the room.
4. **Alternative teaching.** The teachers organise the students into one large and one small group, in a way that best suits the needs of the students, and each teacher instructs one of the groups.
5. **Taking turns.** Both teachers share complete ownership of the lessons and students and take turns with delivering instruction through team teaching.
6. **Analysis of student behaviour.** With the 'one teach, one observe' approach, detailed observations of student behaviours, participation and engagement are observed and analysed by both teachers.

Mentoring strategies

A mentor acts as a kind of broker, accessing different strategies to address the goals of the mentee, and there are a range of different mentoring strategies to promote and enhance effective professional practice.

Collaborative teaching

One valuable strategy is collaborative teaching, or co-teaching, which involves practitioners working together in a number of different ways (Figure 6). It can involve a mentor and mentee planning and teaching a lesson together. When this approach is used, the reasons for co-teaching must be clear to the mentee, who should play a full part in the planning – the key point is that this is a collaborative activity and the mentor should not dominate. For a new teacher it provides a supportive environment to ease them into teaching, but it can also be used to help introduce an experienced teacher to a new approach. Collaborative teaching is particularly useful when a teacher is using a demanding resource, such as GIS, for the first time, or managing a complex class organisation, such as in a role play or thinking skills activity. The shared experience can improve working relationships between colleagues and the direct involvement of both parties can lead to better reflection and analysis.

Structured observation by a mentee

The rich learning experience of observing experienced teachers can be very useful at different stages of a teacher's development. It is an important way of developing a teacher's ability to observe, analyse and evaluate professional practice. A mentor can model specific practice for a mentee to observe; it can also be appropriate for a mentee to observe expert teachers in subjects other than geography. However, being observed can be demanding: it requires the experienced teacher to analyse and explain practice that may have become instinctive or internalised over time. The mentor must be able to articulate the reasons for a particular practice: the observer cannot understand what makes the teaching good simply by watching it.

Three stages are central to the observation process – preparation, observation, and discussion.

Preparation

Both mentee and observer must be aware in advance of the context of the lesson: the class, their previous work and the lesson's place in the scheme of learning, their prior knowledge, learning expectations, teaching strategies, expected timings, and how individual needs will be met. The amount and type of contextual information will vary, but it should give the mentee an insight into the decisions taken by the teacher during the lesson. The specific foci for the observation, such as aspects of classroom management, teaching techniques, the geographies of the lesson or how different students approach a task, should also be agreed beforehand.

Observation

Observation should be an active process for the mentee, who should make notes on agreed foci and identify questions to follow up. For example, one trainee geography teacher observed in other teachers' lessons particular students they were struggling to teach. This led the trainee teacher to notice that one student responded much better in oral than written tasks. The trainee adapted her subsequent lessons accordingly. Student shadowing also offers the opportunity to see the effect on students of other teaching styles. For example, a trainee teacher was impressed by student responses in performing arts lessons and began to incorporate more active learning into his own lessons.

Discussion

Discussion after the lesson is essential to help a mentee understand how expert teachers evaluate their teaching and the effectiveness of the learning that took place. The shared lesson experience is a good basis for the mentee to ask, and the mentor to answer, questions. Experienced teachers can make it look deceptively easy and trainee teachers, in particular, may not always be aware of the complexity of the process unfolding before them. The teaching profession, as a whole, tends to underplay the highly skilled nature of many strategies they use in the classroom. This is unhelpful in many ways, not least for trainee teachers striving to emulate the good practice they are observing: it can be extremely useful to deconstruct a sequence of events.

Mentor-mentee meetings

Professional dialogue (Lofthouse and Hall, 2014) is an essential component of mentoring and there should be regular scheduled meetings in addition to the time spent chatting informally. Meetings should be both professionally challenging and supportive, providing opportunities to explore a mentee's ideas and understandings in depth, raise their awareness, develop plans and commit to future activities. A mentor should listen actively, as well as offer guidance and direction. While it is most important that a mentee contributes fully to the meeting, the mentor is the expert practitioner in the partnership and should be bringing new ideas or materials to the discussion. In many situations a good rule of thumb for an hour's meeting is to allocate 25 minutes to review and discussion, 25 minutes to the introduction of new ideas/materials and 10 minutes to agreeing the targets and plan for the next period.

To ensure the time is used profitably, all meetings between mentor and mentee require careful preparation. This generally means both mentor and mentee should collect items for discussion – readings, resources, targets, plans and lesson observation records – and review them in advance. The meeting should have clear objectives so talk does not drift off into discussion of day-to-day or organisational matters. In the increasingly pressurised atmosphere of a normal school working day, it is important to focus on the developmental nature of mentoring, so the meetings should be held in a place that is conducive to a private discussion where you will not be interrupted.

Observing a mentee's lesson

Mentors observe a trainee teacher's lessons as part of the formal assessment process, but the majority of lesson observations by mentors are purely for professional development. Here it is helpful to have agreed in advance the main focus for the observation and the mentor's role in the lesson. In informal situations, there may be opportunities for the mentor to act as a classroom support, perhaps as a teaching assistant, or to sit quietly and unobtrusively. It is often easy for mentors to focus on generic skills when mentoring or coaching teachers. Margaret Roberts (2011), in her role as an external examiner to ITE schemes, observed geography lessons where school-based mentors judged the lessons as good 'because of progress in particular standards, when the teaching and learning of geography was very poor'. Remember that you are observing a geography lesson as a subject specialist, and you should consider both the geography content of the lesson and the resultant student learning. Equally, in lessons where impressive geography is taught and learnt, be careful not to overly criticise aspects such as a lack of pace or plenary (Roberts, 2011).

Figure 7: Comments from geography mentors on lessons by PGCE trainees.

> **A year 12 lesson using internet-based independent enquiry**
>
> 'The more independent learning in a lesson, the more the teacher needs to provide a structure for that learning in order to ensure the students achieve the learning objectives. Have you developed a sense of place or could this be an economics lesson?'
>
> **A year 9 lesson on Japan**
>
> 'It is extremely important that you set the geographical context prior to the activities. Would the provision of photographs have helped here? Be careful about over-simplifying complex geographies.'
>
> **A year 9 lesson on Ghana**
>
> 'The atlas exercise is difficult without an explanation of different scales and brief guidance on "reading" an atlas.'
>
> **A year 8 lesson on the geographies of iPhones**
>
> 'Contemporary, effective and innovative geography – you have set very challenging geographies for the students, but do the resources present a purely negative picture?'
>
> **A year 10 lesson on UK rainfall**
>
> 'Your own subject knowledge needs work and you need to think more carefully about how to communicate abstract concepts via real-world examples.'

Figure 7 gives some examples of geography mentors' comments, which themselves prompt a range of possible responses both from the perspective of the mentor and the mentee.

There are several approaches to recording what takes place in a lesson. For example, schools may use an agreed observation recording form – for teacher trainees, this is usually related to the Teachers' Standards. Some schools have developed scoring systems to provide a number or grade for a lesson, but this can lead to mentees fixating on the 'grade' rather than qualitative comments. A better approach for professional development purposes is for a mentor to act as a 'research assistant' in a lesson, gathering descriptive evidence of what happened in the form of a detailed narrative, without evaluative comment. This non-judgemental mode of observation is a rich source for analysis and a good basis for a post-lesson discussion with the mentee.

Post-lesson discussion/feedback

Whichever observation and recording approach is adopted, the most important part of observing lessons is the post-lesson discussion. Here the mentor and mentee discuss the lesson in detail and review how it went. It is an opportunity for the mentor to be aware of how the lesson appeared from the mentee's perspective, as well as to discuss the mentor's observations. The post-lesson discussion should be conducted in an atmosphere of openness and mutual respect, preferably in an environment conducive to effective reflection. A useful starting point is to ask the mentee 'How did you think the lesson went?' and 'If you were to teach the same lesson again, is there anything you might do differently?' Such an approach will help the mentee to reflect and self-assess. Equally, rather than making an immediate judgement, an approach based on open-ended questions about the lesson content is likely to lead to a more useful discussion. For example: 'Do you think the students understood the differences between weathering and erosion? How could we improve their understanding?' There is a danger that a mentee can be overwhelmed by criticism (however constructively intended), so it is important to be selective, conveying the key messages rather than commenting on everything.

Personalised written feedback is useful because it can be reflected on and referred to later by both parties. It is also very important in ITE because it provides evidence of a trainee teacher's progress and indicates future targets. Records that are simply checklists of superficial yes/no judgements are inappropriate for professional development purposes.

Self-reflection and evaluation

A mentor should ensure that self-reflection and analysis are embedded in a mentee's professional practice. As Sheila King says:

> 'reflective practice goes beyond any common-sense approach. It is a deeper and constructive process which encourages both inexperienced and experienced professionals to reflect explicitly and critically so that practice is improved' (King, 2010, p. 36).

Mentors should assist a mentee to critically analyse their teaching and should always strive to provide a model of good practice in the way they review and evaluate their own lessons; for example, when they are discussing lessons where they have been observed. A mentee should be encouraged to look at examples of good evaluative writing about teaching and learning. The GA journal *Teaching Geography* is a good place to start. The best lesson evaluations examine both the effectiveness of the planning and the success of the learning that occurred. To help mentees develop evaluation skills, they need to take the lead in the post-lesson discussion and to reflect first on the learning outcomes, rather than their teaching or the behaviour of the students. Figure 8 provides a list of possible prompts.

An appropriate way to encourage evaluation and reflection is for mentees to keep a diary (a video diary or a journal) to record their thoughts. Their reflections need to be frank and honest and analyse both strengths and weaknesses.

Using video

Video is an accessible option for recording what happens in classrooms (assuming the school permits this). It is an objective witness and helps a teacher to see things they would often miss. It enables relevant episodes of a lesson to be replayed and this can assist the mentor and mentee to discuss and understand what took place. It is often best if the mentee watches the video first, on their own, and prepares for the subsequent discussion with the mentor. Lofthouse *et al.* (2010) have used this approach at Newcastle University to help trainee teachers evaluate their practice. The trainee teachers:

- video a lesson
- transcribe a short section (e.g. an explanation or questioning to develop students' understanding)
- annotate their transcript
- write a reflective commentary.

Alternatively, a mentor could do a similar review, so the mentor and mentee each select a section they want to watch together and discuss. The process of reviewing small incidents together can help the trainees to 'really understand what is happening… [and] learn so much from small bits of lessons' (Lofthouse and Leat, 2006, p. 130).

- Did you feel students understood the relevance of the learning objectives?
- Did they achieve what you expected them to?
- Was the lesson content challenging enough?
- What do you think the students have learnt in the lesson? What did they not learn? Why?
- Were all students engaged in the task? If not, why not – and what were they doing?
- Did you assess students' learning effectively? What different ways could you have used?
- Were you confident in your subject knowledge about this geography topic? Were you comfortable teaching it?
- Did you pitch your geography explanations and questions at the correct level for these students? How do you know?
- Were all the students catered for effectively within this lesson? Would you change anything?
- Were the resources effective? How do you know? Were there alternative resources you could have used?
- On reflection, did you choose the best teaching strategy and learning activities for this geography topic? What alternatives could you have used?
- Did you manage timing/transitions/ student behaviour effectively? Are there any changes you would make?
- Did you achieve everything you planned to do?
- If you taught this lesson again what would you change?
- What could you do to enable the same geography content to be taught to a less/more able class?
- Was the way you taught this lesson more/less successful than with previous classes? Why?

Figure 8: Prompts to encourage reflection and evaluation.

Setting targets

Review, target setting and action planning are all essential components of mentoring for professional development. Targets should arise from a mentee's specific needs and be shaped, through discussion, to deal positively with areas that need improvement. Targets should be challenging but they also need to be achievable. The mnemonic 'SMARTER' outlines the characteristics of effective targets, as shown in Figure 9.

Mentees should have an action plan comprising specific targets and these should be reviewed regularly in discussion. The action plan provides a medium-term agenda for mentees and gives them a sense of achievement when they succeed.

Specific
with a clearly stated outcome for the mentoring activity.

Measurable
so that both mentor and mentee can identify that actual change has happened.

Agreed
by both parties, so there is commitment to achieving the target.

Realistic
and achievable by the mentee.

Timed
i.e. have a target date when it should be achieved (you may agree milestones to help monitor progress towards achievement).

Exciting
i.e. challenging and stimulating for the mentee and linked to their professional development needs.

Reviewed
i.e. agree a time to review targets and adjust if necessary.

Figure 9:
Smarter targets.

Lesson planning

Be clearer over learning objectives on the lesson plan.

Be explicit about the students' skills to be developed.

Be clear about how individual tasks relate to the accomplishment of learning objectives.

Geographies

Be explicit about the wider geographies of the lesson.

Familiarise yourself with local school geographies.

Provide concrete examples to illustrate abstract concepts.

Build on the students' known world.

Relate abstract statistics to the students' known world.

Provide appropriate geographical contexts during the lesson.

Ensure a sense of place is developed during the lesson.

Pedagogies

Aim for greater impact when introducing the geographies.

Enrich the geography by leading the learning.

Provide structures for independent learning to ensure students can achieve the learning objectives.

Develop/be explicit about success criteria for extended activities.

Management

Scan the room when talking to individuals.

Follow school discipline procedures implementing appropriate sanctions.

Establish effective approaches for gaining students' attention prior to giving instructions/explaining tasks.

Figure 10:
Common targets for trainee geography teachers.

Trainee teachers working to meet the Teachers' Standards have a good deal to cover. To make it manageable a mentor should identify steps or short-term targets. These should be set weekly and mentors should recommend tasks and activities that will help the trainee teacher to achieve these targets. An action plan for a trainee teacher should identify the in-school activities and experiences that will help them to meet specific targets and develop as an effective teacher. As a subject mentor, the targets you set should identify clearly the geography actions the mentee should take. Figure 10 shows some examples of geography targets that have been set for PGCE trainees.

Conclusion

Mentoring is a critical element in the professional development of teachers. Effective mentoring has very real benefits for both mentors and mentees, irrespective of the stage of their professional career, and is an essential element in ensuring that high-quality, critically reflective geography teaching occurs in the classroom.

References

Bott, G. (2012) 'How to mentor beginner teachers', *Teaching Geography*, 37, 3, p. 119.

Centre for the Use of Research and Evidence in Education (CUREE) (2005) *Mentoring and Coaching CPD Capacity Building Project: National framework for mentoring and coaching*. Available at: www.curee.co.uk/files/publication/1301587364/MC%20Framework%202010.pdf (last accessed 14/11/2016).

Charteris, J. and Smardon, D. (2013) 'Second look – second think: a fresh look at video to support dialogic feedback in peer coaching', *Professional Development in Education*, 39, 2, pp. 168–85.

Friend, M. and Cook, L. (2010) *Interactions: Collaboration skills for school professionals* (6th edition). Boston, MA: Allyn and Bacon.

GA (no date) *How to be an effective geography mentor*. Available at: www.geography.org.uk/ (last accessed 14/11/2016).

Honey, P. and Mumford, A. (1986) *Using Your Learning Styles*. Maidenhead: Peter Honey.

King, S. (2010) 'Reflecting critically on practice' in Brooks, C. (ed) *Studying PGCE Geography at M Level*. Abingdon: Routledge, pp. 1–10.

Lofthouse, R. and Hall, E. (2014) 'Developing practices in teachers' professional dialogue in England: using coaching dimensions as an epistemic tool', *Professional Development in Education*, 40, 5, pp. 758–78.

Lofthouse, R. and Leat, D. (2006) 'Coaching for geography teachers', *Teaching Geography*, 31, 3, pp. 130–32.

Lofthouse, R., Leat, D., Towler, C., Hall, E. and Cummings, C. (2010) *Improving Coaching: Evolution not revolution*. Available at: www.ncl.ac.uk/cflat/news/documents/CoachingSkillsTWFinalwebPDFv3.pdf (last accessed 14/11/2016).

Lord, P., Atkinson, M. and Mitchell, H. (2008) *Mentoring and Coaching for Professionals: A study of the research evidence*. Available at: www.nfer.ac.uk/publications/MCM01/MCM01.pdf (last accessed 14/11/2016).

Roberts, M. (2011) *What makes a geography lesson good?*. Paper based on a lecture given at the 2011 Geographical Association Annual Conference. Available at: www.geography.org.uk/projects/makinggeographyhappen/teachertips (last accessed 14/11/2016).

Teaching Schools Council (2016) *National Standards for school-based initial teacher training (ITT) mentors*. Available at: www.gov.uk/government/uploads/system/uploads/attachment_data/file/536891/Mentor_standards_report_Final.pdf (last accessed 14/11/2016).

Recommended key readings

Bott, G. (2012) 'How to mentor beginner teachers', *Teaching Geography*, 37, 3, p. 119.

This short article discusses geography mentoring from first-hand experience.

Tapsfield, A. (2015) 'Resourceful geography mentoring', *Teaching Geography*, 40, 1, pp. 8–11.

This article considers the key part that that mentoring and coaching play in teachers' professional development and discusses where to start, and the skills you will need, if you are asked to be a mentor.

Chapter 23

Leading the geography department

Catherine Owen is Head of geography at The King Alfred School, Highbridge, Somerset

Introduction

Subject leaders, and teachers aspiring to be 'Head of Geography', appreciate the complexities and challenges that this role demands today. At a local level, the school's job specification, with details of the departmental and whole-school responsibilities, is one interpretation of the role. While there may be variation between schools in what is expected of a subject leader, all have seen a significant re-interpretation of the role in recent years. Previously, literature on the subject described the tasks involved in 'running' the geography department (Bailey, 1974) or offered advice on how to successfully 'manage' it (Wiegand, 1989). However, with increased emphasis on departmental self-evaluation (Cambers, 1996; King, 2000) the role of a Head of geography has become one of leadership rather than management (Kinder, 2005; Kent, 2006). Increased accountability, as a result of the performance culture that now pertains in schools and academies, is a prominent feature of this middle leadership role.

In reality the concepts of leadership and management overlap: subject leaders perform, often simultaneously, the roles of 'manager', 'administrator' and 'leader' while still carrying out their daily teaching commitments. Careful management of resources, budgets, curriculum and staff (both teaching and non-teaching), is of course important: but leading a geography department also requires a strong sense of moral purpose and the ability to create a collaborative culture while coping with what Busher and Harris (1999) have identified as the tensions of this middle leadership position. This chapter, written from a practitioner perspective, examines the elements that make up subject leadership, from co-constructing a shared vision, through ongoing departmental evaluation and cultivating leadership in others, to knowing how best to promote the subject and department both within and beyond the school.

Sharing a vision

'Establishing and articulating a vision for geography is one of the key responsibilities of subject leaders. This vision should ensure that the geography curriculum is stimulating, current, relevant, challenging and worthwhile. Above all, it should clearly be seen to contribute to a high-quality educational experience – and attainment – for all students' (Balderstone and Lambert, 2006, p. 530).

Ensuring that a geography department has a clear, shared vision of what constitutes high-quality geography continues to be central to a subject leader's role today (see Figure 1). While a department's policies and practices should have their roots in the school's vision, to promote consistency between subjects, the geography department's shared vision should reflect the culture and ethos of the geography team. Of course, individual teachers will have their own style and approach to teaching, but it is important that all agree to work within the context of the departmental vision to maintain consistency of student experience.

A vision statement on the departmental website, in the departmental handbook or displayed in every classroom publically announces what geography means in the context of your school or educational setting. If it is written as a list (and it need not be) the order in which it appears will say something about the values and priorities of

	Key characteristics of a subject leader	Ofsted (2013) guidance for outstanding quality of leadership in, and management of, geography
Vision and subject expertise	Articulating your department's view of geography in the curriculum; what students should gain from their geographical experiences at key stage 3, GCSE and post-16. Planning for, securing and benefiting from ongoing professional development for yourself and members of your team.	'Leadership in geography is informed by a high level of subject expertise and vision.' 'There is a shared vision and effective strategies to share good practice and update teachers' subject knowledge through high-quality professional development in the subject.'
Curriculum review and out-of-classroom learning	Having an informed understanding of how to respond to and implement curriculum change. Updating teaching and learning approaches, including fieldwork and other out-of-classroom learning, to meet the requirements of new specifications and to ensure that students are successful in their learning.	'There is a strong track record of innovation and success.' 'Out-of-classroom learning is seen as an entitlement within the subject and is highly promoted by the subject leaders.'
Reflection and evaluation	Evaluating your department's performance: • What aspects of practice require improving and how do you know? • What aspects of practice are good and how do you know? • How can these be improved further? • How will you achieve this as a department?	'Subject reviews, self-evaluation and improvement planning are well informed by current best practice in the subject and in education generally.'
Inspiration and connections	Encouraging, supporting and mentoring/coaching colleagues in the department. Communicating your enthusiasm for and commitment to geography, to your department, the wider school community and beyond. Connecting and collaborating with other colleagues in the school, across schools and in the wider geography community.	'Subject leadership inspires confidence and whole-hearted commitment from pupils and colleagues.' 'Geography has a very high profile in the life of the school and is at the cutting edge of initiatives within the school.' 'The subject makes excellent contribution to whole-school priorities, including consistent application of literacy and numeracy policies.'

Figure 1: The role of the subject leader.

the departmental team. Vision statements are likely to include a reference to student attainment, but they are also an opportunity for the department to celebrate aspects of their work they are particularly proud of, or which make them stand out from other departments in the school. For example, showing a departmental aim for lessons to relate to students' lives and experiences, helping them to make sense of a complex world, emphasises the importance of 'personal geographies'. In your school you may make particularly effective use of GIS or give students an opportunity to participate in a wide range of fieldwork experiences. A vision statement also enables you to share what is important to your department with your students and with the wider school community (see Figure 2).

Figure 2: Geography department vision statement.

Our geography department aims to:
- support students in achieving their potential in public examinations
- raise students' awareness of global issues
- encourage students to play an active role as global citizens
- foster students' love of geography.

Our vision for the geography department is:
- for all students to achieve or exceed their target grades
- for our department to be rated first in our county for GCSE performance
- for 50+% of students in the cohort to opt to study GCSE geography each year.

Our geography students will:
- be aware of and appreciate the diversity of our world
- act with sensitivity, tolerance and empathy
- think independently
- prepare to be active citizens in a time of change.

Subject expertise

Ofsted (2013) stipulates that for a school to meet the criteria for outstanding geography provision, subject leadership should be 'informed by a high level of subject expertise and vision'. Subject knowledge is one dimension of this expertise, and as well as ensuring that their own subject knowledge is as good as it can be subject leaders are responsible for supporting colleagues – especially non-specialists – in this respect. Sound subject knowledge is at the heart of good lessons. Confident in their subject knowledge, teachers can select from a wide repertoire of teaching approaches to make a particular geographical theme, issue or process accessible to all learners. They can take ideas presented by students and run with them, using questioning to extend students' learning. An additional dimension of geographical knowledge is its dynamic nature: teachers need to keep up to date with geographical events and new theories and developments in academic geography.

Continuing professional development (CPD) opportunities provided by the Geographical Association (GA) through their website, publications (including journals), courses and the Annual Conference are extremely useful in keeping up with developments in geography, in terms of both content and pedagogy. In addition, participating in conferences and workshops at local universities is an opportunity for teachers to make links with academic geography. Establishing and maintaining school–university links offers mutual benefits to students, teachers and those working in higher education (see Hill and Jones, 2010; Butt and Collins, 2013). Finally, where a geography department includes non-specialist teachers, subject leaders must make sure that their subject knowledge is at an appropriate level. Clear schemes of work making use of high-quality resources will help in this respect. Regular communication through email alerts is also useful, for example emailing a couple of weeks before the end of a half-term to explain what teachers will be teaching next half-term and suggesting websites where they can read up on the topics.

Leading curriculum review

Subject expertise is also essential in developing the curriculum vision, particularly when responding to external changes; for example, implementing different versions of the geography National Curriculum, adapting to changing GCSE and GCE specifications and embracing new courses such as Travel and Tourism and other qualifications such as BTECs. In other subjects, some teachers maintain that such changes make little difference to them, as the core knowledge in their subject stays the same regardless of the different incarnations of the curriculum. For geography teachers, however, curriculum change can make a radical difference. Additionally, geographical events and academic research require continual updating of the curriculum, although of course this 'topicality' is a major strength, as well as a challenge.

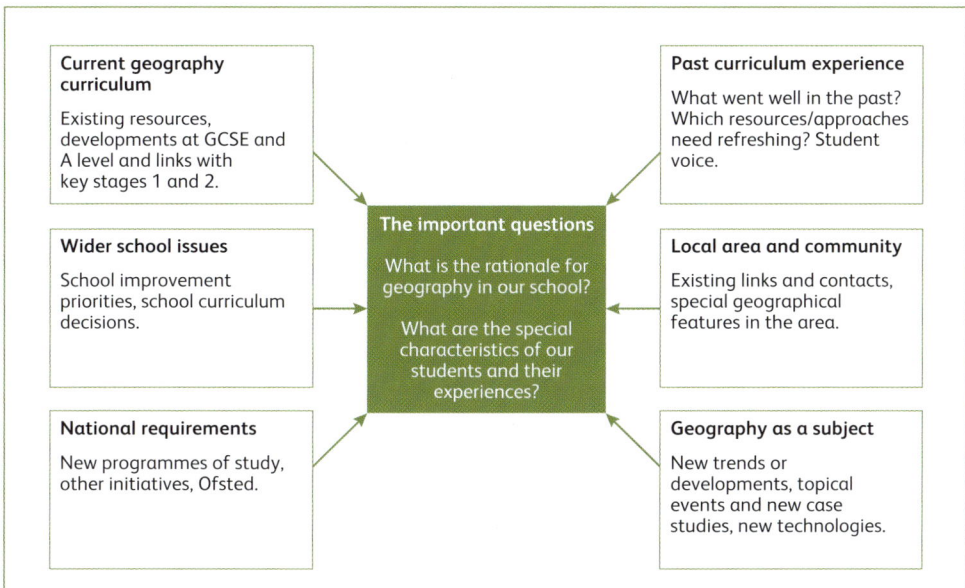

Figure 3:
Factors to take into account when designing a new curriculum. **Source:** Kinder, 2013, after Rawling, 2007.

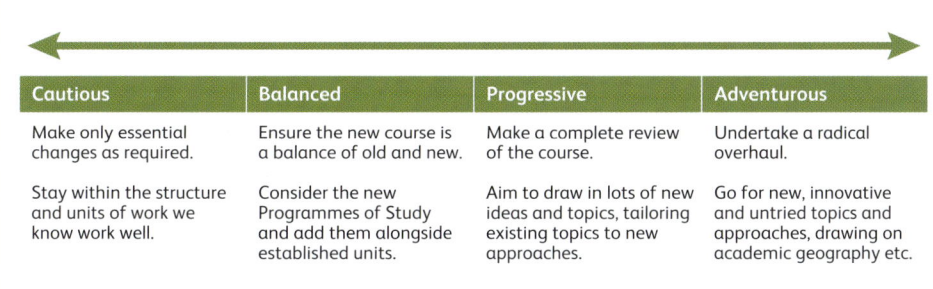

Figure 4:
Types of curriculum planning. **Source:** Kinder, 2013, after Rawling, 2007.

Kinder (2013), drawing on Rawling's (2007) key stage 3 curriculum planning advice, suggests a number of elements to consider when designing a new curriculum (see Figure 3). At the heart of curriculum planning, of course, is the department's shared vision/rationale for geography. The diagram then breaks down the complex process of curriculum planning, showing how external factors – for instance school improvement priorities – should be taken into account. National requirements, such as the focus on 'writing at length' at key stage 3 (DfE, 2013) or on core knowledge at GCSE and A level, should also be incorporated. At a local scale, a scheme of work featuring a local issue – for example, there may be a town centre regeneration project that you could make the subject of an enquiry – can powerfully engage students.

When reviewing an existing curriculum, Kinder (2013) refers to Rawling's (2007) typology, which describes four types of curriculum planning ranging from cautious to adventurous (see Figure 4). Which approach is adopted will depend on the regulatory context and the make-up of the department, as this example will show. In my school, prior to the implementation of the concept-led National Curriculum (QCA, 2007) in September 2008, key stage 3 schemes of learning had been adapted and 'patched' for several years. However, the move to a two-year key stage 3 and the arrival of a new Second in the department gave us the opportunity for a radical overhaul of the key stage 3 curriculum, and we wrote and resourced new topics, incorporating a number of innovative approaches. Of this 'adventurous' approach to curriculum review, teachers in the department commented '…as well as receiving better results for assessments than in the past, classes [were] also behaving better, …motivated by the engaging and relevant new schemes of work' (Owen, 2008, p. 113).

However, five years later, tighter time constraints and a different staffing situation called for a more 'balanced' response to the National Curriculum content requirements (DfE, 2013). The new course we introduced in September 2013 was a balance of old and new. We added aspects of the new key stage 3 programme of study to existing 'strong' units, for example integrating the requirement to teach geological timescales into an existing unit on the landforms of the Somerset coast. As these two examples show, subject leaders must decide which approach to curriculum review and planning will be of greatest benefit to their department, taking account of different teachers' views and strengths. A radical overhaul of the curriculum based solely on the Head of department's own ideas and preferences may result in a maverick, rather than an adventurous, curriculum!

While the Head of department will take the lead, it is important to engage other members of the team in the curriculum review, recognising their different ideas and strengths. Ideally, Inset time can be used to look at new curriculum requirements as a team. Starting from the shared vision of the department and the requirements of the curriculum, the team can draw up a long-term plan for the implementation and delivery of the new curriculum, showing which units will be taught and at what point in the course. At this stage it is important to review the coherence of the curriculum, and where it is 'fit for purpose' (Rawding, 2013) as a team. The team can roughly plan the outline of each unit before individual members of department take responsibility for developing the scheme of work for different units, working on an area in which they are confident of their subject knowledge. A scheme of work should clearly show the objectives for each lesson, the learning activities that are proposed to enable students to achieve these objectives, which resources are needed for the lesson and how the lesson can be differentiated to meet the needs of different students. Individual teachers can then produce their own short-term plans for each lesson based upon the particular needs of their students.

Good subject leaders are aware of the strengths and weaknesses of the departmental team, and must introduce new initiatives and curriculum reviews carefully. Some teachers will relish the opportunity to work on new schemes of work, while others may feel threatened by curriculum change. Where individual teachers struggle with an area of professional practice it may be possible to play to their strengths by timetabling them to teach certain groups. However, this may not be to the advantage of their long-term professional aspirations: a more developmental approach is to help them learn new skills or subject expertise by providing CPD opportunities or using a 'buddy' system to pair them with a teacher who is confident in that area.

New schemes of work should be supported by high-quality resources. Resources can be made in-house, although time constraints can limit opportunities to both plan the new schemes and create the supporting resources. Buying published resources (such as the GA's *Geography Teachers' Toolkit* series) or schemes of work for some units can reduce this pressure, but ready-made resources should always be adapted to meet the needs of the individual department. Another way to reduce the burden of curriculum planning is to share ideas, resources and schemes of work with other schools, whether through face-to-face meetings or online. There are enormous benefits to be had from online networks and from accessing resources posted online by other geography teachers and departments. However, it is important to bear in mind Parkinson's (2013) question: 'Do we spend too much time… passing on materials, with only superficial engagement with the messages and challenges that such materials present?' (p. 201). A departmental team should 'keep a watch' on how a geographical theme, event or issue has been represented in the downloaded resource before adopting or adapting it to an existing scheme of work.

However, changing specifications and programmes of study should not be the only things to prompt curriculum review:

the opportunity to reflect on existing schemes of work should be built into departmental development plans. Equally, subject leaders should not rely solely on teachers' experience of the curriculum: wherever possible, the student voice should be part of the review. As Ferretti (2007) helpfully reminds us, 'teachers' perceptions of what makes geography attractive may differ from their students' perceptions' (p. 147). Taking account of the student voice could mean using an online survey package; a more dialogic approach is running a focus group, which allows you to probe lines of enquiry and clarify students' responses with them. For an ongoing student evaluation of the geography curriculum, homework schedules for some key stage 3 topics can include reflection exercises. A less formal approach is to ask past students who drop in to say 'hello' to tell you which geography lessons they feel they learnt most from – their responses are sometimes not the ones you would expect!

Monitoring and intervention

A well-planned curriculum should ensure that students enjoy and are stimulated by their geography lessons, but it is also important that they make progress in their geographical studies. It is the role of the classroom teacher to monitor and intervene with students in their lessons, but to make this job straightforward and achievable the Head of department needs to ensure that an effective 'monitoring and intervention' system is in place. It is equally important to overview the whole intervention programme at regular intervals to make sure it remains 'fit for purpose'.

Regular, rigorous assessments of students' progress should feed into a monitoring system that is likely to involve the use of some sort of spreadsheet or database, and the Head of department may work with a member of the Senior Leadership Team (SLT) or the school's Data Manager to set this up. The system needs to be simple enough for teachers to add data easily and identify patterns and trends in attainment; for example a traffic light system to show if students have achieved, exceeded or failed to achieve their target for each assessment.

A subject leader oversees the use and effectiveness of intervention strategies, ensuring consistency across teachers in a department. A school may prioritise interventions according to year group or have a particular area of concern such as students whose attainment is at a particular grade border or students who are not making the expected progress between key stages 2 and 4. Individual teachers should identify students in their classes who would benefit from interventions. This process is most effective when co-ordinated by the Head of department; if students from several classes are struggling with, for example, map skills, they could all be invited to the same after-school session rather than working only with their own teachers. Student participation in intervention activities should be recorded on an appropriate tracking system and the effectiveness of intervention strategies discussed in departmental meetings.

Observations and departmental reviews

Subject leaders are 'gatekeepers of standards and innovation; they are the leaders closest to the classroom' (DfES, 2005, p. 2). As such, they may be involved in lesson observations for several reasons: they may have a PGCE student or newly qualified teacher in the department, be involved in an appraisal or be carrying out a departmental review. These different types of observation can be focused on a particular aspect of professional practice or have a specific purpose as part of coaching or mentoring. Where observation involves 'making judgements' against different criteria it is important that the teacher being observed knows what criteria are being used and how they can meet them. Figure 5 provides some headings used in different types of observation, but consider how useful these would really be to both the observer and the person being observed. Terms such as 'learning' and 'progress' need both clarification and exemplification to be of value in the observation process.

Teachers will worry about lesson observations and what the observer has 'seen' and 'heard' in the lesson, so it is important to provide good quality feedback as soon as possible.

Figure 5: Possible criteria for lesson observations.

Possible criteria for lesson observations:

- Quality of teaching (including examples of reshaping tasks and explanations to improve learning).
- Students' learning and progress.
- Effective use of assessment and feedback.
- Inclusion of effective approaches to developing students' literacy and numeracy.
- Promotion of Spritual, Moral, Social and Cultural (SMSC) development.
- Promotion of positive attitudes, behaviour and safety.
- Teacher's areas of strength.
- Teacher's areas for development (including practical advice).
- Evidence of students' progress over time in books/lesson.

However, it is also important to make sure there is enough time to feedback properly, so sometimes the feedback may not be immediate. If a teacher is seen to be struggling during a lesson observation they will need to be given support to improve. This support could be from other members of the department; alternatively, some schools have 'learning and teaching teams' made up of outstanding teachers from different subject areas who have an aptitude for working with others to develop their practice.

It is important for a department to demonstrate good learning on a daily basis, so in addition to formal, timetabled observations, which favour teachers who can pull a fantastic lesson 'out of a hat', subject leaders may carry out occasional 'learning walks'. This involves walking around the department and dropping into lessons for a short time, taking note of aspects such as the learning environment and student engagement. Learning walks help Heads of department understand what is going on in their department on a day-to-day basis.

Many departments participate in annual self-reviews. Throughout the year 'focus weeks' provide an opportunity for subject leaders to carry out lesson observations, student voice work, scrutiny of students' work, and reviews of student performance in recent assessments. The outcomes of focus weeks can feed into a departmental development plan cycle and support work towards achieving the GA's Secondary Geography Quality Mark (SGQM). In some schools, self review has been replaced by a 'team review' approach. This process starts with the Head of department and the link member of SLT carrying out a joint review of the department, identifying an area for development and breaking this down into a series of questions. A team of teachers from other departments then investigates these questions, using student interviews, interviews with non-specialist teachers, scrutiny of books and learning walks around the department. Following feedback, the geography subject leader and SLT link member produce an action plan. One benefit of the team review process is that it can produce useful ideas to move the department forward without involving the subject leader in significant work. Of course, geography subject leaders will contribute to team reviews in other subjects; but seeing how other departments deal with, for instance, intervention with underachieving students, can result in useful adaptations to departmental practice.

Preparing for inspection

Subject leaders need to be up to date with the latest guidance and criteria covering both school inspections and subject survey visits. If a departmental team has excellent subject knowledge, has planned its curriculum carefully and has put in place an effective programme of monitoring and intervention they will be in a good position if Ofsted come to call. Heads of department need to ensure that practice within their department reflects Ofsted requirements.

A portfolio produced for the SGQM can provide useful evidence to show inspectors. It is also a good idea to keep a file of important documents on the department's area of the school computer system so that they can come quickly to hand during an inspection or for other interested visitors. These documents can include: departmental vision, aims and objectives, policies on supporting whole-school

Method	Description	Why not…
Classroom and corridor displays	Displays may relate to topics students are studying, or to recent fieldwork, visits and competitions.	…include examples of students' work and guidance about why these pieces of work are particularly good?
		…show how geography is contributing to whole-school policies such as literacy and numeracy?
Geography in the news	Show relevance of the subject using a notice board or section of a website or blog.	…put students in charge of updating the display or blog, saving you a job and giving them increased ownership?
Geography Club	Students meet regularly to take their learning further in areas that interest them.	…use a vertical structure so younger students learn from older ones?
Celebrations of excellence	Break or lunchtime displays of the best assessments.	…invite pastoral staff and members of the leadership team to celebrate with you?
Competitions	Organised externally (e.g. GA Worldwise Quiz) or internally.	…ask a local business to suggest a competition and provide a prize?
Handouts at parent consultation evenings	Sheet showing what students will study that year.	…make suggestions for home activities to enhance learning?

Figure 6: How to raise awareness of the geography department in school.

priorities, e.g. literacy, numeracy, Spiritual, Moral, Social, Cultural (SMSC) and Sustainable Futures, assessment policy including year-on-year tracking of students' progress, annual reports from student voice sessions and learning walks, fieldwork reviews, past students' university destinations and employment (where geography-related), partner primary school transition activities, and records and impacts of teachers' CPD.

Raising awareness of geography

With careful planning, a geography department committed to self-review and a 'curriculum making' approach is likely to produce a geography curriculum that is 'stimulating, current, relevant, challenging and worthwhile' (Balderstone and Lambert, 2006, p. 530). This in turn creates an opportunity to raise awareness of geography among students, teachers, the SLT, parents and governors within a school. As Alastair Bonnett (2008) reminds us, a lot of people 'stumble over the question "What is geography?" (p. 1). Whereas for geographers 'geography is a fundamental fascination' (Bonnett, 2008, p. 1), members of the school community, and beyond, may not share this view; indeed, they may labour under misconceptions as to what geography is about. These need to be tackled if we are to help others to see the relevance, dynamism and utility of the subject. Promoting a positive image of geography within school (see Figures 6–8) may also boost the number of students choosing to study geography post-14 and post-16 and keep them motivated during their studies.

It is also possible to play a part in raising awareness of geography beyond the school community: locally, regionally, nationally or even internationally. Linking with the local GA Branch, participating in joint Inset days with local schools or working with partner primary schools to support them in developing their geography teaching will strengthen your local links. Your own school may provide opportunities for raising awareness of geography – this could be through taking part in a regional programme for sharing good practice or establishing a link school in another part of the UK, or even another country. The GA is very keen to involve practising teachers in its work, which could involve: writing an article for one of the GA's journals, attending the Annual Conference, or joining a Phase Committee or Special Interest Group.

Figure 7: Corridor display: 'Literacy in geography', at The King Alfred School, Somerset. **Photo** © Catherine Owen.

Recognising and accrediting excellence

With so many geography departments across the country providing high-quality geographical experiences for students, it is important that both the department and the school take the time to have this hard work acknowledged. Schools can be accredited by the GA as part of the SGQM, which is awarded at two levels – the SGQM and a higher 'Centre of Excellence' award (see Figure 9). The framework has been developed 'to enable subject leaders to raise the standards of geography in school, supporting the teaching of quality geography and promoting department leadership and management' (GA, 2014). Participating in this process is a good way to celebrate the excellent work done by departments across the country and also shows students and parents that a certain standard has been achieved. Once awarded, the SGQM logo can be used on letterheads and displays, promoting both the school and the subject.

It is, however, the work that goes on behind the scenes in a department applying for the SGQM that constitutes the real value of this scheme. The process involves schools providing evidence that they have fulfilled certain criteria on the SGQM framework. The SGQM process can support a department, both in developing a shared vision and in planning. Gathering a portfolio of evidence on aspects such as literacy and SMSC also provides useful documentation in the event of a visit by Ofsted.

Within a department, individual teachers may be interested in applying for Chartered Geographer (Teacher) status, a scheme run by the Royal Geographical Society with Institute of British Geographers (RGS-IBG). This accreditation recognises teachers for their geographical knowledge and skills and their commitment to ongoing professional development. Students are usually only aware of what goes on in geography lessons in their own school, leading to a tendency to take the work we do for granted. Participating in the GA's SGQM and RGS-IBG's CGeog (Teacher) schemes can show students that they and you are part of something special.

Networks

'Local solutions emphasise the ability of teachers themselves, with appropriate challenge, stimulus, leadership and support, to find solutions to curriculum and pedagogic issues' (Balderstone and Lambert, 2006, p. 532).

In recent years, teachers from secondary schools and academies in Somerset, as in other parts of the UK, have held joint Inset days (see Figure 10). This is an opportunity for teachers from different subject areas to meet up at schools across the county for a programme of talks, workshops and networking opportunities. Face-to-face meetings enable real connections to be made; these connections can then be maintained virtually through email, Twitter or online forums.

The future of subject leadership

Much of this chapter has emphasised the positive impact that a subject leader can have on the nature and status of geography, on colleagues' expertise, morale and ambition, and on the quality of the students' experience of geography. However, as the role of Head of department has changed its focus from management to leadership, tensions have crept in. Busher and Harris (1999) identified four different functions of the Head of department role that contribute to this situation:

- translation of SLT/whole-school initiatives and policies at a departmental level
- fostering collegiality through shared vision
- improving staff and student performance
- liaison/representative role.

Heads of department could adopt a 'transactional' approach to these roles – simply carrying out tasks or 'transactions' within the school's hierarchical culture. In this model, whole-school initiatives are translated into working agreements to suit the requirements of the SLT, and resources are managed to support departmental colleagues in the practical application of this process. Increasingly, however, where the leadership role is viewed as 'transformational', the emphasis is on Heads of department having clear moral values and the ability to use power with, or through, other people, instead of controlling them. Transformational leaders have the potential to make a difference to departmental performance and to influence whole-school development. A good example of this is fostering departmental collegiality through the development of a shared vision; this gives a transformational leader the opportunity to

'To celebrate Geography Awareness Week and raise our profile in school my department set out to run as many geography-linked activities as possible. These ranged from a daily brain teaser on the tutor time bulletin to a week of challenges based on the Mission:Explore concept. The challenges included writing a poem to a tree and creating a time-lapse journey film. It was a fantastic week with a real geography buzz around school. It motivated students to be more interested in the world around them, raised the department's profile in school and gave my team the chance to get our geographical juices flowing!'

Jenny Denton, Head of Geography, The Blue School, Wells

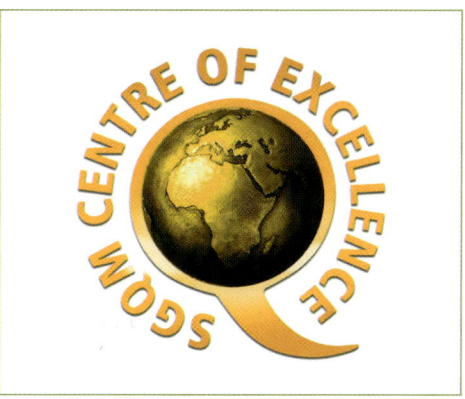

Figure 8: Geography Awareness Week.

Figure 9: SGQM Centre of Excellence logo.

empower others and to change the culture of the department, rather than simply dealing with a series of transactions.

Bennett et al. (2007), in their systematic review of empirical studies published between 1998 and 2005, found two key tensions in the middle leadership role. First, there may be a tension between a subject leader's loyalty to their department and the expectation that they have a whole-school role. Second, in schools with a hierarchical line management culture, middle leaders have to grapple with the potential gulf between the rhetoric and reality of collegiality. Running through these tensions were three issues:

Figure 10: Ben Totterdell from Exmoor National Park leading a workshop session at the 2014 Somerset Geography Common Inset Day. Photo © Catherine Owen.

- the concept of collegiality
- concepts of professionalism, authority and monitoring
- questions of authority and expertise.

Their research found that a collegial approach to leadership was preferred. Heads of department were not comfortable monitoring colleagues' work for quality control reasons, but would do so if they felt that the members of the department were learning from each other. This collegiality rested on deep trust between teachers who were willing to work together towards shared goals, but still looked to their Head of department for leadership. However, Bennett *et al.* (2007) note that a lack of collegiality between different subjects and territorialism can result where there is no sense of the school as a collegium.

Monitoring colleagues to improve staff and student performance can cause tensions if the process is seen by individual teachers as a challenge to their professional status; they may feel that surveillance is replacing the trust of collegiality. If the department recognises that 'everyone has something to learn from and something to teach their colleagues' (Bennett *et al.*, 2007, p. 459) collegiality may be strengthened rather than undermined.

Ability to deal with such complex situations will depend on the Head of department's expertise in human relationships, in their subject and in teaching. As a 'leading professional' they need to be able to build an environment of trust, protect their department from being overwhelmed by too many initiatives and ensure that other departments and senior leaders value the department. This 'representative role' (Busher and Harris, 1999) requires integrity and the ability to analyse and evaluate often complex and competing interests before making decisions.

Conclusion

The interpretation of subject leadership presented here suggests a geography teacher leading a team of colleagues within a hierarchal school structure. However, more distributed models of leadership, or where geography teachers find themselves leading and teaching several subjects in school-specific thematic or competency-based approaches, present additional challenges. What is certain is that for schools with hierarchical structures and individual subject departments, subject leaders will continue to have an important middle leadership role.

The role of subject leader requires a strong sense of moral purpose, subject expertise and the ability to lead a geography team through an increasingly complex and changing educational landscape. To ensure a sustainable vision, and the daily practice of quality geographical experiences, aspiring and new subject leaders need to be encouraged and supported.

References

Bailey, P. (1974) *Teaching Geography*. Vancouver, BC: Douglas, David and Charles Limited.

Balderstone, D. and Lambert, D. (2006) 'Sustaining school geography' in Balderstone, D. (ed) *Secondary Geography Handbook*. Sheffield: Geographical Association, pp. 524–33.

Bennett, N., Woods, P., Wise, C. and Newton, W. (2007) 'Understandings of middle leadership in secondary schools: a review of empirical research', *School Leadership and Management*, 27, 5, pp. 453–70.

Bonnett, A. (2008) *What is Geography?* London: SAGE.

Busher, H. and Harris, A. (1999) 'Leadership of school subject areas: tensions and dimensions of managing in the middle', *School Leadership and Management*, 19, 3, pp. 305–17.

Butt, G. and Collins, G. (2013) 'Can geography cross "the divide"?' in Lambert, D. and Jones, M. (eds) *Debates in Geography Education*. Abingdon: Routledge, pp. 291–301.

Cambers, G. (1996) 'Managing the departmental team' in Bailey, P. and Fox, P. (eds) *Geography Teachers' Handbook*. Sheffield: Geographical Association, pp. 273–78.

DfE (2013) *National Curriculum in England: Geography programmes of study*. London: DfE.

DfES (2005) *Secondary National Strategy for School Improvement: Middle leaders' self-evaluation guide*. London: DfES.

Ferretti, J. (2007) 'What influences students to choose geography at A-level?', *Geography*, 92, 2, pp. 137–47.

GA (2014) *Secondary Geography Quality Mark*. Available at: www.geography.org.uk/cpdevents/qualitymarks/secondaryqualitymark (last accessed 14/11/2016).

Hill, J. and Jones, M. (2010) '"Joined-up geography": connecting school-level and university-level geographies', *Geography*, 95, 1, pp. 22–32.

Kent, A. (2006) 'Innovation, change and leadership in geography departments', *Geography*, 91, 2, pp. 117–25.

Kinder, A. (2005) 'Leading the geography department', *Teaching Geography*, 30, 2, pp. 101–104.

Kinder, A. (2013) 'Geography from 2014: back to the future', *Teaching Geography*, 38, 3, pp. 98–101.

King, S. (2000) 'Evaluating geography departments and their staff' in Kent, A. (ed) *Reflective Practice in Geography Teaching*. London: Paul Chapman Publishing, pp. 141–53.

Ofsted (2013) *Geography Survey Visits: Generic grade descriptors and supplementary subject-specific guidance for inspectors on making judgements during visits to schools*. Manchester: Ofsted.

Owen, C. (2008) 'Developing the international dimension at KS3', *Teaching Geography*, 33, 3, pp. 110–13.

Parkinson, A. (2013) 'How has technology impacted on the teaching of geography and geography teachers?' in Lambert, D. and Jones, M. (eds) *Debates in Geography Education*. Abingdon: Routledge, pp. 193–205.

Rawding, C. (2013) *Effective Innovation in the Secondary Geography Curriculum: A practical guide*. Abingdon: Routledge.

Rawling, E. (2007) *Planning Your Key Stage 3 Geography Curriculum*. Sheffield: Geographical Association.

RGS-IBG (2014) *Chartered Geographer*. Available at: www.rgs.org/OurWork/CharteredGeographer/Chartered+Geographer.htm (last accessed 14/11/2016).

Wiegand, P. (1989) *Managing the Geography Department*. Sheffield: Geographical Association.

Recommended key readings

Kent, A. (2006) 'Innovation, change and leadership in geography departments', *Geography*, 91, 2, pp. 117–25.

Ashley Kent's article draws on his long-standing professional interest in subject leadership. His research across a number of secondary schools in London identified the geography subject leader as a key player in curriculum innovation and change. Kent identified the need for more support for subject leaders to reflect on and research their role.

Rawding, C. (2013) 'How do you know if your geography is fit for purpose?' in Rawding, C. *Effective Innovation in the Secondary Geography Curriculum: A practical guide*. Abingdon: Routledge, pp. 78–102.

This chapter raises important questions for geography departments evaluating the geography curriculum in school and provides guidance on how to critique existing schemes of work.

Chapter 24

Belonging to a subject community

Alan Kinder is Chief Executive of the Geographical Association

'…a dynamic subject community is built on participation and innovation' (GA, 2014a, p. 6)

One of the fundamental beliefs on which the work of the Geographical Association (GA) is founded is that our subject community requires sustained contributions from many individuals and organisations in order to function. In this chapter I will examine why a subject community needs such activity, why teachers of geography should 'belong to' and contribute towards a wider community of practitioners (and others with subject expertise), and what individual and collective benefits might result.

Becoming, and developing as, a geography teacher

The idea of teaching as a profession may seem familiar – we talk routinely of 'joining the profession' or 'acting professionally' – but defining what it means to be a professional geography teacher remains elusive. While expert knowledge is often regarded as one of the fundamental dimensions of professional identity (Armstrong, 2013), the nature of a teacher's expertise and the means by which it is acquired are as contested as the idea of teaching itself. At one extreme, the notion of teaching as a craft and teachers' knowledge as a kind of practical wisdom over-emphasises knowledge gained through first-hand experience without recognising that this can be made explicit and shared more widely. At the other, the view of teachers as executive technicians who need only follow protocols about 'best practice' established elsewhere overlooks the importance of interpreting evidence or deciding how best to apply it in unique educational settings. Winch *et al.* (2014) introduce a more useful way of thinking about the expert knowledge needed for teaching (see also Figure 1). Professional interaction and communication are essential to this model, as they enable teachers to combine practical, technical and theoretical aspects of knowledge and to make their reasoning and underlying assumptions explicit in doing so. The model therefore conceptualises pedagogy as not simply the act of teaching, but as 'the discourse which informs and justifies the act of teaching' (Alexander, 2004, p. 11).

Professional identity and practice is also distinguished by moral understanding and purpose. Plato argued that a professional requires not only mastery of knowledge and practical skills but also 'moral excellence', implying that attitude, behaviour and an altruistic approach matter as much as technical expertise (Armstrong, 2013). Moral, ethical and values dimensions underpin the teaching of geography in many ways. They have long been prominent elements of curriculum debate in geography and are widely regarded as legitimate criteria for the selection of teaching content (Bailey, 1975; Morgan, A., 2011; Morgan, J., 2011; Hicks, 2014), although this is not an uncontested view (see Standish, 2012). The GA's position is that our profession needs teachers with a clearly-developed view of the purposes, including the moral purposes, of geography in education (GA, 2014c). Within the process of 'curriculum making' (GA, no date, 2005), for example, the complex choices teachers make about content and pedagogic approaches are 'guided ultimately by a sense of purpose or educational vision translated into curriculum goals' (Lambert, 2011, p. 244). Designing a curriculum therefore 'is not just a technical matter, specifying objectives and a course of study to meet them. It is a moral concern, and should reflect what we think we should be teaching' (GA, 2009, p. 27). Just as the recent crisis in the financial sector was a salutary lesson in what can happen when a profession loses its collective moral compass,

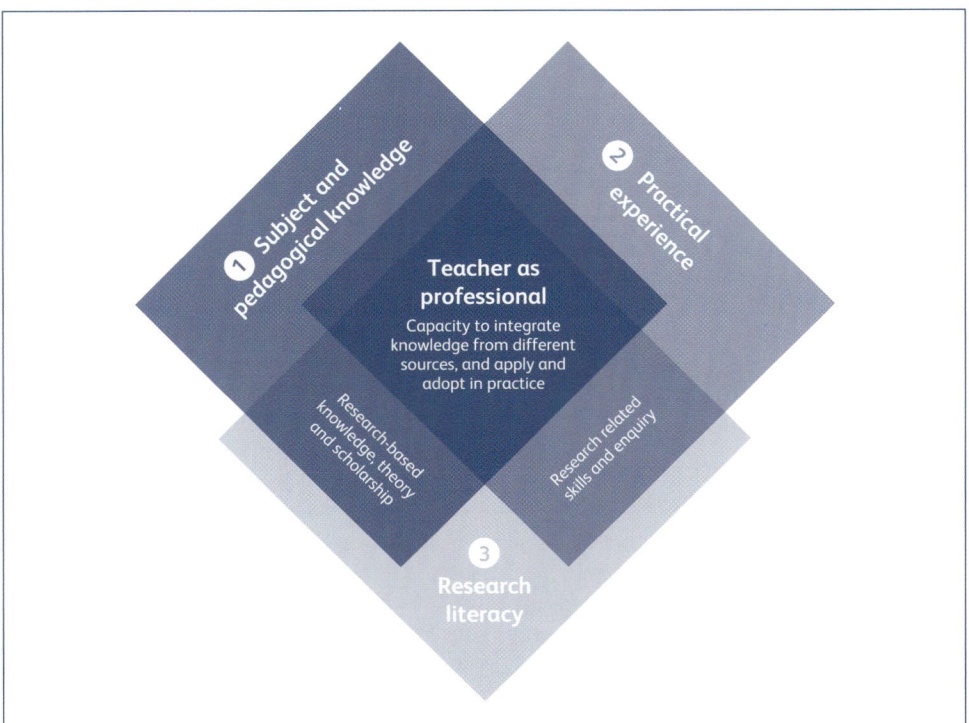

Figure 1: Dimensions of a teacher's professional knowledge. **Source:** BERA, 2014.

Morgan and Lambert (2005) sound a warning about 'moral carelessness' in geography teaching and argue that truly moral geography lessons are concerned not with teaching a specific moral code (e.g. 'correct behaviours' for environmental sustainability), but with addressing the ways in which individuals and groups make judgements about right and wrong and how worthwhile distinctions between the two can be made. These are complex challenges; they require collective and personal critical engagement and are not likely to be satisfactorily addressed by individual teachers working alone. For this reason, many of the GA's curriculum support materials include the 'why' as well as the 'how' of teaching and place considerable demands upon teachers to think and reason for themselves and with others.

Continuing professional development (CPD) also demands rich interaction between individuals and their community. The Teachers' Standards (DfE, 2013) place the emphasis on the individual by requiring teachers to take responsibility for their own professional development, maintain their knowledge and skills, and remain self-critical. However, in order for professional development activities, whether provided for or created by teachers, to provide professional *education* – that is the 'valuable learning… which leads to improved and more intelligent understanding' (Pring, 2011, p. 98) – they must acknowledge the role of interpersonal connections. Theories of learning such as social constructivism, for example, emphasise the role of other people in helping us to create new knowledge and make sense of the world, and show that we do this by discussing how we understand things with other people (Roberts, 2013). As Chalmers and Keown (2006) point out, not only does learning begin in a social context, but 'internal reflection and "monologues" follow on from previous social interactions' (p. 109). Effective professional development therefore involves more than direct instruction; it includes 'immersion in inquiry, analysis and synthesis; problem-solving and role play; planning, practising, experimenting, adapting, reviewing and debriefing' (CUREE, 2012, p. 12). Put simply, teachers must work actively together to achieve professional development rather than be passive recipients of information about 'what works'.

The benefits of belonging

So far, we have considered the significance of connections between teachers of geography, emphasising the effect on the individual. But we can also think of the teaching community as a collective resource – a reservoir of expertise and support that amounts to more than the sum of its parts. Most professional communities seek to express their shared expertise through formal structures, such as professional associations, which carry out two key functions:

1. Disseminating the knowledge base on which professional practice rests and incorporating new knowledge based on practice.
2. Defining, developing and maintaining standards of knowledge and standards for applying this to practice in an ethical manner (PARN, 2014).

In geography, subject matter and pedagogy are continually developing, and these developments take place within an increasingly fragmented educational landscape. With authoritative sources of support such as the Qualifications and Curriculum Development Agency (QCDA) largely replaced by a diverse range of voices, judging the accuracy, relevance and applicability of ideas and information becomes ever-more difficult for teachers. Of course, the GA upholds teachers' freedom to make appropriate choices over curriculum content, contexts for study and the organisation of teaching. However, this role is neither self-evident nor straightforward: it requires specialist knowledge and training, so part of the subject community's role is to provide a reliable source of specialist content and pedagogical knowledge. Research and inspection evidence support the view that specialist expertise plays an essential role in challenging and supporting teachers' professional development (Ofsted, 2011; Teacher Development Trust, 2014). Peer-to-peer networking complements specialist support by facilitating the sharing of practice and experience, and providing a reference point for our own unique circumstances. Knowing that others face similar (or different) circumstances and challenges to ourselves not only *feels* good, but widens our knowledge of professional practice and allows a degree of 'benchmarking' against which we may adjust our own expectations and future decisions. Some sources of support, such as the GA's journals, disseminate established professional knowledge and share emerging professional practice by providing a balance of theoretical and practical resources for teachers.

The GA's mission to provide 'a trusted voice for geography in education' (GA, 2014a) references the idea that subject communities also possess the power to establish norms and expectations within their field. Articulating the purposes of geography teaching, and establishing the terms of reference against which professional practice is subsequently understood or measured within and beyond the community, creates what social realists term *context-independent knowledge*: knowledge that has an objective existence located in and regulated by the specialist communities who produce it (Standish, 2012; Firth, 2013). This means more than simply exerting greater influence by speaking with a collective voice, or making a powerful case to policy makers on behalf of the community, and involves the community defining what it *means* to teach and learn a subject like geography. The GA has made several significant claims about the importance and nature of geography in education, through publications such as *A Case for Geography* (Bailey and Binns, 1987) and *A Different View: A manifesto from the Geographical Association* (GA, 2009). The GA's Geography Quality Marks may be understood as a more direct attempt by the subject community to set its own standards for teaching, learning and leading geography in schools, drawing on both expert judgements and classroom practice to do so (Owens, 2013).

Geography networks and communities

Let us now look in more detail at the operation of networks and communities of geography professionals, at scales from the local to the global, examining the way in which individuals and organisations work together and the significance of their interactions.

Face-to-face teacher networks

We live increasingly in an online world, yet face-to-face groups and networks continue to flourish and to play an important role in the geography community. Informal human contact is credited with relationship building and the spontaneous sharing of ideas. As one teacher

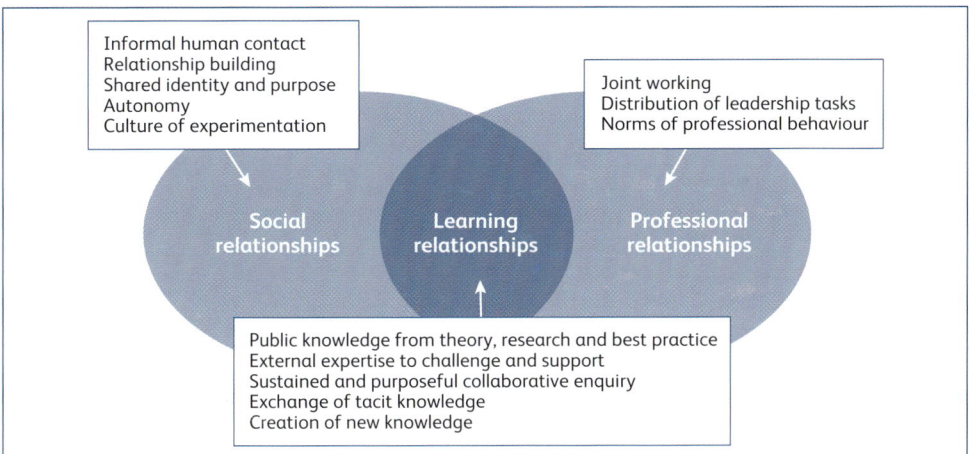

Figure 2:
Developing learning relationships.
After: Stott et al., 2006, p. 20.

put it: 'You need to see people… there is nothing like being face to face and sitting with somebody… there's a livelier debate I think… better interaction, because things are off the cuff' (Stott et al., 2006, p. 21). In the world of global finance, Sassen (2012) cites the role of 'breakfast meetings, lunches… cocktail parties and… health clubs' in building relationships of mutual trust and shared motivation, which consequently support risk taking (p. 192). Within education, formal face-to-face networks are seen as generating a shared identity or sense of purpose, creating autonomy and a 'safety in numbers' effect in which network members give one another permission to do things differently, and encouraging a culture of experimentation that can lead to 'deep and consequential change in classroom practice' (Coburn, 2003, p. 4).

An important distinction should be made here between *networking* – the unpredictable tapestry of 'sharing-exchanging' relationships in which joint activities are made and unmade for a wide variety of purposes – and *networked learning*, which involves groups of individuals in 'sharing-exploring' (Huxham and Hibbert, 2008). In the latter, face-to-face engagement allows professional as well as personal relationships to flourish, as members of a network learn to work with one another, establish norms of professional behaviour and distribute leadership tasks. This combination of personal and professional relationships provides the foundation for learning relationships, in which tacit (difficult-to-codify) knowledge is exchanged and new professional knowledge is co-constructed (Figure 2). In this sense, educational networks can be regarded as providing the 'shared space' needed for knowledge creation identified by researchers in the field of organisational knowledge (see Nonaka and Takeuchi, 1995).

In recent years, organisational changes within education, particularly the emergence of school chains and 'system-leading' schools such as Teaching Schools, have encouraged networks of schools to replace one-off or intermittent CPD experiences with localised, school-led 'joint practice development' (JPD), on the understanding that sustained and purposeful developmental activity makes the greatest impact on professional learning (Jackson and Temperley, 2006; CUREE, 2012). This shift has been accompanied by rhetoric in support of school autonomy, a trend towards in-house training and some mistrust of expert-led professional development (Teacher Development Trust, 2014), yet the goal of local professional autonomy is not free of risks and limitations. Brooks (2012) shows how, as schools have become more preoccupied with generic skill development and student engagement, they have become less subject-focused in terms of discussion and debate and therefore less inclined to look outwards to subject experts or others for the broader or critical perspective required to improve practice and ultimately empower teachers. Unbridled educational localism risks creating parochialism, and can run counter to the need for educational expectations to be consistent. An over-emphasis on local needs or interests can also conflict with our desire for education to be based on and help promote universal values: witness the confusion following the removal of geography National Curriculum levels in 2014.

The most effective local networks therefore operate not in glorious isolation but with reference to a wider community, for example by accessing theory, research and professional practice (e.g. via the Geography Education Research Collective – GEReCo) or by using face-to-face external expertise to challenge and support local collaborative enquiry (Stott *et al.*, 2006; Weston, 2013). So-called 'spoke and hub' approaches have been adopted to good effect within geography education, for example by the GA's Quality Mark scheme, whereby a national moderation team provides expert advice to hub schools, which in turn provide support and advice to their local networks. As a result of these connections, individual departments are encouraged and supported when seeking accreditation for excellence through the Quality Mark scheme (Figure 3).

Online networks and communities

> 'In Britain teachers are for the most part too scattered and too busy to come together frequently for discussion. They require a medium through which they may readily communicate with one another, exchange experiences and learn the progress that is being made in method or in appliances in our own country or abroad' (Freshfield, 1901, p. 1).

Writing at the turn of the twentieth century, Freshfield could scarcely have imagined the digital resources now available to the 'networked teacher' (Figure 4). The explosion in the range of lateral, non-hierarchical and collaborative connections between teachers has created what some commentators call the network society, in which networking has become the dominant social-cultural paradigm (Castells, 2000). What is as yet unclear is whether 'online' is replicating, replacing, reinforcing or removing earlier forms of community for geography teachers, or indeed producing new ways of interacting and creating professional knowledge.

At a basic level, online tools allow rapid and low-cost sharing of ideas and resources and the reduction of duplicated effort, and so for many teachers the internet remains primarily a medium for browsing and downloading teaching ideas and resources produced elsewhere, a level of engagement that tempts us to conclude that online activities 'aren't better than face-to-face contact, they're just better than nothing' (Shirky, 2008, quoted in Staines, 2010, p. 16). The world's 'largest online community', TES Connect, which supplies 4.5 million resource downloads per week to around 6 million teachers (Rogers, 2014), could be described more accurately as a resource exchange, while many 'social' media such as Twitter are used mostly as a means of consuming information and ideas produced by particularly energetic individuals or organisations (see, for example, @The_GA or @richardallaway on Twitter). The internet also permits teachers to share ideas with and seek the advice of a very large number of their peers in the UK and elsewhere, allowing them to benefit from colleagues' experimentation and avoid their pitfalls; there is evidence that as little as 75 minutes per month discussing professional practice in this type of arena can be transformational (Parkinson, 2013). Geography teachers have embraced this potential with great enthusiasm. One of the best known online communities in geography education, the Staffordshire Learning Net (SLN) forum *(http://learningnet.co.uk/geoforum)*, has received over 40,000 posts across 8000 topics since it was established in 1999, and professional exchange now occurs through many other avenues, such as Twitter or virtual TeachMeets.

There is also an emerging sense that something richer and deeper is evolving online, not limited to transmission and consumption but about interacting, repurposing and co-creating (Mason and Rennie, 2009). Wood (2007) tentatively identifies a new form of professional learning or 'communal constructivism' through the use of geography blogs, in which collaboration occurs organically through strings of comments, associated resources and websites, all of which assist geography teachers to construct their own knowledge from their interaction with the emergent and archived knowledge of others. Similar features can be seen in more recent forms of collaboration, such as through geography wikis, LinkedIn pages and slideshare collaborations (e.g. *http://sharegeography.co.uk/collaborate*) and through initiatives dedicated to quality online debate (see, for example, *www.greateducationdebate.org.uk*).

Nevertheless, Parkinson (2013) raises some important questions about the impact of online communication on our capacity to sustain professional dialogue; he wonders whether we 'spend too much time connecting and collaborating and passing on materials, with only superficial engagement [with] the messages and challenges that such material presents' (p. 201), and questions whether the difficult job of mediating, curating and sourcing material responsibly online should be added to the teachers' job description, or fall to organisations such as the GA. Rather than comparing and contrasting online with face-to-face interaction, perhaps it would be more productive to ensure virtual networks support face-to-face activity, particularly where the obstacles of time and distance mean infrequent meetings, as is the case with Primary Geography Champions networks (see Figure 5).

The national community of practice

The geography education community at the national scale is both complex and dynamic. Opportunities do exist for teachers to connect with one another in a range of ways, although some of these may not always seem as readily accessible as those available locally. Networking and the exchange of resources for teaching is most certainly part of the national picture – witness the sharing of ideas, information and contact details routinely undertaken by delegates at the GA Annual Conference. The national subject community has the capacity to create new knowledge through 'networked learning' at this scale. Consider, for example:

- the collaborative enquiry undertaken by the GA's Phase Committees (Early Years and Primary; Secondary, and Post-16 and HE) and Special Interest Groups (Assessment and Examinations, Sustainability and Citizenship, Fieldwork and Outdoor Learning, Physical Geography, ICT, Independent Schools, Welsh, International, and Teacher Education) in co-designing and leading workshops at the GA Annual Conference

- Participating in or organising a GA Worldwise event or other local geography competition.
- Sharing resources with other colleagues, perhaps via a website.
- Planning and hosting a CPD event for primary and/or secondary colleagues.
- Guiding another school or cluster of schools through the Quality Mark process.
- Establishing a school-based GA Branch.
- Developing email links with schools in other areas/countries to compare experiences and share good practice.
- Video-conferencing with a geographical theme.
- Producing a regular geography newsletter distributed to colleagues.
- Leading CPD sessions for Associate Teachers.
- Fostering and maintaining links with HE institutions.

Figure 3: Secondary Geography Quality Mark requirements for Centre of Excellence community/network activity.

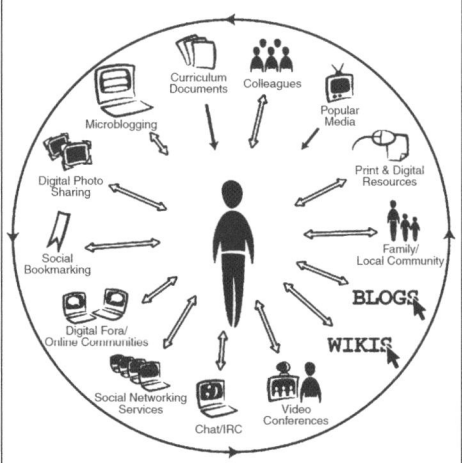

Figure 4: The networked teacher. **Source:** Dr Alec Couros, University of Regina, Canada.

- the efforts of the GA's National Curriculum Development Group in producing curriculum proposals, responding to consultation responses and influencing government policy in the run-up to the 2014 National Curriculum *(www.geography.org.uk)*

Figure 5: Case study of the Primary Geography Champions network.

The Primary Geography Champions network began in 2006 as part of the GA's work on the government-funded Action Plan for Geography. Around 50 Champions now support local geography educator networks across England, Wales and the Republic of Ireland, shaping their own mix of face-to-face and online engagement. The enduring success and widening reach of their work is reflected in the steady growth of online memberships, which now number over 2700.

Primary Geography Champions initiate and lead network events and discussions, moderate online exchanges, act as curators of online content or as trusted advisors. They can also facilitate the activities of others within networks. Champions were originally drawn from the primary teacher educator community, but very quickly the value of drawing from a range of settings became apparent. Today, the mixture of participants is significant, allowing ITE students to exchange ideas with subject or senior leaders, and primary teachers to discuss issues with secondary colleagues. The network model offers autonomy as well as collegiate support at every level; participants use face-to-face and/or online communication to network with local and distant colleagues. The permeable boundary of each network allows Champions to widen and deepen valuable conversations about transition from primary to secondary education, initial teacher training to the classroom, and from newly-qualified status to subject leadership *(http://geographychampions.ning.com)*.

- the innovative curriculum development undertaken by teachers and young people through the Young Peoples' Geographies project *(www.youngpeoplesgeographies.co.uk)*
- the way in which the 'guerrilla geographers' of the Geography Collective 'make events, books and other things…' *(http://thegeographycollective.wordpress.com)*.

If we consider the common cause underpinning these examples of networked learning, we come closer to the idea of a *community of practice* – a group of people 'who share a concern or a passion for something they do and learn how to do it better as they interact regularly' (Wenger-Trayner, 2007). In communities of practice, collective learning is situated in the various conversations in which individuals take part, and professional competence is measured by the degree of an individual's involvement in the community: participation accords more status than an individual's acquisition of knowledge. Communities of practice need not be hierarchical in a formal sense, since individuals may choose the degree or intensity of their involvement; they can therefore accommodate diverse networks, which can act as 'potentially maverick entities that exist outside formally established structures and hierarchies' (Stott *et al.*, 2006, p. 4). In practice, organisational structures are often present to allow complex large-scale communities to function, although the most effective communities promote easy entry and navigation – supporting wide participation – while deploying expert resources to maximum effect. The Global Learning Programme for England was designed along these lines, being founded on the operation of local school-to-school networks, with expert centre/lead practitioner hubs supported by both regional and national structures in order to meet the ambitious project aim of engaging half the schools in the country (Figure 6).

The broader national geography education community is not of course a project that has been designed, but a patchwork of overlapping local, regional and national networks – real and virtual, formal and informal – which has evolved over time. I like to think of this community, with the GA at its heart, as possessing the features both of a series of networks and of a community of practice, with its true worth being a kind of collective intelligence, an ability to 'face up to problems that confront us collectively and to develop collective solutions' (Lacey, 1988, p. 94). Navigating the complexity of this landscape – knowing where to go and how to become involved – is a challenge in itself.

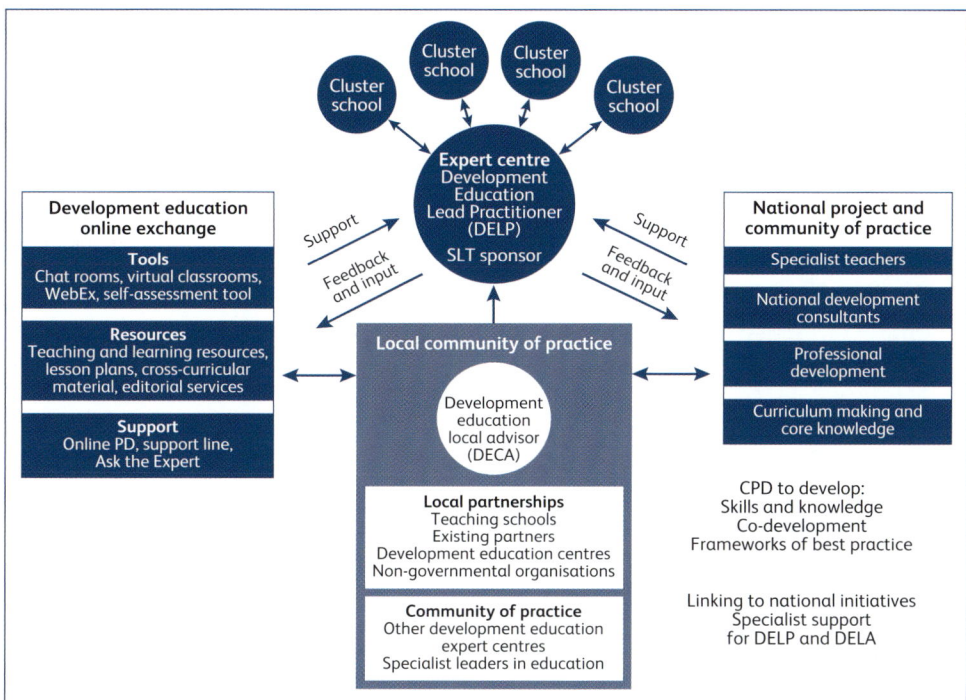

Figure 6:
The Global Learning Programme (England) community.

Figure 7 should give every reader encouragement (if simply buying and reading a publication or visiting a website gains us entry to this community) but it also provides an opportunity for a collective pause for thought (are we unintentionally excluding any teachers and how do we widen and deepen participation?)

International communities

With many organisations increasingly acting from an international or even global perspective, and policy makers undertaking international comparisons using data from jurisdictions around the world, geography educators find themselves in the intriguing position of not only critically analysing the notion and processes of globalisation, but experiencing the phenomenon directly. In response, international geographical communities play vital roles in advocating for geography, building international understanding and sharing ideas and research evidence.

Within Europe, interaction often occurs at the level of the individual or their institution, for example with significant numbers of European geography educators attending the annual UK-based Geography Teacher Educator's conference. European-funded projects also provide opportunities for joint working (see, for example, http://i-use.eu). At the continental scale, the European Association of Geographers (EUROGEO) has as its principal aims advancing the status of geography and the European dimension within geographical education. It pursues these aims by organising events, producing publications and by lobbying at European level on the role that geography and geographers play in realising the potential of spatial skills and geographical information (www.eurogeo.nl).

At the global scale, the International Geographical Union's Commission on Geographical Education (IGU-CGE) (www.igu-cge.org) promotes geographical and environmental education, by:

- organising international conferences and research projects
- publishing an international research journal (*IRGEE*), newsletters, conference proceedings and policy documents
- co-sponsoring the International Geography Olympiad (iGEO) for young people.

Figure 7: Engaging with the GA subject community.

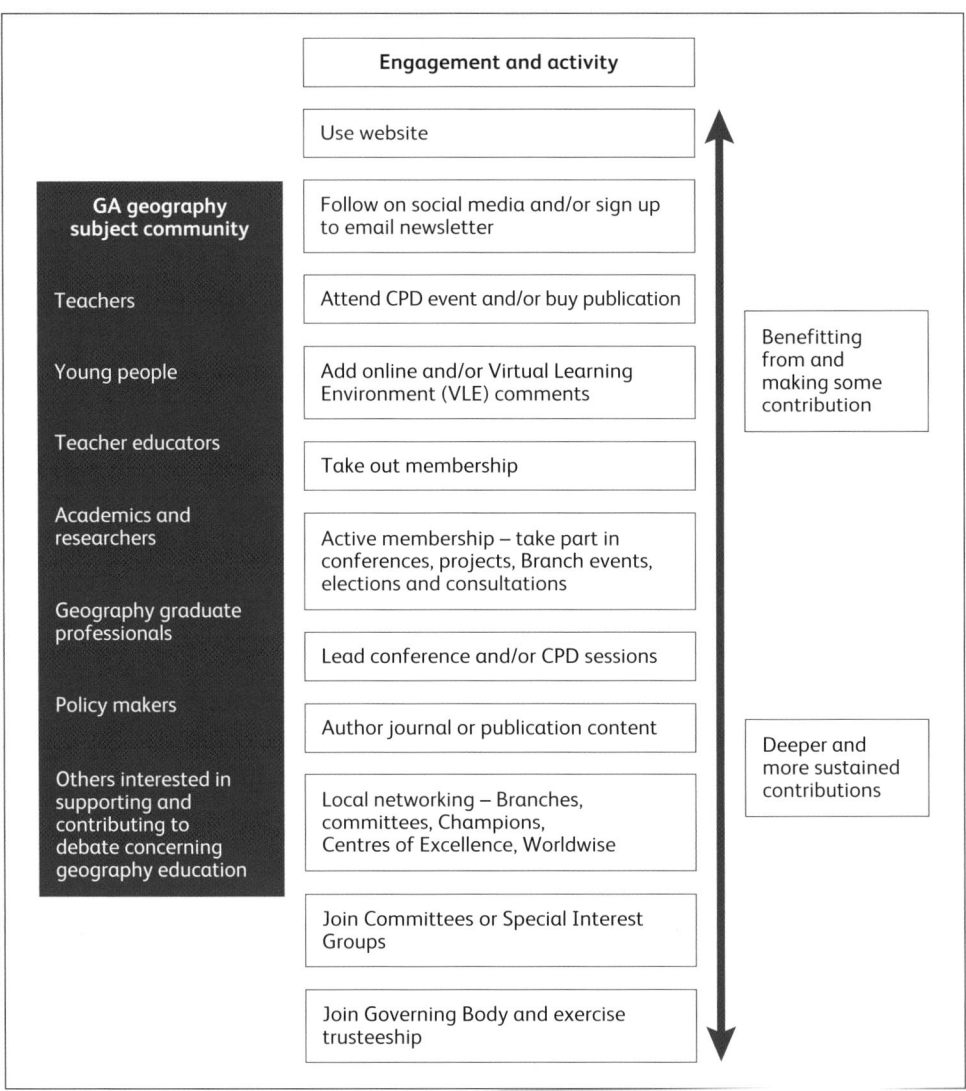

The GA is also active at this scale. Its International Special Interest Group is responsible for developing the international dimension of the GA's work and establishing links, both with international geographical and educational organisations and between schools and individuals. The group administers an International Initiatives Fund (GAIIF) and uses this to promote educational initiatives between individuals and associations concerned with geographical education across the globe, for example by sponsoring delegates from the global South to attend the GA Annual Conference.

The time and cost associated with face-to-face contact are obvious barriers to international collaboration. International communities can also face particular difficulties in terms of language. The IGU-CGE steering committee and regional contacts, for example, display a bias towards English-speaking countries (Figure 8), while the GA's strongest international links, in terms of associate members and collaboration with other subject associations, are also with English-speaking former colonies such as Australia.

Balancing the need for strategic impact with democracy and plurality is an additional

Chapter 24: Belonging to a subject community

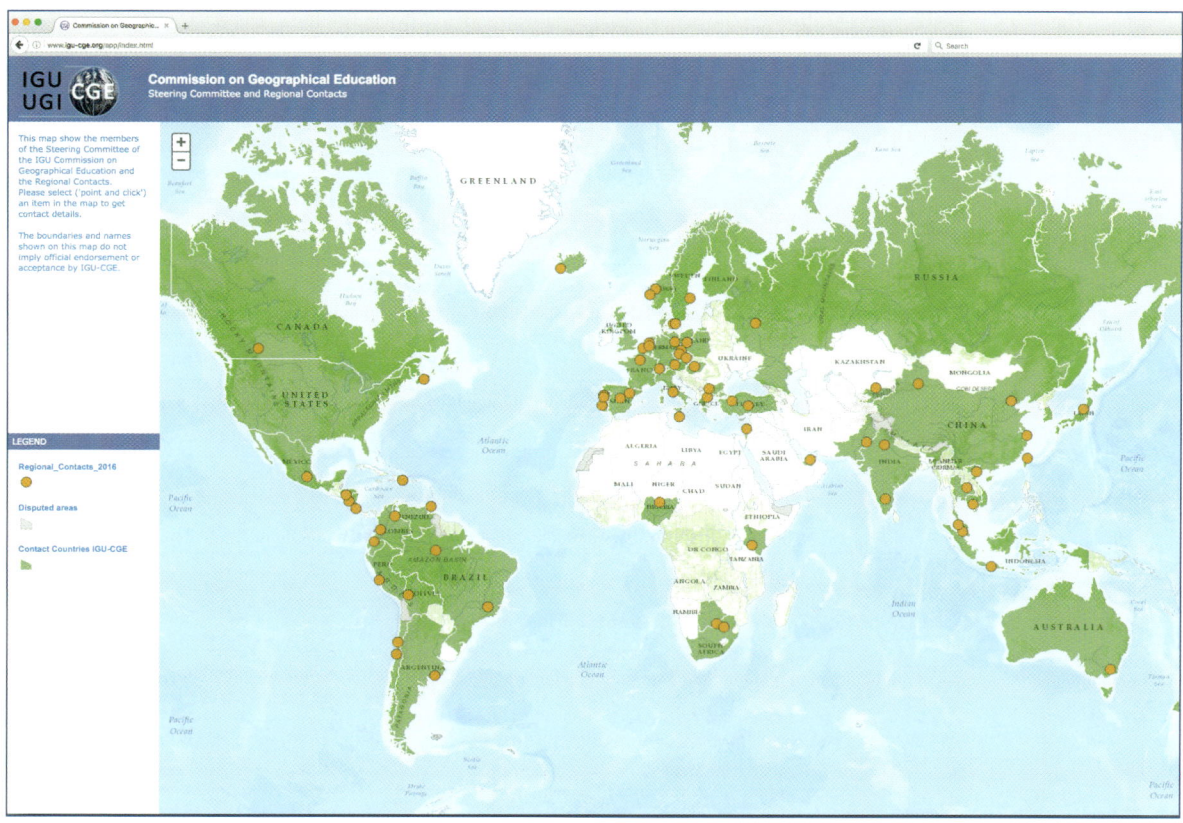

Figure 8: Map of IGU-CGE contacts and steering committee members. **Source:** www.igu-cge.org/

challenge, which is why interaction at this scale is often most successful when a careful balance is struck between respecting and understanding local circumstances and building commitment to a common cause (see, for example, the International Charter of Geographic Education – *www.igu-cge.org/charters_1.htm*). Part of this challenge is rooted in the fact that geography and geography education mean different things in different countries. With geography positioned in different parts of the world as a spatial science, social science or with the humanities, the pedagogic and curriculum challenges can be diverse and international comparisons rather tricky (see, for example, the 'Wikigeo' at *www.igu-cge.org*).

The GA: past, present and future

The GA's strapline – 'the leading subject association for all teachers of geography' – reflects its identity over more than a century of activity. It was formed by five geographers at a meeting in Oxford in 1893 in order to share ideas and exchange resources – lantern slides being the technology of the day (Balchin, 1993). From these relatively humble beginnings, the pursuit of its charitable mission to 'further geographical knowledge and understanding through education' has led the Association to undertake an extraordinary range of initiatives with and on behalf of geography teachers (Figure 9). In doing so, it has developed a deep knowledge of teaching, learning, leadership, curriculum, standards, progress, assessment and teacher education in geography; knowledge expressed within its published output (journals, publications, website and conference papers) and shared across the community by its members, volunteers and contributors.

Today, the GA remains an independent association, with its core activities financed principally by membership subscriptions, the sale of educational resources, CPD events and externally-funded curriculum development project work. Like the subject community it serves, it is a rather complex entity which

339

Figure 9: Selected highlights from the history of the GA. **After:** Balchin, 1993.

Year	GA event/initiative	Function/impact
1894	First policy proposal – to exam boards.	Recognition of geography within examinations.
1901	Published first journal – *The Geographical Teacher*.	Sharing professional knowledge of geography, curriculum, pedagogy.
1904	First local Branch – South London.	Local networks affiliated to and supported by the national body.
1905	Publishes A.J. Herbertson's article 'The world's major natural regions' in *The Geographical Teacher*.	Helps define the subject of geography in education and the public mind.
1910	Publishes first book – *Guide to Geographical Books and Appliances* by H.R. Hill.	Bespoke publishing house for geography education, focused on professional knowledge and practice.
1918	First Standing Committees – Exhibitions, Regional Surveys, Syllabuses and Examinations, Books/Maps/Atlases.	Expert committees address educational challenges and disseminate ideas to members.
1921	First Spring conference – Southampton.	National conference of events for showcasing practice and debating issues of the day.
1930 (and 1960, 1996)	Land Utilisation Survey of Britain – led by Professor Sir Dudley Stamp.	Public awareness of geography as a major contribution to civil society.
1932	First *Handbook* for geography teachers.	Comprehensive account of professional knowledge.
1947	Prof. S.W. Wooldridge lecture 'On taking the "ge" out of geography'.	Advocacy for geography and its place within the curriculum.
1967–1969	Committee and conference focus on quantitative revolution.	Maintains the link between disciplinary developments in HE and school geography.
1975	Launches *Teaching Geography*.	Practical professional journal for teachers.
1987	Publishes *A Case for Geography*.	Instrumental in securing the place of geography within the National Curriculum.
2006–2011	Action Plan for Geography.	National programme (with RGS-IBG) for professional and curriculum development and support, credited with reviving the fortunes of geography.
2012–2016	Policy discussions on the National Curriculum, GCSE and A level.	Shapes new geography curriculum and criteria 5–19.

enjoys the support not only of teachers, but of a wide range of geography professionals (e.g. teacher educators and others in higher education) as well as schools. Rather than attempting to impose a single model of professional community the GA seeks to build a shared sense of professional practice from a multitude of contributions, allowing professionals to 'associate' with one another in a variety of ways, both formal and informal, online and face-to-face, through peer-to-peer and expert connections and by receiving and/ or contributing professional knowledge. While it is usually thought of as a national organisation, in fact the GA operates at all scales, from local to global. Its affiliated Branches are shaped by local circumstances and priorities, while the global reach of the Association can be

Figure 10: What members of the GA community believe the GA 'does well'.

illustrated by its membership (in more than 60 countries), delegates to its Annual Conference (typically from over 30 countries) and access to its online materials (worldwide).

The future success of the Association rests on its ability to meet the professional and educational needs of the next generation of teachers and to demonstrate the value of geographical education as widely as possible. As is the case for many membership organisations, membership recruitment has become more challenging over the years. From a high point of around 12,000 in the late 1990s, the membership of the GA declined throughout the noughties, before stabilising in recent years at around 5500 members (personal and institutional). The rise of digital technology presents both a threat and an opportunity. On the one hand, as we have seen, teachers now have instant access to a huge range of ideas and resources, much of it for free. In response, the GA has developed products and services online, and the growth of its website and social media traffic suggests that it continues to meet the demand for professional support, as well as for quality teaching resources (Figure 10). Unfortunately, this activity does not always lead to the richer relationship represented by membership of the Association. The challenge is therefore to draw more teachers into a sustained professional conversation, widen participation to reflect the full age range and ethnic diversity of the teaching workforce, and nurture a new generation of contributors.

There is an equal and ongoing need to remake the case for the importance of subject expertise in teaching, for the sake of geography education as well as the GA as an organisation. Marketisation and the removal in 2010 of a National Curriculum authority have contributed to greater complexity and uncertainty in the education sector, while also encouraging schools to innovate at a local level. The GA's 2014–19 strategic plan emphasises the need to play a key leadership role in defining the purpose and value of geography in education, draw on the evidence of research and classroom practice, and work in partnership with school leaders and other organisations in order to make sure our authoritative subject voice is both heard and heeded. Within its marketing and communications, the Association has tended to emphasise its tangible products and services rather than its impact on curriculum and policy. However, 'thought leadership' is already a significant and valued feature of our work and is likely to become more important in the future (GA, 2014a, pp. 6–7).

Returning to the GA's fundamental belief in participation and innovation, we should acknowledge a certain irony: it is difficult for a teacher of geography to operate as an *autonomous professional*, able to make sound judgements about practice (e.g. interpret a curriculum framework rather than simply implement it) by pursuing this goal in isolation. Rather, teachers need to articulate and reflect upon their own experience in the light of evidence and experience from elsewhere, share in a discourse that covers the 'why' as well as the 'how' of what they do, and engage with the values, purposes and acquired wisdom of the wider profession. A rich and sustained level of interaction with other subject specialists is an essential element of all of this: a teacher who is unable or unwilling to engage may be doomed to repeating or reproducing a narrow range of technical procedures, whether appropriate to their own context or not, and is unlikely to equip their students with a framework for understanding themselves in the world.

Conversely, a profession lacking interaction and debate would soon cease to be a profession at all, since it would lose its collective intelligence as well as its sight of any shared (even if contested) moral purposes, technical practices or evidential base. The underpinning functions of our subject community – to incorporate and disseminate professional knowledge and define standards of knowledge and practice – produce both tangible and intangible benefits that flow in both directions. Just as transport systems provide the physical infrastructure for safe and reliable travel between places, so subject communities provide a form of social infrastructure, helping to chart the means of communication and exchange between individuals. At the same time, the long-term capacity of our community to produce and share new knowledge or exert influence depends upon the support and participation of the many, not the few.

References

Alexander, R. (2004) 'Still no pedagogy? Principle, pragmatism and compliance in primary education', *Cambridge Journal of Education*, 34, 1, pp. 8–33.

Armstrong, J. (2013) 'Introduction: The importance of professionalism' in *Towards a Royal College of Teaching: Raising the status of the profession*. Available at: www.teachingleaders.org.uk/wp-content/uploads/2013/05/Towards-a-Royal-College-of-Teaching.pdf (last accessed 14/11/2016).

Bailey, P. (1975) 'Editorial: New geography – new schools', *Teaching Geography*, 1, 1, pp. 4–5.

Bailey, P. and Binns, T. (eds) (1987) *A Case for Geography*. Sheffield: Geographical Association.

Balchin, W.G.V. (1993) *The Geographical Association: The first hundred years, 1893–1993*. Sheffield: Geographical Association.

BERA (2014) *Research and the Teaching Profession: Building the capacity for a self-improving education system. Final report of the BERA-RSA inquiry into the role of research in teacher education*. Available at: www.bera.ac.uk/wp-content/uploads/2013/12/BERA-RSA-Research-Teaching-Profession-FULL-REPORT-for-web.pdf (last accessed 14/11/2016).

Brooks, C. (2012) 'Changing times in England: the influence on geography teachers' professional practice', *International Research in Geographical and Environmental Education*, 21, 4, pp. 297–309.

Castells, M. (2000) 'Toward a sociology of the network society', *Contemporary Sociology*, 29, 5, pp. 693–99.

Centre for the Use of Research and Evidence in Education (CUREE) (2012) *Understanding What Enables High Quality Professional Learning: A report on the research evidence*. Coventry: CUREE. Available at: www.curee.co.uk/files/publication/%5Bsite-timestamp%5D/CUREE-Report.pdf (last accessed 14/11/2016).

Coburn, C. (2003) 'Re-thinking scale: moving beyond numbers to deep and lasting change', *Educational Researcher*, 32, 6, pp. 3–12.

DfE (2013) *Teachers' Standards: Guidance for school leaders, school staff and governing bodies*. Available at: www.gov.uk/government/uploads/system/uploads/attachment_data/file/301107/Teachers__Standards.pdf (last accessed 14/11/2016).

Firth, R. (2013) 'What constitutes knowledge in geography?' in Lambert, D. and Jones, M. (eds) *Debates in Geography Education*. Abingdon: Routledge, pp. 59–74.

Freshfield, D. (1901) 'Introduction', *The Geographical Teacher*, 1, 1, pp. 1–3.

GA (no date) *Curriculum making*. Available at: www.geography.org.uk/ (last accessed 14/11/2016).

GA (2005) *The Action Plan for Geography: Executive summary*. Available at: www.geography.org.uk/download/GA_APGproposals.doc (last accessed 14/11/2016).

GA (2009) *A Different View: A manifesto from the Geographical Association*. Available at: www.geography.org.uk (last accessed 14/11/2016).

GA (2014a) 'The GA's 2014–9 strategic plan', *GA Magazine*, 27, pp. 6–7.

GA (2014b) *About the GA*. Available at: www.geography.org.uk (last accessed 14/11/2016).

GA (2014c) *Carter Review of Initial Teacher Training (England): Call for Evidence Consultation Response. Submission from the Geographical Association September 2014*. Available at: www.geography.org.uk (last accessed 14/11/2016).

Hicks, D. (2014) 'A geography of hope', *Geography*, 99, 1, pp. 5–12.

Huxham, C. and Hibbert, P. (2008) 'Manifested attitudes: intricacies of inter-partner learning in collaboration', *Journal of Management Studies*, 45, 3, pp. 502–29.

Jackson, D. and Temperley, J. (2006) *From professional learning community to networked learning community*. Paper presented at the International Congress for School Effectiveness and Improvement (ICSEI) conference, Fort Lauderdale, 3–6 January. Available at: www.innovationunit.org/sites/default/files/From%20professional%20learning%20community%20to%20networked%20learning%20community.pdf (last accessed 14/11/2016).

Lacey, C. (1988) 'The idea of a socialist education' in Lauder, H. and Brown, P. (eds) *Education: In search of a future*. London: Falmer Press, pp. 91–98.

Lambert, D. (2011) 'Reviewing the case for geography, and the "knowledge turn" in the English National Curriculum', *The Curriculum Journal*, 22, 2, pp. 243–64.

Mason, R. and Rennie, F. (2009) 'Social networking as an educational tool' in Arthur, J. and Davies, I. (eds) *The Routledge Education Studies Reader*. Abingdon: Routledge.

Morgan, A. (2011) 'Morality and geography education' in Butt, G. (ed) *Geography, Education and the Future*. London: Continuum, pp. 187–205.

Morgan, J. (2011) *Teaching Secondary Geography as if the Planet Matters*. Abingdon: Routledge.

Morgan, J. and Lambert, D. (2005) *Geography: Teaching school subjects 11–19*. Abingdon: Routledge.

Nonaka, I. and Takeuchi, H. (1995) *The Knowledge-Creating Company: How Japanese companies create the dynamics of innovation*. Oxford: Oxford University Press.

Ofsted (2011) *Geography: Learning to make a world of difference*. Available at: www.gov.uk/government/publications/geography-learning-to-make-a-world-of-difference (last accessed 14/11/2016).

Owens, P. (2013) 'More than just core knowledge? A framework for effective and high-quality primary geography', *Education 3–13: International Journal of Primary, Elementary and Early Years Education*, 41, 4, pp. 382–97.

Parkinson, A. (2013) 'How has technology impacted on the teaching of geography and geography teachers?' in Lambert, D. and Jones, M. (eds) *Debates in Geography Education*. Abingdon: Routledge, pp. 193–205.

Pring, R. (2011) 'What is education for?' in Little, B. (ed) *Radical Future: Politics for the next generation*. London: Lawrence & Wishart, pp. 98–102.

Professional Association Research Network (PARN) (2014) *Professional Body Sector Review 2014*. Available at: www.parnglobal.com/2014-professional-body-sector-review-out-now (last accessed 14/11/2016).

Roberts, M. (2013) *Geography Through Enquiry: Approaches to teaching and learning in the secondary school*. Sheffield: Geographical Association.

Rogers, L. (2014) 'A letter to the TES Resources Community', *Times Educational Supplement*, 5106, 1 August, pp. 16–17.

Sassen, S. (2012) *Cities in a World Economy* (4th edition). London: SAGE.

Staines, J. (2010) *Excited atoms: an exploration of virtual mobility in the contemporary performing arts*. Available at: www.on-the-move.org/files/news_files/excited_atoms_final.pdf (last accessed 14/11/2016).

Standish, A. (2012) *The False Promise of Global Learning: Why education needs boundaries*. London: Continuum.

Stott, A., Jopling, M. and Kilcher, A. (2006) *How Do School-to-School Networks Work?* Available at: http://citeseerx.ist.psu.edu/viewdoc/download?doi=10.1.1.577.7676&rep=rep1&type=pdf (last accessed 14/11/2016).

Teacher Development Trust (2014) *Annual Report 2014*. Available at: http://tdtrust.org/teacher-development-trust-annual-report-2014-2 (last accessed 14/11/2016).

Wenger-Trayner, E. (2007) *Introduction to communities of practice: a brief overview of the concept and its uses*. Available at: http://wenger-trayner.com/introduction-to-communities-of-practice (last accessed 14/11/2016).

Weston, D. (2013) *What Do Grassroots Teachers Need? Towards a Royal College of Teaching: raising the status of the profession*. Available at: www.teachingleaders.org.uk/wp-content/uploads/2013/05/Towards-a-Royal-College-of-Teaching.pdf (last accessed 14/11/2016).

Winch, C., Orchard, J. and Oancea, A. (2014) 'Philosophical reflections on the contribution of research to teacher education' in *The Role of Research in Teacher Education: Reviewing the evidence*. Interim report of the BERA-RSA inquiry. Available at: www.thersa.org/globalassets/pdfs/reports/bera-rsa-interim-report.pdf (last accessed 14/11/2016).

Wood, P. (2007) 'Advances in e-learning: the case of blogging in school geography', *GeogEd*, 1, 1.

Recommended key readings

Chalmers, L. and Keown, P. (2006) 'Communities of practice and the professional development of geography teachers', *Geography*, 91, 2, pp. 109–16.

Chalmers and Keown describe the context in which a community of practice has been developed, present evidence for its effectiveness in professional development and argue for serious consideration of the 'community of practice' approach more broadly.

Lambert, D. (2010) 'On being a professional geography teacher' in Brooks, C. (ed) *Studying PGCE Geography at M level*. Abingdon: Routledge, pp. 9–22.

This chapter opens up a discussion on teaching as a professional activity, with particular reference to teaching geography in primary and secondary schools in England. It examines the complex role of the teaching professional and the relationship between individuals, their community and their wider environment.

Index

A

A level
- continuity and progression, 45
- curriculum, 34, 260–1, 321
- and enquiry, 49
- exam preparation, 272–3
- fieldwork, 232–3, 242, 260
- GIS, 248
- human geography, 78, 80, 82, 85
- individual projects, 66
- issues-based teaching, 69
- physical geography, 68, 71
- place knowledge, 124
- reforms, 272
- specifications, 263, 265

accountability, 33, 59, 185, 310, 318
accrediting excellence, 326–7
Action Plan for Geography, 8, 279, 286, 336
action research, 297–8, 300
aerial photography, 159, 248
affective learning, 232, 240, 293
affective mapping, 125
AfL (assessment for learning). *see* formative assessment
agriculture, 76–8, 84, 87, 90, 103
Amazonian stories, 100–4
analogies, 219, 220
analytical writing, 202, 203
Anthropocene and nexus studies, 66
application of knowledge, post-16, 260
'Arab Spring,' 84
ArcGIS, 249, 252–4
AS level, 242, 260, 261
Asia, rise of, 14
assessment, 56, 182–97, 323
- government policy, 182–6
- for learning (AfL). *see* formative assessment
- performance outcomes and, 190
- planning for, 186–8
- progression and, 46–7, 191–6
- students' prior knowledge and, 189

atlases, 124, 156, 159, 314
audio and video resources, 160–2
awareness of geography, 325
awe and wonder, 73

B

behaviour management, 308, 316
belonging, 330–43
bias, 151, 225, 338
Brazil, 100–3, 129, 132
BTECs, 320

C

capabilities approach, 25–6, 109
capitalism, 92–3, 95, 109
carbon cycle, 66, 70, 260
case studies, 123, 124, 143
censuses, 159–60
choice, student, 168, 180
cities. *see* London; urban studies
citizenship, 17–18, 79, 106, 107, 110
classrooms
- activities, 55, 56
- environment as resource, 162–3
- formative assessment, 182, 186
- speaking and listening, 199

climate, 27, 70, 271
climate change, 63, 92–3, 271
coaching, 278, 282, 284, 306, 310–11
collaboration, 266, 267, 338
- and GA, 335
- online, 334–5
- teachers', 281, 282, 290, 312–13, 322, 327

collaborative learning, 319
collegiality, 327–8
Common Agriculture Policy (CAP), 87
communication, 36, 52, 192
communication systems, 27
communities, 14, 129
communities and networks, geography, 282–7, 332–9
computer models and simulations, 66, 67
concept maps, 178–80, 270
connections, 23, 28, 58, 84, 87, 114
constructivism, 41–2, 43, 48–9, 122, 331
- GIS, 249–50, 251

consumption, 26, 41, 90, 96, 128, 301
content, post-16, 264–5
country studies, 123, 124, 176
countryside, 81
coursework, GCSE, 183, 242
CPD (continuing professional development), 278–91, 331
- leadership, 320, 322
- whole-school focus, 8
- *see also* professional development; research

creative writing, 205–7
critical thinking, 114, 115, 117, 272
cross-curricular liaison, 226
cross-curricular projects, 210, 215
cultural contexts, practices/behaviours, 85
cultural geography, 49, 120, 121
cultural studies, 86–7
curriculum, 30–9
- definitions and debates, 6, 31–4

development, 335–6
EfS (education for sustainability), 98
   of engagement, 27, 118
   global learning, 106–8
   ideologies, 135–6
   making, 24–5, 37, 140, 143, 264
   organising concepts in, 26
   planning, 34–7, 321
   post-16, 260–2
   review, 319, 320–3
   for sustainability, 92–3

D

DARTs ('Directed Activities Relating to Texts'), 154, 205, 209
data, 49, 50, 54, 74, 143, 159–60
   collection, 233–4, 289
   handling, 67–8, 112, 216, 217, 218, 220–4
   . see also GIS (geographical information systems); maps; statistics
debate, 199, 201, 342
debriefing, 220, 221
departmental development, 319, 323, 324, 325
departmental mentoring, 308–9
description, 295, 296
desertification, 103
development, 109–10, 112, 117
   . see also global learning
diaries, 58, 199–202
differentiation, 166–81
   approaches to, 169–73
   for EAL students, 169
   learning environment for, 166–8
   for least and most able, 167–9
   literacy, 204–5, 206
   strategies for, 173–80
digital mapping, 245, 256–7
digital resources, 150–64
disabilities, students with, 167, 168
discourse, professional, 342
discovery, fieldwork, 236–7
discussion, 145, 147, 302, 313
displays, 214, 326
   wall, 162–3, 167, 208
distant places, 108, 112, 123, 126, 129, 131
diversity, 106, 108
Dragons' Den, 179

E

EAL (English as an Additional Language) students, 167, 169
Earth education, 237–8
Earth system science (ESS), 65–6
Earth viewers, 244, 245, 248, 255–6, 257
Eco-schools, 263
eco-tourism, 16
Education for Sustainable Development (ESD), 98
Education Reform Act, 1988, 31

emotion, geographies of, 125, 301
English as an Additional Language (EAL). see EAL
English Baccalaureate (EBacc), 185
enquiry approach, 36–7, 48–59, 115, 167
   characteristics, 48
   fieldwork, 220, 234–6, 239–40
   GIS, 246, 249–50, 256
   and global learning, 111–13, 114, 116
   justification, 48–9
   and lesson planning, 134
   place, 122
   planning for, 44, 50–9
   post-16, 266–71
   . see also questions
environment, 27, 28
environmental education, 96–8
environmental ideologies, 94–5
environmental issues, 68
environmental knowledge, 13, 14–16
environmental science, 15, 64
equality/inequality, 236, 301
e-readers, 153
essays, 205, 206, 272
ethical issues, 27, 87, 100, 111
   rights, 85, 107
   . see also global learning; sustainability; values
ethnogeographies, 122
Europe, subject community initiatives, 337
evaluation, 171, 181, 323
   of CPD, 288
   in mentoring, 314–15
   of performance, 187, 319
   resources, 113, 143
Every Child Matters, 33, 34
everyday geographies, 23
examination boards, 31, 93, 183, 234–5
examinations
   and enquiry, 49
   focus on, 8
   post-16, 261, 262
   preparation, 272–3
   specification, 50, 153
exclusion, 79, 82
EXIT model, 209, 210
experiments, 163
exploration, geography as, 15–16, 18

F

farming, 76–8, 84, 87, 90, 103
feedback, 170, 188, 314
   fieldwork, 240–1
   in formative assessment, 193–5
   students', 147, 289, 323
female genital cutting (FGC), 85
field excursions, 232–3
fieldwork, 228–43, 319

approaches to, 232–8
data-handling, 218, 220
definition, and places for, 230–1
physical geography, 67
post-16, 260–1
preparation and objectives/outcomes, 238–40
purposes and benefits, 228–30, 242–3
sustainability, 231, 241–2
and travel, 15–16
films, 92, 160–2
Five Key Points strategy, 54
flipped classroom, 139
flooding, 38, 67, 69, 103, 264
food, 76–8, 84, 85–7, 89–90
food security, 78, 88
forests and deforestation, 45, 100–3, 163, 219
form tutors, role of, 46
formative assessment, 46, 56–8, 184, 186, 187
    feedback as, 193–5
futures dimension, 27, 49, 113

G

GA (Geographical Association), 20, 21, 34, 37, 52
    on assessment, 186
    belonging to a subject community, 330–43
    CPD, 279, 283, 285, 286, 320
    curriculum making, 24–5, 262
    A Different View, 22, 24, 27, 37, 116, 138, 332
    literature, 7
    mentoring, 307, 315
    and numeracy, 226
    post-16, 263–4
    Secondary Geography Quality Mark (SGQM), 324, 326
    Valuing Places, 125
games, 163
GCE, 8, 87, 217, 224, 248
GCSE, 33, 321
    enquiry approach, 49, 59
    fieldwork, 242
    GIS, 248, 252
    global learning, 108
    human geography, 80, 87
    numeracy, 217, 220, 224
    physical geography, 68, 71
    progression from, 263, 266
    and school performance, 183
    and skills, 145
    specification, 8, 45, 124
Geographical Association. *see* GA (Geographical Association)
geographical enquiry, 25, 33, 36–7, 111–13
geographical imaginations, 18, 81–2, 128
geographical terminology. *see* vocabulary
geographical thinking. *see* thinking geographically
geography, 8, 12–19, 84
Geography Collective, 283, 284

geology, 14–15, 70, 73
GER (geography education research), 292, 293, 297, 298, 301–3
GIS (geographical information systems)
    benefits for research, 88
    digital mapping, 256–7
    geospatial technology, 157, 244–6, 255–6
    online, 252–5
    physical geography, 66, 67
    in schools/curriculum, 247–55, 258
    'true,' 246–7
glaciers, 68, 71, 254
global citizenship, 17–18, 114–15, 117
global issues, 64
global learning, 23–4, 106–19
Global Learning Programme (GLP), 107–8, 110, 336
global links, distant places, 129, 131
global positioning systems (GPS), 244
global systems and governance, 78, 80, 260
globalisation
    differential impact of, 83–4
    and governance, 80
    and interdependence, 110–11, 114, 117
    as key concept, 108
    and sustainability, 64
good geography lessons, 134–9
Google Earth, 67, 157, 244, 255, 256
graphs, 215, 221–2, 224–5, 248
group work, 54–5
grouping, and differentiation, 167, 170

H

higher education, 63, 70–1, 78–9, 87–8, 213
    . *see also* research; universities
historical geography, 53, 81, 86–7, 101–3
HIV/AIDS, 85
homework, 139
hotboards, 163
human development, 109–10, 112, 117
human geography, 14, 76–91
    nature and, 100
    vs physical geography, 72–3
    post-16, 260
    research on learning, 42
human graphs, 222, 238
human rights, 85, 107
humanistic tradition, 111, 120–1
hydrology, 66, 67, 69
hypothesis testing, 233–4

I

ICT, 41, 272
    . *see also* data; GIS (geographical information systems)
identity, and environment, 27
ideologies
    capitalist, 92–3

curriculum, 135–6
   of sustainability, 94–5
imperialism, 18, 23, 81
inclusion. *see* differentiation
independent learning, structured, 180
inequality, 236, 301
informal learning, 32
Inset, 146, 280, 325, 327
inspections, 145, 324–5
   . *see also* Ofsted
interdependence, 108, 110–11, 116, 117
International Geographical Union's Commission on Geographical Education (IGU-CGE), 337, 338
international subject communities, 337–9
internet, 14, 16, 126, 334
   . *see also* digital resources
interpretivism, 120, 121
interviews, 240, 294
investigative skills, 26, 40, 41, 49, 193
issues-based teaching, 63, 69–73, 100, 106

J

joint practice development (JPD), 333

K

key concepts, 144, 264–5
key stage 2, 45, 107, 257
key stage 2/3 links, 45
key stage 3, 8, 191, 321–2
   continuity and progression, 45
   enquiry approach, 59
   evaluation, 323
   fieldwork, 242
   GIS and ICT, 248, 252
   global learning, 107, 116
   non-specialist teaching, 6, 34
   numeracy, 214, 215, 217, 218, 221, 222
   Ordnance Survey (OS), 257
   on place, 124
   planning for progression, 44
   reduced time for, 33, 34
   textual resources, 153, 154
key stage 4, 34
knowledge
   core, 8, 17, 20–1, 22, 33–4, 164, 265, 321
   fieldwork, 229
   international and environmental, 13–15
   key concepts, 144
   neglect of, 68, 114
   scaffolding, 141
   scientific, importance of teaching, 69, 71, 72, 73, 74
   students' prior, 52–3
   world, 40–1
   . *see also* enquiry approach
'knowledgeable' approach, 116–17

L

landscapes
   fieldwork, 16, 67, 238
   human and physical processes, 63, 88, 93
   models, 236
   systems and evolution, 15, 70, 71, 72, 73
layers of inference, 173–5
leadership, of subject, 283, 318–29
learning
   principles, 191–2
   theories, 41–2, 47, 48–9, 140, 331
learning activities, 141–3
learning environments for differentiation, 166–8
learning grids, 270
learning logs, 58
learning objectives, 56
Learning Outside the Classroom Manifesto, 229
learning styles, 141–2
   post-16, 265–71
   teachers,' 309
learning support staff, 167, 168, 170
least able students, 167–8, 171, 176
lessons
   and assessment, 193
   observations, 323–4
   planning and structuring, 134–9, 152, 153, 316
   . *see also* differentiation
listening, 167, 199–200
literacy, 198–211
   and cross-curricular projects, 210–11
   geography and, 144, 198
   reading, 207–9
   speaking and listening, 199–200
   writing, 199–207
literature, subject-specific, 7
lived experiences, 23, 126
local issues, 84, 112
local places, 126–9, 130, 220, 230
localism, 281
localism, educational, 333
locational knowledge, 121, 124–5
London, 81, 82, 83, 235–6, 237
   fieldwork, 239, 257

M

maps, 129, 144–5, 156–9, 160, 215, 221–4
   atlases and, 124, 156, 159, 314
   memory and sketch, 42, 125, 127, 128, 130, 131, 205
   mind maps, 56, 138, 189
   . *see also* GIS (geographical information systems)
marking, 168, 169, 193, 194
Marxist, 88, 109
mathematics. *see* numeracy
measurable outcomes, 36
media, 38, 152, 160–2
   . *see also* resources

media literacy, 151, 164
memory maps, 125, 128, 130
mentoring, 282, 284–5, 306–17
metacognition, 169, 201, 280
migration, 86, 87, 90, 152, 153
Millennium Development Goals (MDGs), 109, 110, 126
mind maps, 56, 138, 189
Mission:Explore, 236, 237, 284
mixed ability, 167, 174, 177
models
    for curriculum planning, 35–7
        physical, 150, 163, 236. *see also* simulations
    for thinking, 20
modernity, 14, 17, 18, 62
moral issues. *see* ethical issues; values
most able students, 168–9, 171, 173, 180
motivation, 147, 180, 187, 189, 194, 197
multicultural education, 85, 106
mysteries, 299, 300

N

national community, 335–7
National Curriculum, 8, 17, 20, 28, 49, 341
    and assessment, 183, 190
    concept-led, 286
    development of, 31–3
    on differentiation, 166
    on GIS, 248
    and global learning, 106, 108, 111
    human geography, 80
    on ICT, 247–8
    key concepts, 143
    levels, 185–6, 195–6, 334
    and locational knowledge, 124
    map skills, 156, 157
    on numeracy, 213, 214, 217
    physical geography, 68, 162
    and return to 'tradition,' 115, 124
National Foundation for Educational Research (NFER), 190, 229, 230
National Numeracy Strategy (NNS), 213, 214
National Standards, initial teacher training (ITT), 307
National Strategies, 8, 33, 34, 134, 171
    CPD, 278, 279
    for differentiation, 167
national subject community, 335–7
nature, 84, 95, 99–100
'nature deficit disorder,' 242
'need to know,' 174
networks and communities, geography, 282–7, 332–9
new teachers. *see* NQTs
non-specialist teachers, 6, 34, 310, 320
NQTs, 281, 306, 308, 309
numeracy, 212–27
    cross-curricular, 214–15
    in geography, 144, 215–27

    standards, 213
    . *see also* data

O

objectives, post-16, 262–4
observation, 146, 312–16, 323–4
Office for National Statistics (ONS), 159–60, 220
Ofsted, 20, 33, 34, 36, 59, 145, 183, 310
    on CPD, 274, 287, 288
    on fieldwork, 242–3
    on GIS, 248
    on global learning, 108, 116
    on leadership, 319, 320
    on learning activities, 265
    on National Strategies, 134
    on numeracy, 217
    on post-16 geography, 272
    preparing for, 324–5
Olympics 2012, legacy, 236
online communities, 283
online networks, 322, 334–5
optimal flow theory, 250, 251
Ordnance Survey (OS), 157–9, 224, 256–7
Orientalism, 82

P

pedagogy(ies)
    concept of, 330
    and curriculum, 37, 140
    emphasis on, 7, 265, 278
    and global learning, 114
    mentoring and coaching, 311, 316
    and resources, 150–1
    and subject knowledge, 20–1, 24–5
peer review, teachers,' 309
peer teaching, 138, 141, 169, 170
peer-assessment, 46–7, 188, 193, 272
    applying criteria, 58, 192, 195
performance, outcomes, 190
performance, schools', 183, 185, 187
performance culture, 318
personal geographies, 53, 112, 125, 127, 128, 139, 140, 319
photographs, 154–5, 156, 157, 175, 238
physical geography, 14–15, 62–75
    definitions and history, 62–3
    vs human geography, 72–3
    key directions, 63–6
    nature and, 100
    post-16, 260
    renewed emphasis on, 162
    research on learning, 42
    scientific knowledge, teaching of, 68, 69, 71, 72, 73, 74
place(s), 41, 120–33
    academic perspectives, 120–2
    approaches to teaching, 123–32
    case studies, 108

definition, 79
investigations and schemes of work, 126–32
as organising concept, 26, 28
people and, 79, 80
pre-modern relationship to, 14
scale and locational knowledge, 124–5
subjective/emotional aspects, 125
. see also distant places; space
planning, 42–5, 47, 50–9, 186–8
. see also differentiation
planning the curriculum, 32, 35
plurality, 338
poetry, 205, 206–7
political ecology, 101–4
population, 43, 72
growth, 65, 78, 103, 219
positivism, 120, 121
post-16, 260–75
aims and objectives, 262–4
approaches to learning, 265–71
curriculum change, 260–2
exam preparation, 272–3
school-university divide, 274
subject content and concepts, 264–5
post-structuralist approaches, 110
poverty, 81, 126, 236
poverty reduction, 107, 108, 110
praise, 194
process model, 36–7
processes, 173, 229, 264
professional development, 106, 114, 274, 278–91, 320, 322, 333
mentoring for, 309, 314
and numeracy, 214
. see also CPD (continuing professional development); research
progression in learning, 40–7
fieldwork, 231–2
planning, 42–5
planning/identifying, 191–5
recording, 195–6
students' and CPD, 288
teachers'/CPD, 281
. see also assessment
projects, 180
publish research, 303

Q

QCA (Qualifications and Curriculum Authority), 92, 107
QCDA (Qualifications and Curriculum Development Agency), 93, 332
QUADS grids, 204, 209
qualitative research, 294
qualitative skills, 79, 240, 261
quantitative research, 294
quantitative skills, 213, 216, 232, 233–4, 240, 261

quasi-experimental designs, 299–301
question grids, 267–8, 269
questions, 25, 26, 173, 193, 267–70
about images, 155, 158
and differentiation, 168, 169–72
enquiry approach, 48, 51–2, 55–6, 57, 235–6
in formative assessment, 193
and lesson objectives, 137–8, 139
students', 174, 189, 196

R

rainforests, 100–3
Randomised Control Trials (RCTs), 296–7
read research, 302–3
reading, 207–9
real events, 38
real world, GIS, 250
received curriculum, 32
reflection, 36, 48, 58, 192, 194–5, 323
teachers', 279, 289, 314–15, 319
relational thinking, 25, 26–8, 81–4, 121
relevance, 38, 70–1, 164, 261, 278
remote sensing (RS), 244
research, 292–305
CPD, 289–90, 302–3
cross-disciplinary, 87–8, 301
GIS enquiry, 249–50
on leadership, 327–8
on learning, 41–2, 47, 249
skills, 144, 204
research methodology, 36
resources, 150–65
CPD, 285–6, 287, 289
creating, 152–3
data and statistics, 159–60
and differentiation, 168
for enquiry, 54, 58
evaluation, 113, 143
games and simulations, 163–4
images, 154–6, 168, 175
maps and atlases, 156–9
online, 132, 283, 334–5
and pedagogy, 150–1
place(s), 125–6, 132
post-16, 263–4
schemes of work, 322
selecting, 138, 151–2
teacher as a resource, 164
textual, 153–4
video and audio, 160–2, 286, 287
revision, 196, 298
RGS-IBG, 285–6
Rio Earth Summit, 98
risk assessment, 238, 239
role play, 179
Royal Geographical Society, 252, 263–4, 279

S

SATS (standard assessment tasks), 184
scale, 41, 170
   and connection, 28, 114
   human geography, 81, 87
   maps, 223–4
   physical geography, 64, 66, 67
   and place, 121, 124
schemes of work
   distant places, 129, 131
   expertise and curriculum, 320, 322–3
   global learning, 108, 109
   local places, 126–9
   maps, 222
   numeracy, 226
school performance/targets, 183, 185, 187
school-linking programmes, 113, 333
school-university links, 274, 297, 302, 303, 320
self-assessment, 46–7, 188, 193, 272
   applying criteria, 58, 192, 195
SEN (Special Educational Needs) students, 167, 168
sense of place, 79, 108, 125, 230, 256
sensory experiences, fieldwork, 230, 237–8
shared views, 176–8
shared vision, 318–19, 327
simulations, 67, 163–4
sketch maps, 127, 131, 205
skills dimension, 144, 145
   fieldwork, 229
   global learning, 114
   and map use, 156–7
   post-16, 260–1, 265
   progression, 41, 44, 45
   . see also data
skills-based curricula, 6, 33, 34
slavery, 81, 86
social constructivism. *see* constructivism
social justice, 109, 114
social media, 286–7
social networking, 68, 155
social realism, 117
social science, 84, 121
social theory, 88–9
social/personal development, 229
socio-economic/political processes, 121
software
   GIS, 249, 252–4
   for statistics, 160
   for websites, 161
space
   and connection, 114
   as organising concept, 26–7, 28
   and society, 79, 81
   . see also place(s)
spatial literacy, 248–50
speaking and listening, 167, 199–200
Special Educational Needs, 167, 168
Spiritual, Moral, Social and Cultural development (SMSC), 324
Staffordshire Learning Net (SLN), 334
standards, 183, 184, 190, 192
statistics, 159–60, 215, 216, 224–5, 261
stereotypes, 14, 124, 132, 174
story maps, 252, 254
storyboards, 175–6
stress, 266, 273, 308, 311
structured independent learning, 180
student experience, 7, 25, 52–3
   . see also personal geographies
student-centred approach, 164, 232, 233, 242, 265, 266
student-led learning, 48, 138
subject community, 330–43
subject expertise, 8, 320
subject leadership, 318–29
subject-specialist teachers, 20–1, 24, 146, 272
subject-specific support (LA), 74
summative assessment, 46, 58, 186–7, 195, 196
sustainability
   agri-food system, 76, 90
   Amazonian stories, 100–4
   definitions, 93–4
   environmental education, 96–8
   fieldwork, 231, 241–2
   ideologies, 94–5
   political controversy and, 92–3
   studies, 64–6
   types of geography teaching for, 99–100, 106
sustainable development, 106, 107, 108, 109

T

talking essays, 205, 206
target-setting, 316
taxonomies of cognitive objectives, 171, 172–3
teacher-led approach, 232, 233, 265, 266
teachers' networks, 282–7
teacher's role
   in enquiry, 50–1
   in process model curriculum, 37
   resource or facilitator, 164
Teachers' Standards, 331
teaching, post-16, 265, 272
teaching approaches, 37–8
   literacy, 210
   physical geography, 66–73
   . see also pedagogy(ies)
TeachMeets, 287
test outcomes, 196
textbooks, 152, 153–4
thinking geographically, 20–9
   connections, 23, 28, 90
   curriculum making, 24–5
   enquiry, 44, 48, 51, 111–13

global, 23–4, 116
  knowledge, 21, 22, 143, 164
  relational, 26–8
thinking skills, 33, 141–3, 267, 270–1
  metacognition, 169, 201, 280
  research, 299–300
Thinking Through Geography (TTG), 299–300
three lamps model, 121–3, 132
time, 27, 144, 157, 264
tourism and travel, 16, 177, 178, 320
'traditional' approach, 115–16, 117
trainee teachers, 306–8, 309, 313, 314, 316
trust, 328

U

UN Food and Agriculture Organisation, 78
UNESCO, 106
United Nations Development Programme (UNDP), 109, 110
United Nations Millennium Development Goals (MDGs), 64, 110
universities, 272, 274, 297, 302, 303, 320
  . *see also* higher education; research
urban studies, 49, 72, 80, 129, 163, 240, 242
  . *see also* London

V

values, 49, 106, 114
  and content, 145, 330–1
  fieldwork, 230, 234
  post-16, 263
  in research, 297
  . *see also* ethical issues

Valuing Places, 125
video, 160–2, 286, 287, 315
vision statement, 318–19, 321, 327
vocabulary, 25, 172, 191, 208
  . *see also* knowledge
vocational curriculum, 70, 74

W

wall displays, 162–3, 167, 208
weather, 69, 144, 171, 180
  data, 157, 160
whole-class teaching, 54
word mats, 208
workplace geographies, 301
world systems theory, 101
writing, 121, 199–207, 321
writing frames, 168, 175, 204–5

Y

Young Lives study, 126
Youtube, 160–1

Z

zone of proximal development (ZPD), 140–1